# The Daily Telegraph

# Golf

## Chronicle

THIS IS A CARLTON BOOK

Text copyright © 2000 The Daily Telegraph/Ted Barrett
Design copyright © 2000 Carlton Books Limited

First published in 1994
by Carlton Books Limited
20 Mortimer Street
London W1N 7RD

10 9 8 7 6 5 4 3 2 1

A CIP catalogue record for this book
is available from the British Library

ISBN 1 85868 950 3

Project editors: Martin Corteel and Chris Hawkes
Project art editors: Robert Fairclough and Paul Oakley
Production: Garry Lewis and Bob Bhamra
Design: Steve Wilson

Printed and bound in Dubai

AUTHOR'S ACKNOWLEDGEMENTS
The author would like to acknowledge the use of extracts from reports and articles by, among others, Michael Williams, Donald Steel, Lewine Mair, Michael Calvin, John Campbell, Leslie Edwards and Bill Meredith that have appeared in the "Daily Telegraph" and "Sunday Telegraph".

The burdens of picture research were greatly relieved by assistance rendered by Russell Cheyne, and the patient labours of Michael Hobbs. Special thanks are due to Elizabeth Price-Fisher, Gary Prior for what is surely the best "reaction" picture of 1993 and to "Telegraph" librarian Alexandra Erskine and her staff, who could scarcely have been more supportive.

The publishers would like to thank the following sources for their kind permission to reproduce the pictures in this book:

Allsport UK Ltd./Simon Bruty, David Cannon, Chris Cole, J.D.Cuban, Tony Duffy, John Gichigi, Elsa Hasch, Harry How, Rusty Jarrett, Craig Jones, Ross Kinnaird, Vincent Laforet, Andy Lyons, Don Morley , Stephen Munday, Gary Newkirk, Doug Pensinger, Mike Powell, Steve Powell, Andrew Redington, Todd Rosenberg, Richard Saker, Paul Severn, Ezra Shaw, Jamie Squire, Todd Warshaw, Nick Wilson
Allsport Historical Collection/MSI
Corbis/Bettmann
Peter Dazeley Photographer
Hobbs Golf Collection
Hulton Getty/Joseph McKeown
Mark Newcombe/Visions in Golf Picture Library
PA News

Every effort has been made to acknowledge correctly and contact the source and/copyright holder of each picture, and Carlton Books Limited apologises for any unintentional errors or omissions which will be corrected in future editions of this book.

*Following page:* Jack Nicklaus, in 1998, unveils a plaque
honouring his achievements at Augusta.

# The Daily Telegraph

# Golf
## Chronicle

## Ted Barrett

**CARLTON**
**BOOKS**

# CONTENTS

# CONTENTS

# INTRODUCTION

The aim of this book, after touching upon the origins of golf, is to present newspaper-style snapshots, year on year, of its great championships and a glance at some of the myriad events spawned by the oldest established, and still most sought after title, the Open first contested at Prestwick in 1860.

This expanded second edition is updated a mere six years, during which the only unchanging elements seem to be Colin Montgomerie's domination of European golf (seven years the leading money-winner on the European PGA Tour), José Maria Olazabal being helped into a another Green Jacket at Augusta after chronic foot pain almost ended his career in the mid-1990s, and the endless battle between the ruling bodies of golf and makers of clubs and balls. Space-age materials such as thermoplastics used in ball casings allow professionals to cut the longest courses down to double figures under par. Weather permitting, that is. Fearful conditions at the 1999 Carnoustie Open brought tears from Sergio Garcia, pushed every 72-hole score over par and led the links to be renamed Carnastie.

In calm air, courses are more and more vulnerable to the march of golfing science. Jack Nicklaus, 100 victories to his name, calls it "a crazy spiral ... we're just running out of golf". The main culprit, in Nicklaus's eyes, is the ball. The news that several holes at St Andrews were to be lengthened to shore up "the Old Lady's" defences was greeted with dismay by Seve Ballesteros, who thought it the rape of an international treasure. But it had perforce been done before. In any case, a greater threat to St Andrews might be posed by developers, accused by Dr Frank Riddell, chairman of St Andrews Community Council, of wanting to turn St Andrews into "a golf-related theme park".

Two solutions offer themselves to the threat to par: that the USGA and R&A clamp down on technological upgrading, or that courses, especially for major championships, be "tricked up". The first solution is full of dangers for the ruling bodies. Bruising encounters with lawyers defending ever-more explosive ammunition or the shape of extra-spin generating grooves on their clients' iron clubs have made the law-givers cautious.

**Seve Ballesteros: dismayed at Old Course renovations.**

The second option has brought the wrath of the leading players down onto the United States Golfing Association, whose executive director, David Fay, said before the US Open of 1998 at Olympic, San Francisco, that the Association were "entirely comfortable with the golf equipment on the market today". The course is 300 yards short of the usual (these days) 7,000+, and 1990s equipment was clearly capable of shattering all records. But the USGA-style rough, and pin positions that were, said Tiger Woods "borderline illegal" produced a winning score (by Lee Janzen) of par, only once exceeded in four Opens at Olympic, and then by an "outsider" – Jack Fleck, with his 287 in 1955. Drivers were not in general use.

It is true that Nicklaus warned long ago that golf was never meant to be a fair game, but there are occasions, in the view of Peter McEvoy, who generals British international amateur teams, when unfairness is evident and course trickery crosses the line. Tiger Woods played as accurate a third shot as he is ever likely to play, having laid up at Valderrama's par five 17th in the final round of the 1999 Amex World Championship. He pitched well onto the green, but his ball rolled slowly back off the green and down a steep, shaven slope into the lake below. Result, a seven. Getting an approach to stop in the optimum position for putting, below the hole, carried an unacceptable degree of risk. Woods won a play-off with Miguel Angel Jimenez, but the feeling of unfairness lingered, especially as another sad trend in the last years of 20th century golf surfaced: Jimenez's Spanish supporters applauded Woods's misfortune at the 17th.

Surely time, thinks McEvoy, that ball and clubs were "wound back". There is not enough spare yardage round many of the game's classic courses to withstand equipment improvements.

How ironic that the most prominent purveyor of big-headed, big-hitting clubs, Eli Callaway, moved into the golf industry from previous successes in textiles and wine-making by taking over a small enterprise that specialised in reproduction hickory-shafted putters.

There is a market for such ephemera: the English chapter play at Rye, and Sam Snead at a nine-holer near Greenbrier in West Virginia, where his old friend Lewis Keller holds the record at 37 with Penfold gutties made in England. Like Nicklaus, Snead blames the modern ball for current golf ills.

**Improved technology has placed a number of courses under threat.**

Another unvarying cause of dissension is dress: the world's richest man, Bill Gates, was asked to leave a fashionable Californian country club because he was wearing a tee-shirt. He determined to set up his own club, but should be warned of Karsten Solheim's experience. He bought the club at which he and his wife were asked to stop playing because they had offended the starting times schedule. Even when he became the owner, Solheim was unable completely to reset the timetables to his personal preferences.

Shirts with collars are obligatory at most clubs, yet David Duval's black outfit in the Bob Hope 2000 classic was collarless. Evidently there is one rule for billionaires and one for millionaires, even though it seems to turn on its head the old saw about one law for the rich and one ...

The great trouser suit controversy may well at last have been settled, at least as far as Britain is concerned, in the first days of 2000 by the Birmingham Employment Tribunal. Judy Owen, married to a policeman and mother of two children, left her job at PGA headquarters in England's West Midlands after an official told her to wear a skirt. She accused managers of harassment and bullying because she was a woman, and won her case, with damages. Julie Mellor, Equal Opportunities Commission chairman, called on employers to scrap "old-fashioned dress codes".

British men looked forward to the 21st century with some misgivings on the equal opportunities front. The government decided to outlaw all-male clubs. Private clubs were exempted from the Sex Discrimination Act, but ministerial opinion was that this was an "anachronism".

Another small victory for English women was the removal from the foyer of the East Sussex National club of Nick Deans's five-foot bronze of "Young Girl removing her blouse".

Year 2000 began with the promise of a handful of the most starry young talent at top level, though youth does not rule unchallenged: surprisingly the average age of golfers reaching the US PGA Tour through success on the Nike Tour is 33.

Tiger Woods has already felt the pressure of Sergio Garcia's talents. Bright as they are, the feat of an 18-year-old Australian amateur, Aaron Baddeley, in holding off a much-restored Greg Norman and Nick Faldo to win the Australian Open Championship was even more striking, not only for its execution, but also for Baddeley's composure as he became the youngest ever winner in the event's 95-year history, and first amateur winner for 39 years. He is taking the gentle Garcia route to the professional path, using invitations to pro events as an amateur to acclimatise. Justin Rose, whose introduction at 17 to the pro Tour was so prolific in missed cuts after his third place triumph as an amateur in the 1998 Birkdale Open, won his card back for Year 2000, and pocketed a cheque right away in the South African Open. Trevor Immelman of South Africa is another high-achieving amateur tracking Garcia.

Casey Martin has his card on the US PGA Tour, finishing high on the Nike Tour which has been renamed, in the on-line spirit of Y2K, Buy.com. He was soon touring the fairways in his golf cart, gaining that dispensation on account of the degenerative state of his right leg. His successful appeal was based on the American Disabilities Act, the outcome of which the Tour authorities and many players are not inclined to accept as final.

Everyone is tracking Tiger Woods, or trying to. Like Gary Wolstenholme, the on-course leader of British Isles amateur golf triumphs, he has benefited from laser surgery making contact lenses obsolete. He began 2000 by beating Ernie Els in a play-off at the climax of a crossfire of eagles and birdies in the season-opening Mercedes Championship in Hawaii, having won his last four starts in 1999. He lost the first World Championship event, but won the other three. His final World Ranking total was the highest ever, 19.98, and his margin over David Duval in second place a record 6.83. His ten wins in 1999 were worth $7.2million (£4.5million).

Two outstanding players died in 1999: Gene Sarazen, the first player to win all four of the modern majors, in Naples, Florida, aged 97, and reigning US Open Champion Payne Stewart, 42 – the victim of a bizarre plane crash. The Payne Stewart Award will be given at the end of the year 2000 to the most worthy upholder of the golf professional's standing and of the Tour's charity efforts.

**Aaron Baddeley: one of a group of exciting youngsters tracking Tiger.**

# EVIAN GOLF LINKS.

**Evian-les-Bains. Lake of Geneva. 35 minutes from Lausanne.**
**Frequent Steamboat service.**

Season
May
to
September

Near the
ROYAL
and
SPLEN-
DIDE
Hotels
under
RITZ
manage-
ment.

CLUB HOUSE.

Motor Car Service to the Links.
Ladies and Gentlemen's Monthly Medal and
Bogey Competitions.

**Open Meeting for the Championship of Savoie,
2nd, 3rd and 4th September, 1909.**

Head Professional, **ARNAUD MASSY.**

*All further particulars can be obtained from*
Mons. J. BOHY, Secretary,
Chalet du Golf, Evian-les-Bains.

# Origins of the game set in Scottish mists

THE ORIGINS of golf, despite mighty efforts by the scholars of the game, have remained hidden by the mists of time. The case for supposing that those mists are Scottish is overwhelming.

The Oxford English Dictionary makes no bones about it: "A game of considerable antiquity in Scotland in which a small hard ball is struck with various clubs into a series of small cylindrical holes made at intervals usually of a hundred yards or more ... with ... the fewest possible strokes."

If it is true that the cross-country game we recognize as golf today is a Scottish variant of the Dutch game "het kolven", or the French "jeu de mail", or the Flemish "chole" or the French "soule", then it must be admitted that it is a variant which has radical new features, to say the least. Further, as the Dictionary goes on to point out, "none of the Dutch games have been convincingly identified with golf".

Moreover, though many believe that "golf" derives from "kolf", the stick or bat used in the Dutch game, no Scottish form of the word beginning with a "c" or a "k" has been found. There is, however, a Scottish dialect word "guwf" – "a blow with the open hand", which also serves as a verb "to strike". The Scots pronounce the name of the game as "gouf", and the author can vouch for the fact that in some quarters, as The Oxford English Dictionary states, English players imitate that sound.

Earlier references to golf-like activities include the game of "paganica", played by the Romans, with a ball of leather stuffed with feathers which was struck with a bent stick. But little else is known about how they played.

29.—THE "MASHIE." — 42.—THE PARISH MINISTER. — 30.—NEW WOMAN. — 23.—A DUFFER'S STROKE. — 41.—THE BRASSEY.

**Seen on the links: the "Mashie", the Minister, the New Woman, the Duffer and the "Brassey".**

# Continental variations on a golfing theme

THE DUTCH GAME, sketched by Rembrandt, among others, was played upon ice, or, more usually, in a courtyard – a "kolf-bann" or court, often one of the attractions of an inn. Kolf was sometimes played in a church, in the days before pews when the church interiors were unencumbered, in the churchyard or even in the street. But this practice angered unsportsminded citizens and attracted prohibitions, as at Naarden in the middle of the 15th century.

The object of kolven was to strike the ball, much larger and weighing about two pounds more than a golf ball, so that it struck a post first at one end and then the other end of the court or playing area with the least number of shots. A well-directed shot striking one post hard full on could give the player a good start towards the other post.

There have been claims that kolven played upon ice was the forerunner of golf, but in pictures such as those painted by Pieter Brueghel, the same posts and large ball appear. There seems to have been a notorious absence of any Scottish Brueghels, but on the other hand we know that golf was being played long before such pictures were produced.

The French game of jeu de mail, a favourite at the French court, resembles golf even less. The game of chole, which stands as a halfway house between hockey and golf, is to judge by legal references to it in the 1350s, older than either golf or kolven.

The targets here are not holes or goal-nets, but doors or gates, perhaps as far off from the starting point as a mile or more. The players divide into two teams and undertake to hit the target in a given number of "turns" of three strokes each. After each turn the opposing side are allowed a stroke with which to strike the ball away from the target and into any inconvenient spot they can find.

This stroke is called a dechole, and the principle behind it certainly conflicts with one of golf's major tenets, that a player may not interfere with his opponent's ball. Indeed, such interference has always led to penalties in golf.

The word "tuitje" – meaning a small heap of earth upon which the ball was placed for the initial stroke – has been cited as the origin of the golfing term "tee". However, the early Scottish rules of golf make it clear that the tee (the teeing ground) is actually the place from which the game is started.

**Rembrandt sketch of het kolven in a kolf-bann at an inn c.1654.**

# Lure of the linksland proves greater than that of battlefields

ROBERT BROWNING quotes in his *A History of Golf* from the Liber Pluscardensis a passage which might provide a clue as to how continental chole could have been carried into Scotland and there perhaps refined into a linksland setting.

The relevant incident occurred in 1421, when the forces of King Henry V of England, after winning the battle of Agincourt, were consolidating their territorial gains. Henry's brother, Thomas, Duke of Clarence, was laying siege to Baugé. The French asked for help from the Scots, who sent 7,000 men. By this time the Peace of Troyes had been signed, and Catherine of France was married to Henry.

The English broke an Easter truce at Baugé with a surprise attack on Easter Sunday, at a time when the Scots were "playing ball and amusing themselves with other pleasant or devout occupations".

The historian of the events of that Easter Day makes it clear that three Scots, whose names he gives, were "men of note" playing close to the crossing of a river. They saw the English advancing under cover of the woods, sent back to Baugé for help and pre-

*James III: repeated his father's ban on "unproffitable sportis" such as "Golfe".*

pared to defend the crossing. Clarence and his knights had got ahead of their archers and had to dismount to try to force the crossing. Many of the English fell, including Clarence and several other noblemen, and the Scots secured important prisoners, too. The theory is that the game the Scots were playing, providentially for their cause, was chole.

Thirty-six years later, in 1457, James II of Scotland's parliament declared that "the futeball and golf be utterly cryed downe and not usit". In a decree issued soon after the Baugé incident, only the playing of football was proscribed, and golf was not mentioned.

Clearly golf must have gained in public popularity in the intervening years, and by 1457 was considered by the authorities to be equally damaging to the practice of arms, and hence to the defence of the kingdom against the old enemy, England. James II was engaged in a long conflict with the English at the time.

The two games became no more popular with governments as the 15th century drew to a close. In 1470 James III repeated the football and golf prohibitions and in 1491 James IV's parliament passed a statute ordaining that "in na place of the Realme there be used Fute-ball, Golfe, or uther sik unproffitable sportis", since such activities were held not to be favourable to "the commoun good of the Realme and defense thereof".

The links between golf and archery grew in the 1500s — and not just the fact that, in the king's

eyes, time spent playing golf meant that archery skills were impaired. In 1502 there are the earliest references of bowmakers making golf clubs and James IV bought "Gowf clubbes" from a bowmaker in Perth.

Though it has been generally accepted for many years, there came in 1552 confirmation of the rights of the townspeople of St Andrews to play golf on the links. This came in the form of a license issued by Archbishop John Hamilton.

In time it would become a game for the common man. Yet no game under the sun comes near to golf as a favourite of kings and princes – and latterly, presidents too. White House incumbants Taft, Harding, Eisenhower, Ford and Clinton spring most readily to mind as keen golfers.

**"Golf is a game in which you try to put a small ball in a small hole with implements singularly unsuited to the purpose."**

WINSTON CHURCHILL.

**"Clearly kolf is no more golf than cricket is poker."**

ANDREW LANG.

Winston Churchill and (right Lloyd George) playing in Wales.

9.—ANDREW LANG.
"The Laureate of Golf."

**Andrew Lang: known as the laureate of golf.**

President Dwight D.Eisenhower and Arnold Palmer.

President Taft keeps swinging
in retirement.

# How Royalty began to warm to the game

THE SUDDEN change in royal and governmental attitudes that encouraged the growth of golf in the 16th century was a by-product of dynastic moves to end the age-old enmity between Scots and English, and which did take much – but not all – of the heat out of border feuds.

Three years into the new century, at Holyrood in Edinburgh, there was celebrated one of the most important of royal marriages, that between James IV and Margaret Tudor, eldest daughter of Henry VII of England. The marriage, and a peace treaty with England, had been agreed the previous year.

It is known that James played golf with the Earl of Bothwell. He does not look the part of a monarch of the fairways, and he cannot possibly have been the first Scot to swing a golf club, but James IV of Scotland is the first golfer whose name is known to history. The royal patronage of the game had begun.

The treaty of 1502 was intended to set up a perpetual peace between the warring nations, but almost exactly ten years after his marriage, James was killed at Flodden at the head of one of the biggest armies ever put together by Scotland, consisting of about 20,000 men. His intention had been to strengthen the bonds of the Scottish alliance with France with a massive border raid. England was at the time set on the encirclement of France

with the aid of Spain. Attempts to act against the English in concert with the French became more and more futile, and James V, like an increasing number of his subjects, turned to the game of golf as a relaxation.

His daughter Mary was born as he was on his deathbed in 1542, so she became Queen of Scots when she was only a few days old. Her connection with golf proved the fallacy of the contention that there is no such thing as bad publicity.

Her early life was dominated by one projected dynastic marriage after another. The first, by the regent Arran, promised her to Prince Edward of England, but the Scots parliament would have none of it, which was the cause of more fighting with the English.

Mary, at six years of age, went to spend a decade at the French court where she was educated. In 1558 she married the dauphin, the French king's eldest son, who in turn became king the following year, dying in 1560. The death of Mary's mother in Scotland necessitated her return home in 1561 to a volatile political situation complicated by Catholic/Protestant power struggles.

More marriage plans were mooted and abandoned, and Mary's unexpected marriage to Lord Darnley in 1565 brought an end to conjecture. His part in

*Continued overleaf*

Mary Queen of Scots returning from her golf – a reconstruction.

# Golf gradually wins the hearts of Royalty

James IV – the first golfer whose name is known.

*Continued from page 11*

plots against the Catholic interest favoured by Mary led to an estrangement. Divorce was in the air, but Mary and Darnley seemed subsequently to be moving towards reconciliation She left him late on the night of Sunday, February 9, 1567. Soon after midnight Darnley's house was blown up with gunpowder. His corpse was found in the garden.

All too shortly afterwards, it is alleged, Mary was seen golfing at Seton. To compound her insensitivity, her detractors asserted, she played golf with the Earl of Bothwell, suspected by many of complicity in Darnley's murder. The record does show that Bothwell was acquitted of the murder in what many consider to have been a whitewashing show trial and carried Mary off to Dunbar. He had recently married, but obtained a divorce, and in little more than three months after Darnley's death he and Mary were wed.

Whether Bothwell had been her golfing partner or not, her supporters voted, so to speak, with their feet. Her army vanished, and eventually she had to throw herself on the mercy of the English queen, Elizabeth.

This act of desperation brought her only a life sentence of imprisonment, ended by her execution after a final flurry of plots, real or invented. The sad example of this beautiful and accomplished woman – she sang pleasantly, spoke or read in six languages and wrote and collected poetry – had no discernible effect on the increasing popularity of golf among all classes.

Late 16th-century church records are proof of this, since golfers in many areas, from St Andrews to Banff were charged with the offence of playing on Sundays. Fines were often levied for playing "in tyme of sermonis". However, the right of golfers to enjoy their sport on Sundays once their religious duties were complete received confirmation at the highest level from James VI of Scotland, the son of Mary Queen of Scots, when he became James I of England on the death of Elizabeth in 1603.

# King James I gets princes in the swing

JAMES I was undoubtedly biased in favour of golf, but his unanswerable question was: "When shal the common people have leave to exercise, if not upon the Sundayes and Holydayes, seeing they must apply their labour, and winne their living in all working dayes?"

This was in 1618, and James's second son, King Charles I, drove home his father's point of view in 1633 by instructing justices "to see that no man doe trouble or molest any of our loyall and duetiful people, in or for their lawfull recreations, having first done their duetie to God".

Once established in England (he promised to go back to Scotland every three years, but more than a decade passed before he did), James I had both his sons swinging golf clubs at an early age.

He had himself begun playing at Perth, and had given a lifetime appointment as royal club-maker to William Mayne of Edinburgh. James's eldest son, Henry, died of a fever aged 18; hence the accession of Charles I. When the crowns of England and Scotland were united in 1603, James I settled in Blackheath, on the edge of London. Royal Blackheath Golf Club is said to date from 1608.

Charles I seldom enjoyed peace of mind from the moment – on the Leith Links – that news arrived of a rebellion in Ireland. Accounts differ as to whether he withdrew from the match, or finished it after the fashion of Francis Drake on Plymouth Hoe. Leith Links itself has a famous place in the game's Royal and ancient history. The Gentlemen Golfers of Leith later changed their name to the Honourable Company of Edinburgh Golfers, whose home is at Muirfield.

The House of Stuart did not desert golf. Charles I had little opportunity to play further, except at Newcastle when a prisoner of the Scots. Charles II, crowned as such by the Scots at Scone on the first day of 1651 in defiance of Parliament after his father was executed, exercised himself at the Scottish game. His invasion of England foundered at Worcester, and off went Charles to nine years of relative poverty in exile in the lands of soule and kolven.

Royal golfing times were happier when Charles was restored to the throne, notably for his brother James, Duke of York. Arguments about who should get the credit for golf had evidently already begun, because James, a frequent visitor to Leith Links in the 1680s, set up a foursome to settle a dispute with two English nobles.

The Duke was very well advised in his choice of partner – John Patersone, a humble shoemaker. A tradesman and a nobleman in sporting partnership was not an unheard-of alliance in this game of relative classlessness. James and John were too good for the English. The shoemaker received a generous share of the match stakes and, with the proceeds, built a house which stood in Edinburgh till 1961. But, with

19. — CHARLES I.
A Royal and Ancient Golfer.

**Charles I.**

the expulsion of James II in 1688, and the arrival of William of Orange, ironically from the land of the kolf-bann, the royal connection was ended. It had extended through every ruling Stuart monarch from 1502.

William III did make use of a notable golfing terrain – as an embarkation point on his way to the Battle of the Boyne, namely Hoylake in Cheshire. Not for the best part of 200 years was a more sporting royal part played in the game than by William IV.

**Charles I receives news while playing golf on Leith Links of the Irish Catholics' rebellion.**

# Royal patronage puts game on firm footing

ST ANDREWS, the oldest club of all (1754) barring the Honourable Comapny of Edinburgh Golfers, found the decision of William IV in 1833 to honour the Perth Golfing Society (formed in 1824) as the first "Royal" club hard to bear. Besides, King William was also Duke of St Andrews; in 1834 he was petitioned to become a St Andrews patron and grant the unique title of Royal and Ancient, which he duly did.

Queen Victoria followed with various "royal" entitlements for golf clubs, and while Edward VII and George V only dabbled at the game, both George V's sons played keenly, the younger, the Duke of York, with more natural skill than the Prince of Wales, who played in many parts of the world. The Duke of York hit one of the best shots seen from an incoming captain when he drove himself into office as captain of the Royal & Ancient the future Edward VIII seemingly did not.

The present Duke of York, Prince Andrew, brings the royal link up to date, 300 years on from the victory of that other Duke and

Prince Andrew, Duke of York, himself a keen player, presents the Curtis Cup at Hoylake in 1992.

The Duke of York – the future King George VI – opened one of the Richmond Park municipal courses in Surrey in 1927.

the shoemaker. The thought arises that Frederick, a 19th-century Duke of York, who marched his men up and down the hill, would have been much better employed at the golf in the manner of his forebears and successors.

All the foregoing had to do with the amateur. What gave golf its worldwide pre-eminence, most importantly in America, was the emergence of the professional. The golf professional was early on the sporting scene, but considerably later than such paid men as the gladiators of ancient Rome and the servant of the huntsman and the angler – the gillie.

# Nature plays its part in golf's evolution

LEITH LINKS, upon which the Duke of York and his shoemaker partner triumphed, were typical of the natural golfing ground that gives the Scottish game its unique characteristics.

No earth-shifting equipment or pick and shovel brigades created these courses, but the movement of the waters over the ages which left the sandy, grassy rolling wastes that were fertile only for golfers. Rabbits and grazing animals nibbled back the grasses, and winds and animal hoofs tore holes in the turf that became natural bunkers: Leith Links was the course of the Honourable Company of Edinburgh Golfers.

These courses were without many of the features we associate with golf today, such as neatly marked off tees or clearly defined fairways or greens (the whole course was known as "the green", which explains "green keeper" and "green committee"). They had bunkers, rough, gorse and other delights, supplied by

Hell Bunker, one of the most feared landmarks at St Andrews.

nature, but no defined fairways, and, certainly until 1744, there were no written rules.

All this changed when Edinburgh town council provided a silver club to be competed for annually over the Leith Links, the winner to assume the title and duties of "Captain of Golf", the

duties to include settlement of all disputes on points of play.

The competition was rather grandly offered to "Noblemen or Gentlemen or other Golfers, from any part of Great Britain or Ireland", but the entry list of 12 contained only local players, of whom only ten competed on the

day. Stroke play had yet to be invented. Match play was the thing, and five pairings were drawn from a hat, the biggest winner by way of holes up to receive club and captaincy. The champion proved to be a surgeon named John Rattray, who also won in the second year.

The Honourable Company drew up a set of rules – their membership conveniently included members of the legal profession well able to take on such a task – because they had hoped that the total number of entrants would be swollen by players from near and far, and confusion over playing conditions was to be avoided.

The pattern of club competition as a catalyst for the foundation of golf clubs was followed elsewhere, notably ten years later at St Andrews, on May 14. Royal & Ancient as the club based at St Andrews is, it is not as ancient as the Honourable Company, now

*Continued overleaf*

# 18 holes, and a set of Rules

*Continued from page 13*

based at Muirfield, nor, as we shall see, was it the first royal club. The Royal & Ancient followed the Honourable Company's lead as to a code of rules, and took as their guide much of the Edinburgh wording, as follows:

*1 You must tee your ball within a clublength of the hole.*

*2 Your tee must be upon the ground.*

*3 You are not to change the ball which you strike off the tee.*

*4 You are not to remove stones, bones, or any break-club for the sake of playing your ball, except upon the fair green, and that only within a clublength of your ball.*

*5 If your ball come among water or any watery filth, you are at liberty to take out your ball and throw it behind the hazard six yards at least; you may play it with any club, and allow your adversary a stroke for so getting out your ball.*

*6 If your balls be found anywhere touching one another, you are to lift the first ball until you play the last.*

*7 At holing you are to play your ball honestly for the hole, and not to play upon your adversary's ball, not lying in your way to the hole.*

*8 If you should lose your ball by its being taken up or any other way, you are to go back to the spot where you struck last and drop another ball and allow your adversary a stroke for the misfortune.*

*9 No man at holing his ball is to be allowed to mark his way to the hole with his club or anything else.*

*10 If a ball is stopped by any person, horse, dog or anything else, the ball so stopped must be played where it lies.*

*11 If you draw your club in order to strike and proceed so far with your stroke as to be bringing down your club, if then your club should break in any way, it is to be accounted a stroke.*

*12 He whose ball lies farthest from the hole is obliged to play first.*

*13 Neither trench, ditch, or dike made for the preservation of the links, nor the Scholars' Holes, nor the Soldiers' Lines, shall be accounted a hazard, but the ball is to be taken out, teed, and played with any iron club.*

The St Andrews course, eventually to become "The Old Course" as others were formed alongside, had 12 holes at this time, but they were played – and some replayed – in such an order that a round consisted of 22 holes. Golfers played 11 holes out, turned to play 10 of the 11 in reverse order and then took on a lone hole near the start.

In 1764 the Society of St Andrews Golfers converted the first four holes into two. This also meant that the last four holes became two holes – leaving 18 holes in all.

As St Andrews moved slowly towards its present eminence, latterly alongside the United States Golf Association, as arbiter of all things in golf, the course became more fashionable than any other,

**A bunker made by nature at Westward Ho! in Devon.**

and the somewhat arbitrary number of 18 holes for a round was accepted worldwide.

The foundation in 1766 of the first English club followed a competition at Blackheath for a Silver Driver. The second, Old Manchester, founded in 1814 by William Mitchell, was not active

until four years later on Kersal Moor, Salford. The founders were nine businessmen, several in textiles. The club still exists, but lost its course in 1960, and sold up everything but its trophies, which are still played for on neighbouring courses by its limited membership.

# Choose your weapon: the golf ball takes shape

GOLF, its professionals and its amateur adherents are and always have been profoundly affected by the nature, performance, supply and price of the

**Early golf balls: featheries from the 1840s.**

golf ball. The first notable professional, Allan Robertson of St Andrews, was the grandson of a feathery-ball maker and the son of a caddie – a word which the

game undoubtedly owes to that same Mary Queen of Scots, on account of the young noblemen (cadets) she brought to Scotland from the French court. The word was amended and put to disparaging uses at first by the Scots. It came to mean "hanger-on", later "porter" and then, in a purely golfing sense, "club or bag carrier".

The Robertsons had been engaged in making featheries for 100 years. A hatful of feathers stuffed into a leather sphere is a simple concept, but demanded great skill to produce, especially in large quantities. Robertson's business turned out more than 2,000 annually.

They were expensive, because even the best maker could manage only three or four a day. In optimum conditions

they were gratifyingly lively projectiles as they sprang off the club face. A Royal & Ancient gold medal winner of the 1820s is credited with a drive of 361 yards with a feathery, though he had the advantage of a hard, frosty surface and the wide open space of St Andrews.

Featheries were soon damaged by clumsy players, and were not at their best in wet weather, tending to burst when saturated. It was in the manufacture of featheries that Robertson, helped in his kitchen "factory" by Tom Morris and Willie Lang, was prospering when in 1848, the year of revolutions across Europe, this, the main industry of St Andrews, was threatened by a new product, the gutty.

This ball, made of the coagulated and moulded juice of the

gutta-percha tree, happened almost by accident. The first gutties were fashioned from strips of gutta-percha used to protect a fragile item sent from India by a missionary. They served better and were not so dear as the feathery, and it was possible to remould a damaged gutty. The first gutties, moulded by hand, were smooth and traced an erratic path through the air. Professional Willie Dunn noticed that

old, scuffed gutties flew straighter than new ones. Soon the gutty was being hand-punched in regular patterns and later machine-moulded.

Moreover, the gutty was not only more robust, but featheries cost half a crown (12 ½ pence) – a great deal of money in mid 19th-century Britain. Robertson could see his business going out of the window, metaphorically speaking (he had actually sold featheries

out of his kitchen window close to the links). Other makers were also alarmed, but Tom Morris differed on the subject, and the partnership broke up when Robertson found Morris playing with a gutty. The newcomer soon proved itself a boon to the professionals, though it was several years before the feathery was phased out. The cheaper ball made golf more accessible to the less well-heeled, and sales of

balls and clubs began to move ever more quickly. Robertson was not to enjoy the fruits of this golfing boom. Jaundice carried him off in 1859 at the age of 44.

He had begun to use the gutty himself while Morris went off to work as green keeper at the new Prestwick course south of Glasgow, not surpassingly rich with an income of £50 a year. In 1851 Tom's wife gave birth to Tom junior.

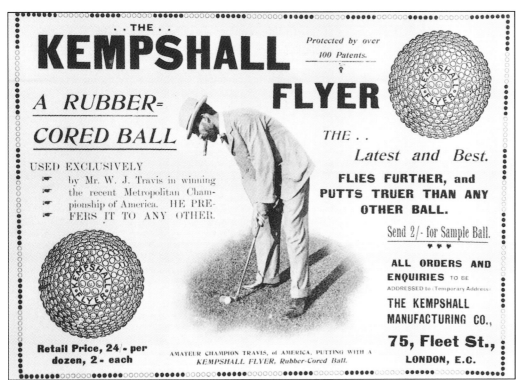

Walter Travis with an early rubber core.

## TEE TALK

### "It's nae gowff."

ALLAN ROBERTSON,
of the gutty ball.

Allan Robertson.

# St Andrews' uniqueness makes it a shrine

THE EXTRAORDINARY basic fact about St Andrews is that in 1552 the right of citizens to play on the links "at golff, futball, schuteing at all gamis with all other maner of passtime ..." was confirmed by the licence granted by the Archbishop of St Andrews, John Hamilton.

This confirmation of rights long enjoyed by the citizens specified that no impediment to these rights should be imposed "in any tyme coming", though this did not extend to those who played when they should have been at their devotions, and who were fined for their transgressions.

These rights were repeated at intervals and, even after parts of the links were sold 200 years ago, the new owner was bound not to plough up any part of the links "in all time coming" but to reserve them for the comfort or amusement of the inhabitants and others.

"Others" has come to mean golfers from every part of the world, so that a round at the headquarters of golf is no longer free, and permission and a tee-time have to be arranged.

St Andrews' Old Course foundation date is given as "circa 1400" in the *Sunday Telegraph* golf course guide, which warns the visitors that tee-times are allotted by ballot, so massive is the demand. When blocks of tee-times were sold to a major travel agent and ticket agency, local hotels suffered and the idea was soon dropped.

The most successful golfer of all time as far as the number of major events won is concerned, Jack Nicklaus, explained his fascination with St Andrews rather differently. It was, he said, the only course he knew that started in the

middle of town, went out into the country and then came back again.

Bobby Jones, another of the game's immortals, had an awful first experience of the course, departing from the scene with round unfinished. But he came to love the place.

Another unique property of the course is that, because of the narrowness of the strip of land upon which it winds away from, and then back to, the city, there are six double greens, each with two holes, which serve the 2nd, 3rd, 4th, 5th, 6th and 8th on the way out, and the 10th, 12th, 13th, 14th, 15th and 16th on the way home. Since the golfer starts from the tenth tee, it is from the peculiar St Andrews pattern of play that the terms "out' and "home" are derived, and which are thus highly inappropriate for

the thousands of courses that have loops of nine holes beginning and ending at the clubhouse. The course also pioneered separate fairways and greens for each

## TEE TALK

### "Oh, sir, ye see, onybody can teach thae laddies in Latin and Greek. But gowf, ye see sir, gowf requires a heid."

ST ANDREWS CADDIE,
to a professor of literature struggling on the links.

# Quest for a champion leads to the Open

THE UNDERLYING reason for the creation of the Open championship, it was said, was the need, because of Robertson's death, to settle who was the new champion.

He was, without doubt, the outstanding player of his day, though the claim that he was never beaten must be taken with a bigger pinch of salt than the Scots use with their porridge. He and Tom Morris triumphed in a number of foursomes for sizeable stakes, though Robertson seems to have avoided taking on Morris in single combat for serious money.

The pair of them beat Willie and Jamie Dunn in a £400 series over three courses. Robertson acted with commendable caution in taking on Tom Morris, in view of the subsequent career and titles of the postman's son who became, as "Old Tom Morris" the most respected figure in Scottish golfing history. Robertson was not a big hitter but, like every great player since, constantly discouraged opponents by putting his approach shots close to the hole. In the feathery days he used the wooden baffing spoon to flick the ball up. With the gutty, he began to employ an iron club to nip the ball up and, so adept was he at these strokes, that his lifetime eclectic score at St Andrews – that is, the total of his best scores on each hole over the years – was 56. The year before his death he became the first man to break 80 there.

Robertson's legacy to the game is a great one, however. He is credited with having laid out ten holes at one of Scotland's most famed courses, Carnoustie.

It was dropped from the Open Championship rota for 23 years because of lack of facilities, notably accommodation, but by 1999 a new hotel and other improvements brought back the Open – won by Scotland's first resident champion for 106 years, Paul Lawrie.

Young Tom Morris, who would go on to win four Opens.

Old Tom Morris: Grand Old Man of golf.

St Andrews pictured in the 1850s: Tom Morris extreme left, Allan Robertson third from right.

# Stroke play becomes the championship norm

STROKE PLAY is a relatively modern invention, succinctly defined in 1759 by a St Andrews ruling that their Silver Club competition founded five years earlier would be won by whoever "puts in the ball at the fewest strokes over the field, being 22 holes". The ruling also reiterated the "play the ball as it lies" principle. This was the system employed for the game's first major event, the Open competition signposted in the late 1850s by an inter-club foursomes competition suggested by Prestwick.

Eleven pairs competed at St Andrews. The winners at match play were Blackheath's George Glennie and Lieut. J.C.Stewart. St Andrews was well known to both men, who represented the only English club to enter in July 1857. The following year a singles event, forerunner of the British Amateur championship, was held, also at match play, and won by Robert Chambers. He beat "Old Wallace" in the final, his phlegmatic and easy-going nature proof against the frustrations of the pace at which Wallace played, which was funereal. The problem of slow play has outlasted him by over a century.

This amateur series continued with victory for Robert Condie of Perth in 1859, when Allan Robertson died. The innovators of Prestwick then turned their minds to the question of a competition for professionals.

George Glennie: Blackheath winner at St Andrews.

# Scotland's sporting legacy to the world at large

SCOTLAND'S next great contributions to the growth of golf included the first women's club – founded at St Andrews in 1867 – and the spreading by its citizens of the game throughout the world. Many of the early members of the first English club, Blackheath, were Scottish exiles. Britons on holiday prompted the construction of the first continental golf course at Pau, in France, close to the Pyrenees.

Among the oldest established clubs overseas are Calcutta, 1829, and Bombay, set up 14 years later. Both were later granted royal status. The Indian clubs quickly took up the idea of a national championship, and the first amateur title there was won by F.J.McNair in 1892, making the championship the oldest amateur event of its type apart from those in the British Isles.

Courses proliferated all over the East, but not until early in the 20th century was the first Japanese course opened. The post-1945 explosion of Japanese golf has made up for the late start in a country notoriously short of suitable golfing land. Most golfers there have to limit their golf activities to driving ranges. Entry fees to clubs and green fees are prohibitive for the majority. The Japanese will go a long way to play golf – and they do, regularly, to Hawaii and Australasia. Their businessmen overseas play at such Japanese-owned courses as Old Thorns in Hampshire, with its palatial Japanese restaurant.

Canada's senior club, Montreal, was established in 1873, 15 years before golf began to take a permanent hold in the United States. Within a decade of this, golf clubs had been established in every part of the British Empire.

Golf at Pau, in France, the first continental course, constructed by holidaying Britons.

Founder member of the oldest English club, Royal Blackheath, with caddie. Golf bags were not invented till the late 19th century.

# The rebirth of golf in the New World

THE BIRTH, or more properly, rebirth of golf in the United States has been well recorded. Early flickers of activity, mostly to be detected from newspaper advertisements, faded out long before the setting up of America's own St Andrew's club in Yonkers, New York, in 1888.

Scottish army officers golfed in the same area more than a 100 years earlier, during the Revolutionary War, and in the last decades of the 18th century American newspapers carried notices of golf clubs formed (those responsible being mainly Scottish merchants) and the availability of the Dutch game at a kolf-bann. These traces vanish soon after 1800.

H.B.Martin, in his "Fifty Years of American Golf" believes that golf at Harleston Green in America's south went on for about 25 years before ending, not altogether surprisingly, at the time of the War of 1812 when British troops burned down the White House.

American distrust of sports imported from Britain was long-lived, according to George Peper's article on the "Birth of an American Passion" in "Golf in America".

Cricket had never taken a

strong hold; the nation was struggling to cope with westward migration and the death and destruction caused by the Civil War. America was a nation of spectators, not players, says Peper, and baseball and football cast their spells.

Salvation was at hand, though America took a good deal of nudging before embracing the game that was to enliven a billion weekends and provide the United States with many of its greatest sporting glories.

Despite the slow start, America was the world's dominant golfing nation within 40 years. So it has remained, with only the briefest interludes of doubt or defeat for the stars and stripes, amateur or professional, men or women.

Dunfermline, north of Edinburgh, can take a good deal of credit for re-lighting the golf flame – aptly enough, on George Washington's birthday, February 22, 1888.

The link with the home of golf was direct. Robert Lockhart, a New York linen merchant, was from Dunfermline, and so was his friend and neighbour in Yonkers, John Reid, who managed an iron works. They had gone to school together in Scotland, and Lockhart had played as a youth on the links at Musselburgh outside Edinburgh.

He often went back to Scotland after settling in New York and, before the epoch-making golf enterprise, he had brought tennis rackets and balls, but the Yonkers' set did not take to the court game.

How different the welcome given to the golf clubs – made by Old Tom Morris himself – that Lockhart brought back in 1887 from Fife. Tom was by this time resident professional at St Andrews.

Lockhart's purchases were six clubs and 24 gutties. The clubs were a driver, a brassie (two wood), spoon (three wood) and three irons, including a putter. The whole lot cost only a few dollars. Today, at auction they would command many thousands.

Lockhart tried them out in a park. Some say he was arrested for playing in Central Park, some that one shot almost took the ear off an ice-man. Lockhart's son, Sydney, recalls that a mounted policeman got down off his horse to have a go and produced an excellent drive at the first time of

asking. Then he whiffed four times, and departed "with a look of disgust on his face".

The mood was far more progressive on Washington's birthday the following February. Reid, recognized as the father of American golf, and five friends laid out a three-hole course on pasture land. He and John Upham played a match: all present were instantly hooked.

Larger pastures were soon resorted to and, before the new converts reached their permanent home at Hastings by the Hudson, they were for some time playing on land studded with apple trees, which led to their being nicknamed the "Apple Tree Gang".

Indeed, some members were not a little upset when a supposedly new and better location had no apple trees, and players lost the challenge of flying them, which some considered the acme of golfing skill. Would it be altogether too fanciful to imagine

**John Reid: acknowledged father of American golf.**

that the American penchant for the high-flying shot dropping on to the target was born here?

The United States Golf Association was formed in 1894 and the game in America expanded rapidly, as did the USGA's horizons, which brought some early disagreements with the Royal & Ancient, particularly on the rules and equipment.

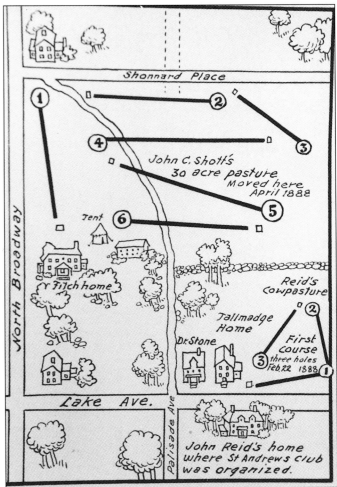

**Early layouts of the American St Andrew's.**

# Golf triumphs in the United States

BY THE end of 1888 a club had been formed, St Andrew's by name, complete with apostrophe, as distinct from the original, which has no such adornment.

The romance of the name certainly had its effect, because the activities of Reid and his friends attracted far more interest, and imitators, than, for example, the Oakhurst Club founded in western Virginia in 1884.

More importantly, the St Andrew's club was present at the formation of the United States Golf Association in 1894, along with Newport, Shinnecock Hills, The Country Club of Brookline, Massachusetts and the Chicago Golf Club, where Charles Blair Macdonald was the driving force in the game.

Macdonald was insistent that there was a real need to discover who was the best amateur player in the country. He got his way and, at Newport, went on to win the first US Amateur championship, beating C.E.Sands 12 & 11. Macdonald went on to build a deserved reputation as a designer and builder of fine golf courses.

This was the year of the setting up of the Morristown, a nine-hole course, by a group of New Jersey women, an emancipating event even though men soon took over the running of the club, and the year when the Spalding company sold the first American-made club.

The moment was ripe for an explosion of golf in an era of experiment and invention, the age of Carnegie steel, Edison's electric light and Henry Ford's first automobiles.

If one man can be set alongside Reid as chief begetter of America's fixation with golf, it is Harry Vardon, master golfer of the era.

His Spalding-sponsored tour, undertaken when he was reigning British Open champion in 1900, turned fledgling American enthusiasm into a relentless search for the perfect, elegant control of the ball that Vardon, at his best, demonstrated.

There was also the example of J.H.Taylor to admire. Taylor had twice won the Open championship and won it again later in the year to draw level with Vardon at three titles apiece.

American golfing tastes have tended always towards stroke play rather than the match play that dominated the early period of golf development. This is illustrated by the diminishing appeal of the US PGA, which from its inception in 1916 was until 1958 a match play event.

**Charles Blair Macdonald, first official US Amateur champion.**

**Social whirl at The Country Club, Brookline, in the 1890s.**

**Harry Vardon: missionary work in the United States.**

# Willie Park takes championship belt in Prestwick 'Open'

AT THEIR spring meeting on May 30, 1860, Prestwick Golf Club agreed to Major J.O.Fairlie's suggestion that "a private subscription should be opened with a view to procure a Medal for professionals to be competed for under regulations submitted to the meeting".

Five guineas were subscribed right away at the meeting, but since other clubs did not join in this initiative, Prestwick took on the administration of the event.

A challenge belt of red morocco leather adorned with silver plates and costing 30 guineas was to be the prize, and not the medal originally envis-

aged. The belt was to become the permanent property of any player winning it three times in succession.

Eight players, seven hailing from Scottish clubs and one from Blackheath – the only English golf club apart from the Old Manchester – took part in the contest held at Prestwick on Wednesday, October 17.

Willie Park of Musselburgh won by two strokes from Tom Morris of the host club over 36 holes – three rounds of Prestwick's 12 holes. The scores, not considered to be outstanding by any means, included a 21 at one hole.

The 1860 champion wearing the belt, the original trophy.

**Willie Park Senior, winner of the first (all-pro) "Open".**

## Old Tom 13 strokes ahead

TOM MORRIS SENIOR, who was 39 years old at the time of the first championship, won the 1862 Open at Prestwick by 13 strokes from Willie Park. His 36-hole total was 163, as in the previous year.

The rivalry between the two men was beginning to add spice to the Open. Amateur chal-

lengers, who must have thought they could do at least as well as the professionals after the poor scoring in the first championship, found the going tough in the third event. James Knight of Prestwick was 23 strokes behind Tom Morris, and J.F.Johnstone, also of the host club, 45 strokes adrift of the winner.

## Second Open is truly 'open'

PRESTWICK'S 1861 spring meeting responded to pleas, after Park's victory the previous year, that amateurs should be eligible to play for the belt, naming eight clubs whose members might enter, including Blackheath.

Clubs who were not named protested and, on the eve of the championship, which was played on September 26, the committee unanimously decided that "the belt to be played for tomorrow and on all future occasions until it be otherwise resolved, shall be open to all the world".

So Tom Morris senior won the second competition for the championship belt, and with it the first Open, pushing Willie

Park into second place by achieving the lowest score of the day on the final 12 holes, which he completed in 53 shots, six better than Park, who was four shots behind overall.

Park was a daring player and, like the late Allan Robertson, an innovative shot-maker. Park went down as the man who said: "A man who can putt is a match for any man."

But he lacked Tom Morris's ability to avoid error and paid dearly, according to a report by the "Ayrshire Express", for trying to cross Prestwick's formidable "Alps" hole in two shots. This misadventure added three shots to his score.

# Willie Park levels score

WILLIE PARK could not equal Tom Morris's two belt-winning totals of 163 but took his second championship at Prestwick in 1863, returning 168 for 36 holes. He had the satisfaction of winning £10 to add to his trophy, from the biggest field yet in the event, 14 competitors having been attracted by the addition of prize money.

## SCORECARD

**1860 scores (full details not recorded)**

| | | | | |
|---|---|---|---|---|
| Willie Park Snr (Musselburgh) | 55 | 59 | 60 | 174 |
| Tom Morris (Prestwick) | 58 | 59 | 59 | 176 |
| Andrew Strath (St Andrews) | | | | 180 |
| Bob Andrew (Perth) | | | | 191 |
| Daniel Brown (Blackheath) | | | | 192 |
| Charlie Hunter (Prestwick St Nicholas) | | | | 195 |
| Alexander Smith (Bruntsfield) | | | | 196 |
| William Steel (Bruntsfield) | | | | 232 |

**1861: final total**

| | | | | |
|---|---|---|---|---|
| Tom Morris Snr (Prestwick) | 54 | 56 | 53 | 163 |
| Willie Park (Musselburgh) | 54 | 54 | 59 | 167 |
| William Dow (Musselburgh) | 59 | 58 | 54 | 171 |
| David Park (Musselburgh) | 58 | 57 | 57 | 172 |
| Robert Andrew (Perth) | 58 | 61 | 56 | 175 |
| Robert McEwan (Bruntsfield) | 56 | 60 | 62 | 178 |
| William Dunn (Blackheath) | 61 | 59 | 60 | 180 |
| Col JO Fairlie (Prestwick) | | | | 184 |
| George Brown (St Andrews) | 65 | 60 | 60 | 185 |
| Mr Robert Chambers Jnr (Prestwick) | | | | 187 |
| James Dunn (Blackheath) | 63 | 62 | 63 | 188 |
| Charles Hunter (Prestwick) | 67 | 64 | 59 | 190 |

**1862: leading totals**

| | | | | |
|---|---|---|---|---|
| Tom Morris Snr (Prestwick) | 52 | 55 | 56 | 163 |
| Willie Park (Musselburgh) | 59 | 59 | 58 | 176 |
| Charles Hunter (Prestwick) | 60 | 60 | 58 | 178 |

# Tom Morris completes hat-trick

TOM MORRIS SENIOR, who had come so close to retiring the championship belt the previous year, gained his third Open championship win at Prestwick in 1864, this time with Andrew Strath from St Andrews as his closest rival.

Willie Park could do no better than fourth place, ten strokes in arrears, his worst showing in five attempts. He could not recover after a disastrous 67 over the middle 12 holes of the event. It amounted to his worst return by seven shots.

Young Tom Morris was also drawing crowds. He was 13 when he made his first public appearance at a tournament in Perth. He was too young to enter the senior event, but played an exhibition match against another promising youngster, William Greig, a member of the local club.

Young Tom was reported to be "born and bred to golf" and possessed of all the steady, sure qualities that had brought his father repeated Open success. Greig lost heavily against Young Tom, watched by hundreds who must have wondered at the brilliance of the precocious pair.

# Park lands third crown

TOM MORRIS travelled back to his old stamping grounds at Prestwick for the seventh Open in 1866, but had to give best to Willie Park, whose score, though seven shots worse than Strath's the previous year, was good enough to give him title number three, which Morris had achieved two years earlier. Another of the Park family, David, was two strokes away second, with Robert Andrew a respectful five shots further back, two ahead of Morris senior.

The seventh Open was the first occasion on which official scorecards were used.

## SCORECARD

**1863: leading totals**

| | | | | |
|---|---|---|---|---|
| Willie Park (Musselburgh ) | 56 | 54 | 58 | 168 |
| Tom Morris Snr (Prestwick) | 56 | 58 | 56 | 170 |
| David Park (Musselburgh) | 55 | 63 | 54 | 172 |
| Andrew Strath (St Andrews) | 61 | 55 | 58 | 174 |

**1864: leading totals**

| | | | | |
|---|---|---|---|---|
| Tom Morris Snr (Prestwick ) | 54 | 58 | 55 | 167 |
| Andrew Strath (St Andrews) | 56 | 57 | 56 | 169 |
| Robert Andrew (Perth) | 57 | 58 | 60 | 175 |
| Willie Park (Musselburgh) | 55 | 67 | 55 | 177 |

**1865: leading totals**

| | | | | |
|---|---|---|---|---|
| Andrew Strath (St Andrews) | 55 | 54 | 53 | 162 |
| Willie Park (Musselburgh) | 56 | 52 | 56 | 164 |

**1866: leading totals**

| | | | | |
|---|---|---|---|---|
| Willie Park (Musselburgh) | 54 | 56 | 59 | 169 |
| David Park (Musselburgh) | 58 | 57 | 56 | 171 |
| Robert Andrew (Perth) | 58 | 59 | 59 | 176 |
| Tom Morris Snr (St Andrews) | 61 | 58 | 59 | 178 |

# Andrew Strath breaks big two's stranglehold

ANDREW STRATH born in St Andrews and a resident in the town of his birth, won the sixth championship staged by Prestwick in 1865 and broke the stranglehold Tom Morris and Willie Park had gained on the title.

Strath's 36-hole total of 162 was the lowest yet, one stroke fewer than Morris had achieved in 1861 and 1862. Strath improved his score by one stroke each round, beating Park by two. He left three-times champion Morris 12 strokes behind.

Morris had been tempted back to St Andrews by the Green Committee's offer of £50 to take charge of the course.

He was presented with his symbols of office – a barrow, spade and shovel – and was offered a labourer to do the heavy green-keeping work.

**Members gather outside the R&A Clubhouse soon after its opening.**

# Great year for the Morrises

TOM MORRIS SENIOR proved two strokes too good for Willie Park at Prestwick in 1867 and was, at 46 years of age, able to buckle on the belt for the fourth time. Andrew Strath was third and young Tom Morris fourth, five shots behind his father.

In a tournament at Carnoustie, Young Tom, now 16, also defeated all the leading professionals, including Willie Park and Robert Andrew in a play-off. Andrew, twice as old as Young Tom, was Perth's sporting hero and rejoiced in the nickname of "The Rook".

He played many matches against the Morrises, whose partnership became as effective in big money matches as that of the elder Morris with Allan Robertson, who had won many a hard-fought match with the Dunn brothers. Andrew got the better of the Morrises on one occasion in spectacular style; his ball finished inches from the hole after knocking off a spectator's top-hat.

The continuing rivalry between the senior Tom Morris and the senior Willie Park went in its earliest days much in favour of Park, thanks to his 1860 win and his victory in the first challenge match in which the two of them met.

Though Morris lacked Park's mercurial brilliance, he had greater staying power, and went on to get the better of their frequent clashes. All the same, Park was never out of the first four in the first eight years of the Open, scoring three wins.

Old Tom Morris, winner of the first true Open.

Musselburgh caddie "Fiery", so called because of his ruddy complexion.

## SCORECARD

**1867: leading totals**

| | | | | |
|---|---|---|---|---|
| Tom Morris Snr (St Andrews) | 58 | 54 | 58 | 170 |
| Willie Park (Musselburgh) | 58 | 56 | 58 | 172 |
| Andrew Strath (St Andrews) | 61 | 57 | 56 | 174 |
| Tom Morris Jnr (St Andrews) | 58 | 59 | 58 | 175 |

**1868: leading totals**

| | | | | |
|---|---|---|---|---|
| Tom Morris Jnr (St Andrews) | 50 | 55 | 52 | 157 |
| Robert Andrew (Perth) | 53 | 54 | 52 | 159 |
| Willie Park (Musselburgh) | 58 | 50 | 54 | 162 |

**1869: leading totals**

| | | | | |
|---|---|---|---|---|
| Tom Morris Jnr (St Andrews) | 51 | 54 | 49 | 154 |
| Tom Morris Snr (St Andrews) | 54 | 50 | 53 | 157 |
| Mr S Mure Fergusson (Royal & Ancient) | 57 | 54 | 54 | 165 |
| Bob Kirk (St Andrews) | 53 | 58 | 57 | 168 |
| David Strath (St Andrews) | 53 | 56 | 60 | 169 |
| Jamie Anderson (St Andrews) | 60 | 56 | 57 | 173 |

## St Andrews trio make their mark

ALL TOP SIX players in the 1869 Open at Prestwick were from St Andrews.

Young Tom Morris retained his title by three strokes from his resurgent father. Old Tom equalled his son's record 157 of the previous year, but young Tom set another mark by completing his final round of Prestwick's 12 holes in 49 strokes – one over fours.

Mr S.Mure Fergusson of the Royal & Ancient Club made the best showing so far by an amateur in the championship, though he was 11 strokes behind in third place.

## St Andrews open first women's club

VOTES FOR WOMEN were a long way off, but golf for women was an established fact long before. In the same year as Tom Morris captured his fourth championship, the ladies of St Andrews formed the world's first ladies' golf club.

## First hole in one to Young Tom

YOUNG TOM MORRIS gained his first Open title at Prestwick in 1868 and lowered the record for the 36 holes by five shots to 157. He was the youngest champion so far.

In the process he performed the first hole in one in the history of the championship, at the eighth hole. Robert Andrew was two shots adrift, but had the consolation of being the only other golfer to break 160 since the championship began. Willie Park came third, while Morris senior took, amazingly for a four-time winner, 21 strokes too many. He was sixth, four behind John Allan from Devon, England's first links course, founded four years earlier. The elder Morris had been closely involved with the setting out of Westward Ho!, as he was with Royal Dornoch, Carnoustie, Royal County Down, Nairn and Lahinch.

# Young Tom and Old Tom

## The Morrises dominated golf in the Victorian era: the son's brilliant career was curtailed by a tragic early death, the father's steady skills spanned two generations

**The Morrises, father and son.**

TRIUMPH AND TRAGEDY were never more poignantly juxtaposed than in the brief and glorious career of Young Tom Morris, who remains the only golfer to win the Open Championship on four consecutive occasions, and is still the youngest Open champion of them all, at 17 years. His glittering talent was lost to the game before he had attained his quarter century. The game's consolation was that his father, for Old Tom became golf's most revered figure at St Andrews, lived on into the 20th century to witness the flowering of a sport he and his son had done so much to inspire.

### Golfing stalwart

It is difficult to discover a word written or said against Old Tom. He was still a useful golfer at 80, and though steady was the name of his game, putting was some-

times not. He took part in every Championship (winning four times) from 1860 to 1896, the year Harry Vardon won the first of his six titles. Between them, father and son Morris won eight Opens in the first 12 years of the competition's existence.

What the father achieved by application and an enviable capacity for keeping his ball out of trouble, the son achieved in shorter time with an astounding series of attacks on course records, and the pockets of those who ventured to bet against him. Young Tom's most celebrated performance earned him his hattrick of Opens in 1870 and thus the Championship Belt to keep.

### Peerless performer

It is a pointless exercise to compare players of one era with another, but one can say for Young Tom that his 1870 score of 149 for 36 holes was not equalled while the gutty ball was in use, so that his performance was not matched for a generation. Moreover, reckoning Young Tom's score as an average of 74.5 strokes for 18 holes, then not for 34 years, until the advent of the

livelier rubber-wound ball, did an Open champion cut his average per round to 74, which was Jack White's winning performance at Royal St George's in 1904.

Young Tom piled up these scores on rough and natural terrain. He was not spoken of as a particularly smooth swinger, but his game had no weakness, especially with the touch shots round greens. Leonard Crawley, the former English Amateur champion and for many years golf correspondent of the Daily Telegraph, used to say that a golfer was either born with quick hands or he wasn't. Such was the decisive power of the young Morris's fingers and wrists that he was reputed to have snapped shafts merely by the force of his preparatory waggles. His Scots bonnet would fly off at such moments too.

He developed the use of the mashie, and gave a fine exhibition of its powers in matches with Arthur Molesworth, an amateur from Westward Ho! making the ball bite and stick on a wintry day on the small areas of grass round the holes which had been cleared of snow.

After his fourth Open title in a row, which made him the first

winner of the present silver claret jug trophy at the age of 21, his play lacked its former dominance, though he was highly placed in both the 1873 and 1874 Opens.

### Family tragedy

All ended sadly in 1875. A telegram called him home to St Andrews from North Berwick, where he and his father were playing a challenge match against Willie and Mungo Park. His wife was in labour and dangerously ill. To save time, rather than journeying by way of Edinburgh, father and son sailed home across the Firth of Forth in a yacht belonging to John Lewis, an Edinburgh golfer. Shortly after he left the boat, Young Tom received a second telegram. Mother and child were both dead.

Legends have embroidered the story of Young Tom's death three months or so later: he had resorted to the bottle in his grief, some said, others that his heart was broken. The autopsy had it rather more prosaically that he had burst a blood vessel in a lung. He was found dead in bed on Christmas morning, 1875.

**Young Tom's Memorial**

| **SCORECARD** |
| --- |
| British Open |
| |
| **Young Tom** |
| 1868 (Prestwick, Scot) |
| 1869 (Prestwick, Scot) |
| 1870 (Prestwick, Scot) |
| 1872 (Prestwick, Scot)* |
| *1871 no championship took place |
| |
| **Old Tom** |
| 1861 (Prestwick, Scot) |
| 1862 (Prestwick, Scot) |
| 1864 (Prestwick, Scot) |
| 1867 (Prestwick, Scot) |

## TOM MORRIS' 1870 RECORD CARD

| Hole | Name | Yards | Bogey | Score |
|---|---|---|---|---|
| 1 | Back of Cardinal | 578 | 5 | 3 |
| 2 | Alps | 391 | 5 | 5 |
| 3 | Tunnel (Red) | 167 | 3 | 3 |
| 4 | Stone Dyke | 482 | 5 | 5 |
| 5 | Sea He'therick | 460 | 5 | 6 |
| 6 | Tunnel (White) | 350 | 4 | 3 |
| 7 | Green Hollow | 165 | 3 | 3 |
| 8 | Station | 162 | 3 | 3 |
| 9 | Burn | 298 | 5 | 4 |
| 10 | Lunch House | 290 | 4 | 3 |
| 11 | Short | 97 | 3 | 4 |
| 12 | Home | 359 | 4 | 5 |
| Total | | 3799 | 49 | 47 |

## SCORECARD

**1870: leading totals**

Tom Morris Jnr (St Andrews)  47 51 51 149

Bob Kirk (Royal Blackheath)  52 52 57 161

David Strath (St Andrews)  54 49 58 161

Tom Morris Snr (St Andrews)  56 52 54 162

**Selected totals**

Willie Park (Musselburgh)  171

Jamie Anderson (St Andrews)  174

John Allan (Westward Ho!)  176

**1872: leading totals**

Tom Morris Jnr (St Andrews)  57 56 63 166

David Strath (St Andrews)  56 52 61 169

Mr William Doleman (Musselburgh)
 63 60 54 177

Tom Morris Snr (St Andrews)  62 60 57 179

David Park (Musselburgh)  61 57 61 179

# Young Tom retires the belt

YOUNG TOM MORRIS succeeded in 1870 where his father had so narrowly failed seven years earlier by knocking his gutty ball round Prestwick's 3,799-yard, 12-hole layout three times for a total of 149 strokes. His victory, by 12 strokes, from Bob Kirk of Royal Blackheath and Tom's great friend, David Strath, meant that the championship belt of red morocco decorated with silver

*A mid-19th century club and hand-hammered gutta-perch ball.*

plates became the permanent property of Tom Morris junior. His father missed his chance of retiring the belt when Willie Park edged past him in 1863.

It was not only the capture of the belt that distinguished Young Tom's triumph, but also the remarkable first round that put him ahead to stay. He was round in 47 strokes, two under par, beginning with an awesome three at the 578-yard first hole. Four under par after ten holes, he must have been nettled when he dropped a shot at the 11th (called Short, of 97 yards) and the 12th, Home Hole, of 259 yards. Having got one hand on the belt, the champion allowed no-one to make a meaningful challenge in rounds two and three, both of which he completed in 51 strokes, a better score than any other player achieved in the entire championship, with the shining exception of David Strath's 49 in the second round.

# Champion Tom sets another record

THE NEW Open trophy and gold medal were expected to attract a bigger entry to Prestwick in 1872, but only eight competitors turned up – the same number as at the first championship 12 years earlier.

Another feature had not changed either – the winner was Young Tom Morris. Although his score was 17 shots higher than two years before, mainly because of severe weather, his fourth consecutive win was another record.

David Strath was again runner-up, this time on his own, three strokes behind. Strath was five shots ahead of the champion with one round to go, but faded to 61 at the death.

An amateur from Musselburgh, William Doleman, who was a regular in the Open, gained renown for taking two strokes fewer than the elder Morris.

The new trophy was in fact not to be presented for another 12 months because the silver claret jug, only recently commissioned, was not completed in time for the 1872 event. The medal served as a temporary presentation and the trophy was engraved at a later date.

**David Strath: refused to play off with Bob Martin in 1876.**

# Tom Kidd breaks the mould in a high scoring Open win

TOM KIDD'S victory in the first St Andrews Open, in 1873, was by virtue of the highest winning score yet recorded. The weather was good, but scoring on the Old Course was not easy, even for the locals among the record entry of 26. Not surprisingly, Kidd and five other golfers in the top seven were St Andreans. The driving rain from Thursday to Saturday may have served to reduce the number of anticipated entries.

Four of the 26 competitors bore the now hallowed name Morris. Young Tom of that ilk was third, three behind Jamie Anderson, whose 89 in the final round was one too many to catch Kidd.

Old Tom took ten shots too many and, well down the final order, were Old Tom's second son, J.O.F.Morris, and his nephew, Jack, who had three years before taken up the position of professional at the newly founded Hoylake Club on the Cheshire coast. Jack, like Old Tom, was a link with the pre-championship days.

On one occasion Allan Robertson had given him a sixpence. "That was a lot of money for a poor boy in those days," said Jack.

As for the mystery of the high scores that week, local newspapers reported that the weather could not be blamed. 'The putting greens were in fine condition,' reported one publication. "New holes had been cut. But pools of water on the greens added considerably to the hazards and militated against good scores."

"The Field" recorded that the course was "rather damp and in many places covered with water". Lifting the ball from casual water at this time was done under penalty of one shot.

Kidd would earn a living as a St Andrews caddie. The best caddies would earn up to 1/6d for a round. It meant that Kidd could not afford to travel far on such meagre earnings. He did, however, find enough wherewithal to defend his title at Musselburgh the following year, finishing a highly respectable eighth.

One aspect of competition play at this time was the speed of play, which would not start until almost 10.30 a.m. — leaving them very little October daylight to complete 36 holes.

# Big Three fill trophy gap with silver claret jug

TOM MORRIS, the triple champion, went on beating all comers – he once wagered he could score 83 every day for a week at St Andrews (no small task) and won the bet.

Meanwhile Prestwick's committee looked about them for a means of reviving the Open after a blank 1871 brought about by the permanent departure of the original trophy to the Morris household.

The solution was found in an alliance with the Royal & Ancient Club and the Honourable Company of Edinburgh Golfers. These three clubs bought a silver claret jug, and there was also to be a gold medal awarded each year for the Open champion. But he would have to hand back the silver jug, for this was to be a perpetual trophy.

The organizers clearly had their eye on the reigning champion, who had three Opens under his championship belt at 19 years of age, and looked all too capable of another hat-trick.

A further major change in the championship was the decision to stage the event in rotation over the links of Prestwick, St Andrews and Musselburgh, to which the Honourable Company, Bruntsfield and Edinburgh Burgess golfers had moved from Leith and Bruntsfield.

A number of high profile challenge matches were taking place between the leading players. One such duel fought between Young Tom Morris and

David Strath in 1873, took place over six rounds in three days at St Andrews. Young Tom ran out the winner of this epic, 4 & 3.

## TEE TALK

> "An amateur golfer truly moves heaven and earth."
> ANON.

**Old Tom Morris plaque at St Andrews.**

# Parks land brotherly double at home

MUNGO PARK beat Young Tom Morris by two shots to win the first Open to be played at Musselburgh, his home course, in 1874.

Like many golf professionals, Mungo Park, brother of Willie, the first champion, could not earn a living from playing the game.

Mungo was a seafaring man before getting his name added to golf's roll of honour. Another Musselburgh player, George

Paxton, was a stroke behind Young Tom, whose father, now 53, faded to joint 18th, alongside David Strath.

Willie Park, restored to his best form, gained his fourth championship the following year when the Open returned to Prestwick and for the first time the name of Morris did not appear among the challengers for the title – and this in the same year as Young Tom's untimely death.

# A tie and trouble at St Andrews

BOB MARTIN of St Andrews became the 1876 champion on his own links after a thoroughly mismanaged event which involved the leading players in the first serious dispute to disrupt the championship.

This cannot have impressed King Leopold of the Belgians, who played himself in as Royal & Ancient captain at the club's autumn meeting. Leopold was a golfer, having taken up the game at the instigation of his physician, who had played a round at Carnoustie and thought that golf might benefit the prince's health.

The Open followed and contenders found themselves having to share the links with weekend players, the event being contested on Saturday, September 30.

This was the second Open to be contested at St Andrews, but there was enough untoward incident to suggest that it was an apprentice effort. At least the administration could not be blamed for the weather, which was bad, or the scores which, accordingly, were high.

David Strath's total of 176 was compiled in exactly the same fashion as Martin's 86+90. Strath's first-round total included an improbable missed putt from two inches at the 15th. All the same, his total offered him his best chance yet of the title, but a muddle over the rules cost him dearly.

Martin finished first, and Strath's inward progress, avidly watched by a huge gallery, was interrupted when, as he played the Long Hole In, his ball hit the forehead of an upholsterer playing out on an outward hole. The injured man recovered well enough to be able to walk home, but Strath, shaken, dropped a shot, and another at the next. He needed fives at the last two holes to win: a good third shot to the 17th brought him his first five, but he had a six at the last, so the scores were tied.

A protest was entered that Strath's well-directed approach to the 17th had arrived there before the players in front had cleared the green. The inference was that his ball had been prevented from going on to the Road, though this point seems never to have been resolved.

The Royal & Ancient had omitted to appoint a referee to settle such a dispute. The committee ordered a play-off for the following Monday, but Strath held that the protest should be settled before the play-off since, if he lost the verdict, a contest would be superfluous.

On the appointed day Strath was absent, Martin walked the course and walked off with the title. Strath was awarded the second prize of £5, bringing the whole conduct of the committee into question. Martin seems to have become champion on the basis of Strath's having committed no more than a breach of etiquette.

Bob Martin's contentious first Open victory.

# Universities tee off

YET ANOTHER St Andrean spreader of the golfing gospel made his mark on the game's progress in 1875, when W.T.Linskill founded the Cambridge University Golf Club. Cambridge had, much earlier, been a prime mover in the development of soccer, putting together the first written laws, but efforts on the golfing front, despite inter-college play in the late 1860s, were less successful. The Open remained the only fixture of note, and the amateur championships that had preceded it 20 years before had not been staged again.

An Oxford club was also formed in 1875, and land around a college cricket ground was put into service as a course. However, it could be used only out of the cricket season. These pioneer efforts were rewarded on March 6, 1878, when Oxford won the first University match at the Wimbledon course of the London Scottish club. Cambridge lost all four of the singles matches that made up the event, Oxford winning by 24 holes overall, though W.Adams did well to lose by only three holes against Horace Hutchinson, in a troublesome breeze. Hutchinson was outstanding among amateurs of the day.

Cambridge got their own back in 1879. Oxford's transport arrangements were not conducive to thoughts of victory despite the continued presence of Hutchinson, beaten by F.G.H. Pattison after being three up with five to play, and Stuart.

H.G.Hutchinson, university golf pioneer.

# Three course hat-trick

JAMIE ANDERSON, who had been knocking at the Open door for several years, reached the top of his profession with a trio of titles, won at Musselburgh, Prestwick and St Andrews in turn, to round out the 1870s.

Only the second golfer to win three Opens in a row, he was, significantly, like Willie Park, a consummate putter. He did not share Park's dashing approach through the green, but he did provide an astounding finish in gaining his second title at Prestwick.

J.O.F.Morris, who had taken Young Tom's place in challenge matches in partnership with their father, had finished in 161. Anderson had therefore to cover the last four holes in 17 shots in order to win: he thought he could do it in 5, 4, 3 and 5.

In the event he holed a full iron shot for a three at the first of the four finishing holes, keeping to his plan with a four at the next, though it required a huge, across-the-green putt. Then he played his ace at the Short, where he overhit his tee shot, but his ball trickled back off a mound at the back edge of the green and rolled into the hole. A five at the last meant he had covered the closing four holes in 13 strokes – three better than Young Tom Morris with his marvellous 47 in 1870.

Even this bravura finale was only just good enough, for Bob Kirk was threatening to catch Anderson at the last gasp, and had a sizeable putt at the last for a four to tie. He hit the hole, but

Thomas Hodges's 1880 sketch of Jamie Anderson, Open champion.

the ball would not go underground, and Kirk in his anguish or frustration missed the little one back, and so lost by two shots.

The threat of Scotland's monopoly of the title being broken by golfers from south of the border became ever more apparent as the 1870s drew to a close. John Ball, a 14-year-old amateur from Hoylake, was in joint fourth place in 1878, and James Allan from Westward Ho! was joint runner-up in 1879. There was a record entry of 46 this year.

Anderson would prove a great role model for the following generation's players. One youngster, from Earlsferry, 12 miles from St Andrews, watched his idol entranced. "I followed him around like a little dog", the nine-year-old would recall in later years. Anderson took time to make the boy's acquaintance and watched him hit a few balls. He told the lad that, if he paid attention to his game, he, too, might become Open champion one day. That youngster's name? James Braid.

# Women's clubs multiply

MUSSELBURGH and Wimbledon founded women's clubs in 1872. The Musselburgh fish ladies had long been active golfers, with a Shrove Tuesday match in which the "marrieds" are reputed always to have beaten the "unmarrieds". These initiatives came five years after the first such club, at St Andrews. Westward Ho! were second in 1868.

Carnoustie followed their lead in 1873, and Pau in France in 1874. This did not mean that women golfers were to be granted equal playing facilities with their menfolk. "Ladies links", in the opinion of Lord Westwood, in "Badminton Golf", "should be laid out on the model, though on a smaller scale, of the 'long round' containing some short putting holes, some longer holes admitting a drive or two of 70 or 80 yards ... the posture and gestures requisite for a full swing are not particularly graceful when the player is clad in female dress."

Miss A. M. Steward in "The Gentlewomen's Book of Sports", held that "a damsel with even one modest putter in her hand was labelled a fast and almost disreputable person".

An early (patented) golf bag and stand.

The R&A medal, won in 1875-7 by Leslie Balfour-Melville.

# Amateurs regain centre stage

AS WITH Prestwick's initiative in setting up the British Open championship, the Amateur championship was a gift to golf by a single innovative club, this time English. It was founded in 1869 on the Cheshire coast south of Liverpool, which was the name, after some changes of mind, finally decided upon by the members.

The land, at Hoylake, still in use as a racetrack for some time after the club came into being, was the place from which William III, some 200 years earlier, had embarked his 10,000 men for the Irish campaign that ended with the defeat of that royal golfer James II.

The club had gained the "Royal" prefix by the time its committee announced a tournament "open to all amateur golfers" to be played from April 20 to April 23, 1885: entry fee, one guinea.

It was won by a Scot, Allan MacFie, who was a member of the host club, and played under a curious set of rules that were not employed the following year, when Royal Liverpool suggested the event should be taken under the wing of the Royal & Ancient.

MacFie was one of three semifinalists surviving from an entry of 48. Matches level after 18 holes were not to go to extra holes, but were replayed. Byes were not eliminated in the first round, so with an entry of 48, three men reached the semifinals.

MacFie got a bye into the final, and beat Horace Hutchinson, also of the home club, by 7 & 6. MacFie was lucky to get his bye at the penultimate stage, but less so earlier when he had to play three 18-hole matches against Walter de Zoete of Blackheath before progressing from the fourth round, on account of the no sudden-death ruling.

He was helped in his third confrontation with de Zoete by holing his tee shot at "The Rushes" hole, and went on to win by two holes.

Hutchinson won at St Andrews in 1886, when straight match play was the order of the day. Two of the 44 entries were disqualified because they had acted as caddies, and were deemed professionals.

The definition of "professional" is already, and no doubt will continue, causing contro-

**Allan MacFie, first British Amateur champion.**

**TEE TALK**

### "Nothing handicaps you so much in golf as honesty."

ANON.

versy. Douglas Rolland was ruled out of amateur play because he had accepted prize money as runner-up in the 1884 Open.

It looked as if John Ball's amateur status would go the same way because he had accepted ten shillings for a high finish in the Open. However, he avoided loss of status because he took the cash before his 16th birthday.

St Andrews, 1886, marks the formal launching of the Amateur championship. The event, won by MacFie at Royal Liverpool, was not immediately recognized as being an official competition for the Amateur championship of Great Britain.

Hutchinson won again when the Amateur returned to Hoylake the following year, getting home at the 18th against the formidable John Ball, who had lost in the semifinal at St Andrews. The number of entrants declined to 33.

**Horace Hutchinson gets his tee shot away, watched by youthful caddies.**

# Ferguson's fourth Open title slips away

HARDLY HAD the cheers for Jamie Anderson's run of three Open championships died away, than Bob Ferguson, the strongly built Musselburgh golfer, who had been winning prize money from the age of 18, started on a hat-trick that came within a whisker of being a four in a row sequence to equal Young Tom Morris's record.

Ferguson had been too good to the tune of four holes against Young Tom at Prestwick, in a challenge match in which the two men used only a cleek – for Ferguson it was something of a magic wand.

His skill, strength, calm demeanour and ability to play his game in the most unhelpful weather made him invincible in the 1880, 1881 and 1882 Opens, and in many other competitions. His 1881 win was achieved against the background of one of the worst storms ever to strike Scotland, in which scores of fishermen lost their lives in the disaster.

Ferguson's star faded after his narrow defeat by Willie Fernie at Musselburgh in 1883, a decline hastened by a bout of typhoid.

Willie Fernie had signposted his challenge, as so often happens in golf, by advancing to runner-up at St Andrews the previous year, when Jamie Anderson subsided to joint third place in company with John Kirkaldy, Bob Martin and an amateur, Fitz Boothby. A curious point about Fernie's win was that his play-off against Ferguson, the first in Open history, was reached by virtue of a 36-hole total of 159, which included a ten.

Ferguson's route to the play-off proves his unshakeable temperament: the requirement for tying with Fernie was threes at each of the last three holes. Ferguson got them.

The play-off was a knife-edge affair, with nothing much in it for 35 holes, at which point Ferguson was a stroke to the good. He got his par four at the last, but lost his title because Fernie drove the green and inserted a lengthy putt for a two.

Fernie certainly worked hard to get his hands on the silver jug, and he was second again in 1884, jointly with Douglas Rolland of Elie and one stroke behind Jack Simpson, Carnoustie's first champion.

Bob Martin regained the trophy at home at St Andrews in 1885, after a nine-year interval since he had won over the same course.

It was horses for courses again in 1886, David Brown of Musselburgh holding off other locals, Willie and Ben Campbell, with steady scoring. He was the first to break 80 in both rounds over the course.

Bob Ferguson: three Opens in a row.

Johnny Laidlay gets his short game in order.

# Johnny Laidlay, golfer by moonlight

JOHN BALL was not to be denied in 1888, defeating Johnny Laidlay 5 & 4 at Prestwick. Laidlay, who was also an excellent cricketer, had been taught by Bob Ferguson, at Musselburgh, on moonlit nights, it is said, while absent without leave from Loretto School.

Laidlay's record outside the major events is full of remarkable feats of low scoring, with a 70 at North Berwick and 77 at St Andrews, where Open leaders were commonly scoring in the 80s. Laidlay came back to take the Amateur in 1889 and, just as with Old Tom Morris and Willie Park, the rivalry between the two Johnnies, Ball and Laidlay, and Horatio Hutchinson, fired public imagination. Royal Liverpool's reputation as a nursery for winners was made, with MacFie and Ball. Hutchinson and Laidlay were members at Hoylake, though it was not their home club.

**"A man who can't putt at Hoylake – can't putt."**

Said of the turf at Royal Liverpool.

**"One can feel so lonely at St Andrews missing a putt."**

ANON.

# Blackpool's loss is Lytham and St Anne's gain

A LONE FIGURE could be seen playing on the sand dunes at St Anne's on the Lancashire coast off and on during the mid-1880s, and on February 23, 1886, he took steps to obtain some company. The figure was that of Alexander Doleman, a Scots exile, who had tried to arouse an interest in golf among the sportsmen of Blackpool, and was now trying again a little further south, with the letter in the panel (right) to likely recruits.

The letter was signed by J.T. and J.S.Fair, but the club's historian is in no doubt that they had been encouraged by Doleman.

*"Dear Sir,
It is proposed to form a Golf Club in this district, to be called 'The Lytham and St Anne's Golf Club.' Very suitable 'Links' can be obtained close to St Anne's station. A meeting for furthering the above scheme will be held at the St Anne's Hotel on Saturday next, the 27th inst, at 8 pm, which you are earnestly requested to attend."*

The club was duly established that Saturday by 19 founder members, who fixed the annual subscription at one guinea.

"Ladies introduced by Members and subject to the will of the Council to use the Links on payment of five shillings per annum." Caddie charges were to be nine pence for 18 holes, but this was considered too much and soon reduced to six pence.

It was decided to open the links on the following Saturday, March 6, weather permitting. Remarkably enough, this was achieved.

The St Anne's Hotel became the clubhouse and, by arrangement with the railway company, a bell was installed which rang to signal the arrival of a train.

This would give the golfer just enough time "to finish his glass, collect his hat and coat, say goodbye to his friends and reach the platform, just across the road".

The first tee was only 50 yards from the station, a crucial factor in locating a golf course in the ever more prospering age of the railway. And the relationship between the railway and golf courses is evident elsewhere in the country.

27.—J. E. LAIDLAY.

25.—J. BALL.
A Celebrated Golf Ball

24.—HAROLD HILTON.

**Amateur heroes on cigarette cards: Johnny Laidlay, John Ball and Harold Hilton.**

# The financial rewards

DAVID BROWN'S CAREER was further proof of the poor financial pickings in contemporary golf. He played only when the building trade was short of work, or when prize money was available close to home.

Jack Burns, the 1888 champion, was a plasterer and, though he obtained a golfing position at Warwick, later preferred more regular work plate-laying on the railway. This explained his reply to questions about his golf to the effect that he had not been off the line for years. Willie Park junior, son of the inaugural Open champion, was the winner either side of Burns, and proved himself a man of parts, since he was a considerable businessman, and club designer.

He sold many thousands, and did his best to provide weapons that would deliver lesser players from hooks and slices. His "lofter" club was described thus:

"Without being either a lofting-iron or a mashie, it partakes of the nature and characteristics of both; its shape brings the upper part of the blade, which is very concave, nearer to the ball and so, while less turf is taken, a very considerable backspin is put upon the ball, which is sent very high in the air and falls almost without any roll."

Park also played in many big money matches, one of the most famous being the one in which he beat the St Andrews' favourite Andrew Kirkaldy, this in the same year as he outscored Kirkaldy by five shots in a play-off for his second Open.

Among his greatest strengths was his putting. He followed the fashion for having names for favourite clubs: his putter was "Old Pawky" – an accurate summing up of its capabilities, for "pawky" in Scotland means "sly", "arch", "quiet", "dry".

# The club flourishes

THE FIRST competition at Lytham and St Anne's was held within two months of the club's inception and, surprisingly, won by captain-to-be John Mugliston, since he was not one of the two competitors who were the only ones who, up to six weeks previously, had so much as seen the game played. This was a typical whirlwind creation of a club, as the game began to take a firm hold in England, greatly encouraged by the foundation of the Amateur championship. Club founders were usually businessmen with an eye to the main chance, as witness the election to honorary membership at Lytham and St Anne's of two individuals at the opening prize-giving dinner. One of them owned Headroomgate Farm, over which many of the holes were played.

Also typical was the decision to hold no further meetings till the autumn, since golf was very much a winter game. In two years the membership had reached 57.

By the end of the 1880s it was organizing a professional tournament, the principal meeting for prize money (£53 was on offer) apart from the Open itself. First prize went to Willie Fernie, with a fair showing of Open "regulars" in pursuit, including the Kirkaldys, Willie Park, Sandy Herd, Jack Morris (the professional at Royal Liverpool) and his uncle, Old Tom Morris, now in his 69th year. The bookmakers had it right, with Fernie and the runner-up, Archie Simpson, as favourites.

Doleman was the Lytham captain in 1888-89. No Scot did more to spread the game than he did. Born in Musselburgh in 1838, he trained as a teacher and also served in the army. He taught at Sedbergh school, then founded one of his own in Blackpool. A member of both Royal Musselburgh and Royal Liverpool, he had played with feathery and gutty, and watched the celebrated match between the Dunns and Allan Robertson and Tom Morris in 1849. Apart from being a violinist of talent, he was a fair golfer, and came ninth in the 1870 Open.

**Willie Fernie: two at the last forces Open play-off with Bob Ferguson.**

## SCORECARD

**Open**

1880, Musselburgh: Bob Ferguson (Musselburgh) 162

1881, Prestwick: Bob Ferguson 170

1882, St Andrews: Bob Ferguson 171

1883, Musselburgh: Willie Fernie (Dumfries) 159 (after play-off with Ferguson 158-159)

1884, Prestwick: Jack Simpson (Carnoustie) 160

1885, St Andrews: Bob Martin (St Andrews) 171

1886, Musselburgh : David Brown (Musselburgh) 157

1887, Prestwick: Willie Park Jnr (Musselburgh) 161

1888, St Andrews: Jack Burns (Warwick) 171

1889, Musselburgh: Willie Park Jnr 155 (after play-off with Andrew Kirkaldy 158-163)

**Amateur**

1885, Hoylake: AF MacFie bt HG Hutchinson 7 & 6

1886, St Andrews: HG Hutchinson bt H Lamb 1h

1887, Hoylake: HG Hutchinson bt J Ball 1h

1888, Prestwick: J Ball bt JE Laidlay 5 & 4

1889, St Andrews: JE Laidlay bt LMB Melville 2 & 1

## TEE TALK

**"A man who can putt is a match for anyone."**

WILLIE PARK SENIOR.

# Amateur John Ball bursts into Scots' charmed circle

IT FINALLY happened at the 1890 Open championship at Prestwick. It had taken 30 years for an amateur to outplay the Scottish professionals and, when one did, it turned out that he was an Englishman into the bargain – John Ball from Royal Liverpool. He left Willie Fernie, now established at Troon, and Archie Simpson three strokes behind with two rounds of 82, and Willie Park a further three adrift.

Ball achieved another first by becoming Amateur and Open champion in 1890, but then he had got into the winning habit early in life.

At eight, he had won the Boys' medal at Hoylake. His great golfing advantage in life – apart from a rich vein of talent – was that his father, John senior, owned the Royal Hotel, the original Royal Liverpool clubhouse.

Ball first competed in the Open championship in 1878 at the age of 17, and finished in fourth place.

Bernard Darwin of The Times was not the man to lavish praise unduly, but he waxed lyrical about the delights of watching the play of this slight, stooping idol of the galleries. He said: "I should get more aesthetic ecstasy watching him that Bobby Jones and Harry Vardon together."

**John Ball: first amateur to win the British Open championship, and first to win Open and Amateur titles in the same year – 1890.**

### TEE TALK

## "Hitting my drives the right height for the day."

JOHN BALL,
on how he won the 1890 Open.

Ball's modesty was more than a byword – it was a definite barrier to journalists, to whom he did not grant interviews. His method was all his own and he used the old fashioned grip, both hands well under the shaft, but there was no impression of tension in his swing and, as with Bob Ferguson, close pursuit by other players was unlikely to shake him out of a winning position.

Hugh Kirkaldy took the trophy back into the keeping of the Scottish professionals in 1891, with Andrew Kirkaldy in second place along with Willie Fernie.

A Scottish amateur, Mure Fergusson of the Royal & Ancient, played a good hand, only four shots behind the winner.

**Willie Park junior on the tee in a match with Andrew Kirkaldy (far left).**

# Prize money up but amateurs prosper

THE MOVE of the Honourable Company of Edinburgh Golfers to Muirfield, further to the east of Edinburgh, was followed by radical changes in the Open championship from 1882. This was the first 72-hole championship – 36 holes per day.

The prize money almost quadrupled to £110, but there was a small entry fee. And the 1890s, rapidly becoming the golden age of amateurism, had another unpaid champion to applaud, and another Royal Liverpudlian too, Harold Horsfall Hilton. To add to the professional loss of face, John Ball was joint second with the 1891 champion, Hugh Kirkaldy, and Alex Herd, a professional with Huddersfield.

Hilton would amuse the crowd when, as often happened, his cap fell off as he swung through the ball. But his scores were not so amusing to his opponents, especially in this, his finest season to date. Not only was he Open champion, but he came

**Willie Auchterlonie: succeeded Old Tom Morris as pro at St Andrews.**

within a whisker of repeating John Ball's unique Open/ Amateur double of two years earlier. However, John Ball himself got the better of Hilton in the Amateur final at the 17th hole.

**Willie Auchterlonie: made the clubs he won the Open with in 1893**

**Johnny Laidlay missed the 1893 Open by two strokes.**

Like Ball, Hilton had lived close to the Hoylake links and, before he reached the age of 20, he was taking on John Ball senior in his first attempt at the Amateur, and next time out giving best to John Laidlay only on the last green.

Hilton had only a day's intensive practice before his Muirfield victory. He was eight behind at halfway, having faded to 81 in round two, but 72 in the third round was worth second place, and he stood on the 72nd tee having played 68 strokes. An eight would have won the vase. Hilton took six.

This was the year of the first match known to have taken gate money: it was between Jack White and Douglas Rolland. The Open remained one of the best free shows on offer, and now there were four rounds to watch.

Professionals were back in charge at Prestwick in 1893, Willie Auchterlonie of St Andrews taking the trophy, though he had only two strokes to spare over the leading Scots amateur of the day, Johnny Laidlay of the Honourable Company.

Auchterlonie won with clubs of his own making. Alex Herd advanced to third place, and the names of Harry Vardon and J.H. (as he was always known) Taylor were on the entry list for the first time.

# 1893 – emancipation and innovation

ST ANDREWS LADIES' club had attracted 500 members, but there was no "Event" with a capital E to test their skills.

Issette Pearson, first and foremost, was the pioneer who thought very little of the depressingly small pitch and putt courses to which women were usually restricted, with male club members looking on occasionally and somewhat patronizingly. Such courses were dismissed as "nice little hen-runs" by the writer Eleanor Helme.

So it was that, at Issette Pearson's urging, in June 1883, 35 brave spirits converged on Royal Lytham and St Anne's for the first Women's Amateur championship. This was two months after the foundation of the Ladies' Golf Union, with Issette Pearson as secretary.

The successful launch of the championship, won by Lady Margaret Scott from Minchinhampton in Gloucestershire, a slender, dark 18-year-old, who photographed well, provided great satisfaction for Miss Pearson and her committee.

The LGU had asked a leading male golf official for his advice about planning their championship, and his reply had been both depressing and infuriating:

"1. Women never have and never can unite to push any scheme to success...

2. They will never go through one Ladies Championship with credit. Tears will bedew if wigs do not bestrew the green.

3. Constitutionally and physically women are unfitted for golf. They will never last through two rounds of a long course in a day ... the first ladies' championship will be the last ... the LGU seems scarcely worth while."

This pessimist might more truly have said that women's clothes were totally unsuited to golf: stockings, chemise, boned corset, garters, drawers, two petticoats, a long-sleeved blouse fitting closely at the wrist, a long skirt, boater and gloves were the order of the day.

All this did not restrict the playing skills of Lady Margaret, who was as far ahead of her rivals as Allan Robertson or Young Tom Morris had been in their day. Moreover, she had recently come off best in a men's tournament at Cheltenham.

Lady Margaret Scott (in black bobble hat) with rivals, caddies and championship trophy.

Issette Pearson was a most capable opponent for Lady Margaret in the final, but did not have a good temperament in competition.

Moreover, her concentration cannot have been helped by her cares as championship organizer, and she lost 7 & 5. Lady Margaret's father proudly walked the course as his daughter became inaugural champion.

It was the same story the following year when the LGU proved that the one-championship theory was well wide of the mark and Lady Margaret beat Issette Pearson again, this time 3 & 2, at Littlestone in Kent. Lottie Dod, a Wimbledon lawn tennis champion, made her first attempt at the golf title at Littlestone.

In 1895 the LGU staged their championship in a setting still beyond the imaginings of the Royal & Ancient – Royal Portrush in Ireland. Lady Margaret completed the hat-trick, beating Elisabeth Lythgoe 3 & 2.

In 1899, May Hezlet won at 17, the event again being played in Ireland. Edith Orr was the winner when the championship first ventured north of the border, to Gullane, in 1896.

May Hezlet: champion at 17.

# City of the Dead puts life into Woking golf

WOKING GOLF COURSE was built on land that became available at most reasonable cost as a by-product of an 1852 Act of Parliament passed to remedy a pressing health problem in the rapidly growing City of London. The problem was that the inner-London cemeteries were filling up.

The chosen solution was a bold one: the founding of the Necropolis Company, with 2,300 acres of common land costing the company £14 an acre, on which to lay out cemeteries well clear of London's narrow, crowded streets. Trains were run daily from a specially constructed London station to the new cemeteries.

On the front page of the Daily Telegraph on October 6, 1860, Necropolis advertised as follows:

| First class | |
|---|---|
| funeral complete | £17. 4s |
| Second class | £10. 18s |
| Third class | £3. 15s |
| Fourth class | £2. 5s |

Funerals could be ordered from any of six London offices.

Necropolis (meaning "City of the Dead") had land to spare, but found it difficult to sell for building until the turn of the century, when cheap suburban train fares transformed Woking into a dormitory area.

Thus Woking Golf Club acquired land extremely cheaply, and their lease began – rent one shilling – on Christmas Day, 1892. The club was soon on a sound financial footing, and had every reason to be, since it was very much a City of London creation, discussed at a meeting there, in the midst of the world's greatest financial centre. The would-be founders stipulated that there was to be no club unless 100 members of the bar subscribed.

Deal (Royal Cinque Ports) also came into being in 1892, five years after its near neighbour, Royal St George's, on the sand dunes of the east Kent coast.

It was thought in 1893 that there were some 300 courses worldwide. Royal Calcutta, which was the first overseas course, had by then been in existence for over 65 years.

# USGA tackles muddle over Amateur and Open

THE USGA'S main task was to put an end to the title muddles and hold an Open and Amateur event in an orderly fashion. A start was made at Newport in 1895. Evidence of varying attitudes to the professional and amateur games was gleaned from the fact that the Amateur took two or three days in the early years, with the one-day professional event tacked on at the end on the same course.

Macdonald at last got satisfaction. He became amateur champion with a 12 and 11 thrashing of a relative novice, called Charles Sands, of Newport.

Immediately afterwards, the professionals who (and not only in America) were thought to be rather lower down the social scale, competed at match play for the Open title. Better players, indeed, but as newspaper coverage reflected, they were mostly exiled Scots difficult to comprehend and sometimes overly addicted to the wine of that far-off country.

The inaugural US Open was played on October 4, 1895. This and the Amateur had been postponed from September because of a clash with the vastly more important – in most Newport eyes – America's Cup yacht races.

Horace Rawlins, 19, an English professional, became the first Open victor, beating Willie Dunn by two shots with a total of 173 after four rounds of Newport's nine-hole layout by ten professionals and one amateur, a Mr A.W.Smith from Toronto, who came joint third with James Foulis. Rawlins got $150, a $50 gold medal, and the

One of the powerful amateurs from Hoylake, Harold Hilton, who pipped James Braid in the 1897 Open.

Open cup, to take back to his club. Foulis took the prizes the following year over the 18-hole Shinnecock Hills course. Rawlins was runner-up – and Mr Smith again joint third in what the USGA record book describes as, like the first Open, "a side-show to the Amateur".

Open No 3 went to Chicago, Foulis's club, but this time an Englishman won – Joe Lloyd, professional at the Pau Club in the winter, and at the Essex County Club, Massachusetts, in the summer. This was Willie Anderson's first attempt at the US Open, and he led at halfway, but an 84 cost him victory by a stroke.

## TEE TALK

**"Golf does not seem somehow to take such a grip in America as does the other Scotch game, curling … now and again we get from some American papers very queer accounts of the game of golf, so queer that we do not wonder the Yankee does not guess it to be worth his while."**

AMERICAN COMMENTATOR, in 1892.

# America makes it official

NEWS OF the growing popularity of golf in the United States came thick and fast in 1892. Shinnecock Hills built the first clubhouse in the nation, the St Andrew's Club acquired its new nickname of "The Apple Tree Gang" when it moved to a four-acre orchard to the north of its present course, and American industry began to take notice of the game.

An emissary of the sporting goods company, A.G.Spalding & Bros, brought back across the Atlantic an assortment of clubs and balls, as vacation golf venues began to be constructed in Virginia, Florida and California.

The media did their best to hasten the spread of the game, and as early as 1891 Harpers, a new monthly magazine, was gushing about golf's conquest of America and Colorado's sporty course, and grumbling about too many rattlers and cacti in New

Mexico. Nearly all of Long Island is a links, it was reported. Shinnecock Hills was favourably compared to British linksland and it was noted that the holes at Chicago were the same length as those at St Andrews.

Spalding sold the first US-made golf balls in 1894, when it all became a matter of record with the founding of the United States Golf Association.

This did not happen until December, too late to prevent well-meant but muddled attempts to stage national championships.

Three months earlier a band of players, mostly novices who soon dropped out as their scores became almost uncountable, had struggled on the Newport course in Rhode Island in a would-be national amateur championship. Charles Blair Macdonald, who had set up the course in Chicago, was, as befits a former habitué of Tom Morris's shop at St Andrews, a relentless pioneer in the cause of golf.

But he lost this time to a Newport man, William Lawrence, 188 to 189. A stone wall had caused him plenty of trouble, and he considered such hazards as "not golf." St Andrew's put on a match-play event a month later, Macdonald losing again, this time to Laurence Stoddard of the host club.

Lawrence Curtis, prime mover in the formation of The Country Club, Brookline, Massachusetts, joined with

**Charles Blair Macdonald, a hard man to please.**

Henry Tallmadge, one of the original St Andrew's players in Yonkers, and called together five rival clubs to dine at the Calumet Club on Fifth Avenue, New York City. St Andrew's, Chicago, Shinnecock Hills, The Country Club and Newport gave birth to the USGA, with Theodore Havemeyer (Newport) as president.

Havemeyer went on to present a trophy worth $1,000 for the winner of the Amateur competition.

## Coburn Haskell winds up Bounding Billy

PATENT RIGHTS were granted to Coburn Haskell and Bertram Work in 1898 on their invention of a rubber-cored golf ball.

This had a balata cover and inside was a hollow core in which the inventors tried various substances, including compressed air. Rubber strips were wound under tension around the core. The ball, it was claimed, left the club face with greater velocity, and made more ground once it landed.

Some players found it too lively a performer, hence the derivation of the nickname "Bounding Billy".

## SHORT PUTTS

● Golfing terms diverged after the invention in 1899 of "birdie" for one less than par for a hole by golfers at Atlantic City, one of whom, George Crump, put his second shot inches from the hole on a par four after his ball hit a bird in flight. Eagle and double eagle inexorably followed. Britain stuck to bogey.

# New Jersey ladies make their point

IT WAS TO BE expected that John Reid's St Andrew's Club in Yonkers would hold the first mixed foursomes event at the rebirth of American golf in 1899, but such opportunities were rare, and golf was a man's world.

It was equally to be expected that independently minded American women, many of whom were free to expend much time and money on leisure activities as late-19th century technology and the opening up of the west multiplied the numbers of the well-heeled and educated classes, would take measures to end this unemancipated state of affairs even more rapidly than their sisters in Britain.

The women of Morristown in New Jersey met to further this aim, and set up a 6,030-yard course, the Morris County Club,

in 1893. The experiment did not last long, and men soon took over the running of the course, but the women's game was given an important boost by the men who ran the game, the USGA, which was considerably more than the Royal & Ancient could be said to have done in Britain.

The first US Women's Amateur championship was staged – at stroke play for the first and only time – at Meadowbrook, New York, in 1895 and won by Mrs Charles Brown, from Shinnecock Hills, by 132 (69-63) to Miss N.C.Sargent's 134. They had played nine holes morning and afternoon.

Morristown ladies were rewarded in some degree for their earlier initiative, for the second championship, now at match play, was held at their pride and

joy, temporary though their proprietorship had proved. It was won, as it was for the next two years, by America's first dominating woman golfer, Beatrice Hoyt, whose first title came at a mere 16 years of age.

The entry more than doubled at her second victory, to 61, and attracted a huge following from New York – by train, horseless carriage and phaeton they arrived. Miss Hoyt was a smart dresser, and had long hair and a long swing to match, but an accurate game withal.

English clubs remained men's citadels for the most part. Woking decided in 1895 that ladies might subscribe at two guineas per annum (one guinea for members' wives), but they were not to play at weekends and during holidays.

# English takeover gathers strength as Taylor captures Sandwich Open

J.H.TAYLOR won the Open at his second attempt in 1894 on the links of Royal St George's at Sandwich, where the first Open outside Scotland was staged. No English professional had achieved this before, and Taylor was very conscious of the severity of the blow to the Scottish pros, and proud to be leading the English charge.

The following year at St Andrews, Taylor, who was professional at Winchester, proved by finishing at the head of a field including all the Scots and English contenders of note that his first success was by no means just a "home win".

He beat Alex Herd at St Andrews by four strokes, Andrew Kirkaldy by six, Willie Fernie by 15, and the brothers Tom and Harry Vardon, down in joint ninth place, by 16.

Muirfield, 1896, merely brought a different Englishman the title. Harry Vardon, who had moved from Bury to the Ganton club in Yorkshire, tied with Taylor with a total of 316, and won the play-off by two shots, 157 to 159 over 36 holes. To add to the pain for the Scottish professionals, amateur Freddie Tait, of the Black Watch, shared third place with Willie Fernie.

Amateurs were first and third in 1897 at Royal Liverpool, Harold Hilton returning to his best form with a total of 314, one better than James Braid, a Scottish professional based at Romford to the east of London, and three in front of Tait, joint third. This was Hilton's own course, being used for the Open for the first time, but Hilton was as far away as ever from winning the Amateur title despite his two Open successes.

Vardon's second and third

**Champion Freddie Tait.**

Opens at the end of the 1890s meant that the decade had brought him more wins than the entire establishment of Scottish professionals.

Willie Park junior failed to catch him by a stroke at Prestwick, where he led going into the fourth round and shared with Vardon the honour of being first to break 80 in all four rounds.

It was clear, even from Yonkers, that Vardon was the man of the moment, and in 1898 the far-sighted St Andrew's members guessed what an appearance by the great man would do for golf's good health in the United States.

Many of the Scottish professionals employed in America were not of the highest class with a club in their hands, and the story goes that, so keen were clubs to obtain a "fashionable" Scots professional from the land of the game's birth, that they would grab the first immigrant they could find with the right accent.

Nothing came of a St Andrew's (of New York) plan for the leading American clubs to subsidize a Vardon/Braid tour but, since Vardon was still champion the following year, a further approach was made, backed by the Spalding Company, who were about to bring out a new golf ball. The usual claims were made about its superiority over all other gutties. It was to be called the Vardon Flyer. To publicize it, Spaldings sponsored an exhibition tour by Vardon, to begin early in the year 1900.

**Harry Vardon and (right) J.H.Taylor: they took a grip in the 1890s.**

# Record start for Vardon mission

BRITISH OPEN champion Harry Vardon began his American tour in February in New Jersey, moved on to Pinehurst, North Carolina, where he broke the course record with a 71, and proceeded to set up records galore, attracting galleries of more than a thousand at most stops.

Vardon faced an itinerary of 20,000 miles and, after returning home to defend his Open title – he was second to J.H.Taylor at St Andrews by eight strokes, with James Braid a further five shots behind – he returned to win the US Open at the Chicago Club, the first foreign-based professional to do so. Taylor came second in Chicago, beaten by two strokes, though Vardon missed a tiny putt on the final green.

Bernard Nicholls was the only man to beat Vardon in singles play on the tour. The match was played on a course in Ormond, Florida. Most of his matches were played against the best ball of two golfers, yet Vardon lost only 13 out of 87 such matches, for he assessed his form as the best of his life. He was called the "apostle of perfect timing."

Clubs were already multiplying at lightning speed: there was one in every state by this time, 1,000 at least in all, against a mere handful in 1890, and there were now upwards of 200,000 players.

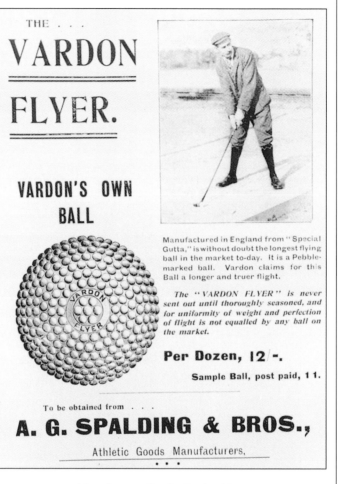

Advertisement for the Vardon Flyer.

## SHORT PUTTS

● Walter J.Travis proved an exception to the rule that champions usually make an early start at the Scottish game when he won the US Amateur at the age of 38. He had not played the game at all till he was 34, which is why he quickly acquired the nickname of "The Old Man." He was born in Australia and came to America as a child.

● Beatrix Hoyt looked a sure thing to win her third Women's title at her home club, but lost to Margaret Curtis – who found Frances Griscom, a deadly putter from the Merion Cricket Club, too much of a handful in the final, going down 6 & 5. Hoyt, now 20, retired.

# Hilton wins at last as golf mourns Tait

HAROLD HILTON, who had lost three Amateur championship finals in the 1890s, at last carried off the title at Royal St George's. There were big gaps in the field, for the game was mourning the loss of Freddie Tait, a favourite of the crowds in the major amateur events, who was killed in February at the head of his company of the Black Watch regiment, attacking a Boer position at Koodoosberg. Tait, aged only 30, was buried beside the Riet River. Reigning champion John Ball had already volunteered for service, at the age of 37, with the Denbighshire Hussars as a trooper.

Tait's outgoing personality and never-say-die attitude in match play were the virtues that made him so watchable. His father was a professor of natural history at St Andrews University, and published a paper which held that a ball would not travel further than 190 yards on a calm day.

Tait junior's experiences on the tee tended to contradict this claim, for he was a prodigious hitter, a useful talent which helped towards his first Amateur win, when he beat Hilton in the final, after dismissing John Ball, Horace Hutchinson and John Laidlaw.

**Freddie Tait of the Black Watch.**

**Professor Tait: golf theorist.**

Laidlay was the true progenitor of the grip ascribed to Vardon but no doubt it became asociated with the now triple champion because he made better use of it than any of his peers.

Frederick Guthrie Tait was forever on the go – his 1898 diary records 99 days of golf, nearly all of 36 holes. Lytham members put a memorial box holding the Tait medal and a list of the members who subscribed for it in their clubhouse.

## TEE TALK

**"If profanity had an influence on the flight of the ball, the game would be played far better than it is."**

HORACE HUTCHINSON.

# James Braid breaks Taylor-Vardon grip

JAMES BRAID had been making it clear for years that he would be strong competition for J.H.Taylor and Harry Vardon, who had won five of the previous six Open championships. He made good his threat to the English pair, and the final reckoning at Muirfield on June 6 resulted in this order – Braid 309, Vardon 312, Taylor 313 – exactly the reverse of the top three in last year's Open.

Braid was born at Earlsferry in Fife, so the Scottish galleries at last had one of their own to cheer. It was their first chance to do so since Willie Auchterlonie's win at Prestwick eight years before. Braid was tall and renowned for his length off the tee, no matter how boisterous the wind. He was the archetypal laconic Scot, with a long, leisurely, mile-eating stride and the ability to stay calm, no matter how uncooperative the weather or aggressive his opponents. Added to his long driving was the sec-

**James Braid: held off Vardon.**

ond crucial element for success, getting up and down from just off the green.

Braid had left his native land early in his career to cross either the border or the Atlantic, and was now professional at Romford in Essex. He had been accustomed to using a cleek for putting for some time, failing by a fraction to tie with Harold Hilton when the great amateur won in 1897. His putting improved when he gave up using the cleek, and changed to an aluminuum putter.

He started the 1901 Open badly, hooking out of bounds. Out in 43, he recovered with 36 home, and he won despite a last round of 80. The scoring was less impressive in the US Open at the Myopia Hunt Club in Massachussetts. Willie Anderson and Alex Smith, tied on the highest 72-hole finishing total yet, 331. Anderson won the play-off over 18 holes by a stroke with an 85, and with it his first US Open.

# Hilton at the double after his long wait

HAROLD HILTON found that a long sought-after ambition, once achieved, is not so difficult to duplicate. So he won his second Amateur championship off the reel at St Andrews.

He was the first to retain the title since Horace Hutchinson in 1887. He was now 42, but clearly far from a spent force, as John Low discovered in a final which was fought down to the last hole.

Hutchinson achieved great renown as a writer on a variety of outdoor sports, golf naturally, plus cricket and tennis. His instructional series "Golf: The Badminton Library" went into its seventh printing this year. Success at amateur golf seemed to fan the flames of writing talent: Walter Travis the American Champion, also put out an instructional book, Practical Golf.

# Travis proves virtues of 'Haskell'

THE VIRTUES of the rubber-cored ball, patented by Coburn Haskell three years before but not yet taken up by the majority of players, were made clear to all by that deep thinker among golfers, Walter Travis, in the US Amateur championship at the Country Club of Atlantic City, New Jersey.

On September 14, a week later than scheduled because of the death of President William McKinley, the championship ended with victory for Travis over Walter Egan from Onwentsia by 5 & 4 in the final.

So Travis emulated the British Amateur Harold Hilton in retaining his title, a feat only previously performed in the United States by H.J.Whigham, son-in-law of the first winner, Charles Blair Macdonald.

Entries for the women's event rose to a healthy 84, Baltusrol in New Jersey being chosen as the venue for the first time. Press opinion was hot for Margaret Curtis to go one better this time, but her sister Harriot lost to her first opponent. Neither could Margaret stay the course, but Genevieve Hecker could, and did, prevailing over Lucy Herron in the final.

Margaret's 204-yard effort in a long-driving competition was some small consolation.

**Walter Travis: emulated Harold Hilton.**

## SCORECARD

**British Open** (Muirfield, Scot)
J Braid 79 76 74 80 309

**US Open** (Myopia Hunt Club, Mass)
W Anderson 84 83 83 81 331
(Anderson beat A Smith in play-off 85-86)

**British Amateur** (St Andrews, Scot)
H Hilton bt JL Low 1h

**US Amateur** (Atlantic City CC, NJ)
WJ Travis bt W Egan 5 & 4

**British Women's Amateur** (Aberdovey, Wales)
M Graham bt R Adair 3 & 1

**US Women's Amateur** (Baltusrol, NJ)
G Hecker bt L Herron 5 & 3

# Haskell makes a winning mark

COBURN HASKELL'S two-piece ball reached even deeper into professional and public consciousness. It had soft rubber intestines, but was not at all queasy about air travel and was very lively upon landing.

On both sides of the Atlantic it was the winning ball in the Open championship. In June, at Hoylake, Alexander "Sandy" Herd used it to hold off Harry Vardon and James Braid by a stroke.

In October Laurie Auchterlonie at Garden City used it and became the first to break 80 in all four rounds of the Open. Herd, a noted club waggler at address, had not intended to waggle at a Haskell ball until persuaded to have a go with one just before the championship. The resultant lengthy drive converted him to Haskell on the spot. His was the only non-gutty ball in Open play. It was expensive, because still scarce. But Herd's was a bargain, and he made it last throughout the championship.

Though outshone so often by the Vardon/Braid/Taylor trio, Herd, professional at Huddersfield in Yorkshire, was nevertheless constantly in action with them, playing with Braid against the English pair in many an "international" challenge. He was no slowcoach despite his waggling, which many copied as a loosener before hitting.

Auchterlonie was not pressed over the final 18 holes, winning by six strokes from Stewart Gardner and Walter Travis, both of the New Jersey host club. As if to prove the consistent qualities of the Haskell, both Opens were won with the same 307 total.

All was not completely plain sailing with the Haskell. It was not an instant success. Like the early, smooth gutty it had an uncertain flight path until the right dimpled pattern was found for the balata cover to correct its vagaries. Moreover, Haskell had to face patent problems in court, dealing with British claims that the concept of the rubber-wound ball had been registered a generation ago.

Laurie Auchterlonie: easily held off closest pursuers.

Sandy Herd: "Haskell" convert.

## James the last beats Travis to become James the first

LOUIS JAMES got the last match play place in the US Amateur at Glen View, near Chicago, with the highest score of the 64 qualifiers, but finished the winner by beating Eben Byers in the final: Walter Travis was joint top qualifier, but his title hat-trick hopes ended in round three.

At the age of 53 Charles Hutchings deserted the gutties he had used all his life in order to defeat Sidney Fry in the British Amateur at Royal Liverpool. Fry used the same ball but lost the final by one hole.

May Hezlet, one of three Irish golfing sisters, carried off the British Women's title at Royal Cinque Ports, Deal, and Genevieve Hecker kept her US title, prevailing by 4 & 3 in the final against Louisa Wells, who shared top qualifying place with Margaret Curtis. They were the first to break 90.

# Vardon struggles to secure fourth Open

HIS FOURTH Open did not come easily for Harry Vardon. He felt so ill during the championship at Prestwick that he came close to having to withdraw. His fourth round of 78 was his worst, but it still left him six shots clear of his brother Tom. Afterwards, Vardon was diagnosed as suffering from tuberculosis and spent periods of time in sanatoriums.

He had been either first or second in the event for seven of the past eight years. Despite his illness, and growing suspicions that his putting stroke was failing him, he had outdistanced all three of his colleagues in the leading "Quartet" – Taylor, Braid and Herd – by upwards of nine strokes.

Willie Anderson's second US Open was gained, like his first, by way of a play-off. After tying with David Brown on a total of 307, Anderson setting a record 73 in his first round, Anderson became champion by two shots, 82-84.

# Ambassador Adair

RHONA ADAIR, so striking with her red hair and white skin, added a second British Women's Amateur to her four consecutive Irish titles and made a tour of American courses that echoed in a minor key Harry Vardon's role as golfing missionary in 1900.

Adair played at Merion in an invitation event with a strong field, short only of the reigning American champion, Bessie Anthony, and won easily. She reported glowingly on the excellence of courses in the United States and on the rising standards of play.

Bessie Anthony's first championship was gained at the Chicago Club, the furthest west the event had been staged.

She beat J.A.Carpenter by the record margin of 7 & 6. Genevieve Hecker did not travel west to attempt her hat-trick of titles.

**Rhona Adair: United States tour.**

# The Old Man makes it three out of four

WALTER TRAVIS returned to putting invincibility and his third US Amateur at the Nassau County Club, Glen Cove, Long Island, where the losing finalist was again Eben Byers from Allegheny. The event was in Royal & Ancient fashion, all match play.

This was the third Amateur Championship to fall to Travis in four years, and apart from a close call in the quarter-final against G.T.Brokaw of Deal, whom he beat at the 18th, he was never called upon to play the last, winning 5 & 4 against F.O. Reinhart in the semi-final and 5 & 4 again in the final against Byers. Reinhart was champion of the Intercollegiate Golf Association. He came from Princeton, but the dominant force in collegiate golf continued to be Harvard.

**"The fine spirit of their game enlightened the golfing community of America and did much to bring the various warring factions in the States together..."**

CHARLES MACDONALD, of the Oxbridge tour.

## SCORECARD

**British Open** (Prestwick, Scot)
H Vardon 73 77 72 78 300

**US Open** (Baltusrol, NJ)
W Anderson 73 76 76 82 307
(Anderson bt David Brown 82-84 in play-off)

**British Amateur** (Muirfield, Scot)
R Maxwell bt H Hutchinson 7 & 5

**US Amateur** (Nassau CC, NY)
WJ Travis bt E Byers 5 & 4

**British Women's Amateur** (R Portrush, Co Down)
R Adair bt F Leigh-Walker 4 & 3

**US Women's Amateur**, Chicago Ill)
B Anthony bt JA Carpenter 7 & 6

● Oxford and Cambridge Golfing Society, led by a prominent amateur, John Low of Cambridge and Woking, toured the United States, sailing on a ship called the Mayflower, and did not lose a match, in a whirlwind trip of 33 days with ten matches and several stroke play events. Low beat Walter Travis 3 & 2 the week before Travis won the US Amateur.

● Alex Smith, professional at the Nassau Club, venue for the Amateur, won the well-established Western Open at a sodden Milwaukee, needing 318 strokes, a record high-winning total.

● Robert Maxwell, a member at Muirfield, won the British Amateur there with a crushing 7 & 5 final victory over Horace Hutchinson. For the second year in succession Maxwell was also leading amateur in the Open. Not his least remarkable feat had been performed in the 1897 Amateur, when on his first day in major competition he accounted for John Ball and Harold Hilton, also at Muirfield.

● Emsley Carr of the "News of the World" newspaper offered £200 for a match play championship. The PGA accepted and places were allocated to the various PGA regions and James Braid beat Ted Ray in the final, played at Sunningdale. Braid got £100, and there were seven other prizes.

● First international was played at Prestwick, where Scotland beat England 9-8. This followed the setting up of the British PGA the previous year.

● Willie Park senior, winner of the first British Open, died aged 69.

**Willie Park, the first Open champion, dies at 69.**

● First Seniors golf organization set up at the Apawamis Club, Rye, New York.

● Mungo Park, the 1874 British Open champion, died

● Amateur champion Chandler Egan lost his gold medal match in the St Louis Olympic Games to George Lyon, Canada. Though Canada had a club – Royal Montreal – which had been active longer by 15 years than any in America, the first Canadian Open was held nearly ten years after the inaugural US Open. J.H.Oke, professional at Royal Ottawa, won it – at Montreal – with 156 for 18 holes.

● Australia's first Open was won by an amateur Briton, the Hon. Michael Scott, in Sydney.

● Walter Travis lost his US title when in the last eight George Ormiston holed a cleek shot for an eagle.

### SCORECARD

**British Open** (Royal St George's, Kent)
Jack White 80 75 72 69 296

**US Open** (Glen View, Ill)
W Anderson 75 78 78 72 303

**British Amateur** (Royal St George's)
W Travis bt E Blackwell 4 & 3

**US Amateur** (Baltusrol, NJ)
HC Egan bt F Herreshoff 8 & 6

**British Women's Amateur** (Troon, Scot)
L Dod bt M Hezlet 1h

**US Women's Amateur** (Merion, Pa)
G Bishop bt Mrs EF Sanford 5 & 3

**Lottie Dod: lawn tennis and now golf champion.**

# Travis upsets British hierarchy

WALTER TRAVIS raised a few hackles, eyebrows, and many American golfing spirits when he travelled to England and became the first overseas golfer to export the British Amateur championship – this from Royal St George's in Kent.

At 42, he beat former champions Horace Hutchinson and Harold Hilton as well as James Robb, twice a finalist, and went on to take the final by 4 & 3 against Edward Blackwell, who constantly outdrove him by 50 yards.

Travis played in Scotland first, then developed a mood as black as the cigars he was forever drawing upon because, of all things, his putting deserted him just before the Amateur began.

Since putting was his main strength, Travis clearly considered himself to be in deep trouble. Though he was very straight through the green, he was also relatively short, and played many approach shots with a wooden club. A friend suggested that he use a centre-shafted Schenectady putter, patented a year before by Arthur Franklyn Knight, of Schenectady, New York. Suddenly all was well, although he had few anxious moments reaching the final, which was effectively a massive hitter against a dead-eye putter. Willie Park senior's axiom about a man who can putt was never more clearly proven, as Travis continued his relentless holing out of putts of up to 20 yards.

Travis, a taciturn soul, found the English hard to get on with, and the feeling was reciprocated, especially among those who thought this odd putting instrument was in some way unfair. Yet Travis had never used one before he got to Sandwich. All the same, the incident rankled and eventually centre-shafted putters were banned in Britain.

**Walter Travis: putter problems.**

# Jack White first to break 300

JACK WHITE, the Sunningdale professional from North Berwick in Scotland, succeeded at Royal St George's where an admittedly ailing Harry Vardon had failed at Prestwick the previous year, by breaking 300 for four rounds of the British Open.

In doing so, White, with an average of 74 per round, put up, at last, a performance half a stroke better than Young Tom Morris had managed with the gutty over 36 holes 34 years ago. White's achievement was a fine one because, unlike Young Tom, he was being pursued by Taylor, Braid and both Vardons, Tom and Harry, the four of them finishing behind him in that order. He scored better each round, finishing with a wonderful 69, while Taylor scored 68 – failing by a stroke to force a tie.

To Braid fell the honour of being first to break 70 in the Open, with 69 in the third round and, indeed, his last 36 holes in 140 was one better than White's. James Sherlock's second round of 71 was, for a few hours at least, an Open record.

Willie Anderson ensured that it was "as you were" in the US Open, and this time, without the need for a play-off, he became champion for the third time, five shots ahead of Gilbert Nicholls from St Louis.

**Jack White: talented pack in pursuit as he set a record score.**

# Willie Anderson moves way ahead

A FOURTH US Open for Willie Anderson, and his third in a row, were his unique achievements, created by a 314 total at the Myopia Hunt Club, Hamilton, Massachusetts on September 22. Born in North Berwick, the son of a green keeper, Anderson was a wanderer. He was professional at ten clubs in the United States, having left his native land aged 17.

His clubs were, for the most part, at the upper edge of fashion, notably Apawamis, Baltusrol and Ontwentsia. Though he was the first dominating player in America in the 20th century, his swing was right out of the 19th, for at the top of the back-swing his left arm was bent round his right shoulder and the plane was flat. His strengths were, however, off the tee and in his approach shots, and he proved time and again that there is no more fruitful combination. Like J.H.Taylor, he was at his most dangerous with a five iron in his hands.

He is often portrayed as the dourest of dour Scots, but he got on well with his fellow pros, though he cost them plenty of prize money, notably in the Western Open, of which he was a multiple winner. Hope of an Anderson hat-trick seemed remote at Myopia, since he used up 161 strokes on the first two rounds, five behind Alex Smith and Stewart Gardner.

A good start in the third round – two under par after four holes – encouraged him, somewhat uncharacteristically considering his reputation for the laconic, to say "That's the championship." His confidence was totally justified when, with two holes remaining, he had a four-stroke cushion, and though his lead was only two shots over Alex Smith at the end, his victory was comfortable enough.

**Willie Anderson: US hat-trick.**

# Women international trailblazers

THE BRITISH Women's Amateur at Cromer, in Norfolk, was the initial target of the Curtis sisters, Margaret and Harriot, and other leading American players when they sailed to Britain.

The trip provided the opportunity for the first international between the two countries, Britain winning 6-1.

The American party included their 1900 champion, Frances Griscom, Philadelphian and all-round sportswoman, who was a good shot, dashing carriage and four driver, angler and a pioneer of the automobile. There was also the 1904 champion, Georgiana Bishop, and Mary Adams. The British Women's title went to Bertha Thompson.

Back in the States, the autumn battle between Pauline Mackay and Margaret Curtis in the Amateur final at Morris County, New Jersey, was the closest fought yet, Mackay clinching her first title by one hole.

# Braid first but Massy stakes record claim

THE OLD Course sent totals back over the 300-mark after the record low scores at Sandwich in Jack White's Open. James Braid moved up one place for his second Open title, five shots clear of J.H.Taylor, so regaining the trophy although troubled by the fencing along the railway which skirted the closing holes. Seven strokes behind came the first continental player to make a big challenge, Arnaud Massy of France. Braid also won the PGA Matchplay title at Walton Heath, his second victory in three years.

## Egan double

CHANDLER Egan, a Harvard man, enjoyed his golf in Chicago, where he retained the Amateur title at the Chicago club, and beat his brother Walter for the Western Open at nearby Glen View.

**Harriot (left) and Margaret Curtis.**

## SCORECARD

**British Open** (St Andrews, Scot)
James Braid 81 78 78 81 318

**US Open** (Myopia, Mass)
W Anderson 81 80 76 77 314

**British Amateur** (Prestwick, Scot)
AG Barry bt Hon O Scott 3 & 2

**US Amateur** (Chicago, Ill)
HC Egan bt DE Sawyer 6 & 5

**British Women's Amateur** (Cromer, Norfolk)
B Thompson bt ME Stuart 3 & 2

**US Women's Amateur** (Morris Co, NJ)
P Mackay bt M Curtis 1h

# Open at last for Alex Smith

ALEX SMITH could have chosen no more spectacular way of ending his years of frustration chasing Willie Anderson for the Open championship of the United States than by becoming the first to break 300 – and this he did by five strokes at the Ontwentsia Club, Illinois, a stroke better than had been achieved in the much more closely contested British Open of 1904.

Alex left his brother Willie, working as professional in a new outpost of golf, Mexico, seven strokes behind. Alex was the eldest of the three Smith brothers from Carnoustie, Macdonald the youngest.

Alex's progress at Ontwentsia was regal, for he led from the first round and was no doubt in a hurry to get a stranglehold on the championship, as he had been so close so often right from his first attempt eight years before. Since then he had lost a play-off to Anderson, finished fourth and been runner-up nine months before he finally landed the prize, the Open having been moved back to June.

Alex Smith and his Open spectacular.

## Braid on top at Muirfield

FOR THE third time in seven years the names Braid, Taylor and Vardon head the final scores of the British Open, this time at Muirfield.

But this was the first time that the Great Triumvirate, as they were now respectfully known, appeared in this particular order.

Braid's score of 300, with an improved return every round, brought him his second Muirfield victory.

## Harriot edges out her sister

THOUGH Margaret Curtis was generally considered a better player than her sister Harriot, and had as evidence two runner-up places in the American Women's Amateur, Harriot was first to receive the trophy, with its picturesque golf scenes around the cup. Harriot beat Mary Adams in the final at Brae Burn, near Boston, at the 17th.

# Golf indebted to Balfour

ARTHUR JAMES Balfour gives up the seals of office as prime minister, but continues to rejoice in the honorary title of "Father of English golf".

The game has reason to be grateful to him, as had the country for his part in ending the Boer War. Even if the Royal & Ancient had been in a position to make a conscious choice of a distinguished public figure, intellectual and respected sportsman to promote and encourage golf, and effectively to act as unpaid head of public relations, they could not have done better than obtain the services of A.J.Balfour.

Golf has always had its detractors, but Balfour gave the game an aura that dispelled ridicule. He was an all-round sportsman of talent who became chairman of the Conservative Party, was nephew to Lord Salisbury and a noted scholar.

Like Walter Travis, he took up golf relatively late in life, but was soon the best player among members of Parliament. When out of office, he is reputed to have golfed every weekday. Because of his eminence in so many fields his often expressed

Balfour: golf's best friend.

love and approval of golf swayed many minds. He became captain of the Royal & Ancient, and always did his best to oblige when asked, which he often was, to open new courses, usually in company with leading professionals.

## SHORT PUTTS

● Eben Byers, after twice finishing second in the American Amateur, beats George Lyon in the final at Englewood, New Jersey; 1906 consolation for Canadian Lyon was his fifth national amateur title over New Yorker Douglas Laird by 5 & 4 at Ottawa.

● Robert Trent Jones born in Lancashire, England.

● George Lyon lands a nap hand of Canadian titles with 5 & 4 win over a New Yorker, Douglas Laird, at Ottawa.

## SCORECARD

**British Open** (Muirfield, Scot)
J Braid 77 76 74 73 300

**US Open** (Ontwentsia, Ill)
A Smith 73 74 73 75 295

**British Amateur** (Prestwick, Scot)
J Robb bt CC Lingen  4 & 3

**US Amateur** (Englewood, NJ)
EM Byers bt GS Lyon 2h

**British Women's Amateur** (Burnham, Bucks)
Mrs W Kennion bt B Thompson 4 & 3

**US Women's Amateur** (Brae Burn, Mass)
H Curtis bt M Adams  2 & 1

# Arnaud Massy makes it an Open à la française

**Arnaud Massy scores a first for France.**

ONE OF the first thoughts of the French champion, Arnaud Massy, after becoming the first player from outside the British Isles to be British Open champion was to dash home, where his Scottish wife had given birth to a daughter during Open week, and name the child Hoylake, after the links of the Royal Liverpool Club.

There it was that Massy, a Basque who was said to have the soul of a Scotsman, had two strokes to spare over J.H.Taylor, five over Harry Vardon and six over James Braid.

Also six behind was Ted Ray, a big hitter who had taken over Harry Vardon's old job on the beautiful Ganton course in the Vale of Pickering, Yorkshire.

This Open was the longest yet, because the committee had felt obliged, so popular was it becoming, to introduce qualifying. Massy led that as well. So his total over the six rounds was six better than anyone else's. The prize-money was still in (low) three figures. American champion Alec Smith tried for the title, but was 20 shots behind Massy.

The British professionals went over to France to try to part Massy from the French title but they had no luck there, either. Indeed, another Frenchman came second.

## TEE TALK

**"It's good sportsmanship to not pick up golf balls while they are still rolling."**

MARK TWAIN.

# Margaret Curtis — US champion

MARGARET CURTIS took the US Women's title everyone had been expecting her to win for years past – ironically, at the expense of the reigning champion, sister Harriot. Margaret had been trying for the championship from the age of 13.

Now she not only had the best qualifying score at the Midlothian Club, Blue Island, Illinois, but steam-rollered her way through the rounds, with successive margins of 7 & 6, 9 & 7, 3 & 1, 6 & 4, and finally 7 & 6, over her sister. This was the first instance of a final between sisters. Margaret had excellent qualifications for match play, hitting long off the tee and putting soundly.

Earlier the sisters toured Britain again, Harriot's penchant for feathered hats proving out of place in the wind and rain at Newcastle, County Down. Here another sisterly battle ended with May beating Florence Hezlet 2 & 1 for her third Amateur title in nine years.

# Alex wins the battle of the Brothers Ross

ALEX ROSS was a very hot golfer, even hotter than his rivals in blistering conditions when the US Open made its first visit to the Philadelphia Cricket Club. It was played over the old St Martin's course. Ross's total of 302 was two better than Gil Nicholls, who had to be content with second place for the second time.

Alex's brother Donald was in tenth place. As an impecunious son of a Dornoch stone mason, he had left his native town nine years before, and was engaged in developing the golf complex at Pinehurst, in the North Carolina sandhills.

Perhaps unnerved by being the first to hole in one in the championship, Jack Hobens, from the Englewood club, soared to over 80 in the final round, and finished seven behind Alex Ross, who had travelled down from the Brae Burn club, near Boston.

# Travers triumphant in a one-sided final

JERRY TRAVERS, 20, won his first American Amateur championship at the Euclid Club, Cleveland, Ohio, on July 13 with a crushing final win over Archibald Graham from New Jersey.

The Old Man, Walter Travis, had for the fifth time had the best qualifying score, but fell at the quarter-final stage to William Fownes from Oakmont.

Travers squeaked through to the last four one up, and reached the final by putting out the reigning champion, Eben Byers, by 6 & 5. He was to repeat that margin emphatically, with his victory in the final.

## SCORECARD

**British Open** (Royal Liverpool)
A Massy (France) 76 81 78 77 312

**US Open** (Philadelphia Cricket Club, Pa)
A Ross 76 74 76 76 302

**British Amateur** (Royal Liverpool)
J Ball bt CA Palmer 6 & 4

**US Amateur** (Euclid, Ohio)
JD Travers bt M Behr 6 & 5

**British Women's Amateur** (Newcastle, Co Down)
M Hezlet bt F Hezlet 2 & 1

**US Women's Amateur** (Midlothian, Ill)
M Curtis bt H Curtis 7 & 6

## SHORT PUTTS

● John Ball, for the first time since his Boer War service, won the British Amateur at St Andrews, beating C.A.Palmer 6 & 4 for his sixth title over a span of 18 years. Ball had not played much golf in the new century and his ability to come back to top-class competition amazed his peers. The entry was a record 200.

● Henry Cotton was born on January 26 in Holmeschapel, Cheshire.

● Joe Dey born in Norfolk, Virginia.

# St Andrews welcomes the ladies and says farewell to Old Tom Morris

THE BRITISH Women's championship, being staged for the 16th time, at last gained a foothold at St Andrews. Old Tom Morris, still welcoming one and all to his shop next to the links, said that he had always hoped to live to see a ladies' championship at St Andrews.

Two days after Maud Titterton became champion at the 19th hole of the final against Dorothy Campbell from North Berwick, Morris was dead, at the age of 86, after suffering concussion in a fall downstairs at the New St Andrews Club.

Born at St Andrews in 1821, he had outlived his son, Young Tom, by 33 years. Both won the Open four times, but only the son ever managed it four years in succession. His father competed in the championship every year from 1860 to 1896. He was green keeper to the Royal & Ancient from 1865 up to his retirement in 1904, holding an honorary position till his death. The 18th at St Andrews is named after him.

Old Tom had tipped Dorothy Campbell to win, and her 22nd hole win in the semi-final against Hilday Mather suggested she had the right competitive credentials to succeed.

Maud Titterton had accounted for a difficult opponent in Cecil Leitch, 17, who possessed a swing that was shorter than most but smooth and forceful.

She adopted more practical, lighter clothing for the game than was previously the fashion, which did no harm to her strong iron play.

The final, despite poor visibility, attracted a huge crowd, and turned Titterton's way at the 18th, where she drew level after enjoying a touch of luck getting over the Swilken Burn. Par at the 19th gave her the title.

## SCORECARD

**British Open** (Prestwick, Scot)
James Braid 70 72 77 72 291

**US Open** (Myopia Hunt Club, Mass)
F McLeod 82 82 81 77 322
(McLeod bt W Smith in play-off 77-83)

**British Amateur** (Royal St George's, Kent)
EA Lassen bt HE Taylor 7 & 6

**US Amateur** (Garden City, NJ)
JD Travers bt M Behr 8 & 7

**British Women's Amateur** (St Andrews, Scot)
M Titterton bt D Campbell 19th

**US Women's Amateur** (Chevy Chase, Md)
K Harley bt Mrs TH Polhemus 6 & 5

## SHORT PUTTS

● Horace Hutchinson became the first Englishman to captain the Royal & Ancient.

● Margaret Curtis won the Women's National Lawn Tennis Doubles title with Evelyn Sears, and was thus the only American ever to have held national titles in both golf and lawn tennis.

● The Royal & Ancient decreed that golf was not suitable for the Olympics, so the game was excluded from the London Games of 1908.

Old Tom Morris: dies at 86.

---

## Tiny Fred McLeod is US champion

THE SCORES were huge, but the winner was tiny. Fred McLeod from the Midlothian Club weighed in at only 108 pounds when he beat Willie Smith 77-83 in a play-off at Myopia, after they had tied at 322.

McLeod, like Dorothy Campbell, hailed from North Berwick, where he was born in 1882, the year before she was. He had come over to the United States in 1903 and soon became a force to be reckoned finishing fifth in the 1907 Open Championship.

McLeod: Mighty battler.

## Medallist Travis falls to Travers

A MEETING between Jerry Travers, the new champion, and Walter Travis was bound to come sooner or later with two such fierce competitors about, and it took place at Garden City, New Jersey. Travis was the leading qualifier for the sixth time, but lost the semifinal at the 17th to Travers, who went on to retain his title 8 & 7 against Max Behr.

Travers beat William Fownes of Oakmont 7 & 5 before accounting for Travis.

## Braid runs away with fourth title

JACK WHITE'S record 296 of four years ago was shattered at Prestwick by James Braid, with 291, spread-eagling the field and earning his fourth Open championship. Tom Ball from west Lancashire was a distant second with 299.

Braid had a firm grip on the event at halfway, which he reached in another record of 142 strokes. It was a good year for him to publish his instructional book "Advanced Golf".

# Dorothy Campbell's transatlantic double

HAVING BEATEN Florence Hezlet at Birkdale in the British Women's Amateur, Dorothy Iona Campbell travelled to the Merion Club in Pennsylvania to land a unique double on October 9 by winning the American title from Mrs Nonna Barlow, 3 & 2. She began with a 10 & 8 trouncing of Mrs C.W.McKelvey, and was thereafter never taken past the 17th hole.

This was a self-taught golfer, who made a friend of her clubs to the extent of giving them names. An especially useful implement, which she called "Thomas", was a goose-neck five-iron. She could get up and down from 50 yards and occasionally, to the consternation of opponents, hole a run-up of that length – a powerful factor in her game. Her putter, "Stella," starred in many a match.

Ironically, the one title Campbell could not capture this year was that of her native Scotland, in which she finished runner-up to E.Kyle over the Machrihanish course at Campbeltown. She had enjoyed great success in previous years, winning the Scottish title in 1905 on her home course, North Berwick and winning again in 1906 and 1908.

Dorothy Campbell: starred with 'Stella' the putter.

## SCORECARD

**British Open** (Royal Cinque Ports, Kent)
JH Taylor 74 73 74 74 295

**US Open** (Englewood, NJ)
G Sargent 75 72 72 71 290

**British Amateur** (Muirfield, Scot)
R Maxwell bt C Hutchison 1h

**US Amateur** (Chicago, Ill)
RA Gardner bt HC Egan 4 & 3

**British Women's Amateur** (Royal Birkdale, Liverpool)
D Campbell bt F Hezlet 4 & 3

**US Women's Amateur** (Merion, Pa)
D Campbell bt Mrs Nonna Barlow 3 & 2

## TEE TALK

### "I'll no. Yon's a freak shot."

SCOTS PROFESSIONAL, to an American lady who asked to be taught how to perform Dorothy Campbell's mystically accurate run-up shot.

# American talent threat to imports

THE DAY for an American to end the run of US Open winners from the old country appeared to be at hand at Englewood, New Jersey, when, on June 24, Tom McNamara, from the Wollaston Club, near Boston, reached the halfway stage five clear of the field. He was the second player ever to break 70 in the tournament, with a second round 69. Dave Hunter had a 68 in the first, but faded to 84 in the second.

McNamara prompted George Sargent, an English-born professional playing out of Hyde Manor, Vermont, to press on next day to the lowest total yet in the championship – 290. McNamara took 77 in the final round, against Sargent's 71, and was runner-up four strokes in arrears.

J.H.Taylor was back in charge at the Royal Cinque Ports Club, Deal, in Kent, with six shots to spare over James Braid. Ted Ray was again prominent in sixth place. Taylor's victory was his tenth finish in the top three in 16 years. It was achieved with three 74s and a 73 for 295. Darwin wrote of Taylor as "the acknowledged head of his profession."

J.H.Taylor: six shots to spare.

# Maxwell's match to remember

ROBERT MAXWELL gained his second British Amateur, and again victory came at Muirfield, at the last hole, against Cecil Hutchison, a course architect.

Bernard Darwin wrote: "They produced a never-to-be-forgotten match by those who saw it. The golf was so faultless, the speed at which it was played so great, that they seemed to be playing not a championship final but one of the friendly, almost casual games which they had played together on the links of the Lothians."

## SHORT PUTTS

● Golf Illustrated inaugurated their Gold Vase, a one-day, 36-hole competition, at Royal Mid-Surrey, where it was won with a 146 total by C.K.Hutchison.

● President Roosevelt unsuccessfully advised his successor William Taft not to play golf, which he considered undemocratic and "sissy".

# Gardner, man of many talents

THE US AMATEUR champion must have turned a good many of his contemporaries green with envy. Quite apart from becoming, at 19 years and five months, the youngest ever to lift the title, Robert Gardner was handsome, sang well and was a national record-breaker in the pole vault.

He was level with Chick Evans as leading qualifier at the Chicago Club, Wheaton, Illinois, beat Walter Travis in the quarterfinals, and Chandler Egan, who had won in 1904 and 1905, in the final, 4 & 3. Yet Gardner had not been a threat before this impressive string of victories in any significant event, and had only just finished his freshman year at college.

# 'No' to Cup offer

THE offer of a Cup as a trophy for an international team match made by the USGA was not accepted by the Ladies Golf Union, on the grounds that it would be difficult to field a team.

# Casting the first stone – on Woking's 13th

THE CAMPAIGN for women's suffrage began to impinge on golf. Greens were damaged and windows broken at clubs, which many suffragettes, with some reason, saw as bastions of male domination.

The struggle came close to home for the Woking club in Surrey, in particular, for among their lady members – and lady members, in the spirit of the times, were still merely temporary members – was Ethel Smyth, the writer and composer, who had studied at Leipzig, and wrote a mass and symphonic and choral works. She lived close to the course, and was a friend of Emmeline Pankhurst, founder in 1903 of the Women's Social and Political Union, whose highly militant campaign Smyth joined, and for which she composed a battle song, "The March of the Women."

Just before the WSPU embarked on a widespread window-smashing campaign, Smyth invited Mrs Pankhurst to Woking, for stone-throwing practice, it is believed, on the 13th fairway. The practice was sorely needed, since at her first attempt Mrs Pankhurst almost hit her hostess's dog. The pair were on target in serious action in London, and were jailed in adjoining cells at Holloway prison, Smyth having received a sentence of three months, though she served only three weeks.

A more sporting manifestation of the battle of the sexes came at Walton Heath in Surrey on October 11, when Cecil Leitch, who made such an impression on the St Andrews galleries the previous year, took on former Open winner Harold Hilton.

The match was from the men's tees, and the challenge for Hilton severe, as he was to give a half-stroke per hole. Leitch (christened Charlotte Cecilia Pitcairn Leitch) began nervously, but was only one down at the end of the first 36 holes of the confrontation. Big crowds hemmed the players in, and many a bet was struck.

The second 36, at Sunningdale, ended with a victory for Leitch at the 71st hole overall. Over the final 17 holes of the match she had taken 77 strokes, Hilton 75. Women's golf in general, and the reputation of the Ladies' Golf Union in particular, were definitely not harmed by this, while the suffragette movement edged inexorably forward.

Bold hitter: Cecil Leitch.

## John Ball back with seventh title

JOHN BALL resumed his position at the top of the amateur game, gaining his seventh British title at the Hoylake course of his own Royal Liverpool club, needing only 27 holes to rout C.C.Aylmer, which added up to the first double figure victory, 10 & 9, in championship history.

The US Amateur title at the Country Club, Brookline, went to a member of one of America's distinguished golfing families, William C. Fownes, who played his golf at the daunting Oakmont course.

### TEE TALK

## "Golf is a good walk spoiled."

MARK TWAIN (died 1910).

### SHORT PUTTS

● Willie Anderson dies at his home in Philadelphia aged 31.

### SCORECARD

**British Open** (St Andrews, Scot)
J Braid 76 73 74 76 299

**US Open** (Philadelphia CC, Pa)
A Smith 73 79 73 73 298
(Play-off, A Smith 71, JJ McDermott 75, M Smith 77)

**British Amateur** (Royal Liverpool)
J Ball bt CC Aylmer 10 & 9

**US Amateur** (Brookline CC, Mass)
WC Fownes bt WK Wood 4 & 3

**British Women's Amateur** (Westward Ho!, Devon)
G Suttie bt L Moore 6 & 4

**US Women's Amateur** (Flossmoor, Ill)
D Campbell bt Mrs GM Martin 2 & 1

## Braid makes it five out of ten

JAMES BRAID cheered Scottish hearts with his fifth Open championship in the first decade of the new century. Moreover, he had assembled his nap hand of Opens before either J.H.Taylor or Harry Vardon. None of his victories was by fewer than three shots.

This time Alex Herd was runner-up, with George Duncan third. This was the first time that the 300 mark had been broken at the home of golf.

Braid's dominance in this decade was the result of two developments – better putting with an aluminium club, and the sudden discovery that he could drive the ball a long way. As he expressed it: "It was just the same as if I went to bed a short driver one night and got up a long driver in the morning. It was then, and is still, the greatest golfing mystery that I have ever come across." A thunderstorm forced the abandonment of the first round at St Andrews. Only the 60 leaders were permitted to play the final 36 holes; prize money at this Golden Jubilee Open was raised to £125.

James Braid: five in the decade.

## McDermott's all-American Open

THE DAY OF complete British supremacy ended on June 24 at Chicago Golf Club, Wheaton, Illinois, where Johnny McDermott became the first American-born winner of the US Open championship.

It was not easy. Having recovered from a shaky start (81) he put together three rounds in the 70s to total 307.

That figure was also achieved by Mike Brady and George Simpson, with four below-80 rounds. McDermott belied his lack of years – he was the youngest champion yet, at two months short of his 20th birthday – and carried off the cup with 80 in the play-off, two better than Brady and five better than Simpson.

## Vardon just holds on

THOUGH EVEN his most fervent supporters considered that Harry Vardon was never as impressive a player after his bout of tuberculosis, he held his game together at Royal St George's for 107 holes. Then Arnaud Massy conceded at the 35th hole of a play-off that gave Vardon his fifth Open, and equality with James Braid. Vardon was well placed after three rounds, then faded to 80, which led to the play-off.

## Macdonald's masterpiece

NO ONE had done more to stir the America into golfing action than Charles Blair Macdonald, the first amateur champion, and a keen supporter of the need for an authoritative ruling body, a campaign that led to the founding of the USGA. In 1911 he opened of the National Golf Links of America, at Southampton on Long Island, New York.

### TEE TALK

**"It wasn't just replacing the turf – more like returfing the place."**

REASON FOR GIVING UP GOLF.

# Hilton lands most elusive double of all

AT 42, Harold Hilton, second only to John Ball as the outstanding player among Royal Liverpool's crop of conquering amateurs, won his third British Amateur, then sailed away to take on the best of American amateurs at Apawamis, not far north of New York City.

He began in menacing fashion with the best score (150) in qualifying and began to skim along at the top of the draw, with 8 & 6 and 10 & 9 wins on the way. He was never taken beyond the 16th, even by Jerry Travers in the quarterfinals, till he reached the trophy match.

Here on September 16 he met Fred Herreshoff (Ekwanok) who had been a losing finalist against Chandler Egan.

Hilton got a firm grip on affairs and, with 13 to play, he was six holes up. Herreshoff got them all back by the 16th, and missed winning chances from middling range on the next two holes. His luck was out and Hilton's definitely in at the first extra hole, where his wooden approach shot took a kindly deflection off a bank, and par gave him the transatlantic double which had never before been achieved. Hilton stood only 5 feet 7 inches (and used an unusually short-shafted putter), but was well built and "hit for all he was worth", according to Bernard Darwin. "He was master of himself and the ball."

Cassidy's sculpture of Harold Hilton.

### SCORECARD

**British Open** (Royal St George's, Kent)
H Vardon 74 74 75 80 303
(Vardon bt A Massy in play-off – conceded)

**US Open** (Chicago, Ill)
JJ McDermott 81 72 75 79 307
(Play-off, McDermott 80, M Brady 82, G Simpson 85)

**British Amateur** (Prestwick, Scot)
HH Hilton bt EA Lassen 4 & 3

**US Amateur** (Apawamis, NY)
HH Hilton bt F Herreshoff 37th

**British Women's Amateur** (Portrush, Co Down)
D Campbell bt V Hezlet 3 & 2

**U S Women's Amateur** (Baltusrol, NJ)
M Curtis bt L Hyde 5 & 3

### SHORT PUTTS

● Dorothy Campbell regained her British title against Violet Hezlet at Portrush, in Ireland, and retained her Canadian title, but she fell to Margaret Curtis in the American semifinal. Curtis went on to her second convincing triumph at Baltusrol, beating Lillian Hyde 5 & 3.

● In conjunction with the Portrush event, a British team took on an "American and Colonial" selection, and won 7-2. This unofficial match indicated a growing desire to found a series.

● Consolation for Arnaud Massy came in the shape of his third French championship.

● Ralph Guldahl was born on November 22 in Dallas, Texas.

**Margaret Curtis: regained title at Baltusrol.**

# John Ball, the 'Greatest Amateur'

JOHN BALL drove home his status as the "Great Amateur" by winning his eighth British title over the classic Westward Ho! links of the Royal North Devon Club.

Great things were expected of Abe Mitchell, his opponent in the final, but he missed a four footer on the 36th hole for the title, which Ball won on the 38th.

Ball was good at staring defeat in the face, and surviving. He had been five down and seven to play in the fifth round.

He also seemed able to take golf or leave it, for not only did he come back to win titles after his Boer War service, but his motorcycling and gardening hobbies were equally important at times.

He had, however, found time to captain England from 1902 to 1911. Through nearly all his long competitive career there was to be seen in his wake his faithful caddie Jones, who was almost but not quite a deaf mute. Few players have equalled Ball in the ability to flight the ball low into the wind, a skill essential at his home course of Hoylake.

Margaret Curtis retained the US women's Amateur title at her home course, Essex Country Club, Massachusetts.

John Ball: the "Greatest Amateur."

### SCORECARD

**British Open** (Muirfield, Scot)
T Ray 71 73 76 75 295

**US Open** (Buffalo, NY)
JJ McDermott 75 74 74 71 294

**British Amateur** (Westward Ho!, Devon)
J Ball bt A Mitchell 38th

**US Amateur** (Chicago, Ill)
J Travers bt C Evans 7 & 6

**British Women's Amateur** (Turnberry, Scot)
G Ravenscroft bt S Temple 3 & 2

**US Women's Amateur** (Essex Co, Mass)
M Curtis bt Mrs RH Barlow 3 & 2

## McDermott beats unlucky McNamara in biggest US Open

JOHNNY McDERMOTT'S second US Open title in a row underlined native American talent, for the runner-up was the unlucky Tom McNamara, who had almost pulled off the American first trick three years ago, and now closed with a superb 69 – still two too many to force a tie. Tom Vardon, now with the Ontwentsia Club, was placed far back.

For the first time, more than a 100 players took part. Another first was the venue, the Open being staged at Buffalo, in upstate New York.

## Ted Ray breaks into winners' triangle

TED RAY'S four-stroke British Open win at Muirfield was only the second occasion in eight years when Vardon, Braid or Taylor did not carry off the silver claret jug. Like Vardon, Ray was born in Jersey in the Channel Islands. His pipe was as permanent a feature of his equipment as Walter Travis's black cigar. He also reached the PGA match-play final for a second year.

Ted Ray: "hit it harder."

## President 'bumble puppy' Taft

AMERICA'S FIRST rabid Presidential golfer ended his term, having used the charisma of his office whenever possible to spread the gospel of golf. He held it to be a game "that makes you ashamed of your profanity".

Francis Drake had nothing on Big Bill Taft. He reacted to the news that a foreign head of state was arriving with: "I'll be damned if I will give up my game to see this fellow." Taft termed his own game "bumble puppy golf".

The Press certainly gave him coverage during his Presidency that owed more to his office than his skill on course. He enjoyed his mashine but his putting was, according to one contemporary account, "problematical." As he weighed nearly 300 pounds (over 20 stone), Taft could be described as a great golf enthusiast in more ways than one.

## Hilton loses US title

RETURNING TO DEFEND his American Amateur title, Harold Hilton was top qualifier in company with Chick Evans, but fell to Charles Waldo in the first match play round. In the next round Walter Travis lost, as in the 1908 semifinals, to Jerry Travers, who went on to beat Evans in the final by 7 & 6.

The USGA had issued a national handicap list six months before the Championship, naming 471 players eligible to enter with handicaps of six and below. Only 85 entered. Hilton did achieve considerable success with his book "The Royal and Ancient Game of Golf" written in collaboration with Garden C. Smith.

### TEE TALK

## "Hit it a **** sight harder, mate."

TED RAY,
tip for achieving greater length.

# Francis Ouimet beats the invading giants

FRANCIS DE SALES OUIMET was 20 when, at his fourth attempt, he gained entry to the US Open championship, held in September at the Country Club, Brookline. Just across the road from the club was the Ouimet family home, around which was a miniature course Francis played on as a child.

Later he worked as a caddie at the Country Club, won the state Amateur title and remained an amateur, earning his living in the sales office of Wright and Ditson's, a store that sold sports equipment. A couple of weeks before the Open, Ouimet qualified for the national Amateur championship, with a score one better than that of veteran medallist, Walter Travis, but lost in the second round to the eventual champion, Jerry Travers.

Johnny McDermott, twice US Open champion, was the chief American hope to repel the powerful two-pronged challenge from England – Harry Vardon, who had won at his only previous attempt at the US Open in 1900, and Ted Ray, 1912 British Open champion, and runner-up to J.H.Taylor earlier this year.

Amazingly, Ouimet forced a play-off with the invading giants, playing the last six holes in two under par. The play-off attracted a crowd of 10,000 as the Open went into an unprecedented fifth day. Play began in a downpour. The trio were level after nine holes, then the Englishmen three-putted the next and Ouimet was ahead to stay.

Vardon most uncharacteristically – and unwisely for one who had suffered from tuberculosis – lit a cigarette during the play-off. The Times man, Bernard Darwin, was marking Ouimet's card, and began to change his allegiance to the young American as Ouimet stuck to his daunting task.

Vardon's daring at the dog leg of the 17th undid him. Bunkered, he took five. Ouimet, on for two, sank his putt for a birdie three for a lead of three shots. This he expanded to five at the 18th, to make sure of becoming the first amateur to win the title.

Ouimet was front page news in Boston, and earned the accolade of "World's Golf Champion" in the New York Times. Press coverage had ever favoured the amateur game, blessed by high society and so played mostly by well-heeled men and women in exclusive private clubs. But here was an amateur to whom the public at large could relate – not

Vardon, Ray (right) and Brookline's conquering hero.

Incongruous: Ouimet and his young caddie, Eddie Lowery.

to mention his caddie, Eddie Lowery, aged ten, who had his own battle to fight and win when it was suggested that a more experienced caddie should accompany Ouimet in the play off. Lowery won and his constant advice to his player to keep his eye on the ball was profitably

heeded. Walter Hagen, also 20, a professional from Rochester, New York, also made his first appearance in the Open, and finished three shots behind the leading trio. He had started his final round 6, 7, 5, 2, 3, 3. A double bogey seven on the 14th killed his chances.

# Tearing the greens

THE SUFFRAGETTE, edited by Christabel Pankhurst, was unrepentant about damaged inflicted upon golf courses by militant seekers after votes for women: "What have golfers ever done for the Suffrage Cause, and what will they ever do if they are left to play their game in peace?"

There were also arson attacks; a house being built for Lloyd George at Walton Heath was blown up; and insurance cover was provided for the St Andrews clubhouse. Woking club members encouraged their womenfolk to make it clear to the suffragettes that violence used against club property could only rebound to the disadvantage of lady members.

## Big 3: 5-all

J.H.TAYLOR'S eight-shot win in the British Open at Royal Liverpool brought the championship score to five apiece for Taylor and the other two members of the Triumvirate, Braid and Vardon. Taylor's score increased on every round, but then the last round was played in a full gale.

### SCORECARD

**British Open** (Royal Liverpool)
JH Taylor 73 75 77 79 304

**US Open** (Country Club, Brookline, Mass)
F Ouimet 77 74 74 79 304
(Play-off, Ouimet 72, H Vardon 77, E Ray 78)

**British Amateur** (St Andrews, Scot)
HH Hilton bt R Harris 6 & 5

**US Amateur** (Garden City, NJ)
JD Travers bt JG Anderson 5 & 4

**British Women's Amateur** (St Annes, Lancs)
M Dodd bt E Chubb 8 & 6

**US Women's Amateur** (Wilmington, Del)
G Ravenscroft bt M Hollins 2h

### TEE TALK

## "I'd put you at scratch with the late Alexander If I was a Keats – but I ain't."

GRANTLAND RICE'S
ODE TO OUIMET.

# The Great Triumvirate

In that glorious era of British golf before the First World War these three men reigned supreme and added lustre to the game with their triumphs at home and abroad

F OR THREE unassuming professional golfers such as Harry Vardon, John Henry (J.H.)Taylor and James Braid, the collective title of "The Great Triumvirate" sounds perhaps a little grandiose, though it should be remarked on their behalf that their reign lasted a great deal longer than that of the Triumvirate of ancient Rome, since Augustus Caesar was soon rid of Mark Antony and Lepidus.

## Outstanding record

In the 21-year period from 1894 to 1914, when Vardon, uniquely, won his sixth British Open championship, the Triumvirate gained 16 Opens between them – five each to Taylor and Braid. On three of the five occasions upon which they did not win during those years, one or other of the Triumvirate was within one stroke of the champion.

The number of high finishes they achieved is equally remarkable. Only Jack Nicklaus, with 17 top three finishes, has outdone them. Vardon and Taylor had 12, and Braid 11. Taylor was in the top half-dozen 18 times, one better than Nicklaus. Apart from Peter Thomson, who had seven, Nicklaus and Vardon share the highest total of consecutive top three finishes – six.

Their characters and methods were as far apart as their birthplaces, Vardon, a Channel Islander from Jersey, Braid a Scot from Fife not far from St Andrews, and Taylor from Devon, though all three shared the enviable ability to keep their games together over many years, Vardon despite periods of treatment for tuberculosis after his Prestwick victory in 1903.

Indeed, he was the only one of the three to have a solid chance of winning a major championship after the First World War – the US Open of 1920 at Inverness when, despite high winds during the last round, his total was inferior only to that of Ted Ray. He was then 50, 20 years on from the US Open title he won on his epoch-making Spalding tour in which he proved to be an unrivalled evangelist for golf.

The Vardon grip, used by almost every leading golfer of modern times except Jack Nicklaus, was the brainchild of

Clement Fowler's famed study of the Triumvirate: Vardon drives, watched by Taylor (left) and Braid.

*Personnel of many of an exhibition foursome – the Triumvirate (from left) Taylor, Braid and Vardon, with Sandy Herd (seated right).*

Johnny Laidlay, a Scottish amateur. In Vardon's huge hands the overlapping principle – which Vardon thought of as a marriage between the golfer's hands – advertised itself to the whole golfing world.

Vardon was what present-day American professionals would call a "cherry-picker" – he took the ball cleanly off the turf. So the stories that the main danger he faced in the afternoon round was the likelihood of his driving into the pitch marks he had made on his morning round are apocryphal.

Another story illustrating his accuracy is true. Giving an indoor exhibition on tour, he found that by hitting a valve on a wall some distance away he could start a sprinkler. Before he could become very good indeed at this it was suggested to him that the practice was not good for the fabric of the building. How appropriate that the trophy awarded annually for the professional with the lowest stroke average is named after Vardon.

## Serene champion

Above all Vardon had a smooth, unhurried swing ("a beautiful, free movement", said Bernard Darwin) and an equable temperament to match. The first Duke of Wellington once said, when he held high office at a time of great unrest in Britain, that he made a point of not worrying, and never lay awake doing so. There are few men – the Duke certainly was one – from whom such sentiments can be seriously entertained. Vardon's long reign at the top of his profession suggests he was not exaggerating when he claimed that nerves never troubled him.

Andrew Kirkaldy, who never managed to win an Open or defeat Vardon, though he beat all the other leading players of the day, supports this view of the serene Vardon: "He smiles as he plays, but it is not a broad smile, just a faint flicker ... what you might call the Vardonic Smile. Nothing ruffled him. He was the perfect picture of an athlete and golfer, with not an ounce of superfluous fat on his body; good-

looking, bronzed, healthy, and supple as cane."

Apart from Walter Travis, few significant golfers have taken up the game so late in life as Vardon. He played scarcely at all in his teens, and might never have turned to golf but for his brother Tom's winning money, which led to his taking up a professional post at a nine-hole course in Yorkshire. Only when established in the game did he start to think about technique. His natural gifts were clearly enormous, but his powers of adaptation and innovation were just as important. Above all, he had the air of not seeming to care what the opposition were doing. Darwin again: "He could fight, if need be, without appearing to be fighting at all." Moreover, he did it all with six clubs. Leading players between the wars used five times as many until the 14-club rule was adopted.

## Taylor the great pro

Taylor's career after the war was not dissimilar to that of Vardon, seldom being in contention in major events. His place in the game's history was assured in 1894 when he became the first English professional to take the major prize, yet his greatest achievements were in the first decade of the 20th century. He was a selfless worker for the status of the professionals, a leading light in their trade association and, in his own unflamboyant way, did the ground work that Walter Hagen was to embellish in such colourful fashion in the 1920s and 1930s. After retiring from major events in 1925 he was victorious captain in the Ryder Cup team of 1933.

Pupils came from far and near to seek the secret of his accurate mashie play, high or low according to the demands of the situation and the weather. One such was Tommy Armour, who asked Taylor how he managed to stop the ball so efficiently. Taylor's answer was to the effect that when Armour showed some signs of getting the ball up to the hole he would tell him.

Long before an American-born golfer had won the US Open, Taylor said: "But American golf is rapidly improving, and ere long American players will be able to hold their own in the best company." This was highly prophetic in Taylor's case, for he held brief Open championship leads over Hagen in the 1920s, but lost them.

Sports ever thrive on head-to-head battles and, with three such

players as the Triumvirate, their fame was spread by print, photography and oil paint, too. Punch magazine joined in with this contribution:

"Nine tailors, says the adage,
must you take,
To form a man of average degree,
T'would need nine very special
men to make,
Another Devon Taylor such
as he".

Artisan golfers – he began with the Northam artisans at his Devon birthplace – had much to thank Taylor for, and he was the moving force behind the public courses in Richmond Park, Surrey.

Taylor won the French Open in 1908 and 1909, and the German in 1912. He had ten holes in one, not altogether surprising in a player of such judgment with approach shots, and received a silver salver from the Royal & Ancient on his 90th birthday, for he was last to arrive and last to go of the Triumvirate.

Braid's reputation was that of a mighty hitter, an ability, as he many times admitted, that came upon him suddenly and for no reason that he could adduce. His approach play was frequently beyond criticism. He won half the Opens in the 1900s, four match play championships, and the French Open in 1910. Later he was busy as a course architect, notably originating or revamping such celebrated layouts as Gleneagles, Carnoustie and Rosemount in Scotland, and Bournemouth's delightful Queen's Park.

The war added too many years and not enough top-level competition to the Triumvirate, and as they declined the next great trio of players, Hogan, Snead and Nelson, were growing up in Texas and Virginia.

## TEE TALK

OFF-FORM HARRY VARDON:
### "What on earth shall I take now?"
CADDIE:
### "Well, sir, I'd recommend the 4.05 train."

### "The story of J.H.'s life might be called, like that of the Mayor of Casterbridge, the 'Story of a Man of Character'."
BERNARD DARWIN, of Taylor.

### "This putting is wicked. It is sinful."
BRAID at the 1900 Open.

# Harry Vardon's sixth 'best of my achievements'

Two qualifying rounds on the American pattern, rather than one, was a new feature of the British Open at Prestwick, but the name of the winner was familiar enough, as Harry Vardon earned his record sixth championship at the age of 44.

He led J.H.Taylor and James Braid by a stroke after one round, but Taylor was two ahead at the three-quarter mark. The rest of the field had faded away, so the event had all the makings of a two-horse race in the wind and rain.

A final 78 proved good enough for an ailing Vardon, who reported that he almost fainted several times during the last 18 holes. A disappointing and disappointed Taylor slid to an 83 and a three-stroke defeat. Vardon considered this record-breaking Open as his best effort.

This was the first Open to be covered by newsreel cameras.

## SCORECARD

**British Open** (Prestwick, Scot)
H Vardon 73 77 78 78 306

**US Open** (Midlothian, Ill)
W Hagen 68 74 75 73 290

**British Amateur** (Royal St George's, Kent)
JLC Jenkins bt CO Hezlet 3 & 2

**US Amateur** (Ekwanok, Vt)
F Ouimet bt JD Travers 6 & 5

**British Women's Amateur** (Hunstanton, Norfolk)
C Leitch bt G Ravenscroft 2 & 1

**US Women's Amateur** (Glen Cove, NY)
Mrs H Arnold Jackson bt EV Rosenthal 1h

Harry Vardon: ailing champion but a wonderful victory.

### SHORT PUTTS

● After threatening to do so for years, Cecil Leitch finally gained her first Amateur title. The championship was making its first visit to Hunstanton on the sometimes forbidding Norfolk coast, and Gladys Ravenscroft, who had won the American title a year back, lost to Leitch on the 17th.

● Mildred "Babe" Didrickson was born on June 26 at Port Arthur, Texas.

● Eleven days after Canada entered the war raging in the fields of Flanders, Karl Keffer won his second Canadian Open, at Toronto.

## Ouimet gets his heart's desire

FIFTEEN days after his vain pursuit of Hagen, Francis Ouimet realized the great ambition of every American amateur. He won the Amateur title at Ekwanok, Vermont, by beating an outstanding player, Jerry Travers, who already had four titles to his name.

This was another distinction for Ouimet, since he was the only player to have the Open and Amateur to his credit, added to which he had gone to Europe in the summer, and had returned with the French Amateur. Previously, in the British Amateur, he impressed no one.

# Walter Hagen US champion as guns open up in Europe

Local papers at Walter Hagen's Rochester base ignored Ouimet's Open win once Hagen had slipped out of contention on the last nine holes at Brookline, but he made them sit up and take notice when he led throughout the Open at Midlothian. It was a narrow squeak in the end when Charles "Chick" Evans's pitch to the 72nd hit the hole and jumped out, killing his chances of becoming amateur No 2 to win the Open.

Hagen's good showing at Brookline had convinced him that golf and not baseball was his future. It certainly looked that way after the first round, for Hagen broke the course record with a 68, but was only one ahead of Francis Ouimet. He was still one ahead of both Ouimet and Tom McNamara after the second round. This, for the first time, was now played on the second day of the Open proper, with the final 36 to follow on the third day.

Hagen, 21, kept his nerve and equalled the 1909 champion George Sargent's record score of 290. Editors spared little space for his triumph, with the war raging in France to distract their attention.

Walter Hagen: held off Evans.

# Jerry Travers outplays the professionals

JERRY TRAVERS, already in possession of four American Amateur titles, emulated Francis Ouimet's feat of having both major US titles on his career record. He had to play the last six holes at Baltusrol, New Jersey, in one under par to carry off the Havemayer trophy. This pushed the perennial bridesmade of US Open golf, Tom McNamara, from Boston, into second place – for the third time. Walter Hagen began well, and was only three shots behind the eventual winner after 36 holes but, like Chick Evans and Ouimet, he found the last few furlongs beyond him, both the amateurs fading into the 80s.

Alex Smith, who taught Travers to play, confessed that he could never tell from his demeanour whether he was winning or losing. He was certain that Travers was the greatest competitor he knew. Travers was, rather after the John Ball fashion, no slave to golf, and seemed able to take it or leave it, sometimes inactive for long periods. He was an infuriating prospect for opponents, who often felt that some dreadful Travers tee shot or approach was about to gift them the hole, only to discover at next shot that Travers had holed an outrageous putt or put the ball stiff from a rubbish pile – all this without a flicker to acknowledge that he had played good, bad or indifferent golf.

As a lad of 17 he had beaten Walter Travis shortly after Travis won the British Amateur, and did it by switching to that same type of putter, the Schenectady, that the "Old Man" had turned to almost in desperation at Sandwich. Playing against Travis as often as he did was a fairly foolproof way of honing Travers's competitive instincts.

Robert Gardner gained the Amateur title at the Country Club of Detroit, six years after his first victory in the event. Francis Ouimet, the defending champion, fell in his second match, as did Travers.

*Jerry Travers added the Open at Baltusrol to his four Amateur titles.*

# British clubs begin to count the cost

WITH A.J.BALFOUR as their first captain, Worplesdon, not far from Woking in Surrey, looked in 1913 to have a brilliant future. They had to delay buying the land to lay out the course because of Lloyd George's "People's Budget," which had added land value duties of 20 per cent on increments of land value, when sold.

The land was bought a few weeks before the war began, and members were soon playing their first rounds. For many of them, it proved to be their last: 31 members were killed in 1915, mostly service personnel.

Officers had been offered free membership; soldiers mobilized on the outbreak of war could become members for one guinea. Entry fees were suspended. The net result was that club income fell from £3,000 in 1914 to £1,336 in 1915. Sheep were brought in to graze on the course – as they were on the other side of London at Chelmsford, a club founded in 1893, whose course was originally, like Hoylake, laid out on a race track, at Galleywood.

A.J.Balfour, ever willing to advance the cause of golf, was first vice-president. Tom Dunn, architect, or so he claimed, of 137 courses, designed Galleywood's nine holes. He had a speedy method of persuading would-be founders of clubs that they should get on with it. "God," he would say, "always meant this to be a golf course."

James Braid was called in to appraise another site at Widford in 1910, which he deemed suitable for an 18-hole course, even if it was next to the workhouse. Play began on the new course on the day of King George V's coronation – June 22, 1911.

By the time the war began membership was 241. There were immediate problems as the steward, A.E.Konter, was called up for military service, and his wife took over the job, soon to be cut back as meals were no longer served in the clubhouse, and the bar was opened only on Wednesdays and weekends.

Ploughing took place on courses up and down the country, though steps were taken to protect greens.

Golf took a back seat. and course maintenance and club finances were at risk as the war dragged on.

## SCORECARD

**U S Open** (Baltusrol, NJ)
JD Travers 76 72 73 76 297

**US Amateur** (Detroit, Michigan)
RA Gardner bt JH Anderson 5 & 4

**US Women's Amateur** (Ontwentsia, Ill)
Mrs CH Vanderbeck bt Mrs WA Gavin 3 & 2

(British championships suspended following the outbreak of war)

# Ouimet loses amateur status: double for Evans

**Chick Evans: stylish double.**

ON JANUARY 14, the USGA ruled that players who traded on their golfing prowess in their business careers would be deemed professionals. On January 15 Francis Ouimet, former Open and Amateur champion, made it clear that he would open a sporting goods business.

Ouimet had been in the sports goods business, though not on his own account, before his Open championship win over Harry Vardon and Ted Ray had made him a celebrity.

Nevertheless, the anxious guardians of simon-pure amateurism, led by USGA president Frank Woodward, had their way, and Ouimet attended to business while his Open/Amateur double was now performed, uniquely, in the same year by Charles "Chick" Evans.

Evans had given fair notice of his quality six years before, coming top of the Western Open, which professionals were beginning to look on as next best thing to the national Open.

His Open victory at Minikahda, Minneapolis, was gained in style: a record total of 286, two under par, with professional Jock Hutchison two strokes behind. Jerry Travers did not defend, yet the amateurs had found another champion; indeed, they had taken the Open for the third time in four years.

Evans's golf career, which like Ouimet's began in the caddie shack, proved that it was not necessary to belong to the moneyed country-club set to attain the heights at golf. He did not over-burden himself with equipment, though he did routinely carry seven clubs – one more than Harry Vardon's usual armoury.

Unlike Ouimet, he earned his living in the money markets and so was not troubled by Woodward's rulings. Evans vanquished the reigning champion Robert Gardner, in the Amateur final. Gardner had beaten a little-known 14-year-old called Robert Tyre Jones from Atlanta in the quarter-finals.

Jones had got through two rounds of match play, knocking out a former champion, Eben Byers, in the first.

**Bobby Jones at 14.**

## Alexa Stirling the serene champion

WITHIN A MONTH of Chick Evans's landing his unrivalled double, Alexa Stirling, a childhood companion of Robert Tyre Jones won the Women's Amateur title at Belmont Springs club near Boston. Indeed, six years previously, at the age of 12 she had beaten Jones at a garden party (he was only six), but Jones made off with the small trophy they had played for.

Like Jones, she was taught by Stewart Maiden, the Scottish professional at the East Lake, Atlanta, course. Stirling had red hair, and everything about her had an aura of cool, graceful athleticism.

## Professionals organize

FIFTEEN YEARS after the founding of the British Professional Golfers Association, America's paid performers followed their lead – with the appropriate election of a St Andrews (Scotland) man as president, Robert White.

A benevolent fund was set up. Underlying the move for organization was a feeling that the professional was worth his hire and that the widely held perception of the pro as footloose, sometimes inebriate and certainly not a gentleman was unfair and should be improved. To this, and other ends, the first meeting of the USPGA was held at Minneapolis at the time of the Open championship. The association also set up a competition of their own, and James Barnes, "Long Jim" as he was known on account of his prodigious hitting, beat Jock Hutchison in the final at Siwanoy, New York. The entry was 31 and the trophy and prize money were the gift of a wealthy encourager of the profession, Rodman Wanamaker.

The amateurs continued to get the better showing in the newspapers. The weakness in the standing of the PGA championship was that the finalists in October had been second and third to amateur Evans in June, and they had trailed in the wake of amateurs in three Opens in the last four years.

### TEE TALK

**"If Evans could putt like Travis it would be foolish to stage an amateur tourney in this country."**

JERRY TRAVERS,
speaking about Chick Evans.

# Walter Hagen points the post-war way

AMERICAN GOLF was quicker off the mark than was feasible in an exhausted Britain when the carnage had finally run its course.

America's entry into the war in 1917 and its vast shipments of men and materiel to Europe did not bring a complete shutdown of competition at home.

Jock Hutchison won a tournament similar to the Open with a total of 292. It was held in aid of Red Cross charities at Whitemarsh Valley, Chestnut Hill, Pennsylvania, in June 1917. Bobby Jones and Alexa Stirling formed a travelling foursome with another Atlanta player, Perry Adair, and Elaine Rosenthal of Chicago, runner up in the 1914 national championship. They raised $150,000 for the Red Cross.

## Carefree Hagen wins the Open

WALTER HAGEN reached new peaks of self-assurance in the Open at Brae Burn in June 1919.

He took a young lady to the theatre in Boston the night before beating Mike Brady in a play-off. Later they socialized with the star of the show, Al Jolson, and Hagen went out to face Brady after about three hours' sleep. He had forced the tie with a four at the 72nd.

On the green for two, he had Brady come out to watch him putt for the title. His ball spun out and hung on the edge.

Alexa Stirling: partnered Bobby Jones in charity events.

**SCORECARD**

1919

**US Open** (Brae Burn, Mass)
W Hagen 78 73 75 75 301
(Play-off, Hagen 77, MJ Brady 78)

**USPGA** (Engineers' Club, NY)
J Barnes bt F McLeod 6 & 5

**US Amateur** (Oakmont, Pa)
S Davidson Heron bt RT Jones 5 & 4

**US Women's Amateur** (Shawnee on
Delaware, Pa)
A Stirling bt Mrs WA Gavin 6 & 5

"Long Jim" Barnes: trophy.

## Herron outplays Bobby Jones at Merion

BOBBY JONES reached his first national Amateur final but ran into in a formidable opponent in the shape of Davey Herron who, playing at his home club of Oakmont, Pennsylvania, was four under fours and beat Jones 5 & 4 in the final. Francis Ouimet's amateur status had been restored in the first few days of 1918. The USGA, under their president Frank Woodward, underlined their rigorous attitude to amateurism by defining a professional as "Engaging in any business connected with the game of golf wherein one's usefulness of profits arise because of skill or prominence in the game of golf." Not everyone agreed, with the Western GA supporting Ouimet.

# Counting the cost: Graham killed in action

CHAMPIONSHIP GOLF should have restarted in Britain in October 1919 with the Women's Amateur at Burnham, but a rail strike got in the way. Accordingly, play in all major events had to wait another year, although Abe Mitchell won a victory tournament in 1919 that was an Open in all except name. The Open was to be the Royal & Ancient's responsibility from now on.

For thousands, however, there was no restart. One of the saddest losses was that of Jack Graham, with Ball and Hilton one of the powerful Hoylake trio, and reckoned to be the best player never to win the British Amateur. He was killed in the battle for Hooge, fighting with a battalion of the Liverpool Scottish regiment. Graham was an all-rounder, and played rugby for Liverpool. The PGA lost their secretary, F.H.Brown, who died on active service with the Honourable Artillery Company.

Madge Neill Fraser, who played for Scotland, worked as a nurse in Serbia, and died there.

Chelmsford lost seven members out of their 1914 total of 241, and their professional, Robert Finch, died of wounds in France in 1917. Their steward, Konter, returned safely. Subscriptions were trebled.

J.L.C.Jenkins, last prewar winner of the British Amateur, was injured in the fighting and never regained championship form. Ernest Jones, an English pro, lost a leg in the war, but made a new career for himself with the first indoor golf school in New York City. Tommy Armour, who was born in Edinburgh, returned to the golf course from his service as a tank commander with only one eye, and with metal plates inserted in his head and shoulder.

Woking's finances were left in turmoil by the loss of subscriptions, and it was drifting into debt. The club had appealed to the Necropolis Company to cut their rent, and received a timely 1916 Christmas present in the form of a rent reduction of £500.

Worplesdon men passed resolutions which put their women members back where they had been before the war and the grant of the vote in 1919 to women over 30. "No ladies' match may ever play at weekends or a on a Bank Holiday unaccompanied by a male member," was the message from a meeting just before Christmas 1919.

**SHORT PUTTS**

● A.D.Locke was born on November 20, 1917, in the Transvaal.

● "Long Jim" Barnes published instructional book — the first to use photographs for the task.

# George Duncan's turnabout Open

GEORGE DUNCAN, vintage 1883, son of an Aberdeenshire policeman, carried off the first postwar British Open from the Royal Cinque Ports course at Deal in Kent. He did so by virtue of the biggest turnabout in Open history. After two rounds he was to all intents and purposes sunk, for his total was 160. That might have been a winning score 30 years ago but not now, at halfway, in the days of ever-improving equipment, in particular the rubber-wound ball. Much livelier projectiles, the Haskell and its derivatives were causing many a club to call in the architect to move hazards back a little and so protect their par against the continually increasing length of golfers' shots.

Abe Mitchell was in the lead, having got round twice in 147 strokes. Duncan now set another record by covering the final 36 holes in 143 (71 + 72), and got home two ahead of Alex Herd and three clear of Ted Ray. Duncan was the first Open champion to earn three-figure prize money – exactly £100 out of a total purse of £225.

George Duncan: bad start but...

## 'I'll be back,' says Hagen

WALTER HAGEN did not thrive on this most natural of links. He arrived as reigning US Open champion, and was an immediate magnet for the crowds. Hagen often travelled in a procession of two large cars, he in the first, his manager in the second. A hired Rolls Royce was his usual transport in Britain.

He changed fashions in golf as radically as Vardon had changed playing methods. The Triumvirate had progressed to functional garb radically different from the top hats and red coats of pioneer days. Knickerbocker suits, flat cap or trilby, and, invariably, a tie, were the widespread rule. Hagen gave up the hat in the cause of showing off his sharply parted, gleaming black hair. He also went in for much lighter garb, in paler colours.

At Deal Hagen's first round score was five worse than Duncan's, upon which he was deserted by his gallery. He improved the second time round to 84, but finished 55th. "I'll come back," he promised .

## Tolley's two is trump at 37th

ROBERT GARDNER, the former American Amateur titleholder, fought out a marvellous British Amateur final on June 11 against Cyril Tolley at Muirfield.

George Greenwood described in The Daily Telegraph how Tolley, who seemed well in control as the second 18 holes of the final moved to a climax, suddenly looked vulnerable when Gardner put together three threes on the 11th, 12th, and 13th, with par, birdie and eagle.

At the 17th Tolley still led by a hole, but Gardner, who reached the green on this 530 yard hole with his second, sank a five-yard putt for another three. Tolley, "groping on his knees for a line to the hole", followed the American in from three yards to protect his lead in a most precarious fashion.

On the 36th hole, with a gusting wind blowing across the fairway towards "prickly and tenacious rushes on the right," Gardner's slightly hooked drive held up against the wind. Tolley's drive went into a villainous-looking clump of spikes, so on went the match to the 37th. This 204-yard par three, defended by bunkers left and right and with a stone wall beyond it, brought fine shots on to the green from both men. Gardner's ball finished 15 yards past the flag, to the left, Tolley's five yards short. Gardner missed his putt, Tolley did not.

A crowd of 3,000 cheered the two men, both war veterans, off the course. Tolley had been a prisoner of war; Gardner had fought as an officer in the US Army.

**Cyril Tolley and (right) Bernard Darwin.**

## Old guard still keeps control

TED RAY became the oldest player to win the US Open Golf championship when he held off Harry Vardon, Jack Burke, Leo Diegel and Jock Hutchison by a stroke at Inverness, Ohio. Vardon, 50, was giving seven years away to Ray, and appeared to be handing Ray a beating, too, since he led by five strokes with seven holes to go. Up came a strong northerly, and Vardon had fives at each of those holes as the pack closed on him, and Ray slipped past.

The two leading amateurs, Chick Evans and the 18-year-old Bobby Jones, were only three and four strokes respectively away from Ray, and both of them were ahead of the reigning champion, Walter Hagen.

Ray, whose pipe was seldom absent from between his clenched teeth, was, like Vardon, a Channel Islander from Jersey. Ray's Open marked a definite step up in the social perception of the professional golfer. For the first time, the players at Inverness were allowed to make use of all the clubhouse facilities.

# Hutchison scrapes in, wins out

JOCK HUTCHISON, one of the better immigrant Scots professionals, won the USPGA title by one hole in the final, gaining entry to the event only as a substitute. The losing finalist was a British born professional, J. Douglas Edgar. A week later Edgar, victor by 6 strokes over Harry Vardon in the 1914 French Open, became the first player to win the Canadian Open two years in succession. In the autumn he went on to win the Southern Open – and a few months later was found dead on an Atlanta street. He bled to death from a thigh wound, probably inflicted by a mugger. Good judges considered Edgar a matchless and innovative stylist.

# Ethel Smyth smooths Woking waters

DESPITE THE granting of the vote to women at the end of the war, there were still prickly men versus women scenes at many clubs.

At Woking Ethel Smyth, imprisoned before the war for suffragette militancy, helped to bring peace after a difference of opinion over starting times for women, still temporary members, and over days when women were permitted to lunch at the club. The rift was papered over with the help of a diplomatic Smyth resolution.

## SCORECARD

**British Open** (Royal Cinque Ports, Kent)
G Duncan 80 80 71 72 303

**US Open** (Inverness, Ohio)
E Ray 74 73 73 75 295

**USPGA** (Flossmoor, Ill)
J Hutchison bt J Douglas Edgar 1h

**British Amateur** (Muirfield, Scot)
C Tolley bt RA Gardner 37th

**US Amateur** (Engineers' Club, NY)
C Evans bt F Ouimet 7 & 6

**British Women's Amateur** (Newcastle, Co Down)
C Leitch bt M Griffiths 7 & 6

**U S Women's Amateur** (Cleveland, Ohio)
A Stirling bt Mrs JV Hurd 4 & 3

# Alexa's three in a row

ALEXA STIRLING, the first southerner to break into the American Amateur roll of honour, took the trophy for the third time in a row at the Mayfield club, in Ohio. Her final opponent was Dorothy Campbell Hurd, 11 years on from her capture of the two major amateur titles. Stirling also won the Canadian title.

Mrs. Hurd: still a contender, 11 years on from her unique double.

# Evans wins classic final

All the British challengers, including Cyril Tolley, failed to qualify for the US Amateur at the Engineers Club, New York, leaving the field clear for the outstanding Americans of the day, Chick Evans and Francis Ouimet, to fight their way into the final, Evans winning 7 & 6. Evans' iron play was at its most potent and as he also putted well, not even Ouimet could prevail against him.

Evans also won his fifth Western Open. The entry for the national title soared in the postwar boom, with 235 players trying for 32 matchplay places.

The Reddy Tee.

## TEE TALK

"Give me a man with big hands, big feet and no brains and I will make a golfer out of him."

WALTER HAGEN,
who had slender, sensitive hands.

# Hutchison spins the Auld Mug to America

JOCK HUTCHISON, who was, appropriately, St Andrews born and bred, won the British Open there on June 25, taking the silver claret jug trophy on its first trip to the United States, where Hutchison, an apprentice clubmaker, had sought fame and fortune 20 years before. Hutchison, unlike many of his fellow countrymen and profession, was of a talkative and nervous disposition. All the same, he planned his assault on the Open with care: he had two strong cards to play.

First, he had relatives in Fife, arrived there well before the championship, and got to know the course thoroughly. Secondly, he carried deeply grooved pitching clubs that pulled the ball up on the most resilient of billiard table-like surfaces.

This factor soon began to elicit the same mutterings of discontent that had followed Walter Travis's conquest of the Royal St George's greens with his Schenectady putter.

Hutchison's opponents might have added, in an unguarded or ungenerous moment, that he was a touch lucky, for he came within a fraction of the billion to one combination – two holes in one in a row. As it was, in the first round, at the course's celebrated "loop" at the far end of the links, he aced the eighth and came with an inch or two of another at the ninth.

His total was 72 and, though he faded to 75, then 79, over the next 36 holes, a 70 in the final round gave him a play-off with amateur Roger Wethered, which he won by nine strokes.

Here again good fortune favoured Hutchison, for Wethered would not have been required to play off had he not incurred a penalty for accidentally stepping on his ball during the third round.

Bobby Jones, making his first attempt at the British Open, found St Andrews a puzzle and, after an unhappy time round the "loop", he did not complete his third round.

Jones later denied the calumny that he had torn up his card, but it had taken the Atlanta prodigy till the end of the war to cast off his earlier tendency to tantrums.

**Jock Hutchison: careful campaign in Fife.**

# Jim Barnes holds off the Haig

**Jim Barnes receives Open trophy from President Harding.**

THE SILVER JUBILEE of the American Open was a triumph for Jim Barnes. He led every round at the Columbia Club in Maryland, and had the trophy presented to him by the US president, Warren Harding.

Barnes came to the United States in 1906 from his native Cornwall in England, where he had been born at Lelant in 1887. He had shared fourth place in Ouimet's Open eight years ago, and now outpaced the ebullient Walter Hagen and left him and Fred McLeod a distant second. He scored 69 to Hagen's 79 in round one. Barnes had already won the first and second PGA championships but, though his career was based in the United States, he would not give up his British citizenship.

American amateur talent was such that Chick Evans was fourth and Bobby Jones fifth.

# Graham beats Jones but not Hunter

ALLAN GRAHAM experienced extremes of triumph, tragedy and defeat in Amateur championship week at his home club, Royal Liverpool.

Allan, brother of Jack who was killed in action in the war, defeated Bobby Jones 6 & 5, and marched on all the way to the final, on the eve of which his father died.

Quite apart from Jack, a Hoylake player thought by many to be the equal (certainly in stroke play) of fellow members John Ball and Harold Hilton, and who lost only twice in ten appearances for Scotland, the Grahams of Hoylake had a distinguished golfing record. In 1901, Molly Graham, who also played at Wimbledon, beat no less a player than Rhona Adair for the British Amateur title.

Allan Graham's heavy defeat (12 & 11) by Willie Hunter in the final must be weighed against the shock of the loss of his father.

Four months later in the American Amateur at St Louis, Missouri, Hunter beat Jones at the penultimate hole, but lost in the quarterfinal against Robert Gardner, the hero in defeat at Muirfield 15 months earlier. This time Gardner was not given the chance to engage in play-off excitement, for Jesse Guildford saw him off by 7 & 6.

The choice of St Louis as the Amateur Championship site was a novelty: never before had the title been decided west of the Mississippi. Francis Ouimet led the qualifiers with 144.

The idea of Olympic golf did not meet with acclamation from America's amateurs. Only two leading players, Bob Jones, who got through only two rounds at St Louis, and Max Marston, beaten by his first opponent, Ouimet, agreed to go to the summer games in Antwerp, so the idea of a United States team was dropped.

# Leitch vengeance for Wethered defeat

Cecil Leitch (headband): got the better of Joyce Wethered at Turnberry in the British Women's Amateur final.

JOYCE WETHERED could not part Cecil Leitch from her British title as she had parted her from the English title a year before. This time, at Turnberry, Leitch won easily, three holes from home. She was recognized as the leading woman player of the day, and had been since before the war.

Wethered beat her opponents almost apologetically. The powers of concentration that she had demonstrated so chillingly at Sheringham the previous year were such that, rather after the Jerry Travers fashion, her demeanour of hardly noticing what the opposition was up to was an extremely powerful weapon, though her natural reserve and graceful manners precluded any complaints from friend or foe. Moreover, her swing was a thing of beauty, a thing apart.

Leitch was a far more forth-right character, attacking the ball fiercely as no woman before her had done. Aggressively punching her iron shots, She brought a new athleticism to the game, but Leitch did not possess the equable temperament of her most celebrated opponent. Their rivalry quickly became a big crowd puller, as they fought their way to several final confrontations.

One of golf's extroverts, Marion Hollins, ended Alexa Stirling's run of victories – she was in line for a unique fourth consecutive US Amateur Championship till she met Hollins in the final at Deal, New Jersey, and foundered 5 & 4. Hollins was a respected big hitter and excellent iron player, however, and the biggest shock of the event was probably the defeat early on of Cecil Leitch, British champion for the second year, by Mrs F.C.Letts.

## US win first "international"

Hoylake, as perhaps the most celebrated hotbed of amateur golf, was the fitting venue for the first international meeting (without benefit of trophy as yet) of British and American amateurs. The visiting Americans won by 9-3 (4-0 in foursomes and 5-3 in singles). Although the British team included Cyril Tolley (who beat Chick Evans 4 & 3), and the Scot, Tommy Armour, the "engine room" of the American team – Bobby Jones, Francis Ouimet and

William Fownes – made sure that Britain struggled almost from the moment Jones stepped on to the tee and drove the first ball of the day – "before the cheers had died away or the movie cameras had begun to work," according to the club historian, Guy Farrar.

He added: "It was obvious that certain members of the British team were suffering from an acute attack of nerves. America did not play unbeatable golf . . . we obligingly dug our own graves."

## John Ball's farewell to the Amateur

THE 1921 British Amateur was not only staged at the runner-up's own club, but at that of the eight times winner of the event, John Ball.

He chose this year – at the age of 61 – to compete for the last time for the trophy he first won 43 years before. He reached the sixth round, too.

Bernard Darwin pictured him "with the blue-jerseyed fishermen and indeed the whole population of Hoylake tramping prayerfully and proudly behind him." A unique and moving sight, Darwin thought. Harold Hilton was still going strong, too

John Ball: swansong at 61.

"At his best, Wethered had a game which few amateurs have ever equalled ... a grand iron player with a 'power of cue' if the phrase may be permissible."

BERNARD DARWIN.

"It's a shame but he [Bobby Jones] will never make a golfer – too much temper."
ALEX SMITH.

Bobby Jones: found St Andrews a puzzle; Roger Wethered (right) disappointment.

● Open Champion Jim Barnes was not allowed to have it all his own way in America, and met his match in the USPGA final at Inwood, New York, losing to Walter Hagen 3 & 2. This was another first for Hagen, the first American-born player to win the PGA.

● Bobby Jones was given a rusty blade putter by Jimmy Maiden, brother of his teacher Stewart, after missing too many putts in a heavy defeat by Francis Ouimet. Jones at once began to sink everything with this weapon, which Jimmy had named "Calamity Jane." Since Jones's form with it was anything but a calamity, the humour of the situation appealed to everyone, and the name stuck.

● The USGA and the Royal & Ancient ruled that the ball must be not more than 1.62 ounces in weight and 1.62 inches in diameter.

● Cary Middlecoff was born on January 6 in Tennessee.

# Hagen, Fownes and Co make it America's year

WALTER HAGEN became the first American-born professional to win the British Open at Sandwich in June, 1922. Two months later William Fownes's team beat Great Britain and Ireland in the inaugural Walker Cup match. The shift of world golfing power to America was now undeniable.

The truly remarkable achievement was the relatively short amount of time that it had taken for the United States to aggregate such a long list of talented players, from a mere handful of clubs 30 years before. How right H.K.Vanderbilt had been – "a game I think would go well in our country." Hagen was at the head of nearly two million American golfers.

His triumph at Royal St George's, after his abject failure two years ago down the road at Deal, was sweet and complete. Moreover, two more Americans were in the first four – Jim Barnes, level in second place with George Duncan, and in fourth place, Jock Hutchison, who had won 12 months before. All were within three strokes of Hagen. J.H.Taylor, a golfer from another age it seemed, was sixth, four strokes behind.

But no-one was within a country mile of Hagen as a publicist for golf, and on his return to America he set off on one of the exhibition tours (usually in company with the Australian trick-shot artist, Joe Kirkwood) that served to finance his love of the good life – and the fair sex.

He would play at least seven exhibitions a week, performing double headers often enough at weekends. His fee – the gate money at a dollar a head: his attraction – his penchant for breaking course records; his business partner – bon viveur and canniest of sports promoters, Bob Harlow, who continued on and off to ply his original trade of journalist.

*Generations apart but together: Walter Hagen and Harry Vardon.*

## Gene Sarazen lands US pro double

At the first US Open to be held at the Skokie Country Club, Illinois, which was also the first at which gate money was charged, a fresh and intriguing personality became one of the giants of the game, though he was a giant in reputation, not in stature, since he stands 5ft 4in, and has small hands. For good measure, Gene Sarazen followed his Open win by beating Emmet French four weeks later in the PGA final at Oakmont, Pennsylvania. Hagen had declined to defend his PGA title – he had an exhibition to play. So, by way of a hat-trick, though the final leg was an unofficial event, Sarazen defeated the newly crowned British Open champion 3 & 2 in a so-called world championship over 72 holes at the Westchester-Biltmore club, Rye, New York.

The victory might easily have cost Sarazen his life, for he played in great pain towards the end, and immediately afterwards had to have his appendix removed. Born at Harrison, New York, at the age of ten Sarazen walked to work as a caddie at Rye for Apawamis club members, and had escaped death before only a couple of years before his Open success when he had severe problems with fluid on the lung.

Sarazen's name was his own invention, for he thought his real one (Saraceni) was suitable for a violinist, but not for a golfer. A Haig-like shot, a bold approach with a wood to the final green as Bobby Jones, Bill Mehlhorn and Hagen headed the chasing pack, gave Sarazen a birdie and the Open championship – at 20.

*"Wild Bill" Mehlhorn.*

*Gene Sarazen's big 1922 moment.*

## Joyce Wethered takes over the leadership

WITH THE BIGGEST margin of victory – 9 & 7 – since the final was extended to 36 holes in 1913, Joyce Wethered gained the title Cecil Leitch had denied her a year since. The match at Prince's, Sandwich, was all square till the second round, when Wethered's relentless long and accurate hitting destroyed even Leitch's hard-hitting, aggressive style. Not many men, it was thought, could equal the Wethered brilliance, an opinion Bobby Jones shared. A third English Amateur title in a row added to Wethered's fame.

Glenna Collett, from Rhode Island, proved herself to be the outstanding new talent in American women's golf by breaking the Amateur qualifying record at the Greenbrier Club, White Sulphur Springs, West Virginia, with 81. On she went to the final, where she defeated Mrs William Gavin, from England, 5 & 4.

# Into the breach with Bernard Darwin

BERNARD DARWIN went to America to report the first official Walker Cup match between the United States and Great Britain and Ireland, and finished as a winning hero in a losing cause. He replaced the captain, Robert Harris, who fell ill, as a player and as captain too, at the National Links, New York.

His team lost 4-8, which was better by a point than Britain and Ireland had achieved in the unofficial inaugural match at Hoylake the previous year.

Darwin had a lucky escape on the practice ground, where he was hit in the chest, but was able to tee off against the opposing captain and former US champion, William Fownes, and beat him 3 & 1.

Cyril Tolley and Roger Wethered were no match for Jesse Guilford and Bobby Jones respectively in the top singles, while Francis Ouimet beat C.C.Aylmer 8 & 7. Wethered and Aylmer won their foursome and, apart from Darwin's, the other British points were won by W.W.Mackenzie (6 & 5 against Max Marston) and in unique fashion, as far as the Walker Cup is concerned, by C.V.L.Hooman. He was level with Jess Sweetser after 36 holes, and there were to be no extra holes, but the two players did not seem to realize this, and had gone off on No 37 before anyone could stop them. Hooman won and the result was allowed to stand.

**Bernard Darwin.**

# Jess Sweetser trounces Bobby Jones at Brookline

BOBBY JONES suffered one of the worst beatings of his career when Jess Sweetser of the Siwanoy Club, Bronxville, New York, knocked him out at the semifinal stage of the American Amateur at The Country Club, Brookline, by 8 & 7.

Sweetser secured another distinguished scalp in the title round, defeating Chick Evans 3 & 2.

## SHORT PUTTS

● The Worplesdon mixed foursomes, inaugurated in 1921, was an immediate success and a big draw for men and women from all round the London area, and before long brought pairs from much further afield. Roger and Joyce Wethered, who had been beaten the previous year by Eleanor Helme and T.A.Torrance, won in October, which became the invariable month of the event, by 2 & 1 in the final against Mrs Patey and E.N.Leyton.

● The Prince of Wales drives himself in, not too well, as captain of the Royal & Ancient.

● The United States Golf Association continued in its opposition to the use of steel-shafted clubs in championship play.

## SCORECARD

**British Open** (Royal St George's, Kent)
W Hagen 76 73 79 72 300

**US Open** (Skokie CC, Ill)
G Sarazen 72 73 75 68 288

**USPGA** (Oakmont, Pa)
G Sarazen bt E French 4 & 3

**British Amateur** (Prestwick, Scot)
E Holderness bt J Caven 1h

**US Amateur** (Brookline,)
JW Sweetser bt C Evans 3 & 2

**British Women's Amateur** (Prince's, Kent)
J Wethered bt C Leitch 9 & 7

**U S Women's Amateur** (Greenbrier, W Va)
G Collett bt Mrs WA Gavin 5 & 4

**Walker Cup** (National Links, NY)
US bt GB & Ireland 8–4

# Birdie hunt

BERNARD DARWIN'S conclusions about the defeat of Britain and Ireland in the Walker Cup inaugural led to an experiment on Boxing Day at fashionable Worplesdon, southwest of London. He said: "We played well, but the other men played better ... when, very rarely, I keep close to the par score I expect the other man to break up. Not so with the American golfer; he takes the par score in his stride; it is the 'birdies', the holes done in under par, that he thinks about."

Worplesdon therefore staged a competition against par standard, as applied in the United States. Par was set at 71 (bogey had been 79) and R.H.de Montmorency had scored 33-37=70 for a course record the previous year.

# Dame Ethel Smyth and the short cut

A WONDER CAME to light as 1922 passed into 1923, when the name of Ethel Smyth, the window-breaking suffragette of yesteryear, appeared in the New Year Honours list. She was to become a Dame of the British Empire. Dame Ethel herself was convinced that the honour was the outcome of the friendship of Lord Riddell, lawyer, newspaper proprietor and a member of the Woking golf club, with Lloyd George, the prime minister.

His lordship knew that Smyth had averted another clash of the sexes at Woking golf club with her successful motion about a vexed short cut certain women members persisted in taking between general club rooms and the women's section, and which led past the men's changing rooms. There was even talk, Smyth had heard, of a ban on women playing at the weekend at all.

She told a Ladies' committee meeting that none could doubt that it was in the taking of this short cut, "given the modesty of the British male," that their chief crime lay. This raised a laugh, all but three unashamed short-cutters voted to abandon the route.

Dame Ethel, though she was credited with being a straight driver, on occasion she sent her caddie to the Greenkeeper's yard to borrow a sickle to trim a patch of heather in which her ball was apparently lost.

# Jones's 'famine' is ended at Inwood

THE NEW YORK sporting public were privileged to witness the first major championship victory of Bobby Jones, the Atlanta amateur, who won at the Inwood club, Long Island. Though his game at all points dazzled the critics, he had till now always managed to find a way to lose promising positions,.

He nearly did it again this time, stumbling into an unlooked for play-off with a double bogey six at the 72nd hole. There was a three-shot swing against him there, since Jones dropped two shots and Bobby Cruickshank, chasing hard, saved one.

The play-off next day was settled at the same hole, for the pair were level after 17 holes. Cruickshank's drive went too far left, forcing him to lay up short of the lagoon in front of the green. Jones shook off all doubts with a 200-yard shot on to the green and, by two strokes, 76 to 78, he was Open champion. It is scarcely appropriate to add "at last," as only four months had passed since his 21st birthday. He had, though, been trying for a major since he was 14.

The USGA were now dependent for most of their revenue on Open gate money. This lends a certain irony to their situation, in that their sure-fire gate improver was an amateur, and there has never been a suggestion that, while engaged in serious competition, Jones was anything else.

This Open was a week-long production. Qualifying required four days and the Open proper two, plus play-off.

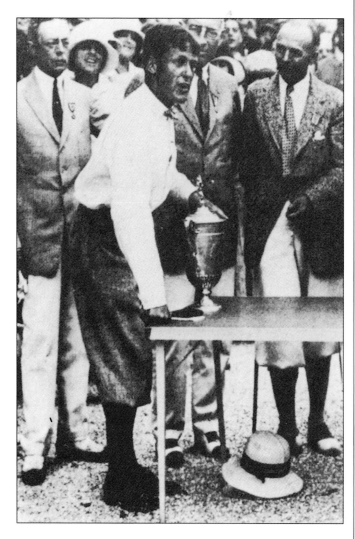

Bobby Jones: attained his majority in 1923, and his first "major," the US Open at Inwood after a play-off.

# Havers keeps the silver mug at home

ARTHUR GLADSTONE HAVERS made his name reverberate even more than usual by beating a star-studded field, cincluding Walter Hagen by a stroke and Macdonald Smith by two for the British Open on the Ayrshire links at Troon.

He was still young, at 25, but had first qualified for the Open proper nine years previously, though he had never done better than fourth, three behind Jock Hutchison, in 1921.

With his reputation established by lifting the Auld Claret Jug, Havers added icing to his cake by beating Bobby Jones over 16 holes and Gene Sarazen over 72 on a tour of the United States.

Open Winners together: Sandy Herd(left) vintage 1902, with Arthur Havers 1923. Macdonald Smith (right) went close at Troon.

# Fresh faces behind women's trophies

AMERICAN WOMEN'S golf could not fail in the postwar years to gain the attention of the smart magazines as well as that of the sports reporters. One graceful eye-catching beauty after another took the major prizes. Auburn-haired Alexa Stirling's reign had bracketed the war years; Glenna Collett warded off the foreign challenge of Englishwoman Mrs William Gavin in 1922; and then along came Edith Cummings, the very height of 1920s glamour and fashion.

F.Scott Fitzgerald is said to have taken her as the pattern for the character of Jordan Baker in "The Great Gatsby", imbued with a casual elegance to match her golfing skill. Cummings' brother, Dexter, was collegiate champion and the family was numbered among the social elite.

Edith Cummings joined the sporting elite when she defeated Stirling 3 & 2 at the Westchester-Biltmore Country Club, Rye, New York. This went well with the Cummings aura of luxury, grace, space and beauty, for the club offered 400 rooms, 45 acres of beach club, a polo field, a race-track and two 18-hole courses.

Cummings had never been taken past the 16th hole all week, apart from a cliff-hanging win at the second extra hole against Mrs Florence Vanderbeck, who had earlier knocked out Glenna Collett in the second round, by 3 & 2. Edith Leitch tried again, but was routed 6 & 4 by the eventual champion. In the last six championships Alexa Stirling won three times and was runner-up twice.

Joyce Wethered reached the unprecedented heights of four English titles in a row, but neither she nor Cecil Leitch got to the final of the British Amateur at Burnham and Berrow. Doris Chambers, a veteran of Home International play, won.

Chambers, from Birkenhead, was a member of Wirral Ladies on Merseyside. She was like George Duncan in that she played golf at the gallop. Her win at Burnham was achieved in one of the stormiest weeks on record. When she returned to her club, she did a lap of honour there mounted on a shire horse, suitably re-ribboned.

# U S squeeze home in Walker Cup at HQ

THOUGH without Bobby Jones, busy at Harvard, the United States retained the Walker Cup at St Andrews by a point, a result the British and Irish team must always consider an opportunity lost.

They got off to a prosperous start on May 18. Cyril Tolley and Roger Wethered led off with a 6 & 5 win over Francis Ouimet and Jess Sweetser and, though the captain, Robert Harris, and C.V.L.Hooman lost to Bob

Gardner and Max Marston, the home partnerships of Holderness and Hope and Wilson and Murray made the first day score 3-1 against the Americans, who began the singles badly on the following day.

They needed five wins to keep the trophy and six to win outright, but trailed in most matches after 18 holes. George Rotan, who was a new team member, rallied from six down after 14 to win 5 & 4 over Willis Mackenzie, taking

(from the 15th) 11 of the next 12 holes. Fred Wright and Max Marston wrested success from threatened defeat, Wright with a birdie putt at the last, after being two down with three to play.

Ouimet had been obliged to equal the course record of 70 to earn a half with Wethered, and Gardner won by one hole against the British captain.

All rested on Dr O.F.Willing's match. His 2 & 1 victory in the bottom match sent the Cup back

to America. Gardner, the American captain, possessed of an excellent voice, brought proceedings to a close with a song to the crowd from the steps of the Royal & Ancient.

In a sage postscript to the second Walker Cup match, Howard Whitney of the USGA told the executive committee that, "international competition in golf has done as much for the development of the game as any other factor."

---

## TEE TALK

**"Mr Wethered must have an intellect adapted to all known spheres of precise calculation."**

NEWSPAPER CRITIC.

**"I had no reason to be dissatisfied with his play."**

ROGER WETHERED'S SISTER, JOYCE,
keeping calm as usual.

**"I know of no more terrific crack than that of a perfectly struck drive by Mr Wethered; it is like a pistol shot."**

BERNARD DARWIN.

# Stubborn Sarazen holds on to PGA title

WALTER HAGEN'S year 1923 definitely was not, for the master of scrambling finishes, having lost his British Open championship by a stroke, was unable to get his

PGA title back from Gene Sarazen, though he fought down to the 38th hole at Pelham, New York. This was the first extra holes finish for the title.

Gene Sarazen: got the better of the Haig.

# Wethered and Harris keep out US team

THE OMENS FOR the second Walker Cup match had seemed to favour the British at the end of the Amateur championship on the Royal Cinque Ports course at Deal, which immediately preceded the Cup meeting.Two Americans, Francis Ouimet and Douglas Grant, reached the last four, but the final was contested by the Walker Cup captain, Robert Harris, and Roger Wethered, who strolled to his first title by 7 & 6.

Jess Sweetser was parted from his American Amateur title only at the 38th hole of the final against Max Marston at Flossmoor, Illinois. But Marston had to beat Bobby Jones, top qualifier with Chick Evans, and Ouimet.

---

## SCORECARD

**British Open** (Troon, Scot)
AG Havers 73 73 73 76 295

**US Open** (Inwood, NY)
RT Jones 71 73 76 76 296
(Play-off, Jones 76, RA Cruickshank 78)

**USPGA** (Pelham CC, NY)
G Sarazen bt W Hagen 38th

**British Amateur** (Royal Cinque Ports, Kent)
R Wethered bt R Harris 7 & 6

**US Amateur** (Flossmoor, Ill)
M Marston bt J Sweetser 38th

**British Women's Amateur** (Burnham & Berrow, Somerset)
D Chambers bt A Macbeth 2h

**US Women's Amateur** (Westchester-Biltmore, Rye, NY)
E Cummings bt A Stirling 3 & 2

**Walker Cup** (St Andrews, Scot)
US bt GB & Ireland 6½-5½

# Hagen holds nerve for victory

ERNEST WHITCOMBE found out in harrowing fashion at Royal Liverpool's Hoylake links that there was nothing amiss with Walter Hagen's nerve in a tight spot.

Whitcombe, born at Burnham in 1890, played the last nine in the second round in 32 and set a course record of 70. He faded in the final round to 78 for a total of 302, and therefore knew that 77 would give Hagen the title. Hagen knew it, too, and then buckled down to negotiate the last five holes in 21 shots to capture his second British Open title. Poor Whitcombe had a long wait before the roar of the crowd told him that Hagen, over those last crucial holes, had equalled par and beaten him – with the climax a putt on the 18th slightly longer than Hagen was tall – five feet ten inches.

The Haig's style of play had been utterly typical of the man — many a wild shot, mended by rescue efforts that defied belief because of their audacity and Hagen's ability to produce them when all seemed lost, and at precisely the right moment. He needed to snatch a few strokes back here and there; he had started his last round 6, 4, 6.

Perhaps the most remarkable statistic to emerge from the championship was that, if the qualifying scores and the four championship rounds played by J.H.Taylor, now 53, were added together, he had the lowest total of all. His performance in the 72 holes of the Open itself, however, was only good enough to give him fifth place, six behind Hagen. Alex Herd and James Braid were still trying, but finished well down the order.

After his relative drought in the previous year, Hagen was now in his best pot-hunting form, and in the autumn he was beating Jim Barnes by two holes for the USPGA title at French Lick, Indiana.

# Bobby Jones close to 'Pro-Am' double

PROOF OF THE strength of the amateur game in America in the first quarter of the 20th century came with Bobby Jones gaining his first Amateur title a year after beating the professionals in the Open. Francis Ouimet, the first prodigy of US golf had won the Open before the Amateur, too. Chick Evans had won both in the same year.

Jones, putting his salad days behind him, had mellowed, remarkably for a 22-year-old, into the very model of what the world thinks of as a southern gentleman. Whether he was playing professionals or amateurs, the feeling among them was that if they were in touch with Jones, they were in with a chance. When he was beaten, the headlines seldom said: "John Smith won"; they said: "Bobby Jones lost".

Jones came second in the Open in June before he won the Amateur in September. Cyril Walker beat him by three strokes at Oakland Hills, Michigan, designed on the same lines as the Muirfield's two nines in Scotland. Both have graceful clubhouses and quick greens. Walker's prize was $1,000, and the total prize fund $5,000. By 1919 the prize fund had increased from the original $150 of 1895 to $1,745. The growing entry list caused this to be the first Open with regional qualifying, at two centres. It was decided to allow the use of steel-shafted putters for the first time.

Walker, at barely 118 pounds, refused to be blown off course by either Jones's reputation or the gusty wind. "Wild Bill" Mehlhorn was third, one behind Jones, and Hagen, Bobby Cruickshank and Macdonald Smith were bracketed on 303, six behind Walker, a

Cyril Walker: Mancunian making good at Bobby Jones's expense.

transplanted Englishman, from Manchester. He was also as close to being unknown as a golfer can be who has qualified for a national championship. Walker's name had evidently made little impression on the starter at an event he entered a few months later. Unsure which state Walker represented, the starter asked him which one he was champion of. Walker replied, somewhat testily, that he was "champion of the whole goddamned forty-eight." And so he was, winning the Open by dint of a highly effective short game that made up for his short hitting.

# Walker Cup treble by US

Michael Scott: an example not followed.

THERE WAS NO change in the transatlantic balance of power to judge from an American 9-3 victory in the third staging of the Walker Cup at Garden City, New York. The United States were able to put out a team who had all played before in the competition.

Though the score was one sided, none of the Americans won before the 33rd hole. The match was a personal triumph for the Hon. Michael Scott, who was 45 years old and had won the Australian Amateur and Open during the 1900s. His sister, Lady Margaret Scott, had won the first three British Women's Amateur titles 30 years ago.

Against the United States, Michael Scott won in the foursomes (the only Britain and Ireland point on the first day) in company with Robert Scott junior, beating Bobby Jones and William Fownes when Jones was

a few days away from his first American Amateur success.

Then in singles Scott defeated Jess Sweetser by 7 & 6. Scott did not often leave the fairway. Cyril Tolley, the captain, was the only other visitor to disturb the even tenor of America's way in the singles. The celebrated trio of Jones, Ouimet and Evans were seven holes up between them, while Gardner, their captain, Jesse Guilford and Dr O.F.Willing cleaned up in the bottom three matches.

There was no doubt that the match continued to attract a great following and passionate argument, but once a year was felt to be a financial burden, and that going to the Walker Cup well too often might tend to produce ennui. In future, the two sides agreed, biennial matches would be the rule, and 1926 was to see renewal of the rivalry.

# Joyce Wethered carries on, Campbell Hurd comes back

BOTH THE MAJOR women's amateur events were won by British-born players, Joyce Wethered taking the British Amateur and Dorothy Campbell Hurd the American version, Beryl Hawtrey Cautley and Mary Browne being the respective runners-up.

Both were remarkable achievements, Wethered's because in the same year she won her fifth straight English title, Campbell Hurd because, far from being a courtesy competitor at the age of 43, she was, rearmed with the Vardon grip and a remodelled swing, a match for anyone. Considering Willie Park's phrase about putting, she

was more than a match for most. In the final, against a long hitter like Browne, she might have been struggling but for her celebrated knack of getting run-ups to the hole-side and putts underground. Whenever Browne started to rally, Mrs Hurd would exert

pressure with her short game. Eventually it meant a 7 & 6 win. Glenna Collett had fallen to Browne at the 19th in the semifinal. She had broken the qualifying record with a 79 and was rolling along with big wins till she ran into Browne.

Mrs Hurd: a few tips for her son.

Joyce Wethered: Victory at Portrush.

# Ouimet and von Elm take a battering

FRANCIS OUIMET lost 11 & 10 to Bobby Jones in the American Amateur semifinal at Merion, and George von Elm went down 9 & 8 to Jones in the final. It was not unlike Jones to start with conservative margins of victory, then get into gear and win many holes from home.

# Macfarlane's Open after double play-off

WILLIE MACFARLANE proved that there was life in the old-fashioned Scottish professional when, at the end of six rounds in the US Open championship at Worcester Country Club, Massachusetts, he had taken 438 strokes to Bobby Jones's 439. They had tied at 291 after 72 holes, and in the first play-off finished 75 apiece.

In the second, Jones led at the turn by four and they were level after 17 holes. The Scot fought back and on the 18th tee the pair were level again. A four by Macfarlane at the last for a round of 72 was worth the title, Jones taking five, for 73.

Macfarlane, from the Oak Ridge club, Tuckahoe, New York, and born in Aberdeen 34 years ago, was the first champion to win wearing spectacles. He was the first to score 67 in an Open championship, a record he achieved in the second round. Quite apart from the contest between the two principals, this was one of the Open's most closely fought finishes, since Johnny Farrell and Francis Ouimet were a stroke behind Macfarlane and Jones, with Gene Sarazen and Walter Hagen a further stroke back, sharing fifth place. Each of them was in contention tackling the 72nd hole.

Macfarlane took on British Open champion Jim Barnes at Columbia Country Club, near Washington, DC, for the so-called World Championship and was routed 12 & 11.

Willie Macfarlane 438, Bobby Jones (right) 439.

# Long Jim in, Prestwick out

DESPITE VALIANT EFFORTS by Ted Ray and Archie Compston, and almost certainly because an over enthusiastic Scottish crowd ran wild and ruined Macdonald Smith's glittering chances, the Auld Mug went back to America for a second year.

The winner was another expatriate Briton, Jim Barnes, born in Cornwall. He certainly gave himself every chance of winning an Open, achieving regular high finishes in the 1920s. Still a British citizen, Barnes had two USPGA titles and a US Open to his name when he added the British Open at Prestwick to his tally on June 26. The championship was unsatisfactory in that on the last day the vast crowds of Scots who came to cheer Macdonald Smith to his first Open, succeeded only in con-

Alex and (right) Macdonald Smith.

tributing to his defeat. Smith was five ahead after 54 holes, having returned a 69 in the second round, and a 78 in the fourth would have given him the major title he had so often threatened. His chances were lost, as was Smith himself at times, in the massive, jostling, galleries. He took 82 and finished fourth with a total of 303, three behind Barnes. He was the youngest of the three golfing Smith brothers from Carnoustie, and the unluckiest of the trio.

The lack of crowd control led to Prestwick, the club which had been the progenitor and first host of the Open, to be taken off the roster of championship courses.

Silky smooth action: The top of Macdonald Smith's hat and the treetop behind it tell how very still he kept his head until the ball was ...

# Popular champion, unpopular rule

BOBBY JONES had to gain only four victories in the match play section of the US Amateur championship at Oakmont, Pennsylvania. He did so by 11 & 10 against William Reekie, 6 & 5 against Clarence Wolff, 7 & 6 against George von Elm and, in the final, 8 & 7 against Watts Gunn.

He was clearly getting into his stride at 24 years of age.

For the first time stroke play qualifying over 36 holes admitted only 16 players to the match play proceedings. This was thoroughly unpopular and when plans were being made for 1926, the rule was dropped.

Plans for the next year had also to include the provision of a new trophy because the one donated by and named after Theodore Havemeyer, the USGA's first president, was destroyed in a fire at Jones's club, East Lake, in Atlanta, on November 22.

## Hagen beats Mehlhorn in final

WALTER HAGEN kept his USPGA title at the expense of Bill Mehlhorn, one of the major figures in the growth of the fledgling professional tour.

The first shot struck by Hagen in the final at Olympic Fields, Illinois, produced a hole in one. He won far from home.

Mehlhorn was noted for his taste in hats, of the wide-brimmed western variety. He had briefly worked as a bricklayer, the trade followed by his father, who had emigrated from Germany aged 16, to evade the military service he would have had to begin a year later.

Even for such a superb golfer – particularly from tee to green – as Mehlhorn, it was not easy to make a living purely as a player unless, as with Walter Hagen, a national title could be almost always trumpeted to encourage the public to watch exhibition matches.

The tour, based on wintertime events in the (sometimes) sunny south and west, was growing slowly. Even the best of the American professionals had to hustle for their prize money, but they had more opportunities for competition.

Their English brethren tended to be tied to their club jobs, with fewer chances of taking on the best available talent on a wider stage, and the difference between the two régimes was becoming evident when golfers from the two nations were in opposition.

### SHORT PUTTS

● The USGA and Royal & Ancient ban deeply grooved club faces, following criticisms of equipment used by Jock Hutchison in winning the 1921 British Open.

● Deaths of Willie Park junior, Open champion, pioneer golf course architect and strict teetotaller, and putter supreme Walter Travis.

# Joyce Wethered beats both her chief rivals at Troon

JOYCE WETHERED'S star shone brighter than ever. She defeated Cecil Leitch, three times British Amateur champion, for her own third championship victory in the final at Troon, though she did not add to her run of five English titles.

She achieved a highly satisfying victory on her way to meet Leitch, for in the third round of the British Amateur she beat the favourite of the American crowds, Glenna Collett, 4 & 3.

Collett had enjoyed an easy proficiency at every game she tried, including swimming, baseball and tennis, before her father encouraged her to take up golf.

She was taught by the same Carnoustie Smith brother, Alex, who had improved Jerry Travers's somewhat uneven game, and at first Collett's play was in the same category, lacking consistency.

She prospered to the extent of beating Cecil Leitch in a minor event when she was only 18. Her match with Wethered at Troon was proof that Margaret Curtis, still seeking a way to set up a Walker Cup-type event for women, was right in thinking that the women's game would benefit greatly if she could succeed.

Wethered did not enjoy the struggles she and Collett had to get through the crowds anxious to see a British player come out on top, fast becoming a rarity at the upper levels of the men's game, amateur or professional.

Wethered did not disappoint them. Topped drives were costly for Collett, especially one at the ninth after Wethered had missed a short putt and failed to draw level at the short eighth hole, the celebrated Postage Stamp.

Wethered, striking the ball with total concentration and increasing accuracy, put together six birdies, and the match was over after 15 holes.

The final against Cecil Leitch was a much tougher affair, which went to the 37th before Wethered achieved her third British title. Fame did not change her shy nature, and she now retired from major golf.

Collett returned to America to land her second Amateur title, and had to contend with two former champions in the semi-final and final.

First there was the "brilliant blonde", Edith Cummings, celebrated as more beautiful than any Hollywood star, who lost on the final hole, and next there was Mrs Fraser, the former Alexa Stirling, by now living in Canada.

But Collett was at full power, and demolished the talented Georgian 9 & 8.

### SCORECARD

**British Open** (Prestwick, Scot)
J Barnes 70 77 79 74 300

**US Open** (Worcester CC, Mass)
W Macfarlane 74 67 72 78 291
(Play-off, Macfarlane 147, RT Jones 148)

**USPGA** (Olympic Fields, Ill)
W Hagen bt W Mehlhorn 6 & 5

**British Amateur** (Westward Ho!, Devon)
R Harris bt K Fradgley 13 & 12

**US Amateur** (Oakmont, Pa)
RT Jones bt W Gunn 8 & 7

**British Women's Amateur** (Troon, Scot)
J Wethered bt C Leitch 37th

**US Women's Amateur** (St Louis, Mo)
G Collett bt Mrs WG Fraser 9 & 8

. . . well on its way. It was a money-making stroke, but most unluckily not one that would bring him the Open championship he craved.

# Half-crown Bobby Jones is full value for first Open double

BOBBY JONES, known always to his peers as Bob, secured his first British Open championship at Royal Lytham and St Annes on June 25. Fifteen days later he won his second US Open in Ohio. Jones was the first to capture both titles in the same year.

The previous year's crowd control problems at Prestwick led to admission charges being introduced at Lytham on the Lancashire coast south of Blackpool in order to impose a curb on attendance; 10,923 tickets at a half-crown (in pre-decimal currency – about 13p) each were sold over the three days.

One of the tickets was sold to the eventual champion, for Al Watrous and Jones left the course together between the two final rounds to have a rest and a sandwich at a hotel across the road. Jones forgot his player's badge and the commissionaire, no expert at recognizing the leading lights of the game, refused him entry. It is typical of the man that he did not make a fuss, but went over to the public gate and paid his half-crown.

## Four one-putts

Jones and "Wild Bill" Mehlhorn led with 144 apiece after the first two days, with Walter Hagen a stroke behind, one better than Watrous. Jones needed to one-putt the last four greens to make his 72. Hagen was home in 68, then faded to 77 on the second day. On the third, Jones and Watrous were drawn together, with Hagen 90 minutes behind them.

Watrous, out-hit by Jones but not out-putted, led by a stroke with a round to go thanks to a three-yard birdie putt for a three on the 54th hole, where Jones missed his three from about the same distance.

Halfcrown admission charges or not, the stewards were kept busy by the huge crowd intent on watching Jones and Watrous fight it out. With five holes left, Watrous had increased his advantage to two strokes, but three putts on the 14th and 15th cost him his lead.

Jones pulled his drive into the sandy scrub on the 17th, which dog-legs to the left. Watrous was down the middle,

**Bobby Jones: completed a unique Open double.**

and the referee decided he should play next. His ball finished on the front edge of the green.

Jones's ball was on sand, but lying well. He had 175 yards to the green, with nothing but trouble in between. Jones took no time at all over the shot, the rounded swing unaffected by the make or break situation.

## Watrous trapped

His mashie-iron disturbed only a few grains of sand as his ball rose quickly, held its course through the breeze and landed on the green nearer the hole than his opponent's ball.

Watrous putted short up the slope, missed the next, was bunkered on the last hole, and Jones was the leader by two. He

had now to wait for Hagen who, ever the showman, was accompanied by a caddie who was also his valet and kitted out in the same style as his master.

On the par four 18th, where Hagen needed an eagle to tie, he provided the gallery with a shot that came close to trumping Jones's sandy miracle on the 17th. His drive was excellent, and he walked ahead to survey his second. Finally, he sent his caddie/valet forward to hold the flagstick. His ball almost pitched in the hole, but ran on into a bunker.

Instead of two Hagen took six, finishing joint third with George von Elm the American amateur, but he had added usefully to his legend, and departed in an open-topped Rolls, throwing

**Watrous: had to bow to Jones's saving miracle at the 71st.**

golf balls to the crowd. J.H.Taylor, aged 56, finished 11th and scored 71 in his best round, Jones remarking that this was better than he could do.

The General Strike of 1926 had threatened to prevent any of these heroics taking place. Jones had not entered and, after being beaten in the sixth round of the British Amateur, he was almost on the boat home, but was persuaded to stay.

He qualified at Sunningdale for the Open. His first round of 66 there was dubbed by Bernard Darwin the best round of golf ever seen. This was not a putting bonanza: Jones holed only one putt above 20 feet, but he did hit every par four and par five in two shots. He recovered from a bunker for par after his one poor shot from the tee at the short 13th.

All these wonders were performed with Jones's carefully chosen set of hickory-shafted clubs, which turned out, when weighed later, to be perfectly matched. This near-perfect round was played in the year when, in the United States but not Britain, steel-shafted clubs became legal.

# US depart with Amateur trophies

DESPITE a severe attack of what looked like influenza, Jess Sweetser won the British Amateur on May 29, the first American-born golfer to do so.

The effort might easily have cost him his life. He had to be carried on to the boat on the way home, for the problem was tuberculosis, and it took him a year to recover from the resultant lung damage.

At the beginning of June, he and his Walker Cup colleagues kept possession of that trophy despite a Britain and Ireland win in singles – the first they had achieved. But it was by 4-3, with one singles halved, and they had lost the foursomes 3-1. Bobby Jones defeated Cyril Tolley 12 & 11 in the top single, Sweetser winning both his matches.

Minor consolation for British golf came at the newly created Wentworth Club in Surrey, where a professional American team lost 13-1 to a British team in an unofficial international.

From this match the Ryder Cup was born, when Samuel Ryder, who had made his money as a seed merchant, offered a £750 gold trophy for biennial competition between the two countries, to begin next year.

**Jess Sweetser: life-threatening victories.**

# Jones penalty stroke drama at Scioto

OPEN DOUBLE chances seemed to vanish for Bobby Jones in the second round of the US Open at Scioto, Ohio, when in the second round he faltered to a 79, after his ball rolled over as he was addressing a putt and he called a penalty on himself. Jones evidently considered the widespread approval this action provoked was misplaced.

"To praise me for that is to congratulate someone for not robbing a bank," was his retort. A 72nd-hole birdie was the winning coup by Jones, edging out Joe Turnesa, one of the seven golfing Turnesa brothers, by a stroke.

# Von Elm's moment of glory

GEORGE VON ELM, from California, went from strength to strength as the American Amateur progressed at Baltusrol, New Jersey. Bobby Jones, the overwhelming favourite as usual, beat Francis Ouimet 5 & 4 to reach the final, where von Elm achieved his greatest victory, beating the Open champion of Britain and the United States on the 35th hole.

For the first time, native-born Americans had won all the major titles.

**George von Elm: sweet win over America's hero.**

● Walter Hagen, who had begun the year by beating Bobby Jones in a so-called world championship challenge match, outplayed Leo Diegel by 5 & 3 in the PGA final, his third PGA in a row and fourth in six years.

● Bing Crosby won the United States Musicians Championship in California. Crosby, 22, had been playing for ten years, starting as a caddie in Tacoma.

● Walter Hagen presented the champion Bob Jones with a niblick with a face the size of a soup plate at the Lytham Open prize-giving, and left in an open Rolls-Royce bouncing golf balls into the crowd.

● The General Strike that threatened the Open at Lytham caused Glenna Collett, at her father's insistence, to return home without playing in the British Women's Amateur, which was recaptured by Cecil Leitch.

**Alex Herd: winner of the PGA Matchplay Tournament at 58.**

**British Open** (Royal Lytham, Lancs)
RT Jones 72 72 73 74 291

**US Open** (Scioto, Ohio)
RT Jones 70 79 71 73 293

**USPGA** (Salisbury GC, NY)
W Hagen bt L Diegel 5 & 3

**British Amateur** (Muirfield, Scot)
JW Sweetser bt AF Simpson 6 & 5

**US Amateur** (Baltusrol, NJ)
G von Elm bt RT Jones 2 & 1

**British Women's Amateur** (Harlech, Wales)
C Leitch bt Mrs P Garon 8 & 7

**US Women's Amateur** (Merion, Pa)
Mrs G Henry Stenson bt Mrs WD Goss Jnr 3 & 1

**Walker Cup** (St Andrews, Scot)
US bt GB & Ireland 6½-5½

# US professionals make their point

WITH NINE WINS and a half in 12 matches, America's professional golfers proved in the inaugural Ryder Cup international against Great Britain that, like their amateur colleagues, they represented the leading golfing nation.

Walter Hagen captained the United States at Worcester Country Club, Massachusetts, and set his team off on the right foot with a foursomes win in company with Johnny Golden, who was the only member of the team not American born.

This was unlike the unofficial US team beaten at Wentworth a year before, which included several US-based but British-born players. Golden, an immigrant from eastern Europe, also won his single with the biggest margin of the match, 8 & 7.

Hagen won his at the 17th against Arthur Havers, who had edged him out of the British Open at Troon four years ago. Another

big win was registered by Johnny Farrell and Joe Turnesa, by 8 & 6, against golfers of the calibre of George Duncan and Archie Compston.

Hagen and Golden's victims in the top single were the US Open champion of only seven years before, Ted Ray, who was Britain's captain, and Fred Robson, a frequent high finisher in the British Open, and renowned as a club-maker and teacher.

Ray also lost his singles, against Leo Diegel, whose putting troubles and tortures led him to adopt an extraordinary stance on the greens, crouching with chin close to top of grip, with feet far apart and elbows stuck out left and right, like, it was said, a car with both doors open.

This method was widely copied for a while, Bernard Darwin giving it extra life with his conjugation of the verb "to

George Duncan: scored Britain and Ireland's singles point.

Jim Barnes: with the donor of the Ryder Cup, Sam.

diegel" – "I diegel, thou diegelest, he diegels, we all diegel."

Intensely nervous, Diegel would almost run after his ball after striking it, or jump on to the nearest raised object to see where his shot might finish.

His apprehensive nature cost him a great deal of money and fame, and was the implicit proviso in Bernard Darwin's opinion of Diegel as "in a way the greatest golfing genius I have ever seen".

Britain's only doubles victors were Aubrey Boomer, who like Harry Vardon was born at Grouville, Jersey, in the Channel Islands, and Charles Whitcombe, the only unbeaten visitor.

They beat Diegel, whose peace of mind cannot have been helped by being put for the first time in the onerous position of an international team player, and

"Wild Bill" Mehlhorn. The score was 7 & 5. George Duncan had the honour of securing Britain's only singles point by a one-hole victory over Joe Turnesa.

Leo Diegel: elbow room at Worcester Country Club.

## Two in a row for Jones at HQ

PUTTING ASIDE any reservations he may have felt about the vagaries of St Andrews, Bobby Jones retained his title won so thrillingly at Lytham, and did so with a record low score of 285. His first round of 68 was his first under 70 in any Open proper. It gave him a lead he never relinquished.

The field played a round on the Old Course, then a second on an adjoining course by way of qualification. The leading 100 and ties were admitted to the Open proper, and of these, anyone 15 strokes or more behind the leader was eliminated from

the last two rounds on the third and last day.

There was to be no fourth day, because Jones finished six clear of Aubrey Boomer and Fred Robson. Charles Whitcombe, who had shaped so well in the Ryder Cup, came sixth, 11 strokes behind Jones. His brother Ernest was joint fourth with Joe Kirkwood, who didn't win many tournaments but didn't need to, for his armoury of trick shots made him welcome everywhere at exhibitions. His most spectacular was to play off the face of a watch, and he once managed a hole in one using a watch as a tee.

Jones: led all the way at HQ.

# Walter Hagen's fourth PGA

JOE TURNESA made Walter Hagen work hard in the final for his fourth successive PGA title. He was ahead most of the way, but fell behind after 31 holes. Thus Hagen and Gene Sarazen held the title between them from 1921 to 1927 inclusively.

Hagen had now won five PGAs in all, and in doing so lost three matches out of 35. Out of the 10 PGA championships staged since the inception of the event in 1916, Hagen had won half.

He won this one in November, in Dallas. Apart from Turnesa, the player who gave him most trouble was the little-known Jack Farrell, Hagen's first opponent after heading the qualifiers with 72 and 69. Hagen survived a four-hole deficit at halfway, then went on to trounce Tony Manero and get the better of the reigning Open champion, Tommy Armour, 4 & 3. It was his first head-to-head win against Armour. Al Espinosa ruined his semifinal chances against Hagen by three-putting the 36th, where the Haig got his four with a phenomenal chip and a putt. Espinosa erred again with his putter on the 37th.

## Romp for Jones at Minikahda

ONLY A PLAYER from Old Flatbush, Maurice McCarthy junior, took Bobby Jones beyond the 16th green at Minikahda in Minnesota.

Once Jones was launched on the hunt for his third American Amateur title his progress was almost brutally swift, his last three wins being by 10 & 9, 11 & 10 and, in the final, 8 & 7, over Chick Evans.

With no American Walker Cup team on tour, there was an all-domestic British Amateur final at Royal Liverpool, where a member, Eustace Landale, lost the final to Dr William Tweddell, who combined golf with a full-time career in medicine.

Perhaps the most curious statistic of the year was the hole in one that Jones achieved on his own East Lake course in Georgia, curious in that it was the first that this most accurate of strikers had scored.

Tommy Armour: outpaced "Light Horse Harry."

### SCORECARD

**British Open** (St Andrews, Scot)
RT Jones 68 72 73 72 285

**US Open** (Oakmont, Pa)
TD Armour 78 71 76 76 301
(Play-off, Armour 76, H Cooper 79)

**USPGA** (Cedar Crest, Dallas, Texas)
W Hagen bt J Turnesa 1h

**British Amateur** (Royal Liverpool)
Dr W Tweddell bt E Landale 7 & 6

**US Amateur** (Minikahda, Minn)
RT Jones bt C Evans 8 & 7

**British Women's Amateur** (Newcastle, Co Down)
Miss T de la Chaume bt D Pearson 5 & 4

**US Women's Amateur** (Garden City, NY)
Mrs MB Horn bt M Orcutt 5 & 4

**Ryder Cup** (Worcester CC, Mass)
US bt GB & Ireland $9\frac{1}{2}$–$2\frac{1}{2}$

# Armour's Open on Oakmont monster

A BIRDIE by Tommy Armour from ten feet on the 72nd hole of the US Open at Oakmont, gave him a play-off against Harry Cooper, who had at the outset of the 1920s been gifted by no less than Damon Runyon with the nickname "Light-Horse" Harry Cooper, on account of his quick stride and the pace at which he played the game.

Cooper had begun to get into or close to the major winners' circle over the past year or so, but missed a glaring chance here by three-putting the 72nd. Gene Sarazen had the best final round of the leaders, a 74, but missed the play off by a stroke.

Armour won the play-off by three strokes on a course which, with its deeply grooved bunkers and lightning fast greens, sent the leading totals over 301 for the first time since Hagen's second Open in 1919 at Brae Burn, Massachusetts.

Armour had turned professional two years after moving to the United States from Britain in 1922. Cooper, born in England, had a golf professional as a father, who brought his family across to Texas while Harry was still very young.

At 18, Harry won the Texas PGA title, and did it again the next year. Of the British Ryder Cup team who took part, Archie Compston performed best, finishing in a tie for seventh place.

Armour never operated as a full-time professional tour player and always had a job as a professional at some high-society club, where he would often charge up to three figures per hour per lesson.

# Walter Hagen, golf's best, worst and happiest swinger

WALTER HAGEN'S rate of success in the significant stroke play championships of his time was phenomenal and his durability in match play unapproached by any man before or since

He lost his US PGA title in 1928, in the third round at Five Farms Country Club, Baltimore, to the eventual champion, Leo Diegel – but that was his first defeat in 23 starts, since he lost the 1923 final to Gene Sarazen at the 38th hole, then won in the four following years.

Hagen had first gained the title in 1921 and, busy with his interminable and lucrative exhibition tours, did not enter in 1922. Thus he won this event five times in seven attempts, although it must be said that, since Bobby Jones could not play in the PGA, its standing as a measure of greatness is somewhat weakened.

The acid test, however, of a golfer's skill and will to win, as Gary Player has emphasized, is the ability to win abroad. Here Hagen is on undisputed high ground, for in ten tries for the British Open, he won four times in the space of eight years.

## Star quality

His two earliest successes, in his own national Open, were achieved by sheer self-belief and disregard for most of the tenets of latter-day champions, who prize physical fitness, a sensible diet and practice, and employ fitness coaches, sports psychologists, gurus, agents and managers. They also court sponsors and go through schools that teach business management and how to deal with the press.

The list is endless. (Hagen, by the way, found the deadly serious golf school graduates of the late 20th century "amusing".)

Hagen followed this pattern only to the extent of having a caddie (also his valet on occasion), chauffeurs (two or three, perhaps) and a manager, and here he had a great advantage over most modern players, for Bob Harlow was the long-term incumbent. He and Harlow made

Hagen's larger than life personality was a great crowd puller, but beneath the flamboyant exterior was a player with nerves of steel, who managed four consecutive wins in the US PGA

**The Haig's first trophy, 1914.**

a pair. Harlow was a past master as a publicist for the game, and a gourmet.

Hagen just generally liked a good time, wine, women and song, and lively conversation. These interests he pursued well into the night before many a crucial match.

Who has not heard the story of Hagen at Muirfield, scene of his last British Open win? He was celebrating as usual, and why not, for he had just broken the 18-hole record for any Open, with 67, which he considered to be his lifetime best.

All the same, he was still two behind Diegel with two rounds to go on the following day. It was

pointed out to him that Diegel had long ago retired to bed.

"Yeah," Hagen retorted, "but he ain't sleeping." To judge from subsequent events, Hagen may have been right there, for next day Diegel started in a fierce wind with a horrid 82, followed it with 77, and subsided to third place, while Hagen won by six shots.

He could have taught a thing or two to sports psychologists, for though the term was not current in his day, Hagen "psyched out" many an opponent who was a more complete golfer and finer stroke player.

Looking back at the end of a long life (Hagen was born in Rochester, New York, on December 21, 1892, and died on October 6, 1969), he may occasionally have regretted missing a chance to begin the creation of the Hagen legend in 1913, when in a fourth round of spectacular hits but too many misses he failed by three strokes to secure a place in the historic three-way Ouimet/Vardon/Ray play-off.

## Birth of a legend

In 1914 Hagen, who attracted money, and spent it, with equal facility (he claims to have been the first golfer to earn one million dollars and spend two) set off with his friend, Dutch Leonard, to try for the Open at Midlothian, Illinois, bank-rolled by the editor of a Rochester paper, who had talked Hagen out of another ambition of his, to try for major league baseball.

Hagen was troubled by food poisoning on the eve – and morning – of the Open. It would be difficult to imagine a man of Hagen's lavish tastes contracting meat-pie food poisoning: indeed, a lobster was to blame.

Dutch Leonard urged him to make a start despite his pain, and his first two shaky tee shots were converted into pars by early-vintage Hagen recovery shots. He finished in a record 68 en route to the title.

Neither Ouimet in 1913 nor Hagen in 1914 shook the sporting firmament at all severely: baseball and football ruled jointly.

For now, Hagen returned to his club post in Rochester. It was, after all, only two years since the death of three-times British Open champion Jamie Anderson in the poorhouse.

There were ten more majors to come for Hagen, yet they were only the bare beams of his personal hall of fame – which he fitted out in first-class style. His best epitaph is contained in the words of Gene Sarazen: "All the professionals who have a chance to go after the big money today should say a silent thanks to Walter Hagen each time they stretch a cheque between their fingers. It was Walter who made professional golf what it is."

## Larger than life

Hagen touched that chord in the American psyche which is attuned to the sports hero who is larger than life, twice as generous, yet seemingly careless of success. His fans knew he played hard on and off the course, seldom short-changing his exhibition cus-

"Sir Walter's" favourite means of transport – unless he could lay hands on something a little roomier.

tomers. They knew he would not be put down by anyone.

At Deal in 1920, where amateurs and pros had separate luncheon facilities, he hired an aircraft to fly himself and his friends to an inn for their meals. Nor would Royal St George's, two years later, allow him clubhouse facilities, so Hagen's limousine was parked outside to serve as a luncheon and changing room and luxurious resting place in

between his winning rounds. The year after that Hagen was runner-up to Arthur Havers, but rejected an invitation into the Troon clubhouse for the presentation ceremony, and instead stood anyone who felt inclined a drink at a nearby public house. By contrast, full clubhouse facilities had been offered to professionals at the 1920 US Open at Inverness, Ohio.

In this fashion, without pick-

ets, posters or breaking any windows, Hagen rapidly changed the standing of the golf professional.

He decided immediately after his 1919 Open title that he would become that rare being, a tournament professional – not that there were many tournaments. Besides, professionals had still to tend their clubs, source of most, if not all, of their income.

Hagen soon added other strings to his bow, for in 1922 he was the first playing professional of the modern era to form a company under his own name for the manufacture of golf clubs.

## The showman

Hagen was a boon to the golf clothing industry and, as he strolled down the fairways, head tilted at an imperious angle, he brought to life the magazines that encouraged the smart set to wear smartly cut plus-fours and sweaters in bright colours. When asked why he took such care over every shot in his last round when losing at Deal in 1920, he said: "I was scared I might finish fifty-sixth." What Hagen really thought about losing was that being second was little better than coming fifty-sixth, and it is true there wasn't much difference in the financial return. He made his money elsewhere.

Charles was his middle name, but his opponents must have thought it was pronounced "confidence". After losing to the British Ryder Cup player Archie Compston in a challenge match billed to run for 72 holes so heavily that the final 18 were superfluous, Hagen posed for pictures, all smiles, then drove off with Harlow in what became a pointedly prolonged silence. It was broken by Hagen's final reflections on the match: "You know something, Bob? I can beat that sonofabitch the best day he ever had." "Sir Walter" or "The Haig", as he was also known, very soon beat Compston into third place at Sandwich in the Open.

Hatless: Hagen set a trend with his choice of bright clothing.

# Jones – definitely the man to beat

JOHNNY FARRELL underlined the theme of the 1920s – be one (at least) up on the Jones boy and you are flying high. Farrell, from Quaker Ridge, Scarsdale, New York, had to battle through a double play-off to gain his first US Open championship, having forced a tie with Jones after 72 holes with 294 shots, ten over par.

The play-off was raised to 36 holes again, and Jones was left one stroke short of his eighth major. His scores were 73+71=144, against Farrell's 70+73=143. Since the Walker Cup was played in America this year, Jones did not defend his British Open title or try for the only major that had so far eluded him, the British Amateur.

The entry at Olympia Fields, Mateson, Illinois, was over 1,000 for the first time; 1,604 tried to qualify. Walter Hagen was only two shots away from the play-off, which was as close as he ever was in the 1920s, except for 1925, when he finished fifth, also two strokes away from a play-off.

Farrell distinguished himself by being accepted as the best-dressed man in golf, no small achievement with Hagen about. He won plenty of cash to pay his tailor for, apart from many tour wins, he was highly placed in the 1923, 1925 and 1926 US Opens, Farrell always was a help when players were being sought for exhibitions.

But this win against the great amateur was at a different level, and his nerves were equal to sinking a seven-footer on the final hole of the six rounds to win. Farrell was a graceful rather than powerful hitter, and his opponents' disappointments were usually on the green, where Farrell had a Travis-like flair.

Jones's golfing philosophy is well summed up by his answer to the question as to whether there was any golfer he ever wanted to beat for personal reasons. Jones replied: "We were in the final of an important championship, and just before we were to to tee off he came over and said, 'I really don't care who wins this thing, you or I. Let's just go out and have a nice, pleasant, enjoyable round.' I didn't appreciate that. I knew he wanted to win that championship just as much as I did."

Johnny Farrell: best-dressed – and a winner.

# United States amateur domination

AT THE END of August and in the early days of September, the visiting British Walker Cup team in particular and British amateur golf in general were made to feel somewhat inadequate.

First, in the Cup match at Chicago, they lost all four foursomes matches. Next, in the top single, the first meeting between a British champion and his American counterpart, Bobby Jones, who had taken over the captaincy from Robert Gardner, ended in defeat for Phil Perkins by the record Walker Cup margin of 13 & 12.

Earlier, Perkins and Dr William Tweddell were beaten by a mere 7 & 6 by George von Elm and Jess Sweetser.

The only British point was wrested from Chick Evans by Tony Torrance, by one hole. Dr Tweddell captained the visitors, who were without their leading pair, Cyril Tolley and Roger Wethered.

Perkins came into prominence the previous year as English Amateur champion and, before setting off for the United States, brought off a splendid win in the British final against Roger Wethered, whom he beat 6 & 4 at Prestwick.

His troubles were not over yet on his American visit, however, since his reward for fighting his way to the American Amateur final at Brae Burn, Massachusetts, was another huge beating from Jones, this time a marginally less punitive 10 & 9.

Perkins and Harold Hilton are the only Britons ever to reach the final – Hilton was successful, however, in 1911.

The Jones/Perkins match was the first meeting of the two nations' champions in this final. At least Perkins had beaten the qualifying medallist, George Voigt, heavily along the way.

Of the other British Cup players, Edward Storey got through one round and John Beck won twice.

# Walter Hagen adds to Auld Mug's travels

FIVE OF THE FIRST ten in the British Open at Royal St George's were not British, the clearest evidence yet of the growing international nature of the game. Americans Walter Hagen and Gene Sarazen were first and second, another, Jim Barnes, was joint sixth along with José Jurado of Argentina, with "Wild Bill" Mehlhorn ninth. Percy Alliss, joint fourth, represented the Wannsee club, in Berlin, and Aubrey Boomer, another player in joint sixth position, was still working in France as a professional. Moreover, it was now five years since the Open trophy had stayed in Britain.

Regal: HRH The Prince of Wales presents the Auld Mug to Hagen.

# A little light revenge for Leo Diegel

WALTER HAGEN'S extraordinary freedom from defeat in the USPGA came to an end, after 22 wins, at Baltimore Country Club, Five Farms, Maryland, where Leo Diegel gained his first significant success.

Reassuring though this must have been for Diegel, it must have been deeply satisfying also that he should be the man to end Hagen's run in the third round, for he had been subjected to so many embarrassments at Hagen's hands.

One particular instance was in this very championship. Diegel had been four up with five to play, but Hagen, ever ready to stage a great comeback, was only one down on the penultimate green.

Here, before striking a 20-foot putt which could bring him level, Hagen turned and gave his opponent a big smile. Then he sank the putt, and Diegel was at a psychological disadvantage for the rest of the game.

The year 1928 was, however, a profitable one for Diegel, for he also won his third Canadian Open (by two shots from Hagen, too) and the Massachusetts Open, and tied for first in the Long Beach Open.

He was also the first top-class golfer who is known to have sought help from a psychiatrist for the anxiety problems that so hampered his career.

Diegel's opponent in the PGA final was Al Espinosa, who went down 6 & 5. Al and his brother Abe were the first Hispanic players to come to prominence in US golf.

Earlier in the year Abe broke the ice for Hispanics by winning the Western Open, one of the oldest tournaments in the country and still one of the most keenly contested.

Leo Diegel: stopped the Haig's gallop at Baltimore Country Club.

# PGA Tour gets on the road

WHEN HORTON SMITH turned professional in 1926 there were only two other playing professionals he knew of, Walter Hagen and the Australian Joe Kirkwood, who had followed the Travis trail to golfing fame in the United States. Most professionals still earned their living selling clubs and teaching their members, even front-line players like Tommy Armour, and Al and Abe Espinosa.

Jim Barnes recalls informal events during the winter at Florida resorts, before and after the Great War, not regular tournaments, and sometimes with giant layer cakes given by the resort hotels as prizes. The credit

for establishing the cornerstone of the winter tour, the first part of the professional circuit to develop, goes to the rich Texans who in 1922, led by a newspaperman, Jack O'Brien, put up a $5,000 purse for the inaugural Texas Open on a public course at Brackenridge, San Antonio.

Others followed, for professionals in the northerly states and especially the eastern seaboard, where golf was impossible, or at best highly uncomfortable, in the winter months, looked south for gainful competition. Sacramento, California, started a $2,500 event. There was another in San Diego, possessed of one of the most benevolent year-round climates

in the world, and Los Angeles trumped them both with a prize fund of $10,000 for the LA Open.

Players' wives – Estelle Armour, Jo Espinosa, Nellie Cruickshank and others – acted as ex-officio chasers of prize money and places for the players to stay. But of formal organization there was none, apart from the PGA itself, which had more to do with getting deals from golf gear makers for club pros.

Southern holiday resorts became more alive to the fact that by sponsoring winter tournaments, they could make it clear to frost-bound northerners exactly where sunlit fairways awaited them.

# Comeback for hickory – and the Ryder Cup

STEEL SHAFTS were still illegal when the US team travelled to Moortown, Leeds, in Yorkshire to defend the Ryder Cup, won so easily by Walter Hagen's team in Massachusetts two years ago at the first staging of the competition. So the team brought their hickories, with which they had learnt the game and with which they had continued to play until the recent past.

Thus, the British had a double advantage: they were on their own home ground and the Americans had to suffer an enforced change of weapons. But the United States were still favourites – only one British player had won his own national championship in the past eight years.

Sure enough, on a cold and blustery April day, radically different from the winter tour in southern sunshine in which the visitors had been performing, the United States won the foursomes 2-1. Abe Mitchell and Fred Robson were the only British winners, 2 & 1, against Gene Sarazen and Ed Dudley, while Charles Whitcombe, the best Briton in the first Cup match, and Archie Compston, managed a half against Johnny Farrell and Joe Turnesa.

Leo Diegel and Al Espinosa strolled in by 7 & 5 over Aubrey Boomer and George Duncan, and John Golden and the US captain, Hagen, had two holes to spare over Ernest Whitcombe and Henry Cotton, who was the first professional to reach the paid ranks by way of a public school, Alleyn's, at Dulwich, a London suburb.

There was criticism of Hagen for selecting Dudley in place of the in-form Horton Smith, and the next day Hagen ran into more trouble on his own account as the British captain, George Duncan, gave him the biggest beating yet administered in this fledgling event. Duncan's 10 & 8 win in the second singles confirmed that there had been a complete change in the atmosphere, if not in the weather, for Charles Whitcombe won the top match against Farrell 8 & 6.

Compston overwhelmed Sarazen 6 & 4, while Boomer and Cotton had 4 & 3 margins over Turnesa and Watrous respectively. Smith was chosen on the second day, and he beat Fred Robson 4 & 2, while Diegel, thoroughly in form, gave himself a 75 per cent success ratio over the first two Ryder matches by thrashing Abe Mitchell 9 & 8. The sum total was that Sam Ryder's Cup stayed home, with Britain the 7–5 winners. The victors were left with the sad reflection that the Ryder Cup was the only competition in the 1920s in which Britain could claim parity with the United States.

The Royal & Ancient were in a quandary when the Midland club, Sandwell Park, let players use steel shafts in competition and presented a set to the Prince of Wales. The relevant committee at headquarters decided to legalize steel shafts in November rather than disqualify the Prince for use of illegal equipment.

## Jones's romp in play-off

AL ESPINOSA must have been a little surprised to find himself in a play-off with Bobby Jones when the US Open was staged for the first time at Winged Foot, one of designer Tillinghast's masterpieces. He had tied with Jones at 294, and this was in large measure due to Jones's stumbling to a brace of sevens in his final round of 79. Jones, the loser after ties in 1925 and last year, left nothing to chance this time and came out a winner by 23 strokes.

In it goes: Jones holes out to force a play-off against Al Espinosa.

Taking flight: Jones plays an approach at Winged Foot towards United States Open title No. 3.

## Hagen and Co put the record straight at Muirfield

TWO WEEKS after his drubbing in the Ryder Cup, Walter Hagen secured his fourth British Open at Muirfield. The championship was held early in May and thus the American Ryder Cup team were present in force.

It was Hagen's second title in succession and his fourth in eight years. He finished six shots clear of American Open champion Johnny Farrell.

British hopes of a revival of local talent in their national championship were made to look pathetic by the finishing order, in which eight of the top ten were Americans, though there was the minor cavil that two, Jim Barnes and Tommy Armour, were British born.

The British "interlopers", Percy Alliss and Abe Mitchell, shared fourth place, eight in arrears of the Haig, who had a 67 in the second round, finishing with a bravura touch of a kind special to him by hitting the flag with his brilliant approach on the 18th.

He scored 75 in the other three rounds and, what is more, as in his 1928 victory, his scoring owed little to his famed recovery shots.

The world had got a grip on the Scottish game and was not about to hand it back.

# Champion's Nebraskan nemesis

THE RYDER CUP defeat caused more than a few ripples in the golf club bars of America, but was not remotely as severe a shock to the golfing hierarchy and hackers alike as that served up by Johnny Goodman when he beat Bobby Jones in the first round of the US Amateur.

He did so at the final hole at the Del Monte Club, where the spectacular Pebble Beach course strides along the cliff edges of the Monterey peninsula. Goodman was from the Omaha Field Club, Nebraska, and hitched a ride in a cattle truck to this, the first Pacific coast major in the history of American golf. Goodman did not last long, being beaten by a large opponent in William Lawson Little in round two.

Goodman's start in golf had been as different from Jones's as can readily be imagined. He was an orphan of Polish stock and not like Jones born of a patrician southern family and a student at three universities.

Jones had started well, being joint best qualifying scorer with Gene Homans, and showed a liking for the course, since he is credited with a practice round of 67, a course record, including seven consecutive birdies. The title, expected to become Jones's fifth, went instead to Jimmy Johnston (White Bear Yacht Club, Minnesota) who beat Walker Cup veteran Dr O.F. Willing in the final. Apart from this first West Coast major, other novelties for

**Johnny Goodman: together with Bobby Jones.**

American golfers were the pro-am, in which tour pros such as Hagen and Diegel would play with local dignitaries, business-men or stars from other sports, and floodlit golf, Francis Ouimet losing one such match in Massachusetts at midnight.

# Wethered wins women's transatlantic decider

**Thriller: Joyce Wethered and (right) Glenna Collett.**

BY THE END of her victory over Glenna Collett in the British Amateur final at St Andrews, Joyce Wethered had proved, on her return after three years to major championship play, that whatever the failings of Britain's men players, her reputation as the world's leading woman golfer was unassailable.

This was her fourth title, and she had been runner-up once and English champion five times. Now she defeated, 3 & 1 at the home of golf the three-times champion of America after being five holes in arrears after nine holes. During the second round in the afternoon the crowd was, as ever, keener to see every shot than they were to leave the players with enough room to play. Wethered was four up at the ninth, a swing of nine over 18

holes and held on till victory at the 17th.

Collett, returning home, reasserted her dominance on American soil by retaining her title on October 5 by 4 & 3 against Mrs Leona Pressler, at Oakland Hills, Michigan. She was thus the first woman to gain four titles, and the record was not set without anxiety. She beat Mrs Harley Higbie at the first extra hole after being four down with four to play in the quarterfinal.

## TEE TALK

### "Nothing at all."

**GEORGE DUNCAN,**
when asked what he thought about when striking the ball.

## SHORT PUTTS

● Another of many attempts to set up a Britain v United States women's international series failed. Margaret Curtis offered in 1928 to solve the most pressing problem, defraying fares and accommodation. In a letter to Cecil Leitch, Curtis guaranteed $10,000 per match for the first ten matches.

● Horton Smith won eight tournaments on the PGA tour.

● Peter Thomson was born on August 23 in Melbourne, Australia.

● Cyril Tolley ends the 1920s as he began them by winning the British Amateur.

● Leo Diegel retained his PGA title with a 6 & 4 win over Johnny Farrell at Hillcrest, California, a venue demonstrating the spread of the game to the west.

**Still Diegeling – to the USPGA title.**

# Joyce Wethered – simply the straightest hitter of them all

## A superb sense of balance, a straight drive, remarkable powers of concentration and imperturbability – she possessed all the qualities which make a great champion golfer

HENRY COTTON'S era, playing or watching, included Harry Vardon, Walter Hagen, Bob Jones and Ben Hogan, so it meant a good deal when he said of Joyce Wethered: "In my time ... I do not think a golf ball has ever been hit, except perhaps by Harry Vardon, with such a straight flight by any other person."

Jack Nicklaus once declared that it was a fluke if any golfer using a big club managed to hit the ball perfectly straight. The number of compliments aimed at this shyest of golfers yet most intense of competitors suggests that either her swing was close to perfection or that in a first-class career of a decade and a half she was the luckiest player of all time.

### Early skills

Balance being an essential ingredient of success in all ball games as in many other sports, Joyce Wethered's words on the subject may give a clue to the consistent accuracy which made her almost invincible in match play.

Leonard Crawley quoted her in instructional pieces he wrote for the *Daily Telegraph* as defining her thoughts on the subject as follows: "I feel nobody could push me off my right heel at the top of the swing and, at the other end, I feel nobody could push me off my left foot."

She had not fully assembled method or tactics when at 19 she entered the 1920 English championship "for fun". She had been learning the game, with help from her brother Roger, who was to be in a play-off for the Open the following year.

She was in this year still absorbing what she had learnt from watching Harry Vardon and J.H.Taylor play, adopting the so-called Vardon grip, and trying to create a more upright plane to her swing. One great advantage she possessed was to be a member of a well-to-do sporting family (her father, H.Newton Wethered, had a six handicap) with a holiday home near that superior course, Dornoch.

Having beaten Cecil Leitch, the woman who held the English title, Wethered won it again four times. From the start it is clear that she had the knack of appearing to be unfazed by weather, opponent or anything that could disturb the rhythm of her swing, or her concentration on chips and putts.

The following year she got to the British final at Turnberry, but Cecil Leitch, ten years older and renowned as the first woman player with an uninhibited swing of which many men would have been proud, was too good for her.

The final of the British event in 1922 was between the same two players at Prince's, Sandwich, and the two women found themselves on the front pages. This time Wethered did not succumb to the early match nerves that afflicted her to the end of her big match career.

Her relentless accuracy wore down Leitch and the match finished on the 29th hole. Leitch was not to gain the title again till Wethered retired, temporarily at least, after beating Beryl Cautley for the British title in 1924 and Leitch again, at Troon in 1925 in a touch and go affair, at the 37th.

### Dramatic final

George Greenwood's *Daily Telegraph* report of Wethered's comeback in the 1929 final against Glenna Collett, who was in possession of her third American Amateur title at the

Balanced as ever.

time, suggests that while a crowd of more than 10,000 were drawn to the final 18 holes of the confrontation, and often impeded the play, neither of the finalists seemed the least bit distracted.

This is a tribute to both, since they later made it clear how wearing and, at times, disturbing they found the crush and the noise at such moments.

Many Americans came to St Andrews on the night train to support Collett, and Horton Smith

and the other American professionals who had been knocked out of the Yorkshire Evening News Tournament came up from Leeds for the same purpose. (They left Joe Turnesa behind, for he had reached the final, which he won.)

Collett's long and vain attempt to secure the British title and Wethered's determination to stamp her authority on her era made for a match which, Greenwood said, had never, in its excitement. There are few head-to-head matches for the title of world champion, but here were the two leading players, without rival in the two leading golfing nations. The match began badly for Wethered.

## Close rivalry

The Briton, still only 27, had no touch with her approach putts, which cost her the first two holes, with fives against her opponent's fours. The American then reeled off another five fours, including a birdie at the long fifth, 530 yards, where she played two wooden clubs to the foot of the slope leading up to the huge plateau green, pitched to four yards and sank the putt.

She also won the seventh, getting up and down from a green-side bunker, and the eighth with a 25-yard putt for a two. Three putts by Wethered at the ninth brought her to the turn in 39 strokes. Collett needed only 34, and was five up – 4 4 4, 4 4 4, 4 2 4. She had even managed occasionally to drive a yard or two beyond Wethered.

"This," wrote Greenwood, "is the first time I have ever seen any lady keep up with Miss Wethered from a tee, a fact not without significance."

The Wethered supporters believed, prayed, that this would not go on, and at the 12th Collett missed a yard putt that would have put her six ahead.

She now lost three holes of those that remained, three-

**Glenna Collett: Wethered's perennial opponent.**

putting the 16th and 18th after being for the most part so secure on the greens. Her score was still the splendid one of 75, against 77 by Wethered, who now was only two down, however.

## Glorious finale

The crowd trebled in size for the second round. Within 15 minutes, Wethered was level, with a birdie three over the Swilken

Burn on the first and a four at the second. Now ensued a landslide in the opposite direction to the morning's play. Bunker trouble proved costly for the young American at the sixth and seventh, while Wethered was wearing her down with exemplary golf: she reached the turn in 35 strokes with a birdie at the ninth. From the twelfth in the morning to the ninth in the afternoon – 15 holes – Wethered had won nine.

Collett fought back strongly with two threes, to be only two down but was quickly three down thanks to a sliced brassie shot on the 13th.

The long 14th was a disaster for both players, Wethered losing with an eight to a seven after her brassie just caught the edge of Hell bunker, from which she took two to escape.

Two halves in fours brought the game to a climax at the Road Hole, with its seemingly magnetic bunker in the front face of the slope up to the long, shallow plateau green with the road and boundary wall beyond – a recipe for more disaster.

Both were at the foot of the slope in three: Collett putted short, Wethered to two feet for a win by 3 & 1. The American ran across to shake her opponent's hand as the cheers rang out and she declared her pleasure at having taken part in "the most glorious match of my life."

This time the champion did not return to major competition, having played 38 matches in the British Amateur and winning 36

– four titles, one semi-final defeat and one final defeat. She did, however, play on at Worplesdon, managing to win eight times with seven different partners, including such leading amateur lights as Michael Scott, Cyril Tolley, Raymond Oppenheimer and Bernard Darwin, not to mention her brother Roger.

## Later career

A brief spell as a professional in the 1930s included exhibition matches in America involving "Babe" Didrikson, Horton Smith and Gene Sarazen.

In 1937 Joyce Wethered married Sir John Heathcoat Amory, and she and her husband were later awarded the Victoria Medal of Honour by the Royal Horticultural Society, for the remarkable improvements they had made to the wonderful gardens of their home, at Knightshayes Court, near Tiverton in Devon.

Lady Heathcoat Amory lived on well into her nineties at Knightshayes, now one of the National Trust's loveliest properties, and she played an active part in Tiverton's social life. She died in 1997.

### SCORECARD

British Women's Amateur champion
1922, 1924, 1925,1929
English Women's champion
1920-1924 inclusive
Curtis Cup team 1932

### TEE TALK

**"I have not played golf with anyone, man or woman, amateur or professional, who made me feel so utterly outclassed."**

BOBBY JONES.

**"Good swing? My god, mon! She could hit a ball 240 yards on the fly while standing barefoot on a cake of ice."**

WILLIE WILSON,
Scots pro.

A favourite relaxation: foursomes with (left to right) Wanda Morgan, Eustace Storey and her future husband, Sir John Heathcoat Amory

# Year of the impregnable quadrilateral

**Grand slam: Jones's last cup – the US Amateur trophy that completed the sweep.**

THE ODDS AGAINST Bobby Jones winning his first British Amateur championship at St Andrews in Fife were, at 5 to 1, "seemingly cramped". That was the view expressed on May 26 in the Daily Telegraph's summing up of the possible outcome.

"Cramped" was a considerable understatement, for Jones had proved vulnerable in 18-hole matches such as he now faced until the 36-hole final, having lost at Muirfield four years earlier to an unknown youngster from Glasgow, Andrew Jamieson, who dashed up to the links on a motorcycle, and the previous year to another newcomer, Johnny Goodman, in the first round of the American Amateur. Significantly, Jones had lost only one 36-hole match in six years, to George von Elm.

Moreover at St Andrews Jones faced a field that included the best of the Britons, Cyril Tolley and Roger Wethered, and the rest of the US Walker Cup team who, led by Jones, had just ridden roughshod 10-2 over the home team for their sixth win out of six starts. Jones's last stint as captain left him with a 100 per cent singles record and one foursomes defeat in five Cup matches.

The bookmakers might well have scored a wipe-out in the first round, but for the astounding mixture of brilliance and good fortune with which Jones beat Sidney Roper, aged 30, a former miner and now a clerk in the oil business, who played at Wollaton Park, Nottinghamshire. Roper started 4, 4, 4, 4, 4, four pars and a birdie, and was three down. Jones started 3, 4, 3, 2, 4 – birdie, par, birdie, eagle, birdie. Jones's celebrated putter, "Calamity Jane", ran down an eight-yarder at the first for a three and tapped in from two feet for another at the third. The faithful blade had a rest at the fourth, where Jones holed out from a deep bunker with his mashie from 140 yards for a two.

Roper, whose ball lay dead after three shots, managed to smile. Even more wonderful to relate, he was composed enough to halve the long fifth with a birdie. He was two down at the turn, which he reached, playing superbly well, in nine consecutive fours. The match ended at the 16th, Jones having played 61 strokes to that point, Roper having covered himself with glory.

A deeper crisis tested Jones's nerve in the fourth round against Cyril Tolley, whom he beat with the aid of a stymie at the 19th. The players had to contend with a strong wind, and were constantly held up by the crowd, certainly in excess of five figures, rushing wildly about seeking the best vantage points. One spectator helped Jones greatly at the Road Hole where his mashie approach was checked by a mackintosh folded over an arm. His ball finished on the green when it had looked sure to end on the road.

Tolley got a half to stay level by virtue of a superb touch shot over the Road bunker, his tiny pitch (the finest of his career, Tolley thought) just clearing the sand and finishing four feet from the hole. Jones's fate was in Tolley's hands at the 18th, but the Englishman missed for a birdie from 12 feet for the match.

The wind had moderated as the players set off on the 19th where Jones, often outdriven, again had to play his approach first. He hit to within 12 yards of the flag. Tolley's approach was well to the left, and then he pitched to three yards below the hole. Jones, aware that two putts might well be enough, putted carefully a foot short, setting up also the possibility of a stymie, which is what happend. Tolley's attempt, after great deliberation, at lofting the putt failed. "A cruel way to win," Jones conceded.

Jones was again uncertain against fellow American Jimmy Johnston in round six, letting slip a good lead, then holing out from seven or eight feet for par and the match at the last hole, where Johnston's ball lay stone dead for three. Jones was never threatened so severely again, and in the final, in a pairing devoutly wished for and watched by 15,000 paying spectators, he outplayed Roger Wethered by 7 & 6.

**Crowd-puller: In short pants or plus fours, the fans packed round Bobby Jones in Britain.**

## Hagen record goes to Compston at Hoylake

BEFORE he became the second man since John Ball (in 1890) to win the British Open and Amateur in the same year, Bobby Jones was overtaken in the third round by Archie Compston (215-216), with a phenomenal score (for Hoylake links) of 68.

Players had laboured in vain for generations to break 70. The threat faded as Compston slid to a catastrophic 82. A fine 71 left Macdonald Smith two behind Jones's 291, like Leo Diegel, who might have tied but for finding a bunker at the 16th and slipping to 75.

Jones's anxious moments were mostly of his own creation, notably early in the final round. Two strong shots at the eighth, 482 yards into the teeth of the wind, left him with no other obstacle than a small slope up to the green.

He said afterwards that a little old lady with a croquet mallet would have done better. Failing to make the slope first time, he then took four more, missing a putt of 12 inches that would have given him a six.

## Putting in order for US Open

MOVING INEXORABLY, it seemed, to a clean sweep of the major titles for 1930, Bobby Jones finished two ahead of that eternal bridesmaid Macdonald Smith in the US Open at Interlaken, Minnesota, on July 12. He required birdies at three of the last six holes, his last thrust of all being a 40-foot putt on the 72nd hole, which enabled him to post a total of 287, one under par. He had holed out in two strokes fewer in the St Andrews Open of 1927, but this was his best in the American Open.

His grip on the title was powerful at the end of 54 holes, when he had a lead of five, thanks to his third round of 68 with six birdies. Another of those Jones miracles occurred in round two, when he thinned a wooden club approach over the lake on the long ninth hole. His ball played ducks and drakes instead of havoc with his score, reached the other side and the result was a birdie.

Jones was finding the going even harder now, for with three majors under his belt, the tension could only increase. His weight loss during an important championship could reportedly amount to well over a stone (14 pounds).

## The slam – without a crisis

BOBBY JONES achieved the last leg of his grand slam of every one of the four major titles open to him with a minimum of fuss at Merion, Pennsylvania, where he had first competed in the Amateur Championship 14 years earlier.

He did so in a fashion blending the neat, the orderly and the imperious, for he was qualifying medallist, with 142, and in his five match play rounds, the first over 18 holes, the rest over 36, achieved the following margins – 5 & 4, 5 & 4, 6 & 5, 9 & 8 (against Jess Sweetser), and 8 & 7 in the final against Eugene Homans. The crowd of 18,000 people, all eager to witness Jones's historic achievement, overwhelmed cordons of police, marines and course marshals in their excitement.

Before the year was out Jones had become a professional. Equally epoch-making, insofar as the art of the greenkeeper is concerned, was the installation at Merion before the Amateur Championship of an up-to-the-minute watering system.

### TEE TALK

"Bob was a fine man to be partnered with in a tournament ... he made you feel that you were playing with a friend, and you were."

GENE SARAZEN, on Bobby Jones.

September 27: memorable moment at Merion at the Grand Slam's final presentation is made to Bobby Jones.

# Bobby Jones – winner of the Grand Slam

"Like the man in the song, many of Mr Jones's opponents are tired of living but feared of dying. However, their fears are rarely unduly protracted since they usually die very soon after lunch."

BERNARD DARWIN.

"As a young man he was able to stand up to just about the best that life can offer, which is not easy, and later he stood up, with equal grace, to just about the worst."

HERBERT WARREN WIND.

"All he would say afterwards was that he would never, never do it again."

BERNARD DARWIN,
after the 1930 Open.

Thing of beauty: Jones's swing.

A supremely graceful and stylish player whose incredible feat in capturing the British and American Open and Amateur championships in one year ranks him among the immortals of golf

Bobby Jones retired from serious competition at the age of 28 after winning in one year – 1930 – all the major events he was eligible to enter. He was and still is unique not only in this, but because he invented the Masters, which became one of the four major events in world golf.

## One glorious year

He stood alone in so many fields of achievement. The most startling of all, perhaps, was the fact that he played so little and won so much. In his final fruitful year he entered only eight formal competitions. He lost the first, the Savannah Open in February, to Horton Smith, who was enjoying a well-paid winter with seven tour victories. Jones broke the course record in round one with 67. Smith did 66 in the second and Jones 65 in the third, but he lost the event to Smith by a stroke on the final day. This was the last time he was beaten in serious competition.

He next entered the Southeastern Open in Augusta, Georgia, at the Forrest Hills-Ricker course, and finished 13 shots clear of the field, which again included the "hot" professional of the day, Horton Smith. Retaining the Walker Cup at Royal St George's in Kent was the next target, Jones setting off

with his wife Mary and a host of players and celebrities on the liner Mauretania early in April. The Cup safely retained, and Jones, the US captain, still in possession of his perfect Cup singles record, there was time for the Golf Illustrated Gold Vase at Sunningdale, southwest of London, an amateur 36-hole event. Jones won it by a stroke, with a total of 143.

After the Vase, "only" the four majors remained, the Open and Amateur championships of Britain and America, described under the events of 1930. On his return from the British leg of his odyssey, New York welcomed Jones with a ticker-tape parade.

The completion of the Grand Slam on September 27 at Merion made Jones even more of a national hero, if that were possible. Besides, the prowess of this handsome, charming man was much pleasanter to think about than the increasing economic difficulties into which the United States was staggering a year after the great stock market crash.

One important facet of Jones's character was his great honesty. He had twice called penalties on himself in American Opens for the movement of his ball at address, though no-one else saw any such movement. The episode that brought Jones sharply to a stern sense of the golfing proprieties occurred at

the end of his first attempt at the Open in 1921 at St Andrews, where a catastrophically increasing catalogue of dropped shots impelled him to pick up his ball.

## Supreme champion

Like Joyce Wethered, whose play he so admired, Jones was ever a likely winner. He qualified for every event he entered and no-one ever beat him twice in 36-hole match play. His worst effort in his last ten starts in the US Open was finishing 11th in Tommy Armour's year of 1927. Otherwise he was (in order, from 1921) joint fifth, joint second, first, second, loser in a play-off, first, loser in a play-off, first and first. He would not in later years enter into discussions about who was the greatest player of all time, but Leonard Crawley played with or watched all the contenders, and was adamant that Bobby Jones (always "Bob" to his friends) had no peer because he had no weakness.

In a crisis there was, with "Calamity Jane" in hand, no better putter. He is famous for rejecting the "never up, never in" school of putting. He essayed to do something beyond the grasp of normal mortals, which was to reach the hole just before the ball "died."

Jones was an intensely nervous individual and shed pounds

Collectibles: Jones in 1930 with his silverware collection and his biographer O.B.Keeler.

in weight in big events. He seldom lost time over playing his shot, however. All this sounds too good to be true, but Jones was no goody-goody: he smoked a lot and was not a dietary paragon, playing many important rounds on tea and toast. He habitually got rid of tension at the day's end with a stiff Scotch and could enjoy some ribaldry in the locker room with the best of them.

Jones got on well with his professional rivals, and would help them to obtain club jobs. He was that rare being who can consort with all classes and charm them all – a southern gentleman with a universal appeal, who managed the burden of fame with aplomb.

One of the reasons he played so irregularly was his extensive studies, first to gain a mechanical engineering degree at Georgia Tech, then at Harvard to read literature and finally at the Atlanta law school to qualify as a lawyer. He also found time to marry and had three children.

Within weeks of completing the "Impregnable Quadrilateral", the phrase coined by the sports writer, George Trevor, Jones announced that he was turning professional, but that he did not intend to engage again in championship golf.

## Sense of purpose

What he was doing was to make it clear that he was an ex-amateur. He proposed to use his golfing fame to increase his personal wealth. Club makers, ball manufacturers, the press, publishers and radio all wanted a piece of Jones and, with all his playing ambitions satisfied, he was going to make money and follow his other calling as a lawyer.

The most valuable initiative of all was his joint effort with course designer Dr Alister Mackenzie and businessman Clifford Roberts to build Augusta National Golf Course near Atlanta in his native Georgia on 365 acres of what had been a

nursery, with plenty of trees and flowering plants available, and a stream running through it.

To the slopes and quick greens of this new southern jewel of a course, Jones invited winners of important events to play a 72-hole tournament. Though Jones's innate modesty was not at ease with the name the tournament quickly acquired – the Masters – it remained.

Jones was born on St Patrick's Day, March 17, 1902, and had a touch of the luck of the Irish now and then in his career, but never such a kiss from Lady Luck as in 1935, when Gene Sarazen scored a double eagle – or albatross – on Augusta's par five 15th hole, the three shots thus saved enabling him to tie with Craig Wood and beat him in a play-off.

The impact on the golfing and general public, and invitations to Jones's fledgling event, not to mention admission tickets to watch, became as sought-after as membership of the 400. Life

was unkind to Jones in his later years in all but the strengths of the friendships he had forged.

He played in his own tournament, though without any competitive edge to his efforts, until 1947, when shoulder pain led to exploratory medicine, and finally a diagnosis of a spinal disease, syringomyelia, that put him in a wheelchair.

St Andrews made him an honorary burgess in 1958, the second American to achieve this distinction: Benjamin Franklin was the first.

He lived to see his Masters recognized as a major before the US PGA championship. The latter, it was thought, produced freak winners because of its match-play format.

It became a stroke play event in 1958, 13 years before Jones's death in 1971. It could never truly be considered a major while Jones was in championship action.

Moreover, since Jones retired only one amateur has won the US Open (Johnny Goodman, in 1933), and professionals have always won the British Open since 1930, so Jones can be considered to be the leading force in changing the majors – from the Open/Amateur double to the Opens, plus Masters and US PGA.

No-one has accomplished the feat of carrying off all the titles in his new line-up yet.

# USGA approves 'balloon ball' but the arguments continue

OGDEN NASH, the American humorist, wrote a cautionary New Year poem about the clock crouching, black and small, like a time bomb on the wall, which ended:

"Hush, it's midnight, children dear,
Duck, here comes another year."

What was lying in wait for US golfers at midnight on December 31, 1930, was the "balloon" ball, approved by the USGA for use from January 1, 1931.

Its nickname derived from the fact that, far from being black and small, it was white and, though the same size as the previous projectile, not so heavy. The new golf ammunition mea-

sured not less than 1.68 inches in diameter and weighed not more than 1.55 ounces. It had been in use experimentally for two years, but players were not bound to put it into service till 1931 dawned. This was intended to be an "easier and pleasanter ball for the average golfer".

There was also the question of the coarser grasses common on American fairways, upon which, the thought was, this new model would sit better.

Scores of different balls were being produced on either side of the Atlantic, and the Royal & Ancient and the USGA had agreed ten years before to take any step they felt necessary "to limit the powers of the ball with

regard to distance, should any ball of greater power be introduced".

If the ball makers were allowed full rein, the distance to which golfers would be capable of hitting the ball might put half the world's hazards out of business.

For the present, the Royal & Ancient stayed with the formula introduced ten years earlier: 1.62 ounces and not less than 1.62 inches in diameter.

Grumbles soon began about the balloon ball, whose characteristics were well summed up by its name. The change was minute, but produced a ball that, especially in wind, "got away" from even expert players.

# Burke too strong for von Elm at Toledo

WHAT THE 1931 US Open lacked in star quality – from the absence of Bobby Jones – it did its best to make up for in length. An unprecedented eight rounds were needed to settle it in favour of New Englander Billy Burke, aged 31, who defeated George von Elm at Inverness Club, Toledo, in a 72-hole play-off. Von Elm's birdie on the final hole forced the tie at 292, eight over par.

After the first 36-hole head to head proved a stalemate, because von Elm again birdied the final hole, Burke got a stroke ahead on the 31st hole the next day and kept his advantage to the end on the fifth day of play.

# Carnoustie welcome for Tommy Armour

HOW FITTING it was that on June 5 Tommy Armour, now prematurely grey and so graduating from "Black Scot" to "Silver Scot", should win in his homeland the first British Open to be played at one of Scotland's longest and toughest courses, Carnoustie, near Dundee, north of St Andrews, across the mouth of the Tay estuary.

Armour, flourishing at 36 years of age despite his war injuries, had already captured the American and Canadian Opens

and PGA titles, and so became the first to have four national titles to his name. As in his US Open victory, he finished strongly with his best round of the championship, 71, just enough to keep out the Argentine, José Jurado, who was leading after 54 holes by three strokes from Macdonald Smith and Arthur Havers.

Armour later described how, having missed a short putt on the 71st hole, he faced one of a similar distance at the last. "I took a new grip, holding the club as

tightly as I could and with stiff wrists. From the instant the club left the ball on the backswing I was blind and unconscious." It was a wonder the ball dropped!

Armour was a popular figure and talked well. He was often accused of being too deliberate a player, but the eye he had lost in a mustard gas attack during World War I meant that he had no bifocal vision, and so had to line his shots up with greater care than opponents with binocular vision.

# Ouimet back to fill the gap

SIGNIFICANTLY, as soon as quintuple American Amateur champion Bobby Jones was out of the way, with his premature retirement from the game, back came Francis Ouimet (still only 38) to reclaim the title after 17 years.

Ouimet, said by Bernard Darwin to have founded the American golfing empire, comfortably beat Jack Westland in the final 6 & 5.

Back to his Scottish roots, Tommy Armour receives the Auld Mug from tartan-clad host at Carnoustie.

## SCORECARD

**British Open** (Carnoustie, Scot)
TD Armour 73 75 77 71 296

**US Open** (Inverness, Ohio)
B Burke 73 72 74 73 292
(First play-off, Burke 73+76=149, G von Elm 75+74=149)
(Second play-off, Burke 77+71=148, von Elm 76+73=149)

**USPGA** (Wannamoisett, RI)
T Creavy bt D Shute 2 & 1

**British Amateur** (Westward Ho!, Devon)
E Martin Smith bt J de Forest 1h

**US Amateur** (Beverly CC, Ill)
F Ouimet bt J Westland 6 & 5

**British Women's Amateur** ( Portmarnock, Ireland)
E Wilson bt W Morgan 7 & 6

**US Women's Amateur** (Buffalo, NY)
H Hicks bt Glenna Collett Vare 2 & 1

**Ryder Cup** (Scioto, Ohio)
US bt G B & Ireland 9–3

# At last – Curtis dream to become reality

YEARS OF SCHEMING and planning by Margaret Curtis bore fruit when the USGA and Britain's LGU agreed to play biennial matches. The French were to join in whenever they were able. André Vagliano presented the silver Vagliano Cup for the annual competition between England and France. Sir Ernest Holderness, the former Amateur champion, opposed such matches. He said that a married woman with young children could not be expected to win titles. "It would be enough ground for a divorce."

Glenna Collett, now Mrs Edwin Vare, was a clear favourite to lead the US team in such endeavours, though she failed in her attempt to gain an unprecedented sixth Amateur championship at Buffalo, losing the final to Helen Hicks 2 & 1.

With the retirement of Joyce Wethered from championship play, Britain was in need of a dominant new character, and in tall, slim Enid Wilson that need was fulfilled. She had deliberately got herself thrown out of school in 1927 for swearing and settled down to serious golf right away. She wore trousers, smoked cigarettes, was very much her own woman at all times and remained firmly of the opinion that their war service, not the suffragette movement, had won the battle of votes for women.

She soon began to win tournaments. Beaten in the English final in 1927, she won the following year and in 1930, and she reached the last four of the British Amateur three times (1927, 1928 and 1930) before winning at Wanda Morgan's expense, by 7 & 6, at Portmarnock in Ireland. Later in the year she reached the American semifinal, but lost at the 17th to the eventual winner, Hicks.

Wilson, always outspoken as a writer on the game from 1927, was impatient with forward tees for women and players who were not prepared to work hard on their strokes. Her own progress had been checked by an inability to putt.

"I had to get on the green four strokes sooner than the other girl, just to get a half," said Wilson, exaggerating just a little. Then, in the late 1920s, the professional, James Sherlock, gave her a lesson on the mechanics of putting. "In five minutes I suddenly got it," said Wilson. "Soon afterwards I managed 12 single-putt holes in a row at Formby. They were going in from all angles and distances. That lesson changed everything."

Genuine seaside golf.

## TEE TALK

**"How well you play golf depends on how well you control that left hand of yours."**

TOMMY ARMOUR,
who had huge hands.

# US 2-1 ahead in Ryder series

THE THIRD Ryder Cup match ended in 9-3 defeat for Britain at Scioto Country Club, Columbus, Ohio, where a heatwave added to the British team's collection of troubles.

So perhaps did the absence of Henry Cotton, 4 & 3 winner over Al Watrous in 1929, and a golfer who was beginning to figure towards the head of the British Open fields.

Cotton, increasingly a law unto himself, was also Hagen-like in his disinclination to be bound by authority. He missed this Cup match because his request to travel separately from the rest of the team was not granted.

The net result was that America now led 2-1 in Cup matches. Hagen himself captained the winners again and got sweet revenge for the 10 & 9 drubbing he had received from George Duncan at Leeds two years before.

Now he and Densmore Shute beat Duncan and Arthur Havers 10 & 9. Havers won his singles against American newcomer Craig Wood easily enough, by 4 & 3, but five points went America's way by margins of 7 & 6 or more. Abe Mitchell and Fred Robson got Britain's only foursome point against Leo Diegel and Al Espinosa, 3 & 1.

Densmore Shute, who with his captain Walter Hagen trounced George Duncan and Arthur Havers.

Enid Wilson: elementary, my dear Sherlock.

# Gene Sarazen, Sandwich and the sand wedge

THOUGH HE LOST a deal of money in the stock market crash, and the Great Depression was not becoming any shallower, Gene Sarazen experienced a personal boom in 1932.

A better term than boom would be explosion, for Sarazen had been working for a year or two on the problem of bunker play and, early in June 1932, unveiled his solution in the first British Open to be played at Prince's, next to Royal St George's at Sandwich in Kent. Here was the perfect place to test his method of exploding the ball from sand.

Sarazen's theory was born when he was taking flying lessons – Howard Hughes, the aviation pioneer, was a friend – and a thought flashed through Sarazen's mind as he pulled the joystick back and the aircraft's tail went down and the nose went up. It was that his niblick should be lowered at the back. He got a bundle of niblicks from the clubmaker, Wilson, and began to reshape the club with solder, putting a flange on the back of the club so that the flange hit the sand first. Until this point in club manufacture it had been necessary to chip cleanly out of bunkers – otherwise the sharp edge of the chipper became buried in the sand. Sarazen and most other pros at the time were expending too many shots emerging from bunkers, and when they did get out they were not getting near the hole, even from bunkers at close range.

Sarazen was, before long, routinely getting up and down in two. The upshot was that Sarazen, untroubled by the Prince's bunkers, set a record 72-hole score of 283 and won the Open by five shots from runner-up supreme, Macdonald Smith. He hid his sand wedge when off the course, but need not have worried. Though the concave wedge that had recently been in vogue had been banned (it was proved that it hit the ball twice), such a fate never overtook the club Sarazen had invented.

Not many golfers have an idea that puts a club in every golf bag in the world. Sarazen got little out of it – apart from championships – because his equipment company claimed the rights.

The British Open was Harry Vardon's last championship, but he failed to qualify.

It adds up: 28 holes = 100 strokes = Sarazen.

# Hundred strokes that landed Open double

FIFTEEN DAYS after lifting the silver claret jug at Prince's, Gene Sarazen needed only 100 strokes to complete the last 28 holes of the US Open championship at Fresh Meadow, Flushing, New York. His average for the 100 holes was, therefore, just under 3.6 strokes. That turned a deficit of seven into a winning margin of three.

The par was 280, Sarazen's 286 equalling the best previous Open total by Chick Evans at Minikahda in 1916, and making him the second man after Bobby Jones (who did it twice) to win both the major Opens in the same year. Bobby Cruickshank shared second place with Phil Perkins, the former British Amateur champion, who had turned professional in the United States. Perkins had a mixed year in 1932, with its high point in the Open and its lowest when he was shot in the thigh during a gun battle between police and gangsters, the latter using Perkins for cover.

The USGA had bowed to the protests about the balloon ball, and had sanctioned a return to the no smaller than 1.68 inches and no lighter than 1.62 ounces formula.

Gene Sarazen: got his hands on the claret jug again.

## SHORT PUTTS

● A.J.Balfour, who had performed just about every service to popularize golf that a prominent politician could, died at the Woking home of his younger brother, Gerald, in March.

● Virginia Van Wie routed Glenna Collett Vare at Salem, Massachusetts, where she made her third appearance in the Women's Amateur final. Van Wie had twice lost finals to Mrs Vare, who had won in five of her seven appearances, but now Van Wie waltzed home by 10 & 8.

● Enid Wilson lost at the final hole to Charlotte Glutting in the Salem quarterfinals, but won her second successive British final amid the mighty sandhills of Saunton in Devon by 7 & 6 against Purvis-Russell Montgomery.

● Though the four home countries in the British Isles had been holding amateur internationals since 1902, the first official meeting of England, Ireland, Scotland and Wales now took place at Troon, the Scots defeating all three of their rivals. England, who lost 7-8 to the Scots, came second.

● Dr Frank Stableford's system of scoring first used at Wallasey, near Liverpool. Points are awarded for performance against par, with allowance for handicaps, so that alone among games, golf can offer a competitive match between an expert and a duffer.

**Another Enid Wilson victory speech: this time at Saunton.**

# Olin Dutra top, Sarazen out

TWO MONTHS after his joyful June, Gene Sarazen failed to qualify for the PGA championship at the Keller Club, Minnesota. Olin Dutra, who was of Spanish blood, beat Frank Walsh in the final. Though a number of members were in receipt of relief from the PGA as the Depression hit at leisure activities, the total of cash available on the tour reached a record $130,000.

Club professionals and tour players were represented by the PGA, but the divergent interests of the two groups tended to cause friction. Hence the end, in April, of Bob Harlow's stint as tour manager, which he began on a full-time basis in 1929, though he continued as Walter Hagen's manager, in itself a useful post from which to approach sponsors, who were naturally eager to have Hagen the showman teeing off at their tournament. Harlow, a nationally syndicated journalist, finally received a $100 a week salary for this task, one which he was eminently suited to tackle.

Harlow was an expert at getting the ear of fellow journalists and a master at the art of puffing the sport at the least opportunity. He also convinced equipment manufacturers of the wisdom of setting up a fund to guarantee tournament purses. Despite all this, Harlow had to go when the club pro versus tournament pro problems spilled over into a personal differences between the PGA's George Jacobus, defender of the club pros, and Harlow. Not only did Harlow manage Hagen, but Joe Kirkwood, Horton Smith and others too, he also had agreements with sponsors to run their events.

He induced newspapers to publish lists of players in order of their achievements, and all in all was well worthy of being called "The Ziegfeld of the Pro Tour."

## SCORECARD

**British Open** (Prince's, Kent)
G Sarazen 70 69 70 74 283

**US Open** (Fresh Meadow, NY)
G Sarazen 74 76 70 66 286

**USPGA** (Keller GC, Minn)
O Dutra bt F Walsh 4 & 3

**British Amateur** (Muirfield, Scot)
J de Forest bt E Fiddian 3 & 1

**US Amateur** (Five Farms, Baltimore, Md)
C Ross Somerville bt J Goodman 2 & 1

**British Women's Amateur** (Saunton, Devon)
E Wilson bt CPR Montgomery 7 & 6

**US Women's Amateur** (Salem CC, Mass)
V Van Wie bt Glenna Collett Vare 10 & 8

**Walker Cup** (The Country Club, Brookline, Mass)
US bt GB & Ireland 9½–2½

**Curtis Cup** (Wentworth, Surrey)
US bt GB & Ireland 5½–3½

# Brookline battering for Britain

THE SEVENTH Walker Cup match, held in the autumn at The Country Club, Brookline, was no more encouraging for Britain's male amateurs than the Curtis Cup for their women amateurs.

Leonard Crawley was the solitary winner on the visiting team, though three matches were drawn in a 9½–2½ trouncing. Crawley beat George Voigt from Buffalo by one hole.

**Leonard Crawley: solitary Brookline winner.**

# US win first Curtis Cup

JOYCE WETHERED, though sticking to her second retirement from major championship play, could hardly do other than make a comeback on the occasion of the first Curtis Cup match, played at Wentworth, southwest of London, all on May 21. Thus the Cup, offered by the Curtis sisters five years before, could at last be presented, and America's captain, Glenna Collett Vare, was the happy recipient.

She gained a little consolation for her championship defeats at Wethered's hands by partnering Patty Berg in the top single and beating Wethered and Wanda Morgan at the final hole. Helen Hicks, the reigning American champion, and Virginia Van Wie, who was soon to succeed her, beat the British champion, Enid Wilson, and Mrs J.B.Watson at the 17th, and Maureen Orcutt and Mrs L.D.Cheney beat Molly Gourlay and Doris Park by one hole. That made a clean foursomes sweep.

In the singles, Collett Vare fell to Wethered again, 6 & 4 in the top match, but Diana Fishwick was Britain's only other winner, by 4 & 3 over Orcutt, though Gourlay got a half in her match with Opal Hill.

Thus the match, for which the LGU and the US PGA had assumed responsibility, ended in a 5½–3½ victory for America. The 15,000 spectators it attracted must have delighted Margaret Curtis.

## TEE TALK

## "Call every woman 'Sugar' and you can't go wrong."

WALTER HAGEN.

# Densmore Shute three-putts the Ryder Cup away

HERMAN DENSMORE SHUTE allowed Great Britain to level the Ryder Cup series at two-all at Southport and Ainsdale on the Lancashire coast by three-putting the final hole in the last match on the course. His opponent from Devon, Sid Easterbrook, knocked

his putt close, Shute putted his winning chance past the hole, then missed the one back. Easterbrook was left with a three-footer for the whole match, and he holed out to set the huge crowds cheering the home team and their Cup-winning total of 6½

points. Horton Smith beat Charles Whitcombe 2 & 1 in the bottom single, but to no avail.

The Americans had seriously damaged their cause on the first day, when only Ed Dudley and Billy Burke managed to win a foursome, though Gene Sarazen and Walter Hagen did eke out a half again Percy Alliss and Whitcombe.

With the help of Bill Davies, Easterbrook gained a foursome point against Craig Wood and Paul Runyon at the final hole on the first day, while Abe Mitchell and Arthur Havers won at the 34th against Olin Dutra and Shute, who had won both his matches in his first Ryder Cup in 1931. Mitchell, Alliss and Havers also won in singles.

Henry Cotton, now professional at Waterloo in Belgium, was again absent from the side, from which he had been excluded in 1931 because of his plans to travel alone.

His foreign posting, so to say, kept him out now, since the Cup rules stated that only home-born

**Abe Mitchell: won both his Ryder Cup matches.**

players domiciled in their native country could take part. The home side was captained by (non-playing) J.H.Taylor.

He took a stern line throughout the proceedings, including getting his team up for early morning runs.

**Every little helps: Percy Alliss who, with Charles Whitcombe, squeezed a half out of the reigning Open Champion, Gene Sarazen.**

# Ryder villain Shute makes good at HQ

DENSMORE SHUTE, who was not far short of 30 and had turned pro as recently as 1928, proved that he could stand firm in a crisis, despite his poor showing in the Ryder Cup. This he did by beating Craig Wood easily in a play off after a tie earned with four rounds of 73, the first time a champion had put in so consistent a performance.

Syd Easterbrook, his nemesis at Southport and Ainsdale, was third, only a stroke in arrears, in company with Leo Diegel and Gene Sarazen, who looked set to retain his title till he tangled with Hell Bunker in his last round, a risk he need not have taken. Wood proved that his long-driving reputation did not lie by reaching a bunker 100 yards short of the 530-yard fifth hole.

The PGA, happy after the Ryder Cup, were cast down by the presence of five Americans in the first six in the Open.

British journalists were not exactly in transports of delight watching two American pros fight it out for the British Open.

The fact remained that, for ten years – an extraordinary drought – no British player had won his national Open.

**Hand it over: It's tough to smile for Craig Wood as the Auld Mug passes to (right) Densmore Shute.**

# Michael Scott, Amateur champion at 54

THE SAME Michael Scott who had won the inaugural Australian Open in Sydney in 1904 gained the British Amateur title at Royal Liverpool. The Hon. Michael Scott, at 54, is the oldest man to win the title. His sister, Lady Margaret, won the first three British Women's Amateurs before the turn of the century.

Scott was, needless to say, given little chance. Moreover, he was told not to go to Hoylake when, in the pre-championship week, he developed a severe cold. "This will probably be my last chance of winning. I'm going," said he.

His health did not improve and he declared after the first round that, if he had not holed the winning putt on the 18th, he would not have had the strength to play the 19th. George Dunlap, the American Walker Cup player, was greatly fancied to play Cyril Tolley in the final, but Scott grew stronger as the week went on, especially with his long irons, and he beat Dunlap easily, while Bourne surprised Tolley by beating him at the second extra hole of the semifinal. No heroics attended the final, Scott prevailing 4 & 3.

Dunlap, from the Pomonok Country Club of Flushing, New York, returned home to win the American Amateur in September, in the process proving that last can often finish first, for he was joint worst in qualifying. Dunlap went on to beat Max Marston 6 & 5 in the final.

## SCORECARD

**British Open** (St Andrews, Scot)
D Shute 73 73 73 73 292
(Play-off, Shute 149, C Wood 154)

**US Open** (N Shore GC, Ill)
J Goodman 75 66 70 76 287

**USPGA** (Blue Mound CC, Wisconsin)
G Sarazen bt W Goggin 5 & 4

**British Amateur** (Royal Liverpool, Lancs)
M Scott bt D Bourn 4 & 3

**US Amateur** (Kenwood, Ohio)
GT Dunlap bt M Marston 6 & 5

**British Women's Amateur** (Gleneagles, Scot)
E Wilson bt D Plumpton 5 & 4

**US Women's Amateur** (Exmoor CC, Ill)
V Van Wie bt H Hicks 4 & 3

**Ryder Cup** (Southport & Ainsdale, Merseyside)
GB & Ireland bt US 6½–5½

# Augusta National opened

IN DEFIANCE of superstition on Friday, January 13, came the formal opening of Bobby Jones's Augusta National Golf Club in Georgia, on land converted from a former horticultural nursery.

The opening, which was preceded by a parade, was given a touch of Jones's authority when he went round the new course in 69, in not very auspicious weather.

He had a good audience, for the opening was attended by friends from far and near. The moving spirit of the new layout also announced that he would hold a spring tournament there to entertain his former rivals at the end of the winter tour. It would be entitled the Augusta National Invitational.

# Goodman is fifth US Open amateur winner

JOHNNY GOODMAN, the Omaha amateur, became the fifth unpaid golfer to win the US Open by holding off a bunch of resourceful professionals at North Shore, Illinois, including Ralph Guldahl, Craig Wood, Walter Hagen, Tommy Armour, and the Dutras – Mortie and Olin.

He almost didn't shut them out, despite a fast start, in which he totalled 141 (75+66) over the first 36 holes. After round three, which he completed in 70 strokes, Goodman looked home and dry, six ahead. Even more depressing for his pursuers, he began his final round 4, 3, 2, saving three shots in as many holes. But he needed 67 for the remaining 15 holes, and would have been caught had not Guldahl's stroke failed him by a fraction at the final hole, his approach tailing off into a bunker.

Johnny Goodman

# August consolation for Sarazen

JOINT THIRD in the British Open and nowhere in the American Championship, Gene Sarazen looked to be heading for a blank year in the majors when on August 13, he defeated Willie Coggin 5 & 4 in the final of the PGA Championship at Blue Mound, Wisconsin. Sarazen had first won the title ten years before, and this was his third success.

# Bernard Darwin – writer, wit and player

BERNARD DARWIN became Joyce Wethered's sixth different winning partner in the Worplesdon foursomes. She had won with the Hon. Michael Scott two years earlier, and now landed a hat-trick with the help of the distinguished golf writer.

He had started as a general-purpose, and leader, writer on *The Times*, and had a considerable reputation as a player, though nothing he did after 1922 equalled his singles win in the first Walker Cup match, when Britain were a man short because of Robert Harris's indisposition.

Nevertheless, he had three wins for Cambridge University against Oxford, played for England in the first international against the Scots, won the Golf Illustrated Gold Vase in 1921 and reached the semifinal of the Amateur championship in 1909 and 1921.

No doubt Darwin himself enjoyed winning the Oxford and Cambridge Golfing Society's President's Putter in 1924 just as much as anything else he ever achieved.

Darwin could, according to legend, be rather less in control of himself with a club than a pen, as on the day when in an annual medal competition he missed birdie putts from five feet at the first, eight at the second, six at the third and three at the fourth.

Darwin sank to his knees, buried his face in the turf, then looked up and appealed to heaven: "O God, are you satisfied now?"

## TEE TALK

"I say, are those your old school colours or your own unfortunate choice?"

BERNARD DARWIN, at St Andrews to the wearer of an unusually bright outfit.

# Henry Cotton breaks American grip on Open

A STARTLING BURST of scores in the 60s by Henry Cotton at Deal and Sandwich spreadeagled the field in the British Open and ended a whole decade of British failures in the world's oldest championship.

Cotton, born in Cheshire in 1907, scored 66 over the exposed and challenging links of the Royal Cinque Ports club at Deal during qualifying, a performance that gave him great pleasure and instilled confidence. He then started with a 67 in the first round of the Open proper at Royal St George's.

Next day, Thursday, June 28, he improved on this with an epoch-making 65 for the 6,700-yard links that gave him a lead of nine strokes at halfway over Alf Padgham, whose 71+70 would have given him a lead of four shots at halfway the last time the Open was played at Royal St George's in 1928.

Cotton's 36-hole total of 132 took the game to a level of consistency and excellence unseen on either side of the Atlantic.

Cotton's 65:
4 3 3, 4 4 4, 3 4 4 = 33 out
4 3 4, 4 4 4, 3 3 3 = 32 in

Though his third round on the final morning was "only" 72, it increased his advantage over his closest pursuer, now the dogged Macdonald Smith, to ten strokes.

In the fourth round Cotton came close to one of the greatest disasters in major championship history. His start was delayed because of crowd control problems. His unprecedented scoring on the first two days had, not surprisingly, made it a busy day for the gate-men and stewards on the third.

Moreover, as the Daily Telegraph reported, Cotton had gone back to his hotel after the morning round for lunch and had eaten too hurriedly. Before he

had got far on the final round, he was suffering from stomach cramps.

This discomfort on top of the burden of knowing the huge gallery was looking to him to stem the tide of American success made him wonder for a moment whether he could carry on. Soldier on he did, taking 40 strokes to the turn.

Providentially, his putting held up, a part of the game that is often more vulnerable to stress than any other.

Though he could do no better than come back in 39 for a total of 79, he still equalled Gene Sarazen's record low score of 283 at nearby Prince's two years earlier, and took the trophy five shots clear of Sid Brews, whose

second place with 288 was the best effort by a South African.

The American challenge was muted compared to recent years. Padgham was third, Macdonald Smith, the American Scot still searching for that first major, was joint fourth with Marcel Dallemagne (France).

On the final day of the Open Marianne Mayfayre reported in the fashion pages of the Daily Telegraph that all London was at Syon House (formerly a nunnery) for the Duchess of Northumberland's coming out ball.

Nazi bombs were exploding in Austria. Dr Dollfus, the chancellor, said the purpose of the attacks was to ruin Austria's tourist trade. He was murdered later that year.

**Cotton: not always a Dunlop 65 man, as this advert shows.**

## SCORECARD

**British Open** (Royal St George's, Kent)
TH Cotton 67 65 72 79 283

**US Open** (Merion CC, Pa)
O Dutra 76 74 71 72 293

**Augusta National Invitational** (Augusta, Ga)
H Smith 70 72 70 72 284

**USPGA** (Park CC, NY)
P Runyan bt C Wood 38th

**Leading US money winner**
Paul Runyan $6,767

**British Amateur** (Prestwick, Scot)
L Little bt J Wallace 14 & 13

**US Amateur** (The Country Club, Brookline, Mass)
L Little bt D Goldman 8 & 7

**British Women's Amateur** (Porthcawl, Wales)
H Holm bt P Barton 6 & 5

**US Women's Amateur** (Whitemarsh, Pa)
V Van Wie bt D Traung 2 & 1

**Walker Cup** (St Andrews, Scot)
US bt GB & Ireland 9½–2½

**Curtis Cup** (Chevy Chase, Md)
US bt GB & Ireland 6½–2½

## TEE TALK

**"To watch a first-class field drive off must convince everyone that a golf ball can be hit in many ways."**

HENRY COTTON.

Henry Cotton: on the tee at Royal St George's, Sandwich.

# Olin the overtaker wins US Open

Despite having hospital treatment for a painful stomach ailment, and having to come more or less straight from his sickbed to the tee in the American Open, Olin Dutra gained his first title and surprised a group of the nation's leading professionals who had been as many as eight strokes in front of him at halfway.

His most dangerous opponent was undoubtedly the 1932 champion Gene Sarazen, but Dutra had 16 others to get past also. He had taken 150 strokes for the first 36 holes on the East Course at Merion, but improved with scores of 71 and 72 to win by a shot from Sarazen.

# Damp British spirits in Curtis Cup

THE SECOND Curtis Cup match at a very wet Chevy Chase, Maryland, in late September went the same way as the first, only more so, the US team, led by Glenna Collett Vare, winning by four points instead of two. The teams shared the foursomes in a stormy opening session, but Mrs J.B.Walker was Britain's only winner next day just as, with Diane Plumpton, she had been in the foursome play.

# Americans dominate the Walker

THE UNITED STATES' eighth consecutive victory in the Walker Cup took place at St Andrews by a thumping 9-2, with one match halved. For the third time in a row Britain and Ireland emerged with only one singles win.

They did gain a foursomes point, however, which was more than was achieved two years previously. Britain's veteran champion, the Hon. Michael Scott, led the home team against Francis Ouimet, still only 41, and still winning. He crushed Leonard Crawley, Britain's only singles winner in 1932, 5 & 4.

# Lawson Little's "Little slam"

WILLIAM LAWSON LITTLE announced himself as the amateur of the year by winning both the British and American titles, a double dubbed the "Little slam." His victory in the British event at Prestwick over Jack Wallace was by a record 14 & 13 and not unexpected considering the previous perfect record in the event of one visiting Walker Cup American or another. Back in America in September, Little, 24, got through the all-matchplay US Amateur at Brookline despite the presence of nine former title holders. He beat David Goldman in the final after a series of comfortable wins.

Lawson Little: with half of the "Little" slam at Prestwick.

# Record for Jones, but first title goes to Horton Smith

THE FIRST OF Bobby Jones's Augusta Invitationals on the Alister Mackenzie course in Georgia went to the tall, articulate Horton Smith, who had been winning nothing but money, but plenty of it.

He could not equal the course record Jones set up earlier in March, but his 284 was a stroke better than Craig Wood could manage. Jones himself was joint 13th.

Smith's crucial stroke was the birdie putt he put down at the 71st hole. It was from around six yards and gave him a one-stroke lead over Craig Wood, who had finished. A par at the last sealed Smith's victory.

Horton Smith, first at Augusta.

# Runyan top money winner

PAUL RUNYAN, short in stature but a fine holer-out, beat tall Craig Wood for the PGA title, then became first official leading money winner. Chances of the $6,767 he won being greatly exceeded in future years by Runyan or anyone else seemed dim. The Depression still gripped hard, but, on the bright side, Bob Harlow was back in favour with the PGA after the tour had seemed rudderless in 1933. He was busy in 1934 in his capacity as assistant business administrator and tournament-bureau manager.

His tasks included the endless search for more and bigger sponsorships, inventing new publicity wheezes and generally organizing the play itself, with published tee-times. Horton Smith was in agreement with Harlow on many of the rights the tour required if it were to thrive – which that faction of the PGA supporting the club pros would vigorously oppose.

# Van Wie hat-trick

VIRGINIA VAN WIE retired from competitive golf after beating Dorothy Traung 2 & 1 in the final of the American Women's Amateur at Whitemarsh, Pennsylvania. She had beaten five-times winner Glenna Collett Vare in the semifinal. All the British Curtis Cup team entered, but Wanda Morgan was the only survivor to the third round. "A star in the making" was the widely held view of Pamela Barton, at 17 years of age a strong, bold golfer who had been taught by Archie Compston. All the same, she lacked experience and lost to Helen Holm in the British final at Royal Porthcawl.

**"An event will flop unless conducted on a business basis with careful planning and suitable organization."**

BOB HARLOW.

# Henry Cotton – the man who revitalized British golf

As three times victor in the British Open against tough American opposition, and as a teacher, writer and course designer, Henry Cotton was a dominant figure on the professional scene

There was never a greater individualist than Henry Cotton. He was not the most approachable of men, yet he did much to raise the reputation of his profession. He could scarcely have resembled Walter Hagen less, yet like the great American he would brook no hint of an insult to the dignity of the golf professional.

Hagen felt insulted when he was refused clubhouse facilities in Britain, and did much to end such discrimination. Cotton had the stature to make it a condition of his being attached to the Ashridge club in Hertfordshire, as it had been at Waterloo in Belgium, that he should have honorary membership. This is now a widely accepted practice.

He was a public schoolboy who liked to consort with the rich and celebrated, and was at ease when he did so. It has been said – no doubt by the envious – that among his fellow pros he spoke only to champions. Nevertheless, at well past three score years and ten, he could be the life and soul of a pro-am party.

## Unique

He was, understandably for a triple Open championship winner, an expensive golf teacher, yet freely gave a great deal of his time to the cause of the Golf Foundation, which he helped to establish in 1952. The Foundation began with coaching at six schools, and now organizes coaching at more than 2,000 schools and junior groups. How much this initiative is responsible for the general raising of professional and amateur standards in Britain can scarcely be quantified, but cannot be discounted – nor can Cotton's leading role in the enterprise.

His other notable contribution to the cause of encouraging young players was the institution in 1960 of the Rookie of the Year title, which goes annually to the best newcomer on the tour. His part in helping the 1938 Walker Cup team to gain their first success against the United States is another example of his inspirational effect on British golf. His most outstanding service to the

Henry Cotton: Most influential figure in European golf.

nation's game was breaking the American grip on the British Open in 1934, not to mention the majestic way in which he did it, setting up a 36-hole record of 132, not equalled for 56 years until Nick Faldo beat it with 130 in 1992. Cotton held a far more dominating position in English – and European golf – than anyone who followed.

## Triumph

Long before he won the Open, and Cotton did not hide the fact that he proposed to do so, he had made himself known to a wide public, for here was no ordinary golf professional, but a self-possessed, stylishly dressed, articulate member of the upper middle class who intended to make a glittering career from the game.

When he at last won the Open at Royal St George's after several high finishes, his second round of 65 gave the Dunlop company the long-running idea for a new golf ball. Dunlop 65s remained highly saleable for many years after the second world war, though many golfers were totally ignorant of the significance of the number. Millions of them must have found a final resting place in rough or lake, but few of Cotton's suffered such a fate, since his greatest asset was his long, straight driving.

He is one of the few professionals who never tried to plan their way round a course with fade or draw as their chief means of control. His endless practice gave him the means to attempt this daunting tactic, and he succeeded at many important moments in his career – though not in the last round of his Sandwich triumph, when he put up the same sad closing score as in 1933 – but this time, thanks to his meteoric start, it was good enough to give him a five-shot win.

Only two strokes separated Cotton from his closest pursuer, Reg Whitcombe, at the end of his second Open at Carnoustie in

1937, but the weather on the final day was abominable, and the labours of ground staff and volunteers with hastily purchased extra brushes were urgently needed to allow the championship to finish, after a downpour before the final round left pools of water everywhere. Moreover, the assembled ranks of the American Ryder Cup side were nowhere in sight as Cotton scored 71 despite the unhelpful conditions – his best round of the week on the longest championship course. His third Open, at Muirfield in 1948, was like his first won by five strokes. King George VI saw Cotton off from

**Cotton the champion: bunkered in the 1934 Open.**

the first tee, and the round that followed, 66, was certainly worthy of royal patronage.

## 'Concentration'

Thomas Henry Cotton, the son of a successful businessman who owned an iron foundry, was born in Cheshire in 1907, and went to Alleyn's school in Dulwich, London, and made a start on his golf career at 17 in the most determined and methodical way. His father took Henry, aged 13, and his brother, Leslie, to J.H.Taylor to see what the sage thought of their potential as golfers. Taylor's not unprescient response was that Henry "would be the better player as he had more determination and more power of concentration."

Hagen called him "Concentration Henry" and Cotton certainly left nothing to chance in developing his knowledge of club making and all the paraphernalia of the game with several club professionals. Most of all he devoted endless hours to the swing – he was an indefatigable

analyser of everyone else's methods until, he said, he found he could not play as they did, and evolved his own style.

## Masterly skills

In later years in his golf clinics he developed the central theme of his teaching, which was that the golfer's hands could not be too strong – they should be exercised – and that no matter how good the swing the result would be indifferent if the fingers lost control of the club at impact.

He would ask if his audience was wondering whether an old codger like himself, who talked a lot about how to play, could still hit the ball. Well, he could, he said, and turning on his heel would walk towards a ball he had left lying a few yards away. Still on the move, he would hit it high and straight down the practice ground. To emphasize that the hands did the work he would play the same firm mid-iron shots with both feet pointing away from the target, as with both feet pointing towards it. His favourite teaching aid for beginners was a motor tyre, which he encouraged pupils to whip with a golf shaft, then "sting", as he put it, with a normal club. Next he put a ball down and said: "Now! sting that", and away it soared to the amazement of us duffers.

He was reportedly a great deal harder on serious students, but then he had never spared himself and practised to the extent that he needed remedial treatment, for he had practised himself round-shouldered, indeed to the extent of having his right shoulder lower than his left – basically, the position at address.

At 21 Cotton went to America and briefly played in the 1928-29 winter tour, solely to look and learn at what was clearly, on the evidence of recent British Open results alone, the toughest and best competitive régime in the game. The following year he played in Argentina. He visited the United States again in 1948, performed creditably in the Masters and won at Greenbrier. Cotton was, however, first and foremost a European golfer and, to his three Opens in 1934, 1937 and 1948, he added many continental opens.

He stole one march on Hagen, the showman of golf, by putting together a theatrical entertainment in London. He played shots in a 15-minute act with club and ball, visible in a darkened auditorium thanks to phosphorescent paint. Then on came the lights and he fired soft balls into the audience.

## Final honours

Cotton served in the Royal Air Force during the Second World War, but was invalided out, suffering from stomach ailments. After his retirement from regular tournament play in the late 1940s, Cotton took up course design, notably at Abridge, Canons Brook, Megève (France) and above all, the lengthy Penina course in the Algarve, Portugal, where he spent much of his retirement.

This was interrupted when the Portuguese revolution in the 1970s caused his temporary expulsion.

This was scarcely just treatment for the man who was the most influential founder of the sporting feast, so to speak, which had brought, and still brings, so much cash to the area. Cotton received the rare honour, for a professional, of honorary membership of the Royal & Ancient in 1968, and a few days before his death in London in December 1987, he learned that he was to be dubbed knight for his services to the game.

The timing of the award, the first of its kind in golf, was considered by many to be rather late for a man whose own timing had always been impeccable.

# Gene Sarazen's fateful double-eagle

NEVER in the field of sporting endeavour has a shot seen by so few been marvelled over by so many as the four-wood Gene Sarazen struck on the par-five 15th at Augusta National on April 7, 1935. It was his second shot, it went into the hole and he had erased the three-stroke lead of Craig Wood, who was just finishing his final round of 73 for a total of 282. "Now that," Wood must have been fondly thinking, "is surely good enough at last to get me a first place in Bob's new-fangled tournament" ... which, to be pedantic, started out in life as the Augusta National Invitational.

That soda-siphon title was quickly being discarded in favour of the "Masters", a little rich for Jones's blood, but it was a name which stuck. Anyway, it was a tournament for players who had mastered the difficult art of winning.

Sarazen scored par on every hole after his albatross/double-eagle – call it what you will, the effect was electrifying. Caught by a haymaker like this one at the end of the final round, so to speak, not many fighters, even ones as patient and talented as Wood, survive a rematch. So it proved in the 36-hole play-off next day when Sarazen played two par rounds, but that was enough at five strokes better – 144 to 149 – to vanquish Wood, a runner-up with experience in the very best circles, but not the winner's circle.

This near miss in the Masters was particularly disappointing, for he had rallied in an initially disastrous final round to save four strokes on the last eight holes, including a birdie on the 72nd – but all in vain. Wood was left to rue his latest attack of "just miss-itis". Two years ago he was third in the American Open and

lost a play-off for the British. Last year, coming second to Horton Smith at Augusta preceded defeat at the 38th hole of the USPGA by Paul Runyan.

From the start Sarazen did not begin to deny that his shot, though a good one, was distinguished mainly by the luck that blessed it. He had been the only player left on the course who could conceivably catch Wood, already into the photograph and congratulation mode as the dire news of "the shot" came in.

Sarazen had struck his drive about 250 yards to the right side of the fairway, which was grassy and damp. His caddie reckoned that for the remaining 230-odd yards, a three-wood was the club but, because the ball was "down" a little in damp grass, Sarazen let fly with a four-wood. His witnesses were, to say the least, as impeccable as they were few in number, for they included Jones himself, and Sarazen's playing partner, Walter Hagen. Sarazen's shot flew low a little to the right again, but kicked towards and into the hole.

Sarazen's victory catapulted Jones's tournament into the headlines right away. And now he had a Grand Slam of his own – a career record distinguished by both the major Opens, the US PGA and now the happily named Masters.

Gene Sarazen: with the four-wood that dished Craig Wood.

### TEE TALK

**"Mr Gene, you got to hit the three-wood if you want to clear that water."**

STOVEPIPE (Sarazen's caddie), before the double-eagle four-wood.

# Sam Parks comes to terms with the monster

OAKMONT in Pennsylvania continued to be just about the most frustrating layout on the American Open circuit of courses and proved its cussedness again by producing plenty of scores in the high 70s and beyond, and a champion no-one outside the ambit of college golf and the catchment area of South Hills Country Club (a near neighbour of Oakmont) had heard of – Sam Parks.

Parks won with the highest

score, 299, in the Open since Tommy Armour's 301 eight years before – at Oakmont.

He was professional at South Hills, but was well accustomed to the demands of Oakmont, and it was said, not too flatteringly, that he could play any course in the world in 75.

That meant success at Oakmont, for this was a fraction over his average score and, lined up behind him at the finish, were many of the greatest names in

golf – Jimmy Thomson with 301, Walter Hagen 302, Densmore Shute and Ray Mangrum 303, both Gene Sarazen and Horton Smith 306 – and not one of the leaders, including Parks, broke 75 in the final round.

Fast greens and ridged bunkers had done their destructive work again and people said that only the members could play Oakmont. Is it a coincidence that two Oakmont men had won Amateur titles there?

### SHORT PUTTS

● Johnny Revolta and Henry Picard, both members of America's victorious Ryder Cup team, won five tour events apiece, but Revolta finished top money winner with $9,543, and on the way beat Tommy Armour 5 & 4 in the PGA final at Twin Hills, Oklahoma.

● Gary Player was born on November 1 in Johannesburg, South Africa.

# Glenna Vare makes it six

STOCKY, STRONG and full of confidence, Patty Berg made her first appearance in the US Women's Amateur championship at Interlachen, where she had been taught by the professional.

She came up against the nation's most experienced and successful player in Glenna Collett Vare, and went down, not without honour, 3 & 2. So Mrs Vare, now playing in her eighth final, took an unprecedented sixth title.

In the British final, another emerging talent, Pam Barton, appeared again, and again went down to a more battle-hardened opponent, Wanda Morgan, by the same score.

# Perry wins the battle of the Alfreds

ALF PERRY equalled the scoring record of 283 set up by Gene Sarazen and Henry Cotton when he beat Alf Padgham by four strokes at Muirfield in the British Open. Thus the trophy stayed in Britain, and Padgham got closer to it, for he was third at Sandwich. Perry, from Leatherhead in Surrey, scored well with 69 in round one and 67 in round three. Perry's win must be balanced against the absence of a strong United States contingent. Of the Americans present, only Lawson Little (joint fourth) and Henry Picard (sixth) were highly placed.

**Alf Perry: equalled record.**

**Congratulations: for Perry from Herbert Gadd.**

# Little redoubles his "slam"

REPEATING HIS "Little slam" of the previous year, William Lawson Little was not as brusquely dismissive of his opponents in the British Amateur at Royal Lytham as he had been 12 months earlier at Prestwick. This immensely strong American was held up by the dogged resistance of Dr William Tweddell, slight in build but mighty in spirit and an experienced match player.

Four down right away in the final, Dr Tweddell, the 1927 winner, fought back to two down at lunch, after which Little was late on the tee by 20 minutes. He might well have been disqualified – his explanation was he had taken a bath – but on they went, and Little, clearly put off his stroke by his lateness, was caught by Tweddell whose run of 2, 4, 3, 3 squared the match with six holes remaining.

Little struggled to stay level now, and did well to achieve this. He had a fine recovery at the 13th with one of the eight mashie-niblicks he carried – or which his poor caddie did in these days of no limitations on clubs. Tweddell almost got ahead with a birdie here, but instead Little won holes 14 and 15 and, though Tweddell kept the match going with a win manufactured from a fine bunker shot at the 17th, the last hole was Little's, as he putted dead for three, and Tweddell's birdie putt was just off line.

Little was seldom under pressure in the American version of the title in Cleveland in the autumn and vanquished Walter Emery 4 & 3 in the final after beating par in every round.

**Lawson Little: tough going against Dr Tweddell.**

## SCORECARD

**British Open** (Muirfield, Scot)
A Perry 69 75 67 72 283

**US Open** (Oakmont, Pa)
S Parks 77 73 73 76 299

**Masters** (Augusta, Ga)
G Sarazen 68 71 73 70 282
(Play-off, Sarazen 144, C Wood 149)

**USPGA** (Twin Hills, Oklahoma)
J Revolta bt TD Armour 5 & 4

**Leading US money winner:**
J Revolta $9,543

**British Amateur** (Royal Lytham, Lancs)
L Little bt Dr W Tweddell 1h

**US Amateur** (Cleveland, Ohio)
L Little bt W Emery 4 & 2

**British Women's Amateur** (Newcastle, Co Down)
W Morgan bt P Barton 3 & 2

**US Women's Amateur** (Interlachen, Minn)
Mrs EH Vare bt P Berg 3 & 2

**Ryder Cup** (Ridgewood, NJ)
US bt GB & Ireland 9–3

# Britain rationed to two wins

WALTER HAGEN, leading the American Ryder Cup team for the fifth time, won his foursome with Gene Sarazen. Open champion Sam Parks and Craig Wood replaced Hagen and Ky Lafoon on the second day, at Ridgewood, New Jersey.

Parks got a half against the British Open champion but Wood lost to Percy Alliss, who gained Britain's only point apart from the Whitcombe brothers, Charles and Ernest, who won at the last hole against Olin Dutra and Lafoon.

The upshot was another beating for the British by eight to two, with two halved. Cotton was absent in Belgium.

# Pam Barton on top of the world

THIRD TIME LUCKY in the final at Southport and Ainsdale, Pam Barton became British Women's Amateur champion at 19 years of age. She did so with the American Curtis Cup team in the field – and she came out top again in September at Canoe Brook Country Club, New Jersey, in the US final. Only once before had this double been achieved – in 1909 by Dorothy Campbell from North Berwick.

Pamela Barton, born in 1917, was by nature a left-hander but, without evident damage to her psychological health, trained as a right-hander. Archie Compston helped in this and also coached Pam's sister, Mervyn. Pam Barton had an entirely different style of golf to Joyce Wethered. This was power as against the delicate balance of the Wethered swing. Barton's strong leg action and robust grip enabled her to develop a wide arc of swing. Firmly planted on her left foot, she came into and through the ball with great but controlled force. In the words of Enid Wilson, Barton could give the ball "an imperial bash."

At 19, Barton was not an inexperienced competitor, quite apart from her previous near misses in the British championship, the first of which in 1934 earned her a place in Britain's team against France – the youngest girl ever to gain that distinction. Later that year she won the French Open and played in the Curtis Cup team.

Having beaten Bridget Newell 5 & 3 in the British final, Barton sailed across the Atlantic, giving herself time to prepare meticulously for her attempt on the US title. The only significant

Pam Barton: completed double at 19.

American absentee from the field Barton faced was champion Glenna Collett Vare. Barton, who had added a canny short game to her powerful hitting, was never required to play the 18th hole all week except in the morning round of the final on October 3, when she opposed Mrs John D. Crews, and finished off the match 4 & 3.

All Barton's hard work before the Championship had paid off, for she played seven holes each day with 20 balls, then spent more time on putting, driving and iron play.

> ### TEE TALK
>
> **"...wonderful power of concentration and wonderful fighting qualities coming up the home stretch where it matters most."**
>
> ARCHIE COMPSTON,
> of his pupil, Pam Barton.

# Tony Manero record at Baltusrol

OUTPACING ALL the stars and breaking all previous US Open scoring records, Tony Manero surprised the massed ranks of America's best players with a 282 total at Baltusrol. He had won six events on the PGA tour, but no-one took much notice of him in the 40th Open despite his fine 69 on the second day. When he slipped back to 73 on the third morning, he looked like another also-ran, but he went out in 33 in the afternoon, moving within two strokes of "Light Horse" Harry Cooper, whose day, many thought, this was at last to be. Handily for Manero, of Italian stock, Gene Sarazen was his playing partner. Cooper's 284 total, an Open record for an hour or so, proved inadequate as Manero came home in 34 and a total of six under par, beating Cooper by two and the Open record by four – a mark first set by Chick Evans 20 years ago.

The entry grew again, 1,277 players attempting to qualify regionally. One who did, Ben Hogan, got to Baltusrol, but did not survive the second day.

Tony Manero: surprise record-breaker.

> ### SHORT PUTTS
>
> ● Joyce Wethered won her second Sunningdale foursomes with J.S.F.Morrison of the home club, and her eighth Worplesdon foursomes with T.W.E.Coke.

# Birdie, Birdie, Birdie Fischer beats McLean

TWO WEEKS after Pamela Barton lifted the women's title in New Jersey, Jock McLean looked a good thing for a British double in amateur play, for he was one up with three to play against John Fischer from Kentucky in the American Amateur final at Garden City, New York.

McLean was a difficult-to-dislodge matchplayer. He had a hat-trick of Scottish titles and two Irish ones to his credit, and he had just played in his second Walker Cup match.

Fischer laid a dead stymie against McLean on the 34th hole,

for a half, and another half in birdie fours followed. At the 36th Fischer holed a 12-footer for a two, and at the 37th with yet another birdie, a three finished off with a 20-foot putt, he at last got his hands on the Edward Moore trophy.

Two weeks earlier the Walker Cup at Pine Valley in New Jersey came perilously close to a whitewash by the United States, led by Francis Ouimet, this time a non-playing captain. Three halves was the meagre portion of Britain and Ireland, their only glimpse of respectability on the

second day coming from Harry Bentley's half with George Dunlap.

This was the United States' ninth consecutive win and the first time that Britain and Ireland had failed to win one match. The only match that seized the imagination was the fourth foursome on the first day, when Alec Hill and Cecil Ewing, seven down with 11 holes to play, levelled the match on the penultimate hole and would have gained a point against George Voigt and Harry Givan had not the Americans sunk a testing putt on the 36th.

# Padgham finally tops Open ladder

ALF PADGHAM, armed with an easy and much admired three-quarter swing, was British Open champion at Hoylake after being third in 1934 and second last year.

His score was four fewer than Bobby Jones's on the same course in 1930. His cultured swing was, early in his career, let down badly by poor putting, but no-one would have guessed it at Royal Liverpool, or at several other courses Padgham played in 1936, which was for him a richly rewarding year in prize money.

Leslie Edwards, journalist and Royal Liverpool member, said that Padgham's putt at the 17th for a three in the third round was probably the longest known in an Open at Hoylake. The flag was near the back of the green, Padgham's ball only just on the front edge. He therefore holed the undulating putt from all of 30 yards.

Jimmy Adams, a Scot with a ready smile, was second only a stroke adrift, with Henry Cotton another stroke behind, sharing third place with Marcel Dalle-magne, by far France's leading player of the 1930s, with two high placings in the British Open. A 140-pound amateur called Bobby Locke made his first Open appearance at Hoylake.

Only Gene Sarazen, faithful as ever to the British Open, showed the flag for America, and was only four strokes away at the death. A total contingent of thirteen Americans had entered, however.

Alf Padgham: his giant putt was the longest known at Hoylake.

## Smith's two Masters in three years

A WET AUGUSTA NATIONAL was the setting for the third Masters, Horton Smith winning again by a stroke from Harry Cooper. Sarazen took two strokes too many to keep his spectacularly won title.

Denny Shute landed the final major of the year, the second of his career, over the celebrated No. 2 Course at Pinehurst, North Carolina.

# Jessie Anderson forces first Curtis tie

ON MAY 6 Britain and Ireland made some progress towards the Curtis Cup to the extent of a tie on the windy King's Course at Gleneagles in Scotland. The first two matches had been lost. G and, luckily for the home team, Jessie Anderson was equal to the challenge.

The foursomes had been shared, one and a half points each. The top American pairing was an imaginative one, combining the best of two generations, Glenna Collett Vare and Patty Berg. They halved with Wanda Morgan and Mrs Marjorie Ross Garon. Jessie Anderson and Helen Holm got the home point, while Pamela Barton and the heroine of the last cup match, Mrs J.B.Walker, lost to Mrs John Crews and Mrs Leona Pressler Cheney.

The singles were just as much of a cliff-hanger. Charlotte Glutting (against Barton) and Mrs Crews scored last-hole wins, Holm and Mrs Ross Garon replying with victories far from home. It all came down to the last putt, which Anderson slotted in from seven yards to beat Mrs Cheney and square the whole match.

### TEE TALK

**"Expert golf playing is an art, not a trade, and unionization of players doesn't work"**

BOB HARLOW.

## Fred Corcoran takes over the PGA Tour

BOB HARLOW was dismissed again from PGA Tour management, the association's president, George Jacobus, citing "conflict of interest." He managed to get some of his ideas accepted, notably the minimum purse of $3,000, exemption of the best players from qualifying, and entry fees based on $1 for every $1,000 of prize money. At the end of the year Fred Corcoran, highly articulate as befits a New Englander of Irish extraction, was appointed by Jacobus to manage the Tour.

# Henry Cotton's finest hour

WHEN A Briton wins his national Open, he tends to assess the standard of his achievement for the most part in terms of how many top-class Americans were in the field.

By this measure, Cotton's 1937 Open victory was his best, since the US Ryder Cup team had stayed on to try for the title at Carnoustie. Byron Nelson was the nearest of the PGA tour elite to Cotton, who started with a 74 and took one stroke fewer each round, his final 71 leaving him two clear of Reg Whitcombe.

The Carnoustie course, among the longest of championship courses anywhere, would allow of no such liberties as Cotton inflicted on Royal St George's, where he won his first Open. Nelson (296), Ed Dudley, (297), and Horton Smith (299) were the only other "names" from across the Atlantic to beat 300.

Sam Snead, Ralph Guldahl, who had just gained his first American Open title with a record 281, Densmore Shute, Henry Picard and the slender South African amateur, Arthur D'Arcy Locke, were all 300 or more. Cotton's late hitting was the envy of the golf analysts: the wonder was that from his three-quarter swing he generated such power – how difficult it was, said one, to "wait for it" when one does not go back all the way. Yet few could consistently hit as far and as straight as Cotton through the green.

Henry Cotton's way at Carnoustie, the longest Open course: rounds of 74, 73, 72 and 71.

## Byron Nelson states his case in Masters

THE FOURTH Masters went to a player freely tipped to dominate US golf for years to come, the Texan Byron Nelson. He made a quick start towards fulfilling this prophecy, since his Masters win was only his third PGA tour success.

Moreover he showed the nerve of a champion and scored spectacularly just at the point the leader, Ralph Guldahl, was going astray – the 12th and 13th to be precise, where the damage was: Guldahl 5, 6, Nelson 2, 3 – a fatal (to Guldahl) swing of six strokes. He lost by two shots.

## Sweeny beats Sandwich expert

LIONEL MUNN, well acquainted with the vagaries of Royal St George's, Sandwich, was, in the final of the British Amateur championship, no match for the Californian, Robert Sweeny, who won the final 3 & 2.

Sweeny also won the Golf Illustrated Gold Vase at Ashridge, Henry Cotton's club, and did so with the record low score to date – 137 for the 36 holes.

Johnny Goodman from Nebraska had, unusually, to travel west to compete in the American Amateur, which was staged for the first time in the northwest, at Portland, Oregon.

Goodman, the last amateur to win the American Open, beat Ray Billows by two holes in the closely-contested final. The championship this year resumed the previous practice of 36-hole qualifying for the 64 places on offer.

# US tail wags in Ryder Cup victory

GREAT BRITAIN and Ireland flattered to deceive in the Ryder Cup match at Southport and Ainsdale, where they seemed to have a chance till the Americans swept the last four singles for a win by 8–4 – their third in four Cup matches. Significantly, this was the first time that the Americans had been victorious on British soil.

They won the foursomes 2½ to 1½. Henry Cotton, now attached to the Ashridge club in Hertfordshire, was in the home side for the first time in eight years, and his partnership with the Open winner of the previous year, Alf Padgham, looked promising, but melted before a 4 & 2 beating by Ed Dudley and Byron Nelson. Padgham got a worse mauling by Ralph Guldahl in the singles, 8 & 7. The British singles points were well gained, in particular by the stocky Welsh newcomer, Dai Rees. He overcame Nelson 3 & 1, and Cotton was five up with three to play against Tony Manero.

Then came durable Gene Sarazen, new star Sam Snead, in his first Ryder Cup match, and Dudley and Henry Picard to reel off the points to a final 8-4. Walter Hagen was captain, as for all the matches to date, but did not play.

# A year for record breakers

Nice trophy, Ralph: Sam Snead in his first US Open takes a good look at the trophy Ralph Guldahl (right) has won.

TONY MANERO'S US Open record lasted only a year, thanks to the assault on it by Ralph Guldahl at Oakland Hills, Michigan.

Despite Guldahl's win, it was the runner-up, Sam Snead (immediately nicknamed "Slammin' Sam"), who was attracting all the headlines, and was only two strokes behind the winner in his first Open.

Guldahl, a Texan from Dallas, was no more than a missed four foot putt away from a tie with the amateur, Johnny Goodman, in 1933. Guldahl was not a regular on the Tour, spending much of his time as a club professional in Chicago, yet his disappointment in the Masters did not prevent his finishing with great self possession in the Open a couple of months later.

He knew he needed only to par in to equal Snead's total. Instead he soon holed an eagle putt and broke Manero's record by a stroke. Guldahl and four other players beat par in this championship. Byron Nelson, 14 shots behind, won $50.

The numbers of would-be competitors continued to grow ever upwards:1,402 this year. Though the professionals were now pre-eminent, it was a sign of amateur strength in the United States that there were three amateurs in the top ten at Oakland Hills, Johnny Goodman, the winner in 1933, Frank Strafaci and Charles Kocsis. Goodman got the gold medal for the best amateur by a stroke from Strafaci.

Not only did Harry Cooper top the money list with more than $14,000, but he won eight Tour events. The disappointment was in major championships, and after one narrow miss he said plaintively to Bob Jones: "It seems that it was not intended for me to ever win a major".

## SHORT PUTTS

● Bridget Newell, finalist in the 1936 British Women's Amateur, who was a lawyer and the youngest magistrate in Britain, went to Turnberry to practice for the Home Internationals. On the eve of the matches she died suddenly, and the event was abandoned.

● Jessie Anderson, heroine of the Great Britain and Ireland tie in the Curtis Cup last year, gained her first major championship, taking the British Amateur at Turnberry, beating Doris Park comfortably 6 & 4.

● Patty Berg reached the American Women's Amateur final for the second time in three years, seldom being pressed until she reached the final, and lost 7 & 6 to Mrs Estelle Page, from Sedgefield, North Carolina, who topped the qualifiers at Memphis, Tennessee, with a 79.

● The groundswell rose against the stymie rule, which more and more golfers were beginning to see as contrary to the spirit of the game, in that it was the only way in which a player could be hampered by the actions of his opponents.

● The USPGA honoured Harry Vardon, whose death took place at Totteridge, Hertfordshire, on March 20, by naming their trophy for the player with the highest number of positional points after the six-times British Open champion. Cooper, with 500 points, was the first recipient.

● Bernard Darwin was made a Companion of the British Empire for service to literature. His writings were predominantly on golf, but he also wrote on other sports.

## SCORECARD

**British Open** (Carnoustie, Scot)
H Cotton 74 73 72 71 290

**US Open** (Oakland Hills, Mich)
R Guldahl 71 69 72 69 281

**Masters** (Augusta National, Ga)
B Nelson 66 72 75 70 283

**USPGA** (Pittsburgh CC, Pa)
D Shute bt H McSpadden 37th

**Leading US money winner**
H Cooper $14,138.69

**British Amateur** (Royal St George's, Kent)
R Sweeney Jnr bt LO Munn 3 & 2

**US Amateur** (Alderwood, Oregon)
J Goodman bt R Billows 2h

**British Women's Amateur** (Turnberry, Scot)
J Anderson bt D Park 6 & 4

**US Women's Amateur** (Memphis CC, Tenn)
Mrs Julius A Page Jnr bt P Berg 7 & 6

**Ryder Cup** (Southport & Ainsdale, Lancs)
US bt GB & Ireland 8–4

**Densmore Shute: second USPGA title.**

# 'Slammin' Sam' opens the door for Corcoran

FRED CORCORAN'S first year in charge of the PGA was greatly helped on the publicity front by the fact that Sam Snead made his entrance into big-time golf at exactly the same moment. His folksy Virginian accent, with down-home wisecracks (some no doubt supplied by Corcoran, no mean yarn-spinner himself), allied to a swing that was powerful, smooth, and rhythmic to a degree that turned millions green with envy – all these features made Snead good copy on and off the course.

On top of which he won his third PGA tour event, at Oakland, with four rounds under 70, then won the first Bing Crosby Pro-Am, with a 68 in a competition cut by rain.

## TEE TALK

### "In golf, when we hit a foul ball, we got to go out and play it."

SAM SNEAD,
to baseball star Ted Williams.

# The Walker Cup doesn't go west

"THE BRITISH," says the USGA's record book, "were most serious about the Match." This is an understatement worthy to have emerged from beneath the stiffest British upper lip.

The Walker Cup match of 1938 was played at St Andrews on June 3 & 4 and Great Britain and Ireland won it 7-4, with one match halved, after losing every one of the first nine Cup matches, four of them by large margins and the last without winning a single point.

Stern measures were taken by the four home countries. They threw out the old selection committee en bloc.

The outstanding English amateur, Cyril Tolley, chaired the new one, Open champion Henry Cotton was engaged to supervise preparations and trials were held by the captain, John Beck.

John Bruen, 19, from Belfast, Northern Ireland, is however credited by some observers with being the spark that lit the team spirit of the British side.

Bruen was a long hitter with a swing all his own, containing a loop that did not prevent his giving the ball a tremendous wallop. In the lead up to the match, Bruen put together a string of good scores on the Old Course (in eight rounds his best was 66 and worst 69) and generally cheered everyone up. There is little doubt also that Cotton, a hard taskmaster on the practice ground, infected his amateur charges with a little of his own will to win.

The visitors started with the psychological advantage of Charles Yates, who was to play top single for them, having just beaten Cecil Ewing, another Irishman in the home team, in the final of the British Amateur championship.

The top foursome on the first day did not provide John Beck with a point, but Harry Bentley and Bruen demonstrated clearly that they were disinclined to lose. They were three holes down at lunch, to John Fischer and Charles Kocsis, and hit back with a score of approximately 68 to square the match.

Two foursomes were won, Gordon Peters and Hector Thomson, British champion in 1936, striking a crucial blow with 4 & 3 victory against Johnny Goodman, America's outstanding amateur since Bobby Jones's retirement, and Marvin Ward, better known as Bud. Leonard Crawley and J.J.Frank Pennink beat Reynolds Smith and Fred Haas junior, 3 & 1, giving Britain and Ireland a lead they never lost.

Bruen lost his single at the 17th to Yates, but Thomson enjoyed a second win against Goodman by 6 & 4.

Though Pennink and Crawley now failed in singles, Ewing, a powerful figure who played with weighty woods and irons, Peters and the taciturn Scot, Alex Kyle, captured the Cup with wins over Ray Billows, Smith and Haas respectively. Ward's 12 & 11 trouncing of Pennink gave notice of a considerable talent.

## SCORECARD

**British Open** (Royal St George's, Kent)
RA Whitcombe 71 71 75 78 295

**US Open** (Cherry Hills, Denver, Col)
R Guldahl 74 70 71 69 284

**Masters** (Augusta National, Ga)
H Picard 71 72 72 70 285

**USPGA** (Shawnee CC, Pa)
P Runyan bt S Snead 8 & 7

**Leading US money winner:**
S Snead $19,534.49

**British Amateur** (Troon, Scot)
CR Yates bt C Ewing 3 & 2

**US Amateur** (Oakmont, Pa)
WP Turnesa bt BP Abbott 8 & 7

**British Women's Amateur** (Burnham & Berrow, Somerset)
Mrs H Holm bt E Corlett 4 & 3

**US Women's Amateur** (Westmoreland CC, Ill)
P Berg bt Mrs Estelle Page 6 & 5

**Walker Cup** (St Andrews, Scot)
GB & Ireland bt US 7½–4½

**Curtis Cup** (Essex CC, Mass)
US bt GB & Ireland 5½–3½

James Bruen: life and soul of Walker Cup team.

# Reg Whitcombe leads hollow British 1, 2, 3

REG WHITCOMBE and Jimmy Adams showed stamina, skill and dedication to their profession well beyond the call of duty as they fought out the final holes of the British Open at Sandwich in a gale which, early on the final day, made off with everything not nailed down, and in particular the exhibition tent.

Adams, a Scottish professional from Royal Liverpool, finished runner-up for the second time in three years; he had to endure the nickname of "James the Second". Whitcombe won, by two shots, an honour that had eluded his brothers Charles and Ernest, and led a British 1, 2, 3. Henry Cotton was third, though his 74 in the storm-tossed final round was a remarkable feat. The absence of American challengers rather took the gilt off Whitcombe's gingerbread. Their technique underwent the most rigorous test that can be imagined. They were playing partners all the way over the last 36 holes. Whitcombe had a long backswing, yet was able to control it even in these conditions. Adams led by a stroke at halfway from Whitcombe. Cotton was five strokes further behind.

With one round to go, Adams had fallen back to two behind Whitcombe, but there was a big turnabout at the short 16th hole, normally tackled with a seven iron. Against this fiercest of Channel gales, Adams took a one iron, and got his three, Whitcombe his driver, and double-bogeyed.

The players were now level, but Adams's approach to the 17th was blown into a bunker and he took a double-bogey six, while Whitcombe a four, opening a gap Adams could not close. Only these two and Cotton broke 300.

Reg Whitcombe: trouser-flapping Open win.

# Ralph Guldahl again

RALPH GULDAHL performed the rare feat at Cherry Hills in Colorado of winning the US Open two years in succession. Willie Anderson, Johnny McDermott and Bobby Jones were the only players to have brought it off previously.

Though increasing signs of tension in Europe were giving the shipping and armaments industries a nudge, the Depression had been a lowering influence on golf as in many other spheres of American life, and the prize for winning the Open remained $1,000 for the tenth year, though the overall purse rose from $5,000 to $6,000.

Guldahl, now attached to the Braidburn club in New Jersey, compiled a par total of 284, which left him six clear of Dick Metz, from Kansas.

Lawson Little, now a professional, and Sam Snead were alongside each other far down the field 25 shots behind Guldahl, who in April had come within two shots of winning the Masters, but Henry Picard finished off with a decisive 70.

The Open record for the highest number of strokes taken at a single hole was broken by Ray Ainsley when, during his second round, he had a 19 on the 16th (par four). His ball had fallen into a stream, and he expended a sinful number of strokes extricating it, upon which a little girl said (or so the story goes): "Mummy, it must be dead now because the man has quit hitting it."

## TEE TALK

**"The PGA? Well, that just goes to show you that no matter how closely you try to keep in touch with what's happening in Washington, the moment you turn your back the government has created another agency."**

LORD HALIFAX.

# US rally to keep Curtis Cup

AS BEFORE WHEN played in America, the Curtis Cup was contested over two days, the United States winning 5-3, with one match halved, thanks to a withering counterattack in singles after losing the foursomes, in which Great Britain and Ireland dropped only half a point.

Clarrie Tiernan had a fine debut for the visitors at the Essex Country Club in Massachusetts for the visitors, winning the top foursome with Helen Holm against Estelle Page and Mrs John Crews (née Orcutt) by two holes. Jessie Anderson continued her inspiring Cup form in company with Elsie Corlett by beating Glenna Collett Vare and Patty Berg at the final hole.

The next day Frances Stebbins' American side played up a storm, winning five of the six singles, Mrs Julius Page, Berg, Marion Miley and Mrs Vare taking the top four matches. Tiernan revived British hopes by winning her second point against Mrs Crews at the 17th.

All depended on the bottom single, won by Charlotte Glutting who swept the last three holes against another British newcomer, Nan Baird.

The visitors moved on to Illinois for the US Amateur later in September, at the Westmoreland Club, situated near Chicago.

Patty Berg, runner-up in her first two finals, met Mrs Page for the second year and turned the tables to the tune of 6 & 5. Clarrie Tiernan reached the third round, further than any of the other six members of the British Curtis Cup team who qualified.

# Byron Nelson triumphs in double play off

**Byron Nelson: held firm all the way to the winning post.**

BYRON NELSON won a major championship on June 12 – the American Open on the Spring Mill course in Philadelphia – which will ever be more readily remembered because Sam Snead lost it. The climax was a throwback to the days of Bobby Jones when occasionally the favourite just couldn't lose – but did, and won the headlines instead of silverware.

This state of affairs is scarcely congruent with the respect due to Nelson, who got the trophy because he did not succomb to the winning post blues as did Snead and Densmore Shute, and because he shook off Shute in the first play off and Craig Wood in the second with the consistent excellence of his play.

The final nine holes of regulation play were strewn with regrets. Nelson was 12th, five strokes in arrears, after 54 holes, at which point Johnny Bulla was in the lead, one ahead of Snead, Wood and Shute. Nelson now played his best round to date in the championship, 68, on a not particularly long course of 6,800 yards, so his total of 284 was not exceptional. For one well-placed rival after another, it proved impossible to beat

Sam Snead suffered most. He needed two pars for 282, but missed a putt on the 17th for his par. A five at the long last hole would still earn the title, but with Shute and Wood playing behind him, Snead felt he needed a birdie. He drove into the rough then, straining to reach the green, he played into a bunker, took two to emerge and eventually three-putted for a triple-bogey eight.

Wood met the challenge most creditably, since his birdie four at the last put him into the play-off. So did Shute's par at the last, though, as it transpired, he had fatally dropped a shot at the 17th.

Shute was well beaten by his two rivals in the first play-off, at the climax of which Wood was forced into another head-to-head by Nelson's long putt for a birdie at the 18th. In the afternoon Nelson prevailed by three shots, two of them saved at a psychologically damaging moment early in the round, which may have persuaded Wood, if only for a moment, that this was not to be his day. At the fourth, a par four, Nelson holed a one iron for an eagle.

The scene was set for Nelson versus Snead to become a premier attraction. Both were 26, Nelson having been born a little over 100 days before Snead in 1912.

Nelson had won nine Tour events (including the Masters) starting with his first success in the New Jersey Open in 1935.

# Early axe for Ryder and Curtis Cups

THE UNCERTAIN STATE of affairs in Europe caused the cancellation in February of the Ryder Cup match due to be played in America in the summer. The 1940 Curtis Cup was cancelled in the autumn.

Even before Britain entered the war with Germany in September the British PGA lost their secretary, Commander Charles Roe, recalled by the Admiralty to Royal Navy service. He was stationed at the Chatham base in Kent and was able to keep an eye on PGA affairs.

He had changed the thrust of the Association's policies since his appointment in 1934. Previously, like the USPGA, the British organization had concentrated on the affairs of the club professional, equipment supply and similar bread and butter issues, but Roe saw the advantages to be gained by all parties if

the tournament programme could be enriched and enlarged.

It was a slow business and, as Jimmy Adams said of the 1930s, club work was the theme, and the "majors" for British professionals, apart from the Open, were the Match Play, another casualty in 1939, and the Dunlop tournament. Winter golf, in cold contrast to the American experience, hardly existed.

British professionals in Europe were hurrying home, some like Wally Marks, professional at Henry Cotton's old club, Waterloo in Belgium, arriving back with little more than the clothes they stood up in. Competitive golf and the Association's journal were abandoned.

Another casualty was the four home-countries tournament, begun the previous year as a replacement for the England-Scotland matches which started

in 1903 and were played before the Open annually.

While the new four-way tournament was in progress trenches were being dug in London parks – this a year before hostilities began.

As autumn gave way to winter PGA members were taking up national service of one sort or another – eventually nearly half the membership of 2,000 or so.

## TEE TALK

**"Sam [Snead] was born with a natural ability to keep his bar bills as low as his golfscores."**

JIMMY DEMARET.

## SCORECARD

**British Open** (St Andrews, Scot)
R Burton 70 72 77 71 290

**US Open** (Spring Mill, Philadelphia CC)
B Nelson 72 73 71 68 284
(First play-off: Nelson 68, C Wood 68, D Shute 76; Second play-off: Nelson 70, Wood 73)

**Masters** (Augusta National, Ga)
R Guldahl 72 68 70 69 279

**USPGA** (Pomonok, NY)
H Picard bt B Nelson 37th

**Leading US money winner**
H Picard $10,303

**British Amateur** (Royal Liverpool)
AT Kyle bt AA Duncan 2 & 1

**US Amateur** (N Shore CC, Ill)
M Ward bt R Billows 7 & 5

**British Women's Amateur** (Portrush, Co Down)
P Barton bt Mrs T Marks 2 & 1

**US Women's Amateur** (Wee Burn Noroton, Conn)
B Jameson bt D Kirby 3 & 2

# Richard Burton holds off Johnny Bulla

**Dick Burton: Took the brave line at Old Tom Morris's hole to clinch an Open championship triumph.**

JOHNNY BULLA, one stroke away from joining Ralph Guldahl, Craig Wood and Denny Shute in the triple US Open play off a month ago, had to bite on the bullet again at St Andrews, beaten out of the British Open by a stroke by Richard Burton, who was born near the soccer ground of perennial silverware winners, Blackburn Rovers in Lancashire.

Burton's capture of some sideboard decorations of his own was clinched when he took the brave line at Old Tom Morris's hole on the Old Course, sinking the putt for a final birdie and a two stroke victory over Bulla. The pair started level on 219 after 54 holes.

The value of the two big Opens has for long not resided most rewardingly in the prize money (Burton got £100) but in the offers that follow in the way of exhibitions, equipment endorsement and so on, but Burton's door to such riches was quickly slammed by the war.

## 'Chocolate Soldier' wins PGA campaign

HENRY PICARD was dubbed the "Chocolate Soldier" by an enterprising newsman when he was made professional at Hershey (the link is the eponymous chocolate bar). He added the PGA championship to his Masters title of the previous year, beating Byron Nelson, now nearing his peak, at Pomonok's 37th. The year began and finished well for Picard, a New Englander from Plymouth, whose rich vein of form gained him five other first places. Unsurprisingly, his much-admired swing smoothed his way to becoming leading money winner with $10,303. Not the least of Picard's claims to fame is that he alone beat Walter Hagen in a play-off.

## Guldahl, slow master of the fast finish

RALPH GULDAHL, the tall, dark-haired Texan, was self-taught and had a back swing so long that it almost got in front again. He was not the quickest player that ever was born, but he put in a few fast finishes at critical junctures in his career, none more so than in the sixth Masters at Augusta. Sam Snead, by now a prime candidate for understudy to Craig Wood as the nearly man of the 1930s, was the victim of Guldahl's back nine flourish of 33 strokes, for a record total of 279, one ahead of Snead.

This gave Guldahl a phenomenal run, for his haul of honours includes three Western Opens (little behind the Open, the Masters and the PGA Championship in professional estimation), back-to-back Opens, rare indeed, and now a sparkling new mark in the Masters.

**Ralph Guldahl: back nine of 33 was decisive.**

**"But I've never been to New York in my life."**

SAM SNEAD,
on being shown a picture of himself in a New York newspaper

**"The valleys [in the mountains of Virginia] are so narrow the dogs have to wag their tails up and down."**

SNEAD

● Charles "Chick" Evans formally retired from championship play. His gift to golf was a caddie scholarship scheme.

● Sandy Herd, the British Open champion of 1902, played his last Open at the age of 71. His participation in the event spanned 54 years.

● A.D.Locke used a record low 265 strokes in February to become Transvaal Open champion, over the Glendown course, Johannesburg, which at 7,071 yards was only 129 shorter than Carnoustie. Locke finished 26 shots in front of the runner- (or limper-)up. Soon he was to be relinquishing his beloved hickory shafted putter for the joystick of a Liberator bomber.

● Pam Barton regained her British Amateur title at Portrush and, on the outbreak of war, joined a group of players who staged exhibitions in aid of the Red Cross. Before long, Barton was commissioned as an officer in the Women's Auxiliary Air Force.

● Betty Jameson, aged 20, one of the most beautiful women ever to excel in championship golf, won the American Amateur at Wee Burn, Connecticut, against Dorothy Kirby.

# While bombs are falling, players may take cover . . .

EVEN BEFORE the eerie "phoney war" of late 1939 and early 1940 ended abruptly with the Nazi invasion of Scandinavia, the Low Countries and France, golfers in Britain were playing by new and ominous rules, such as being directed to collect bomb and shell splinters to prevent damage to the mowing machines. At Wirral Ladies' club, seven minutes by rail from Liverpool, a prime target for German bombers, it became quite usual for a player to collect a pocketful of shrapnel during a round.

In competition "during gunfire or while bombs are falling, players may take cover without penalty for ceasing play", was another comforting thought. On the other hand, a player whose stroke was affected by explosion

of bomb or shell, or machine-gun fire, was permitted to play another ball from the same place. This was far from being a joke, for German planes were known to attack golfers at play.

Ernie Sewell, an Artisan member at Woking, thought his number was up when two Spitfire fighter planes collided over the course. The pilots, both Polish, baled out, and one of the planes seemed to Sewell to be coming straight at him. It crashed in flames and a hail of exploding ammunition less than 100 yards away.

Chelmsford club, to the east of London, mourned the loss of four members, officers spread throughout the three armed services. Seven members had died in the 1914-18 war. Wirral Ladies'

Doris Chambers, the former British champion, completed a useful double by driving an ambulance for the First Aid Nursing Yeomanry. She had driven one in France during the First World War. Wirral members said that Hitler would not dare to bomb their stern secretary, Maud Henry. But he did, and up went the club house, with 300 sets of clubs, records and trophies in safe keeping for Bromborough, whose clubhouse had been requisitioned as accommodation for nurses.

Financially, as in 1914, the times were disastrous for a lot of clubs, and course maintenance was bound to suffer. Many fairways were not to see a mower for years. Grazing sheep and cattle, as in the First World War, kept

the grass down. Steel obstructions were erected or trenches dug across fairways to hinder landings by hostile aircraft. Turnberry on the Ayrshire coast became an airfield.

In America the majors continued until Pearl Harbor at the end of 1941 and, in two instances, beyond.

What was apparent before 1942 dawned and American war efforts intensified, was the emergence of a thrilling talent to challenge Byron Nelson, Sam Snead and the rest – Benjamin William Hogan. Nelson, Snead and Hogan were all very much of an age, but Hogan had taken longer to impress his powers on the tour. Now he was leading money-winner for both 1940 and 1941, with a total of $29,013.

---

# Six disqualified in Little's Open

LAWSON LITTLE, who had twice performed the "Little Slam" of both major Amateur titles in the same year, reached the top of the professional tree in 1940 at the Canterbury club, near Cleveland, Ohio. He beat Gene Sarazen, now 38, in a play-off. Sarazen would have been the oldest winner of the Open had he prevailed.

A third player, Ed Oliver, also totalled 287, but he and five others were disqualified for starting the fourth round before their appointed time. The other players who broke the USGA speed limit and shared Oliver's fate were E.J.Harrison, Leland Gibson, Johnny Bulla, Ky Laffoon and Claude Harmon. Walter Hagen quit after the third-round.

### TEE TALK

**"Heck, if it wasn't for golf, Sarazen would be back on the banana boat between Naples and Sicily."**

JIMMY DEMARET.

Gene Sarazen: almost made it as oldest Champion.

# Chapman's local knowledge counts

DICK CHAPMAN made mincemeat of "Duff" McCullough in the final of the Amateur at his own club, Winged Foot, New York, winning 11 & 9. The finalists had returned the best qualifying medal score.

Pretty Betty Jameson of San Antonio, Texas, retained her Women's Amateur title, winning this time on the cliff tops of Pebble Beach against Jane Cothran from Greenville, South Carolina. Patty Berg, the talkative and combative youngster from Interlachen, who had been voted woman athlete of the year in 1938, after her Amateur title and Curtis Cup selection, now turned professional. While she raised much money for charity there were few professional events for women. The day before Pearl Harbor a road crash damaged her left knee.

Berg had won three of the four 1941 professional tournaments. First prize for her victory in the Western Open, against Mrs Burt Weil, of Cincinnati, was a $100 war bond.

# Craig Wood double after his years of heartache

ST ANDREW, or whoever controls golfers' fortunes, had been particularly unkind to Craig Wood till, in 1941, everything fell into place – at least, to the extent of winning two majors in the same year.

First Wood finished three ahead of Byron Nelson in the Masters at Augusta, then, two months later, three clear of Denny Shute in the Open at the Colonial Club, Fort Worth, in Texas.

The Masters was a highly satisfying win for Wood, not only because he had been waiting so long for his first major but because, having led for three rounds and then having got caught by Nelson with nine holes to go, he finished strongly (34 to Nelson's 37) to take the trophy in style.

Wood's Open triumph was fraught with pain and anxiety, not to mention stormy weather. Wood was not fit and was obliged to wear a back brace. Indeed, he almost gave up during the first round when he started to spill shots.

Tommy Armour urged him onwards, and Wood followed his scratchy first-round 73 with 71, 70, 70, to beat Shute into second place. Johnny Bulla was third, another two shots back, in company with leading money-winner Ben Hogan.

Craig Wood: braced for success despite back trouble.

**Happy landings: Laddie Lucas at Prince's.**

# Demaret wins Masters

BURSTS OF record low scoring enlived the Masters, the eventual winner, Jimmy Demaret, coming home in 30 on opening day. Lloyd Mangrum's 64 gave him the lead, though.

A poor second round was costly for Mangrum, and Demaret gained his first Masters by four strokes, a record at Augusta, with Byron Nelson third. Demaret had been, briefly, a nightclub singer. Demaret continued to entertain when he bagan to win significantly at golf. sometimes in the company of Bing Crosby. His off-course trademark was his high-heeled Texas boots. In the PGA at Hershey Nelson enjoyed a one-hole win over chief rival Sam Snead to take the trophy.

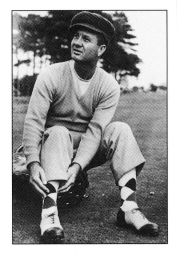
**Jimmy Demaret: home in 30.**

# Vic Ghezzi outlasts Byron Nelson

THE 1941 US PGA championship final was Byron Nelson's third in a row, but he won only one. This time he was caught on the finishing post by big Vic Ghezzi, who was three down with nine holes to play. He finally accounted for Nelson at the 38th.

Ghezzi was not a big hitter, though he stood half a head taller than Nelson, himself no midget. Ghezzi's stock in trade was accuracy and it was this factor that enabled him to get the better of Nelson.

Sam Snead won his battle of supremacy on the Tour, with six wins to Ben Hogan's five.

# Double champion Pam Barton killed in air crash

MELVYN SUTHERLAND-PILCH was living in Calcutta in November 1943 when she had a dream that her sister, Pamela Barton, Britain's outstanding young golfer of the 1930s, was dead. Not long afterwards, a radio news confirmed that Pam Barton had been killed in an air crash. She was a serving officer in the Women's Auxiliary Air Force, and had accepted a lift in a light RAF aircraft to Manston airfield in Kent, near to where a party was being held.

Afterwards her pilot evidently forgot to switch on the fuel supply. The aircraft crashed on take-off and burst into flames. The pilot was not strapped in, and he was thrown clear and survived. His passenger did not, for she was strapped in. Not long afterwards he, too, was killed.

Pamela Barton was 26. She was buried at Biggin Hill Cem-

**Pam Barton: incalculable loss.**

etery close by the airfield over which so many desperate engagements were fought in the Battle

of Britain. At the time of her death she was still British Amateur champion, having won the title in 1939 before the war wiped out competition. She had shown at home and away that her strong game and tough competitive spirit were good enough to beat the best. Beat the best she did, starting with the French championship when she was 17.

She was 19 when, in 1936, she became only the second golfer to win the British and American Amateur championships in the same year. Dorothy Campbell, the Scot from North Berwick, had achieved the feat in 1909. No American had managed it.

Barton's loss to the British game was incalculable. She would have been 28 at the end of the war, and was surely destined to achieve more honours. Enid Wilson, British champion three

times at the beginning of the 1930s, fondly remembers her red hair and outgoing personality. Wilson, also a wartime WAAF officer, says: "The last time I saw Pam was when we played in a "Daily Mail" charity match at Purley in aid of a service fund. The Germans bombed the course while we were playing."

Royal Lytham was well frequented by Americans, whose base at Warton airfield nearby was manned by bomb sight and automatic pilot technicians. One of them, Tom Madden, had the thrill of playing with Bobby Jones in a practice round before a Red Cross match. Jones had not played at Lytham since his Open win in 1926. Next day Madden caddied for Jones and met his future wife at the course, where she was trying to get out of a bunker. Wars can have their consolations.

# Pearl Harbor brings 'Major' cutbacks

BETWEEN THE JAPANESE attack on Pearl Harbor and the end of the war only four major events were played. Byron Nelson won the only stroke play event of the four, the 1942 Masters, and he was in the final of two of the other three, all in the PGA at match play.

He won the first of the four, his second Masters title, at the end of a five-round duel with Ben Hogan, for they tied with 72-hole totals of 280, one stroke more than Ralph Guldahl's 1939 record, and Nelson won the play-off by a stroke with a 69.

Nelson didn't figure in the 1942 PGA, before which Sam Snead, no doubt in his charming southern drawl, sweet-talked his recruiting officer into delaying his naval call-up for a day or so to allow him to try for the title at Seaview Country Club in New Jersey. He beat Jim Turnesa in the final. Both Harold "Jug" McSpaden ("Jug" because of his prominent jaw) and Nelson were not called to the colours because they were unfit, McSpaden through asthma. Nelson was a haemophiliac. Otherwise all the leading professionals were drafted, though Craig Wood was

**Byron Nelson: 11 in a row.**

rejected because he had damaged his back in a road crash; hence his corset in the 1941 Open. Most were in the army, including Hogan and Horton Smith, and Lloyd Mangrum was wounded in the Battle of the Bulge.

For the most part professional sportsmen of all kinds were engaged in what they knew best –

**Sam Snead: into Navy after winning the Seaview title.**

keeping fit themselves and organizing the fitness of others. The golfers also got to play a good deal, especially in charity events. One of the biggest was the Hale America National Open. The USGA had a hand in this, in June 1942 at Ridgemoor, Chicago. Hogan won it, and counted it as an Open, but no-one else did. The PGA tour almost, but not quite,

ground to a halt. Records were not kept, though Nelson won $37,967.69 in war bonds in 1944.

He had much to do with the revival of the tour as peace drew closer. In 1944, when the tour increased to eight events, he lost to Bob Hamilton in the PGA final. Nelson came again in the following year to clinch the PGA, in the middle of an astounding run.

# Nelson dominant partner of Gold Dust Twins

WHAT BYRON NELSON didn't win "Jug" McSpaden did, was the general rule in 1945, when the pair became known as the Gold Dust Twins and Nelson was victorious in 19 professional tournaments, including 11 in a row. Nelson, aged 33, finished with $63,335.66 in war bonds; his opponents finished out of breath.

McSpaden was often second to Nelson, won lots of war bonds but found, as many bond-holders did after the war, that they did not keep their value as well as, say, lots of golf balls. A good prewar ball was fetching $4 in 1945 because of war production restrictions.

Leaving aside arguments about much of the best opposition being absent most of the year, the sheer quality of Nelson's golf and the number of under-par rounds he played cannot be argued away. Anyway, Sam Snead was almost always present, having been discharged with back problems which were not damaging to his swing. He won five times in 1945. Moreover, Ben Hogan was back from the army for the autumn events.

Nelson rivalled Harry Vardon and Henry Cotton among the few genuine, consistent, deliberate straight hitters in the game's history, averaging 68.33 for 120 rounds. He had one run of 19 rounds under 70 and another of winning money in 113 consecutive events. The closer he got to the winning post, the better he played, the average for his last rounds being a fraction over 67.

On the trophy trail: more silver for 'Iron Byron' Nelson.

## Death of Dame Ethel

DAME ETHEL SMYTH, writer, composer, one time stone-throwing suffragette, later pourer of oil on troubled waters at Woking Golf Club, died aged 86 in 1944.

Apart from Dame Ethel's musical work, she also published the autobiographical "Female Pipings for Eden".

Victoria Sackville-West wrote: "Blinkered egotism could scarcely have driven at greater gallop along so determined a road. But although often a nuisance, Ethel was never a bore."

Henry Picard: Masters and PGA winner before the war, forced by ill-health to curtail his tournament appearances in the early 1940s.

## TEE TALK

**"I call my sand wedge my half-Nelson, because I can always strangle the opposition with it."**

BYRON NELSON.

## SHORT PUTTS

● In 1944 Royal Lytham erected plaque in bunker at 17th to commemorate Bobby Jones's decisive shot of the 1926 Open.

● Mrs J.V.Hurd (née Dorothy Campbell), first to win the British and American titles in the same year (1909), was killed aged 63 in 1945 by a railway engine while changing trains at Yemassee, South Carolina.

● British golf moved quickly into postwar gear, and in May 1945 the PGA, with the aid of newspaper sponsorships, speedily arranged five events, including one at St Andrews in the autumn. Charlie Ward won from a field including six Americans, among them Lloyd Mangrum, playing in uniform.

● After five years of trying, in 1943 Babe Zaharias was reinstated as an amateur.

● The United States named their Ryder Cup squad in 1942 in case the war should end before the next Ryder date of 1943. Walter Hagen was named as non-playing captain and the team was to include Ben Hogan, Sam Snead and Byron Nelson, as well as Harold McSpaden.— a lineup to make the British PGA envious.

# A 'National' at last for Sam Snead but it's no dollar bonanza

SAM SNEAD captured his first National Open title, the British Open, when golf returned to as near normal as the after-effects of the war – inflation, equipment shortages and other hindrances – would allow. The prize money now reached four figures exactly, and second prize went to Johnny Bulla, another American, who must have thought that this was where he came in, for he was second in 1939 at St Andrews, which was, appropriately, where the Open resumed. Bobby Locke was joint second with Bulla, four strokes behind Snead.

Henry Cotton, in search of his third Open, clearly had a great deal left in his locker, coming

**Snead: no rich pickings.**

joint third with Norman von Nida from Australia, Dai Rees, a stocky, combative Welsh golfer, and Charlie Ward, a Midlander by birth and by club. Ward did not hit very far, but he was mustard near the green, and achieved scores which were hard to believe in short-course championships, like that at the Palace in Torquay.

Cotton began well, though his less than confident attitude when he got down over a putt was reminiscent of his pre-war Opens. His 70 was equalled by von Nida, the leading qualifier and only Locke, with 69, scored better. Cotton was ahead after 36 holes but Snead handled the windy third day well,

m his rivals scoring in the high 70s. Success for Snead came at only his second attempt. Snead found travelling uncomfortable in postwar Britain, as who didn't.

He was renowned for being careful with a buck, but it is easy to believe his complaint that the expenses of his trip exceeded his prize money, which was about $600. But the title's worth in terms of endorsements and attraction for sponsors is incalculable. Snead's success had another and somewhat bizarre outcome. He went on a South African exhibition tour with Locke and, of 16 matches, lost 12.

This helped Locke decide to try his luck on the US PGA tour.

## Mangrum holds off Nelson and Ghezzi

GOLF HAD CERTAINLY not lost its prewar magnetism for crowds, as was proved when the greatest-ever attendance, at Canterbury, Ohio, watched Lloyd Mangrum, winner of a Purple Heart in the war, beat Byron Nelson and Vic Ghezzi in a second play-off, 72 to 73 apiece, after all three had scored 72 in the first play-off.

Nelson suffered from the pressure of the crowds, if only because in the thick of one gallery his caddie accidentally kicked his ball. It was to be his last season. Like Bobby Jones, Nelson found the mental stress of winning, even with his marvellous talent, ever harder to bear.

Mangrum was impervious to adversity in the second play-off, in which with six holes to play, he was four behind Ghezzi and three behind Nelson. Birdies at three of the six, in a storm, clinched the title and $1,500 from a prize fund of $8,000.

### SHORT PUTTS

● December: retirement of Byron Nelson, 34. who had begun the year with a January victory and had won five other tournaments.

● A rule was introduced limiting players to 14 clubs. Many leading players had routinely carried more than 30.

**Tour stars: Byron Nelson and (right) Henry Picard.**

## Simplicity is the key

BRITISH WOMEN'S GOLF, tragically without the inspirational figure of Pam Barton, was not even close to setting up a professional circuit, what women pros there were being limited to club duties and shopkeeping. The Amateur championship at Hunstanton on the Norfolk coast was a triumph for Jean Hetherington (née McClure), possessed of a swing that for simplicity must have made many of her rivals green with envy. There was nothing about it that could go wrong, or so it seemed ... perhaps because she regularly achieved what golfers are instructed to achieve, but seldom do, which is to swing the club, not try to hit the ball. All the same, she did not get the better of Philomena Garvey, until the last green.

## Bruen clicks

ROYAL BIRKDALE on the Lancashire coast staged its first important event, the British Amateur. James Bruen from Cork in Ireland won it, perhaps five years after he might have done so but for the war, for he was top amateur in the 1939 British Open. He beat the American winner of the 1937 championship, Robert Sweeney, 4 & 3 in the title match.

# Spokane boost for US women pros

THE WOMEN'S PRO TOUR had been a flimsy affair when the war started in 1941, with prize money of only a few hundred dollars. It virtually vanished from sight till, in 1946, Patty Berg and Betty Jameson, both one-time Amateur champions, met in the match play final of the new Women's Open.

This was sponsored by Spokane Athletic Round Table to the surprising extent of $19,700, of which $5,600 (in bonds) fell to Berg, who headed the qualifiers and won the final 5 & 4. The men's Open prize fund totalled only $8,000.

Berg had recovered from her knee injury of 1941, though this had been no easy task, since she had a triple fracture, the injury was not set correctly and the knee had to be rebroken. She then served as a lieutenant in the Marine Corps Reserve until the

**Patty Berg: in the money.**

end of the war. She won four tournaments during the year, her determination mighty, though her stature, at 61 inches, was not impressive.

The Women's Professional Golfers' Association had been set up in 1944, and a number of top-class amateurs joined, but not Babe Zaharias, reinstated as an amateur during the war after years of waiting, and who set off on a winning spree to rival that of Byron Nelson's in the previous year.

Her Olympic fame was still clinging to her, and she added to her laurels and potential at the box office by victory in the Women's Amateur at Southern Hills, Tulsa, where her winning margins were 4 & 3, 4 & 3, 5 & 4, 3 & 2, and, against Mrs Clara Callender Sherman in the final, 11 & 9. She was never headed by

any of her opponents all week. By some counts, her haul had included 13 straight tournament victories.

Other talented girls began to surface during the war, notably Louis Suggs, daughter of a baseball player.

She had piled up several significant amateur victories by VJ Day, and there was a solid reserve of talent in American women's golf that suggested a circuit could be enlarged and enriched.

# 'Dour' Ben Hogan cashes in

BEN HOGAN suffered two sharp disappointments, first in the Masters through three-putting the last green, then by missing the play-off for the US Open by a stroke. He trounced Jimmy Demaret in the semifinal of the US PGA and Ed "Porky" Oliver in the final to capture his first major at Portland, Oregon, and he was leading money-winner again.

When Demaret was asked at

Portland what Hogan, already becoming renowned for his taciturn (not to say dour) manner, had said during the semifinal, Demaret replied that when the two of them were playing Hogan spoke to him on every green. And what he said was: "You're away."

In the final Hogan trailed at halfway, but took only 30 strokes to the turn in the afternoon, and streaked away from Oliver,

whose nickname derived from his generous girth.

A missed 30-incher at Augusta cost Hogan a play-off against Herman Keiser, who had started the final round five ahead of Hogan. Hogan could scarcely hope to rival Byron Nelson's 1945 near monopoly of first prize cheques, but he did win 13 times in the 32-event tour, and was second on seven further occasions.

**Usual silver scenery for Ben and the Babe.**

# Worsham wins in the Year of the Tube

SAM SNEAD'S talent for not winning the US Open reared its ugly head at St Louis Country Club in Missouri. On the course designed by Charles Blair Macdonald, Lew Worsham, professional at the feared Oakmont course, scored 69 in a play-off with Snead and won by a stroke.

Snead's narrow defeat in this event was nothing new, but local television coverage certainly was. Missouri folks equipped with a tube were able to watch Snead torturing himself on the last hole, where in regulation play, that is, at the 72nd hole, he needed to sink an 18-foot birdie putt to equal Worsham's total of 282. This he did, and on June 15 the two players set off to decide the ownership of a brand-new trophy, the one presented to Lloyd Mangrum almost exactly 12 months earlier, having been lost in a fire at George May's Tam O'Shanter club, Chicago.

It all came down to the last hole again. The play-off pair had scored with commendable consistency throughout, Snead's first round of 72 being the highest score of the eight rounds they had played. Worsham's 69 in the play-off was the first below-70 round between them. It might not have been enough but for Snead's missing a three footer on the 18th that would have meant a second play-off.

There was financial consolation for Snead in that, like Worsham, he received a special play-off payment of $500. The winner's prize was increased from $1,500 to $2,000, and the total purse rose $2,000 to $10,000.

An amateur, James McHale set an Open record with his 65 in round three. He was joint 26th.

Lew Worsham: TV champion.

Fred Daly: almost caught by Stranahan.

# Daly emulates Braid

FRED DALY, the Balmoral, Northern Ireland pro from Portrush, won the British Open and the Match Play championship in 1947, which no player except James Braid had ever brought off before. In the Open he defied and profited in turn from Hoylake's winds. He was four clear of Henry Cotton and Sam King at halfway, in unhelpful weather and, though his third round of 78 appeared terminal, he completed his final round (a praiseworthy 72) before the weather really got to work on his opponents' swings and stamina.

Only Reg Horne (Hendon) and Frank Stranahan, an amateur and heir to an American spark-plug fortune, got within a stroke of Daly. Norman von Nida was one of the favourites, but he faded to a final 76, and Stranahan came within an inch or two of upsetting Daly at the very last gasp, since his "two for a tie" shot at the 18th, from 150 yards, missed going down by inches. Daly's prize was £150.

# Bobby Locke's lucrative look round US Tour

SOUTH AFRICAN CHAMPION six times, twice as an amateur, Bobby Locke puzzled and then piqued America's professional golfers on his money-making trip to the United States. Neither Locke nor, in particular, his swing, looked remotely athletic. His scores, and notably his putting with a very prewar looking putter (which war was not readily discernible), earned large amounts of money which were not going into the pockets of US PGA members.

The slim Locke of prewar years, during which he had performed well, even in his teens, had now become comfortably rounded, and proceeded down fairways in a manner that a Roman emperor might have envied. His swing began with a figure eight and was not of the coiled spring variety. "Loose" was more appropriate, and he hooked everything. He even managed to hook his putts, starting his stroke on the inside as Walter Hagen had done.

His way of dealing with a short hole was, at his best, devastating to opponents. He would not take long over the tee shot, which would zoom out to the right and come back safely to the putting surface. On the green there would follow much stately pacing about and close examination of the grain of the grass. A two footer would receive the same care as a 20 footer, and the result was frequently the same – a birdie two. Locke arrived in time for the Masters and finished 14th. He then won, to the stupefaction of American pros, four of the next five events, and missed the play-off in the Open by three strokes.

Even more galling, he was then offered $5,000 appearance money by George May to play in the Tam O'Shanter. Locke won it, for a total take of $12,000. He also won the Canadian Open, scoring a record 268 in Toronto and, with one more first and a second, finished second to Jimmy Demaret on the money list.

Many and vehement were the critics of his style of play, a fair number of them impelled by envy. He was dubbed "Muffin Face" by American detractors and indeed his features did look "lived in" to say the least. But his methods of play were made for prosperity on the US Tour.

# British golfers feel US heat

TEAM OR INDIVIDUAL, this was a victorious year for American golf, both the Ryder and Walker Cups providing crushing wins. The Walker Cup at St Andrews, scene of the Britain and Ireland initial success before the war wiped out the series, was a great blow to the home side. The Americans had agreed to travel, though it was not their turn to do so, and with a team which included only Bud Ward of the beaten 1938 selection, had a comfortable 8-4 win on the Old Course. Leonard Crawley, Alec Kyle, Charles Stowe and Cecil Ewing returned for the home team, who introduced two strong players in long-hitting Joe Carr from Ireland and Ronnie White, a Wallasey man who based his golf on Royal Birkdale. After the foursomes were shared, White, a winner, with Stowe, and Crawley with Laddie Lucas, White and Carr got Britain and Ireland their two singles points. Willie Turnesa and Robert Riegel were the dependables in the visiting team, which was led by Francis Ouimet.

A stronger American Ryder Cup side can scarcely be imagined. They swept the foursomes and could afford to leave Hogan out of the singles, and still win them 7-1. Sam King beat Herman Keiser in the bottom match, all the rest going to the United States, who only once had to play the penultimate hole. Snead beat Cotton 5 & 4.

Louise Suggs: first "Amateur".

Sam King: lone singles win for the British team at St Andrews.

# US gather up the silver

APART FROM Fred Daly at Hoylake and Jim Ferrier, the Australian who beat Chick Harbert in the US PGA final, wherever you looked in 1947, American players stood in the winner's circle.

The outstanding amateur performance of the year was undoubtedly to be witnessed at Gullane, down the road from Muirfield, where Babe Zaharias smashed the ball out of sight and seldom gave opponents a glimpse of the winning post. She was the first American to win the British title.

Her extrovert ways did not suit everyone, and she was asked not to wear red and white checked shorts on the course, but her golf was unstoppable. She was holder of both the major amateur titles at the same time. Now came a film offer which Babe could not refuse, and this time it was a voluntary move into professionalism. It was said that she received more for her exhibitions, managed by erstwhile PGA tour manager Fred Corcoran, than Snead or Hogan.

On the slowly growing US women's tour, Betty Jameson became the first woman to break 300 in a significant 72-hole event, and did so to win the US Open, with a total of 295 at Starmount Forest, Greensboro, North Carolina. This was the first women's Open to be decided at strokeplay.

Louise Suggs won the national amateur title from Dorothy Kirby at Franklin HIlls, Detroit. Both Suggs and Kirby were from Atlanta.

# Demaret's second Masters

A SECOND AUGUSTA victory by Jimmy Demaret, who led from start to finish, put him level on April 6 with double winners Horton Smith and Byron Nelson. Demaret, the one-time dance band singer and permanent snappy dresser, held off "Iron Byron", making a now rare appearance in major golf, by a stroke. Amateur Frank Stranahan shared second place with Nelson.

Shortly before the Masters, the Tour's total prize money for the year was announced as $352,500. Demaret won nearly $28,000, though Hogan had seven Tour wins.

# Abe Mitchell, master of match play

ABE MITCHELL who, in the opinion of J.H.Taylor was the finest player never to win an Open, died. He was fourth to Harry Vardon in 1914, and had other good chances. He won the Match Play championship three times, that form of the game being his strong point.

# 'Quiet' Ben Hogan comes into his own

BEN HOGAN achieved what his followers had been expecting for most of the 1940s when he beat his close friend Jimmy Demaret by two shots for the US Open Golf championship at Riviera in Los Angeles. What is more he did it with a most daunting record total of 276. Only his second round exceeded 70 strokes.

His total was five fewer than the previous best by Ralph Guldahl, and eight below par, another record, and all this on a 7,020-yard lay-out with a testing par of 71. Jimmy Turnesa was a further two strokes back in third place, followed closely by Bobby Locke, with 283, worth $600. Hogan's $2,000 was by now very small potatoes reckoned against his instructional book sales (you had to believe him now) and other endorsements.

His strong (almost) silent style touched a chord with American hero-worshippers who like their athletes to make their reputation by deed not chat. He did not believe in taking chances, but practised instead, giving him such control over the ball that he could carry out his final pro-gramme, course management, and, said Hogan, "Management is 80 per cent of winning."

In other words, he was at the opposite end of the Richter scale of sporting earth-movers from Walter Hagen, a gambler on the course, on or off which he had a genius for communication with his public. Hogan was already in possession of his second major title when he won the Open, for less than three weeks earlier he had routed Mike Turnesa in the final of the US PGA at Norwood Hills, Missouri. Turnesa could hit the ball past Hogan, who hit only as far as was necessary, and whose response with further extraordinary scoring feats was to regain the title he had won in Oregon two years earlier.

Hogan was a tough man to beat all year, winning 10 times. He started with the Los Angeles Open and finished as leading money-winner, with $32,112.

His implacable pursuit of success, which often involved hours or practice before and after a tournament and night-time sessions putting on his hotel room carpet, began to pay off richly.

Ben Hogan: practising and cashing in with his silent approach.

# Henry Cotton's right royal round

KING GEORGE VI, one of the most competent of the many royal golfers through the centuries, was at Muirfield to enjoy Henry Cotton's second round in the British Open.

It was a 66 and the main reason Cotton could afford a 75, 72 final day and still win his third title by five shots from the holder, Irishman Fred Daly. Norman von Nida, an Australian of uncertain temper but unmistakable talent, shared third place six behind Cotton with three others, including Robert de Vicenzo of Argentina.

That dogged American seeker of Open honours, Johnny Bulla, was joint fifth, but no other prominent Americans figured, though Frank Stranahan, Claude Harmon, Bobby Cruickshank and Lawson Little were among those present, as was a Walter Lyle, 23 shots off the pace, from Clober, a course near Glasgow designed by the Lyle family.

Cotton, 41, was now the most influential figure in the European game. He said after this third Open that he missed only four fairways with his driver.

Henry Cotton: third Open.

# US stay ahead in Curtis Cup

ROYAL BIRKDALE was the scene of the first Curtis Cup confrontation between America and Britain and Ireland for ten years, and like all the others, apart from the tie in 1936, it ended in victory for the United States, by 6 1/2 to 2 1/2. Philomena Garvey, an Irish nationalist who refused to play unless Ireland was included in the team badge, fought out the most exciting singles – the top match against American champion Louise Suggs. The home team were 2-1 down in the foursomes and Garvey was two up with two to play. Suggs hit back to halve the match.

She and Grace Lenczyck had lost to Jacqueline Gordon and Jean Donald. This was Donald's debut in the Curtis Cup, which she celebrated by beating Dorothy Kirby by two holes. She was the only singles winner, for Lenczyk, Mrs Julius Page, Polly Riley and Dorothy Kielty swept the bottom four singles.

Back home in September Lenczyk gained her first Amateur title at Helen Sigel's expense at Del Monte, California. Marlene Bauer, the latest in America's long line of glamorous golfers, made her first appearance in the championship and got through two rounds, aged 16.

"If ah didn't have these ah'd hit it twenty yards further."

BABE ZAHARIAS,
on the subject of her mammary glands.

"Ben Hogan would rather have a coral snake rolling in his shirt than hit a hook."

CLAUDE HARMON.

● Bobby Locke came back for another cheque-lined trip on the PGA tour, and had three wins. He managed to set an unlikely-looking record in Chicago by leaving the field 16 strokes behind, two better than even Hogan had managed in 1946.

● A final trophy to come Ben Hogan's way was the Vardon Trophy, in recognition of his stroke average of 69.3.

● The USGA decreed that women would not be allowed to enter the Men's Open.

● Bing Crosby aced the daunting 233-yard 16th at Cypress Point.

Centre of attraction: Bobby Locke wins Chicago Victory Open.

### SCORECARD

**British Open** (Muirfield, Scot)
H Cotton 71 66 75 72 284

**US Open** (Riviera, Los Angeles, Cal)
B Hogan 67 72 68 69 276

**Masters** (Augusta, Ga)
C Harmon 70 70 69 70 279

**US PGA** (Norwood Hills CC, Mo)
B Hogan bt M Turnesa 7 & 6
Leading US money-winner: B Hogan $32,112

**British Amateur** ( Royal St George's, Sandwich, Kent)
FR Stranahan bt C Stowe 5 & 4

**US Amateur** (Memphis CC, Tenn)
W Turnesa bt R Billows 2 & 1

**Willie Turnesa after winning US Amateur.**

**US Women's Open** (Atlantic City CC, Northfield, NJ)
Mrs G Zaharias 300

**British Women's Amateur** (Royal Lytham, Lancs)
L Suggs bt J Donald 1h

**US Women's Amateur** (Del Monte, Cal)
G Lenczyk bt H Sigel 4 & 3

**Curtis Cup** (Royal Birkdale, Lancashire)
US 6½, GB & Ireland 2½

# Caucasian clause causes problems on US Tour

THE US PGA began life in 1916 with a clause in their constitution which banned non-Caucasian golfers from membership. As time went on it was frequently ignored.

Few black players had made much of a fist of the game until after the Second World War, and in 1948 a crisis was reached when two black professionals were in the top 60 of the Los Angeles Open, which gave them the right to enter another Californian event, the Richmond Open. The event secretary accepted their entries, George Schneiter, chief of the PGA tournament bureau, did not.

The position was that the PGA contract with sponsors included an agreement that a sponsor was free to include the first 60 finishers in the most recently completed tournament.

Ted Rhodes had finished 21st and Bill Spiller 34th. Litigation ensued, and by the autumn the case was settled, not altogether to the satisfaction of the plaintiffs, Rhodes and Spiller, who had to make do with an undertaking that blacks would not be refused entry into Open events in future on account of their race.

Neither Spiller nor Rhodes got any money from the PGA for being prevented from engaging in their employment. They also sued Richmond Golf Club for $3,400 (first and second prize money). Nor did they get to play at Richmond. The underlying reason for this unsatisfactory outcome was that the LA Open had a big purse and could dictate to the Tour bureau. Richmond could not. Similarly George May, at Tam O'Shanter, could admit whoever he wanted in his events.

# Harmon's smooth Masterly path

CLAUDE HARMON was not a tournament pro, but beat the leading lights in that category by a street in the Masters. With three rounds of 70 and one (the third, or "money round" as the pros call it) of 69, Harmon had five shots to spare over Cary Middlecoff, and eight over Chick Harbert in third place.

He gave his pursuers (for he led from the second round onwards) something to despair about in the final round, during which he saved four shots against

par in the space of three holes. His margin of victory was a record. The win was no surprise to Harmon, who had been a professional at Winged Foot, which he once negotiated in 62 shots. Moreover he had recently been playing at Seminole with Ben Hogan and won as often as Hogan beat him.

Harmon must have thought the day was his when in the final round, he made par despite having to play out of water at the 13th.

# Babe bounces ahead in the paid game

NOT THE LEAST significant Open championship victory of the year was clinched by Babe Zaharias, who burst clear of the field in June at Atlantic City to win by eight strokes. This, not surprisingly, was a record in the short stroke play history of the event, which now extended to two years. Betty Jameson was second.

Later in the year Louise Suggs turned pro after her British Amateur win (rather handed to her by Jacqueline Gordon's wayward putting on the final green) and so did several other prominent amateurs. The scene was set for the launching of a worthwhile series of events. Bud Ward for one was convinced that it could be done, but regretted that so far the know-how was missing.

Corcoran and the game's two leading women professionals were determined to end this state of affairs, at the same time recognizing the pioneering role played by Hope Seignious, who had put a good deal of her own money in setting up the Women's Professional Golfers' Association.

Corcoran was working for the Wilson Sporting Goods company, and for him, and the leading women professionals the year was a busy one as they sought sponsors to get women's golf on a firmer footing. Corcoran agreed to take charge at an annual salary of just $1 until the tour was more profitable.

# Ben Hogan near death after head-on crash

STARTING THE New Year just as he had started 1948, by winning, Ben Hogan decided to go home for a rest in February. He had two victories in a row at the Bing Crosby Invitational and Long Beach Open; then lost the Phoenix Open to Jimmy Demaret in a play-off.

Home was in Fort Worth. On the way across Texas near the town of Van Horn Hogan's car was wrecked in a head-on collision with a Greyhound bus as it tried to overtake a truck. Hogan threw himself across his wife in the passenger seat and so escaped being crushed by the driving wheel, but suffered fractures to pelvis, collarbone, rib and ankle. Complications ensued, involving tying off veins in Hogan's legs, for there was the threat of thrombosis. To counter this, a month after the accident, he was given emergency surgery at El Paso. Hogan was never very

big or heavy, but back home again he weighed less than 100 pounds. He quickly set about eradicating the effects of his injuries just as relentlessly as he had striven on the practice ground to eliminate his swing faults. Early on in this process even a stroll round the garden would compel him to rest all next day.

Four months later Hogan convinced his doctors that he was fit enough, as non-playing captain, to lead the Ryder Cup team to Ganton in Yorkshire, where he presided over a 10-2 American win in September.

Playing golf was something else entirely, and not until December was there any hint of a return to competition. Every foray to the golf course was a severe test of Hogan's reviving strength. Nevertheless, at the end of the year came the astounding news that a few months after

being struck down at the height of his powers and drifting close to death with crippling injuries, he had entered for the Los Angeles Open in January.

**Demaret: victor at Phoenix.**

# Middlecoff edges out Snead and Heafner

SAM SNEAD'S hopes for a "major" a month (he had landed one in April and another in May) went awry at Medinah Country Club in Illinois on June 11 when Cary Middlecoff took his first US Open title by a stroke from Clayton Heafner and the event's champion active runner-up, Snead.

Middlecoff ("Doc" to his peers, for he was a qualified dentist who had been a professional golfer for only two years) fought it out first with Heafner, who missed a birdie putt on the 72nd hole for a 287 total, one more than Middlecoff. Snead was left with the task of playing the last nine holes in 33 strokes, but failed to get up and down for his par at the penultimate hole and finished level with Heafner, a huge mustachioed man of uncertain temper who had reputedly made a lot of money betting on Bobby Locke.

Later the same month Middlecoff and Lloyd Mangrum were involved in a sudden-death play-off for the Motor City Open, in Detroit. The battle went on for 11 holes, neither able to secure victory, until the pair were declared co-winners.

**Middlecoff: champion by a stroke.**

# Snead off to fast start at Augusta

SAM SNEAD emulated the absent Ben Hogan's capture of two majors in 1948, starting with a mixed performance at Augusta, where he followed a halfway total of 148, compiled in boisterous conditions, with two rounds of 67 and won by three strokes from Johnny Bulla and Lloyd Mangrum. Johnny Palmer, a regular money-winner who was chosen for the Ryder Cup side, and Joe Turnesa were joint fourth.

Snead had eight birdies in his final 67; indeed he holed more birdies than pars. This first Masters triumph was, according to Snead, the result of ridding himself of putting cares.

Less than a month later Snead captured the US PGA title, any other result being unthinkable since the event was in Snead's backyard at the Hermitage Country Club in Richmond, Virginia. He was not short of support. His victim in the final was Palmer, Snead winning at the 34th.

# Springbok Locke is Open champion

BOBBY LOCKE had clearly been lining himself up for a British Open championship since well before the war, and patiently battled away for six rounds finally to achieve his goal at Sandwich in a 36-hole play-off against Harry Bradshaw from Ireland. The now portly Transvaaler, who looked so inoffensive, could be brutal in his demolition of opponents, and won the play-off by 12 strokes.

For all Locke's brilliance in holing out and the inevitability of his finally winning a major championship, it was, as often happens, an untoward event that captured the headlines at Sandwich in the first few days of July.

Bradshaw's second round of 77 was a burden he was unable to shake off, and his unfortunate encounter with a broken beer bottle on the sixth hole was of no help at all.

His second lay in the rough near pieces of bottle glass. He was frightened a fragment might

**Congratulations: Bobby Locke and (right) runner-up Harry Bradshaw.**

fly into his face, and the outcome was dropped shots. A picture appeared in the press purporting to show Bradshaw's ball in the neck of a bottle, but Leslie Edwards, an occasional contributor to the "Daily Telegraph", dis-

covered that a photographer had set this up some time after the event.

The image of ball-in-neck-of-bottle, though it was a lie, was slow to fade from the golfing public's mind.

# Hogan's team recover in Ryder Cup

BEN HOGAN'S Ryder Cup team had their worst ever foursomes experience in the match at the lovely Ganton course, near Scarborough in Yorkshire, where Harry Vardon was once professional. Jimmy Demaret and Clayton Heafner provided their only point.

Next day Bob Hamilton and Johnny Palmer were their only losers, Palmer to Jimmy Adams, who won in foursomes with Max Faulkner, and Hamilton to Dai Rees, who had not been given a foursomes place. Demaret and Heafner both won their single, Chick Harbert and Lloyd Mangrum helping them sweep the bottom four matches in a bravura American finale.

There were no alarms for the American Walker Cup team at Winged Foot, New York, where one foursome point (Joe Carr and Ronnie White) and one single (White again) were all Francis Ouimet's team would allow.

White had contributed four wins in four starts to the forlorn Britain and Ireland cause. His iron play was outstanding, and did not wilt in the wind. Nevertheless, it was clear that in international team play there was as yet no answer to American expertise in approach shots and putting.

**Max Faulkner: winning partnership with Jimmy Adams.**

## LPGA take over in US

THE YEAR of revolution in women's professional golf began with one of the last events run by the Women's Professional Golfers' Association, at Tampa, where Patty Berg won by a stroke from Babe Zaharias. Later the two of them and other interested parties including the Wilson sporting goods company and Fred Corcoran, until lately manager of the men's tour, decided at a meeting in the Venetian Hotel, Miami, that a more active association should be formed. At Corcoran's suggestion, it was to be the Ladies' Professional Golfers' Association. It sounded nicer, he said.

The LPGA took over the Open from the WPGA. Louise Suggs won it at Prince George's Golf and Country Club, Landover, Maryland. She started with a 69 and finished with a record 291, 14 strokes clear of Babe Zaharias. It was the Babe who generally hogged the headlines, however, by virtue of her Olympic beginnings and extraordinary long hitting at golf.

## TEE TALK

**"Show me where it says in the rrool book that you ha'e to tee it oop. Get oot an' play."**

**PETER HAY,**
Scots pro at Pebble Beach during Crosby Event, to Cary Middlecoff who grumbled that he could not tee his ball up on account of the wind.

# Ben Hogan: from glorious failure to Golden success

THAT HE SHOULD be playing at all in the Los Angeles Open in the first week of January was hard to believe, only 11 months after the automobile accident that nearly killed him. That Ben Hogan should go so close to winning in a play-off with 1949's golfer of the year, Sam Snead, stretches credulity even further.

No wonder there was nearly a five-figure gate at the Riviera Club on opening day. His play was, for Hogan, uncertain in the first round, but he followed 73 with three 69s. But for some loose putting he would have escaped a play-off. As it was Snead required birdies on holes 71 and 72 to tie.

The play-off was rained off for a week and, in between whiles at the Crosby, Hogan played below his usual form. A fifth rousing Riviera round was beyond the capacity of his bandaged, battered legs, and he lost the play-off by four shots.

But the strength was flowing back into him: his ball control and course management had never been stronger and, though he slipped to a 76 and joint fourth place (with Byron Nelson) in the Masters, which Jimmy Demaret won for the third time, Hogan reassembled his forces menacingly at the Greenbrier Pro-Am. Rounds of 64, 64, 65, 66, gave him victory and equalled Nelson's 72-hole record for a par-70 course.

Hogan decided against a potentially long week of USGA match play, preparing instead for the Golden Anniversary Open at Merion, where Snead was favourite. His post-accident feats were already bringing him bags of fan mail, especially from accident victims like himself.

Hogan responded in the way he knew best. Like the other fancied players, he took little heed of the record 64 scored by Lee Mackey, who was out of work but briefly in form (he finished 81, 75, 77). First came a 72 (two over par), then a 69 from Hogan, leaving him fifth, with two rounds to face next day. He had not played 36 holes in a day since before the accident.

His third round was another 72. He now showed signs of tiredness, and cramp made him consider withdrawal. He needed to exceed par on the last seven holes by no more than two shots

Ben Hogan: remarkable return to success after crash.

Hogan: practice audience.

in order to win. But he overhit on the 12th, missed a 30-inch par putt on the 15th, parred the difficult 16th, Quarry Hole, but dropped another shot on the 17th. That was his third bogey in six holes, but he got home safely at the 445-yard closing hole with a par for the tie, against Lloyd Mangrum and George Fazio.

Hogan was revitalized by tee time on the Sunday. Fazio was well beaten, five over par, and Mangrum eased Hogan's task by incurring a two-shot penalty for picking up his ball on the 16th to blow away a fly. Hogan fastened down his second Open with a birdie two on the next hole from 50 feet and a par on the last. Little over a year earlier he had spent 58 days lying on his back.

**British Open** (Troon, Scot)
AD Locke  69 72 70 68  279

**US Open** (Merion, Pa)
B Hogan  72 69 72 74  287

**Masters** (Augusta, Ga)
J Demaret  70 72 72 69  283

**US PGA** (Scioto, Ohio)
C Harper bt H Williams  4 & 3
Leading US money-winner: S Snead
$35,758.83

**British Amateur** (St Andrews, Scot)
FR Stranahan bt RD Chapman 8 & 6

**US Amateur** (Minneapolis CC, Minn)
S Urzetta bt FR Stranahan 39th

**US Women's Open** (Rolling Hills G & CC, Wichita, Kans)
Mrs G Zaharias 291

**British Women's Amateur** (Newcastle, Co Down, N Ire)
Vicomtesse de St Sauveur bt J Valentine 3 & 2

**US Women's Amateur** (Atlanta AC, Ga)
B Hanson bt M Murray 6 & 4

**Curtis Cup** (Buffalo CC, NY)
US 7 1/2, GB & Ireland 1 1/2

# US nap hand in Curtis Cup at Buffalo

THE AMERICAN Curtis Cup side, led by Glenna Collett Vare, celebrated their fifth win in six matches with their biggest victory, 7-1 with one match halved, at Buffalo early in September. The return of Jessie Valentine, with her 75 per cent record, was in vain. The visitors' lone win was thanks to Frances Stephens and Elizabeth Price against Helen Sigel and Peggy Kirk.

The most exciting moment on the second day came in the climax of the top singles match between Frances Stephens and Mrs Mark Porter, amateur champions of their respective countries the year before. Stephens won the last three holes to get her half for the visitors.

Otherwise margins against Diana Critchley's team were mostly heavy, the biggest being Polly Riley's 7 & 6 against Mrs Valentine, heroine of the drawn match of 1936. The Cup matches were for the first time played over 36 holes. The visitors' travel costs were defrayed in part by cash raised by Margaret Curtis's "Pam Barton Fund", in aid of which American golfers held fund-raising "Pam Barton Days".

## Stranahan on top at HQ

FRANK STRANAHAN beat Dick Chapman at St Andrews in the second all-American Amateur final, though this was not a Walker Cup year, when the British title had for years been at the mercy of the visitors.

He took his time over it, but compensated for his deliberate methods by finishing off Chapman on the 30th hole.

Back in America in search of one of the game's more elusive doubles, Stranahan was kept hard at it in the American final at Minneapolis Country Club by Sam Urzetta, who won at the 37th.

### SHORT PUTTS

● Curtis Cup player Polly Riley got the better of the pros at the inaugural LPGA event in January at Tampa, Florida.

● Further signs of a rift between club and tournament pros in America came with an attempt by Demaret, Snead, Hogan and others to form a separate division of the PGA for tour players. It was soon abandoned in favour of accepting places on the Association's tournament committee.

● Pennsylvanian Stewart Alexander, a member of Hogan's winning 1949 Ryder Cup side, was badly burned and broke both ankles in a plane crash in Indiana, shortly after gaining fourth place in the Kansas City Open.

● Death of James Braid, five times British Open winner and professional for 45 years at Walton Heath in Surrey, where he regularly beat his age in his late 70s.

**Death of a legend: James Braid, who in his seventies routinely beat his age.**

## Locke sets new scoring standards

BOBBY LOCKE retained his British Open title with the lowest aggregate yet, 279 at Troon, four better than Henry Cotton's mark of 1934. Roberto de Vicenzo was four shots adrift, and Dai Rees was third.

Locke also triumphed again in America, just the once, tweaking the noses of the PGA by winning George May's Tam O'Shanter Tournament near Chicago by virtue of a series of long putts late in the tournament to force a tie with Lloyd Mangrum, whom he beat by four shots with a 69 in the play-off.

The PGA had decided by a majority vote to ban Locke from their championship, the reason given being Locke's failure to honour playing commitments. May had even paid Locke appearance money, together with a contract for exhibition matches. Locke did not endear himself to the American pros (and to some of the public) by his eccentric behaviour. He also made it clear that he had come to the United States to clear a few dollars, asking fees for interviews.

Unlike Hagen, he was unable to convert his amazing scoring gifts into crowd-pleasing, American style. He was known as Muffin Face. His face certainly looked lived in, and his style was indigestible, though scarcely fattening, for the indigenous professionals. The PGA ban was later rescinded, but Locke decided to spend most of his time in Europe.

**Bobby Locke: triumph at Troon.**

## Finest hour of the Vicomtesse

WITH VICTORY in the British Women's Amateur at Newcastle, County Down, over one of Britain's most dominating amateurs in Jessie Valentine (née Anderson), Lally, Vicomtesse de St Sauveur reached a new high point in her career, which in golfing terms began in 1937, four years after Valentine's.

Lally (née Vagliano) was an aggressive but stylish golfer, and another victim of the war in that it wiped out years of potential trophy-winning. At home in France few could match her. She first came to notice by winning the British Girls title in 1937 and two years later won the French Closed Championship, and further success followed the war.

## Babe Zaharias back in charge

EQUALLING THE RECORD set up 12 months previously by Louise Suggs in the LPGA's first presentation of the the Women's Open, Babe Zaharias left Betsy Rawls a very distant nine strokes behind with her 291 at the Rolling Hills Country Club at Wichita.

Miss Rawls, a Texan, was still an amateur, and won two other events this year, including her state title. She did not start playing golf until she was 17 but within four years had won the Texas Amateur.

Fred Corcoran was busily building up the tour but, whereas the men's tour was worth nearly half a million dollars, the women's fledgling circuit was not much more than a tenth as prosperous.

**Zaharias: nine clear in Open.**

# Ben Hogan, 'Wee Ice Mon' on a hot streak

One of the world's greatest, he rose from a humble background and triumphed over injury to win supreme honours, capturing nine major championships in six years

WILLIAM BENJAMIN Hogan failed to qualify for the last 36 holes of the US Open championship at his first attempt in 1936. Between that and retirement, with a tenth-place finish in the Masters of 1967 (and the final flourish of an inward 30 at Augusta), Hogan managed nine major championships, all won during 1948-53 inclusive.

Hogan never had it easy, though, for the Second World War came just as he was learning how to win. Then after the war, just when he had proved he could win at the highest level, and indeed, like Bobby Jones 20 years earlier, was expected to win almost every time he set out, came the road crash early in 1949 that nearly killed him and wiped out that whole year of competition.

Born at Dublin, Texas on August 13, 1912, during his whole life he struggled against adversity. His was a hard upbringing, though the need to make his name in the world did bring him quickly, as a caddie, in contact with the game that was to be his life.

His father, a blacksmith of Irish lineage, died when Hogan was ten, and his mother took the family to Fort Worth where Hogan sold newspapers to help out. Soon, at the Glen Garden Country Club, golf and Ben Hogan were first united.

## Teething problems

Hogan's first swings at a golf ball were made left-handed. He changed to right-handed at a time when theories about how being forced to do this could lead to personality problems were as thin on the ground as left-handed clubs. It meant, at least ,that his stronger left hand would not allow him to fall into the trap about which golfers are warned from the start, of letting the right hand take over the whole operation.

For all that, Hogan's first difficulty with golf was a persistent hook. This he cured, though not speedily. The second was putting, for which he never secured a remission for long but for which he could and did compensate by accuracy from tee to green. Gene

**Ben Hogan: with British Open trophy - his third major of 1953.**

Sarazen held that in this department, Hogan had no peer: "Nobody covered the pin like he did."

There is the story of the young professionals grumbling to Hogan about the huge greens created on long modern courses designed to run alongside resort complexes and endless estates of holiday homes. Such big greens, was their plaint, made three-putt situations all too frequent. "Have you thought," asked Hogan, "of hitting the ball closer to the flag?"

Getting rid of the hook was not easy. He became a professional at 19, and went on the PGA Tour before his 20th birthday. He could not make a living at it because that hook kept popping in between hope and achievement.

These were indeed tough times, for outside the world of golf, and inside it many a time, was the Great Depression. Hogan scraped and soldiered and practised on, and by 1937 was making some sort of hand at the Tour.

## Success at last

The following year he won a tournament, the Hershey Fourball. Not till 1940, however, did the golf game really turn sweet for Hogan. He won five events, including the much sought-after North and South Open and the Westchester Open.

This year and the next two after that he was leading money-winner, pulling in more than $42,000 in prize money alone after ten years of hardship that would have sent another man off to find some less arduous taskmaster than golf.

He was called away for military service in 1942, just when he had begun to hit the ball very close to the hole indeed, because this taciturn loner had stubbornly refused to give in. It is highly probable, in any case, that he was never happier than when, alone on a practice ground, he was hammering away at some delicate variation of the golf swing.

## Refining his skills

Later in his tournament years "alone" was difficult, for his peers and his public were all too eager to watch the master at work. How typical of the mystery of golf that, with all those watching eyes on Hogan's swing over all those years he could still sell his "secret" for $10,000 (some say $20,000) to "Life" magazine.

It was rotation of the left hand near the top of the back swing, wrist and hand forming a V-shape, with the result that it was impossible to shut the club face. Result: Hogan's controlled fade, keeping the ball tethered on its dispatcher's designated flight path as if receiving instructions by radio. Hogan was jealous of the principles he had laboured so long to discover, and sued a publisher and author who had offered him a derisory sum for putting out pictures of him in a book with instructional material not by Hogan, who had not given permission for his picture to be used in the first place. The publisher had earlier put out a book written by Hogan himself, but this latest one cost him $5,000 in court.

## 140 pounds lighter

Hogan also learned how to cut and fade the ball instead of his earlier emphasis on the draw, and his ability to make long approach shots "bite" on the most resilient surfaces was crucial to a man not in possession of Calamity Jane, or Hagen's relaxed yet positive putting stroke.

Hogan was long, though he was not tall, and weighed about 140 pounds at fighting weight. Like Gary Player, who was of similar build, he had to make the most of his physical attributes in order to surpass the brawniest of opponents either with power or

**Alone: Hogan working out the problem he solved better than most.**

guile. His genius for concentrating on the task in hand was not confined to on-course activities, but was lavished on the Hogan club-making business.

He would accept items for market only when he was 100 per cent satisfied of his quality, and turned down so many designs that it caused his backers some disquiet. In the end the business, like Hogan's swing, proved prosperous, no doubt for the same reason – quality.

The accident made him chary of events demanding 36 holes in a day, especially match play which could go beyond two rounds. Yet he played better than ever, though he never thenceforward walked far without discomfort and constant bandaging and soaking of the abused limbs. From tee to green he became

even more controlled, picking his spots on fairways and greens and moving the ball this way and that to obtain optimum position for his next shot. Hogan would have recognized the game plan of snooker champion Joe Davis, for it was much the same.

Popular he was not, for his mien was grim and unapproachable, though he is held to have mellowed with the successes of the post-accident years.

He was respected, held in awe, certainly, as few players have ever been with the possible exception of Bobby Jones, with whom he agreed that there should be no talk of who was the best player of all time, since nobody could do better than be the best in his own era. Hogan was that.

His services to golf extended to an unbeaten Ryder Cup record and, even when out of action in 1949, he limped at the head of a winning Cup team excursion to Yorkshire. Four player of the year awards and four Vardon Trophies also came his way, plus scoring records in the US Open and Masters. He was never afraid of people in authority and let them know when they were, in his view, wrong. The tricked-up Oakland Hills course on which he won the Open in 1951 was not to his liking, so he stalked it in the earlier rounds like a big game hunter, and killed off the "Monster", with a final round 67.

British galleries were again shaken by the majesty of his game when he and Snead went to Wentworth to win the Canada Cup (now the World Cup) in 1956. He shot a course-record 67 there, just as he did with 68 at Carnoustie in winning his only attempt at the British Open three years earlier, and winning the Scots' approbation as the "Wee Ice Mon".

That put him level with Gene Sarazen as winner of all four of the modern majors, except that Sarazen never won three of them in one year. In fact, only Ben Hogan has done that.

**Hogan: portrait of an elder statesman of golf.**

## SCORECARD

**US Open** 1948, 1950, 1951, 1953

**British Open** 1953

**Masters** 1951, 1953

**US PGA** 1946, 1948

Hogan also lost one US Open play-off, and two play-offs for the Masters. Additionally, he had 23 top-ten finishes in the three majors at stroke play, and eight top-three finishes in the US Open.

# Hollywood and Hogan quick off the mark

THE HIGHLY successful film Follow the Sun, Hollywood's version of Ben Hogan's recovery from the terrible road accident of 1949 and return to golfing triumph, opened in Fort Worth, home town of the hero, in March. Glenn Ford and Anne Baxter took the parts of Hogan and his wife.

Within a month Hogan was setting out an entirely different scenario at Bobby Jones's Augusta National course, where he won his first Masters with relative ease from "Skee" Riegel by two strokes, with an eight under par total of 280.

He got nicely into position by the end of round three, one behind Riegel, then, with a final 68, his best of the tournament, went clear. Lloyd Mangrum and Lew Worsham were third, but six shots in arrears.

Sam Snead's game deserted him at the crisis; he needed 12 more shots than Hogan on the final afternoon.

Hogan had decided against further tilts at the US PGA title, since it involved a potential week of 36-hole matches, more than his legs, still painful after 18 holes, would take.

Nevertheless, he faced a stern challenge if he were to retain his Open title at Oakland Hills, near Detroit.

The city was celebrating its 250th anniversary, but the pros, Hogan included, could see little to cheer about in the set-up of the course, which the leading golf architect of modern times, Robert Trent Jones, had "improved". He and the USGA, never eager to hand out many free pars, were soulmates in their desire to stretch players' talents to breaking point.

Like a good many others, Hogan had decided not to make a charge at Trent Jones's course, which had a par of 70 at 6,694 yards. In round one only Snead got within a shot of par. Clayton Heafner and Albert Besselink, a Michigan man, were two above, and Bobby Locke was well placed with 73. Hogan returned a cautious 76.

Round by round thereafter Hogan got to work on Oakland Hills: first 73, then 71 and finally one of his truly great rounds, 67. What is more, he told the referee what he was going to do. After parring the first half, he had three birdies coming home, culminating with a drive and six iron to 15 feet at the last, trickling in the birdie down the slope to beat Heafner, who had a final 69, by two strokes and Locke by four. Heafner certainly deserved his $2,000 prize. Only he and Hogan of the 55-strong field achieved a below-par round.

Hogan was never one to analyse verbally, but his comment this time spoke volumes: "I am glad that I brought this course, this monster, to its knees."

That final round at Oakland Hills ensured, as early as June 16, that Hogan would be golfer of the year for 1951.

Robert Trent Jones: creator of monster course.

## Faulkner breaks the famine at Portrush

ONE OF GOLF'S best-known stories is that Max Faulkner, before becoming the third British golfer to win the National Open since the Second World War, freely signed autographs and added "Open Champion 1951". As a hostage to fortune this set new standards, but Willie Park senior would have smiled approvingly to watch Faulkner's putting, for it made up for all manner of errors committed through the green, a department where Faulkner could usually be trusted to excel.

A colourful dresser, Faulkner was also a great experimenter with clubs and golf gear. He got £300 of the prize money, which totalled a mere £1,700.

Max Faulkner: hostage to fortune.

## Royal & Ancient agree rules with USGA

AT LAST the two major governing bodies of golf, the Royal & Ancient and the USGA, agreed a code of rules for the game worldwide. The central purpose was that "the perspective was to be worldwide, to meet the varying conditions under which the game is now played."

An important principle was agreed under which loss of stroke and distance were prescribed as penalty for ball out of bounds, unplayable, or lost. The stymie was abolished, after centuries of controversy, it seemed, notably the stymie which aided Bobby Jones against Cyril Tolley, who laid it, early in Jones's 1930 quest for the Grand Slam, and another which came between Jock McLean and the American Amateur championship in 1936. It had been briefly dispensed with in 1833 by the Royal & Ancient, but rapidly restored. American golfers had always muttered against it, and indeed it does hit at the root of golf tradition – that a player shall not interfere with an opponent's ball.

The word stymie is believed to derive from an old Scots word, styme. In the phrase "not to see a styme" the meaning is not to see at all. The word appears in a Robert Burns poem:

I've seen me daez't upon a time,
I scarce could wink or see a stymie.

# Pinehurst thrashing for Great Britain & Ireland

THE GLORIES of Pinehurst in North Carolina may have palled a little on Henry Cotton's team, since they were allowed only one foursome and one singles win by an American team led by Sam Snead and including Clayton Heafner, concerned in the only halved match, against Fred Daly. Arthur Lees, a Yorkshireman through and through, won twice, with Charlie Ward against "Porky" Oliver and Henry Ransom, and Oliver again in singles. The heavy American guns of Hogan, Snead, Demaret and Mangrum all won, and so did Stewart "Skip" Alexander, recovered from his air crash of the previous year. Burns had made gripping the club difficult, but he soon got a grip on John Panton, playing his first Ryder single, and beat him 8 & 7.

Leonard Crawley's pre-match judgment was that the British would be out-hit "on this fearfully long course", but he was wrong. They opened their shoulders and their second shots were more accurate but the Americans were superior near the hole.

The story was much the same in the Walker Cup played at Royal Birkdale. Willie Turnesa was captain, while Gene Littler, tipped as yet another "next Bobby Jones" and Ken Venturi made their international debuts. America's amateurs were not quite so severe on their hosts, having to react quickly when they were behind at halfway in all but one foursome. The visitors rallied well and dined with a healthy two wins and two halves, and next day only the (almost) inevitable Ronnie White, against Charles Coe, and Joe Carr, against Frank Stranahan, registered wins. White had yet to lose in Walker Cup play. Harold Paddock exemplified American stubbornness by halving with Ian Caldwell after being three down with four to play, and the final reckoning was 6-3, with three matches halved.

● Babe Zaharias refined her game and reputation. Not a person of the most delicate sensibilities, occasionally descending to the unpolished vernacular, she was on top for most of the LPGA year, winning seven out of the Association's 16 events, against five out of 11 the previous year.

**Betsy Rawls: beat Louise Suggs for the US Women's Open at Atlanta.**

● Betsy Rawls had the best of it in the Open at Atlanta, with a total of 293, two outside the record.

● Francis Ouimet became the first American to be voted Royal & Ancient captain, and duly drove himself in at St Andrews.

● Lloyd Mangrum won the Vardon Trophy with a stroke average of 70.05.

## Consolation for Snead

BEN HOGAN'S place at the head of world golf did not exactly impoverish Sam Snead, but the only major he could win was the US PGA, which Hogan passed up.

Few American golfers, the faithful Johnny Bulla and the amateur Frank Stranahan apart, were trying of late for the British Open, since it was an expensive business, even if the trophy was won, and ownership of the Auld Mug did not create a sense of awe in the American public.

Snead accomplished the US PGA readily enough at the Oakmont course, beating Walter Burkemo 7 & 6.

# All-American at Porthcawl

ANOTHER US Walker Cup team in Britain, another all-American final in the British Amateur – this time Dick Chapman made up for past final frustrations by beating Charles Coe 5 & 4 at Royal Porthcawl. It meant that he had added one of the tastiest titles to his unique collection, which included his national title, the Canadian and three continental championships.

It was the third final in five years for Chapman, who had served in the US Army Air Force during the war.

**Dick Chapman: 5 & 4 rout of Charles Coe at Royal Porthcawl.**

# Locke's third Open in four years

BOBBY LOCKE achieved his third British Open championship in four years at Royal Lytham and St Annes. Moreover, the golfer who looked most likely to end this South African domination appeared to be not British, nor yet American (few players from the United States were now bothering to contest the oldest championship) but an Australian, Peter Thomson, who hunted Locke home and finished only a stroke short. Thomson was 22 and playing in only his second Open.

Not since the days of the Triumvirate had a golfer scored so often in the Open as Locke, whose slow and stately progress was to get him into the Royal & Ancient's bad books here on the Lancashire coast. Norman von Nida, who had been cutting a swathe in many a competition though he was now perhaps five years or so past his best, complained about Locke's taking three and a half hours to get round. In the end, Locke was instructed to get a move on, though the difference this produced in his deliberate gait was not easy to assess.

This deliberation was Locke's way of avoiding tension – in which case Cary Middlecoff deserved to be the most relaxed golfer who ever teed up a golf ball. Locke had played in his company in America, and the pair of them were widely credited

Bobby Locke: three Open titles in just four years.

with being among the first and most consistent of sinners in the developing saga of slow play.

Locke played his final round under stress: he told Leslie Edwards of the Liverpool Post, "They have threatened to penalise me for slow play. I think it very unfair." Edwards considered him without peer on the green, where his detractors said that he was looking for snakes as he appeared to peer into the hole during his pre-putting routine.

Gene Sarazen was back for this Open for the first time since the war. Henry Cotton, too, was back. He had not entered since winning in 1948, and his fourth place, seven behind Locke, showed his lasting quality.

Thomson: so close at Lytham.

# Julius Boros relaxes and wins in a hurry

THERE WAS NO sense of rush and hurry about Julius Boros, but he did step up to the ball smartly and dispatch it without undue delay. He said that was his way of relaxing, because he felt that if he froze over the ball for more than a moment or two he might stay there for ever.

Boros was of Hungarian extraction. He had worked as an accountant and was not a serious golf competitor till he was 30. Within two years of turning professional, here he was, US Open champion. He had been joint fourth behind Hogan the previous year, when he also won the Massachusetts Open. Now he got into the big money, apart from the Open, by winning George

May's conservatively entitled World Championship. He was leading money-earner and player of the year, too.

Ben Hogan had a disappointing final day, since he had set a record with 69 on day one and day two, which equalled the halfway record. Suffering in the heat over the final 36 holes at Dallas, he finished 74, 74. He was pushed out of second place by "Porky" Oliver's 50-foot putt on the final green.

This was not the closest Oliver had come to the title, for he had been disqualified for starting before the appointed time in 1940 (to beat approaching bad weather). His 287 was the same as the eventual winner.

# President Ike, 'golfer in the White House'

SEVERAL AMERICAN presidents have been golfers, but only one can properly be termed a golf nut, and that is President David Dwight Eisenhower, whose 1951 election campaign had been supported by Bobby Jones, a member of Georgia Democrats for Eisenhower (the Republican candidate).

When the USGA helps in the construction of a putting green for you outside your own home, you know that they see you as a person of benevolent interest, and that is what the association did for Ike in the White House garden. His vacations were planned with golfing possibilities in mind, and he was, as Jones's friend, at his happiest when staying at the "Little White House"

near the Augusta clubhouse. An old football injury did not improve the president's leg action, and he was a keen rather than an expert player. The White House press corps made Ike the best reported golfer of his none-too-exalted class in the history of the game.

How much of the boom in purses on both the men's and women's tours can be attributed to the "Golfer in the White House" is uncertain, but the prize money for the year amounted to a fraction below $500,000 for the men, and $150,000 for the women, who were catching up fast, relatively speaking, though the number of WPGA tournaments offered employment for less than half the year.

# DeMoss disaster in Curtis Cup

JUST ABOUT THE strongest side Great Britain and Ireland had put together at last won the Curtis Cup, at the seventh attempt, at cold and blustery Muirfield, a club that had no women members or yet a women's locker room.

The margin was 5-4, and even the most bigoted British supporter would not have wished on their worst enemy the dreadful fate that overcame Grace DeMoss from Oregon in losing the last match, to Elizabeth Price, who was playing in her second Cup single, having lost the first by a distance to Grace Lenczyk.

Now the golf glove was on the other hand. Price was facing a Cup rookie in DeMoss but, approaching the 15th green, it seemed probable that the home advantage wrung out by Price of two holes up was about to be halved. She was in a greenside bunker for three, whereas DeMoss, despite the wind, was just short of the green, which was close to 400 yards for two.

DeMoss must at this point have been thinking of a dream she reported to her colleagues earlier in the week in which her fellow Curtis Cuppers came to tell her that her single would settle the destination of the trophy.

DeMoss did the unthinkable. She hit three consecutive shanks, almost circling the green in the process as the ball shot off to the right each time from the socket of her wedge – this from a player who had twice been a semifinalist in her national amateur championship. Price, who had prevailed in the first foursome the day before with Jean Donald, won the hole with a bogey five, and the match at the next hole.

Scots voices rang out in cheers to acknowledge the first Britain and Ireland win in two decades of trying. The home team was a powerful one, with Donald and two other Scots, Moira Paterson and Jessie Valentine, plus Philomena Garvey from Ireland and the English trio of Frances Stephens, Jeanne Bisgood and Price.

The DeMoss debacle might never have happened had not Dorothy Kirby fought back so staunchly against Donald, who was five up in the top single with 11 to play, but was caught at the 35th, and bunkered at the last, losing to a Kirby par four. Paterson and Garvey won their foursome, and the other home points came from Bisgood and Stephens.

Polly Riley, such a force in singles for the United States, also had a flair for the diplomatic which she displayed at the post-match dinner. There a friend of DeMoss would not drink from the cup when it was passed round full of champagne, as was the custom after these internationals. Riley stuck a flower between her teeth and danced on a table, a timely distraction from a potentially embarrassing moment.

**Curtis Cup at last: Elizabeth Price and (right) Jean Donald who played key roles in long-awaited triumph at Muirfield.**

# Snead survives water treatment at Rae's Creek

SAM SNEAD, as in 1949, showed his flair for keeping his score going when the wind at Augusta becomes boisterous. He needed only 137 strokes over the first 36 holes, then struggled to a 77 as the wind rose. His final 72 was a triumph in the conditions, and left Jack Burke four strokes out of the title. The Australian, Jim Ferrier, shared third with Al Besselink and Tommy Bolt.

The Masters, despite its distinguished founder and list of winners (and losers) was still not on a level with the two Opens, though many considered it the best run event on the most beautiful course. Since Jimmy Demaret had uniquely won three times he understandably had a very high opionion of it, saying it was the "greatest championship in the world".

**Sam Snead: escaped from Rae's Creek to victory.**

## TEE TALK

### "But the fact is I take cheques with my right hand."

BOBBY LOCKE,
after agreeing that his left hand was weak.

# Ben Hogan sweeps three majors

BY A TOTAL of 15 strokes (four in the British Open, five in the Masters, and six in the US Open) Ben Hogan swept three of the four "modern" majors. The fourth, the US PGA, was out of reach because it clashed with the British Open, an indication of the way the oldest championship of them all had lost its attraction for American players. In any case, a potential week of 36-hole matches would be a great strain on Hogan's damaged legs.

The quality of his runners-up is an endorsement of Hogan's achievement: at the Masters, Sam Snead; at the American Open, naturally, Snead again; at the British Open, Frank Stranahan, Tony Cerda of Argentina, the Australian, Peter Thomson, and Dai Rees.

His second Masters, earned with an Augusta record 14 under par total of 274 was, he thought, "the best four rounds of golf in a tournament I've ever played in."

His fourth American Open, putting him level with Willie Anderson and Bobby Jones, was gained on the 6,916-yard Oakmont course in Pennsylvania which most professionals reckoned to be just as much a monster as Oakland Hills after the Robert Trent Jones revamp. There he opened with 67 to lead all the way, keeping a few flourishes for the finale. He drove the penultimate hole, a 292-yard par four surrounded by choice Oakmont bunkers, and two-putted for a three. On the 72nd hole a five-iron to 15 feet offered the chance of a final birdie. Hogan took it. He had come home in 33 for a total of 283, an Oakmont record.

Persuaded by his compatriots, some of whom had won it, that the British Open would complete his legend, or words to that effect, Hogan set off early for Scotland, and got down to a fortnight of his speciality, course management planning. Carnoustie is the sort of course where such preparation pays off, where position off the tee can be ignored only at the golfer's peril.

John Campbell, the former Scottish international who was Scottish golf correspondent of the "Daily Telegraph", told the author just how meticulous Hogan's preparation was and how little he said while doing it. Hitting several balls to gauge best position was professional routine. Hogan also surveyed the greens meticulously, walked the course backwards and generally took its temperature.

The man they called the "Wee Ice Mon" did not disappoint his British fans, reducing his score round by round, with little to say but the odd request for "cigarette" to his caddie. The outcome was, despite raw and windy weather, a record score (282) for a Carnoustie Open (Henry Cotton's 290 before the war was the previous best).

The only significant stroke of luck Hogan enjoyed was his chip in for a birdie from a bad sandy lie on the fifth in the last round. It put him ahead for the first time.

There were echoes of Jones's great year if only because Hogan played less frequently in 1953 than usual. Hogan put a sting in the tail, though. He made some cutting remarks about Carnoustie when he got home to a ticker-tape welcome on Broadway after the British Open, the third leg of his treble, and did not recommend his caddie, Timms, or keep his promise to defend.

Ben Hogan: watched by caddie Cecil Timms at Carnoustie.

## Worsham, 'the Shot' and the Tube

GEORGE MAY, television and Lew Worsham did a wonderful good turn for golf on Sunday, August 9. May had organized a national telecast (the first of its kind) for his "World Championship" at his Tam O'Shanter club. This enabled about two million people to see a shot with even more immediate dramatic effect than Gene Sarazen's double-eagle at the Masters in 1935. Spectacular as that shot was, it did not there and then win the event for Sarazen. Besides, it was seen by only a handful of people.

What the transfixed two million saw was Lew Worsham's 135-yard wedge shot to the final green, which went into the hole for an eagle and gave Worsham a one-shot $25,000-victory over Chandler Harper, a Virginian like that other renowned runner-up, Sam Snead. Harper must have thought Worsham, also a Virginian, a mite unneighbourly.

Yet it could be only for the greater good of the game that in a few seconds a vast host of people became informed of what golf really was – definitely not the waste of time its detractors, from the early Stuart monarchs to Mark Twain, made it out to be.

## Canada Cup goes south

JOHN JAY Hopkins, a Canadian businessman, filled a hole in the annual fixture lists with his Canada Cup, an international professional team championship, two players per team.

Fittingly, the Cup was first up for competition in Montreal, and it stayed in the Americas, but a long way south of the border, Argentina providing not only the best team but the best individual in Tony Cerda. He and Roberto de Vicenzo put up the winning total of 287. Canada were the runners-up. Only seven teams entered the inaugural event over 36 holes – and Bobby Locke played . . . for England.

## SHORT PUTTS

● Betsy Rawls regained the American Women's Open at Rochester, the first to be overseen by the USGA. She beat Jacqueline Pung from Honolulu in a play-off. Amateurs still outnumbered pros 20-17.

● Walter Burkemo performed an astounding salvage feat in the US PGA final at home in Michigan, beating Felice Torza at the 35th after being seven holes adrift at lunch.

● Babe Zaharias was back on the Tour in August after undergoing surgery for cancer in the spring. Patty Berg had a great year winning seven times and beating Betsy Rawls by nine shots in the Titleholders event.

# Joe Carr turns Amateur tide

AN AMERICAN player had either won the British Amateur or reached the final every year since the war. Indeed, Joe Carr's victory in the final over Harvie Ward, the American holder of the title, ended a sequence of three years in which both finalists had been from the United States. Carr had his moments of good fortune during the championship week at Hoylake, but not in the final in which he finished strongly.

Ward got some measure of revenge by beating Carr in the top Walker Cup single in September at Kittansett, Marion, Massachusetts. A particularly strong defending side was put out by the USGA, including Gene Littler (who won the American Amateur a few days after the Cup match), Charles Coe, Bill Campbell, Dick Chapman and Ken Venturi.

As ever, Ronnie White won his single for the visitors, with three birdies in the last six holes against Chapman, but on the first day he had lost his first Cup point He and Carr went down heavily against Sam Urzetta and Venturi.

White was that happy brand of golfer who seems to produce one fine stroke after another, especially with his irons, without noticeable strain. he was not the best of putters, but made up for that through the green by the relentless accuracy of his approaches. He was runner-up to Gerald Micklem in the English Championship at Royal Birkdale.

Ronnie White: a Walker Cup stalwart.

## TEE TALK

**"You'll never get anywhere fooling around those golf courses."**

CLAIRE HOGAN,
to her teenage son.

**"It was like playing a stretch of golfing territory which had lain untouched by any greenkeeping hand."**

BEN HOGAN,
of Carnoustie.

**"Boy, those undulating fairways fair made me feel seasick."**

LLOYD MANGRUM.

# Ben Hogan out, result normal

DESPITE BEN Hogan's absence from the Ryder Cup team travelling to Wentworth, America won 6-5, with one match halved. After losing the foursomes 3-1, Great Britain were in position to win six singles.

They won only four, after Eric Brown had forced a fine win against the visiting captain, Lloyd Mangrum, and Harry Weetman had come back from four down with six to play to beat Sam Snead at the last hole. Wentworth's par five finishing hole proved fatal to home hopes for two new caps, Peter Alliss and Bernard Hunt, suffered agonies there. Alliss took four to get down from not very far and lost by one hole to Jim Turnesa. Hunt took three putts and let David Douglas escape with a half.

Eric Brown: beat US captain.

Jim Turnesa: let off by Alliss.

# Thomson leads as men from Down Under shine

AUSTRALIANS GATHERED such a haul of trophies that if they had all been placed on the same mantelpiece it would have collapsed into the fireplace. To begin with, Peter Thomson, at 24, became the first Australian to win the British Open title. Though Ben Hogan had said at Carnoustie that he would be back, he did not return, and Thomson, at his third attempt and at a new Open venue, Royal Birkdale on the Lancashire coast, beat Bobby Locke, Dai Rees and Sid Scott by a stroke. Another Australian, Peter Toogood, was leading amateur.

But for the war, Birkdale would have hosted the Open 14 years earlier. There was a not very numerous American representation. Jimmy Demaret and the amateur, Frank Stranahan, were among those present, plus Jim Turnesa come to haunt Peter Alliss, who finished one behind the American again, though in a challenging position, four strokes behind Thomson in joint eighth position. Gene Sarazen and Al Watrous represented the previous generation of American stars.

Locke was the favourite, though, and hounded Thomson

**Thomson: first for Australia.**

throughout. There were minor distinctions for home players, Sid Scott scoring a record 67 on the second day. He added a 69 on the third, his short game as usual seeing him through, to lead with Thomson and Rees, whose scores were identical in each of the first three rounds.

In the last both Scott and Rees fell away to 72, and

**Sid Scott: a record round of 67.**

Thomson, in his uncomplicated smiling way, needed a 71 to overtake the pair of them, and did so with a last putt backhanded into the hole, a cavalier manoeuvre which put a few hearts into mouths.

Locke could still win but lost by one because he, of all people, three-putted twice and then left his putt on the 18th a foot short.

# Sam Snead satisfaction

AFTER THE CLOUDS of glory trailing from Ben Hogan had dispersed a little, Sam Snead responded with a Masters victory in a play-off (70-71) against the great man. The first four rounds produced the highest totals yet seen in the Masters, Snead and Hogan tying on 289. They came within one watery shot of being upstaged by an amateur.

That shot was played, fatally for his chances it transpired, by Billy Joe Patton, from North Carolina, receiving his first Masters invitation. He led at halfway, trailed by five at the three-quarter distance, then, thanks in part to a hole-in-one at the sixth and a birdie at the ninth, where he saved a shot every round, he was ahead again with six holes remaining.

He failed in a gamble to fly the water at the 13th, took seven to get down, then had a six at the 15th, and missed the play-off by a

stroke. Another Patton achievement later in the year was to be the first to be top amateur in the Open three years running.

**Patton: gamble failed.**

# Bachli adds to the haul

LORD BRUCE of Melbourne was waiting to take up office in the autumn as captain of the Royal & Ancient in the club's bicentennial year, as Doug Bachli, from the same Melbourne club as Peter Thomson, emulated him in the amateur field by becoming the first Australian to win the British championship, at Muirfield.

Four different nationalities featured in the semifinals, in which Bachli beat Bill Slark 3 & 2, and Bill Campbell of the United States beat Irishman Joe Carr 3 & 2. The Australian team in Britain for the Commonwealth Tournament at St Andrews won that, too, and Harry Berwick, took the St George's Cup at Sandwich.

Thomson then went on to win the Professional Match Play championship.

# Polly and Co regain the Cup

GREAT BRITAIN and Ireland were captained by Mrs John Beck, wife of the man who led his country's men to victory in the Ryder Cup of 1938, but it was Polly Riley and Mary Lena Faulk who set the tone for the Curtis Cup match at Merion's East Course in Pennsylvania in September.

They beat Frances Stephens and 1952's key winner, Elizabeth Price, 6 & 4. A clean sweep of the foursomes was completed by Claire Doran and Pat Lesser, and Dorothy Kirby and Barbara Romack. Both these matches were won 6 & 5.

The visitors drew the singles, but it was a case of too little and too late. Riley (by 9 & 8 against Price) and Doran won their singles too, and Mrs Howard Smith was brought in to beat Jessie Valentine.

British champion Stephens had an exciting match with Faulk, who drew level on the 35th with a birdie two. Back came Stephens with a 24-foot putt on the last for victory.

## SCORECARD

**British Open** (Royal Birkdale, Lancashire)
PW Thomson  72 71 69 71 283

**US Open** (Baltusrol, NJ)
E Furgol  71 70 71 72 284

**Masters** (Augusta, Ga)
S Snead  74 73 70 72 289

**US PGA** (Keller GC, Minn)
C Harbert bt W Burkemo  4 & 3
Leading US money-winner: R Toski
$65,819.81

**British Amateur** (Muirfield, Scot)
D Bachli bt WC Campbell  2 & 1

**US Amateur** (Detroit CC, Mich)
AD Palmer bt R Sweeny  5 & 4

**US Women's Open** (Peabody, Mass)
Mrs G Zaharias  291

**British Women's Amateur** (Ganton, Yorks)
F Stephens bt E Price  4 & 3

**US Women's Amateur** (Allegheny CC, Sewickley, Pa)
B Romack bt MK Wright  4 & 2

**Canada Cup** (Laval-sur-Lac, Montreal)
Australia (PW Thomson & KDG Nagle)  556

**Curtis Cup** (Merion, Pa)
US 6, GB & Ireland 3

# Ed Furgol beats handicap

Ed Furgol: makes light of bent elbow.

THE HANDICAP that Ed Furgol beat in the US Open was a withered left arm, which was shorter than his right. He could not bend it at the elbow because of a joint smashed in childhood. Though the left arm, for a right-handed player like Furgol, is held to be of prime importance to the golf swing, he compensated for its weakness in champion style to finish a stroke ahead of Gene Littler, who had won the Amateur the previous year and led at halfway.

Furgol, 37, kept his head at the last hole, where he drove into the woods. The Open was on the Lower course at Baltusrol. Furgol got out of trouble by playing on to the Upper course, from there achieving the five that gave him the title. Furgol's prize was $6,000, treble that won by Cary Middlecoff only five years previously. Bobby Locke was fifth and Ben Hogan joint sixth because of a 76 in round three.

The USGA had been quick to follow George May's example. This 54th Open was the first to go out on the national television network. The entry reached a record 1,928.

Despite his severe handicap, Furgol had been out of the top 60 on the Tour only twice since the end of the war. He finished 1954 by being named Player of the Year. His triumph at Baltusrol was seen not only on television but by the biggest crowds yet, nearly 40,000 on a completely roped-off course.

Kel Nagle: Thomson aide.

# Nagle helps Thomson to pro double

KEL NAGLE, born in 1920, did not turn pro till 1946, but proved an admirable aide to Peter Thomson as Australia relieved Argentina of the Canada Cup in the second year of the competition, held in Montreal again, but this time at Laval-sur-Lac.

Roberto de Vicenzo and Tony Cerda had won the inaugural Cup tournament over 36 holes. Now they were second in a revamped event, played over 72 holes. The respective scores were 556 to 560. Stan Leonard of Canada took over from Cerda as the individual winner with a score of 275.

**"Sometimes when I putted I looked like a monkey trying to wrestle a football."**

SAM SNEAD.

# Babe's comeback

BABE ZAHARIAS had a busy 12 months, the more onerous because of her need to recruit her strength after her cancer surgery of the previous year. A dispute between the LPGA players and Fred Corcoran had led to Fred's resignation, and Mrs Zaharias, the president, took over his job in February. Betty Hicks in turn took over from her before long.

Meanwhile The Babe started to win tournaments. Her main purpose was to capture a third Open title, and in the heat of summer she made a great start with rounds of 72 and 71 at Salem, Massachusetts, to lead Betsy Rawls by seven shots. On the final morning her playing partner was Mickey Wright, Girls' champion in 1952. Mrs Zaharias returned a 73 and, though her game became more than a little wayward in the afternoon, she still came home with 12 strokes to spare. She said that she wanted to show colostomy sufferers (for her surgery had been for cancer of the bowel) that the operation could return people to a normal life.

The prize money for the LPGA Tour surpassed $100,000. Louise Suggs took a good slice of it, $12,061, winning five times including the Titleholder Championship, in which she finished seven shots clear of the field at Augusta Country Club with a record 293 total.

# Palmer gets home in a thriller

ARNOLD PALMER, playing out of Pine Ridge, Ohio, had his first success in a national event on August 28, beating Robert Sweeny at the 36th hole of a cut-and-thrust American Amateur final at Detroit Country Club.

Palmer, 24, from Latrobe and educated at Wake Forest, had beaten Frank Stranahan 4 & 3 on the way.

Crowd control was now a must at amateur events, too, and this was the first championship at which all the fairways were roped off.

# Babe Zaharias, athlete of the century

**The greatest all-round sportswoman of modern times – Olympic gold medallist in track and field events, tennis and basketball player – she brought to the game of golf the same outstanding skills as to her other activities, winning every major women's title**

I T IS FAIRLY safe to describe Babe Zaharias as the "athlete of the century". Little time remains for another person, man or woman, to set world athletic records and then win major golf titles on both sides of the Atlantic. The Babe did both.

From her teens, Mildred Ella Didrikson, her maiden name, was a blend of versatile talent and confidence that beggars belief. She was born at Port Arthur, Texas, on June 26, 1914, and grew up in Beaumont, where she acquired the nickname "Babe" because, like Babe Ruth, she could clout home runs better than any girl – or boy – the competition could field.

Young Didrikson (her father was Norwegian, and a carpenter, whose name was Didriksen, which his daughter, the sixth of seven children, later amended) could also run, jump and throw. At 16 years of age she broke the world javelin record with 133 feet 3 1/4 inches (40.63 metres).

## Incredible Olympian

It is not fanciful to say that her sports career went downhill from July 16, 1932, the day of the American Olympic trials meeting. She performed all manner of wonders in the years ahead, but after that day of days, what could even the great Zaharias do to trump the following feats?

She entered eight of the ten events staged. She won the 80-metre hurdles, baseball throw, shot putt, long jump and javelin. She was equal first in the high jump and fourth in the discus. She set three world records in the process, and alone won the team competition. Illinois Athletic Club, with a full complement of competitors, came second.

It was scarcely surprising, therefore, that in the subsequent Los Angeles Olympic Games, in which she was allowed to enter only three events, she won gold medals in hurdles and javelin and silver in the high jump.

Her 11.7 seconds for the hurdles final broke the world record which she had equalled earlier in the Games. If she had been com-

**Golden girl: Mildred Didrickson (right) in the Los Angeles hurdles**

peting today, she would also have won gold in the high jump, for she equalled the world record with 5 feet 5 1/4 inches (1.66 metres) but was obliged to forfeit first place because the judges did not approve of her unorthodox head-first technique.

Rhonda Glenn's "Illustrated History of Women's Golf" adds to the Didrikson compendium of life-enhancing skills such items as lacrosse, billiards, diving, fencing, skating, 100 words a minute typing, cooking and sewing. She tap-danced and played the harmonica in vaudeville and, even before the athletics extravaganza, Didrikson was gaining national selection at basketball.

For all this, The Babe's image

in the back of most minds involves a woman of no great size or height out-hitting men from golf tees. She stood five feet seven inches, and was possessed, for her size and inconsiderable girth, of immense strength. This and her undeniably plain features made life difficult for her.

The public were looking for another Glenna Collett – reserved, refined, stylish. Didrikson was none of these things, and many of the golfing set looked down on her for it, especially when she began to out-play everyone in sight.

The question hinted at was one of gender definition, and her greatest golfing years came, significantly, with the support and

devotion of George Zaharias, the wrestler and so-so golfer. This huge and affable man made Didrikson, not very big to start with, look thoroughly petite. She first met him as partner in a pro-am event in 1938 and they were married the same year.

Yet she needed considerable courage to up her game in spite of the early groundswell against her. After losing to her in the state championship final of 1935, Peggy Chandler and her husband Dan reported her to the USGA for rule violation and Didrikson lost her amateur status, for having played other games as a professional (namely, baseball and basketball), not a disqualifying factor nowadays.

She was also declared a professional by the lawn tennis authorities. Her husband's income as a wrestler enabled her to win pro events and refuse the prize money, and so to apply for reinstatement as an amateur. But this application was not granted till well after the United States had entered the Second World War, which meant further waiting to re-enter competitive golf.

## A great professional

In the meantime she made the best of things in the few professional events open to her, and played exhibition matches. It is a curiosity that, while the four greatest male golfers, Vardon, Jones, Hogan and Nicklaus, were never, through the dictates of time, able to measure their best talents one against the other, Joyce Wethered, the woman Jones thought the best golfer, man or woman, he had ever seen, played briefly with Didrikson. Moreover, Didrikson, towards the end of her career, played with Mickey Wright, the third of the leading women players in the game's history, at the beginning of hers.

Wethered played exhibition matches with Didrikson in the mid-1930s in company with Horton Smith and Gene Sarazen. The Englishwoman had long ago given up championship play, and was out-hit by Didrikson but not

### TEE TALK

## "Honey, I don't care if you send it out and get it dry-cleaned."

to a player asking for relief from casual water.

outscored, for the finer points of the game were as yet not within the Texan's compass.

Back into competitive play, she won whole strings of tournaments as her game tightened up, and took her national Amateur title in 1947, following up the next year with the British.

She had become particularly good at not slipping up on the short-to-medium-range putts that make or mar a score. For a woman of great strength, which compensated for her less than classic or complete follow-through, she achieved a most delicate touch in the short game, and with these attributes and her huge length off the tee, none could dispute a newspaper judgment that she was "a crushing and heart-breaking opponent."

## Tour publicist

Professional offers too good to refuse put her back in the paid ranks in 1947. In any case, her next role was inescapable, that of great publicist for the growth of the women's professional tour. Appointing Fred Corcoran as her manager was a purposeful forward step in this endeavour, and Corcoran claimed that she was earning a six-figure annual income.

With Patty Berg, Corcoran and friends Didrikson helped the women's tour on to a steep upward curve by the early 1950s, and she was a prime mover in the foundation of the Ladies' Professional Golfers' Association. Some of her fellow professionals found it hard to take her assumption of stardom. There was a strange and unpredictable mixture of braggadocio and kindliness for her fellow pros, but her effect on gate money was entirely predictable and beneficial. She could and did demand appearance money which, again, did not endear her to players who were unable to command media attention as she always could, but who could on their day beat her.

Didrikson was learning all the time, and her technique became more polished with the help of Tommy Armour's coach-

**Victory ceremony: Didrickson on top, with Evelyne Hall (left), also of the United States, and Marjorie Clark of South Africa.**

**Didrickson speciality: the javelin in which she struck gold.**

### SCORECARD

**US Women's Open**
1948, 1950, 1954

**US Women's Amateur**
1946

**British Women's Amateur**
1947

31 US wins

ing. Though she was a frequent winner, there came a time as the 1950s advanced when Betsy Rawls and the accurate stroke play of Louise Suggs, not to mention the combative Patty Berg, began to push Didrikson out of the leading position in women's golf. At the beginning of the new decade she won the Open for the second time, plus four other tournaments out of a total of 11 on the tour. She won seven events the next year, and four in 1952, beating the Curtis Cup star Polly Riley 7 & 6 in one final.

## Fighter to the end

She had won twice in 1953 then, after much urging, she sought medical advice about stomach pains, and bowel surgery was necessary for cancer. It was not long before she recovered to the extent of setting her sights on another Open, but in the interim, for this formidable athlete to be too weak to last out a round of golf was a psychological blow of a magnitude difficult for the normally gifted to comprehend.

Didrikson conquered her weakness and began winning again in 1954, her rehabilitation reaching a climax, not without some wearying and worrying moments in the final round, with victory in the Open by a distance. She spoke of having 20 more years and of her recovery having meaning for the thousands of sufferers who had written about their illness and hers. She struggled on against the implacable enemy within, winning her last tournament in the spring of 1955. The next 18 months were a patchwork of hospital stays and treatment, and she died on September 27, 1956, aged 42.

Her Fort Worth friend and confidante, Bertha Bowen, tells how on Boxing Day the previous year they drove out, at Babe's request, to Colonial Country Club. In bathrobe and pyjamas the golfer, with difficulty, walked on to the second green and put her palm flat on the grass. "I just wanted to see a golf course one more time," said The Babe.

# Jack Fleck the speechless champion

THE WINNER of the US Open championship a municipal course pro called what? From where? Davenport, Iowa? And he beat Ben Hogan in a play-off? Yes, it was difficult to persuade seekers after news on the evening of June 19 that an unknown from the outback had outplayed the world's greatest golfer, and parted him from what would have been a record fifth Open title.

Jack Fleck, the cause of eyebrow-lifting from Maine to Sausolito, found it hard to believe, too, and was struck so dumb by his victory that the 1954 champion, Ed Furgol, guided him through interviews at the Olympic Country Club, San Francisco, and gave the responses he thought Fleck should make, and Furgol would know, having upset the odds the previous year, when Gene Littler was supposed to win.

Fleck was on his first full year on the PGA tour, though he had turned pro before the war. His victory was not out of that old golfing cliché, beware the sick golfer, but more the golfer whose

game was sick. Fleck's was – up to and including practice rounds. Nor did his first round (76) give many clues. The USGA had gone further than usual in trying golfers' patience this time, with spreading trees and narrower fairways.

The effect of Fleck's second round of 69 was dissipated by his third of 75 and, because Hogan

finished with his best round of 70 on the final afternoon for a total of 287, and nobody of note could be discerned behind him, Open No 5 seemed to be his. Only Fleck, it transpired, had a chance, and at the death he needed a birdie three at the last to tie. A poor drive was followed by a great approach, and Fleck had done it. Next day he was well in

charge by the turn and ground out a lead of three holes. Hogan got back to one stroke behind, then he lost his footing and a catastrophic drive from the 18th tee went into rough, from which he did not emerge and took a six (which was creditable in view of the drive), to lose to Fleck's par four by three strokes. Only seven scores below 70 were returned. Fleck put in three of them.

Hogan can have gained only a modicum of consolation from the ironic fact that Fleck who at 32 was 11 years Hogan's junior, achieved his scores with a set of Ben Hogan golf clubs.

Sam Snead was also into the golf equipment business, giving his name to a device that allowed the adjustment of the club's lie and loft.

Jack Fleck: landed Open with a set of Ben Hogan clubs.

## Peter Thomson smiles for TV

THE LAST DAY of the British Open at St Andrews was covered by BBC television, eight years after the USGA brought the game into the cathode tube age by local coverage of their Open at St Louis.

Peter Thomson smiled as happily as ever, and continued to disguise the fact, as he retained his title, that it was rather more than a stroll, even with his straight driving, unfussy mastery of iron play and dependable putting. With more than half the century gone, Thomson was one of only five players who had won two Opens in succession.

True, the American competition was not overwhelming, though Byron Nelson was on one of his occasional forays into big golf. George Fazio, who had the distinction of losing a play-off with Ben Hogan, Ed Furgol and Johnny Bulla were also among those present, Bulla still grieving perhaps over his near misses just before and after the war.

Henry Cotton, paired with Thomson on the first day, beat him by a stroke with 70 and was only one behind the three joint leaders, Eric Brown, Sid Scott and

Dai Rees, who at once ruined his chances with 79 in round two. Cotton had a poor last day, though, and finished well down the field, level with Nelson and 15 shots behind Thomson.

The Scot, Johnny Fallon, got closest to Thomson in the end, but the champion was seldom in danger of being parted from his title because the players best placed to challenge after round three, notably Frank Jowle and Harry Weetman, both finished with 74s. Furgol, who like Hagen before him was not over-impressed with the clubhouse facilities, was the best placed American, 11 shots shy.

St Andrews is so strewn with hazards that cannot be seen from the tee that even the best professionals have to seek out a caddie who is familiar with every whin and sand-trap. Thomson had the services of one of the best, Wallace Gillespie. Peter Alliss tells how one Thomson drive was found perilously close to a bunker.

Thomson pointed out he was using a golf club, not a rifle, to which Gillespie retorted: "Well you *are* the Open Champion."

## Harvie Ward's majestic final

HARVIE WARD, at 29, hit his finest vein of form in the final of the US Amateur at the James River course in Richmond.

He was five up on William Hyndman III after the first nine holes, which he covered in an approximate 31 shots, and eight up by lunchtime, his morning score being on the 66 mark. Ward was soon home thereafter, by 9 & 8.

Ward was winning at his ninth attempt. Chick Evans was making his 43rd appearance in the championship, which he first entered 48 years before and had won twice. Despite advancing years, he won nearly twice as many matches as he lost.

Jack Nicklaus, aged 15, from Scioto, Ohio, where he broke 70 several years previously, was making his first appearance in the Amateur. He lost in the first round to Robert Gardner.

Jessie Valentine was too good for Barbara Romack in the British Women's Amateur at Royal Portrush, where by 7 & 6 she won her second final. Her first was back in 1937.

# Ryder and Walker go west again

THE GRIM catalogue of failure by Britain and Ireland in both the Walker and Ryder Cup matches was continued, both matches being stamped with the Stars and Stripes after the first day four-somes, which the American amateurs won 4-0 at St Andrews and the professionals 3-1 at the Thunderbird Ranch and Country Club, Palm Springs, California.

Putting failures had cost Bernard Hunt and Peter Alliss their Ryder Cup places, and new cap John Jacobs repaid the selectors with two of the losers' four points, for he and Johnny Fallon beat Melvin "Chick" Harbert and Jerry Barber by one hole, and Jacobs squeezed home again at the last against Cary Middlecoff, the reigning Masters champion.

Arthur Lees was building a good record, he and Eric Brown, who had yet to lose in singles, providing the other two points. However, Tommy Bolt, Harbert, Sam Snead, Johnny Burke and Doug Ford all won several holes from home, and the 8-4 American advantage was comfortably gained.

When hitherto dependable Ronnie White lost in both the top foursome and top single in the Walker Cup match at St Andrews, the home side's number was potentially up, and so it proved, 10-2.

Moreover, the United States had plenty to spare: their losses, to David Blair and Ian Caldwell, were by one hole, their wins as much as 6 & 5. White's conqueror, by that very score, Harvie Ward, was reckoned as the world's leading amateur.

John Jacobs: repaid Ryder selectors with two points.

## TEE TALK

"... the most famous and infamous ... if one built such a hole today you would be sued for incompetence."

PETER THOMSON,
on the 17th (Road Hole) at St Andrews.

"Lay off for three weeks ... then quit for good."

SAM SNEAD,
to a pupil.

Tommy Bolt: Cup success with holes to spare.

# Middlecoff's Masterly 65

CARY MIDDLECOFF got a stranglehold on the Masters with a record-breaking 65 in the second round, and he had no trouble in holding off Ben Hogan, which he did at arm's length so to speak by seven shots at the finish. Sam Snead was third, one behind Hogan.

Middlecoff's second round record was decorated with a 75-foot putt for an eagle at the 13th and a birdie at the 15th.

## SCORECARD

**British Open** (St Andrews, Scot)
PW Thomson 71 68 70 72 281

**US Open** (Olympic CC, San Francisco, Cal)
J Fleck 76 69 75 67 287
(Play-off: Fleck 69, B Hogan 72)

**Masters** (Augusta, Ga)
C Middlecoff 72 65 72 70 279

**US PGA** (Meadowbrook CC, Detroit, Mich)
D Ford bt C Middlecoff 4 & 3
US leading money-winner: J Boros $63,121.55

**British Amateur** (Royal Lytham, Lancs)
J Conrad bt A Slater 3 & 2

**US Amateur** (Virginia CC, Richmond, Va)
EH Ward bt W Hyndman III 9 & 8

**US Women's Open** (Wichita CC, Kans)
F Crocker 299

**British Women's Amateur** (R Portrush, Co Antrim, N Ire)
J Valentine bt B Romack 7 & 6

**US Women's Amateur** (Myers Park CC, Charlotte, NC)
P Lesser bt J Nelson 7 & 6

**Canada Cup** (Washington, DC)
US (C Harbert & E Furgol) 560.
(Individual): Furgol (after play-off with PW Thomson and F van Donck) 279

**Ryder Cup** (Palm Springs, Cal)
US 8, GB & Ireland 4

**Walker Cup** (St Andrews, Scot)
US 10, GB & Ireland 2

Boros: a $63,121.55 year.

# Thomson finds form and lands hat-trick

THREE BRITISH Opens in a row was no small matter when Bob Ferguson was the last to achieve it, in 36-hole competitions, 74 years ago. Peter Thomson's three in a row, completed at Royal Liverpool, was a much more difficult undertaking, achieved against much bigger fields gathering from many lands and playing over 72 holes.

Despite this, Thomson had not at any time in the British Open faced anything like the full firepower of a representative entry of front-rank American professionals.

Moreover, he had just returned from Wentworth where he and Kel Nagle, representing Australia, had been second best in the Canada Cup to two of the outstanding players of the day in the world of golf, Ben Hogan and Sam Snead, who had won by 14 strokes. Hogan took the individual prize while Thomson had suffered an 82. Neither Hogan nor Snead stayed on for the Open.

All the same Thomson, who three weeks before the British Open had finished joint fourth in the US Open, three off Cary Middlecoff's winning pace and one behind joint runner-up Hogan, could not have chosen a more challenging course on which to seek his hat-trick. Hoylake does not look tigerish, but on better, or worse, acquaintance, has several holes which inflict the most severe punishment for small errors in line or length. Thomson's principal rival, Bobby Locke, began with a 76,

and did not survive into round three. Thomson, by contrast the soul of calm consistency, started with a 70, and on the second day rode his luck in the draw, which sentenced early starters to a buffeting and a wetting, but allowed him to tour the course for another 70 strokes in the dry, with a lively breeze as his only distraction. This brought a novel look to the leader board, with Thomson one ahead of two Argentines, Roberto de Vicenzo and Enrico Bertolino.

The two best-known Americans in the field were Frank Stranahan and Mike Souchak, who had scored a 60 en route to a PGA record 257 a year earlier in the Texas Open at Brackenridge Park, a course renowned for playing short and producing spectacular scores. Both were eight behind Thomson at halfway. A third round of 72 strengthened Thomson's position, Flory van Donck now trailing him by three, and in fourth place Henry Cotton, aged 49.

Thomson's cares were much diminished over the last 18 holes when van Donck found the out of bounds right away on the first hole; 37 out and 37 back gave Thomson the Open by three shots from van Donck, whose ball stayed out of the hole several times after he hit the stick. De Vicenzo was third, and a young, small and slight South African called Gary Player finished fourth. A poor round of 76 on the blustery second day had ruined his chances.

Frank Stranahan: strong challenge to Peter Thomson.

# Amateur Venturi lets in Jack Burke

KEN VENTURI, a protégé of Byron Nelson, looked odds on to become the first amateur winner of the Masters till Jack Burke began to close on him over the final nine holes, and a succession of bogeys chipped away at the four-stroke lead Venturi had over the field at the three-quarter mark. His lead over Burke had been eight.

This vanished in no time as Venturi bogeyed every hole but the 13th from the 10th to the 15th. A three at the 17th by Burke was decisive, especially as Cary Middlecoff double bogeyed the 16th. Burke, a consistent money-winner on tour, was born in Fort

Worth, where Hogan made his home.

Burke was second only to Byron Nelson in the matter of a record number of consecutive Tour victories, though Nelson's run extended to 11, Burke's only to four.

The 1956 Masters was the first to be televised and by CBS, not NBC, who had covered on radio from the beginning. This was because CBS were willing to obey the wishes of the organising spirit of the event, Clifford Roberts, who decreed that TV commercials during the Masters should be limited. It showed the event's drawing power.

# Burke plays catch-up again

JACK BURKE added the US PGA title to his haul of victories in very much the same way as he won the Masters in the spring, by making up for early mistakes to overtake his opponents. He was one of a record field of 128, and beat Ted Kroll in the final at Blue Hill Country Club, near Boston. Burke was an unrivalled candidate for player of the year. Kroll's consolation was to be leading money-winner, with more than $70,000.

The total prize money on the Tour soared to $847,000. Far from hustling for layer cake prizes and other insubstantial rewards at a handful of winter events, the professionals were winning large cheques at 36 events throughout the year.

Jack Burke: beat off amateur.

# Frances Smith clinches Curtis Cup

SOMETHING had to give in the last match to finish in the Curtis Cup at Prince's, Sandwich, on June 9. It was between players with perfect singles records in Cup matches, Britain and Ireland's Frances Smith (née Stephens) and Polly Riley.

The previous day, which was cold, wet and windy, the United States had won the foursomes 2-1. Big wins in singles by Jessie Valentine, Angela Ward and Elizabeth Price brought the scores level, Margaret Smith (9 & 8 against Philomena Garvey) and Barbara Romack having won for the visitors.

Frances Smith lost her lead to Riley on the 32nd and 34th, but holed out for par on the last, where Riley went one over, giving Britain and Ireland the single 4-2 and the match 5-4.

Polly Riley, a Curtis Cup regular from 1948, playing in every match, never lost until the Prince's defeat. She was a formidable match player.

**Frances Smith: gained crucial Curtis Cup point.**

**Jessie Valentine: much at ease in the singles.**

# Middlecoff holds off Hogan and Boros

ONE AFTER another Cary Middlecoff's pursuers in the American Open set their sights on his one over par total of 281 at Oak Hill Country Club, at Rochester, New York. First came Ben Hogan, intent on a record fifth Open. His putting, never his strongest suit, let him down. A putt of a little over two feet stayed out at the penultimate hole, and the three pars finish he needed to catch Middlecoff was beyond him.

Boros got those three pars, but lacked the one birdie over that stretch that would have given him parity with Middlecoff. Ted Kroll plummeted to joint fourth through dropping five shots on the last four holes, to join British Open champion Peter Thomson and Ed Furgol. All three had taken four shots too many, and two shots behind them came Arnold Palmer in his best finish yet in a major. Henry Cotton, joint 17th, won $260, two ahead of Sam Snead.

# Ladies make progress

NEARLY 50 YEARS after the granting of female suffrage, relations at Woking between the sexes improved to the extent that at an extraordinary general meeting new rules were promulgated which allowed lady members all the privileges "not expressly reserved by the rules of Woking Golf Club to Ordinary Members, subject to the right of the Committee to restrict the hours when Lady Members may play on the course." The president, Tony Tate, proposed the resolution passed at the meeting and experienced coolness in his relations with one or two of the extreme male reactionaries.

Nevertheless the end of the war had seen improvements in communication between the club and the ladies, who were even consulted about the appointment of the new professional, John Stirling. The women's biggest nettle was their status as "temporary members".

# Zaharias death casts a shadow over the year

THE WORLD of women's golf in the United States was saddened by the death of Babe Zaharias. She had re-entered hospital in the spring, and again in July, continuing her struggle against cancer, but died early on on September 27. She was 42.

The feeling on all sides as she was buried at Beaumont, Texas, where she had grown up was that women's golf in general and the LPGA tour in particular would never replace her star quality, the crowd-pulling magnetism of her bold approach to the game of golf. Moves began to set up a Zaharias Cancer Fund.

As a first move, a Babe Zaharias Cancer Fund Open was staged and won by Betsy Rawls. A tournament was also named after Rawls, and she went to her native Spartanburg, South Carolina, to win it . . . the Betsy Rawls Peach Blossom Open.

Rawls had the tecnhical know-how about how a golf ball should behave: she had degrees in maths and physics.

## SCORECARD

**British Open** (Royal Liverpool, Lancashire)
PW Thomson 70 70 72 74 286

**US Open** (Oak Hill, Rochester, NY)
C Middlecoff 71 70 70 70 281

**Masters** (Augusta, Ga)
J Burke 72 71 75 71 289

**US PGA** (Blue Hill CC, Mass)
J Burke bt T Kroll 3 & 2
Leading US money-winner: T Kroll $72,835.83

**British Amateur** (Troon, Scot)
J Beharrell bt L Taylor 5 & 4

**US Amateur** (Knollwood, Ill)
EH Ward bt C Kocsis 5 & 4

**US Women's Open** (Northland CC, Duluth, Minn)
Mrs K Cornelius 302
(Play-off): Mrs Cornelius 75, B McIntire 82

**British Women's Amateur** (Sunningdale, Surrey)
M Smith bt MP Janssen 8 & 7

**US Women's Amateur** (Meridian Hills CC, Ind)
M Stewart bt J Gunderson 2 & 1

**Canada Cup** (Wentworth, Surrey)
US (B Hogan & S Snead) 567
(Individual): Hogan 277

**Curtis Cup** (Prince's, Sandwich, Kent)
GB & Ireland 5, US 4

## TEE TALK

**"Nobody wins the Open: it wins you."**

CARY MIDDLECOFF.

**"Any player can win a US Open, but it takes a helluva player to win two."**

WALTER HAGEN.

## SHORT PUTTS

● American Curtis Cup player Margaret Smith carried on the tradition of her country's Walker Cup team by providing the winner of the British Women's Amateur championship, beating Mary Janssen 8 & 7 at Sunningdale.

● John Beharrell became, at a few weeks over 18, the youngest winner of the British Amateur at Troon, beating Leslie Taylor, a member of the host club, 5 & 4 in the final. Another first was that the last three rounds were all played over 36 holes.

# Dai Rees & Co turn Ryder tide

BRITAIN AND IRELAND could win only one foursome in the Ryder Cup match at Lindrick, the beautifully turfed Nottinghamshire course, but lost only one single, and gained their first victory in 34 years by 7-4, with one match halved.

The one factor which, for some, marred this long-coveted victory was the partisan quality of support for the home side. The match, sponsored by Sir Stuart Goodwin, attracted enormous crowds. But while Tommy Bolt of the American team declared: "Good relations – don't make me sick", the US PGA president, Harry Moffitt, said that other team members disagreed, and that the crowds had been very fair.

There was no gainsaying the quality of the British response to the reverses of the first day, during which only Dai Rees, the Britain and Ireland captain, and Ken Bousfield won, by 3 & 2 over Art Wall and Fred Hawkins. Bousfield was back in the side after missing two Cup matches. Peter Alliss and Bernard Hunt were also back after their 1953 Wentworth misfortunes, and they lost at the 35th against Masters champion Doug Ford and Dow Finsterwald. Ted Kroll and Jack Burke beat Max Faulkner and Harry Weetman 4 & 3, Christy O'Connor and Eric Brown losing 7 & 5 to the newly crowned American Open champion Dick Mayer and Tommy Bolt.

Brown gave the home team the best of starts by keeping up his 100 per cent Cup singles record, beating Bolt by 4 & 3. After a team debate, Faulkner and Weetman were not called upon in the singles. Weetman issued a statement that he would never again play in a team captained by Rees. This led to his being suspended by the PGA for a year, a sentence later reduced at the insistence of Rees.

Instead, new cap Peter Mills

Dai Rees: a winner first and last for the Great Britain & Ireland in the Ryder Cup.

followed up Brown's effort by beating the American captain Burke 5 & 3 and the Irish veteran, Harry Bradshaw, brought in by Rees as the home team's tail-gunner, got a half out of Mayer.

Apart from Alliss, who again drew blank and was beaten at the 35th by the journeyman tour player Hawkins, the other four singles all finished in favour of Britain and Ireland some way from home. Bousfield won 4 & 3 against Lionel Hebert, Rees 7 & 6 against Ed Furgol, Hunt 6 & 5 against Ford and O'Connor 7 & 6 against Finsterwald. Significantly, no American won twice, and that had not happened for 24 years.

This Cup was a new pinnacle in Rees's career.

## USGA get tough again

JACQUELINE PUNG, a Hawaiian player with a big smile and a comfortable figure, was lowest scorer in the American Women's Open at Winged Foot, New York. But Betsy Rawls was declared champion for the third time when it was discovered that while Mrs Pung's last round total was cor-

rect on her card, marked by playing partner Betty Jameson, her fourth hole score was recorded as a five, but she had taken six. Club members, spectators and officials at once had a whip-round and raised $3,000 for the disqualified Mrs Pung, $1,200 more than the first prize.

---

### SCORECARD

**British Open** (St Andrews, Scot)
AD Locke 69 72 68 70  279

**US Open** (Inverness, Toledo, Ohio)
R Mayer 70 68 74 70  282
(Play-off): Mayer 72, C Middlecoff 79

**Masters** (Augusta, Ga)
D Ford 72 73 72 66  273

**US PGA** (Miami Valley, Ohio)
L Hebert bt D Finsterwald 3 & 1
Leading US money-winner: R Mayer $65,835

**British Amateur** (Formby, Merseyside)
R Reid Jack bt HB Ridgeley 2 & 1

**US Amateur** (Brookline, Mass)
H Robbins bt Dr FM Taylor 5 & 4

**US Women's Open** (Winged Foot, NY)
B Rawls 299

**British Women's Amateur** (Gleneagles, Scot)
P Garvey bt J Valentine 4 & 3

**US Women's Amateur** (Del Paso CC, Sacramento, Cal)
J Gunderson bt L Johnstone 8 & 6

**Canada Cup** (Tokyo)
Japan (T Nakamura & K Ono) 567
(Individual): Nakamura 274

**Ryder Cup** (Lindrick, Notts)
GB 7½, US 4½

**Walker Cup** (Minikahda, Minn)
US 8½, GB & Ireland 3½

---

Philomena Garvey: British Open and Irish Championship Cup winner in 1957.

## Mayer's Open play-off

DICK MAYER from Florida beat Cary Middlecoff in a play-off for the US Open after the professionals were again threatened by amateur Billy Joe Patton, who shared the lead with Mayer at halfway with a record 138.

# Locke blocks Thomson 1-2-3-4

**Bobby Locke: fourth British Open by three strokes.**

THE COLONIAL golf wars continued in the British Open at St Andrews, this time South Africa, in the comfortable shape of Bobby Locke, holding off Australia's Peter Thomson by three strokes. The championship was switched at the last minute from Muirfield because of complications brought about by oil shortages following the British and French invasion of Suez.

American visitors were thin on the ground and relations with the United States were not at their best after Suez. Moreover, the financial incentive to cross the Atlantic was not strong. Still, Cary Middlecoff, runner-up in the American Open to Dick Mayer, came and so did Frank Stranahan. Neither figured in the finale, Middlecoff putting poorly. The Scot Eric Brown started off with a great rush, holing putts from any given distance and scoring threes galore. He and Laurie Ayton led with 67s, but Locke had a 69, and was still nicely placed two behind Brown, one behind Flory van Donck and, more importantly as it turned out, one in front of Thomson after 36 holes.

Locke's putter ruled thereafter, his third round of 68 putting him three clear of Thomson and Brown. Locke had single putts at four holes going out, and though he three-putted the 13th he came home in 36.

Television and the public liked the new format of play, in which, for the first time, the leading players went out last. Thomson was eager to emulate Young Tom Morris's four in a row, but he could do no better than Locke, who followed him in with 70.

Controversy, smoothly defused by the Championship Committee, ensued. Locke had moved his marker to one side on the final hole to give his playing partner a clear putt and then, in the excitement of his victorious moment, forgot to measure the requisite putter-head length back to the original resting place of his penultimate shot. He then two- putted from a yard or so for a four. This was noticed on newsreel film, but the Committee's conclusion was that Locke had gained no advantage. He could have borne a two-stroke penalty. So the result would stand.

**Locke in action at St Andrews: controversial finale.**

# Expenses row rules out Ward hat-trick

HARVIE WARD was in line for a hat-trick of American Amateur titles at Brookline in September, but in June came a bitter blow – the loss of his amateur status.

Ward, who won the British Amateur in 1952 and had plenty to spare in the American finals of 1955 and 1956, was found guilty by the USGA of having his expenses paid by his employer, Eddie E. Lowery, a San Francisco car dealer, at two tournaments in 1954. Lowery gave evidence to this effect to a grand jury in a tax evasion case in May.

Had Lowery increased Ward's salary, no charge could have been levelled against the golfer, widely recognized as the best amateur since Bobby Jones, though he had not managed to win the Open. Johnny Goodman was the fifth and last amateur to do so, in 1933. Two months before the loss of his amateur status, Ward finished fourth in the Masters, five strokes behind the winner, Doug Ford, and one in front of the reigning British Open champion, Peter Thomson.

Harvie Ward's punishment was announced on June 7: loss of amateur status for one year. The Amateur championship was won by Hillman Robbins, at The Country Club, Brookline, Mass. His opponent in the final was Dr Frank Taylor who the previous week had won both his single and his foursome against Great Britain in the Walker Cup.

The media attention given to the case was all the greater since Eddie E. Lowery was a member of the USGA Executive Committee.

Lowery was also the very same Eddie Lowery who, aged ten, carried Francis Ouimet's clubs at Brookline in 1913 when he defeated Harry Vardon and Ted Ray in a play-off for the US Open.

# Palmer's Masters and the million-dollar Tour

ARNOLD PALMER'S arrival as winner of a major title and the fact that the PGA Tour now offered prize money of more than a million dollars, double the 1953 total, cannot be identified as cause and effect. However, by the end of the year his fans may well have believed devoutly that there was such a connection.

Palmer, at 28 the youngest Masters winner since Byron Nelson in 1937, was a hot golfer when he arrived at Augusta. He had started the year with minor placings for a few hundred dollars at Los Angeles and the Crosby, then came second at

Tijuana, missed the cut at Phoenix and Houston, was second at Baton Rouge, third at New Orleans, 12th at Pensacola, won at St Petersburg and lost a play-off by a stroke to Howie Johnson in the Azalea.

Golf galleries had found cheeky Walter Hagen amusing, Bobby Jones inspiring and, more recently, they and the newly opened eye of television looked with awe upon the perfection of Ben Hogan's shot-making.

Now they gazed with mounting admiration and affection upon Palmer, who acted out the battle of man versus golf course

with no attempt to mask his feelings, be they of joy or despair. He always seemed to be on the attack, smashing away enormous drives, bringing off amazing recoveries, in fact a Hollywood and television director's dream of a golfer. It was easy to tell which one Palmer was: he was the one hitching up his trousers every now and then.

Palmer's Masters victory, however, turned on a ticklish point in the rules: whether he was entitled to a preferred lie when his ball was embedded in its own pitch mark on a bank, not fairway, behind the short 12th.

His playing partner, Ken Venturi, who had already won three times on the winter tour, suggested that the ball was not in its own pitch mark. Be that as it may, Palmer played his shot as it lay, then from a preferred lie, getting a five and a three repectively, a ruling to be made later.

Palmer then eagled the 13th and, with birdies on the last two holes and a favourable ruling on the incident at the 12th, beat Fred Hawkins and Doug Ford by a stroke. Palmer went on to make nine more top ten finishes, and become leading money-winner on the Tour.

# Thomson's fourth Open in five years

LIKE ARNOLD PALMER at Augusta, Peter Thomson was, at 28, in most menacing form as he prepared to regain his British Open title at Royal Lytham. He broke the course record of 67 by four strokes in qualifying, and in the Open proper started with a 68. Gene Sarazen, who had played here in 1923 with Harry Vardon, qualified easily, and finished level with Bobby Locke and Max Faulkner on 288, ten behind Thomson.

David Thomas, two behind after 54 holes, started with a bang with a long putt on the first hole for a two and forced a play-off. Brown, Christy O'Connor and Leopoldo Ruiz of Argentina all

blew fine chances of joining the play-off, which Thomson won by four strokes. His improved putting was decisive over the last 11 holes. Thomson was champion again, for the fourth time in five years. Only Young Tom Morris had achieved this, but in the year he didn't win there was no competition, since he had retired the original trophy by winning it three times in a row.

Thomson allowed his son Andrew, five, to take the trophy plinth to show off at school, fearing for the vase itself. The boy returned crying because, "Tommy's father has won five cups and you've only won half of one."

Peter Thomson: four better in Open play-off.

David Thomas: fourth round sprint in vain.

## Finsterwald's PGA title – at strokeplay

THE AMERICAN passion for card and pencil golf turned the fourth "major", the US PGA championship, into a stroke play event after 39 match-playing years. Dow Finsterwald produced the best card at Llanerch Country Club, Pennsylvania, with two 67s to beat Billy Casper by two strokes and Sam Snead by four.

Finsterwald was admired by his peers as he could draw or fade the ball at will. His accuracy brought him consistent success.

## Mickey Wright blooms at Bloomfield

BABE ZAHARIAS'S playing partner during her last Open victory in 1954 was the former Girls' champion, Mickey Wright. The following year, Wright turned pro, with the vow that she would become the best in the world.

In 20 heady June days in 1958 Wright showed that such a lofty goal might be within her compass. On the 8th she beat Fay Crocker by six shots for the LPGA championship at Churchill Valley in Pennsylvania. On the 28th she led after every round of the Women's Open at Forest Lake, Bloomfield Hills, Michigan. Top amateur in the Open was Anne Quast, who a few weeks later won the Amateur title from Barbara Romack.

### SHORT PUTTS

● Ireland's Canada Cup win in Mexico City, where Harry Bradshaw and Christy O'Connor held off the Miguel brothers of Spain, was by the fifth different country in the first six years of the event. Angel Miguel was best individual.

● Margaret Curtis, who did so much to create the Curtis Cup series, received the Bobby Jones award for distinguished sportsmanship.

● Birth of Ian Woosnam and Alexander Walter Barr (Sandy) Lyle.

● 1907 British Open champion Arnaud Massy died aged 81.

# Curtis Cup returns to Britain after tie

THE BRITAIN and Ireland women's amateur team showed their menfolk a thing or two in the Curtis Cup match at Brae Burn Country Club, Massachusetts, by putting on the best show by any amateur team visiting the United States.

They shared the nine points at stake against Daisy Ferguson's team, which meant that they took the trophy back home with them. Mrs Charles Dennehy was the Britain and Ireland non-playing captain and, like Ferguson, she kept the same six players for foursomes and singles. America began badly, losing the top two foursomes to Angela Bonallack (née Ward) and Elizabeth Price, and Janette Robertson and Frances Smith. Their winning pair were Barbara McIntire and Les Johnstone.

America rallied in the singles, and led 4-3 thanks to JoAnne Gunderson, Anne Quast and Barbara Romack. But, crucially, Mrs Bonallack had hit back at Barbara McIntire, who had to concede a half, and Robertson won her single. So all rested on the last match. Polly Riley was one down to Frances Smith on the 18th tee, but lost the hole, bringing the match score level.

**Tommy Bolt: ferocious forte but not at the 1957 Open.**

# Bolt leads all the way

TOMMY BOLT had four strokes to spare in capturing the American Open ahead of a much improved swinger of the golf club in person of the South African, Gary Player, who also took great pains to be the fittest player around. He was always the most travelled.

Ben Hogan, whose dedication to self-improvement was much admired by Player, was suffering from a wrist injury, and finished tenth. Bolt, 39, led after every round at Southern Hills, in his native state of Oklahoma.

# Ike's Trophy unites world amateurs

PRESIDENT EISENHOWER'S steady support of golf received worldwide recognition when the World Amateur Golf Council was founded, after the Royal & Ancient embraced an idea put forward by the USGA for an international amateur team competition.

The Eisenhower Trophy series was started at St Andrews, 29 countries competing in October over four rounds of stroke play. Australia seemed to have the inaugural event won with a total of 918, but a birdie three on the perilous Road Hole by Bill Hyndman III helped America to a tie. Birdies on the 18th by the Australian captain, Robert Stevens, and Bruce Devlin gained the two strokes that won the play-off (222-224).

Doug Bachli and Peter Toogood made up the winning quartet, while Bobby Jones was, at Eisenhower's request, non-playing captain of the American team of Hyndman, Charles Coe, Willie Joe Patton and Dr Frank Taylor. Britain and Ireland were third on 919 (Joe Carr, Reid Jack, Arthur Perowne and Guy Wolstenholme).

Carr held the British Amateur title, won at St Andrews. A long putt on the 12th and a fine four-iron out of a bunker on the next in the final helped him to stay ahead of Alan Thirlwell.

### SCORECARD

**British Open** (Royal Lytham, Lancs)
PW Thomson 66 72 67 73  278
(Play-off): Thomson 139, DC Thomas 143

**US Open** (Southern Hills, Okla)
T Bolt 71 71 69 72  283

**Masters** (Augusta, Ga)
AD Palmer 70 73 68 73  284

**US PGA** (Llanerch, Pa)
D Finsterwald 67 72 70 67 276
Leading US money-winner: AD Palmer $42,607.50

**British Amateur** (St Andrews, Scot)
JB Carr bt A Thirlwell 3 & 2

**Joe Carr: Amateur Champion.**

**US Amateur** (Olympic CC, San Francisco, Cal)
CR Coe bt TD Aaron 5 & 4

**US Women's Open** (Forest Lake CC, Mich)
M Wright 290

**British Women's Amateur** (Hunstanton, Norfolk)
J Valentine bt E Price 1h

**US Women's Amateur** (Wee Burn CC, Darien, Conn)
A Quast bt B Romack 3 & 2

**Canada Cup** (Mexico City)
Ireland (H Bradshaw & C O'Connor Snr) 579
(Individual): A Miguel, Spain (after play-off with Bradshaw) 286

**Eisenhower Trophy** (St Andrews, Scot)
Australia 918

**Curtis Cup** (Brae Burn, Mass)
US 4½, GB & Ireland 4½ (GB & Ire retain)

# Shy Mickey Wright, the supreme stylist

Mickey Wright elevated women's professional golf in public esteem to new heights throughout a career brimming with records, victories and endorsements of her supreme skill.

THE SIMILARITIES between Joyce Wethered and Mary Kathryn Wright, always known as "Mickey", are inescapable, particularly in that both were shy, shunned publicity and earned the most lavish praise from the leading player of their day.

In Wethered's case this meant Bobby Jones saying that when he played with her he felt outclassed. Ben Hogan's simply said that Mickey Wright had the best swing he ever saw, man or woman.

Both were utterly unlike that extravagantly talented extrovert among extroverts, Babe Zaharias, for they attained their lonely pinnacles of fame solely by the application of skill and dedication.

Both retired in a way that suggested the strain of constantly winning events was becoming too much to bear. Indeed, Wright suffered from ulcers, and there were also hints from both women that they were getting bored with winning, and that other pursuits beckoned.

## Soon in the news

Wright's short game was the last part of the necessary armoury of a champion that she acquired. The daughter of a San Diego lawyer who encouraged her sporting ambitions from the start, Mickey Wright was born in San Diego California, on February 14, 1935, and was already golfing at the age of 11. Johnny Bellante was her first teacher and, whether from conviction or an eye to business, he arranged early on for her picture to appear in the local daily with the caption "The next Babe".

Wright was never going to be the next Babe. Those who watched both, including Ben Hogan, would be more inclined to say that she would be the first Mickey Wright. Her development continued with the aid of Harry Pressler, coach of several amateur champions in the Pacific coast area, who took her on after seeing her, at age 13, win the Southern California Girls' title. Throughout her career, Wright

**Plumb centre: Mickey Wright lines up a putt.**

sought refreshment for her technique from leading teachers.

Talent can be unlocked only when the desire to succeed is present, and with such a withdrawn character as Mickey Wright, that desire was not outwardly visible. It was indelibly written on scoreboards, however, and her progress up the ladder

was measured and orderly. Girls' Champion in 1952, she beat Barbara McIntire by one hole in the final (the field included Anne Quast, Margaret Smith and Judy Bell). In the 1954 Open championship she was top amateur, finished fourth and had the educational experience of being Babe Zaharias's playing partner. Later that year she was finalist in the National Amateur, losing to Barbara Romack 4 & 2. There followed a spell at Stanford University reading psychology, but she gave up her studies in favour of becoming a professional late in 1954.

She had outdriven Mrs Zaharias from several tees in the Open at Peabody, Massachusetts, but when she joined the tour in 1955, the major players – Patty Berg, Louise Suggs and Betty Jameson – were in full flow, and for a 20-year-old neophyte the going was even tougher when Wright discovered that, though she could out-hit every other player on the tour, she could not out-finesse them.

Into her second year on the tour, the up and down technique had been polished, and along came her first professional victory. The tall, blond and graceful Californian, aided by the experience and encouragement of the tour's big three, won the Jacksonville Open on March 5, just 16 months into her professional career.

## New standards

Three tournaments fell to her in 1957. In 1958 she won the LPGA title and the Open. No-one had done this before. Nor had anyone taken the Open in successive years, which Wright did in 1958-59, winning three other events in 1959.

In the 1960s she got into full stride. Perhaps the best index of her achievements is the stroke averages with which she won the Vare Trophy for five straight years from 1960. Patty Berg (75.00) was the first winner in 1953, Zaharias the second with 75.48 despite her failing health, then Berg (twice), Suggs,

Beverley Hanson and Betsy Rawls – all of them more than 74. Mickey Wright brought it down to 73.25 in 1960, and the last year she won, in 1964, achieved 72.46. Fourteen years passed before 72 was breached.

Her earnings ($368,770) now look paltry beside the rewards of those who came later, but then inflation and the ever-richer sponsorships attracted by the exposure she gave to the excellence of the tour make nonsense of the figures. Kathy Whitworth, over a longer active period, scored more wins though she never captured an Open title but, apart from Zaharias, no-one played such a big part as Wright in persuading the public that the LPGA tour represented quality and excitement.

Prize money totalled $135,000 when Wright joined the tour in 1955. By 1979, when she lost a play-off in a rare return to the circuit, total prize money amounted to $4,400,000.

Her 82 victories in all included four Opens and four LPGA titles. By winning the Open,

LPGA and the Titleholders, at that time a "major", in 1961, then winning the Titleholders in April 1962, followed by the Western Open, another major of that era, she held briefly all four of the accepted majors at once. She is still the only player to have won the Open and the LPGA twice in a season.

For sheer consistency, 1963 was her best year, in which she won the Open and 12 other tournaments. In both 1962 and 1963 she won four tournaments in succession.

## A shy champion

Since she was the figurehead of the tour, and the stars that shone when she joined the tour were now on the wane, winning was inevitably followed by press conferences, photographic sessions and the whole panoply of sporting success – not Wright's idea of a good time at all. She would seldom accept personal appearance offers, which came in droves, for hundreds of dollars, but true to her studious bent, read a lot and

**Mark up: another winning score for Mickey Wright.**

sought solace from her stressful life in music and angling.

Her ability to pull out a saving shot in a crisis was Hagen-like. Winning her fourth Open, which equalled Betsy Rawls' tally, involved a last hole challenge after her opponent had birdied from three feet. She splashed out of a bunker to six feet, then holed the putt to tie with Ruth Jessen, whom she beat next day 70-72.

Two rounds of 62 stand to her credit. Both came in her annus mirabilis of 1964, first at the long Hunting Creek Country Club course in Kentucky, where she reached the turn in 29, and missed a birdie putt for 61. She thought this superior to a later 62 over a flatter Texan layout called Hogan Park.

## Back to studies

Her first attempt at retirement, resuming psychology studies at Southern Methodist in Dallas, to which she had moved from her native west coast, ended inside a year and she won the Western Open in 1966.

Further encouragement to retire came early in the 1970s in the form of injuries to foot and wrist, in which she was suffering from arthritis.

Her on-off ways continued with a very "on" performance in 1973 at the Colgate-Dinah Shore near Palm Springs, where she was trailing by four before the last 18 holes against Joyce Kazmierski. She won by two strokes with a 68, finishing with a long birdie putt on the final green.

Long periods of inaction followed but, at 44, she was still good enough to force her way into a play-off for the Coca-Cola Classic, against Nancy Lopez – a

five-way play-off in which she finished second to the new star. She was obliged to play in sneakers since foot troubles precluded spiked golf shoes.

## Mickey bows out

Her most active period finished in 1965 when she had to withdraw from the Open in Northfield, New Jersey, because of the wrist injury. Her ability to come back many years later and shoot challenging scores is indicative of the rarest talent. Her career, however, was gradually wound down.

### SCORECARD

**US Women's Open**
1958, 1959, 1961, 1964

**LPGA championship**
1958, 1960, 1961, 1963

**Titleholders** 1961, 1962

**Western Women's Open** 1962, 1963, 1966

### TEE TALK

**"We had some great head-to-head matches. Nine times out of ten she won."**

KATHY WHITWORTH.

**"What are you doing, copying my swing?"**

BABE ZAHARIAS,
on being outdriven by Mickey Wright.

**Definitely the Wright way to swing it . . .**

# Tears to triumph for Gary Player

THE SOUTH AFRICAN, Gary Player, turned away from the final green in tears as the British Open neared its climax at Muirfield, utterly convinced that he had thrown away the greatest chance of his young (23) life. He felt all the worse because he had rallied so well after a dreadful start – his first round of 75 left him seven behind the leaders.

True, the leaders were not expected to stay at the head of affairs, because Arnold Stickley and Fred Bullock were, to say the least not fancied runners, and they were helped by the fact that their early round coincided with the most favourable weather. Peter Thomson was fancied to retain his title, and had done his supporters' faith in him no harm by leading the qualifying.

Player cut six off his score in the second round, but was still in no great shape, and was only two inside the qualifying score of 148, along with Henry Cotton, aged 52, and Bobby Locke.

Thomson was right on the

On his way: Gary Player putting towards his first major at Muirfield.

limit, with Peter Alliss. Player got only one stroke lower at his third attempt, and was still four behind Bullock, who was holding on manfully, and Sam King.

Worse still, there were as many as 13 players with scores equal to or better than his own. Hence his anguish when, out in 34 in the final round, he dropped two shots at the last, bunkering his drive and three-putting: 68 when 66 and the title looked distinctly possible. A cruelly long wait followed – St Andrew's punishment for Player's three-putt sin? But one after another his rivals found Player's 284 total beyond them, and he became the youngest champion since Willie Auchterlonie in 1893.

# Casper raps in the Open putts

BILL CASPER, a large (over 200 pounds), 27-year-old golfer of the Mormon persuasion from San Diego, had a way with putts. Not for him the modern shoulders and arms all-of-a-piece method. His way was very much his own and almost frightening to watch when he was in full flow, and with a wristy, most positive tap sent the ball scudding on its way.

He was among the quickest of players, seldom waiting about once the club was taken from the bag. His brisk methods carried off the American Open at Winged Foot, New York, by one stroke from Bob Rosburg and two from the powerful Mike Souchak and Claude Harmon, pro at Winged Foot. It was a lucrative time for Casper to land his first Open: the prize money had been increased by 20 per cent, Casper's reward being $12,000. Arnold Palmer was one of three players sharing fifth.

Casper's Open was the first where the regulation 72 holes were carried over to Sunday. Thunderstorms on the third day caused such complications that five players, including Art Wall, were awarded $240 prize money each though they did not complete 72 holes.

Billy Casper: in awesome form at Winged Foot.

# Nicklaus by a whisker

MORE EXCITING finishes than the 36th hole of the American Amateur final at Broadmoor, Colorado, on September 19 cannot readily be brought to mind. The holder, Charles Coe, 35, and Jack Nicklaus, survivors from a record entry of 1,696, approached the final hole level, after Coe had led several times.

Coe's third, recovering from long grass, was an inch from registering a birdie. Nicklaus, whose first round opponent was Robert T. Jones III, then holed from eight feet for a birdie and the title. He was at 19 and eight months second only to Robert Gardner (19 and five months in 1909) as the youngest winner of the title. Anyway, Nicklaus could never sing like Gardner.

### TEE TALK

**"No matter how hard I try, I just can't seem to break sixty-four."**

JACK NICKLAUS.

### SCORECARD

**British Open** (Muirfield, Scot)
G Player 75 71 70 68 284

**US Open** (Winged Foot, NY)
W Casper 71 68 69 74 282

**Masters** (Augusta, Ga)
A Wall Jnr 73 74 71 66 284

**US PGA** (St Louis Park, Minneapolis, Minn)
B Rosburg 71 72 68 66 277
Leading US money-winner: A Wall Jnr
$53,167.60

**British Amateur** (R St George's, Sandwich, Kent)
D Beman bt W Hyndman III 3 & 2

**US Amateur** (Broadmoor GC, Col)
JW Nicklaus bt CR Coe 1h

**US Women's Open** (Churchill Valley CC, Pittsburgh, Pa)
M Wright 287

**British Women's Amateur** (Ascot, Berks)
E Price bt B McCorkindale 37th

**US Women's Amateur** (Congressional CC, Washington, DC)
B McIntire bt J Goodwin 4 & 3

**Canada Cup** (Melbourne)
Australia (PW Thomson & KDG Nagle) 563
(Individual): S Leonard, Can (after play-off with Thomson) 275

**Ryder Cup** (Palm Desert, Cal)
US 8½, GB & Ireland 3½

**Walker Cup** (Muirfield, Scot)
US 9, GB & Ireland 3

## Walker triumph for US All-stars

AMONG STRONG American Walker Cup teams the 1959 edition, 9-3 winners at Muirfield, ranks high. Apart from Ward Wettlaufer (who won twice anyway) the team is a Debrett of American golf: Charles Coe (captain), Harvie Ward, Billy Joe Patton, Bill Hyndman, Dr Frank Taylor, Tommy Aaron and Jack Nicklaus, 19, a student at Ohio.

The tale of the match is soon told: United States 4-0 in foursomes, 5-3 in singles. Joe Carr (against Coe), Alec Shepperson and Reid Jack were the only home winners. Deane Beman was brought in for the singles, and beat Michael Bonallack by two holes, Nicklaus bringing up the rear with a 6 & 5 trouncing of Dickson Smith.

Leonard Crawley, not one to go overboard about new faces, rated Nicklaus a prodigious talent. Coe's team displayed the usual flair for strength of shot and purpose over the closing holes: six of the 12 matches went to the penultimate or final green and the Americans won five.

# Art Wall's bravura finish

ON APRIL 5 Art Wall put in one of the astounding finishes for which the Masters was becoming famous. He had started the year with victory in the Crosby, and began the last round at Augusta six behind defending champion Arnold Palmer and the Canadian, Stan Leonard. But neither Palmer nor Cary Middlecoff could do much about Wall's closing salvos.

His final round of 66 included eight birdies, and he saved five strokes on the last six holes, pipping Middlecoff by a shot with a four-yard birdie put on the last, and Palmer by two. This was the high spot of Wall's most spectacular year on the tour. He was player of the year, Vardon Trophy winner and leading earner, with $53,167 of the Tour's $1,225,205 total fund.

**Art Wall: Master golfer.**

**Class of 1959 at Augusta: from the left, Billie Joe Patton, Ben Hogan, Bobby Jones and Sam Snead.**

## Sifford breaks the southern ice

WHEN THE US PGA was founded in 1916 a clause in the association's constitution required members to be of the Caucasian race. That clause was still in force in 1959, but for some years had been ignored, depending on where tournaments were run and who had the final say on entries. The Greensboro Open, North Carolina, was therefore a watershed in the business of racial discrimination in golf because Charles Sifford competed, the first black to play against whites in the south. He was cat-called by five white men, which did not improve his concentration. They were arrested. Sifford faded and finished badly.

Black women's golf was simi-larly circumscribed, though the Civil Rights movement was more active than ever. Ann Gregory was the outstanding black woman golfer of the day, and played in the American Women's Amateur at the Congressional Country Club in the nation's capital, and got through two rounds.

Earlier, however, a veiled threat had been made by a car park attendant to the father of Gregory's first opponent, Carolyn Cudone, and before the event began Joe Dey of the USGA told Gregory that the club were in charge of social events during USGA-run championships, and that the club had barred her from the traditional pre-tournament dinner.

# Snead & Co regain Ryder Cup

THE MAGIC OF Lindrick deserted Dai Rees and his Britain and Ireland team in the Ryder Cup at Eldorado Country Club, Palm Desert, California. Sam Snead returned to lead America to victory by 7-4, with three matches halved. The visitors were not helped when their Los Angeles to Palm Desert flight ran into fearsome weather conditions and dropped like a stone for thousands of feet.

The description of this nerve-shattering happening by Ronald Heager ran: "Anything not strapped down took off and floated to the roof of the plane. It was the brink of calamity."

Peter Alliss and his father, Percy, were still the only father and son to have played in the Cup. Alliss junior was least affected by the aerial shock to the team's system, to judge from his victory with Christy O'Connor senior against Art Wall and Doug Ford and his half in singles against Jay Hebert.

Only Eric Brown got his singles point, beating Cary Middlecoff 4 & 3. His record now was even: four singles wins and four foursomes defeats, which gave him a record superior to most British players, few of whom could point to equality in their struggles against American professionals. US big guns were Snead (6 & 5 over David Thomas), Bob Rosburg (6 & 5 against Harry Weetman) and Art Wall (7 & 6 against O'Connor).

### SHORT PUTTS

● Bob Rosburg, second in the Open, edged out Jerry Barber and Doug Sanders for the US PGA title in Minneapolis. Many thought him an even better putter than Billy Casper. Rosburg needed only 19 putts in the second round of the Pensacola Open.

● Mickey Wright is the first player to win back to back Women's Open titles.

● British Curtis Cup stalwart Jessie Valentine turned professional.

● Death of Dr Frank Stableford, 89, inventor of points scoring system.

# Palmer's two birdies edge out Venturi

REGAINING THE Masters title was a well-organized operation by Arnold Palmer until he ran into a crisis on the last few holes on April 8. He had already won four tournaments when Augusta time came round, and when it did, he started with a 67 for the lead, and stayed ahead with 73, 72.

Now Ken Venturi, with 213, one behind Palmer, played an excellent closing round, taking 70 strokes for a total of 283. In the clubhouse, surrounded by pressmen, Venturi looked a winner all over as news came that Palmer was leaving the 16th green in need of two birdies to edge past Venturi.

Venturi's feelings, as the media deserted him en masse on the arrival of further intelligence to the effect that Palmer had birdied the 17th, can well be imagined. Indifference hurts, because it, and not hate, is the opposite of love.

Palmer's birdie on the last secured his second Masters' green jacket. For Venturi there was nothing but a cheque and disappointment at being runner-up for the second time in five years.

George Bayer and Jack Fleck, the 1950 Open champion, made a different point at this Masters by getting round the course in eight minutes under two hours. And there had been worse scores than Bayer's 72 and Fleck's 74.

**Arnold Palmer on his favourite stage, Augusta National.**

# Nicklaus bags Ike's trophy

JACK NICKLAUS had not retained his Amateur title at St Louis, losing 5 & 3 to Charles Lewis from Little Rock in round four, but two weeks later, on October 1, he was celebrating with his team-mates a massive American win in the second Eisenhower Trophy competition at Merion in Pennsylvania.

Totton P. Heffelfinger captained the quartet of Deane Beman, Robert Gardner, Bill Hyndman and Nicklaus who finished 42 shots clear of Australia, the inaugural winners. Nicklaus's four rounds were 66, 67, 68, 68 = 269, a chilling thought for his likely future opponents.

# Snead's lucky 7

IN 1938, SAM SNEAD won his first Greensboro Open with a score of 272. In 1960 he won his seventh with a total of 270, one worse than his best score in 1950. No-one was willing to bet that Snead, aged 48, and rumoured to have won a million dollars and saved two million, would stop at seven.

# Mighty Palmer reigns in Cherry Hills caper

THERE WERE FEW people who heard Arnold Palmer's vehemently expressed belief on June 18 at Cherry Hills, Colorado, that a 65 in the final round would win him his first US Open championship. Fewer still, if any, believed it. But Palmer thought that a total of 280 was a winning proposition. His score after 54 holes was 215, seven behind Mike Souchak, and five behind Ben Hogan, so something spectacular was required.

The day was hot and sunny and, as Palmer ate a sandwich in the locker room before teeing off for the last round, he chatted with Ken Venturi, Bob Rosburg and two sportswriters. The question for Venturi was could Souchak hold on. Palmer had a different question: "I may shoot 65 out there. What'll that do".

"Nothing," said one journalist. "You're too far back." Palmer set off for a spectacular rebuttal. A good start, he reasoned, would be to drive the first hole, a par four. Palmer had been trying to do so all week, and at his final attempt his ball ripped through some longer grass in front of the hole, and staggered on to the putting surface. He two-putted for his birdie, got five more birdies in the next six holes, scored his coveted 65 and became Open champion. His first nine was a record 30, and his 65 the best finishing round. Coming on top of his theatrical finish at Augusta, this recruited fans to his army of supporters at a great rate. Palmer was top pro all right and there was also no doubt about who was top amateur. Two strokes behind Palmer at Cherry Hills was reigning Amateur champion Jack Nicklaus.

Two strokes behind him was Nicklaus's playing partner, Ben Hogan, who gambled on the 17th, went into the water and took six, and on the 18th, took seven. These late errors robbed Cherry Hills of the prospect of just about the most mouth-watering play-off of the century.

# Nagle's Open: Palmer's shot in the arm

NATURALLY, the Centenary British Open was staged at St Andrews. Naturally, Arnold Palmer, with two 1960 majors to his name wanted to do a Hogan and capture a third. Palmer, like Hogan, was no academic, but he had a sense of history. There was no date clash this time between the British Open and the US PGA, so there was always a chance of that professional quadrilateral. Oh to be one up on Hogan!

Naturally, life being about 6 to 4 against, the bookmakers did well when Kel Nagle from Australia beat Palmer by a stroke. So did Peter Thomson, who had backed his countryman at better than 30 to 1.

There were surprises from the start. Peter Alliss (with never a five on his card) broke the Old Course record of 66 in qualifying for the championship proper, but did not qualify for the last 36 holes. Henry Cotton and Fred Daly, among other champions, did not qualify at all.

Roberto de Vicenzo, out early, turned in 32 and his 67 beat all comers on the first day, Nagle and Fidel de Luca (Argentina) returning 69s and Palmer, among others, 70.

Nagle, Australian champion in 1959, was not a long hitter, but was very straight. At address his driver was always one club head, so to speak, inside the ball, but at impact all was repeatedly well. Moreover, at 39, he had left early putting weaknesses behind him. A critical moment for him was the 15-yard birdie putt he sank on the Road Hole from a position that had three-putt written all over it.

De Vicenzo scored 67 again the second day; Nagle also returned a 67. He was two behind, Palmer seven, and Palmer did three-putt the Road Hole, which in the third round began to haunt a few minds more than usual. Nagle had a three there, Palmer three putts, plus a bogey on the (fairly) straightforward 18th and, with a round to go, it was Nagle 207, de Vicenzo 209, and Syd Scott and Palmer 211. Hardly had round four started than rain first postponed, then wiped out play for the day.

On Saturday neither Nagle or Palmer were giving an inch as others, notably de Vicenzo, weakened. The two principals, Nagle following Palmer, were two under par at the turn. A birdie for Palmer at 13 and a poor approach by Nagle at 15 brought the gap to two strokes. For once Palmer was equal to the Road Hole, getting his four after being short with his second, and running the ball up close.

Palmer's final thrust was a birdie at the last, which his army, flush with new British recruits, hailed loudly. Back on the 17th Nagle sank perhaps the most important putt of his life for par from seven or eight feet.

He finished with a cast-iron par on the last to lift the silver claret jug first won by Young Tom Morris 77 Opens ago, not to mention a replica made to commemorate the centenary, and a cheque for £1,250, the biggest first prize to date. Bernard Hunt, with the day's best score of 66, leapt to third place. Most important of all, Palmer's bold, outgoing character had brought new excitement to the old contest and the old town.

**Seeing double: Kel Nagle with Auld Mug - and replica.**

**Peter Alliss: broke Old Course record in qualifying with 66.**

## SHORT PUTTS

● The state of California challenged the clause in the US PGA constitution limiting membership to Caucasians, and the "all-white" rule was erased.

● Joe Carr was in regal mood in the British Amateur, winning 8 & 7 against the American, Bob Cochran, who, at 47, was even in defeat enjoying his best achievement.

● Betsy Rawls gained her fourth Women's Open at Worcester, Massachusetts, the reigning champion Mickey Wright tumbling to 82 in the final round. Rawls covered the last nine in 35 strokes to beat Joyce Ziske by a stroke. In the third round Rawls scored 68, equalling the record for a single round.

● Judy Torluemke, at 15, became the youngest player to win the gold pin for the lowest scoring amateur.

● Birth of Paul William Azinger at Holyoke, Massachusetts.

● Deaths of Mungo Park junior, course designer, and Lottie Dod, lawn tennis and golf champion.

# Gary Player, world golfer

FOOTBALL MANAGERS are sometimes heard to complain that it is none too easy drawing at home, never mind winning away. In which case, Gary Player from South Africa proved in general in 1961 and in particular on April 10, when he won the 25th Masters at Augusta, that at 25 years of age he had the game to win anywhere – the acid test of skill and nerve.

He was a regular firecracker of a golfer in 1961, not to mention becoming the first foreign Masters winner. Looking avidly for a second major to put beside his British Open of 1959, he could also look back, as 1961 began, on 25 other tournaments won in South Africa, Australia, Japan, Egypt, England and America. Prize money flowed in during the months leading up to Augusta, and throughout the year, for apart from the Masters, he won the Lucky International, the Sunshine Open, the Yomiuri in Japan and the Australian Ampol tournament.

Then there were 16 top ten finishes on the PGA tour, of which half were in the top three. Just before the Masters, Player was ahead in the 1961 prize-money chart, despite Palmer's victories in three of the first eight tournaments.

The pair were all even at halfway: Player scored 69, 68, Palmer 68, 69. Player's advantage was clear with 18 holes to play, for while Palmer struggled to 73, Player had another 69, thanks in part to a gutsy sliced recovery with a four wood from the trees at the ninth.

Sunday play was washed out and on the Monday Player had two bogeys and a double bogey on the back nine. He and his wife Vivienne watched on television as Palmer, one ahead on the 18th tee, hit a superb drive. It took him five more to get down after tangling with a bunker, the same bunker from which Player had escaped earlier to get his par. So, at his fourth attempt, Player was soon wearing his first Masters' green jacket.

Gary Player: first Masters jacket from only his fourth attempt.

## Gene the machine clicks into gear at last

THE LONG-AWAITED flowering of a great golfing talent occurred at Oakland Hills Country Club in Michigan on June 17, when Gene Littler held off Doug Sanders and Bob Goalby by a stroke to take his first US Open. He won in the most admirable fashion imaginable, for his 68 was the lowest score in the last round. He was also the only player of the 57 who qualified for all four rounds to break par twice. Littler was one of 13 leading players all within four strokes as the final round began, with Sanders on 210 at the head of affairs. Littler was three behind Sanders and the other 11 contenders faded. At the climax, Sanders almost holed from off the 18th green, where Littler had dropped a shot reaching 281, one over par.

The crowds totalled nearly 48,000, a record for the Open. Ben Hogan was not in the first ten, his worst-ever finish. He was eight shots adrift, and so was the defending champion, Arnold Palmer. This was Chick Evans's last Open attempt. Amateur Champion in 1953, Littler had begun his professional career with a bang in 1954, winning the first tournament he entered, the San Diego Open in the city of his birth in 1930.

He followed that with second place to Ed Furgol the same year and won five times in 1955. He went off the boil during a period of swing analysis but his troubles went away in 1959, when he had five wins and came second to leading money winner Art Wall.

## Palmer's 73 a miracle in the gale at Birkdale

THE SECOND round of 73 that Arnold Palmer returned en route to his first British Open title looks ordinary in the record book, but amazed those who had the strength to battle through the gale and watch him at Royal Birkdale.

Kel Nagle, defending the title he had snatched from Palmer by a stroke at St Andrews, led with 68 after 18 holes in company with Dai Rees and Harold Henning. Palmer was two behind.

The weather was brutal on the second day and at its violent worst for Palmer. Yet he saved a shot at five of the first six holes, and reached the turn in 34, though conditions were such that he could not reach the 427-yard second with two flat-out woods. His second at the third (416 yards) was to within six inches. The short fourth (212 yards) required a one iron. The 468-yard sixth, perhaps the most difficult on the course, and rated a par 5, he birdied with a drive, a three wood, a wedge and one putt. He putted only 12 times on the front nine. Not surprisingly, he could not keep this up, and dropped shots at holes 10 and 13, getting one back with a four at the 517-yard 14th.

A thinned bunker shot at the 16th led to an apparent six, but Palmer called a stroke on himself because he said his ball moved as he played from the sand, which meant a seven, double bogey, and he finished with a par three and birdie four to total 73 – the best of his life, Palmer thought, although it did not give him the lead.

Next day proved that the gale that produced so many scores in the high 70s and pushed some players into the 80s was just a sample of what was to come, and play was suspended. There now came the ugly threat of a second blank day, damaging to its reputation and Palmer's missionary work in America on behalf of the Open.

Luckily the weather relented and for the second year in succession the Open ended on a Saturday, Palmer's 69 and 72 taking the title by a stroke from Rees, who was three clear of Neil Coles and Christy O'Connor.

"If Arnold asked all of those people to go jump into the river for him, they would march straight to the river and jump."

GARY PLAYER,
of Arnie's army.

"He went for the green."

Palmer's business manager's suggestion to Palmer for the inscription on his tombstone.

## SHORT PUTTS

**Michael Bonallack: crushing final margin for his first British Amateur title**

● Michael Bonallack easily won his first British Amateur title at Turnberry, beating Jimmy Walker 6 & 4 in the 36-hole final.

● Marley Spearman, a former show dancer, who took up the game relatively late, was Women' champion, beating Diane Robb 7 & 6 at Carnoustie. She is reputed to have discovered her gift at Harrods store in London where the resident pro was much impressed when she took a swing or two in the practice net.

● Joe Dey, executive director of the USGA, looked at the press tent on the Monday of Open Week at Oakland Hills and announced that it would not do, and would not withstand a high wind. The local officials bridled at this, but two hours later the skies darkened and the press tent blew down.

● Bob Falkenburg, Wimbledon singles winner in 1948, completed a hat-trick of Brazilian Open titles.

# US win all-change Ryder Cup

Togetherness: Arnold Palmer (right) and Dow Finsterwald at the Ryder Cup.

Victorious: American Ryder Cup captain Jerry Barber.

ARNOLD PALMER returned to Lytham on the Lancashire coast in October, when Jerry Barber led the United States to a 14½ – 9½ Ryder Cup victory over Britain and Ireland.

The format was changed to two series of foursomes on the first day and two series of singles on the second. Palmer and Casper proved unbeatable in foursomes, and so did Art Wall and Jay Hebert. The home side won the second series of singles, but lost the first three series. Palmer was top scorer with 3½ points out of four, Dai Rees was Britain and Ireland's best with three out of four, though Bill Casper and Art Wall were 100 per cent from their three matches.

Walker Cup play at Seattle was a romp for the United States, who won 11-1, equalling their biggest previous margin. Martin Christmas won the visitors' solitary point and Jack Nicklaus, in his last Cup match before turning pro, won twice. He had trounced Dudley Wysong 8 & 6 a month previously for his second American Amateur title.

## SCORECARD

**British Open** (Royal Birkdale, Lancashire)
AD Palmer  70 73 69 72  284

**US Open** (Oakland Hills, Mich)
G Littler  73 68 72 68  281

**Masters** (Augusta, Ga)
G Player  69 68 69 74  280

**US PGA** (Firestone CC, Akron, Ohio)
J Barber  69 67 71 70  277
Leading US Money-Winner:
G Player  $64,540.45

**British Amateur** (Turnberry, Scot)
MF Bonallack bt J Walker  6 & 4

**US Amateur** (Pebble Beach, Cal)
JW Nicklaus bt HD Wysong  8 & 6

**US Women's Open** (Baltusrol, NJ)
M Wright  293

**British Women's Amateur** (Carnoustie, Scot)
M Spearman bt D Robb  7 & 6

**US Women's Amateur** (Tacoma CGC, Wash)
Mrs JD Decker bt P Preuss  14 & 13

**Canada Cup** (Puerto Rico)
US (S Snead & J Demaret)  560
(Individual): Snead  272

**Ryder Cup** (Royal Lytham, Lancs)
US  14½, G B & Ireland  9½

**Walker Cup** (Seattle, Wash)
US  11, G B & Ireland  1

# Jack Nicklaus states his intentions

AMERICAN GOLF'S new wunderkind Jack Nicklaus disappointed no-one except Arnold Palmer's army, who were more numerous than ever at Oakmont, by beating their hero in a play-off for the US Open. Nicklaus had won the Ohio Open at 16, the National Amateur in 1959 and 1961, scored 269 at Merion in the Eisenhower Trophy and been runner-up to Palmer in the 1960 Open. Now, at 22 years of age, he had his first victory as a professional in the US Open.

Palmer's five-year reign was obviously under threat from a most powerful pretender, whose long-hitting and finely tuned putting stroke betrayed a special talent. It was too good for Palmer and riled his fans, swollen by local admirers from Latrobe, his birthplace. The attendance for the three days of regulation play was more than 62,000, far and away a record, beating the previous best of almost 48,000.

Palmer had begun the year in scintillating form, winning two tournaments on the way to another Masters victory in April. Nicklaus wore him down in the Open on America's most feared course, scoring 283 as Ben Hogan had in winning there in 1952.

The denouement, before the event's biggest gallery to date, 24,492, was impossible to predict, six players leading at one time or another. Nicklaus and Palmer were level with five holes to play and still level at the last. Nicklaus finished the 72 holes first, and had a birdie putt for 282 on the 18th. He missed it and so a little later did Palmer with his birdie

Jack Nicklaus: threat to Arnold Palmer's reign.

Arnold Palmer, worn down by newcomer Nicklaus.

chance from slightly further away.

In the play-off Nicklaus went ahead at once, and was four up after six holes. He still had a three-stroke advantage at the end, when an odd incident brought to mind Bobby Locke's inadvertent putt from the wrong spot five years earlier while winning the British Open.

This time Palmer, clearly beaten on the last green, picked up Nicklaus's ball marker in token of surrender. But, since this was stroke play, Nicklaus had to putt out. He replaced his ball and holed the putt. Holing putts was the secret of Nicklaus's success at Oakmont, where the greens are notoriously difficult.

Over the 90 holes he and Palmer played, Nicklaus three-putted only once, Palmer ten times.

# Pied Piper Palmer top at Troon

RETURNING FOR a third year in search of a second British Open title, Arnold Palmer proved something of a pied piper in that this Open at Troon attracted a better representation of US golfers than for some years.

Gene Littler, US Open champion of the previous year, and Phil Rodgers made the trip, not to mention the new US Open champion, Jack Nicklaus. Sam Snead, now 50, but still moving the ball huge distances, was back at the British Open for the first time since he won in 1946.

Palmer's reward was to win with a record aggregate of 276.

He had the satisfaction of beating Kel Nagle into second place by six shots. Rodgers and Brian Huggett were joint third another seven strokes back, 13 behind Palmer. On his own in fifth place came a decided novelty at this level of play, namely a left-handed New Zealander called Bob Charles, whose putting, however, was already causing eyes to open wide.

The condition of the course did not fill the leading contenders with quiet, happy thoughts. It was playing short, but dry weather produced bizarre bounces on the fairways, though it had also

restricted growth of the rough. The 11th, a long dog-leg beside the railway line, caused great problems and Nicklaus once got into double figures there. In six rounds, qualifying included, Palmer was six under par at the 11th.

Palmer began with a conservative 71, one behind Peter Thomson, but got into gear next day with a 69, equalled only by Peter Alliss. No-one had an answer to Palmer's third round 67, and another 69 placed him beyond pursuit. He was the first Open champion to put together three rounds under 70.

# First triple tie in Masters

ARNOLD PALMER'S third Masters in five years was gained the hard way, in a triple tie, the first at Augusta, against Dow Finsterwald and Gary Player, the defending champion.

Arnie's army great enjoyed his fine finishes. In round four he birdied holes 16 (from off the green for a two) and 17 to force the tie, and next day his 68 was the lowest score returned in a Masters play-off. He covered the back nine in 31 strokes.

Palmer had plenty left on the PGA tour, going on to win four more tournaments.

# Gary Player ends drought

FIFTEEN MONTHS had passed without a win when Gary Player arrived at Aronimink in Pennsylvania for the US PGA championship, a couple of weeks after failing to qualify for the final stages of the British Open though he had finished joint sixth at Oakmont. Green and lovely Aronimink cheered him up after the hostile aridity of Troon. He practised hard and followed an opening 72 with 67, putting him a stroke behind the leader. A third round of 69 put him two ahead with 18 holes to play, and though Bob Goalby, his playing partner, cut his lead to one hole on the 72nd tee, Goalby failed with a birdie putt for the tie, and Player had his third major.

The US PGA was played at Aronimink because blacks, many months before the championship date, protested about the course originally chosen, Brentwood Country Club, Los Angeles. Action by a state's attorney, making it illegal for PGA events to be played on public courses if blacks were banned, and the fact that he told his opposite numbers in other states what he was doing, was the final nail in the coffin of the PGA "Caucasians only" clause. Too many rich tournaments were played on public courses for risks to be taken by banning non-Caucasians.

Gary Player: third major at Aronimink to end a lean spell.

## Rookie takes Women's Open

JUST AS Jack Nicklaus had started his professional career by winning at the very top of his sport, so Mrs Murle Lindstrom gained her first pro win in the US Women's Open at Myrtle Beach in South Carolina. She had big deficits after rounds one, two and three, but came back courageously in a rain-soaked final round to rub out a five-stroke deficit and win $1,800.

Mickey Wright was number one in the LPGA Tour for the second year and got off to a quick start winning the Naples Pro-Am in Florida. She went on to win nine more times, including four in a row between August 10 and September 3.

## Curtis crash for Britons

A MUCH-CHANGED British team lost 8-1 at Broadmoor, Colorado Springs, to a US team led by (non-playing) Polly Riley. The course, a tough one, inspired the home players to excellent scoring, only two of the American victories being gained by less than 4 & 3.

The one British victory was by former British Amateur finalist Diane Frearson over Judy Bell who, playing on her own course, lost 8 & 7.

The Ladies Golf Union had mounted a training programme for juniors and five of the British side were making their Cup debuts.

### SHORT PUTTS

● America's foursome of Deane Beman, Labron Harris, Billie Joe Patton and Richard Sikes had a narrow victory in the first Eisenhower Trophy for the World Amateur Team championship to be played in Japan. They had only eight strokes to spare (854-862) over Canada, who had the consolation of fielding the best individual scorer, Gary Cowan.

● Arnold Palmer and Sam Snead held off Roberto de Vicenzo and Fidel de Luca (who had acquired the nickname "Filthy" in Anglo-Saxon company) in the Canada Cup in Buenos Aires, the United States winning with a score of 557 for their eight rounds, averaging just under 70. De Vicenzo was best individual, with 276.

### SCORECARD

**British Open** (Troon, Scot)
AD Palmer 71 69 67 69 276

**US Open** (Oakmont, Pa)
JW Nicklaus 72 70 72 69 283
(Play-off: Nicklaus 71, AD Palmer 74)

**Masters** (Augusta, Ga)
AD Palmer 70 66 69 75 280
(Play-off: Palmer 68, G Player 71, D Finsterwald 77)

**US PGA** (Aronimink, Newtown Sq, Pa)
G Player 72 67 69 70 278
Leading US money-winner:
AD Palmer $81,448.33

**British Amateur** (Royal Liverpool, Merseyside)
R Davies bt J Povall 1h

**US Amateur** (Pinehurst CC, NC)
LE Harris bt D Gray 1h

**US Women's Open** (Dunes G & BC, Myrtle Beach, SC)
M Lindstrom 301

**British Women's Amateur** (Royal Birkdale, Merseyside)
M Spearman bt A Bonallack 1h

**US Women's Amateur** (Rochester CC, NY)
J Gunderson bt A Baker 9 & 8

JoAnne Gunderson: gained third American Amateur.

**Canada Cup** (Buenos Aires, Arg)
US (AD Palmer & S Snead) 557
(Individual): R de Vicenzo, Argentina 276

**Eisenhower Trophy** (Fuji GC, Kawana, Japan)
US 286

**Curtis Cup** (Broadmoor, Colorado Springs, Col)
US 8, GB & Ireland 1

### TEE TALK

## "He (Palmer) is the reason we're playing for all this money today."

KEN STILL.

# Palmer, another word for popular

ARNOLD DANIEL Palmer has what amounts to a genius for pleasing people. At the height of his powers in the early 1960s, for he won no major title after 1964, Palmer could not only withstand the trials, disappointments and, just as important in a sportsman, the heady moments of success, but he could also show a touching regard for the cares of his fellow man.

The late Jack Statter, formerly of the "Daily Telegraph", was a fervent fan and fond of recounting an incident during one of Palmer's British Open wins, when he was about to take a shot but pulled away as a photographer caught his eye. Palmer asked him not to take a picture from that spot.

The photographer vanished, and Palmer got down over his shot again. He pulled away once more and asked where the photographer had gone. Palmer explained to him that he didn't want him not to take a picture, but not to take it there but from over there, where he couldn't see him out of the corner of his eye. Palmer then got down over his ball again, struck a fine shot, the photographer got his picture and Palmer, in the end, his Auld Mug.

Then there was the time that

*Arnold was an outstanding figure in the postwar golfing scene, with fine achievements both as an amateur and professional and a favourite with the crowds on both sides of the Atlantic*

Arnold Palmer: 'boldness' the story of his life.

Palmer, taking on a tricky chip shot at Colonial Country Club, Fort Worth, was disturbed by a little boy talking to his mother. She did her best to quieten her offspring, without much success, and when Palmer turned round again the child was turning red in the face because his mother had her hand over his mouth. Palmer patted the boy on the head saying, "Hey, don't choke him. This isn't that important."

## Media friendly

Turning back to the game, he made a good fist of the chip, and went on to win the tournament.

It was 1962 and Palmer already had two daughters of his own.

Unlike many star golfers, who can be a tetchy bunch, Palmer had decided that the media are a big help and determined to help them help him. Whether or not he had thought out the principle, often overlooked in the world of sports, that sport scarcely exists without the media, the fact remains that, with few exceptions, writers and broadcasters have reacted positively for Palmer the Public Relations Expert (witting or unwitting).

None of this would have mattered had not Palmer possessed

such a dashing way with him, his body language radiating ambition, enjoyment of a good shot, despair as a putt lipped out and a general air of intent to rip the course apart if necessary.

But, while many a golfer affects aggressive gestures, Palmer is meaningfully on the attack with a club in his hands. His long-time business partner, agent, guide, and commercial guru, Mark McCormack, says the one word that perfectly characterizes Palmer is "boldness". It is summed up by the slashing violence of his driving and long irons. He leans into the shot, almost it seems, ready to tear off after it as he follows its flight, his head on one side, with the most intense gaze.

On the subject of gestures, Palmer has one, very masculine, gesture which could have been choreographed for him by a very subtle dance director to ensure he is recognizable from near or from afar – a frequent hitching up of his trousers. He has narrow hips, and the hitching prevents his shirt tail escaping, which would surely not be fitting with his standing as a champion.

Furthermore, he wins a great deal, as his scorecard shows. So much the hero of the modern golf era had he become by 1962, when Jack Nicklaus beat him so clearly in the American Open play-off, that Nicklaus, the greatest golfer of the late 20th century, was actively resented, though he offered the best hope of American golf retaining its stellar quality.

Palmer's magnetism could be a trial to his peers. His army has been gently demobilized over the years, but in full battle order it ringed every green and lined every fairway, often many bodies deep.

Some said Palmer could scarcely miss the greens with this generous back-stop in position. There were, however, problems once the putting started. Young players found it unnerving playing with Palmer, and all his playing partners appreciated the

"His follow-through resembled a duck hunter tracking a teal."

AL BARKOW.

"Under a new USGA rule, anyone using the word charisma in writing about Palmer will be subject to a two-stroke penalty and loss of down."

HERBERT WARREN WIND.

"I'll guarantee you he'll get it in the hole if he has to stare it in."

BOB ROSBURG,
on Palmer's winning putt
in the 1960 Masters.

A "streaky" putter, with plenty of the requisite will-power.

fact that whenever he could, Palmer would make his putt the final putt. Otherwise his partner would be putting as the army noisily thundered off to watch the next hole.

Palmer's career before golf took it over completely is an unusual one for a champion. He was born at Latrobe, Pennsylvania, on September 10, 1929. His father, Milford Deacon (Deke) Palmer, was professional at Latrobe, but the young Palmer never had the free run of the course, and was seldom permitted to play with his father, or anyone else. However, he did get to practise a lot.

He went into the US Coast Guard in 1950 for three years when just out of his teens, deeply shocked at the death in a road crash of Buddy Worsham, brother of 1947 American Open champion Lew, and friend and fellow student of Palmer at Wake Forest University. He took up golf again regularly after a year or so in the Coast Guard and, upon leaving it in 1953, he won the Ohio Amateur, and again the following year, when he first earned national acclaim as Amateur champion.

Palmer's bold nature now

turned to matters matrimonial and, since the family of his girl, Winifred Walzer, had doubts about her marrying a rookie pro golfer with no money, he eloped with her. They need not have worried over much. His first pro victory was the Canadian Open. He earned about $7,000 in his first year. Two tour wins in 1956 were followed by five in 1957, and on to the first of his seven majors at Augusta in 1958.

Palmer's combined career earnings, augmented by his wins in Senior Golf, soared past $3 million by 1990. He was the first (on July 21, 1968) to pile up $1 million in prize money, a pittance compared to the earnings of the companies associated with his name, which soared once he was clear, in 1963, of the restrictions imposed by a contract with Wilson Sporting Goods, a company with whom he was unable to agree a new contract. Much later Arnold Palmer Enterprises was purchased by RCA for many millions.

## 'Charge' the key

Despite his Masters title in 1958, it was not till his explosive assault on Cherry Hills in the 1960 US Open championship that Palmer really got to work on his legend, based on his match strategy of "charge" which is what Palmer is all about.

His habit of making a mess of a strong position was almost as riveting to watch as his forte for winning when the oppposition were seemingly out of sight. He also lost play-offs for the US

First man to a million dollars.

Mark McCormack: Palmer's guide to a fortune.

Open in 1962, 1963 and 1966. His one American Open was won on a course that is a mile above sea-level, where the air is so thin that the ball travels enormous distances. Nicklaus got to the 548-yard fifth with a drive and a seven-iron in practice. That is why the rough was allowed to grow in front of the green on the 346-yard first hole.

Nevertheless, Palmer drove it after failing to do so in the first three rounds, then two-putted for the birdie which set him off on his winning 65. Even then, he was miffed at not reaching the turn in 29. By contrast, the Open of 1966, when he conceded big leads to the eventual champion, Bill Casper, on consecutive days, seemed to take from Palmer the quality that sustained him in 1960.

Palmer was only once ranked in the top 50 after 1973. Tour prize-money was then nine times the $1 million available when Palmer won his first Masters. His career at the very top was short but television and his own brand of man-against-the-world theatre made it a period of mushroom growth in golf.

At the core of all this was Palmer, who between 1958 and 1964 won seven of the 25 majors he entered, in 12 others finishing in the top ten. When not playing or attending to his multifarious business interests he was usually tinkering with his clubs. He also won the Vardon stroke average award four times, and four times led in prize money, a feat now also rewarded, aptly, with the Palmer Trophy.

# Bob Charles, the first of the lefties

IN ALL THE scores of major events, ancient and modern, Bob Charles is the one and only left-handed winner – and of the British Open at that. For those who are fastidious about such things, it should be added that Ben Hogan, and possibly others among users of right-handed clubs, started out in life as left-handers. Just to complete the confusion, Charles is right-handed except when he plays golf.

Some golfers find left-handers disturbing, constantly forgetting that lefties are going to swing "on the other side". What is disturbing about Robert James Charles, who was born in 1936 at Carterton, a few miles north of Wellington in New Zealand's North Island, is his putting. Golfers reaching the green in the same number of strokes as Charles must feel, as opponents of Walter Travis, Bobby Locke and Bill Casper did or do, that the odds are now stacked against them.

Charles is also the only left-hander who reached genuine world class, which is odd in view of the number of lawn tennis southpaws who have lorded it at Wimbledon. The scarcity of left-handers is underlined by the fact that Charles's first win on the American PGA tour in this same year of 1963 was the first tour win by a left-hander. It was by the best score (268) ever recorded in the Houston Classic.

Bob Charles: first left-hander of world-class.

## Triumph at Lytham Open

CHARLES'S putting was not without flaw in the early stages of the British Open at Royal Lytham, which was the first occasion on which the principle of exempting leading players direct into the Open proper was applied.This would clearly attract leading Americans, who would now be sure that, after taking the trouble to cross the Atlantic, they would at least be certain of getting to the first tee in the Open proper.

The holder, Arnold Palmer, who had just lost a play-off in the US Open to Julius Boros, was on parade, with Jack Nicklaus, Phil Rodgers and Doug Sanders, now earning plenty on the tour.

Palmer began badly with 76, Rodgers and Peter Thomson brilliantly with 67s. Thomson reached the turn in an unheard of 29 shots; so did Tom Haliburton, who finished in 68, which was also true of Charles, who would have led but for missing two short putts.

He rued this on the second day, when he was five behind Rodgers, but put regrets behind him with a course record of 66 on the final morning. So the pair of them set out last after lunch, behind Nicklaus and Thomson, since Charles led Thomson by one and Nicklaus and Rodgers by two. Thomson fell away, Nicklaus did not, but he dropped two shots over the last four holes, a hooked second into a bunker at the last hole being particularly frustrating, and totalled 278. The last pair out both beat this by one, for they got their four at the last.

The Saturday play-off was a nice contrast between the extrovert and (let's face it) portly Rodgers and Charles, who was all straight lines and reticence. He did not hit the ball far but, Locke-like, kept out of trouble till he could torture his opponent on the greens. This he now did, with 11 one-putt greens in the morning, including three of more than 20 feet, beating Rodgers 140-148.

## Nicklaus's Augusta-Dallas double

IT WAS AN up and down year for Jack Nicklaus. It started well with a rough weather win in the Masters, though it was only by a stroke from Tony Lema.

Thanks to his tee shot landing in casual water at the 72nd, Nicklaus got a free-drop, found the green and two putts later became at 23 the youngest Master golfer.

The Auugusta National course had never played longer. The management got very close on two different days to calling a halt to proceedings. Nicklaus made his big move with a 66 in the second round, after which he was hard to catch.

Then came the disappointments of not reaching the last 36 holes of the Open at Brookline, and the last hole hook at the British Open that kept him out of the play-off between Bob Charles and Phil Rodgers.

Nicklaus flew back from London to Dallas, and there at Dallas Athletic, despite another last-hole hook, completed a charge from three behind the Australian Bruce Crampton at the three-quarter stage.

He recovered that error at the final hole for a 68 and his first US PGA. But for that hook at Lytham, he might easily have achieved the modern grand slam in only two seasons.

As it was, he was three parts of the way there.

Tom Haliburton: needed only 29 shots for first nine at Royal Lytham, but faded on last two days.

# Boros wins Open at 43

JULIUS BOROS was 43 but younger by 26 days when he won the American Open at windy Brookline than Ted Ray had been in 1920 when he won at Inverness. The Country Club played host to the Open on the 50th anniversary of Francis Ouimet's 1913 win over Harry Vardon and Ray.

This time there was no leading amateur. Like Jack Nicklaus, the defending champion, none of them qualified for the last 36 holes, Nicklaus finishing one over the cut mark of 152.

There was, however, a triple play-off as in 1913, and Jacky Cupit (73) and Arnold Palmer (76) were the losers, Palmer for the second year in succession. Cupit had double-bogeyed the 72nd hole. He, Palmer and Boros could do no better than nine over par over the four rounds. Only 14 scores were achieved under par throughout.

## SCORECARD

**British Open** (Royal Lytham, Lancs)
RJ Charles 68 72 66 71 277
(Play-off: Charles 140, P Rodgers 148)

**US Open** (Brookline, Mass)
J Boros 71 74 76 72 293
(Play-off: Boros 70, JD Cupit 73, AD Palmer 76)

**Masters** (Augusta, Ga)
JW Nicklaus 74 66 74 72 286

**US PGA** (Dallas Athletic, Tex)
JW Nicklaus 69 73 69 68 279
Leading US money-winner:
AD Palmer $128,230

**British Amateur** (St Andrews, Scot)
MSR Lunt bt JG Blackwell 2 & 1

**US Amateur** (Wakonda Club, Des Moines, Iowa)
DR Beman bt RH Sikes 2 & 1

**US Women's Open** (Kenwood CC, Cincinnati, Ohio)
M Mills 289

**British Women's Amateur** (Newcastle, Co Down, N Ire)
B Varangot bt P Garvey 3 & 1

**US Women's Amateur** (Taconic GC, Williamstown, Mass)
Mrs Anne Welts (née Quast) bt P Conley 2 & 1

**Canada Cup** (St Nom-La-Bretêche, France)
US (AD Palmer & JW Nicklaus) 482
(Individual): Nicklaus 237 (63 holes)

**Ryder Cup** (Atlanta, Ga)
US 23, GB & Ireland 9

**Walker Cup** (Turnberry, Scot)
US 14, GB & Ireland 10

Neil Coles: with Christy O'Connor the only fourball winner.

Bernard Hunt: singles winner in Ryder Cup.

# New format, old result

THE FORMAT for the Ryder Cup was enlarged to include fourballs at Atlanta, Georgia: result, the United States won the foursomes (seldom played in America) 5-1, with two halves, and the fourballs, beloved especially of Sunday golfers, by 5-1, with two halves.

Peter Alliss beat Arnold Palmer in the first series of singles, which the visitors won 4-3, thanks also to Brian Huggett, Harry Weetman and Bernard Hunt. Palmer led a 7-0 stampede in the second series and America won 23-9.

Great Britain and Ireland fared rather better in the Walker Cup at Turnberry, losing 12-8, with four matches halved, after leading 6-3 on the first day's play. The losers' best moments came in the first afternoon's singles, with Stuart Murray, Joe Carr and Michael Bonallack among their five winners. The second day foursomes were fatal for the home side: they lost all four matches, putting their opponents ahead.

## SHORT PUTTS

● When Bob Charles and Phil Rogers putted out at the last in the Open at Lytham, the lack of up-to-the-minute scores information meant that neither knew a four would mean they must play off. The American TV commentators had to go cap in hand to ask for the BBC TV version

● Jimmy Tarbuck tells of the fourball practising for the Kenyan Open, Bob Charles among them, which was late on tee and sent off in a hurry by the starter with orders to make up teams or whatever on the green. There it was Charles to putt first: a huge one for birdie. It rolled and rolled and dropped in, at which his three companions shouted with one voice: "Good putt, partner."

## TEE TALK

### "Never saw one who was worth a damn."

HARRY VARDON,
of left-handers.

# Venturi, the hottest Open champion

KEN VENTURI'S victory margin of four strokes in the 64th US Open at the Congressional Club, Washington, D C, makes the championship sound a cut and dried affair. It was anything but, with record scoring, the lead changing hands and Venturi coming through to put years of physical problems behind him and gain his first major in searingly hot weather that threatened to stop him in his tracks.

Venturi was not in a good state as he trudged with difficulty on to the 72nd hole. Still, he was in better shape than in the two previous years, when nerve damage restricted his left side and then began to affect blood circulation in his hands. After getting to within a whisker of being the first amateur to win the Masters in 1956, Venturi made a lucrative career for himself as a professional, despite another Masters disappointment in the year of Arnold Palmer's second green jacket. Then came the physical troubles, and 1963 winnings were down to $3,000.

Venturi had not qualified for the Open for four years, and just managed it this time. Palmer was the only player to break the par of 70 over the 7,053-yard course in round one, with a 68, four ahead of Venturi. Tommy Jacobs, from Colorado, fractured and shredded par in round two with a record-equalling Open score of 64 (Lee Mackey's 1950 mark). Jacobs finished off with a 60-foot putt on the 18th. Venturi, a Californian who had a smoothly orthodox swing which Byron Nelson had helped him to develop, replied with a 66 in round three, but par by Jacobs left him still two strokes ahead, and six clear of Palmer, who was the form horse after his crushing Masters victory. However, he slid to 75 in the "money round", the pros' name for the third round where a good score helps greatly towards a good cheque or a trophy.

Venturi will have wished at this point that the USGA decision to stage the Open over four days had taken effect in 1964, not 1965. Two rounds in the Congressional pressure cooker where the temperature was 100 degrees was cruel for a man not sure of his fitness, and he was treated for heat prostration between rounds.

Despite all these cares, Venturi's technique and nerve were sound, Jacobs crumbled, and Venturi soldiered on, with a doctor and USGA chief Joe Dey walking anxiously alongside him and his playing partner, Bill Casper. Venturi was sustained greatly by a doctor's wet towel and an 18-foot birdie putt on the 13th hole. On the final green, Dey told Venturi: "Hold your head up, Ken, you're the champion now."

He had a ten-footer for a par round at the death, and sank it for his four-stroke win. Venturi said he could remember little about the closing stages. He won $17,500, and was 1964 player of the year.

**Ken Venturi: beat physical problems and heat in US Open.**

# Bobby Nichols' 271 beats the local lad

BOBBY NICHOLS started with a 64 in the US PGA in Columbus, Ohio. Jack Nicklaus, who was born there, finished with a 64, but he and Arnold Palmer ended joint runners-up, three shots behind Nichols, whose winning total of 271 was the best yet returned in the event. Nichols was a considerable athlete until his pelvis was broken along with other injuries in a car crash. He proved his sporting talents by making a lucrative switch to golf. Despite his injuries he was noted as a big hitter.

Consolation for Nicklaus was that this was his first leading money-winner year ($113,284.50), just under $100 dollars more than Palmer.

**British Open** (St Andrews, Scot)
T Lema 73 68 68 70 279

**US Open** (Congressional CC, Washington ,DC)
K Venturi 72 70 66 70 278

**Masters** (Augusta, Ga)
AD Palmer 69 68 69 70 276

**US PGA** (Columbus, Ohio)
B Nichols 64 71 69 67 271
Leading US money-winner:
JW Nicklaus $113,284.50; British: NC Coles
£7,890

**British Amateur** (Ganton, Yorks)
GJ Clark bt MSR Lunt 39th

**US Amateur** (Canterbury GC, Cleveland, Ohio)
WC Campbell bt E Tutwiler 1h

**US Women's Open** (San Diego CC, Chula Vista ,Cal)
M Wright 290
(Play-off: Wright 70, R Jessen 72)

**British Women's Amateur** (Prince's, Sandwich, Kent)
C Sorenson bt B Jackson 37th

**US Women's Amateur** (Prairie Dunes CC, Hutchinson, Kans)
B McIntire bt JP Gunderson 3 & 2

**Canada Cup** (Maui, Hawaii)
US (AD Palmer & JW Nicklaus) 554
(Individual): J W Nicklaus 276

**World Match Play** (Wentworth, Surrey)
AD Palmer bt NC Coles 2 & 1

**Eisenhower Trophy** (Olgiata, Rome)
GB & Ireland 895

**Espirito Santo Trophy** (St Germain, France)
France 588

**Curtis Cup** (Royal Porthcawl, Wales)
US 10½, GB & Ireland 7½

# Palmer's fourth Masters in seven years

THE YEAR had started in a not too confidence-building way for Arnold Palmer, for he missed the cut at the Bing Crosby Pro-Am in January, when at Pebble Beach's short 17th he piled up a lengthy nine.

His army were rejoicing a few weeks later at Augusta where Palmer got the title back from Jack Nicklaus with a neat progression of scores, all under par and three of them breaking 70. He had six strokes to spare over Texan Dave Marr.

Fans of the Palmer persuasion were especially pleased that their man had four Masters titles to Nicklaus's one. He finished second to Nicklaus in the money list and won the inaugural World Matchplay at Wentworth.

# Tony Lema, quick learner

**John White: soccer star.**

IT TOOK Californian Tony Lema a long time to buckle down to serious business on the PGA tour. He was tall, handsome, tanned and liked a good time. In 1962 he made a playboy gesture Walter Hagen would have loved that, ironically, set him back on the road to prosperity after years of drift. He offered champagne to the press if he won a tournament, won it, served out the bubbly and acquired his nickname of "Champagne Tony Lema".

He turned up with Jack Nicklaus, Doug Sanders, Phil Rodgers, Doug Ford, Gary Player, Bob Charles, Peter Thomson but not, this time, Arnold Palmer, to try for the 104th British Open at St Andrews. He also turned up too late for serious practice, unlike Nicklaus who, imbued with a proper sense of the game's traditions, was transparently set on a British Open or three. He was in good form, too, and spent time learning the bizarre geography of the Old Course.

Lema, certainly in the early stages, simply (simply?) hit the ball in the direction his caddie indicated, for he had not had time to learn the whereabouts of Old Course hazards. He also had calmer weather than many starters, scoring 73, but there were tall scores for many (Charles took 79) as the wind rose. Three and even four putts were common, as players were buffeted on the greens. Christy O'Connor and Jean Garaialde, the Basque, were not blown off course (a difficult feat for the most malevolent of winds in O'Connor's case) and led with 71s.

Purists found fault with Lema's easy-looking swing, but the results of his second and third St Andrews' test papers were 68 and 68, better than all the rest, giving him a seven-stroke lead over Nicklaus, who had at last got the measure of the Old Course with a 66. He was a stroke ahead of Bernard Hunt and Bruce Devlin, and two ahead of Roberto de Vicenzo, Harry Weetman and O'Connor. Lema was hitting long (he twice drove the 359-yard ninth) and putting solidly in his second 68.

Though Nicklaus set up another record by completing the last 36 holes in 134, he was five shots shy of his fellow American at the end. One joyous swoop round the loop at the far end of the course in five consecutive

**Tony Lema enjoys his best champagne moment yet at St Andrews.**

threes by Lema was enough to discourage even the greatest. Lema was a pupil of Lucius Bateman, a black pro working in Oakland across from San Francisco. Lema doubtless raised a glass to Bateman as the champagne flowed. Teacher and pupil had radically different lifestyles. Bateman, like other black professionals, earned his livelihood at a driving range. He also taught Dick Lotz, who earned good money on the Tour and reportedly said of himself: "Some people said I could have made it as a pro. But they didn't allow coloured players then."

## "The only guys on the tour were a bunch of dull bastards."

HERB GRAFFIS,
of golf pre-Palmer.

## "The hole in one."

GROUCHO MARX,
on the most difficult shot.

● Soccer star John White, of Tottenham, winner of 22 Scotland caps, was killed by lightning as he sheltered under oak trees at an Enfield, London, club, where he had been playing golf.

● Arnold Palmer, the first winner of the World Match Play championship at Wentworth, sponsored by Carreras Piccadilly, a cigarette firm, had just stopped smoking. He started again, but not on course. His agent, Mark McCormack, became convinced that this was affecting Palmer's ability to win tournaments.

● The first Espirito Santo Trophy for women's amateur teams went to France, in France at St Germain, represented by Claudine Cros, Catherine Lacoste and Brigitte Varangot, by a stroke (588-599) from Barbara McIntire, Carol Sorenson and Barbara White of the United States; 25 nations entered.

**Catherine Lacoste: one of French trio to win the first World Team Trophy.**

● Great Britain and Ireland won their first Eisenhower Trophy in Rome. Michael Bonallack, Rodney Foster, Michael Lunt and Ronnie Shade beat Canada by two shots (895-897).

# Gary Player completes his set of majors

ALL SORTS of firsts were achieved by Gary Player at Bellerive Country Club, St Louis, Missouri, on June 21. None but he from outside Great Britain or the United States (unless you count Harry Vardon and Ted Ray from Jersey in the Channel Islands) had ever won the US Open, and he was the first South African to do so (and Ray was the last foreigner to do so). Player now made a threesome with Gene Sarazen and Ben Hogan, the only previous winners of all four of the modern majors.

The play-off he forced against Australian Kel Nagle, now aged 44, was not the most popular media event ever staged on an American golf course but, after he had beaten Nagle 71-74 in the 18-hole play-off, he gave the assembled press and television reporters (though some had disassembled by this time) a story, for he handed $25,000 of his $26,000 prize back to the USGA: $20,000 was to promote junior golf, $5,000 to fund cancer research.

Player put up the neatest of figures, two 70s and two 71s, but performed rather untidily towards the end of the 72 holes regulation play. He was ahead after rounds two and three, and led by three with three to play. Then a five by Player on the short 16th and a birdie from Nagle at the long 17th brought them level. Player, five up after eight in the play-off, was a comfortable winner. Ken Venturi, hampered by a recurrence of circulatory problems in his hands, did not make the 36-hole cut in this 65th Open, the first one-round-a-day Open.

## Jack Nicklaus sets new Masters low

A RECORD score of 271 by Jack Nicklaus for his second green jacket and a succés d'estime for television commentator Henry Longhurst on his first performance from the box by the 16th green made a splendid combination, since Longhurst wasted words about as prodigally as Nicklaus wasted strokes.

Longhurst always let the television pictures tell the story, and found delight in the fact that common English expressions were a novelty to many American ears, for example, the Lema putt that he described as "missable". Nicklaus equalled Lloyd Mangrum's record 18-hole score of 64, and Arnold Palmer's feat of three rounds under 70.

He had nine shots to spare over runners-up Palmer and Player, the first time that the "big three", as they were imprinted on the public consciousness, had occupied the top three places in a tournament.

Nicklaus's driving was phenomenal. On the 10 par-four holes of his third round (64) he only had a pitch left for his second shot, half of them wedges.

### TEE TALK

**"I just don't know about the guy. He looks like W.C.Fields in drag. But he happens to be the best in the business."**

CBS TELEVISION PRODUCER

## Peter Thomson's fifth Open

ONLY HARRY VARDON'S total of six British Opens lay ahead of Peter Thomson of Australia after he took his fifth at Birkdale by two strokes from Brian Huggett, the bantamweight battler from Wales, and Irishman Christy O'Connor.

The American contingent, with Arnold Palmer present again, was small but influential it could be said, except for one Walter Danecki, 43, a so-called (by Danecki) professional from Milwaukee.

His 100 plus scores in an attempt to qualify were extreme examples of what Leonard Crawley meant when, moustache twitching, he would denounce some nefarious practice or other as "not goff".

Danecki was not really a pro either. Mind you he had made an application to join the US PGA. The kerfuffle all this caused in the offices of newspapers, even the "heavies", was remarkable.

Now that Gary Player had collected his four majors, Jack Nicklaus was more intent than ever on a British Open. This, by the way, is to be the last with two rounds on the final day. An extra day's gate money, not to mention the ever-open eye of television, have changed the habits of 73 years.

Danecki was not the only would-be qualifier in difficulties. Out after 36 holes went Sam Snead, Phil Rodgers, Doug Sanders and Bob Charles.

Tony Lema, a late arrival again, started well in defence of his title with a 68, and led, with Bruce Devlin, on 140 at halfway, when five strokes covered 14 players. A neck strain put Gary Player out by lunch on day three. Nicklaus's 77 (third round) and Palmer's 79 (fourth round) were terminal.

Thomson, with the ball run-

Tony Lema at Birkdale: 5½ Ryder Cup points out of 6.

ning and he hitting straight, was coming through the field, and was one up on Lema and Devlin with 18 holes remaining. Lema played the two par fives that now completed the Birkdale lay-out rather badly, Thomson perfectly in true linksland style. He had birdies at both and beat Brian Huggett, who had the best last round (70) of the leaders, and Christy O'Connor by two shots.

# US singles strength

A US VICTORY in the Ryder Cup was made certain in the singles at Birkdale where, led by Byron Nelson, the Americans halved the foursomes on the first day, won the fourballs on the second day 4-2, with two halves, and the singles on the final day 10 1/2-5 1/2. Tony Lema had a fine match, five points out of six, but the author's sharpest memory of the match is of the two fourballs in which Peter Alliss (who later won both his singles) and Christy O'Connor first lost 6 & 4 to Arnold Palmer and PGA champion Dave Marr, then beat them by one hole in a terrific afternoon scrap.

Who's that with Byron Nelson? Britain's Premier Harold Wilson. (Below) captain Harry Weetman at the Ryder Cup.

## SCORECARD

**British Open** (Royal Birkdale, Lancashire)
P Thomson 74 68 72 71 285

**US Open** (Bellerive CC, St Louis, Mo)
G Player 70 70 71 71 282
(Play-off: Player 71, KDG Nagle 74)

**Masters** (Augusta, Ga)
JW Nicklaus 67 71 64 69 271

**US PGA** (Laurel Valley, Ligonier, Pa)
D Marr 70 69 70 71 280
Leading US money-winner:
JW Nicklaus $140,752.14; GB: PW Thomson
£7,011

**British Amateur** (Royal Porthcawl, Wales)
MF Bonallack bt J B Carr 7 & 6

**US Amateur** (S Hills CC, Tulsa, Okla)
RJ Murphy 73 69 76 73 291

**US Women's Open** (Atlantic City CC, Northfield, NJ)
C Mann 290

**British Women's Amateur** (St Andrews, Scot)
B Varangot bt B Robertson 4 & 3

**US Women's Amateur** (Lakewood CC, Denver, Col)
J Ashley bt Mrs D Welts 5 & 4

**Canada Cup** (Madrid, Spain)
S Africa (G Player & H Henning) 571
(Individual): Player 281

**World Match Play** (Wentworth, Surrey)
G Player bt P Thomson 3 & 2

**Ryder Cup** (Royal Birkdale, Merseyside)
US 19½, GB & Ireland 12½

**Walker Cup** (Baltimore CC, Five Farms Old Course, Md)
US 12, GB & Ireland 12

## SHORT PUTTS

● Gary Player, seven down to Tony Lema after 19 holes of their World Match Play semifinal at Wentworth, was stung by a dismissive remark by a spectator. He fought his way back and beat Lema at the 37th hole; then won the final against Peter Thomson 3 & 2.

● Bob Murphy, 22, from the University of Florida won the first Amateur championship he had entered at Tulsa, Oklahoma. The championship was the first decided at stroke play, on the same lines as the Open championship.

● Bob Dickson, also a student, of Oklahoma State University, inadvertently had a 15th club in his bag for two holes of the second round. It was not his but cost him four strokes. He would still have won but for bogeys at the 71st and 72nd holes.

# Clark ties Walker Cup

EARLIER IN THE year Clive Clark, 20, had lost the British Amateur to Michael Bonallack. In the crucial match of the Walker Cup at Baltimore in September he was one down to Mark Hopkins, who looked safe for a half and victory as his third finished close to the hole on the final green.

Clark then holed from 35 feet for a birdie that halved his contest with Hopkins and the Cup match, too, though the United States, as holders, retained the trophy. The visitors had led by five going into the last series of singles, which America won 6-1, bringing about the first tied match in the 43-year history of the Walker Cup.

Clive Clark: 35-foot putt to tie.

# Dave Marr's finest hour

ARNOLD PALMER, like Jack Nicklaus at Columbus the year before, could not win the US PGA in his own backyard at Laurel Valley, Pennsylvania. Instead Dave Marr, from Texas, without a win since 1962, gained his first major with a courageous last round, threatened as he was by the big guns of Jack Nicklaus and Bill Casper. All went well for 13 holes and, when he got into difficulties, he got out of them with ingenuity and nerve, especially the four iron over the pond at the 15th, and his recovery shots to make par at the 18th. He told Herbert Warren Wind later that he was so confident of winning that he was starting to prepare his acceptance speech on the 14th tee.

# Nicklaus joins modern majors club

JACK NICKLAUS won all his matches at Muirfield in the 1959 Walker Cup. Seven years later he came to the shores of the Firth of Forth determined to conquer the last unattained major, the British Open, and found Muirfield much changed. The Royal & Ancient, now clearly of the USGA persuasion (make them tough it out) had let the rough grow in, narrowing the fairways. Tall grass waved menacingly in the breeze, close to the greens in many places.

Nicklaus won, for all that, and from the best field in years. His influence and that of Arnold Palmer upon the world's leading golfers, who were as usual mostly American, was now producing a championship of great quality, with 18-year-old Bobby Cole, the new Amateur champion from South Africa, and all.

Many players were felt to be capable of winning, but there was no great faith lavished on any of the Britons. This was a mistake, in one case only, that being the shining exception of David Thomas, winner of national titles on the continent of Europe and tournaments at home and loser of a play-off for the 1958 British Open.

He was the sole Briton in the top 15, Irishman Christy O'Connor in joint 13th place being the only other golfer from the British Isles within ten shots of Nicklaus's winning total of 282. Moreover Thomas, born in Newcastle, finished like Doug Sanders only a stroke behind Nicklaus.

Many and varied were the ploys devised to keep the ball on what remained of the fairways, and there is no doubt that

Peter Butler: round of a lifetime ... 65.

Nicklaus's enormous strength and accuracy with his irons, used more and more as the event progressed, was crucial to his success. As often happens, a golfer whom few (rightly, as it turned out) considered capable of a sustained challenge led on the first day. This was Jimmy Hitchcock, the British Ryder Cup player, with a 70, one under par on the 6,887-yard course.

Nicklaus made his move in the second round, with a 67, trumped by 66 from Phil Rodgers, but Nicklaus still led with 137, one ahead of another British Ryder Cupper, Peter Butler, who slipped two ahead of Rodgers with the round of a lifetime, 65. He slipped out of contention with 80 next day, when Nicklaus did not thrive, a patchy short game pushing him two behind Rodgers, who overtook him with a back nine of 30.

Sanders and Thomas had stuck closer to par than most players, for the scores betrayed many ups and downs from day to day, and both were well in contention. So was Palmer, but he took chances with the rough, and faded with 74 to eighth place.

Nicklaus, out last with Rodgers, was making his iron power count. Up ahead Sanders and Thomas set a target – 283. Despite the odd putting and driving error, at the 15th Nicklaus needed to par in to tie. Two irons and two putts at the 17th (528 yards) gave him the birdie he required to force a win, which he did with a tap-in par at the last hole. This Open broke new ground, for it was organized with a Saturday finish.

# Catch-up Casper is Palmer's nemesis

PERHAPS THE greatest disappointment that Arnie's army ever suffered was delivered in two depressing instalments at the Olympic Club, San Francisco, by Billy Casper.

He had become a good deal slimmer since his rookie year, and solved dietary problems with such exotic nutriments as avocado pear and buffalo meat.

There was no denying the validity of his victory, though he was seven shots behind halfway

through the fourth round. The feeling was that Palmer lost taking chances in pursuit of Ben Hogan's record Open score of 276.

His lead dribbled away, Casper holed useful putts and Palmer had problems in merely tying with Casper.

Next day he was four up after nine holes in the play-off, four down at the end, and Casper had his second Open, one more than Palmer.

Billy Casper: the man who saddened Arnie's Army.

# Nicklaus in rules row

COLONEL Tony Duncan offered to withdraw as referee in the morning round of the World Match Play final at Wentworth after he had ruled against Jack Nicklaus at the ninth hole. The British Open champion had hooked into a ditch and had taken a drop under penalty of one stroke.

He then requested a free drop, because of a large advertising hoarding about 60 yards ahead, in line, said Nicklaus, with the hole. Colonel Duncan, a former Walker Cup captain, said no, which Nicklaus is reported to have described as "a bum decision" and Duncan's offer to withdraw was accepted on the next tee. Gerald Micklem, recently chairman of the Royal & Ancient championship committee, took over. Player, who won 6 & 4, is reported to have said, sotto voce, "Shut up and forget." The reaction of Leonard Crawley, was: "No-one lost more by this than Nicklaus himself."

Crawley added that the matter was "not a question of who is right: in match play a referee's decision is final. Nicklaus's comment is therefore irrelevant." Nicklaus certainly had little chance of so much as halving the hole, as Player's second shot was eight feet from the pin.

**Col Tony Duncan: no to Nicklaus.**

# Lema dies in air crash

TONY LEMA and his wife Betty were killed when the small aircraft in which they were travelling from the US PGA championship at Akron to an exhibition near Chicago crashed. Two other people were killed as the plane came down on the seventh green at a Lansing course, sliding on into a lake. More than 1,000 attended the funerals at Oakland, California.

## Cowan leaves it late to catch Beman

GARY COWAN of Canada, a 27-year-old from Ontario, caught Deane Beman over the closing holes of the US Amateur at Merion, and beat him by a stroke next day in the first play-off, since the title was disputed at match play.

Cowan was the first non-American to win the title since Ross Somerville, another native of Ontario, did so in 1932. South African Bobby Cole beat R.D.B.M. (Ronnie) Shade (his initials, it was said with feeling, stood for "Right Down the Bloody Middle") over 18 holes for the British Amateur at Carnoustie. Sea mist made 36 holes impossible.

**Tony Lema: death on the seventh green at Lansing.**

## Nicklaus breaks Masters mould

ON APRIL 11 Jack Nicklaus contrived to retain the Masters title he had won the previous year with his record score of 271. The scoring was less spectacular, but it was the first back-to-back Masters win. If Gay Brewer had not three-putted the 72nd hole, he might have robbed Nicklaus of the distinction. Brewer paid the price in the play-off, not even finishing second, for he scored 78, Tommy Jacobs 72 and Nicklaus 70 for his third green jacket.

# Jack Nicklaus: a major talent

JACK WILLIAM Nicklaus was very like Robert Tyre Jones in that he saw winning major championships as the way to golfing fame, and for much of his career subordinated all other interests to his quest for such prizes. They were certainly unlike in both technique and physique, facts wryly recognized by Jones after Nicklaus had burned up Augusta one day. The great amateur said admiringly that Nicklaus "plays a game with which I am not familiar."

Strangely for such a masterful golfer, with major successes stretching over three decades, Nicklaus took a long time to add popularity to the respect his golf demanded from the start. He could be described as the most successful slimmer who ever lived.

He arrived on the professional scene in 1961, a year after he put up the lowest total ever achieved by an amateur in the American Open, failing by two shots to catch Arnold Palmer. Here was a clear threat to the dominance of Palmer, whose supporters bridled at such impudence, and it can be imagined that they enjoyed dismissing the newcomer as "Ohio Fats" and "Fat Jack". Palmer's British regiments felt much the same, and Nicklaus suffered some cat-calling and, worse, applause when he flubbed a shot.

## Nicklaus the cub

Bulky yes, fat, scarcely, for this well-muscled young man hit every last ounce of his considerable weight, and could outdistance everyone else around from the tee, but only when he felt it necessary.

Who can forget the moment when, against Doug Sanders in the British Open play-off of 1970 at St Andrews, he stripped off his sweater, and signalled as clearly as can be through his body language that he was intent on driving the green, 350 yards away? This he did, and indeed, went slightly beyond it, and got down

There are many opinions about who is the greatest golfer of all time, but Jack Nicklaus has won more major titles than any other player in the world, which surely entitles him to a leading place among the immortals

**First British Open win, at his favourite course, Muirfield.**

in two more for a decisive birdie. Born at Columbus, Ohio, on January 21, 1940, Nicklaus got down to golf earlier in life than most. His father owned a number of chemist shops, and was

comfortably off, so young Jack was a pupil of swing specialist Grout, and a busy country club golfer at Scioto.

He broke 70 when he was 13, with an eagle at Scioto's last

hole, a par five, with drive, two iron and 35-foot putt. That says it all about Nicklaus really, except that neither success, money nor anything else deflected him from maturity. Palmer had won the Ohio amateur at 24. Nicklaus won it at 16 and he was National Amateur champion at 19.

At this time, and well into his professional career, Nicklaus affected a bristly short haircut, often surmounted by a peaked cap. Taken with his name, the overall effect was unmistakably Germanic. A young man of Nicklaus's size and awesome talent could scarcely stay in the shadow of Palmer, but the brilliant aura Palmer's army of fans could see about their hero dazzled sponsors and advertisers, too, so he continued to bring in more business, via mutual agent Mark McCormack, than the new lad.

## 'Pilot' dropped

After Nicklaus's burst of major titles between 1962 and 1966, there was only one more major in the 1960s, though it was no less than the 1967 US Open, and Nicklaus in his second professional decade dropped his commercial pilot, McCormack, and developed the role we know him by now, that of the Golden Bear, the name of his enterprises.

The difference between Nicklaus's appearance in the mid-1960s and the early 1970s was most noticeable. He was still an imposing figure but (and this is where the slimming comes in, or the body reshaping or whatever) he did not look so lumpy and, what is more, his blond locks were longer and stylishly cut so that the crew-cut square-headed impression had vanished.

Nicklaus also learned to charm the press. He got a big chuckle from them when he walked into the interview room at Pebble Beach during the rain-delayed Crosby tournament of 1978. He had not done well earlier in the tournament but, when the weather smiled and allowed some golf, scored an exciting 66 even if he did smash his approach to the 18th over the green.

"Waal," said he, "I didn't think I was going to get to talk to you fellers this week." He was a frank interviewee when asked if he now had a chance of winning. "Not a chance, not with 12 guys in front of me. They won't all slip up." And they didn't.

## The oldest Master

The crowds always know he will provide something of quality and, what is more, the man seems to be inexhaustible. He cheered up the over-forties no end when, in 1986, he added a 20th championship to his honours list. He was 46, and at Augusta on April 13 became the oldest winner to date of the Masters with a final round of 65, consisting of par for the first eight holes, then three birdies in succession, followed by an eagle, three birdies, one bogey and two pars.

Even Nick Price, still in his 20s, who had recorded a 63 the day before, could not keep up with this finishing thrust. Nor could three others of the best players of the post-Big Three era, who finished behind the Bear – Tom Kite, Greg Norman and Severiano Ballesteros.

Throughout the years from his first US Open to that April day at Augusta, Nicklaus has been coming back time and again to challenge at the highest level. His number of majors might easily have been 50 to 75 per cent higher, given the odd putt here and there, for his number of top-three finishes is in the same heady region as his wins.

His strengths are his strength – of mind and of body. Did anyone ever concentrate quite so devotedly as Nicklaus, though his penchant for dwelling over a putt, after taking a good long look at the hole before he adopts his stance, let him in for slow-play brushes with authority.

His long iron-play has set him apart from others, which is one reason for his unique record in the majors, where the USGA and others set up courses that demand long, accurate hitting beyond the norm, which is where Nicklaus's ability to make greens in regulation without his wooden clubs has been so potent.

He cannot be compared as a putter with such as Bill Casper and Bobby Locke, nor as a bunker player with Gary Player, nor as a run-up magician with Tony Lema, but then his long game gave him fewer problems

| | Masters | US Open | British Open | US PGA |
|---|---|---|---|---|
| 1958 | PALMER | Bolt | Thomson | Finsterwald |
| 1959 | Wall | Casper | PLAYER | Rosburg |
| 1960 | PALMER | PALMER | Nagle | J Hebert |
| 1961 | PLAYER | Littler | PALMER | J Barber |
| 1962 | PALMER | NICKLAUS | PALMER | PLAYER |
| 1963 | NICKLAUS | Boros | Charles | NICKLAUS |
| 1964 | PALMER | Venturi | Lema | Nichols |
| 1965 | NICKLAUS | PLAYER | Thomson | Marr |
| 1966 | NICKLAUS | Casper | NICKLAUS | Geiberger |

## SCORECARD

**US Amateur**
1959, 1961

**US Open**
1962, 1967, 1972, 1980

**British Open**
1966, 1970, 1978

**Masters**
1963, 1965, 1966, 1972, 1975, 1986

**US PGA**
1963, 1971, 1973, 1975, 1980

**Four times US Open champion.**

**Getting out of trouble a Nicklaus speciality.**

**The crowds did not fall away as he got older.**

round the greens than his rivals. Like Ben Hogan, he hit the ball nearer the pin.

## Dominant trio

There is no question as to the quality of the opposition he has faced throughout his career, from Ben Hogan and Sam Snead to Norman von Nida, Nick Faldo, Tom Watson, and most of all, in the 1960s, the other members of the Big Three. The accompanying table shows how dominant they were from 1958 to 1966, when between them they held, every year, one, two, three or, in 1962, all of the four majors.

It is in this sort of company that Nicklaus has been player of the year five times, leading money-winner on the PGA tour eight times (and in the top three 15 times), with combined career earnings of more than $6 million. He won all his matches in two Walker Cup appearances, was individual winner in half his six World Cup appearances and played six Ryder Cup matches, in which he teed off 28 times, won 17 and halved three.

Perhaps his keenest disappointment will have been that, after leading his country in 1983 to a narrow win in his first stint as non-playing Ryder Cup captain, four years later Europe gained their first away win against his team and on his most cherished architectural creation at that, Muirfield Village, at Dublin in his native Ohio.

His acquisitive instincts were not blunted as he joined the Seniors Tour, winning his 100th professional event, The Tradition, with a final 65. He gave the youngsters a fright in the 1998 Masters. Aged 58, he finished only four behind winner Mark O'Meara. Hip problems led to an operation, and his amazing run of nearly 150 majors was interrupted.

## TEE TALK

**"To win the things he's won, build courses, be a daddy to those kids, it's phenomenal. Stick a broom in his rear end and he could sweep the USA."**

JACK BURKE,
on father of five Nicklaus.

# De Vicenzo steals Bear's honey

ROBERT DE VICENZO was busy the Sunday before the British Open, playing a match with Jack Nicklaus at Royal Birkdale. Back at the Hoylake links of the Royal Liverpool Club on Monday, he would not divulge the result of the match because it had been filmed for television transmission later. He did give a hint ,though, and used a highly prophetic phrase in the process: "I was stealing some of the Bear's honey."

This the big bald man in the flat cap from Argentina certainly did in the Open that followed, beating the American, who had won the US Open at Baltusrol a month earlier, by two strokes. After years of near misses (four thirds and a second) even de Vicenzo must have been touched by the warmth of public acclamation for his success. Moreover, it was gained in the most courageous fashion.

The course was very dry until a thunderstorm early on the Friday. Nicklaus was now and then driving the ball well in excess of 300 yards in the fast running conditions. De Vicenzo's putting troubles vanished in round three, when he got four long ones down and otherwise holed out sensibly. So with a round to go he led Gary Player by two and Nicklaus by three.

On the raised tenth green the challenge of Player dropped away as he three-putted from ten feet, and de Vicenzo holed from about the same distance for a two-stroke swing. Nicklaus up ahead, in company with Clive Clark, was closing in, though. He failed to get his four on the long 14th, succeeded on the long 16th and birdied the last to set a target at

Roberto de Vicenzo: pride of Argentina at Hoylake.

280. De Vicenzo needed three pars to win, and almost at once played his masterstroke. His tee shot at the 16th was slightly cut, but his second, a three wood over The Field (the practice ground) which was out of bounds, was greeted with a great roar from the stand at the hole-side. The birdie gave him the cushion he needed, his second at the 17th just avoided bunker trouble and he had no further cares. Clark and Player were third, four behind Nicklaus.

Hoylake proved troublesome again to the very best, and de Vicenzo was the first to become champion there with a score of under 70 to his credit. Others broke 70, too, but couldn't keep it up because consistent scoring day after day was never easy, despite Hoylake's flat course and fine greens.

# Newcomer Jacklin tipped for the top

DAILY TELEGRAPH golf writer Leonard Crawley telephoned the author one evening that summer and said that if he would like to watch the next English Open champion, he would be performing the following day in the PGA championship at Thorndon Park, Essex.

Tony Jacklin, born in Scunthorpe in 1944, was Crawley's nomination, and in the first round the author watched him place his drives and strike his long irons to perfection on this tree-lined course.

Only his wife, Viviene, playing partner, caddies and another journalist were with Jacklin, who struck his 64th shot on to the final green ... and then four-putted. At Hoylake he made his first significant showing in a major, finishing on his own in fifth place, seven behind the winner.

Jacklin had not been required to putt on the 16th at Royal St George's during his first British victory in the Dunlop Masters. He holed his tee shot, and for the first time the feat was caught by the television cameras.

Another youngster to take the eye was Brian Barnes, 22, who turned professional in 1964 after winning the Youths' Championship, and in three years reached 11th in the Order of Merit. He was also one of a group called the Butten Boys, at a residential golf school at Sundridge Park, Kent, founded by Ernest Butten, who was intent on producing an Open champion.

In the case of the long hitters Barnes and Tommy Horton this did not seem a mere pipedream. Self-discipline and good behaviour were the boys' watchwords.

Brian Barnes: at 22, the lofty, big-hitter looked the part.

Milestone: TV caught Tony Jacklin's hole-in-one.

# The great debate: 1.62 or 1.68?

LEONARD CRAWLEY had been thundering away in the "Daily Telegraph" for years that Britain should turn from the small (1.62-inch) ball to the American-sized

**Leonard Crawley: insisted that 1.68 inches was the right calibre for every golfer.**

ball (1.68 inches). The comprehensive Ryder Cup defeat (23½-8½) inflicted on Britain and Ireland at Houston brought this broadside from the sage of Worlington: "We must face facts and admit that American golfers are superior ... the big ball, upon which they are brought up, requires more control and a better method of striking and they are far superior on and around the green.

"It cannot be said too often that is is easy to go from the big to little ball, but to go from the little to the big one requires months of hard work and experience."

Ben Hogan had led America (playing the small ball at Houston) to the biggest Ryder Cup win to date, and all this without Jack Nicklaus, as yet ineligible under the PGA's five-year probation.

Harry Weetman, still smarting from his 1957 dispute with Dai Rees, refused to join the official party under Rees's jurisdiction.

## Nicklaus lowers Open record

TELEPHONE NUMBERS for gates (88,414) at the US Open at Baltusrol, New Jersey, and prize money, now well on the way to $200,000, but not for Jack Nicklaus's scores. They included a 67 and a final round of 65, and were the lowest yet for the championship, beating by one Ben Hogan's 276 of 1948.

This was the Bear's second Open and seventh major title in six years. Arnold Palmer was four shots away in second place, and the rest at a respectful distance. The galleries were much taken with Lee Trevino, a Mexican-American with a store of one-liners and off-the-cuff quips.

Trevino finished fifth, eight behind Nicklaus, with a tidy sequence of scores, 72 70 71 70. By the end of the year he was 44 places behind Nicklaus in the money list, with $26,000 against $188,988. That was due to Trevino taking advantage of invitations offered by tournament sponsors on the strength of his high finish in the Open.

## Lacoste upstages the pros

CATHERINE LACOSTE had unequalled sporting antecedents. Her father was lawn tennis champion René Lacoste, her mother, the former Simone Thion de la Chaume, a star of European amateur golf in the 1920s.

Catherine became the new toast of France. She won most titles in sight as a teenager and, with Claudine Cros and Brigitte Varangot, gained the World Team title in 1964. On July 2, at Hot Springs, Virginia, aged 22 she became the first amateur to take

the US Open title. All was not light and joy, because Catherine, though loquacious, did not communicate well with her peers in these new surroundings. However, she did communicate with the press, and said that other golfers were not very nice to her.

Louise Suggs, and then Beth Stone, certainly did their best to catch Lacoste, who led by seven at one time in the final round, but by only a stroke at the 17th. Here a bold birdie sealed the fate of the title.

## Tour pros threaten boycott

Not for the first time in recent years, American tour pros threatened a boycott. The huge cash-raising potential of television, from which the tour pros thought the PGA was reaping too much benefit, was re-opening the quarrels of prewar years, when Bob Harlow was in and out of office as tour manager, as the long-standing club versus tour pro wrangle rumbled on. The

prospect of tournament pros setting up their own organization could clearly not be ruled out.

Unlike the inter-war professionals, many of whom had known hardship, the post war generation were better educated and had wider ambitions. They had no intention of acting the respectful forelock-touching club pro while they could make a fortune touring.

**Charlie Sifford's 19 years of trying paid off in the Hartford Open.**

# Goalby's Masters, De Vicenzo's regrets

SCORING WAS consistently good at the Masters right through to the final on April 14, except in one sense, that of putting numbers down on paper.

An error by Roberto de Vicenzo's playing partner, Tommy Aaron, who put down a four on the Argentine's card instead of a three on the 71st hole, was fatally compounded when de Vicenzo signed for it. The error gave Bob Goalby from Belleville, Illinois, the Masters.

Everyone, including a vast television audience, saw de Vicenzo hole his third shot on the penultimate hole, a five-foot birdie putt, but the relevant rule makes it clear that if a player returns a score higher than actually achieved, the score as returned shall stand.

That meant that instead of a 65 that would have given de Vicenzo a play-off, he was stuck with a 66 for 278, one too many.

This was almost as unfortunate for Goalby as it was for de Vicenzo, for whom there was a vast upsurge of sympathy. For Goalby, who had after all finished in 66, there was much faint praise and worse, such as noises about his not deserving a green jacket.

Goalby himself was quick to say that he would rather not have won in this fashion, but would have preferred to battle it out in a play-off. De Vicenzo said in that charming way many Latins have: "I am a stupid."

De Vicenzo had perhaps been rushed into error by being escorted quickly away after putting out at the 72nd to be interviewed on television.

He refused to take out his disappointment on Aaron. At the Press conference he said: "It's my fault. Tommy feels like I feel, very bad. I think the rule is hard." It was not a very happy birthday, that last day of the Masters, for de Vicenzo.

There was one positive outcome to this unhappy incident, perhaps the saddest for 90 years, since the British Open was first held at St Andrews. Bob Martin got the title then after a thoroughly mismanaged rules mix-up culminating, by an ironic coincidence, in David Strath's refusal to participate in a play-off.

After the Masters mix-up, a special score-check area was to be set up, with rigorous scrutiny before any signing of cards was done.

Just above de Vicenzo's signature on the fatal Masters' card were printed the words: "I have checked my score hole by hole." Soon he was winning at Houston, checking his card again, and again ...

Goalby's Masters: thanks to the card that de Vicenzo didn't check.

# Boros robs Palmer of PGA chance

ADVANCING YEARS have never bothered Julius Boros, who became the oldest winner of a major championship in modern times at Pecan Valley, San Antonio, in Texas, on July 21.

Arnold Palmer, who had won all the other majors, just failed to get the missing item from his collection when he and New Zealander Bob Charles failed by a stroke to equal Boros's 281. It was a close finish, with George Archer and Marty Fleckman, a Texan, just two behind Boros.

Boros's rich year did not end there, for three weeks later he won the US Tour's biggest first prize, $50,000 at the Westchester Classic in New York. But even that could not topple Billy Casper at the top of the money list with a total in excess of $200,000.

# Tour pros get their own way

THE ILL-FEELING between the PGA and the American tour professionals finally flared into open warfare. Television had made the pros bigger stars than ever. They were bent on getting a better return from their stardom on the small screen. Too much, they thought, was going into the general fund and, since most members of the PGA were club pros, that did not suit at all. The tour men wanted to steer their own ship.

The PGA wanted to maintain control, with both hands on the purse strings. The truth was that the tour players could well do without the PGA, who had seldom made the well-being of the tour their major concern. Thanks to the deeds and colourful expertise of stars like Palmer, Trevino, Nicklaus and the rest, big business saw golf more and more as a means of selling major products. It was no longer simply a matter of the local chamber of commerce puffing the attractions of their city through a golf tournament.

When push came to shove, and the PGA's intransigence overcame even Arnold Palmer's opposition to breaking up the old regime, the tour players had no difficulty in running up a rich tour schedule of their own. The pros called the golf green the dancing floor: a player can't dance a victory jig on it till he gets there. The tour players were the dancing girls and wanted their crock of gold.

On August 23 the players, led by Gardner Dickinson and Nicklaus among others, announced the formation of the American Professional Golfers, and – bull point – the APG had a $3.5-million, 28-event 1969 tour lined up. The PGA appealed to sponsors: no good, they didn't want a tour without stars, and neither did the television compa-nies, and Sam Snead was the only "name" that was not in the APG camp. The "compromise" that was speedily reached was in essence utter surrender by the PGA. A new division was set up within the PGA to run the tour, with a ten-man policy board at the top, made up of four players, three PGA officials and three businessmen. Joe Dey took over as commissioner of the new set-up, appointed by the touring pros and only by them. They had won.

## TEE TALK

### "Yes, but why you no hit it?"

ROBERTO DE VICENZO, softly to Brian Huggett, who had been lamenting about a foot mark at the previous hole where he had missed a two-foot putt.

# Player hits awesome three-wood

GARY PLAYER won on three continents, but his high spot came in midsummer when he struck one of the best shots of his life at not-so-summery Carnoustie to regain the British Open title, his first major since 1965. The course was fearsomely set-up at a massive 7,252 yards.

"The shot" came at the 14th in the last round. Player had never been ahead till the sixth hole and now, with Bill Casper and Bob Charles level with Player at two under, his playing partner Jack Nicklaus hit a marvellous recovery. Player bested it with a three wood two feet from the pin which had even Henry Cotton jigging with excitement. The shot, which gave Player a crucial eagle, was played completely blind, and he had also to fly the menacing, deep pair of bunkers known as the Spectacles.

Nicklaus managed 'only' a birdie. On the next hole Player protected his lead with a fine recovery from the rough.

**Bob Charles: pressed Gary Player hard in Carnoustie Open.**

## SHORT PUTTS

● Tony Jacklin, having won his first British tournament last year, persevered on the American circuit where he had first played in 1967, and won the Jacksonville Open, finishing 29th in the PGA money list.

● Despite the opposition from ball-makers who had the monopoly of the 1.62-inch ball, the 1.68-inch ball was to be played for a trial period of three years in all professional tournaments on the British circuit.

● Henry Cotton was made an honorary member of the Royal & Ancient.

● Arnold Palmer was the first player to pile up $1 million in prize money.

● Death of Tommy Armour aged 72. He had followed his successes in the two big Opens with a long, lucrative career as a most authoritative teacher and writer of best-selling instructional books. He invented the word "yips" to describe the tension that afflicts the nervous putter.

● Craig Wood and Lawson Little also died in 1968.

## SCORECARD

**British Open** (Carnoustie, Scot)
G Player 74 71 71 73 289

**US Open** (Oak Hill, Rochester, NY)
L Trevino 69 68 69 69 275

**Masters** (Augusta, Ga)
R Goalby 70 70 71 66 277

**US PGA** (Pecan Valley, San Antonio, Texas)
J Boros 71 71 70 69 281
Leading US money-winner:
W Casper $205,168.67;
GB: G Brewer £23,107

**British Amateur** (Troon, Scot)
MF Bonallack bt JB Carr 7 & 6

**US Amateur** (Scioto CC, Ohio)
B Fleischer 73 70 71 70 284

**Bonallack: third Amateur.**

**US Women's Open** (Moselem Springs GC, Pa)
S Berning 289

**British Women's Amateur** (Walton Heath, Surrey)
B Varangot bt C Rubin 20th

**US Women's Amateur** (Oakland Hills CC, Mich)
Mrs J Gunderson Carner bt Mrs A Quast Welts 5 & 4

**World Cup** (Olgiata, Rome)
Canada (A Balding & G Knudson) 569
(Individual): Balding 274

**Gunderson: fifth US Amateur.**

**World Match Play** (Wentworth, Surrey)
G Player bt RJ Charles 1h

**Eisenhower Trophy** (Melbourne, Australia)
US 868

**Espirito Santo Trophy** (Melbourne)
US 616

**Curtis Cup** (Royal Co Down, N Ire)
US 10½, GB & Ireland 7½

# Lee Trevino the sixties shooter

LEE TREVINO'S caddie, it is said, had a bet that his boss would break 70 in every round of the US Open championship at Oak Hill, Rochester, in upper New York State. His first three rounds were 69, 68, 69. On the 72nd hole Trevino hung his ball out a little too far to the left (his usual flight started out as if it was going to hook, then it self-corrected). On this occasion he was in some unhealthy-looking rough. He didn't get the ball out first time.

He had shots to spare and did not play safe. He hit his next on to the green and holed the putt: another 69, and his caddie had landed his gamble. Trevino had, all the same, only equalled Jack Nicklaus's record aggregate of 275. But he was the first to beat par and 70 every round.

It seemed, when the last round started, that he was in for a tough battle with Bert Yancey, the Floridian with a smooth swing as different as could be from Trevino's idiosyncratic (some unjustly said, rural) swing.

But Trevino's chipping and putting were his strength, for no more delicate manipulator of the ball ever chipped to the hole-side.

Yancey had covered the first 54 holes in a record 205, but holed out poorly in a final 76. Nicklaus turned that around, but his 67 still left him four behind the wily Trevino, who had four strokes to spare over Nicklaus, who was without a major title for only the second year since turning pro in 1962.

# Jacklin turns US experience to account

Tony Jacklin: giving the Auld Mug a warm welcome in 1969 at Royal Lytham and St Annes with the help of wife Vivienne.

Henry Longhurst: had the right word for Tony Jacklin's final drive at Lytham – "a corker".

HAVING A BRITISH Open champion for the first time since Max Faulkner in 1951 was reward indeed for the faithful and, despite lack of success by British players, ever-increasing Open galleries. Tony Jacklin's win at Royal Lytham and St Annes added the bonus of victory against one of the strongest fields ever assembled for the oldest Open, including a powerful array of Americans, none of whom finished in the first five.

No one doubted that they would be back to exact revenge for this slight, or that they were capable of doing so, but for the moment all was sweetness and light, particularly because of the manner of Jacklin's win, which was a matter of calm command over the course and over his opponents.

They included possibly the best cross-section of American talent yet seen: Jack Nicklaus, Miller Barber, Gay Brewer, Orville Moody (the new American Open champion), Bert Yancey, Bill Casper, Ray Floyd and Lee Trevino. Gary Player, Peter Thomson, Kel Nagle and Coby Legrange, the promising South African, were all present. Arnold Palmer was not.

The experience Jacklin had gained in the fires of competition on the American circuit had a part to play in his eventual victory. The most persistent challenge he faced came from the New Zealander, Bob Charles, winner here six years earlier, when a moderate breeze on the first day died away for the rest of the championship. Now the wind from the northwest seldom relented, and the final rounds were a great test of ball control. Charles started with 66, followed by a 69, but even then was only a stroke ahead of Christy O'Connor, whose record-breaking 65 in the second round was scored in one of his bursts of putting infallibility, for he covered the second nine (par 36) in 32 shots, and putted only ten times.

Jacklin put in two solid rounds, and stood three behind Charles, who in the third round drove indifferently in the wind, scoring 75. When Jacklin strayed off line, his short game came to his rescue. He had not yet gone over par on either half of the course, and led Charles by two, and Roberto de Vicenzo and Thomson by three. Jack Nicklaus, carrying the millstone of a opening round of 75, had come up through the field with a 66, and so had Brian Huggett with a 69. The pair of them were five behind Jacklin.

Setting out on the final round with Charles, Jacklin started with two pars and two birdies, but dropped a shot on the fifth and another on the eighth. However, he got out of trouble on the long sixth, where the wind shift had made it impossible to fly the bunkers on the left of the fairway. A tree did not make his stance easy to take up for his second shot, but he got his five, and birdies on the seventh and ninth put him four clear of Charles at the turn.

Jacklin's bogeys at the 13th and the trickiest par fours on the course, holes 15 and 17, where he three-putted for the first time, were counterbalanced by Charles's errors.

On the 18th tee, not the least difficult driving hole here, Jacklin was two ahead. Charles drove into the left rough, but was not badly placed. At this supremely testing moment in his career Jacklin showed precisely the same mastery with the drive that he had shown at Thorndon Park when the author first saw him. No longer or straighter drive was seen all week. "A corker" said Henry Longhurst on television (in colour for the first time).

Charles put his second on the green. Jacklin put his second inside it as if to rubber-stamp his victory. Jacklin appeared on the green with one shoe on and the other in his hand. It had been torn off in the scrum that formed after he played his approach shot. He two-putted for a two-stroke win, four under par, with never a six all week, and agreed with Nicklaus that it was marvellous to be able to play so well when he was so excited. Nicklaus knows about such things.

Jacklin's prize, besides the maelstrom of deals and endorsements coming his way, was the claret jug, being awarded an OBE, and £4,250, which is £2,550 more than the entire prize fund in Faulkner's year.

De Vicenzo and Thomson were third, three adrift, and Nicklaus and Atlanta pro Davis Love were the leading Americans, joint sixth behind O'Connor.

At last: a British champion to take the Open applause.

## TEE TALK

**"It's always been my contention that the winners of major tournaments are the true champions, although at times some luck may play a part in the victory."**

TONY JACKLIN.

## SHORT PUTTS

● George Archer, escaping with a par from the water at the 15th at Augusta, wins the Masters by a stroke from Tom Weiskopf, George Knudson and Bill Casper.

● Catherine Lacoste of France became the third player to win both the British and American Amateur titles in the same year. No American had managed it, for the previous Little Slam winners were a Scot, Dorothy Campbell, and Pam Barton, the English international. Lacoste also won the French and Spanish Amateurs this year.

● On October 6 Walter Hagen died from throat cancer at the age of 76. Arnold Palmer was one of the pall bearers at the funeral in Michigan.

● Joe Dey, an executive director of the USGA, took up his post as PGA tour commissioner in January.

● Kathy Whitworth equalled Mickey Wright's feat of winning four tournaments in a row on the LPGA tour. Wright did it twice.

## TEE TALK

**"The Clubhouse at Lytham is an ominous gabled structure of brick and wood, undoubtedly the former residence of Count Dracula. But you don't get really frightened until you see the golf course. The rough will hide golf balls, bags and small caddies ..."**

ART SPANDER.

# US Open of nervous leaders

ORVILLE MOODY, after long army service and two years on the PGA tour, won the American Open at his second attempt, an Open that no-one else seemed bold enough to seize.

Eight players, led by Deane Beman, Al Geiberger and Bob Rosburg who were one behind the surprising winner with four others, including Arnold Palmer, two behind, all spurned their chances. Moody's secure long game offset his poor putting, for which the slow greens helped to compensate. While established players almost always won the Masters, ever and anon an unknown took the Open, because, it might be, that playing safe on the narrow, punishing Open set-ups paid off occasionally for lesser players, and frustrated the leading exponents.

Moody: took the US Open prize others feared to grasp.

## SCORECARD

**British Open** (Royal Lytham, Lancs)
A Jacklin 68 70 70 72 280

**US Open** (Champions GC, Cypress Creek, Texas)
O Moody 71 70 68 72 281

**Masters** (Augusta, Ga)
G Archer 67 73 69 72 281

**US PGA** (NCR, Dayton, Ohio)
R Floyd 69 66 67 74 276
Leading US money-winner: F Beard $164,707.11;
GB: W Casper £23,483

**Floyd: US PGA winner.**

**British Amateur** (Royal Liverpool, Merseyside)
MF Bonallack bt W Hyndman III 3 & 2

**US Amateur** (Oakmont, Pa)
S Melnyk 70 73 73 70 286

**US Women's Open** (Scenic Hills, Fla)
D Caponi 294

**British Women's Amateur** (R Portrush, Co Antrim, N Ire)
C Lacoste bt A Irvin 1h

**US Women's Amateur** (Las Colinas, Texas)
C Lacoste bt S Hamlin 3 & 2

**World Cup** (Singapore)
US (O Moody & L Trevino) 552
(Individual): Trevino 275

**World Match Play** (Wentworth, Surrey)
RJ Charles bt G Littler 37th

**Ryder Cup** (Royal Birkdale, Merseyside)
GB & Ireland 16, US 16 (US retain Cup)

**Walker Cup** (Milwaukee, Wis)
US 13, GB & Ireland 11

# Nicklaus's courtly gesture

TONY JACKLIN and Jack Nicklaus were the principals in the most exciting Ryder Cup finale yet at Royal Birkdale in September. The match – new British Open champion versus the greatest golfer of the age – would have drawn the crowds in any case. Another piquant touch was that Nicklaus, despite his mighty list of victories, was a Cup rookie, thanks to his PGA's probationary rules about Cup selec-

tion. But on top of all that the match score was 15 1/2 apiece as the pair of them drove off the final tee. Nicklaus hit from the fairway first, his ball finishing ten yards from the hole. Jacklin had to putt first from the back of the green and finished 18 inches short. Nicklaus gave his birdie putt to win the entire match

every chance, but it went three feet past.

The 20,000-odd crowd held its breath as Nicklaus crouched over the putt ... and holed it. Then he picked up Jacklin's marker, and told him: "I am sure you would have holed, but I was not prepared to see you miss." With the score at 16 all, the Cup

went back to America.

Captain Sam Snead had perhaps been handicapped by too many newcomers in his side. Jacklin had a wonderful Cup match, beating Nicklaus in the first series of singles before the half in that climactic last match. Previously, he had dropped only half a point in four matches. He had restored British golf to an altogether higher plane: the Cup was now sponsored.

167

# Gary Player, the golfer who never gives up

## South Africa's most valuable contribution to the world of golf is a man whose skills have remained undiminished through the years

A GOOD DEFINITION of a professional is a player who soldiers on no matter how hopeless the prospects of winning, or even of avoiding last place. Gary Player, by a distance South Africa's finest golfer, fills the bill here. When he had beaten Tony Lema at the 37th hole in the semifinal of the World Match Play championship at Wentworth, Surrey, in 1965 after being seven down with 17 holes to play, he said that the episode "contains my whole life story". He went on to win the final.

We should all take notice of Player's recipe for happy, healthy jet aircraft travel, because he does a great deal of it and still wins oceans away from home. All his major wins (apart from such trifles as 13 South African Opens) have been on his far-ranging world tour. Other trifles include seven Australian Opens and five World Match Plays. His game plan on jet liners is no alcohol, tea or coffee – and get to sleep. His autobiography published in 1975 is aptly entitled Gary Player, World Golfer.

### Early successes

Born in Johannesburg on November 1, 1935, Player first achieved international recognition when he won the British Open at Muirfield in 1959.

His great achievement has been to be up there with Gene Sarazen, Ben Hogan and Jack Nicklaus with a complete set of the four modern major titles (Nicklaus has three sets). Player has more than 40 top-ten finishes in major championships.

A fervent Christian, he does not pray for victory at golf. The other players are very likely doing that, he says. His fellow pros like to joke about Player's inclination (some might call it an obsession) to make the best of every situation. Player's philosophy is right out of the pages of the positive-thinking gurus. Dan Gleason has written that "Were he to land in hell ... he would probably immediately start talking about what a wonderful place it is."

Player insists that he could see, on the big leader board at the 1965 US Open at Bellerive, St Louis, what no-one else could see – "Gary Player" on the list of champions posted there. Everyone was convinced a few days later, and Bellerive, where Player spent a good many spare moments reading Norman Vincent Peale's The Power of Positive Thought, is the name he gave his ranch back home.

### Fitness and skill

Player is also famous for his insistence on good diet for health and exercise for fitness. He has been obliged to develop his strength, for he is, at five feet seven inches, smaller than most of his rivals. So he runs and does weight training.

As to technique, he had plenty of critics when he first visited Britain. Everyone has a golfer in mind of whom they will say that, if all they owned depended on sinking a five-foot putt, they would choose that man. The author's man is Player, and there

Gary Player: the man in black.

**On the tee, sometimes the odd hook, but ...**

**... a supreme bunker artist.**

**On the Swilken Bridge.**

must be something about South Africans and putters, for his second choice would be, historically speaking, Bobby Locke.

As to bunker play, he is a legend in his own footmarks. Michael Williams, the former Daily Telegraph golf correspondent, tells how he and Player were in partnership at Sun City when it fell to Williams to get down in two putts from a fair distance to save the day against two first-class South African amateurs, because Player was in a bunker a long way from the green. Or so Williams thought, because Player put his explosion

shot within "gimme" range of the hole. He met suggestions that he couldn't do that again by putting his ball back in the bunker. This time he got down in one.

## Sand sage

At Wentworth, when part of a team designing the magnificent Edinburgh course, Player gave a demonstration of how different methods of raking traps (i.e. with toothed rake, coat-hanger type or brush) alter the way a ball leaves sand. One of the most quoted of all golfing axioms is Player's "The more I practise the

luckier I get." The author's first sight of a PGA tour event in America was at Oakland Hills, Michigan, in 1972, where Player struck what he said at the time was one of the two best shots of his career. The other was at Carnoustie in 1968.

At Oakland Hills the final day of the US PGA championship was showery and breezy, with Player being pressed hard by the local favourite, Jim Jamieson, not to mention Tommy Aaron, Ray Floyd, Bill Casper and Sam Snead. Despite the rain, the greens were quick and Player came to the 16th hole, a par four, only one ahead and in need of a birdie in order to breathe more easily.

Not long before the author had seen Rae Johnstone, playing out of Garden City, run up an 11 here. The drive is up an avenue of trees, and those who are long and straight enough then have a shot over a lake to a wide but shallow green that comes straight up out of the lake, with the added refinement of bunkers behind it, so that those who catch their ball a little too thinly from the sand have a splendid chance of getting into the lake. Johnstone pumped three approach shots into the lake, convinced that he had the right club. Player's drive was not perfect and in wet grass. He could not see the flag for the last of the trees, and took his line on a seat stick on the far side. He had taken account of the fact that he was likely to get a flier from the damp grass, and the result was a 150-yard nine iron that finished three feet from the pin.

All this after death threats against him had resulted in a police presence on the fairways. He rattled into the interview area on a trolley and told of his plans to encourage black golfers back home. He also helped to arrange for the black golfer, Lee Elder, to visit South Africa, this and other initiatives bringing scant reward, in that Player was still at times, simply because of his birthplace, reviled as a racist. Yet there were regularly, well before the abolition of apartheid, many more black golfers on circuit in South Africa than in the United States.

Untypically for a man who won the World Match Play title five times, Player's play-off record on the American tour was poor: three wins, 11 defeats. He gained parity in majors, beating Kel Nagle for the Open, losing to Arnold Palmer for the Masters.

## Pit of despair

Player's don't-give-in lifestyle

underwent a severe test in 1973, when his New Year was blighted by medical insistence that he should have an operation for a blocked urethra, a duct leading to the bladder, at once. This was at a moment when his wife, Vivienne, was a month away from giving birth. His condition involved the dangerous side effect of kidney damage.

Rehabilitation was long and slow, and all the more frustrating since he had been third on the world money list the previous year. Now there was to be no Augusta, and when he was given leave to start playing in May, his returns were minimal. He had gone back to the office too quickly for his own good.

## Back to the ranch

He reckons that July 1973 marked the bottom of the pit, even to the extent of his wondering if his professional career as a golfer was over. Back to the ranch was the sensible course, and he took it. There, working around the place and getting more slowly into gear with the occasional round of golf, he found that his touch returned. Back on the tour later in the year, the tie he earned for seventh place in the Greater Hartford Open was all the sweeter because, Player says he was now confident of never hooking again, thanks to a tip from a friend.

Player welcomed another tip, from a British policeman, as to the dreaded hook and, shortly afterwards at Wentworth, he got a good long one into the crowd on the left of the slope facing the first tee. Incidentally, in October 1973, Player beat Graham Marsh at Wentworth's 40th hole for his fifth World Match Play title. The following year, he won the Masters and the British Open.

Player is doubtless still searching for an anti-hook serum, among other golf nostrums. Who would put it past him to find one or two?

# Jacklin's US Open by seven strokes

HAZELTINE NATIONAL golf course was long, difficult, windy and hated by almost everyone except Tony Jacklin, the British Open champion, who won by seven shots. He led from start to finish and was the only golfer under par. No-one had won by such a distance since Jim Barnes's 11 in 1921. No Briton had won since Ted Ray the year before that.

The first round scoring, with winds over 40 mph, was extraordinary, in that Jack Nicklaus's card was his worst (81) in an Open by three shots. Arnold Palmer scored 79 and Gary Player 80. Jacklin returned 71, his worst round numerically, but in the tough, windy conditions, 71 was crucial to his eventual success, for no-one else could better 73, and many other fancied opponents were carrying horrid first-round totals.

The lengthy course (7,151 yards) featured a large lake, many ponds, big dog-legs with the elbows guarded by large trees and a good many young trees, which made the course look a touch immature. It had been the brain child of Totton P.Heffelfinger, a former Eisenhower Trophy captain, and Robert Trent Jones, the leading architect of the day, since Tot, as he was known, feared in the late 1950s that freeway developments might threaten his previous club, Minikahda.

Start to finish US Open winner Tony Jacklin.

## TEE TALK

**"Naturally, after I won the British Open, I entertained some suspicious thoughts about luck, but when I won the US Open this was all dissolved"**

TONY JACKLIN

The layout had been praised, or so the weighty (one pound nine ounces) 1970 Open programme said, by the players in the 1966 Women's Open. No such luck in 1970, when "cowpatch" and other indelicate phrases filled the air, in particular from Dave Hill, who finished second and who was fined $150 for his criticism. He called Trent Jones an idiot.

Jacklin, playing out of the Cloisters Club, Georgia, rapidly moved out of sight with three 70s. He could do little wrong. He did drop shots on the seventh and eighth in the final round, then had a huge putt for a birdie on the ninth. Going at the rate of knots, it hit the back of the cup, jumped into the air and fell into the hole. A birdie on the last clinched a comprehensive win.

# Billy Casper a Master golfer at last

AT HIS 14TH attempt Billy Casper became Masters champion, sweet consolation after his final round collapse in the previous year. His double bogey seven on the eighth hole helped Gene Littler gain a play-off, but in this Casper just about single-putted Littler to extinction, winning 69-74. He became player of the year.

The event had crept into the sporting public's consciousness by now as the fourth major championship. Its founder, Bobby Jones, did not think of it as a championship and, on hearing it described as such on radio asked: "Championship of what?"

He had a point, since the event was invitational. But his brainchild was strong and very theatrical, the stage beautiful. It had become, willy nilly, a championship.

At his 14th try, Billy Casper the Masters Champion.

# Bonallack completes nap hand

MICHAEL BONALLACK, Britain's Walker Cup captain, brought added lustre to Royal County Down's first British Amateur championship by beating Bill Hyndman again for a record third title in a row and fifth in all.

Hyndman, 54, tired quite noticeably after leading at the lunch interval in the final.

Two years earlier, Bonallack had won his fifth English Amateur, staged at Ganton, Yorkshire, in which he scored an unmatchable 61 in the final.

Bonallack was a good all-round player blessed with a wonderful short game.

# Satisfaction for Nicklaus but only despair for Sanders

THE FIRST DAY of the British Open at St Andrews will long be remembered for the atrocious luck Tony Jacklin had with the weather.

Still more memorable was the fourth day, with its vivid mental picture of Doug Sanders on the vast last green missing the four-footer that would have given him the title.

There was more to come on a Sunday, for the first time in 110 years of Open play, when Jack Nicklaus gambled with a mighty drive and won at that same hole against the massively disappointed Sanders.

Jacklin started his title defence with three birdies, and holed a nine iron for an eagle on the ninth. The author remembers the words of Jacklin's caddie three years before: "When this lad gets a short iron his his hands he's upset when he doesn't hole it, never mind get near the pin."

He started home birdie, par, then suffered a par that really hurt because his drive, bound for the green, was checked by an official. But at the long 14th, Jacklin, disturbed by a shout of fore, put his second into the gorse, and that was it for the day, since hail and lightning forced a halt, and Jacklin had to mark his ball.

Next day, with a penalty shot, the hole cost six and his total after the cold restart was a mere 67. Neil Coles led with a 65, setting a record for the Old Course, on which 47 players broke 70.

That missed putt? It was this length, says Doug Sanders.

Lee Trevino was ahead at halfway, with a second 68, with Jacklin (70) and Nicklaus one behind. Two further back was a whole bunch of players including Sanders and Coles, all one ahead of Palmer and Christy O'Connor.

There were no easy pickings in the third round as the wind rose, but Trevino, from windy Texas, stayed ahead, two clear of Jacklin, Nicklaus and Sanders.

The wind was worse still, swinging and gusting, on the Saturday. Trevino and Jacklin could not keep up with Nicklaus, who set the target at 283, which Sanders looked well placed to beat, thanks to possibly the best sand save of his life to within a foot of the pin out of the deadly little pit known as the Road Bunker.

This admirable par left him needing a four at the easiest par four on the course, Old Tom's 18th, to become the first pre-qualifier to win the Open.

His tee shot was fine, his second a pitch too far. His approach putt down and then up the slope from the back of the green finished no more than four feet short.

This for the Open – every golfer's dream, and nightmare. How many times has the tele-

vision eye seen a putt slide right of the hole from this position? Sanders, in mid-putt so to speak, bent down to remove a wisp of grass Then, as many a golfer was saying to himself: "Step back and start again", Sanders pushed the putt right of the hole.

There was more action next day which a scriptwriter with an over-active imagination could not have bettered.

The play-off, now cut to 18 holes, favoured Nicklaus at first and he was still four ahead after 13 holes. Sanders birdied the next, and there was a two-shot swing on the 16th, where Nicklaus went through the green, and Sanders got another birdie – only one down.

Both played the Road Hole immaculately, then Sanders was little short of the 18th with his drive, Nicklaus famously in fluffy grass beyond it with a hit exceeding 350 yards.

Sanders's run up offered a makeable birdie putt. Nicklaus had a tough shot, but got to within three yards, then holed for a birdie and flung his putter in the air.

Sanders must have been surprised that his ill fortune did not extend to the club beaning him on the way down.

Doug Sanders: play-off frustration at St Andrews.

## SCORECARD

**British Open** (St Andrews, Scot)
JW Nicklaus 68 69 73 73 283
(Play-off: Nicklaus 72, D Sanders 73)

**US Open** (Hazeltine National, Chaska, Minn)
A Jacklin 71 70 70 70 281

**Masters** (Augusta, Ga)
W Casper 72 68 68 71 279
(Play-off: Casper 69, G Littler 74)

**US PGA** (S Hills, Tulsa, Okla)
D Stockton 70 70 66 73 279
Leading US money-winner: L Trevino
$157,037.63;
GB: C O'Connor Snr £31,532

**British Amateur** (Royal Co Down, N Ire)
MF Bonallack bt W Hyndman III
8 & 7

**US Amateur** (Waverley CC, Oreg)
L Wadkins 67 73 69 70 279

**US Women's Open** (Muskogee, Okla)
D Caponi 287

**British Women's Amateur** (Gullane, Scot)
D Oxley bt B Robertson 1h

**US Women's Amateur** (Darien, Conn)
M Wilkinson bt C Hill 3 & 2

**World Cup** (Buenos Aires, Arg)
Australia (B Devlin & D Graham) 545

**World Match Play** (Wentworth, Surrey)
JW Nicklaus bt L Trevino 2 & 1

**Eisenhower Trophy** (Club de Campo, Madrid)
US 857

**Espirito Santo Trophy**
(Club de Campo, Madrid)
US 598

**Curtis Cup** (Brae Burn, Mass)
US 11½, GB & Ireland 6½

## SHORT PUTTS

● Great Britain and Ireland began well in the Curtis Cup match at Brae Burn, Massachusetts, where they had managed a draw in 1954. Now they won the foursomes, but faded in singles. Mary McKenna made her debut.

● Woking's long-standing rule against ladies wearing trousers in the dining room was amended in face of changing fashions. Trousers suits were allowed, and soon afterwards, trousers.

● Lanny Wadkins beat Tom Kite by a stroke in the US Amateur, at Waverley, Oregon, both players beating the event's scoring record.

● Lee Trevino declined an invitation to the Masters, saying Augusta did not suit his game.

# Joker Trevino's quickfire Open treble

THREE OPEN championships in consecutive weeks gave Lee Trevino a unique niche in golfing history. First he beat Jack Nicklaus in a play-off for the US Open, then won a play-off for the Canadian Open in Montreal, followed by a one-stroke victory for his first British Open – all this in a total of 24 days from tee-off at Merion in Pennsylvania to third title at Royal Birkdale. Only Bobby Jones, whose death came at the close of the year after his long struggle against a paralysing disease, Gene Sarazen and Ben Hogan had put American and British Opens together in the same year, but not with a Canadian Open sandwiched in between.

Merion was hosting its 13th Open. It has always been regarded, especially when the USGA are calling the shots, as a demand-ing, narrow layout, calling for the cleverest wiles of the manipulating shot-maker. Trevino's style grated with the purists, but the control his slashing style exerted in a low-flying, wind-cheating long game, and his chipping and putting skills, came together in a protracted spell of consistent scoring on tough courses.

His play-off win against Nicklaus, with Trevino in control for the most part, will always, infamously, be remembered for Trevino's prank on the first tee. If the Golden Bear had been suffering from a sore head, he might well have subjected the joker to a bear-hug, or worse, when Trevino produced a rubber snake from his bag and threw it in the general direction of his oppo-nent. The consensus is that this was a spur of the moment jape. Surely if Trevino had thought about it for more than two sec-onds, it would have occurred to him that it might be construed as a piece of jejune, if not tacky, gamesmanship.

Jim Simons, an amateur from Pennsylvania, gave the pros a run for their money, for he was third-round leader with 71, 71, 65, then fell to 76 for joint fifth place. No amateur at all had qualified for several recent US Opens.

In Montreal, Trevino gained the suppport of French Can-adians in the galleries, happy perhaps to see a winner who, like themselves, was from outside the Anglo-Saxon-American establish-ment. He won with a birdie on the first extra hole after catching Art Wall with three late birdies.

Lee Trevino: driving towards first British Open at Birkdale

All smiles: it's Lee Trevino's US Open after play-off with Jack Nicklaus at Merion Cricket Club, Pennsylvania.

## Trevino trumps Lu hat-trick at Birkdale

THE BRITISH OPEN had now become, thanks mainly to Arnold Palmer and Nicklaus, a major major, with everybody who was anybody entering, since the title,

**"You don't know what pressure is until you play for five bucks with two bucks in your pocket."**

LEE TREVINO.

apart from playing values, meant so much commercially.

Tony Jacklin had played no part in the final stages at Merion, having missed the cut like so many American champions before him. At Birkdale he was one of the four first-round lead-ers on 69, with Trevino, Howie Johnson and Vicente Fernandez from Argentina.

Liang Huan Lu from Formosa was among the crush of players one behind, and his polite habit of raising his colourful pork pie hats in response to applause made "Mr Lu" into a media figure at once: the press were quickly into full Lu and cry.

Trevino broke a stroke clear

of Jacklin and Mr Lu on the third day, with the rest falling back, though Peter Oosterhuis, after a bad start, had stated his chal-lenge by breaking the course record with 66.

Trevino held a three-stroke lead over Mr Lu on the 71st tee but his chances nose-dived as his drive on the 510-yard hole stuck on one of Birkdale's precipitous dunes. He escaped at the second attempt, only to land in the rough across the fairway. The double-bogey seven that followed still left him a stroke ahead, Mr Lu failing to get up and down for a birdie four from just short of the green. So the best attempt by an Asian fell one stroke short.

Mr Lu and hat in the shrubbery.

**British Open** (Royal Birkdale, Merseyside)
L Trevino  69 70 69 70  278

**US Open** (Merion, Pa)
L Trevino  70 72 69 69  280
(Play-off: Trevino 68, JW Nicklaus 71)

**Masters** (Augusta Ga)
C Coody  66 73 70 70  279

**US PGA, PGA National** (Palm Beach Gardens, Fla)
JW Nicklaus  69 69 70 73  281
Leading US money-winner:
J W Nicklaus $244,490.50;
GB: G Player £11,281

**British Amateur** (Carnoustie, Scot)
S Melnyk bt J Simons 3 & 2

**US Amateur** (Wilmington CC, Del)
G Cowan  70 71 69 70  280

**US Women's Open** (Erie, Pa)
J Gunderson Carner  288

**British Women's Amateur** (Alwoodley, Leeds)
M Walker bt B Huke 3 & 1

**US Women's Amateur** (Atlanta, Ga)
L Baugh bt B Barry 1h

**World Cup** (Palm Beach, Fla)
US (JW Nicklaus & L Trevino) 555
(Individual): Nicklaus 271

**World Match Play** (Wentworth, Surrey)
G Player bt J W Nicklaus 5 & 4

**Ryder Cup** (St Louis, Mo)
US 18½, GB & Ireland 13½

**Walker Cup** (St Andrews, Scot)
GB & Ireland 13, US 11

## Nicklaus wins first early bird major title

THE AMERICAN PGA had taken up residence in a splendid clubhouse at Palm Beach Gardens near Miami by arrangement with multi-millionaire John McArthur. Part of the deal was that the PGA championship should be held in this southern Florida winter resort in February. Jack Nicklaus won it, beating Bill Casper by two shots, with his fast start of 138 over the first 36 holes offsetting his 73 finish. The victory meant Nicklaus possessed a second set of the four major titles.

The February date was neither popular nor lucrative, and the PGA told McArthur they would not repeat the experiment, so they had to leave their headquarters. This retreat was, as far as the Tour professionals were concerned, another example of how the PGA spent their hard-earned dollars on enterprises that gained no reward.

# Ryder selection switch

THE FIRST SIX in the visiting team for the Ryder Cup match at Old Warson, St Louis, were chosen on the basis of the order of merit. The other half dozen, though, were the selections of a committee, namely Eric Brown, Dai Rees and Neil Coles. This was to make room for such as Tony Jacklin, now spending much time away from Britain.

The Americans stuck to their points system over two years. The result was no great change, the United States winning by five clear points. The match was soured when Bernard Gallacher's American caddie, unbeknown to Gallacher, asked Arnold Palmer what club he had used on the short seventh.

Palmer and his partner Gardner Dickinson consulted a referee, and Gallagher and Peter Oosterhuis lost the hole, because of the illegal request for advice (which Gallacher did not hear or follow), and the match, 5 & 4. Oosterhuis later beat Palmer in singles.

**Peter Oosterhuis: Birkdale course record-breaker.**

# Coody returns to glory

CHARLES COODY, as so often happens, had to learn how to lose the Masters, which he did two years earlier by bogeying the last three holes at Augusta, before he could win it. This he achieved on April 11 by saving a shot over the water at the 15th, and another by the lake at the short 16th, before parring in to beat Jack Nicklaus and Johnny Miller, the tall, blond 23-year-old from San Francisco.

Coody, a Texan, was gaining his third Tour success and went on to win the World Series, a tough 36-hole event at Akron, Ohio.

● A stroke literally out of this world, a six iron on the Moon, no less, was played by Astronaut Alan Shepard during the Apollo 14 expedition. His television audience far outnumbered that of any golf star who ever lived.

● Michelle Walker, at 18 years and six months, became the youngest British Women's Amateur champion in the modern era, beating Beverly Huke 3 & 1 at Leeds's Alwoodley Club.

● America found another of their most glamorous champions, and at 16 their youngest, in slim, blond Laura Baugh, who beat Beth Barry for the Amateur at Atlanta, and rejected offers to become a Playboy magazine centre-fold.

● John Hudson scored consecutive aces in the Martini Tournament at Royal Norwich, at the 11th (195 yards) and the par four 12th (311). His total was 72 ,however, and he finished ninth to Bernard Gallacher.

● Julius Boros won the American PGA Seniors title only three years after winning the US PGA itself.

# Marsh three iron settles it

GREAT BRITAIN and Ireland won the Walker Cup match at St Andrews, the scene in 1938 of their only other victory in 23 starts. It was a seesaw of a match, the home team starting with a 4-0 rush in the first series of foursomes. Michael Bonallack, their captain, led from the front with Warren Humphreys. They beat Lanny Wadkins and Jim Simons.

This was to be Bonallack's only win and, of the eight singles later on the first day the Americans won all but two. They also won the next day's foursomes, 2-1 with one halved match, to go two ahead overall.

A counterattack in the final series of singles carried the day for Britain and Ireland, the clinching stroke a beauty. It was a three-iron second fired on to the Road Hole Green by Dr David Marsh, an England international 10 times since 1956.

It made him dormy against Bill Hyndman, and he went on to win the match to make victory certain 13-10, Tom Kite beating Geoffrey Marks to bring up the final reckoning of 13-11.

# The Half Slam and the Golden Bear

JACK NICKLAUS caught up with Arnold Palmer on the roster of Masters champions at four apiece, winning his fourth green jacket by three shots from tall Tom Weiskopf. This was a high-scoring affair and so was the US Open at Pebble Beach in California, where the USGA proved that no matter how tough a course might be, they could make it tougher. Nicklaus won again.

The British Open at Muirfield was, therefore, target number three towards the professional Grand Slam, still unachieved a year after the death of Bobby Jones, who achieved the Grand Slam, old style (both major Opens and Amateur titles), in 1930. Nicklaus would be the defending US PGA champion at Oakland Hills in August (the February experiment with the fourth major had been dropped), and with the first three under his belt would take some stopping.

Nicklaus had earlier been paid a compliment by Clifford Roberts, Augusta's autocratic ruler, when he had two bunkers inserted to the left of the landing area of the drive at the 18th. This, it was deduced, was to deter the great man from booming his drives to that neighbourhood so that they bounced away onto the practice area, from which he could reach the green with a wedge.

**Augusta Master: a fourth green jacket for Nicklaus.**

# Gary Player wins it for father

THE US PGA championship at Oakland Hills in Birmingham, one of the more salubrious suburbs of Detroit, had reached the 70th hole and Gary Player, leader by a stroke after the third round, was still only one up and not yet fully in control of the situation. He had made a call home to South Africa that morning, and been instructed by his father to "Win it for me, Gary."

Player confounded his pursuers with shot against all the odds on the 16th from wet grass with the pin hidden by a tree. His nine iron soared over the lake guarding the green and offered a three-foot birdie putt. That was enough to win by two shots from Tommy Aaron and Jim Jamieson, who had recently won his first tour event, the Western Open, by six shots.

The US PGA was the first American tour event the author attended and, despite Player's coup, the best golf on the final day was played by Sam Snead, 60 years old in May, who returned the lowest score, 69, in miserable conditions. Snead calculates that a 69 last round in all his US Opens would have won him seven of them. His swing was impervious to age, it seemed. He was in jovial playing partnership with his nephew, Jesse.

One memorable shot, a five-iron approach, was smoothly dispatched on to the green, though Snead's wayward drive had obliged him to play it from the peak of a bunker, both feet below the ball, one in sand and the other in damp grass. It could not have looked easier if he had been playing it off a peg on the tee.

Nicklaus's chances of landing the Grand Slam, even if he had won at Muirfield, would have been problematical. The big story before the US PGA began was whether an injured hand would permit him to play. It did, but he finished six behind Player.

One shot, unwisely played as it turned out with a wooden club from a bunker, made only a few yards out of the sand, and revealed his desperate quest for a birdie or two to retain the PGA title and so take a third major in a year, as Hogan had done in 1953.

# Nicklaus's happy homecoming

A THIRD TITLE for Jack Nicklaus when the American Open was held for the first time at the scenic but unnerving clifftop Pebble Beach course was a matter of horses for courses. Nicklaus won the second of his two US Amateur titles here, and in January beat Johnny Miller in a play-off for the Bing Crosby Pro-Am.

The furniture had been moved around a little in the 11 intervening years, and the course had been set up in such demanding fashion that breaking 80 was beyond all but 48 players in the first round. Strangely, Jerry McGee and Bobby Mitchell both aced the eighth, the first holes in one at the Open for 16 years. Nicklaus led or had a share of the lead all the way.

# Trevino chip stuns Jacklin

JACK NICKLAUS'S strategy at Muirfield was to follow the pattern that helped him to his first Open there six years earlier, which was to use irons from the tee, though the rough was now less severe. Yet Nicklaus missed seven fairways on the first day, and at halfway he was one behind Tony Jacklin and Lee Trevino, defending champion.

With Nicklaus were Gary Player, Johnny Miller, Peter Townsend and Peter Tupling, a former Walker Cup player from Yorkshire who had led by one from Jacklin after 18 holes, and who was not shy of admitting that he had no thoughts of being able to stay at the head of affairs.

Jacklin continued in fine form, his game through the green often exemplary, but after three rounds he was still one behind Trevino, who must have begun to believe at times that his quip about God being a Mexican might be nothing but the truth.

Trevino made little progress before huge putts at the 14th and 15th scored birdies and, at the short 16th, he got another from an almighty fluke. He was in a trap, thinned his splash out, and the ball hit the pin hard and went underground. One more birdie, less fortuitous, at the 17th, gave him a 66 and the lead by a shot.

Nicklaus had slipped to five behind Jacklin. Determined to conquer or perish, Nicklaus unleashed his driver on the final day. Conquer the first half of the course he did, in 32, catching both Trevino and Jacklin at the turn. Two holes, and two birdies, later he was ahead. The 16th was less kind to Nicklaus than to Trevino the day before, and he took three to get down from the rough. A pulled drive cost him the birdie he needed so urgently on the 17th, and his 66 equalled the record but ...

The 17th proved fatal to Jacklin's chances in the cruellest fashion. Trevino was all over the place, his fourth shot on a fluffy bank behind the green. Jacklin was 20 yards short for two, and chipped short. Trevino chipped in, Jacklin three-putted.

A haphazard par beat a tortured bogey. This for Jacklin was a last straw of steel girder proportions, and another shot dropped on the last cost him second place. The final reckoning was Trevino 278 (first winning total here under 280), Nicklaus 279 and Jacklin 280.

Tony Jacklin: solid through the green but ...

Lee Trevino: lunging swing that earned second Open.

Johnny Miller: best second round at Muirfield with a 66.

## European Tour under way

THE PRIZE MONEY and points from European tournaments were now included in the PGA's order of merit, effectively launching the European tour. John Jacobs, author of Practical Golf, had taken over as director-general a year ago, when prize money was starting to soar from a base of only £250,000 compared to the American tour's $7,500,000.

All the same the future looked bright, and prize money almost doubled for the 1972 Tour with its newly-acquired continental dimension. The administrative costs of this were met by raising the entry fees, first to £6 per player, then to a rate of £1 per £1,000 of prize money. Jacobs assumed wide powers and was answerable only to the Advisory Council.

### SHORT PUTTS

● Former long serving secretary of the British PGA, Charles Roe, died aged 91. He had worked devotedly to promote tournament golf in Britain.

● Michelle Walker retained the British Women's Amateur title against Claudine Rubin of France.

● The US Congress brought in legislation to equalize opportunities for female athletes, including golfers.

● Gene Littler, 1961 US Open champion, had never been out of the top 60 on the US Tour since turning pro in 1954. In April he underwent surgery for cancer of the lymph glands under the left arm but in October was back to gain a top ten finish in the Pacific Masters.

### TEE TALK

### "Go to Mexico with some friends and play golf."

LEE TREVINO, describing his perfect vacation.

### "Little worm burners."

Trevino's term for the low-flying iron shots into the pin that were his trade mark.

# Trevino: his clubs also speak volumes

A great player who rose from humble beginnings to bring his own distinctive style to the game and set up an all-time golfing record by winning three Open championships in just three weeks

LEE BUCK TREVINO, Super Mex, is at five feet seven inches two inches shorter than Ben Hogan. On the face of it, the swarthy, talkative Trevino and taciturn Irish-American Hogan could scarcely be more different. Yet in many ways they are very alike, and the similarities are not simply a matter of both men being Texans.

Certainly, both had a hard upbringing, Trevino almost certainly the harder of the two. Born at Dallas, Texas, on December 1, 1939, he and his mother lived in his grandfather's shack in Dallas which had no running water or electricity. He became a caddie at eight years of age and, as he lived close to a country club, knocked balls around with the greenkeeper's son when coast and course were clear.

A school-leaver at 14, he helped out at a driving range, and later assisted in building a pitch and putt course. Then he spent four years in the Marines, and met, on course, none other than Orville Moody, future Open champion, and on Okinawa none other than Mr Lu. But first-class golf was scarcely in Trevino's mind as yet.

## Hogan's way

Back in Texas, his life was changed when he watched Hogan practising, as usual, at his Fort Worth club, Shady Oaks. Both men had started out in golf hooking the ball, and it was a long and costly business for poor, young, struggling tour pro Hogan to get rid of his over-enthusiastic right-to-left tendency. Trevino saw the light when he witnessed Hogan's slight fade keeping a tight rein on the ball, so avoiding the dangers that a hooked ball presents, since, well after landing, overspin propels it ever onwards into all sorts of trouble.

He worked away on this idea in his own way, finally producing, with his distinctive low, lunging swing and big extension through the ball, left hand in control, the low shots that are his trademark. They do not lack

A man with a method – and a robust and reliable method – uniquely his own.

## "I thought I'd blown it at the 17th green when I drove into a trap. God is a Mexican."

Muirfield, 1972.

## "Don't move, hole!"

uttered while playing an approach shot.

He had evidently not heard Henry Longhurst's statement:

## "I've never once seen the cup move towards the ball."

length but do nudge out towards the left, then drift right on to the short grass. His style was equally useful for bringing the ball in to the pin from the left and, not least, in stopping it when it arrived. Every ball, so to speak, has an address label, fastened on by spin.

All the same, he made no inroads on the tour, nor many attempts, in his first six years as a pro, to invade even its lower echelons. Like the old Scots pros, he played matches for cash. With a Trevino-esque twist all his own, he took on opponents using a loaded, taped pop bottle as a club. He could get round Hardy's pitch and putt course in two or three over par, and seldom lost a wager against opponents using golf clubs, who were asked to give him half a stroke a hole.

Trevino started to move up when offered a series of games at El Paso, followed by a professional's post at the Horizon Hills club there. His first try at the Open followed, but he got through only 36 holes. The next year brought him up to fifth. Then there was a win in Hawaii and he was on his way.

Trevino's method had seen him safely through two American Opens, two British Opens, and two PGA championships, which he secured a decade apart. His distinctive methods have prospered in lucrative years on the Seniors tour. There he won seven events in his first (1990) year, when he was Seniors player of the year and rookie of the year all at once. Jack Nicklaus, on his debut, won only three times.

Trevino has also won the Vardon Trophy for best stroke average five times. Nicklaus has never won it, and is to some degree responsible for Trevino's success, since he persuaded him that he was a much better player than he imagined.

## Storm and surgery

Trevino was forced, like Hogan and Player, to come to grips with a major physical problem in mid-career. From the year of his first American Open win he was earning between $100,000 and $200,000 a year in prize money alone.

The sequence came to a painful end in 1977, for in June 1976 during the Western Open near Chicago he, Jerry Heard and Bobby Nichols were knocked over by an unheralded flash of lightning. A brief stay in intensive care followed for Trevino, and in three weeks he was back on tour, but far from the golfer he had been. The fall, or the intensity of the shock, had injured his back, and the damage was compounded a year later when he lifted a heavy object without the due care that patients with back pain must observe throughout their lives, and an operation for disc trouble was ordered.

He was back on tour early in 1977, but his prize money earnings for the year plummeted to $85,103, and his position on the money list to 33rd, though he still contrived to win the Canadian Open, the centrepiece of his unique burst of national Opens in 1971.

He has a fine Ryder Cup record, well into the black, and never played on a losing side, but was non-playing captain in the 1985 defeat.

## One-liner King

Trevino's fame, despite his consistent stroke-saving expertise and nonchalance in a crisis, derives to a great extent with the mass of golf followers from his one-liner skill, and one wit has credited him with "more lines than the Illinois railroad." He can be cruel, once remarking of an amateur's attempt to feather, Trevino style, an iron shot: "If that's featherin', I'd hate for you to pluck my chickens."

He can be kind, too, though it was not a one-liner he delivered at the 1980 Muirfield Open when his playing partner, Ken Brown, who was briefly in contention, had a murderous little shot to play out of heavy grass a few

**Imparting trademark low flight with biting spin.**

steps from the hole. Brown somehow got the ball up, light as thistledown, and it floated down and rolled to within a few inches of the pin. The applause for this little miracle was muted, so Trevino gave the gallery a piece of his mind about what a brilliant shot it was, and that they should give their man (a Scot, after all) a big hand. They did.

Bert Yancey had reason to thank Trevino for his quick thinking while they were duelling for the 1968 Open. Trevino had holed a birdie putt, before which Yancey had moved his marker sideways to clear Trevino's line to the hole. Then he put his ball where his marker was, without making the necessary adjustment. "Hey, did you move the coin back?," Trevino demanded. "I forgot," said Yancey, and did the necessary. But for Trevino, the error could have ended Yancey's leading part in the Open, if not acknowledged before the signing of his card.

At the press conference afterwards, Trevino the champion gave a frank answer to Mark McCormack question: "What does this moment mean to you, Lee Trevino?" After a pause, came: "I don't know. One thing it means is a bunch of money." Some of that money he gave away – notably $5,000 of his Birkdale prize to an orphanage, for which he also sold his clubs.

Neither Trevino nor anyone else could vie with Doug Sanders in the fashion plate stakes and, when he and his manager resorted to evening dress for a London occasion they resembled, in Al Barkow's evocative phrase, tan penguins.

**Like Gary Player, a Houdini of bunker escapology.**

## An honorary Scot?

Trevino's victories in the British Open may be the result of his instant love affair with linksland golf. Before playing in the 1981 Open at Royal St George's he said: "I don't care if I shoot 88. I'll always play over here." Like Hogan, he found that his fade and low flight could be potent weapons in seaside breezes, just as they were in the windy plains of Texas. Unlike Hogan, he could nurse putts in across the slippery slopes of courses like Muirfield, his favourite in Britain.

He told the locals that he could bump and run the ball better than any native. "If you believe in reincarnation, I probably was a Scotsman 250 years ago." He had trouble with the language at first. How was he to know a "marquee" was a tent, and a '"burn" a stream? Not that much of a Scot really, though he eventually got a caddie that solved all such difficulties – Willie Aitchison, who had looked after Roberto de Vicenzo and Tony Lema. The trouble with Aitchison, according to Trevino, was that he talked too much. Trevino would know. He has been accused of being the only man who talked on his back swing.

# Burke's boys recover in first Scottish Ryder Cup

THE FIRST VISIT of the Ryder Cup match to Scotland was working out beautifully on the first day for Bernard Hunt's Britain and Ireland team. They led 5-2, with one half, after the four foursomes and four fourballs at Muirfield.

The following morning, an attack of food poisoning ruled Bernard Gallacher out of the second day's play. He and Brian Barnes had set the ball rolling in the top foursome by beating Lee Trevino and Billy Casper by one hole, and they won yet again, in the top fourball against Tommy Aaron and Gay Brewer, by 5 & 4.

The format was the same for the second day. Peter Butler, called to replace Gallacher, did not have the sort of preparation professionals require to "get themselves up" as the pro phrase goes, for an important match. He was wakened at 8 and on the tee at 9.30.

He and Barnes lost both their matches, despite a morning ace by Butler. Gallacher's absence cast a pall over the recently bubbling spirits of the home side, and the Americans, always dangerous when threatened, levelled the match at 8-8.

The lack of depth in Hunt's team was laid bare Though Hunt was a man short, he did not feel enough confidence in John Garner to give him a game, and three of the players who had been picked from lower regions of the top 12 in the order of merit – Garner, Eddie Polland and Clive Clark – were not employed in singles. Brian Huggett was, and beat Homero Blancas.

It is true that Jack Burke's US team included Ryder rookies, but Tom Weiskopf (who had recently beaten everyone at Troon in the Open), Blancas, Lou Graham and Chi Chi Rodriguez were regular earners on the world toughest circuit.

Besides, Trevino and Jack Nicklaus were in the side, both of whom looked upon Muirfield as a home from home, both having won Opens there, plus Walker Cup victories by Nicklaus.

Tony Jacklin and Peter Oosterhuis played a match of the highest quality in their first day fourball against Brewer and Casper, who survived an opening burst of seven birdies in a row by the English pair, and got back to one down, but lost a spectacular struggle 3 & 1.

Recalled for the singles, Gallacher lost to Weiskopf. He was not at his best after his day in bed, but he was nevertheless called upon a second time and, not surprisingly, subsided 6 & 5 to Brewer.

Lack of depth in Hunt's team was even clearer in singles, and the Americans, with Jesse Snead beating Barnes twice and Jacklin beating Aaron and losing to Casper, swept ahead to a 19-13 win. Oosterhuis enjoyed the final day: he halved with Trevino and beat Palmer 4 & 2. Nevertheless Burke, who led against Dai Rees's Cup victors in 1957, could breathe again.

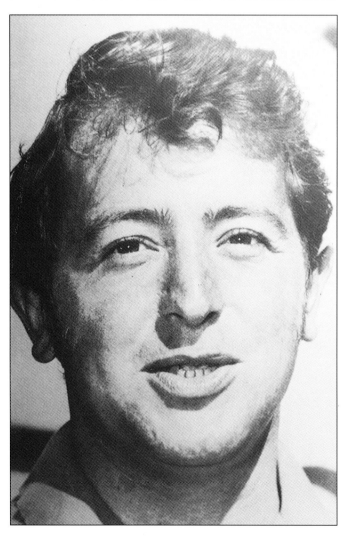

Bembridge: earned 2½ points in partnership with Brian Huggett.

Huggett: beat Homero Blancas.

# Whitworth top again

THOUGH SHE had as yet failed to win the Women's Open, Kathy Whitworth continued to pile up victories on the LPGA tour. She was leading money-winner again this year, as she had been since 1970, and player of the year for the seventh time. Her best Open finish was still runner-up in 1971. The title went to Susie Berning for the second year in succession and third in all, at Rochester, New York. Berning had broken new ground at Oklahoma City University, where she was the first woman to compete on the men's team.

## TEE TALK

### "Nothing has changed."

TOM WEISKOPF,
as his eight-yard putt stops halfway to the hole after he drove a par four hole at Gleneagles.

# US masters in foursomes

BRITAIN AND IRELAND made a solid defence of the Walker Cup at Brookline, Massachusetts, but lost their grip on the trophy in the foursomes. Overall, the Americans won 14-10. Michael Bonallack set up a record 25 matches played. The outcome for a matchplay expert, was less impressive: W8, L14, H3.

## SHORT PUTTS

● Richard Siderowf became the 16th American winner of the British Amateur, beating Peter Moody by 5 & 3 at Royal Porthcawl.

● After eight years at stroke play, the American Amateur returned to single combat, Craig Stadler surviving all challenges including that of David Strawn in the final, which Stadler won 6 & 5 at Inverness, Toledo.

● The PGA opened the first tour school for golfers who wished to play on the American circuit. It involved tuition in the skills and business knowledge proper to a tour pro, and eight rounds to determine the razor-keen few ready to spend their Mondays trying to qualify for the following Thursday's tournament.

● Worplesdon captain Alec Justice took the club's pro, Alan Waters, in a buggy with him during the club's celebrated Mixed Foursomes, but near the short tenth, which is all carry over a pond, the buggy capsized, spilling the pro into the water. This happening was named "The Meeting of the Waters" and is the only known occasion on which the professional went into the pond.

**Tiny Marlene Streit, from Alberta, former US and British Amateur champion, won her 11th Canadian Amateur title.**

# Miller massacres Oakmont

OAKMONT, PENNSYLVANIA, the course that had been terrorizing golfers for generations until partly tamed by Ben Hogan and Jack Nicklaus, was put in its place on June 17 by Johnny Miller.

His first three rounds of the US Open had been unexceptional – 71, 69, 76, – so he started the last round six behind four men, John Schlee, Arnold Palmer, Julius Boros and Jerry Heard. He birdied the first four holes. Five more birdies, a bogey and eight pars later he was champion by a stroke from Schlee. Tall enough to make his strong build look slim, the blond Californian's towering iron shots dropping close by the flag were riveting to watch.

His stunning final round of 63, the lowest ever played at the climax of the Open, shot him to the stardom that had been signalled from the days of his junior championship in 1964. True, some of the most daunting features of Oakmont had been softened somewhat, notably the ridged bunkers, but Miller's round, especially in closing, remains an awesome achievement.

Sam Snead set up another sort of record, overtaking Gene Sarazen's 26 attempts at the title, winning none, though he had been second three times.

# Troon a cruise for Weiskopf

FOR A PLAYER without a major win, Tom Weiskopf was fancied by many punters for the British Open at Troon, though the full panoply of world's golfers were there to dispute it with him. Weiskopf was winning fortunes on the tour back home, and at Troon led after the first round by a shot from Jack Nicklaus and Bert Yancey with a 68; then scored a 67 to stay ahead.

Johnny Miller briefly went ahead in the third round, then Weiskopf, who had from the start played the more difficult homeward half against the wind better than his rivals, hit back to lead by a stroke from Miller. Nicklaus and Arnold Palmer had 76s against their name, and were out of it.

Weiskopf's stately swing continued to propel the ball huge distances, and the fact that he never three-putted made it tough for Miller to cope, and he had to share second place with Neil Coles, whose final effort was 66.

Gene Sarazen responded in spectacular fashion to Sam Snead's record longevity in the American Open by playing at Troon, where he had failed to qualify half a century before.

At 71, he holed his tee-shot at the 126-yard eighth, which from its pulpit tee does justify its name "Postage Stamp", for it appears much smaller in area than the five bunkers around it.

Next day, as befits the inventor of the sand wedge, Sarazen holed out from the bunker there for two. Using only three strokes in two attempts without so much as taking out his putter he certainly trumped Snead.

Arnold Palmer, winner here in 1962, had a less happy time, running up a seven at the eighth careering from bunker to bunker.

**Tom Weiskopf: avoided the deadly three-putt.**

# Player proves he's back to full power

GARY PLAYER says that he went to Augusta strong in the belief that he could win the Masters again. That goes almost without saying for this man of iron will, but his sentiment proves he had wiped out the doubts his illness had prompted just over a year before.

Hale Irwin, the former football star, gave Player plenty to think about with a Masters record of five birdies in a row in the second round, from the short 12th at Rae's Creek. All the same, Dave Stockton led at halfway with a 66 for 137, five ahead of Player, who was taking too many putts, averaging two a hole.

In round three the putting suddenly came right, and Player equalled Irwin's birdie run and on the same holes, too. On the 18th, as Player got ready to putt for a birdie three, a spectator at the edge of the green collapsed. (It later transpired that he died.) Player, his composure shaken, missed the putt, for a 65.

Jack Nicklaus made threatening moves on the Sunday, but Player, adding to his solid, long game a rediscovered flair for holing birdie chances, got two ahead with a birdie on the 17th (that nine iron again, this time to 12 inches, though this was not his favourite hole in previous Masters). He clung to that advantage over Stockton and Tom Weiskopf to win his second green jacket.

The winning cheque for $35,000 for this, his seventh major title, brought Player over the million dollar mark in tour money. His wife and five of their six children were present to see father carry off the booty.

Hale Irwin: Masters' record five birdies in a row.

# Irwin conquers slippery slopes

EVEN JACK NICKLAUS, a trustworthy putter in a crisis, found the greens at Winged Foot in the US Open beyond him. The undulations were, he said the most severe he had known. Hale Irwin gained his first major (only the second champion besides Willie Macfarlane [1925] to wear spectacles) because his straightness gave him the best chance to get the better of this tight course with its small, glassy greens, where patience with his putter paid dividends. His fizzing backspin helped too.

Even Irwin could not manage par, but he alone kept the damage to seven lost strokes, Forrest Fezler having his best golfing moment a stroke behind in second place. Tom Watson had a one-stroke lead after three rounds, but faded to a 79. This increased "Watson's a choker" talk, for he had lost good positions the year before.

Player's hope of a Grand Slam vanished when he finished eighth, with 293 strokes. Fewer than one player in six beat 75 on the opening day. A putt by Tony Jacklin sticks in the mind. On a sloping green it just crept to the hole, spun round it, and rolled to the fringe at a snail's pace.

Tony Jacklin: found putting a trial in the US Open.

**Deane Beman, Joe Dey's successor as US PGA Tour boss**

● Joe Dey, tour commissioner, was succeeded by Deane Beman, winner of both US and British Amateur titles, and tour regular.

● Jack Nicklaus won the inaugural Tournament Players championship at Atlanta Country Club. Another attempt at inventing a fifth major?

● The Curtis Cup was held on the Pacific coast for the first time, but for the 14th time America won. Carol Semple was on the winning side. She almost did the British/American Amateur title double, beating Angela Bonallack at Porthcawl, but losing to Cynthia Hill in Seattle.

● Californian Nancy Lopez, 17, won her second US Junior title.

● Tom Watson won first tournament, Western Open, with a final round of 69.

● Death of Richard Burton, the Lancashire-born last British Open champion before the Second World War.

**Dick Burton dies: last winner of British Open before the war.**

# Gary Player, perfect at last?

GARY PLAYER'S consoling thought as he recovered from his illness of 1973 was that he had at last found out how to avoid the hook. Nevertheless he claimed, on reaching Royal Lytham for the British Open, that he had at last got the swing business right. His opponents, as at Augusta, could not be sure that he had achieved perfection. They only knew they could not overtake him for all his 38 years.

He was never headed at Lytham for his third British Open, which he reached from Augusta via the Spanish Open at the splendid La Manga complex, a Japanese event, a rest period at home in South Africa, a win in Tennessee and disappointment at Winged Foot. He brought with him "Rabbit" Dyer, his usual caddie in the United States, who was strongly supportive when Player was depressed during his long recuperation 12 months earlier.

John Morgan, who was enjoying scant success on the British circuit, shared the lead with Player for a few hours, both scoring 69 in the first round, but Player followed with a 68, Morgan with 75 and, until the last round, no other golfer broke 70.

The reason was twofold. First, the 1.68-inch ball was now obligatory, and many of the home players were not yet in control of it. Secondly, even the Americans were troubled by the boisterous wind.

Player's long irons were the key to his 68 that gave him a grip on affairs, for he was five clear of Peter Oosterhuis and Bobby Cole at halfway, with Tom Weiskopf and Mr Lu nearest of the big names, and they were seven adrift.

Cole caught Player briefly during the third round, when he slipped to a 75, but Cole, Nicklaus and Oosterhuis all made errors on the more difficult inward half, and Player was still three ahead

as the final day dawned. He had shots to spare as he hit off the 71st tee, but there was a desperate search for his ball when it vanished into thick matted grass near the green. What relief when a marshall found it, with 60 seconds of the five-minute allowance left, though the lie cost a bogey. Now surely all would be plain sailing. But no: his approach to the last was too

strong, and he had to play it back left-handed from next to the clubhouse wall. His 70 still beat Oosterhuis by four and Nicklaus by five, and the quartet who shot 69 in the last round – Donald Swaelens (Belgium), the Lancastrian John Garner, David Graham and Peter Townsend – would not have beaten Player, British Open champion for the third time, if they had shot 59.

**Peter Oosterhuis: second to Gary Player at Lytham.**

## Miller adds cash to kudos

JOHNNY MILLER, having made his name with the golfing public with his Open-winning 63 at Oakmont last year, was diligent throughout 1974 in making himself popular with his business and bank managers. He became player of the year without winning a major title. He gave the impression of winning everything else at times, or so his rivals must have thought as he piled up a record $353,021.59 in prize money.

Bad weather at the Bing Crosby Pro-Am gave him a flying, if soggy, start, for his 208 won the money, a fourth round being impossible. He then won at Tucson and Phoenix, and had high finishes in many others, winding up with eight wins in all. In the course of his blistering start to the tour, he never exceeded par in 24 consecutive rounds.

**"From grass you expect him to pitch close. From a bunker you're afraid he'll hole out."**

JACK NICKLAUS,
of Player.

## Lee Elder finds a way

THE MASTERS had not yet invited a black player to take part. There was criticism when tournament winner Charlie Sifford was passed over by Clifford Roberts, the autocratic boss of Augusta. Further criticism led Roberts to say a place would be offered to any black player winning a tournament between one Masters and the next, and right

after Player's win, Lee Elder won a tour tournament.

Roberts neglected his career in high finance to improve the Masters and his much-copied scoreboards kept fans informed with red figures for players under par, green ones for those above par. He gave the media free lunches but forbade them to mention prize money.

# Nicklaus lands fifth green jacket in a white-hot Masters

TOM WEISKOPF and Johnny Miller lost the Masters to Jack Nicklaus by a stroke. The reactions of Augusta's galleries suggested that this was the best green jacket shootout of them all.

The three golfers who dominated the Masters had the best of credentials for favouritism (with apologies to Hale Irwin; even a last round 64 was not enough to fire him into contention). Weiskopf, second in two of the previous three years, clearly had the game to win. Nicklaus was Nicklaus, and Miller had begun the year with an even more extraordinary burst of low scores than he had achieved on the previous year's winter tour en route to record prize money.

Miller fomented New Year revolutions in stroke-saving. He was 24 under par at Phoenix, where he won by 14 shots, and 25 under par at Tucson, though he won there by only nine.

Miller's first round at Augusta was, however, a 75, which immediately cut him out of most people's calculations. Nicklaus, by contrast, started with 68, one ahead of Weiskopf. Miller made little progress in the second round, with a 71, against Nicklaus's 67. Weiskopf fell back to a 72 for 141 at halfway, six behind Nicklaus, then came thundering back in the third round with 66.

He now led Nicklaus by one and stood four ahead of Miller, who had recaptured his January form with a 65, reaching the turn in a record 30 strokes, with six consecutive birdies from the sec-

**Johnny Miller: set new standards in scoring on the Winter Tour.**

ond hole. Sunday's excitement on the final nine holes was almost suffocating.

Nicklaus and Weiskopf, who was playing a hole behind, were level at the turn, Miller chasing hard all the time. Weiskopf's birdies on holes 14 and 15 put him ahead, and he watched from the tee at the short 16th as Nicklaus drew level with a two, holing a scenic-route putt of about 45 feet. Tom Watson, Nicklaus's playing partner,

scored seven. This green beside the lake was one of the Golden Bear's favourite dance floors. He performed a golfer's gavotte, club waving overhead. A Weiskopf waltz did not follow, for his tee shot left him a longer putt than Nicklaus's for a birdie. He missed and missed again ... bogey.

Miller caught Weiskopf with a birdie at the 17th, so the pair of them were one behind Nicklaus with a hole to play. Neither could sink their birdie chances on the

18th, and Nicklaus was champion for the fifth time, overtaking Arnold Palmer's four.

Miller's 131 for the last 36 holes was unique. Irwin's 64 shot him into fourth place, which he shared with Bobby Nichols, four behind Nicklaus. Weiskopf found it all hard to take. This was his fourth second place at Augusta. Black golfer Lee Elder was the first of his race to tee off in the Masters but was never in contention. Prize money was $235,700.

**Brian Barnes: discounted his two victories over Nicklaus.**

## Barnes yes, G B & Ireland no

JACK NICKLAUS'S reputation, especially in a year when he added two majors to his haul of titles, means that the Ryder Cup match at Laurel Valley was chiefly celebrated in Britain because Brian Barnes beat him twice on September 21, by 4 & 2 and 2 & 1.

Though Barnes refused to make a song and dance about it, his feat was no small one if only because Nicklaus had recently won his fourth PGA title and, the week before the Ryder Cup, the so-called World Open, which led

him to say he thought he was playing the best golf of his life. But he could not reproduce the magic when he tackled Barnes.

The Cup matches, mainly because America nearly always won, did not in any case create many media waves in the United States. This is a poor return for the efficient way in which Arnold Palmer's team got a grip on the match on the first two days, which meant that their narrow win in the two series of singles on the final day lacked dramatic effect.

**"Eighteen holes of match play is not a lot different to sudden death, and two wins like that do not mean as much to a professional as they would to an amateur."**

BRIAN BARNES,
of his two Ryder Cup wins over Jack Nicklaus.

**"Every day I try to tell myself this is going to be fun today. I try to put myself in a great frame of mind before I go out, then I screw it up with the first shot."**

JOHNNY MILLER.

## Graham holds off Watson

LOU GRAHAM, a fine putter and straight hitter, had the right recipe for US Open success, though at the halfway stage at Medinah in Illinois he was 11 strokes behind Tom Watson, whose total of 135 was unequalled.

Watson's second 36 (155) has been equalled all too often, and his reputation as "choker" grew. Even then, at the death, he was only three strokes shy of Graham, from Tennessee, who set up victory with a 68 in round three.

He had to seek the trophy in a play-off, though, against John Mahaffey, a shortish hitter but consistent tour earner. Ben Crenshaw's double bogey on the 72nd hole cost him the title. Graham's play-off 71 was enough to make him champion and $40,000 richer.

For all that, Graham's earnings were well short of the $226,118 of Johnny Miller, with whom he later won the World Cup for the United States at Bangkok.

# Watson's at last

A DEPRESSING series of titles thrown away by late fade-outs was ended by Tom Watson, from Kansas City, who defeated Australian Jack Newton by a stroke in a play-off for the British Open at Carnoustie.

One of the few golfers to succeed at their first challenge on a British links, Watson had, unlike Jack Nicklaus, not prepared at all

Watson: past failures forgotten at Carnoustie.

diligently. Three calm days brought splendid three-round aggregates, Bobby Cole from South Africa leading with 204, a shot clear of Newton and two of Miller, four of Watson, and four of a quintet by no means out of it, namely Hale Irwin, Jack Nicklaus, who had been scoring brilliantly in practice, Andries Oosthuizen (pronounced "Oosthazen"), John Mahaffey and Neil Coles.

All Scotland was at this point mourning the third-round score of that large and equable pro from North Berwick, David Huish (pronounced "Hush"), who had stumbled to 76 after 69, 67. Watson's closing round was a hit and miss affair, particularly in the closing stages, missing the short 16th by miles and pitching and putting for his par at the next. The 18th settled it, for he holed a 15-footer for a birdie, his total of 279 edging out both Nicklaus and Miller. Cole had a birdie putt for 279, but missed. Newton ran into trouble at the Barry Burn on the 17th, but still had a putt on the last to win. He missed, too, and next day the 18th proved decisive for Watson needed no more than a par there as Newton bogeyed.

# British pros' new deal

BRITISH PLAYING PROS, after much debate and sundry threats of a split in the PGA, got much of wanted they wanted in August, which was to a great degree what the American tour players had got seven years before – a fair degree of autonomy.

The new PGA constitution established a general division as well as a tournament players' division, each with three representative sitting on a board of management with an independent chairman. Michael Bonallack took up this role, the original player members of the board being Neil Coles, Dai Rees and Peter Butler.

Peter Butler: board member.

# Fourth 'double' by Nicklaus

FOR THE FOURTH time Jack Nicklaus achieved two major championships in a year, adding the US PGA title to his Masters, despite the challenge of Australian Bruce Crampton, who

returned a 63 in the second round on the tough Firestone course. Strangely, Nicklaus had never won the Canadian Open and failed again at the first extra hole against Tom Weiskopf.

**British Open** (Carnoustie, Scot)
T Watson 71 67 69 72 279
(Play-off: Watson 71, J Newton 72)

**US Open** (Medinah, Ill)
L Graham 74 72 68 73 287
(Play-off: Graham 71, J Mahaffey 73)

**Masters** (Augusta, Ga)
JW Nicklaus 68 67 73 68 276

**US PGA** (Firestone, Akron ,Ohio)
D Stockton 70 72 69 70 281
Leading US money-winner:
JW Nicklaus $298,149.17;
Europe: D Hayes £20,507

**British Amateur** (Royal Liverpool, Merseyside)
MM Giles III bt M James 8 & 7

**US Amateur** (Richmond, Va)
FS Ridley bt K Fergus 2h

**US Women's Open** (Atlantic City CC, NJ)
S Palmer 295

**British Women's Amateur** (St Andrews, Scot)
N Syms bt S Cadden 3 & 2

**US Women's Amateur** (Brae Burn, Mass)
B Daniel bt D Horton 3 & 2

**World Cup** (Bangkok, Thai)
US (J Miller & L Graham) 554
(Individual): Miller 275

**World Match Play** (Wentworth, Surrey)
H Irwin bt A Geiberger 4 & 2

**Ryder Cup** (Laurel Valley, Pa)
US 21, GB & Ireland 11

**Walker Cup** (St Andrews, Scot)
US 15½, GB & Ireland 8½

● Lee Trevino, Bobby Nichols and Jerry Heard were struck by lightning in the Western Open near Chicago a week after the Open at Medinah, which had also been endangered by an electrical storm. Heard finished his 72 holes, but they all had back problems. Trevino later needed surgery.

● Jane Blalock of the LPGA won a legal battle with the association in a court case which had been simmering for three years, since she was disqualified after being accused of cheating in the placement of her ball on the green. A seven-year suspension was imposed, but Blalock won an injunction against this ruling, and finally gained damages of $13,500, plus costs. A few days later she won an LPGA tournament.

● Nick Faldo, at the record age of 18 years and eight days, won the English Amateur championship.

● Australian Bruce Crampton won the Vardon Trophy for the best stroke average, to thwart Jack Nicklaus.

# 'Seve' emerges but it's Johnny Miller's Open

**Young Seve: gave it the full treatment at Royal Birkdale.**

**Manuel Pinero: Seve's partner in Spain's World Cup victory.**

A MIGHTY phalanx of American golfers formed up at Royal Birkdale for the British Open in the hottest summer of modern times. The greens were pale in colour, but fierce in pace, though Johnny Miller, who attracted many bets despite Jack Nicklaus's presence, was capable of using the Ben Hogan method of avoiding putting tortures, that is, by hitting the ball close to the stick.

This he did after a duel with the tall, smiling Severiano Ballesteros, born 19 years before at Pedrena on the northern coast of Spain. They were playing partners for the last two rounds, and the contrast of extreme youth and experienced tour pro – dark, handsome Latin versus powerful blond star of the west – began to monopolize the attention of the crowds, upstaging even such as Nicklaus.

The nine-syllable name of the Spaniard first reached the author's ears three years earlier, when Michael Williams, Leonard Crawley's successor on the "Daily Telegraph", rang from Spain to tell of a conversation he had just had with Ramon Sota, also Pedrena-born, and a winner in Europe and South America. They had been talking of the improvement of various Spanish players. Sota took Williams to the practice tee. He indicated a tall, dark 16-year-old with a totally uninhibited swing, stroking the ball away prodigious distances. "The best of all", said Sota.

This was "Seve", as he prefers to be known, now leading the Birkdale Open after three rounds, with 69, 69, 73, by two from Miller, four from Horton and five from the Australian Graham Marsh, Nicklaus and Ray Floyd, the reigning Masters champion from North Carolina. The Spaniard had not yet won a trophy. Miller had won two already this year. His iron tee-shots ruled in the end, though Ballesteros went three ahead on the first hole, where Miller hit two straight shots but went through the green and took five. The Spaniard was twice in rough, criss-crossing the fairway, found the green and holed a huge par putt.

This Walter Hagen/Jerome Travers type game did not hold up thereafter. Miller's confidence, and use of the driver, increased and a seven by Ballesteros at the 11th and a chip-in eagle by Miller on the 13th were conclusive. The youngster even congratulated Miller at this point, but the American, thinking like the pro he is, told his partner to get down to it and improve his finishing position. This he did, sharing second position with Nicklaus, six behind Miller, who let the young Spaniard make the final putt. The noise was deafening.

● Ballesteros's fine showing in the Open encouraged him to become the youngest European tour winner at the Dutch Open. Next he won the Lancôme Trophy, and later the World Cup for Spain, with Manuel Pinero.

● The European Tour opened its first tour school, after the US PGA model. In the same way Sunday finishes and pre-tournament Pro-Ams were introduced. John Jacobs and his tournament-planning team had worked European Tour purses up to beyond the million pound mark, with 30 events arranged for 1977.

● Jenny Lee Smith, from Newcastle-upon-Tyne, became the first holder of the Women's British Open, scoring 299 at Fulford, York. She gained the title while still an amateur. The new event grew out of the Open Amateur Stroke Play event, and the women professionals were initially few and of such a standard that the best amateurs were a real threat.

● Judy Rankin first to earn £100,000 in a year on the LPGA tour.

● Death of tiny Fred McLeod (94), a North Berwick Scot who beat Willie Smith in play-off for US Open in 1908.

**"Hit it as far as you can, find it, get it on the green and then try to one-putt. Never mind the bunkers and the rough. You're used to them."**

PETER ALLISS,
summing up Ballesteros' philosophy.

# 'Memorial' launched

JACK NICKLAUS staged the first Memorial Tournament, an official tour event, on the Muirfield Village course he designed and built at Dublin near his Columbus birthplace in Ohio. Though it is more reminiscent, with its great rolling slopes between trees and its water hazards, of Augusta than the original Muirfield (first planned by Old Tom Morris), Muirfield Village proved well able to protect itself from humiliation.

Small greens with bunkers close by help to make par a battle even for the best. The trap set for the unwary by Bobby Jones at Augusta National's short 12th, across Rae's Creek, is repeated at Nicklaus's lay-out at the same number hole. It is all carry over water, followed by a bunker just above the water-line letting almost at once on to a shallow green.

Boldness can win its rewards at the par-fives and Roger Maltbie did make par but only just, with 288, to set up a play-off in which he beat Hale Irwin at the fourth extra hole.

**British Open** (Royal Birkdale, Lancashire)
J Miller 72 68 73 66  279

**US Open** (Atlanta AC, Duluth, Ga)
J Pate 71 69 69 68  277

**Masters** (Augusta, Ga)
R Floyd 65 66 70 70  271

**US PGA** (Congressional CC, Washington, DC)
D Stockton 70 72 69 70  281
Leading US money-winner:
JW Nicklaus  $266,438.57;
Europe: S Ballesteros £39,504

**British Amateur** (St Andrews, Scot)
R Siderowf bt JC Davies  37th

**US Amateur** (Bel-Air CC, Los Angeles, Cal)
W Sander bt C Parker Moore  8 & 6

**British Women's Open** (Fulford, Bristol)
J Lee Smith  299

**US Women's Open** (Springfield, Pa)
J Gunderson Carner  292 (after tie with S
Palmer)

**British Women's Amateur** (Silloth, Cumbria)
C Panton bt A Sheard  1h

**World Cup** (Palm Spring, Cal)
Spain (S Ballesteros & M Pinero)  591
(Individual): E Acosta (Mexico) 282

**World Match Play** (Wentworth, Surrey)
D Graham bt H Irwin  38th

**Eisenhower Trophy** (Penina, Portugal)
GB & Ireland  892

**Espirito Santo** (Vilamoura, Portugal)
US  605

**Curtis Cup** (Royal Lytham, Lancs)
US 11½, GB & Ireland 6½

**Dave Stockton: US PGA
champion.**

# Floyd, every bit of the way

DOMINATING is a weak word with which to describe Raymond Floyd's Masters victory. This son of an army family, born at Fort Bragg, had won the St Petersburg Open at little over 20. That was 13 years before he coasted through his first Masters, equalling Nicklaus's record aggregate of 271 and beating Nicklaus into third place 11 shots in arrears. Ben Crenshaw was second, a mere eight shots adrift of Floyd, who began 65, 66, and added a couple of 70s while his rivals fought out minor placings.

He said afterwards: "The game was easy for me as a kid and I had to play a while to find out how hard it is." Floyd's early career, like that of the late Tony Lema, was too focused on generally having a good time. A hint as to his changed attitudes may be gleaned from the date of birth of his first child: September 1974.

**Ray Floyd: utterly dominant in the Masters.**

# 'Play it as it lies' plea

COLONEL TONY DUNCAN, golf administrator and former Welsh champion, in a letter to the Daily Telegraph lamented the weakening of the "sacred principle" of playing the ball where it lies. The "insidious teeing up of balls on the fairway" was reasonable but only as long as it was done for course preservation. "The fascination of golf is a delicate balance between physical and mental aspects." The right policy was to hit good shots and not be discouraged by bad bounces.

His letter produced radically different responses from readers, but Duncan stuck to his guns. He felt that modern trends were all directed towards removing the element of chance. If target golf was required from perfect lies, mark out areas on a polo field, he said. A parting shot was to observe: "What a pity the PGA contract out of the Royal & Ancient rules from time to time."

# Jerry Pate's shining 72nd

LIKE JACK NICKLAUS, Jerry Pate made the US Open his first professional win, the year after coming out top at the PGA tour school. He slammed the door on Al Geiberger, Tom Weiskopf, Butch Baird and John Mahaffey in the most satisfactory manner, with the bravest and best shot of the year, a five iron to two feet from rough over the lake which fronts the 18th at Atlanta Athletic Club.

Pate, aged 22, from Georgia, was a member of the routinely successful US Walker Cup team at St Andrews. he went on to win the Canadian Open, in which Jack Nicklaus was once again the bridesmaid, Pate winning by four shots. His $153,102 winnings that year was a record for a rookie.

# US women quick off mark

BRITAIN AND IRELAND could count the Curtis Cup lost after the first day at Lytham. Beth Daniel had a superb four out of four points match, and Nancy Lopez, in her first Cup match, won twice in two starts. Dinah Henson (née Oxley), former British and English champion, and Tegwen Perkins, the Welsh champion, got most of the home team's points, but they amounted to only 6½ against 11½ for the United States, for whom Beth Daniel led off in the top match in all four sessions with a win.

# Britain takes Ike's Trophy

A SECOND VICTORY for Britain and Ireland in the World Amateur Team championship, for the Eisenhower Trophy, came at Penina, the course designed in Portugal by Henry Cotton. They had only two strokes to spare over Japan, who had also been second in Kuala Lumpur in 1974. The key to victory was Ian Hutcheon's gritty final round of 71. His companions were John Davies, Stephen Martin, the Scottish Strokeplay champion, and Mike Kelley, from Yorkshire, a boy, youth and full international.

# Tom Watson takes centre-stage

TURNBERRY'S FIRST British Open presented two wonders to the huge galleries, which were, at 92,200, a record for Scotland. First was the varied and spectacular beauty of the Ayrshire coast in the west of Scotland, which Robert Louis Stevenson might surely have equated with Monterey as a great meeting place of sky, sea and land.

Turnberry has two items Monterey lacks. Out to sea, thrusting skywards, lies the brooding spike of rock called Ailsa Craig; and the lighthouse, on the cliff's edge, opposite the daunting carry over rock and rough water to the ninth fairway. Second was the way in which Tom Watson and Jack Nicklaus fought for the title in a storm of record low scores, a battle in which the rest of the field had only the most academic interest, since the best of them, Hubert Green, the US Open champion no less, was the only player apart from the two principals who beat par for the 72 holes. Green returned 279, but that was 11 strokes behind the winner.

Peter Alliss and David Thomas, now into course architecture, were asked to make improvements to the course, which had been an RAF Coastal Command training airfield during the war, but the money was not available to make better, and more forbidding, use of this superb piece of coastline. Even so, only two players did much damage to the par of this course, named Ailsa, after the Craig.

A less well-known name, at least in golfing circles, caused press tent panics and rewrites galore on the first evening by

Tom Watson and (right) Jack Nicklaus: leaving the Turnberry field floundering.

coming in almost in the dark to lead, with 66. The "guilty" party's father was Ted Schroeder, a lawn tennis champion. John of that ilk finished in the gloaming, and led Martin Foster from Bradford by one, and Nicklaus, Watson and Lee Trevino by two.

Californian Roger Maltbie led after two rounds, with 137, so Nicklaus and Watson, both 68+70, set out together on round three. Both scored 65, so when the final round began there was no trace of hot breath on their necks, and no trace of a young Australian, Greg Norman, who had just won the Martini tournament in Britain, and made the 36-hole cut here, but not the one at 54 holes.

In between the feats of the two gladiators (and an Open record of 63 on the second day by Mark Hayes) came the evocative image of them sitting peacefully on rocks at the water's edge, waiting for an electrical storm to pass.

With nine holes left, Nicklaus led by a stroke, as this private two-man Open reached its climax, in which the short 15th provided the first heart-stopping moment. Nicklaus hit the green, Watson was in light rough, whence he putted in for a two. Nicklaus could not respond. The match, for that is what it had become, was all square.

Almost at once there was another crisis on the 17th, 500 yards. Watson reached the green with his second before Nicklaus, whose mighty drive had left him only a seven iron, hit the ball fat. His little Scottish run up was four or five feet strong. He missed the one back: only a par, and Watson was ahead. It stayed that way at the last, but in the most nail-biting fashion.

Nicklaus pushed his drive into trouble, and his second finished many yards from the hole, Watson's being no more than two feet or so from the pin. He said afterwards, as befits a graduate in psychology, that mentally he gave this 15-yard putt to Nicklaus who, amazingly, did indeed sink it. Watson put his down for the title. A birdie apiece, and Watson, 27, had beaten the reigning world leader, 37, head to head over 36 holes, 65+65 to 65+66, an Open record by eight shots.

Perhaps the golfing crown had changed heads. There was no doubting which nation led the world. Tommy Horton, British Ryder Cup player, was joint ninth; otherwise the top 12 were all American. The top 20 all got four-figure prizes.

# Faldo offers only hope in unhappy Ryder reshuffle

ONLY 20 POINTS were played for in the Ryder Cup match at Lytham. The home side led by Brian Huggett lost by five points, spectators lost patience because the few matches were so far apart in time and distance and, horrors, television didn't like it either.

The format, and the lack of depth in British Isles golf producing one defeat after another – both needed amendment.

England had found promising new material, but still not enough of it. Nick Faldo, rookie of the year, made his Cup debut at 20 and won his foursome and fourball with Peter Oosterhuis. They beat Jack Nicklaus and Ray Floyd in the fourball.

Then Faldo defeated Masters and British Open champion Tom Watson in singles. Oosterhuis, too, was 100 per cent, but American mastery in foursomes and fourballs made parity in singles fruitless.

## SHORT PUTTS

● The death occurred of Fred Corcoran, a key figure, in the footsteps of Bob Harlow, in the growth of the American PGA tour. He was manager of (among many others) Babe Zaharias and baseball stars like Stan Musial.

● Cecil Leitch, winner of four British, five French, two English and one Canadian Women's Amateur titles, also died. Her rivalry with Joyce Wethered was the outstanding feature of British golf in the 1920s.

● The British PGA under their secretary, Colin Snape, moved to their new headquarters alongside the new Belfry course, almost in the centre of England. Their old London offices at Surrey Cricket Oval had become inadequate.

● The Tournament Players' Division remained in the capital under Ken Schofield, who had taken over as secretary and executive director when John Jacobs stood down in 1975.

● Al Geiberger holed an eight-foot putt on the final green of the second round in the Memphis Classic to record the one and only 59 scored at a regular full-length tour venue. He had 11 birdies and an eagle, and took 23 putts. He also won the tournament.

● Nick Faldo won his first professional tournament, the Skol Lager.

● Clifford Roberts, of Augusta National, died by his own hand in September. He left a note apologising to his wife, together with details of his doctors' opiinions that his illness was terminal. He was given the title "Chairman in Memoriam".

# Watson's Masters, and it's no choke

TOM WATSON'S FIRST big battle of 1977 brought him his first Masters at last, his 67 on the final day holding off a weighty charge by Jack Nicklaus, whose 66 was two too many. Watson's hopes of setting up stage two of a Grand Slam campaign were wrecked in the American Open. Hubert Green squeezed home a shot ahead of the 1975 champion, Lou Graham. Green's split-handed putting stroke worked for him on the 72nd hole when it came down to "This for the US Open". "This" was a three-foot putt. Green sank it.

**Hubert Green: his split-hand putting worked in US Open.**

## TEE TALK

**"It is vital to widen the selection procedures if the Ryder Cup is to continue to enjoy its past prestige."**

JACK NICKLAUS.

## SCORECARD

**British Open** (Turnberry, Scot)
T Watson  68 70 65 65 268

**US Open** (S Hills, Tulsa, Okla)
H Green  69 67 72 70 278

**Masters** (Augusta, Ga)
T Watson  70 69 70 67 276

**US PGA** (Pebble Beach, Cal)
L Wadkins  69 71 72 70 282
(Wadkins bt G Littler in sudden-death play-off)
Leading US money-winner:
T Watson  $310,653.10;
Europe  S Ballesteros £46,436

**British Amateur** (Ganton Yorks)
PM McEvoy bt HM Campbell  5 & 4

**US Amateur** (Aronimink, Pa)
J Fought bt DH Fischesser  9 & 8

**British Women's Open** (Lindrick, Notts)
V Saunders  306

**US Women's Open** (Hazeltine Nat, Minn)
H Stacy  292

**British Women's Amateur** (Hillside, Lancs)
A Uzielli bt V Marvin  6 & 5

**US Women's Amateur** (Cincinatti, Ohio)
B Daniel bt C Shark  3 & 1

**World Cup** (Manila, Phil)
Spain (S Ballesteros & A Garrido)  574
(Individual): G Player (S Africa)  289

**World Match Play** (Wentworth, Surrey)
G Marsh bt R Floyd  5 & 3

**Ryder Cup** (Royal Lytham, Lancs)
US  12 1/2, GB & Ireland  7 1/2

**Walker Cup** (Shinnecock Hills, NY)
US  16, GB & Ireland  8

# Bing Crosby, the 'fun' golfer

BING CROSBY, founder in 1937 of the "Clambake" or, more properly, the Crosby Pro-Am (first winner, over 18 holes, Sam Snead), died suddenly at a Madrid golf course immediately after playing a fourball, which included Manuel Pinero.

Crosby was a single-figure "fun" golfer, though he did play in both the American and the British Amateur championship (in which he started birdie, par, birdie at headquarters, but lost).

He is one of the rare beings to have scored a hole in one on the 16th at Cypress Point, one of the most photographed of holes, with its 210-yard carry over the Pacific Ocean and where tour pros have been known to get into double figures and lose fortunes.

**Bing Crosby: keen golfer to the end. Here he enjoys a pipe, and the company of Dai Rees (left) and friend.**

# Gary Player's winning exercise at Augusta

ON THE NIGHT of the champions' dinner early in Masters' week at Augusta, Gary Player already a winner of two green jackets, did not get back to his hotel until nearly 11 o'clock. At 42 with, at that stage, eight major championships to his name, it was perhaps time for a nightcap and more reminiscence. Instead, Player spent until midnight doing his daily exercises. He was doing them again on Sunday, after his extraordinary third Masters win.

With a record-equalling final round of 64, he beat among others, Hubert Green, whom he had trailed by seven strokes going into the last day. The above is how the "Daily Telegraph" golf correspondent, Michael Williams, saw Player's feat on the morning after his third victory at Augusta.

Player's success was unique. To start with, he was the oldest winner. He had caught up only two strokes by the turn in the final round, then tore past the rest of the field with birdies at the 10th, 12th, 13th, 15th, 16th and 18th where, he said "I hit a drive and six iron to 15 feet [pause] and nearly missed it." He came home in 30.

Green, Watson (who was betrayed by the treacherous 14th green, where a six-foot birdie chance turned into a five, not to mention a hooked drive at the last), and Jack Nicklaus – all had chances. Green was unluckiest of all. He was disturbed by a radio commentator as he got over his tying three-foot putt at the 72nd hole He missed, and would blame only himself.

Peter Oosterhuis reached the turn in 33, that is, as close to Player as Green was, but faded.

Peter Oosterhuis: British best again in the Open at St Andrews.

Most notable British feat was certainly that of Peter McEvoy, the Amateur champion, the first British amateur to go the distance in the Masters (and pass the first part of his law examinations, too).

Rod Funseth, an inexorable winner of money, but not of tournaments, hung on well after sharing the lead with Lee Trevino at halfway, and shared second place with Watson and Green. All three missed equalizing putts, ending a 30-minute wait for Player before he knew that another green jacket and $45,000 (£22,000) were his.

Severiano Ballesteros, who came to Augusta having led Spain to a World Cup double, was ahead briefly on the third day, but like Bill Rogers, Nicklaus, Tom Kite and all the others had no answer to Player's sprint.

## SCORECARD

**British Open** (St Andrews, Scot)
JW Nicklaus 71 72 69 69 281

**US Open** (Cherry Hill, Denver, Col)
A North 70 70 71 74 285

**Master** (Augusta, Ga)
G Player 72 72 69 64 277

**US PGA** (Oakmont, Pa)
J Mahaffey 75 67 68 66 276
(Mahaffey bt J Pate and T Watson on second hole of sudden death play-off)
Leading US money-winner:
T Watson $362,428.93;
Europe: S Ballesteros £54,348

**British Amateur** (Royal Troon, Scot)
PM McEvoy bt P McKellar 4 & 3

**US Amateur** (Plainfield CC, NJ)
J Cooke bt S Hoch 5 & 4

**British Women's Open** (Foxhills, Surrey)
J Melville 310

**US Women's Open** (Indianapolis, Ind)
H Stacy 299

**British Women's Amateur** (Hollinwell, Notts)
E Kennedy bt J Greenhalgh 1h

**US Women's Amateur** (Sunnybrook, Pa)
C Shark bt J Oliver 4 & 3

**World Cup** (Hawaii)
US (J Mahaffey & A North) 564
(Individual): J Mahaffey 281

**World Match Play** (Wentworth, Surrey)
I Aoki bt S Owen 3 & 2

**Eisenhower Trophy** (Fiji)
US 873

**Espirito Santo** (Fiji)
Australia 596

**Curtis Cup** (Apawamis, NY)
US 12, GB & Ireland 6

# Nancy Lopez: Rookie and Player of the Year

NANCY LOPEZ shook the firmament of American women's professional golf, starting right away with a victory in the Bent Tree Classic in Sarasota, Florida. Lopez, 21, from New Mexico, won eight more tournaments, including the LPGA championship. This major event she took as part of a nap hand of five consecutive victories.

She had all the right qualifications in the amateur field. Since Mickey Wright, no golfer had shown the flair of a true gallery hynotizer. Despite Kathy Whitworth's multiple tournament wins and huge winnings, the coming of Lopez created a heightened level of publicity for the LPGA just when it was most needed.

By the end of her first year on the tour, Lopez had won $189,813, a record. But there is more to being a golfing superstar than winning money: Like another Latin gallery favourite, Seve Ballesteros, Lopez had a smile, that to say the very least, was winning.

## TEE TALK

**"Don't worry, man, I want to tell you I can get them."**

GARY PLAYER,
when someone said jokingly that he needed only eight birdies to win the Masters. He got nine.

**"He can get up and down from a parking lot."**

AMERICAN WRITER,
of Ballesteros.

# Nicklaus resurgent at HQ

AFTER THEIR Olympian duel at Turnberry, Jack Nicklaus and Tom Watson were inescapably favourites for the British Open at St Andrews. Yet a New Zealander, Simon Owen, chipped in at the 15th to go seven under par and take the lead from playing partner Jack Nicklaus with three holes remaining. The pair of them had started the final round two behind Peter Oosterhuis and Tom Watson. Owen began poorly, but suddenly came alive in mid-round, preceding his lucky break at the 15th by excellent stroke-saving manoeuvres at holes 9, 10, 12 and 14.

The change in the atmosphere was almost tangible. Surely this young man with no better than a German and New Zealand Open to his name was not going to upset all calculations?

The 16th was his undoing, for he went through the green and was short with his return over a choice assortment of St Andrews humps and bumps: a five. Nicklaus holed a birdie putt from three yards and was ahead. He was further ahead after the Road Hole, where Owen gambled, went on to the road and lost another shot to Nicklaus.

Another fine approach putt at the last warded off a final challenge from Owen, who in any case missed his birdie chance, and had to share second place with Ray Floyd, Ben Crenshaw and Tom Kite. Oosterhuis was British best, on his own in sixth place.

The Road Hole enjoyed a rich harvest of lost strokes and abandoned hopes. Tom Weiskopf, out in 31, birdied the tenth, but had a

**Jack Nicklaus: so happy to have won at St Andrews.**

**Owen: brave challenge.**

six on the Road Hole. By far the worst sufferer was Tommy Nakajima, from Japan. His approach putt was the merest touch weak. It wandered heartbreakingly into the tiny, deep Road bunker.

It took him some time to emerge and the resultant nine ruined an otherwise excellent Open, in which he finished level with Severiano Ballesteros, seven behind Nicklaus, and one behind Watson, Masashi Ozaki of Japan and Mark Hayes. A third Japanese, Isao Aoki, made a great impression on the galleries. He seemed almost to chip his putts, performed with toe of putter in air. He led after 18 holes with 68.

## SHORT PUTTS

● America's favourite golf commentator from his eyrie at Augusta's 16th hole, former German Amateur champion and Member of Parliament, and perennial master of the after-dinner speech and golf essay, Henry Longhurst, died after a long struggle with cancer.

● The deaths also occurred of two celebrated British amateurs, Cyril Tolley, twice winner of the French Open, and Mrs Frances Smith (née Stephens), key Curtis Cup player during the 1950s in a rare run of British success.

● American PGA prize money soared above the $10 million mark, while women professionals were looking at purses totalling nearly $4 million. European Tour cash stood at more than £1 million.

● Severiano Ballesteros, still only 20, won his first tournament on the American circuit, the Greater Greensboro Open.

● Tom Watson broke the earnings record set by Johnny Miller with $362,428, had the best stroke average for the Vardon Trophy and most tour wins (five), all these feats for the second year running.

**Miller: record broken.**

● Simon Owen came close in another summit, the autumn World Match Play championship at Wentworth, in which he lost 3 & 2 to another player who had excelled in the British Open at St Andrews, the Japanese, Isao Aoki.

● Nick Faldo won first major European title, the Colgate PGA championship.

# North's Open chance nearly goes west

SIX-FOOT FOUR-INCH Andy North from Wisconsin won the US Open at Cherry Hills with rather less éclat than Arnold Palmer with his last-round 65 18 years before. North built on a two-stroke lead after three rounds, and was four ahead with five holes remaining.

Then he started to shed shots and needed a bogey five at the last to win. He played it most conservatively, but still managed to put his third into a bunker, coming out to four feet. After several false starts he finally put the ball away for his second win since joining the tour in 1973. North's score was one over par. Jesse Snead and Dave Stockton were joint second at two over.

Jesse Carlyle Snead, though suffering the frustration of being referred to repeatedly as the nephew of Sam, was a considerable athlete. He gave up baseball in favour of golf in 1964, played in three Ryder Cups had been Australian champion and won six Tour events.

**Andy North: nervous finish**

# Rocky Ryder Cup start for Europe

A STREAM of untoward events did nothing for either the good name of golf or for the constructive idea of making all Europe's golfers available for selection in the biennial teams to contest the Ryder Cup with the United States.

Britain and Ireland had lacked on all but three occasions since 1927 the depth of playing strength needed to beat America, a nation able to call upon the leading players in golf's most competitive series of events, the US PGA tour, itself based on a golfing population approximately equal to that of the rest of the world.

Jack Nicklaus, aided by British PGA president Lord Derby, had been the prime mover in bringing about the change. They feared the Cup matches would die from lack of interest in the one-sided series unless something could be done to make them competitive.

The Cup got little media attention in America, though it did well in Britain, mainly because the golfing public were eager to seize the chance every four years of seeing the best golfers in the world playing as a team.

The irony was that at the palatial Greenbrier club, Virginia, the outstanding European player of the day, British Open champion Severiano Ballesteros, lost four of his five matches, including his single. Larry Nelson was his bête noire every time. When drawn against Fuzzy Zoeller and Hubert Green, Ballesteros and his compatriot, Antonio Garrido, won 3 & 2.

The untoward events began before Europe flew from Heathrow, where Mark James turned up not wearing the approved uniform for the trip. John Jacobs, one of the chief begetters of the European tour, had been most aptly chosen to be captain, and thought of sending James home.

During the flag-raising ceremony he must have regretted his clemency, for the lounging attitudes adopted by James and the young Scot, Ken Brown, amounted to rudeness, to both hosts and comrades. They were also seen out shopping when Jacobs was holding team talks.

The only British newcomers were Des Smyth, from Ireland, Michael King and Sandy Lyle, the identity of whose opponent in singles was a further cause of contention.

James was injured, and since the format had been changed so that all 12 team members were to play in singles, both captains, Billy Casper and Jacobs, were asked to name in a sealed envelope the player they would stand down if no opponent was available.

On the final morning the Americans asked that their odd man out be changed from Lee Trevino to Gil Morgan, (shoulder injury), who had played in only one game, which not surprisingly prompted talk of "moving the goalposts" from the British camp.

Jacobs agreed and Trevino beat Lyle. Morgan versus James was listed as a half, though not played. Brown made it clear from the start that he wanted no one but James as his partner, but James was hurt in the first fourball in which he and Brown lost

to Trevino and Fuzzy Zoeller. Brown, assigned to play with Smyth, now behaved in highly uncomradely fashion towards the Irishman. They lost 7 & 6.

Though Casper's team had eight new men, including the first black golfer in the Cup, Lee Elder, they proved as competent as ever. Elder and the huge Andy Bean, another fresh recruit, knocked off eight shots from par in beating Nick Faldo and Peter Oosterhuis on the first morning, when only the old faithfuls, Bernard Gallacher and Brian Barnes, won.

The two Spaniards were the sole afternoon winners, and a mighty rally was needed on day two.

It came in the second series

of fourballs and foursomes, won 5-3 without the participation of Brown, and the singles started with America only a point ahead, 8½ – 7½. Gallacher won the top match, but Nelson again had Ballesteros to rights.

Faldo and, ironically, Brown, were the only other winners in an 8½-3½ trouncing, Oosterhuis losing his 100 per cent singles record to Green. Tom Kite's sharp response, expressed in birdies, when he fell behind Tony Jacklin typified the visitors' dependable skills.

Brown was fined £1,000 and banned from international play for a year; James was fined £1,500. The match was lost, and the recalcitrant pair had played a none-too-admirable part in that.

Andy Bean: in wonderful form.

Ken Brown: won his Ryder Cup single but Europe were trounced.

## RYDER CUP

(Greenbrier, White Sulphur Springs, WVa) **US 17, Europe 11**
Captains: US, W Casper; Europe J Jacobs

**FIRST DAY Fourballs: Morning**

| US | | Europe | |
|---|---|---|---|
| L Wadkins & L Nelson 2 & 1 | 1 | A Garrido & S Ballesteros | 0 |
| L Trevino & F Zoeller 3 & 2 | 1 | K Brown & M James | 0 |
| A Bean & L Elder 2 & 1 | 1 | P Oosterhuis & N Faldo | 0 |
| H Irwin & J Mahaffey | 0 | B Gallacher & B Barnes 2 & 1 | 1 |

**Foursomes: Afternoon**

| | | | |
|---|---|---|---|
| H Irwin & T Kite 7 & 6 | 1 | K Brown & D Smith | 0 |
| F Zoeller & H Green | 0 | S Ballesteros & A Garrido 3 & 2 | 1 |
| L Trevino & G Morgan | ½ | S Lyle & A Jacklin | ½ |
| L Wadkins & L Nelson 4 & 3 | 1 | B Gallacher & B Barnes | 0 |

First day: US 5½; Europe 2½

**SECOND DAY Foursomes: Morning**

| | | | |
|---|---|---|---|
| L Elder & J Mahaffey | 0 | A Jacklin & S Lyle 5 & 4 | 1 |
| A Bean & T Kite | 0 | N Faldo & P Oosterhuis 6 & 5 | 1 |
| F Zoeller & M Hayes | 0 | B Gallacher & B Barnes 2 & 1 | 1 |
| L Wadkins & L Nelson 3 & 2 | 1 | S Ballesteros & A Garrido | 0 |

**Fourballs: Afternoon**

| | | | |
|---|---|---|---|
| L Wadkins & L Nelson 5 & 4 | 1 | S Ballesteros & A Garrido | 0 |
| H Irwin & T Kite 1h | 1 | A Jacklin & S Lyle | 0 |
| L Trevino & F Zoeller | 0 | B Gallacher & B Barnes 3 & 2 | 1 |
| L Elder & M Hayes | 0 | N Faldo & P Oosterhuis 1h | 1 |

Second day: US 3; Europe 5. Match aggregate US 8½, Europe 7½

**THIRD DAY Singles**

| | | | |
|---|---|---|---|
| L Wadkins | 0 | B Gallacher 3 & 2 | 1 |
| L Nelson 3 & 2 | 1 | S Ballesteros | 0 |
| T Kite 1h | 1 | A Jacklin | 0 |
| M Hayes 1h | 1 | A Garrido | 0 |
| A Bean 4 & 3 | 1 | M King | 0 |
| J Mahaffey 1h | 1 | B Barnes | 0 |
| L Elder | 0 | N Faldo 3 & 2 | 1 |
| H Irwin 5 & 3 | 1 | D Smyth | 0 |
| H Green 2h | 1 | P Oosterhuis | 0 |
| F Zoeller | 0 | K Brown 1h | 1 |
| L Trevino 2 & 2 | 1 | S Lyle | 0 |
| G Morgan | ½ | M James | ½ |
| (Match not played) | | | |

Singles: US 8½; Europe 3½

## Tree irony

HALE IRWIN'S 40 strokes on the last nine of the American Open at Inverness was still good enough to beat Jerry Pate and Gary Player by two shots. Leading money-winner Tom Watson did not make the cut.

The USGA showed pretty footwork, or rather spadework, after Lon Hinkle found a short cut on the long eighth hole. He hit his drive on to the 17th fairway. Next morning a tree had been planted in the gap through which Hinkle had driven. Voices were raised against changing the course after the championship had started ...

David Graham of Australia took the last major of the year, the US PGA at Oakland Hills but only after seeming to have thrown it away.

He needed a par on the 72nd hole for a 63 which would have meant a record total for the event of 270 and a two-shot win. Instead he made double bogey, putting his approach through the green and needing two chips and two putts to get home.

For the third year in a row the event went to a play-off. Graham atoned with two long putts on the first and second holes to stave off defeat by Ben Crenshaw before winning on the third with a two to a four. The American was runner-up two weeks after a second at Lytham.

## SCORECARD

**British Open** (Royal Lytham, Lancs)
S Ballesteros 73 65 75 70  283

**US Open** (Inverness, Toledo, Ohio)
H Irwin 74 68 67 75  284

**Masters** (Augusta, Ga)
F Zoeller 70 71 69 70  280
(Zoeller bt T Watson & E Sneed at 2nd extra hole in sudden-death play-off)

**US PGA** (Oakland Hills, Mich)
D Graham 69 68 70 65  272
(Graham bt B Crenshaw in sudden death play-off)
Leading US money-winner:
T Watson $462,636;
Europe: S Lyle £49,232

**British Amateur** (Hillside, Lancs)
J Sigel bt S Hoch  3 & 2

**US Amateur** (Canterbury CC, Cleveland, Ohio)
M O'Meara bt J Cook  8 & 7

**US Women's Open** (Brooklawn CC, Fairfield, Conn)
J Britz 284

**British Women's Open** (Southport & Ainsdale, Lancs)
A Sheard  301

**British Women's Amateur** (Nairn, Scot)
M Madill bt J Lock  2 & 1

**US Women's Amateur** (Memphis, Tenn)
C Hill bt P Sheehan  7 & 6

**World Cup** (Glyfada, Greece)
US (J Mahaffey & H Irwin)  575
(Individual): Irwin 285

**World Match Play** (Wentworth, Surrey)
W Rogers bt I Aoki  1h

**Walker Cup** (Muirfield, Scot)
US 15½, GB & Ireland  8½

# Ballesteros: from car park to immortality

THE SEVERIANO BALLESTEROS of the 1970s was not the most relentless player of percentages ever to step on a tee. So his scores in winning the British Open at Royal Lytham were what you might expect, with ten shots difference between his second and third rounds.

His total of 283 was three better than Ben Crenshaw and Jack Nicklaus, four better than Mark James, five better than the Australian, Rodger Davis, and six better than Hale Irwin, US Open champion, who had looked well capable of landing the big Open double – until Ballesteros got to work on him, that is.

Lytham's centenary book quotes Newsday writer Joe Gergen: "Ballesteros forged a new path to glory. It hooked left and then sliced right. It dipped and detoured through sand and scrub. It meandered through bushes and across cart tracks and even into a parking lot ... " In cold figures, the Spaniard hit the fairway once in nine attempts with his driver.

To be fair, he had in practice tried shots from the not very severe rough, to get better approaches to the greens. But on the 16th he drove so far right that he landed where BBC folk had parked their cars.

It was not out of bounds ... no owners about to move the cars, so Ballesteros got a free drop, and whacked a sand wedge to within 15 feet of the pin.

Jack Nicklaus, who alone could steal the trophy from the Spaniard, was contemplating his chances of a birdie from the middle of the 18th fairway.

He was two over, and two behind. There came a great roar from the 16th, rapidly followed by another as a red "1" appeared by the name of Ballesteros on the scoreboard by the 18th. He had got down in two from the car park. Nicklaus hit his second into a trap. He saved par but was runner-up for the seventh time.

So the first Spanish British Open champion, and the first from the continent since Arnaud Massy in 1907, received the silver claret jug.

## TEE TALK

**"I play good from the rough; I have plenty of practice. Bunkers no real problem: I am the best bunker player."**

SEVE BALLESTEROS.

Ben Crenshaw: close to a major at last, but lost to David Graham in US PGA play-off.

# Nancy Lopez, radiant rookie to superstar

During a meteoric rise to stardom she won numerous major tournaments, established a remarkable earnings record and displayed a talent which remains as fresh as ever

Nancy Lopez: youngest golfer ever to reach a million dollars in prize money.

MOST CHAMPIONS have to learn how to lose before they find out how to win. For Nancy Lopez, aged 20, starting her first full season as a professional on the LPGA Tour, winning came naturally ... nine times, including the LPGA championship.

Not even Jack Nicklaus burst upon the golfing scene with such reverberating impact. It is a safe bet that in the near or distant future no one will again, in the same season, become rookie of the year and player of the year (with the exception, naturally, of Seniors Golf, in which Lee Trevino has already brought off this particular double).

That is one measure of the Lopez achievement. Stated in prize money terms, it came to $189,821, a record for the LPGA Tour. A distinguished, though brief amateur career suggested Lopez would not go hungry on Tour. Five years after her professional debut, she reached a career earnings total of $1million by virtue of a sixth place in the Nabisco Dinah Shore. That made her the youngest golfer, male or female, to reach a million in prize money.

## Focus for Tour

Her 1978 start in professional life was what made her, and to some extent, remade the Tour, which was at the time much in need of a new focus of attention to succeed the great Mickey Wright. The mid-1970s were times of some discontent, the purse for the Women's Open causing particular disappointment, for it was about a fifth of the men's Open sum. There were even mutterings about a boycott.

The women's Tour had plenty of competition for newspaper and television coverage from lawn tennis, this being the era of Martina Navratilova, Chris Evert and Billie-Jean King.

The Tour was not short of improvements in sponsorship as the decade wore on. David Foster of Colgate-Palmolive determined to make women's golf work for his company, and the recently appointed chief executive, Ray Volpe, made good use of Foster's enthusiasm, notably with the European Open and Far East Open in Australia, to which LPGA fields were flown en masse.

But people, and least of all television people, will not pay to watch sponsor's money being paid out. Lopez provided the other ingredients. Not only did she quickly become the player to beat, but unlike Nicklaus, she did not have the misfortune to suffer early rejection problems because she was upstaging an established favourite. Moreover, with her dark glossy hair, shining brown eyes, and youthful five-foot five-inch figure, she was the picture of health. She also smiled in a most beguiling way, and made the sale of admission tickets and television rights suddenly much easier.

She had turned pro in July 1977, and in five late season starts gained one second place, in the Colgate European Open at

Sunningdale. Two weeks earlier, in her first appearance as a professional, she had again come second by two strokes in the US Women's open, to Hollis Stacy, having already been runner-up as an amateur. Once embarked on 1978, she quickly dominated the LPGA Tour, even commandeering media space that was usually a male preserve. Magazine and book covers were her natural habitat.

Her second victory, the Sunstar Classic in Los Angeles, woke up the golf fans. Her first, at Sarasota, might have been beginner's luck, but two wins suggested a serious competitor. Before long she had run up five consecutive tournament victories in six weeks. She didn't play the other week, which she used to get ready for the LPGA championship at the Jack Nicklaus Golf Center in Ohio. She won spectacularly, shooting 66 in the second round and totalled 275, 13 under par, beating Amy Alcott by six shots.

## A year of victories

Mickey Wright had won four tournaments in a row twice, Kathy Whitworth had done it once, but the Lopez five was breaking new ground. In all,

Lopez won nine tournaments in 1978, Wright retaining her record of 13 wins in 1963, but Lopez set another record by producing a stroke average below 72. The new target for LPGA members was 71, 76.

Marriage to a sports broadcaster, Tim Melton, in January 1979, had no effect on the Lopez production line of tournament first-place cheques. In 19 starts in 1979, she finished in the top ten 16 times, winning on eight occasions. Her prize money total rose to $197,488, her stroke average fell to 71.2. In the eight years that she can realistically be described as the No.1 player of the Tour, though she was not always leading money-winner, prize money tripled from $3 million to $9 million.

## California girl

Nancy Lopez was born of Mexican-American parentage in Torrance, California, on January 6, 1957. Her father, Domingo, was a keen golfer, and got down to three handicap. He is credited with being her only instructor, though hers is one of the game's great natural talents. Her precocity outdoes even Bobby Jones's, for when the family moved to

New Mexico, she became state champion at 12. She had been playing since eight and her mother gave up playing so that Nancy and her sister Delma and their father could play. Four golfers were not within the family's financial reach.

US Girls' champion at 15 and 17, she gained a Colgate-Palmolive scholarship to Tulsa University, and at 18, in the 1975 Women's Open, she finished joint second to Sandra Palmer, needless to say as top amateur, in company with JoAnne Gunderson Carner and Sandra Post. The following year, in between collegiate victories, she played at Royal Lytham in the Curtis Cup in Barbara McIntire's team.

She was given two matches only, beating Suzanne Cadden 3 & 1 in singles and partnering Barbara Barrow to a 4 & 2 victory over Anne Stant and the experienced Mary McKenna, towards an American win by five points. A place in the nation's team for the World Amateur Team championship for the Espirito Santo Trophy was inevitably gained. America beat France into second place by 17 strokes at Vilamoura in Portugal. Lopez had the best single round and aggregate (72 & 297).

British galleries were soon in thrall to Nancy Lopez. After 54 holes in the Colegate European Open at Sunningdale in 1979 she was 15 under par, and began her victorious final round by saving shots at two of the first three holes.

Nearly two months later, at Dallas, Lopez surmounted a crisis in her golfing life with an extraordinary victory in the Mary Kay Classic, which rescued her from a very depressed state of mind. "Mentally, I was falling apart", she said, which is why, for the first time, she asked another pro for a lesson. Buddy Phillips flew in at her request from Oklahoma, and suggested a realignment of her feet to ward off an attack of the duck hooks.

Lopez started her second round with six birdies in seven holes at the Bent Tree Country Club. Later stumbles led to a 66, but a 67 on the third day, and a confirming 70 on the last, to win by two from Sandra Post, three from rookie of the year Beth Daniel and 11 from Jan Stephenson, fairly summed up the era's balance of power. A major factor in Lopez's dominance was her putting. Bold, and seldom leaving the ball short on the slowest of greens, she had that talent on the greens to see her through when, as the 1980s

**Quickly into professional stride.**

began, her hook reappeared now and then.

## Married again

In 1982 she got married again – to Ray Knight, a sports star in his own right as a World Series baseball player. Golf became less important as they raised three daughters. Yet the enduring strength of her game was proved again in 1985, when she returned to win five tournaments and become player of the year for the third time. Two years later she was inducted into the LPGA Hall of Fame with 35 career victories, among them one major, the LPGA championship.

She won on the LPGA Tour every year (1978-93) inclusive, apart from 1986, when her second daughter was born. One recurring disappointment was her failure to win the US Open, though she never stopped trying, notably in 1997, when on the par 71 Pumpkin Ridge Course in Oregon, she shot four rounds in the 60s – a record. But her total was one more shot than the 274 of Alison Nicholas, the five feet tall British Solheim Cup player.

**Player of the Year four times, plus three LPGA titles.**

| SCORE CARD | |
|---|---|
| **US LPGA** 1978, 1985, 1989 | |
| **Colgate European Open** 1978, 1979 | |
| **Colgate Far East Open** 1978 | |
| 48 LPGA Tour victories. **Solheim Cup**, 1990. **Curtis Cup**, 1976. **Espirito Santo** (winners), 1976 | |
| **US Rookie of Year** 1978 **Player of Year** 1978, 1979 ,1985 ,1988 | |

# Seve breaks the Masters mould

ACCEPTED WISDOM on the Masters championship at Augusta is that it doesn't really start till the last nine holes on Sunday afternoon. Jack Newton, from Australia, and all the pack chasing Severiano Ballesteros on April 13 must have thought the event was definitely over by the turn. Ballesteros reached that point in 33 strokes, ten ahead overall, having started with birdies at the first, third and fifth holes.

As every golfer knows, once one stroke is lost others often follow, and so it was with Ballesteros. Three putts on the tenth, followed by a watery double bogey at the short 12th and a bogey at the 13th where he went into the creek again, put into every head, especially that of Ballesteros, thoughts of a last-day collapse of appalling proportions. Besides, Newton was saving three strokes from 10th to 13th and Gibby Gilbert from Chattanooga saving four, while Ballesteros was dropping four. Thus Newton was three behind now and Gilbert only two.

Ballesteros said that as he came off the 13th green he gave himself a good talking to. "What are you doing?" was doubtless the least scathing of his self-interrogatory remarks.

Having called himself to order, Ballesteros rescued his par at the 14th despite getting himself into trouble in the trees, then gave a clear "Oh, no you don't" signal to his pursuers; with the four-iron approach he rifled over the water at the 15th. Two putts for a birdie there gave him repose and, though his final round of 72 was his worst by three shots, it was four too good for both Newton and Gilbert.

This was a different player from the fearless young man who had cut through great swathes of rough as he turned one errant tee shot after another at Lytham into birdie chances and won the British Open. His swing was more compact, certainly shorter, and he gave himself much less to do by way of recovery shots.

David Graham of Australia shared the lead with Ballesteros after the first round, the eventual winner covering each half in 33, with seven birdies. His putting, as during his second-round 69, was almost flawless. The "Daily Telegraph" went so far as to term it "beautiful if not sensational".

It helped on the 35th hole to achieve a Lytham-type birdie, Ballesteros holing from 15 feet for a three after hooking from the tee and getting a free drop from the seventh green. He followed this with a 68 to set a daunting last-day task for as strong a field as ever assembled at Augusta, including for the first time the Scot, Sandy Lyle, who lasted the course, but finished 19 behind Ballesteros. Amateur Peter McEvoy, who had played all four rounds two years earlier, and European Ryder Cup player Mark James missed the cut.

The course specialist, Jack Nicklaus, 40 in January, had endured a winless 1979 and did not excel in the wake of Ballesteros, who takes Nicklaus's place as the youngest Masters winner (at 23 years and four days), and is also the first European to gain the title.

His uninhibited stroke play had been reined in a little, a wise move since back trouble has been a threat to his game almost from the start of his professional career. He travels with a trapeze, from which he can hang upside down from doorways, relieving pressure on his much-abused spinal discs.

## Evans the Welsh giant

DUNCAN EVANS, 21, and six feet five inches tall, became Wales's first British Amateur champion in the 95 years of the event. He won in Wales, too, at Royal Porthcawl, beating David Suddards of South Africa by 4 & 3 in the final. Suddards, twice a South African stroke-play champion, has the distinction of being runner-up in his national Open to Gary Player in 1976.

In the early morning driving rain Evans soon got ahead with his long iron shots. Conditions were often appalling, but he was only four over par for the holes played.

Seve Ballesteros: regrouped at Augusta's 14th after the bulk of his ten-shot lead had evaporated.

Isao Aoki: a big bonus but no US title.

Jack Nicklaus: his opening 63 silenced critics at Baltusrol.

# Big Jack fights off advancing years and Aoki

JACK NICKLAUS was the subject of plentiful rumours at the American Open at Baltusrol in New Jersey after his eclipse in the Masters, which had been followed by failure to qualify at Atlanta.

Tom Watson added to the rumours by relaying the impression he had gained that, if the great man could swell his total of major pro titles to 16 with a fourth Open, he might well call it a day. And then again, he had reached the age at which those afflicted with the figures 4 and 0 are consoled with the falsehood that that is when life begins.

An opening 63, equalling Johnny Miller's closing round in the 1973 Open at Oakmont, dispelled notions about Nicklaus being over the top. He was just on top of everybody else ... except – for a few hours at least – Tom Weiskopf, who also returned 63.

Both men were out late,

Weiskopf, then Nicklaus arriving at the 18th in search of a birdie for a 62 to trump Miller, not to mention $50,000 dollars offered by "Golf Magazine" of America for a fresh, low 18-hole mark. Weiskopf visited trees and a bunker, but not the magazine's pay-out window. Nicklaus had the best chance, missing his putt for a birdie four from a yard after two hefty blows and a good chip. Not afraid to face the truth about this putt, Nicklaus admitted "chickening out".

Isao Aoki, the slim Japanese with the killing putting stroke, was least overawed by these two 63s. Besides, Nicklaus cooled down considerably after this, though his 71 for a 36-hole total of 134 was still an Open record, and so was his 204 for 54 holes. Aoki, only three years younger than Nicklaus, also returned 204, however, scoring 68 every time, so the stage was set for a transpa-

cific duel to remember. The pair played together all four days as it happened. Tom Watson started only two strokes adrift of the leading pair, having returned a threatening 67 on Saturday.

Masters champion Severiano Ballesteros could take no part in all this: he had been disqualified for being late on the tee for round two on Friday morning. Traffic problems were the unacceptable reason. When he reached the tee both his partners, Hale Irwin and Amateur champion Mark O'Meara, had played their second shots.

Champions, from the days of Old Tom Morris and Harry Vardon onwards, often lose their putting stroke first. Nicklaus was massively deliberate over putts as he and Aoki fought it out, but gave nothing away on the greens. He could scarcely afford to against an opponent who used an average of only 28 putts per round.

Nicklaus had to bear down

hard on the tenth to hole a three-foot birdie putt after Aoki had chipped in for his birdie. The same applied at the 17th, where Nicklaus was further from the pin than Aoki but still equalled his birdie, and finished with another at the 18th.

This time his total score earned the magazine bonus, since his 272 was three strokes better than his own Open record. Aptly, Aoki's 274 was good for the bonus, also. It would have won the Open in any other year but this. Watson had faltered round the turn, and perforce left the front pair to fight it out.

Nicklaus clearly found the emotions of the moment overwhelming. He had won his fourth US Open, so equalling the record of Willie Anderson, Ben Hogan and Bobby Jones, and it was to Jones's memory that this Open was dedicated, 50 years after his victory on the way to his Grand Slam.

# Masterly Watson in the money

WITH THREE PGA Tour wins and high placings in both the Masters and the American Open, Tom Watson had to be favoured to gain a third British Open at Muirfield. The weather was mostly favourable, the greens holding and further assaults on a major Scottish course, on the scale perhaps of the indignities suffered by Turnberry in 1977, were forecast.

Horacio Carbonetti from Argentina did not disappoint on day two. His 64 was a course record. Unhappily, his total was sandwiched by two 78s, and he did not survive the second cut, imposed after 54 holes.

Isao Aoki's turn came next, and he broke the record again in the third round with 32 + 31 = 63:

Aoki: 4,3,4, 3,4,4, 3,3,4, = 32:
4,3,3, 3,3,4, 3,4,4, = 31
Par: 4,4,4, 3,5,4, 3,4,5, = 36:
4,4,4, 3,4,4, 3,5,4, = 35

Tom Watson did not break the course record on the third day, but came home in an unrivalled 30 for a round of 64, and a total of 202, four ahead of Lee Trevino and Ken Brown, the young Scot who had seemingly left his salad days behind him. Aoki's record round served only to bring him within nine strokes of the leader, alongside Jack Nicklaus.

Listening to Watson run through his third round in the press tent sounded like the sort of thing St Andrew might have put forward as a counsel of perfection: "Drive and two iron, two putts, drive and wedge, made the putt", and so on to the 17th. "Two drivers to 55 feet, two putts (birdie), and then I made a mistake on the 18th." At this all present straightened up – so he is human after all.

His drive had not been straight, and he had played his second off the bank of a sand trap, from grass not sand. He had, it seemed, over-compensated for the degree to which his feet were not level with the ball, ending up in a bunker on the right of the green. He got his par four for all that, and was in such supreme form this week that he did not bother to mention that his bunker shot had missed providing him with another birdie, and hence a 63, by an inch or two.

Aoki's 63 reminded many of those present of Johnny Miller and his closing 63 at Oakmont to win the 1973 US Open. Next morning the caddie he employed when in England gave the author a lift into Edinburgh. Miller had not qualified for the final day. "We can't buy a putt", was the caddie's lament. There was a general feeling that there was something more basic in Miller's decline than that.

His commercial value began to be turned into hard cash, as quickly as any player's had ever been, after Oakmont, and he had

**Ken Brown: close on Watson's heels with Lee Trevino.**

performed more scoring miracles, and gained a second major at Birkdale soon afterwards. But, from heading the US PGA money-list in 1974 to being second the following year, he had subsequently been no better than 14th and in 1978 as low as 111th.

The widely held Saturday-night opinion as the rain poured down that no-one would get near Watson on the Sunday was totally vindicated. He won, easing up, with 69, still four in front of Trevino. Ben Crenshaw was third, six in arrears, and Jack Nicklaus, a further three shots away, was fourth. Carl Mason was the sole Englishman in the top eight.

**Tom Watson: home in an astonishing 30 at Muirfield.**

# Jack is back with a vengeance at Oak Hill

BY WINNING the US PGA championship from Andy Bean by seven strokes at Oak Hill, Jack Nicklaus underlined the truth of the message on the Open scoreboard at Baltusrol in June: Jack is back.

Nicklaus, with advice on his short game from Phil Rogers, had, after two unfruitful years, spent the winter in renewing his swing and polishing the bits and pieces of his game. After Oak Hill he also thanked his son for a putting lesson which, he said, had helped greatly on such quick greens. Nicklaus's long game had never been in doubt, nor his powers of concentration, for he could have given lessons to Norman Vincent Peale on the power of positive thinking. Most of all, he had the mental and physical attributes capable of creating a strategy to unlock an intricate problem like a championship golf course.

This he certainly did at Oak Hill, starting off 70, 69, 66. With nine holes to go he led by five, with Andy Bean and Lon Hinkle struggling in rough and trees. When Nicklaus did falter, he at once steadied his round, as at the eighth with a bunker shot to three inches, and the seventh, where he laid up after a poor drive, pitched to 15 feet and holed the putt.

Nicklaus, with 17, has now won more major pro titles than Arnold Palmer and Gary Player together. He has also won more majors than the combined total of Lee Trevino, Tom Watson, Hale Irwin, Johnny Miller, Tom Weiskopf, Hubert Green and Lanny Wadkins.

# Watson and Crenshaw, the late, late men

CAPTAIN PADDY HANMER, secretary of the Honourable Company of Edinburgh Golfers, whose Muirfield links had just hosted the 109th British Open championship, was incensed to hear, several hours after Tom Watson had been presented with the silver claret jug for the third time, that unauthorized persons were playing in the gloaming on the course, now with the giant stands deserted, the galleries gone from the roped walks, the clamour of the tented village and hospitality complexes stilled.

Captain Hanmer, Royal Navy, retired, was secretary of a select club and a man sternly resolved to keep it that way. There were stories of its inaccessibility even to players of impeccable credentials. Jokes were of this sort: would it be all right for Lieutenant So-and-So to have a round, he being plus one, ex-Eton and Brigade of Guards, member of Royal St George's and Boodles? "Oh [grudgingly], all right, let him have nine holes." This conversation, apocryphal needless to say, would, it was alleged, have taken place at a time when the course was empty of players.

On this Sunday night Tom Watson and Ben Crenshaw decided to play a match down the 10th and back up the 18th using hickory-shafted clubs and gutties that golfing historian Crenshaw brought along.

This was watched, the Daily Telegraph reported, by Tom Weiskopf, Tony Jacklin, Bill Rogers, Andy North and Tom Kite, the entourage complete with a bagpiper playing popular Scottish airs. Sand tees were used, but the tenth had to be abandoned because the supply of gutties proved unequal to the powerful game of the two Americans.

Back down the 18th they came, Watson achieving his second, though more muted, triumph of the day, with a bogey to a double bogey, having overshot the green in three, chipped back and sunk his putt. Watson then left for further refreshment in Greywalls, the hotel immediately behind the 18th, while Crenshaw, who had failed to exit first time from a bunker at the 18th, stayed to practise his short game.

Now Captain Hanmer arrived and told Crenshaw in no uncertain terms, in best quarterdeck fashion, that this sort of behaviour was not acceptable and that he must never darken etc., etc. – all this on Sunday night, by the way, well past dinnertime. But outraged feelings soon subsided, and the captain was before long standing "Gentle Ben" Crenshaw a drink.

**Ben Crenshaw: in trouble after hours at Muirfield.**

# US majestic, Europe divided, in Ryder Cup

IT IS REMOTELY possible that by the recruitment as honorary Europeans of, say, the Australians, David Graham and Greg Norman, Gary Player from South Africa and Isao Aoki from Japan, Europe might have beaten the United States in the Ryder Cup at Walton Heath, Surrey, in September.

As it was, the Europeans were handicapped by not fielding two players to whom much was owed and from whom much could be expected, namely Severiano Ballesteros and Tony Jacklin, the only Europeans of the era to have won a major title on both sides of the Atlantic. The

**Manuel Pinero: promising newcomer for Europe.**

Spaniard's absence stemmed from what the European Tour deemed to be his lack of support. A row blew up after Ballesteros reassessed his worth following his new-found pre-eminence in the world game.

He considered himself, as a British Open and Masters champion, well qualified to be paid appearance money, and certainly as much of a draw card as any American. If they were enticed to big European events in this way, he should receive the same respect, and cash.

He did not immediately get his own way. For a while it seemed he would appear only in

the British Open, and there was the possibility of his resigning his membership of the European Tournament Players division. Moreover, he did not respond to an impassioned plea from John Jacobs, who was again captain of Europe, to play in the Carrolls and Benson and Hedges tournaments as a peace-making gesture. The team as a whole opposed his selection.

Jacklin had remained a contender among leading players during the early 1970s despite his disappointments in 1970 at St Andrews and 1972 at Muirfield, but his performance at the latter and, many people said, the way his career had been tilted away from winning tournaments towards winning contracts had dulled his competitive edge, and he had even taken a year off for tax purposes. Crucially, in the run-up to Ryder Cup team selection, he had not performed well.

Peter Oosterhuis, who had just beaten Bruce Lietzke, Andy North and Jack Nicklaus by a stroke to win his one and only US PGA tour event, the Canadian Open, got one of the two places to be filled outside the top ten in the money list. Mark James, 11th in the list, got the other place, to the disgust of Jacklin, who had a clear recollection of James's unhelpful behaviour at the Greenbrier during the first United States versus Europe Cup match.

There were four new players

**Dave Marr: victorious Ryder Cup captain.**

in the team, all showing the greatest promise, namely the German, Bernhard Langer, two Spaniards, José-Maria Canizares and Manuel Pinero, and the Scot, Sam Torrance, so the absence of the experienced Ballesteros and Jacklin was all the more unfortunate.

Despite these self-inflicted wounds, Jacobs's team went ahead by a point in the first day's foursomes and four-balls. But Marr's team, which included the holders of the Masters (Tom Watson), of the British Open (Bill Rogers) and of the US PGA title (Larry Nelson, a late but much-to-be-feared recruit on previous Cup form), turned this round in a big way on day two, in a 7-1 spree.

Now that they had the measure of this mature heathland Walton Heath course to the southwest of London, they stamped the European challenge underfoot 18½ to 9½, notably by winning the singles 8-4.

What the European team were up against was encapsulated in the way Sandy Lyle performed, all in vain, against Tom Kite, a 31-year-old Texan who had been rookie of the year in 1973, and had banked the best part of $1,500,000 in tour prize-money, though he was still short of a major.

When Lyle and Kite had played 11 holes, both men were six under par and the match was level. Lyle was still six under par when he lost 3 & 2 to Kite, who was ten under at the death. Europe were also up against their Cup jinx, Nelson, who won all his matches, and whose Cup record now stood at nine without loss.

**Larry Nelson: a late recruit but made it nine out of nine wins in the Ryder Cup.**

## RYDER CUP

(Walton Heath, Surrey) **Europe 9½, US 18½**
Captains: Europe, J Jacobs; US, D Marr

**FIRST DAY Foursomes: Morning**

| Europe | | | US | |
|---|---|---|---|---|
| B Langer & M Pinero | 0 | | L Trevino & L Nelson 1h | 1 |
| A Lyle & M James 2 & 1 | 1 | | W Rogers & B Leitzke | 0 |
| B Gallacher & D Smyth 3 & 2 | 1 | | H Irwin & R Floyd | 0 |
| P Oosterhuis & N Faldo | 0 | | T Watson & J W Nicklaus 4 & 3 | 1 |

**Four-balls: Afternoon**

| | | | | |
|---|---|---|---|---|
| S Torrance & H Clark | ½ | | T Kite & J Miller | ½ |
| A Lyle & M James 3 & 2 | 1 | | B Crenshaw & J Pate | 0 |
| D Smyth & JM Canizares 6 & 5 | 1 | | W Rogers & B Lietzke | 0 |
| B Gallacher & E Darcy | 0 | | H Irwin & R Floyd 2 & 1 | 1 |

First day: Europe 4½; US 3½

**SECOND DAY Four-balls: Morning**

| | | | | |
|---|---|---|---|---|
| N Faldo & S Torrance | 0 | | L Trevino & J Pate 7 & 5 | 1 |
| S Lyle & M James | 0 | | L Nelson & T Kite 1h | 1 |
| B Langer & M Pinero 2 & 1 | 1 | | R Floyd & H Irwin | 0 |
| JM Canizares & D Smyth | 0 | | J W Nicklaus & T Watson 3 & 2 | 1 |

**Foursomes: Afternoon**

| | | | | |
|---|---|---|---|---|
| P Oosterhuis & S Torrance | 0 | | L Trevino & J Pate 2 & 1 | 1 |
| B Langer & M Pinero | 0 | | JW Nicklaus & T Watson 3 & 2 | 1 |
| S Lyle & M James | 0 | | W Rogers & R Floyd 3 & 2 | 1 |
| D Smyth & B Gallacher | 0 | | T Kite & L Nelson 3 & 2 | 1 |

Second Day: Europe 1; US 7
Match aggregate: Europe 5½; US 11½

**THIRD DAY Singles**

| | | | | |
|---|---|---|---|---|
| S Torrance | 0 | | L Trevino 5 & 3 | 1 |
| S Lyle | 0 | | T Kite 3 & 2 | 1 |
| B Gallacher | ½ | | W Rogers | ½ |
| M James | 0 | | L Nelson 2h | 1 |
| D Smyth | 0 | | B Crenshaw 6 & 4 | 1 |
| B Langer | ½ | | B Lietzke | ½ |
| M Pinero 4 & 2 | 1 | | J Pate | 0 |
| JM Canizares | 0 | | H Irwin 1h | 1 |
| N Faldo 2 & 1 | 1 | | J Miller | 0 |
| H Clark 4 & 3 | 1 | | T Watson | 0 |
| P Oosterhuis | 0 | | R Floyd 1h | 1 |
| E Darcy | 0 | | JW Nicklaus 5 & 3 | 1 |

Singles Europe 4; US 8

# David Graham approaches perfection to land US Open

GOLF HAS always been able to make even the greatest players look pathetic on occasions, and few of them ever claimed to play many strokes in a round exactly as they would wish. On June 21 David Graham put together a round to win the US Open at Merion in Pennsylvania without a stroke he could have greatly regretted, and his 67 allowed him to steam past George Burns and become the first Australian to win the title, and the first foreign-born player to do so since Tony Jacklin in 1970.

Graham, with 273, seven under par, was a stroke away from Jack Nicklaus's record for the event. He had started three behind Burns, whose 203 for 54 holes was the best Open effort ever, and finished three in front of Burns and Bill Rogers.

Graham's final round was remarkable for its lack of error. Even when he missed a fairway, as he did marginally and for the only time at the first, he got a birdie. He also birdied the second and, by the fourth hole, he had caught Burns. A rare error by Graham, three putts on the fifth green, put him behind again, but Burns erred on the tenth, and Graham took full advantage.

He had in each of the first three rounds driven with a three wood at the 14th, a curving 414 yards, and secured two pars and a bogey, but only after struggles with sand and rough. Now he took his driver and hit a perfect shot, followed by an equally good seven iron to six feet. He sank his putt for a birdie, and did so again at the 15th, where a one iron and an eight iron left him ten feet from the hole.

Burns dropped another shot on the 16th. Graham parred in, his game under total control, suffering only the minor frustration that his birdie putt on the 18th to equal Nicklaus's record aggregate hit the hole and spun out.

**George Burns: outlasted by David Graham.**

**David Graham: classic final round in victory at Merion.**

**Howard Clark: singles win over Masters champion Watson.**

# Rogers wins at Sandwich rebirth

BILL ROGERS, a steady earner but scarcely spectacular winner on the US PGA Tour, surprised all and sundry on July 19 by winning the British Open at Royal St George's, at Sandwich on the Kent coast, to where the oldest major had returned after an absence reaching back to Bobby Locke's win of 1949. The narrow

### TEE TALK

**"The only equivalent plunge from genius I can think of was Ernest Hemingway's tragic loss of the ability to write. Hemingway got up one morning and shot himself. Nicklaus got up next morning and shot a 66."**

IAN WOOLDRIDGE,
describing Jack Nicklaus's 81, 66 start in the British Open.

road leading to the course over a toll bridge was the difficulty. Sandwich residents, including the Daily Telegraph cricket correspondent and Royal St George's member, E.W.Swanton, had been eager to see a Sandwich bypass built in order to prevent fine old buildings in the town from being damaged by the thundering of heavy traffic, and to readmit the Open to the course, rated the toughest of Open tests by Seve Ballesteros.

Even more remarkable for those who had suffered previous frustrations at Sandwich was the achievement of the Kent police in organizing highly effective one-way traffic flows, for the approach roads from the bypass are not remotely of freeway standard.

The deed was done and the club, which had always had oceans of room for such facilities as the tented village, and whose officials had most farsightedly made provision for huge car parks, looked forward to a duel between the likes of Masters champion Tom Watson, Jack Nicklaus, Hale Irwin, Ben Crenshaw, Johnny Miller, Bernhard Langer, Nick Faldo and Isao Aoki. Nicklaus made headlines of the "Bobby Jones loses" category on the first day, when he returned

an 81, with a run of 6, 5, 6, 5, 7 from the turn, which involves four double bogeys. Next day he went round in 66 and qualified. He finished alongside Watson, Arnold Palmer and Tony Jacklin, 14 shots behind Rogers.

Nearly everyone made the mistake of ignoring the tall slim Texan Rogers, 29, who had been so close behind the peerless David Graham at Merion and who had won the World Match Play at Wentworth two years earlier. He shot a two over par 72 to start with, then 66 and 67, to lead Langer and Mark James by five shots, and Aoki and Ray Floyd by a further three.

Langer got to within a stroke of Rogers, who double-bogeyed the long seventh in round four. Rogers's response was that of a champion: three birdies in the next four holes, with the sort of recovery that won him the Heritage tournament earlier in the year, despite a six-stroke lead dribbling away to one.

Mark James, joint third with Floyd, again proved his British Open pedigree, becoming top-finishing Briton for the third time. Bernhard Langer, in second place, had even more clearly announced himself as a potential champion.

### SHORT PUTTS

● Jerry Pate, a repeated disappointment since winning the US Open in 1976, kept a promise at the Memphis Classic. After sinking a birdie putt to make sure of winning, he handed his caddie putter and visor, and jumped in the lake by the 18th hole, as he said he would if he won his first title since 1978.

● Kathy Whitworth became the first LPGA member to total $1 million in prize money when she came third in the Women's Open. She led after three rounds, but lost in a 66-68 round-four struggle with Beth Daniel.

● Arnold Palmer, 52, won the American Senior Open in a nostalgic play-off against Billy Casper and Bob Stone. The age limit for Seniors play had been cut from 55 to 50.

● Wilma Aitken lost to Belle Robertson at the first extra hole of the British Women's Amateur final. Aitken had won back five consecutive holes to reach that stage.

● Isao Aoki and Peter Oosterhuis had their clubs stolen before the World Series of Golf in Akron, Ohio. Much publicity later, a phone call to their hotel advised "Take a look in your own back yard." And there were the clubs.

## US take over in the stretch to land Cup at Cypress

AS USUAL when threatened with defeat, the US Walker Cup team at Cypress Point on the Pacific coast reacted positively. They ran out 15-9 winners after Britain and Ireland had hit back to win the second series of foursomes 3-1 and close to 7-9. It was the first time California had staged the event.

In the singles everything changed, only Richard Chapman gaining a point, by one hole, from Hal Sutton, the American champion. Jay Sigel and Jodie Mudd had huge wins against Paul Way and the Scot, Colin Dalgleish, respectively.

Ronan Rafferty, at 17 the youngest ever Walker Cup player, had a great start, winning the opening foursome with Philip Walton, 19, against Hal Sutton and Jay Sigel, and finishing by holing two chip shots.

**Bill Rogers: made the response of a champion to secure the Open title at Sandwich.**

# Nat Crosby does father Bing proud on the road to victory

NATHANIEL CROSBY survived as many narrow escapes in winning the US Amateur championship as ever father Bing (who had died suddenly in 1977 after a round of golf in Spain) did in one of his "Road" films with Bob Hope.

Young Crosby, only 19, won on the Lake Course of the Olympic Club, San Francisco, less than 20 miles from his home at Hillsborough. Crosby certainly dragged out the drama almost every day, for he was trailing in four of his six matches. The American and British Walker Cup teams were in the field, and the defending champion, Hal Sutton, lost to Public Links champion Jodie Mudd.

Ireland's promising youngster Ronan Rafferty, aged 17, had an exciting championship, losing at the 20th hole, in the round before the quarterfinal, to David Tentis.

Crosby's closest call was in the semi-final, against Willie Wood from Oklahoma, who was three up after eight holes. The match was level, with three holes remaining, and at each of them Crosby brought off bunker shots of Gary Player quality to save par and win by two holes.

In the final, Brian Lindley, also based in California, was three holes up on Crosby with seven to play. He lost the 12th and 13th, but chipped in for a birdie at the 14th to go two ahead again.

The finalists halved the 15th in birdie twos, and Crosby scrambled a par and a win on the long 16th. A bogey was enough to give

**Nat Crosby: stretched out the Olympic Club drama**

him the 17th, and pars on the last left it all square. On the first extra hole, a par five, Lindley had a short putt for par, but Crosby sank his birdie putt of 20 feet to take the title though, true to his week of suspense, the ball waited on the lip for a heart-stopping moment before disappearing.

It was the first US Amateur championship to go to extra holes since 1950.

Crosby did not perform well against par, though the weather was not helpful, but as a last-gasp winner of matches he proved supreme.

However, not all the Lake Course spectators (and the magic of the Crosby name attracted a great many) approved of the new champion's punching the air at moments of exhilaration.

# Crawley, all-rounder of style

LEONARD CRAWLEY, former golf correspondent of the Daily Telegraph, a post he took up after the Second World War, died on July 9, aged 77.

He excelled at many sports, having played for Cambridge University, Essex and Worcestershire at cricket, scoring nine first-class centuries, and toured the West Indies with the MCC in 1925, though he did not gain a Test cap. His tour average was 29.95.

Six years later he won the English Amateur Golf title. He had a better Walker Cup record than most, winning half his six matches against the Americans, and enjoyed the rare experience

of being on the winning side in 1938.

No one campaigned harder for the British game to switch to the American size ball and, though other factors in the improvement in British golf can be identified, there has been a different atmosphere since the change was made.

Crawley was also an excellent shot, ice skater, and rackets and lawn tennis player. One golf rule change he did not appreciate was the outlawing of "croquet" putting, since, like many other good strikers of the ball, he found that the problems of putting made the game ever more difficult for him.

# Tom Watson, critic and Master

THE LENGTHENING of the first and eighth holes at Augusta came in for criticism from Tom Watson before the Masters began. "It has become too much of a big hitter's course now," he said.

Big-hitter Seve Ballesteros was soon out of contention with a 78. "Just a bad day, nothing wrong, it's a strange game," he remarked. The Daily Telegraph said his round was strangest over the last 12 holes, where he dropped six shots.

Too long or not, Watson kept very calm on the course in the final round, which he began one stroke ahead of Jack Nicklaus and ended two ahead, for an eight under par total of 280 and his second green jacket.

The final round was not without its dramas for Watson, who put his second into Rae's Creek at the par-five 13th.

Johnny Miller, who had started the year well with his fourth career win at Tucson (adding another at Los Angeles), continued his revival after a number of, for him, anonymous years by finishing alongside Nicklaus in second place.

Sandy Lyle was disappointed to miss the top 24 and an automatic invitation for 1982, and Duncan Evans, the British Amateur champion, had begun with a depressing 81.

## SHORT PUTTS

● When Ray Floyd chipped dead for a par three at the first hole of a sudden death play-off for the Tournament Players' championship against Curtis Strange and Barry Jaeckel, son of the film and television actor Richard, he did more than merely win the tournament for the first time, he set a prize-money record. His victory meant a total take of $376,000, [about £170,000] in two weeks: $54,000 for winning the Doral Open in Miami the previous week, $72,000 for the TPC, and a bonus of $250,000 for winning two of the three Florida events. Tom Kite won the first.

● Larry Nelson holed a 15-yard bunker shot on the last green of the Greensboro Open, the curtain-raiser to the Masters, to force a play-off with Mark Hayes, which Nelson won. The sand save cost Nick Faldo £2,730, the difference between third place and joint second.

## SCORECARD

**British Open** (R St George's, Sandwich, Kent)
W Rogers 72 66 67 71 276
B Langer 73 67 70 70 280
R Floyd 74 70 69 70 283
M James 72 70 68 73 283
S Torrance 72 69 73 70 284

**US Open** (Merion, Pa)
D Graham 68 68 70 67 273
W Rogers 70 68 69 69 276
G Burns III 69 66 68 73 276
J Cook 68 70 71 70 279
J Schroeder 71 68 69 71 279

**Masters** (Augusta, Ga)
T Watson 71 68 70 71 280
J Nicklaus 70 65 75 72 282
J Miller 69 72 73 68 282
G Norman 69 70 72 72 283

**US PGA** (Atlanta AC, Ga)
L Nelson 70 66 66 71 273
F Zoeller 70 68 68 71 277
D Pohl 69 67 73 69 278
**Leading US money-winner:**
T Kite $375,698; Europe: B Langer £81,036

**British Amateur** (St Andrews, Scot)
P Ploujoux bt J Hirsch 4 & 2

**US Amateur** (Olympic Club, San Francisco, Cal)
N Crosby bt B Lindley 37th

**US Women's Open** (La Grange CC, Ill)
P Bradley 279

**British Women's Open** (Ganton, Yorks)
D Massey 294

**British Women's Amateur** (Gwynedd, Wales)
B Robertson bt W Aitken 20th

**US Women's Amateur** (Portland, Ore)
J Inkster bt L Coggan 1h

**World Cup:** not played

**World Match Play** (Wentworth, Surrey)
S Ballesteros bt B Crenshaw 1h

**Walker Cup** (Cypress Point, Cal)
US 15, GB & Ireland 9

# Larry Nelson's first major

THERE WAS bad news for Europe's Ryder Cup players on August 9 when the last major of the season, the US PGA, went to their hoodoo golfer, Larry Nelson, a man who just did not seem to know how to lose a Cup match.

Nelson, the home-town boy in the championship, held at Atlanta Athletic Club, thus gained his first major and late Cup selection, replacing the unfortunate Howard Twitty, who had already been measured for his Cup outfit. Nelson established his grip on the tournament with second and third rounds of 66, giving him a four-stroke cushion for the final round.

# Watson's great little shot to savour

Tom Watson: celebrates the chip that won the title.

TOM WATSON'S celebrated chip for a two on the short 17th at Pebble Beach won him the US Open title on June 20 and rates as one of the three most timely, opposition-scattering, spectacular shots of the 20th century. It is certainly fit to rank alongside Gene Sarazen's three-wood shot that gave him an albatross, or double eagle, and eventually the Masters in 1935, and Lew Worsham's wedge shot that eagled the last hole and gave him the so-called world championship of 1953. Worsham's shot was shown on the first nation-wide telecast of golf ever transmitted.

Watson's immediate reaction was that his two at the 17th "meant more to me than any other single shot of my whole life". Most golf nuts in possession of a television set saw Watson's shot, too. It was quite the wrong moment to take the eye from the screen.

Jack Nicklaus, who had finished his final round, watched on a monitor as Watson played from the 17th tee. Two pars (three and a five) by Watson would mean a play-off for Nicklaus. Anything worse meant an unprecedented fifth Open title for Big Jack and

another missed opportunity for Watson, who coveted an American Open above all others to go alongside his three Opens won in Britain and his two Masters titles.

When Watson's shot from the 17th tee missed the green with a two iron, his ball finishing in fluffy grass long and to the left, 18 feet from the hole, Bill Rogers reckoned Watson's chances of holing the chip at 100 to 1. Nicklaus reckoned them at 1,000 to 1. "At the very worst, I thought I was in a play-off," he said.

As he sized up the shot, Watson's instincts were all positive, as befits a psychology graduate. He told his caddie: "I'm not going to try and get this close. I'm going to hole it." His lie was not as bad as it might have been. It was a bold chip, with his sand wedge, that Watson struck.

He expressed it thus: "Playing the shot with an open club face, I hit it just on to the green and watched it break to the right, hit the flagstick dead centre and drop in the hole for a birdie two and a one-shot lead."

Uncharacteristically, the normally reserved Watson jigged joyfully on to that 17th green, arms spread in acclamation. Who

could blame him?

The finale at the 18th may seem staid compared to what had gone before. Watson had put together a solid last round, missing only one fairway. He had started it tied for the lead with the reigning British Open champion, Bill Rogers, who was his playing partner. But as he faced the final challenge, needing a par five to win along the wild cliff edge of Pebble Beach, he played conservatively.

His strategy demonstrates how clearly he was thinking as the winning post loomed up. His three wood from the tee, aimed between the two trees on the right side of the fairway (away from the Pacific Ocean) left him well placed, 265 yards down this 548-yard hole. Watson determined to change his game plan for the first time in the round. Instead of laying up with his usual five iron, he chose his seven, which would land in a wider part of the fairway.

He was also intent on having a full nine iron into the green, or at least a full wedge. His planned nine iron finished 20 feet past the pin. He thought he had hit the

lightning-fast, downhill, left-to-right birdie putt too hard. But when it was two feet from the hole, "it hit me that I had won ... I'd had a little magic in me, and I was the National Open champion" (with a six under par total of 282, by two shots over Nicklaus and four over Rogers, Dan Pohl and Bobby Clampett).

Two versions of Nicklaus's conversations with Watson as he came off the final green were reported in the Daily Telegraph. One came from Nicklaus, who said he said: "You son of a bitch, you're something else." Watson's version was: "You son of a bitch, I'll beat you yet."

Before landing this coup, Watson had been considering an idea for a book, an instructional work on how to save shots round the green. It emerged as "Getting Up and Down". He did just a little better than that at Pebble Beach for the most satisfying win of his life.

For Nicklaus a record fifth American Open was as far away as ever. This was his fourth runner-up finish, a record shared by Arnold Palmer and Bob Jones, and endured by Sam Snead.

Jack Nicklaus: chipped out of the title at Pebble Beach.

# Kitrina Douglas earns Curtis Cup chance

A NOISY BRITISH Women's Amateur final (thunder but little rain) ended in victory for Kitrina Douglas, the tall player from Bristol, and a place in the Curtis Cup team to play the United States in Denver in August.

Douglas, with only four and a half years' experience of golf, has in that time won the county title

in Gloucestershire three times. She qualified for the match play section of the championship only because the number of qualifiers was doubled from 32.

After a nervous start in the final against Gillian Stewart of Scotland, a member of the 1980 Curtis Cup team, Douglas went from three down to two up in five

holes. Her chipping and bunker play were both in particularly fine order, while Stewart missed a chance of hitting back by three-putting the 12th. The final margin was 4 & 2.

Belle Robertson, 46, is recalled to the Cup team after a ten-year absence, and Mary McKenna plays her seventh

match against the Americans. Balanced against this experienced pair are players like Janet Soulsby, 18, and Wilma Aitken, who a year previously in a Scottish competition achieved a remarkable run of nine consecutive birdies and 11 in all at Hamilton, near Glasgow, in a round of 64.

# Double for Watson as Price feels the heat

ONLY FOUR MEN in the history of the game won the US and British Open championships in the same year before Tom Watson did the trick at Troon, by a stroke, from Nick Price, of South Africa, and Peter Oosterhuis.

The select group Watson is now associated with comprises Bobby Jones (1926 and 1930), Gene Sarazen (1932), Ben Hogan (1953) and Lee Trevino (1971).

Oosterhuis may have been a little surprised to find himself second again, for he was never realistically in a winning position, and caught Price with a birdie on the 72nd hole. By contrast, Price was simply dismayed and disgusted with himself for finishing second.

As clearly as Watson won the American title at Pebble Beach four weeks previously, Price lost the British Open at Troon on the Ayrshire coast. It meant a fourth victory for Watson, all of them

gained in Scotland. Price, 25, was not well placed at 86th on the European money list, but with six holes to play was three strokes ahead of the Open field. His £19,300 prize shot him up the list, but those last six holes did dreadful things to his self-esteem, especially in view of the birdies he had scored at the 10th, 11th and 12th holes, giving him a lead of three over Watson, despite the American's eagle (with a yard putt) at the 11th hole.

His card makes ghoulish reading:

Par 4,4,4, 5,3,5, 4,3,4 = 36:
    4,5,4, 4,3,4, 5,3,4 = 36: 72
Price 3,3,4, 6,3,5, 3,4,5 = 36:
    3,4,3, 5,3,6, 5,4,4 = 37: 73

A slight hook from the 13th tee, after an excellent series of drives, left him unable to get up to this 468-yard hole in two. Just short of the green, he was able to putt his third shot, but left it short: stroke gone. Worse came at the 15th, 457 yards with a hidden

**Nick Price: fell back in disastrous last nine at Troon.**

green. Another hooked drive added grave difficulty to his second shot, which raced across the fairway and finished in a deep trap 50 yards from the green. His recovery touched the lip, but at least he escaped the sand, though not by very much. He pitched short and two putts later he had lost his lead.

Three pars were now needed just to tie with Watson who, after finishing his round in 70 for a total of 284, was able, with mounting disbelief, to watch the title sliding in his direction.

Price was not done yet, and came within a whisker of a birdie at the 16, but hit his tee shot fat at the 17th (223 yards), came up short and just missed again. His putt to tie with Watson at the 72nd was from 25 feet, and proved beyond him. "Three ahead and six to play," said Price, adding, not with absolute candour, perhaps: "I guess I should be happy to have finished second."

The first two days at Troon had been almost as dramatic as the last, for Tony Jacklin started with a 77 and failed to qualify. Jack Nicklaus, too, began five over par, but improved to be placed only four behind Watson.

In the lead on day one and two, to universal surprise, was Bobby Clampett, who posted the best 36-hole score, 67 + 66, since Henry Cotton's 132 in 1934. New names are seldom given much chance, but Clampett, leading by five from Price and seven from Watson, had splendid credentials, for he stood 20th in the American money list and had held on in the Open at Pebble Beach to share third place. He still led at Troon after three rounds, despite a 78, but began to falter again as his

playing partner Price made his bold start to the final round.

Ray Floyd had the best final round (67), but Nick Faldo was not far behind with 69 to share a joint multi-national fourth place with Ireland's Des Smyth, Tom Purtzer from America and Masahiro Kuramoto of Japan.

The final thrilling day was blessed with sunshine, and Troon, which had lagged behind the 1980 Muirfield attendance figures, was now ahead with 133,299. Of the 25,000-odd players and spectators at Troon on the day of the fourth round, none was prouder than Malcolm Lewis from Henbury, near Bristol, who with 300, the same score as Gary Player, won the Silver Medal as leading amateur. In five of the previous ten years no amateur had played through 72 holes and qualified for the award.

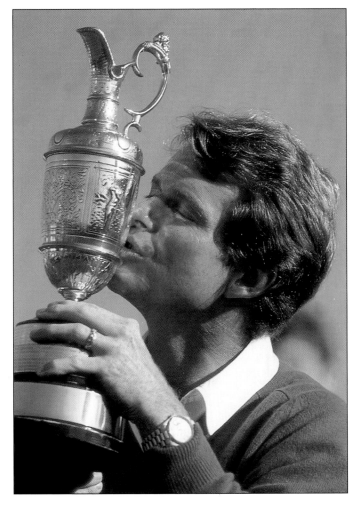

**Tom Watson: out of the rough to glory at Troon.**

**Peter Oosterhuis: nipped into second place with Nick Price.**

# 'Walrus' Stadler takes tough Masters

THOUGH CRAIG STADLER, from San Diego, did not possess the most equable temper among tour professionals, he kept control of himself and his game sufficiently to win at Augusta despite foul weather and his own last-round frailties.

It was inevitable that a man of ample girth (200 pounds, or more than 14 stone) with a large moustache should be nicknamed "The Walrus". A former Amateur champion and with a perfect, though limited, Walker Cup record, Stadler had a hard time of it on the tour in the latter half of the 1970s, but began to pick up wins in the 1980s.

He began with a 74 in the Masters, bad weather requiring the first round to be finished on the second day. Scoring continued to be difficult and, what with cold hands and fast greens, not a single player was under par at

halfway. Stadler was level par though, and his 67 in the "money round" on Saturday gave him the advantage, which he increased to seven strokes with six holes to play.

Disaster nearly followed, for he slid back to the extent of needing a par to win on the last, where he three-putted and went into a sudden-death play-off with Dan Pohl. This was a really big hitter, heading the tour statistics during the first two years such figures were kept. Last year he managed a fraction over 280 yards. But he had not won a tournament in three years on tour.

Nor was he to do so now, despite Stadler's profligacy, for Pohl could not match Stadler's par on the first extra hole. Severiano Ballesteros and Jerry Pate were offered great chances by Stadler's fourth round decline but, by one stroke, they both

missed the play-off. Victory brought Stadler $64,000. For Pohl, who had won only $6,000 in 1982 prior to playing at Augusta, the reward was $39,000.

**Craig Stadler: beat Dan Pohl in Masters play-off.**

# Ray Floyd first and always at Tulsa

RAY FLOYD has the grip of a bulldog once he gets his teeth into a tournament and, just as in his Masters win of six years earlier, he led the US PGA championship from start to finish at steam-heat Southern Hills, Tulsa, starting with a bang.

His 63 was the lowest ever returned in the event, also the lowest for any round in the event, and his 36- and 54-hole totals were records, too. He missed the

record aggregate of 271 because he took two strokes too many on the 72nd hole. The blond Australian Greg Norman, increasingly in evidence on final days on either side of the Atlantic, pressed closest to Floyd, his playing partner, until his putting let him down.

Fred Couples mounted a brief challenge with four shots saved in five holes, but Floyd always had an answer, and his final 72

was enough, by three shots, from Lanny Wadkins, the 1977 champion, who charged home in 67. Nick Faldo was looking good at halfway with 137, but Saturday's 73 was unhelpful and a final 72 gained no ground, though it did yield a high finish.

He was certainly the best British player on the US PGA Tour, and regularly commanded a place in the top eight of the order of merit at home.

# One-sided Curtis causes worries

THE SAME cares that had impelled the United States to fall in with the idea of a European, as distinct from a British, Ryder Cup team were afflicting administrators of women's golf after the August Curtis Cup match at Denver, Colorado.

Maire O'Donnell's team won the Golden Jubilee Cup match 14 1/2 to 3 1/2.

Janet Soulsby had a splendid first day for the visitors, but no-one else did, apart from her partner in foursomes, Kitrina Douglas, another new selection, for they got a half against Kathy Baker and Lancy Smith.

Soulsby went on to beat Judy Oliver by two holes in the afternoon singles. Juli Inkster had a splendid Cup for the US team, the only player to be engaged in all

four sessions and win every time, helped in the foursomes by another former Amateur champion in Carol Semple. But every American who played contributed to their points total.

Only two more points could be ground out next day, by the oldest player, Belle Robertson, and Mary McKenna in foursomes, and by Robertson again in her single against Lancy Smith.

This was the biggest defeat for 18 years, when America won 8-1, and the format of 36-hole matches, foursomes first day, singles second, was changed. How to redress the balance?

Sandy Tatum, former USGA president, has even suggested that in the men's Walker Cup, which has been almost as one-sided, nobody should be allowed

to play under the age of 25, "for then we really would know whether they were amateurs and likely to remain amateurs".

Strangely enough, Inkster was coached by Leslie King at his Knightsbridge, London, clinic. It was not inevitable that the Americans should win by about 5 to 1 in points, though they had five times as many players to call upon as their opponents.

The event was a social success at any rate, all 47 available former players attending a reunion to mark the event's 50th anniversary, including Glenna Collett Vare, Maureen Orcutt and Dorothy Higbie from the original (1932) American side, and Enid Wilson, former Daily Telegraph golf writer, of the British pioneers.

**British Open** (Royal Troon, Scot)
T Watson 69 71 74 70 284
P Oosterhuis 74 67 74 70 285
N Price 69 69 74 73 285
TW Purtzer 76 66 75 69 286
N Faldo 73 73 71 69 286
M Kuramoto 71 73 71 71 286
D Smyth 70 69 74 73 286

**US Open** (Pebble Beach, Cal)
T Watson 72 72 68 70 282
JW Nicklaus 74 70 71 69 284
B Clampett 71 73 72 70 286
D Pohl 72 74 70 70 286
W Rogers 70 73 69 74 286

**Masters** (Augusta, Ga)
C Stadler 75 69 67 73 284
D Pohl 75 75 67 67 284
(Stadler won play-off at first extra hole)
S Ballesteros 73 73 68 71 285
J Pate 74 73 67 71 285

**US PGA** (S Hills, Okla)
R Floyd 63 69 68 72 272
L Wadkins 71 68 69 67 275
F Couples 67 71 72 66 276
C Peete 69 70 68 69 276
Leading US money-winner:
C Stadler $446,462; GB: S Lyle £86,141

**British Amateur** (Deal, Kent)
M Thompson bt A Stubbs 4 & 3

**US Amateur** (Brookline, Mass)
J Sigel bt D Tolley 8 & 7

**US Women's Open** (Del Paso, Sacramento, Cal)
J Alex 283

**British Women's Open** (Royal Birkdale, Merseyside)
M Figueras-Dotti 296

**British Women's Amateur** (Walton Heath, Surrey)
K Douglas bt G Stewart 4 & 2

**US Women's** Amateur (Colorado Springs, Col)
J Inkster bt C Hanlon 4 & 3

**World Cup** (Acapulco, Mexico)
Spain (M Pinero & JM Canizares) 563;
(Individual) Pinero 281

**World Match Play** (Wentworth, Surrey)
S Ballesteros bt S Lyle 37th

**Eisenhower Trophy** (Lausanne, Switzerland)
US 859

**Espirito Santo Trophy** (Geneva, Switzerland)
US 579

**Curtis Cup** (Denver, Col)
US 14½ ,GB & Ireland 3½

Seve Ballesteros: needed an extra hole at Wentworth's Burma Road to beat Sandy Lyle in World Match Play.

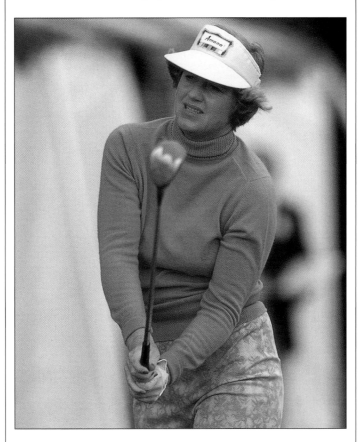

JoAnne Carner: Bob Jones Award for sportsmanship.

**"I have never been given a championship in this way before. I feel very much for Nick. I know I cried after Medinah but I also know that it made a better man of me. I learned from it, and I am sure Nick will too. He is a strong, aggressive player. He had six birdies yesterday: that is quite something."**

TOM WATSON,
of his Troon Open.

**"Just what I need to get my putts up to the hole."**

HACKER,
hearing that carbon-shafted clubs gave greater length.

## Paul Way's fast start as pro nets Dutch win

PAUL WAY, who crowned his amateur career with Walker Cup honours and the English Open Stroke Play title 12 months earlier, won the KLM Dutch Open by equalling the Utrecht course record of 65, and finished 12 under par with 276.

Way, not yet 20, liked Utrecht because it was much like Sunningdale, and confessed: "I regularly travelled up from my home in Kent to play Sunningdale and the other Surrey courses, always with a card and pencil, and sometimes when I should have been at school."

Despite a spectacular finish in 66 shots, rising Welsh star Ian Woosnam finished in joint third place with Ulsterman Eddie Polland, behind David Feherty from Ireland and Vicente Fernandez of Argentina who, despite a limp, was earning good money on the European Tour.

# Great White Shark starts to bite

GREG NORMAN was beginning to justify the hype of his nickname "Great White Shark". His rivals in the Dunlop Masters at St Pierre certainly knew they had been bitten.

Norman's 267 was three strokes better than Bernhard Langer's total there two years earlier. He won by eight strokes (from Langer), a record for the event, played both his final rounds in 65, a course record, and became the first man since Bernard Gallacher (1974-5) to take the Masters in successive years.

Nick Faldo finished ten off Norman's heady pace. It is difficult to compete with so powerful a striker as Norman when, as he said, "every shot was coming right out of the middle of every club", and his longest club for a shot to the green at any of the par fours was a seven iron. The European tour's cosmopolitan nature was amply demonstrated by the trio sharing third place with Tommy Horton: Manuel Pinero, Spain, Hubert Green, United States, and Graham Marsh, Australia.

# Tom Watson, golf's consummate competitor

Nine years elapsed between Tom Watson's 32nd and 33rd US PGA Tour win. It came in 1996, most satisfyingly at Jack Nicklaus's Memorial Tournament, Dublin, Ohio. He must have been wondering if the Senior Tour, then three years away, held out his best chance of another win, though he had won the Hong Kong Open in 1992, and was to gain a 34th US Tour success at Colonial in 1998. It all goes to re-prove the point that class persists, as it has done for legends of the game from James Braid to Raymond Floyd.

More importantly, certainly in Watson's view, he led the US Ryder Cup team to victory at the Belfry in 1993. He did so shortly after coming fifth in the US PGA Championship won by Paul Azinger. Right after that he chose Ray Floyd and Lanny Wadkins as his wild cards for the Cup. Floyd reckoned, with some justification, that he should have picked Thomas Sturges Watson.

## Pioneer stock

His family is a distinguished one. They were among the pioneers who pushed westward and his grandfather, a lawyer, helped rid Kansas City, Tom Watson's birthplace, of the corrupt political machine built by the infamous Pendergast. He acquired the

During the 1970s and early 1980s Watson was a leading figure in world golf, with a succession of victories which included five British Opens, the US Open and two Masters

Player of the Year from 1977 to 1980.

**Five-time winner of the Open Championship.**

double-barrelled nickname of "Huckleberry Dillinger", the invention of his high-school coaches. His freckles and a mop of reddish hair, allied to the boyish appearance he still possesses, could achieve no other result, added to which he was a determined competitor and all-round sportsman of talent. After gaining a degree in psychology at Stanford University he at once began his professional career, much helped at stressful moments by the guidance of Byron Nelson. The first time the author saw Watson in the flesh was at San Diego where,

although he was reigning leading money-winner, he was upstaged by a second-round 62 by the tournament-winner, Jay Haas. Watson has always given the impression of being a short compact man. But he is five feet nine inches tall, and weighs 160 pounds (over 11 stone).

His powerful upper body and forearms generate enormous strength. His driving length increased slightly in the mid 1990s according to Tour statistics, and his putting has improved.

He says he no longer plays enough to become a truly competitive putter: "I have a hard time concentrating, a hard time focusing, a hard time seeing the

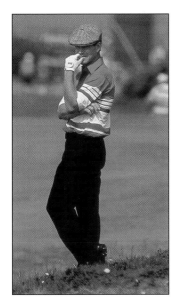

In reflective and
calculating mood.

line of a putt. I think that's a matter of concentration. But when you've been dodging the bullets for 20 years, then your nerves get plenty frayed."

Seve Ballesteros, after finishing 4,3 at St Andrews to win the 1984 Open by two shots from Watson, who finished 5,4, said "I think I could have finished Tom Watson."

The American, with a sixth Open in his sights, had been level with two holes to go, but hit a two iron at the Road Hole, the 17th, against the wall at the back of the green. Since then, close as Watson has been to another major, Ballesteros's opinion has proved correct.

## A career launched

A competitive putter Watson certainly used to be, for it has been written of him that to make a Watson par it was necessary to drive into the left rough, hack out into a greenside bunker, come out within six feet of the hole and sink the slippery putt.

His early career was plagued with accusations of choking, to which his response was that "a lot of guys who have never choked, have never been in the position to do so." They persisted, even after his initial major victory at Carnoustie, but ceased when at the age of 27 he defeated Jack Nicklaus, then 37, in almost match-play situations for the 1977 Masters and British Open.

From that point on he dominated world golf till the mid-1980s. He was player of the year six times, four in succession during 1977-80. For 20 years he has

earned a six-figure sum in tour prize money. His 42 Tour victories add up to well in excess of $9 million.

## Chip to remember

Though he has picked out the 1993 Ryder Cup as the greatest moment of his career, the one that did his reputation most good was his last nine holes in the 1982 Pebble Beach US Open, culminating in his most celebrated shot, a birdie chip from the rough at the short 17th, after which another birdie at the 18th to double his margin over Jack Nicklaus was merely icing on the cake.

His book on the short game (the author knows of no more useful instructional publication) followed not long afterwards. It has a description of those last nine holes at Pebble Beach, which included several very special putts, two bogeys and four birdies. With masterly understatement, Watson says: "I was extremely intense."

He also earned the praise of friend, and former Stanford student, Sandy Tatum, who said Watson was "the consummate competitor". Tatum had done his best, as a former USGA president, to make it tough for Watson at Pebble Beach. He had a bunker on the 16th made deeper. Watson went into it from the tee and it cost one of those bogeys.

That was the high point in many ways of his entire playing career, but there are a considerable number of people, even in Britain, who, if a British player cannot win his national Open, would like to see Watson do it and emulate Harry Vardon with his six titles.

## Personal critics

Watson's reason for lack of tournament successs, a falling-off in his putting, was not good enough for many people. It is not only the British press who build a sporting hero up for, apparently, the pleasure of knocking him down again. Watson was accused of being a drunk, of having a failed marriage and quarrelling with his business manager (who happens to be his brother-in-law).

Watson found it necessary to issue a public denial. The marriage is a nice blend of shy Tom and lively Linda, and they have a daughter, Meg, and a son named Michael Barrett Watson.

In years to come he may be gratefully remembered for the way he tackled his task as US

captain at The Belfry, where he had ready vital information such as the yardages of the carries on the 18th – so damaging to the Americans in 1989, when they didn't have those figures.

## Philosophical view

Watson had one special worry on his mind: "I'm not taking issue with the way Dave Stockton approached his team as our captain [on Kiawah Island in 1991] but I think the mentality of camouflage hats and war by the shore was wrong. That's not what the Ryder Cup means. I think that lessened the dignity of the event ... Sure, it's a partisan event, but the game of golf, the etiquette of the game, shouldn't be trampled over with the partisanship displayed by the crowd and some of the media as it has been in the last few Ryder Cups. You play golf the way you should live your life, by the rules. We don't go out to see what we can get away with. Ours is the only pure game left." His words are a fair summation of the way he has lived his golfing life — quietly, unassumingly and gentlemanly.

There is plenty of golf left in Watson, to judge by the way he added $195,000 to his winnings with first place in the Bank One Championship, 15 days after reaching his 50th birthday and thus qualifying to join the Seniors Tour. His final round at Bent Tree, Dallas, was 62 (10 under par), the best of his career by one. His total of 196 was 1999's lowest.

### SCORE CARD

**British Open**
1975, 1977, 1980 ,1982, 1983

**US Open**
1982

**Masters**
1977, 1981

Born Kansas City, Missouri, September 4, 1949.

### TEE TALK

"There is nothing like winning the Ryder Cup. It beats everything else because you are playing for someone else besides yourself and it means more."

After leading the winning US team.

"Watson scares me. If he's lying six in the middle of the fairway, there's some kind of way he might make a five."

LEE TREVINO.

Dominated world golf for a decade from 1977.

# Close finish to the Ryder Cup

WITH NEVER more than a point between the two sides, the US retained the Ryder Cup 14½ to 13½ at PGA National, Palm Beach, Florida. In the 56-year history of the Cup, mainly American-dominated, there had never been such a close match in the States.

The teams were level at 8-8, just as the Walker Cup teams were in May. This time the United States could not dominate the singles, but they squeaked home 6½ to 5½.

To say that the match was the

mula work, and so nearly brought off a famous victory. The next match, in England, would clearly present the United States with a formidable challenge.

It would also provide both the US PGA and the British PGA with a new money-spinner with rich sponsorship possibilities. To start with, there was £300,000 to come over the next two years from Bell's Scotch whisky.

Europe also had Seve Ballesteros back on the strength. During the Open at Birkdale Jacklin had persuaded the

own Open champion, would be faced by Masters champion Seve.

The scores demonstrate the fluctuating fortunes of the match in which, for the most part, Jacklin's strategy was to place his strongest players at the top, while Nicklaus placed his at the bottom of the draws.

Jacklin's most interesting pairing was superstar Seve with up-and-coming Paul Way, six years his junior. This pairing failed first time out against Tom Kite and the ruler-straight hitter of the era, the black pro Calvin Peete.

Ballesteros felt he was merely performing a hand-holding function. That, Jacklin explained, was the idea. The Way-Ballesteros partnership was not beaten thereafter, gaining 2 1/2 points from 3. Europe led on day one by a point, and lost by the same margin on day two; hence the 8-8 tie on the third morning.

Nick Faldo and Bernhard Langer had been a potent pairing for Europe, and Waites and Ken Brown had successfully replaced off-form Sandy Lyle and Bernard Gallacher. Tom Watson got three points, first with Ben Crenshaw, then with Jay Haas and then with Bob Gilder, but in a second round with Gilder ran into Ballesteros and Way, and lost 2 & 1.

It all came down to 13-13, with José-Maria Canizares battling against Lanny Wadkins and Bernard Gallacher against Watson. Canizares had lost a three-hole lead, and at the last underhit his pitch. Wadkins hit a beauty to three feet for a half: match level with only Watson versus Gallacher, one down on the 17th tee, to come.

Gallacher's three-iron to this 191-yard hole bounced through the green, which Watson then missed on the right. Both men fluffed their chips, but Watson's second effort was close, Gallacher's second chip four feet away, from where he missed and lost 2 & 1.

Jacklin said he felt this loss more than being pipped on the post at Muirfield for the Open in 1972.

"If onlys" were expressed on all sides, and Nicklaus said it should have been a tie. One big "if only" was Ballesteros's half with Fuzzy Zoeller after leading by three holes, thanks to four birdies on the trot.

Seve atoned to some degree by his third shot, with a three wood, from a bunker at the 578-

**Paul Way: innovative pairing with Ballesteros.**

yard 18th. His shot from the sand finished pin-high, having travelled 240 yards, and jaws dropped all round at the sight. He chipped and single-putted to save his half. Jacklin had insisted on first-class treatment all round for the team: it extended to travel by Concorde. It could not be denied that both teams had provided first-class entertainment.

**"So I had this four footer for a half, and I still think to this day that I hit a good putt. There was a subtle break but I missed and that was it, two and one."**

BERNARD GALLACHER, of his putt that missed at the penultimate hole of the Ryder Cup.

**"Too many times in the past the Cup had been run, it seemed, more for the officials than the players. Priorities had been in the wrong places. If I was to be captain it would be run and organized with the players in mind."**

TONY JACKLIN.

**Bernard Gallacher: crucial Cup defeat at 17th.**

most exciting is a pale travesty of the truth, for right down to the final two matches the destination of the Cup was in doubt. It was clear that extending the selection of the team to face the Americans to include the whole of Europe was providing sufficient depth to ensure a close and absorbing contest.

Europe had marshalled their resources much more efficiently than in 1981. For one thing, they had in Tony Jacklin a captain of experience and inspiration. Thinking back to the tied match of 1969 at Southport, and its breathtaking climax on the final green between Jacklin and Jack Nicklaus, it seemed most appropriate that Nicklaus should be the opposing captain.

Jacklin's omission from the 1979 team had puzzled and angered him. Now he bent every effort to make the European for-

Spaniard that participation in the Cup matches was the way forward. Seve had, like Jacklin, suffered the traumas of exclusion, and there was possibly a little fellow feeling on Ballesteros's part that inclined him to join Jacklin now.

Paul Way, now 20, Gordon J.Brand, canny Brian Waites (well seasoned at 43) from Notts, and the stocky, long-hitting Welshman, Ian Woosnam, were other newcomers. The Americans had five new Cup men – Craig Stadler, Curtis Strange, Jay Haas, Calvin Peete and Bob Gilder. Because the American team was chosen on the basis of points awarded over two years, Larry Nelson, the scourge of European Cup teams, was absent.

This surely says something about the absurdity of selection schemes that lack flexibility, for the United States, minus their

## RYDER CUP

(PGA National, Palm Beach Gardens, Fla ) US 14½, Europe 13½
Captains: US, JW Nicklaus; Europe, T Jacklin

**FIRST DAY Foursomes: Morning**

| US | | Europe | |
|---|---|---|---|
| T Watson & B Crenshaw 5 & 4 | 1 | B Gallacher & S Lyle | 0 |
| L Wadkins & C Stadler | 0 | N Faldo & B Langer 4 & 2 | 1 |
| R Floyd & R Gilder | 0 | JM Canizares & S Torrance 4 & 3 | 1 |
| T Kite & C Peete 2 & 1 | 1 | S Ballesteros & P Way | 0 |

**Four-balls: Afternoon**

| G Morgan & F Zoeller | 0 | B Waites & K Brown 2 & 1 | 1 |
|---|---|---|---|
| T Watson & J Haas 2 & 1 | 1 | N Faldo & B Langer | 0 |
| R Floyd & C Strange | 0 | S Ballesteros & P Way 1h | 1 |
| B Crenshaw & C Peete | ½ | S Torrance & I Woosnam | ½ |

First Day: US 3½ Europe 4½

**SECOND DAY Four-balls: Morning**

| R Floyd & T Kite | 0 | N Faldo & B Langer 3 & 2 | 1 |
|---|---|---|---|
| L Wadkins & G Morgan 7 & 5 | 1 | S Torrance & JM Canizares | 0 |
| R Gilder & T Watson | 0 | S Ballesteros & P Way 2 & 1 | 1 |
| J Haas & C Strange 3 & 2 | 1 | K Brown & B Waites | 0 |

**Foursomes: Afternoon**

| C Stadler & L Wadkins 1h | 1 | K Brown & B Waites | 0 |
|---|---|---|---|
| C Peete & B Crenshaw | 0 | N Faldo & B Langer 2 & 1r | 1 |
| G Morgan & J Haas | ½ | S Ballesteros & P Way | ½ |
| T Watson & R Gilder 5 & 4 | 1 | S Torrance & I Woosnam | 0 |

Second Day: US 4½; Europe 3½
Match aggregate: US 8; Europe 8

**THIRD DAY Singles**

| F Zoeller | ½ | S Ballesteros | ½ |
|---|---|---|---|
| J Haas | 0 | N Faldo 2 & 1 | 1 |
| G Morgan | 0 | B Langer 2h | 1 |
| R Gilder 2h | 1 | G J Brand | 0 |
| B Crenshaw 3 & 1 | 1 | S Lyle | 0 |
| C Peete 1h | 1 | B Waites | 0 |
| C Strange | 0 | P Way 2 & 1 | 1 |
| T Kite | ½ | S Torrance | ½ |
| C Stadler 3 & 2 | 1 | I Woosnam | 0 |
| L Wadkins | ½ | JM Canizares | ½ |
| R Floyd | 0 | K Brown 4 & 3 | 1 |
| T Watson 2 & 1 | 1 | B Gallacher | 0 |

Singles: US 6½; Europe 5½

# Ballesteros leaves nothing to chance in Masters

STARTING his final round birdie, eagle, par, birdie, Severiano Ballesteros left first Tom Watson and Ray Floyd, then Tom Kite and Ben Crenshaw in no doubt that he meant business at the climax of the Masters on April 11, a Monday, because rain had forced an extension to the tournament.

As Ballesteros set off, the weather had relented, the sun came out and there was little breeze. Only four strokes separated Craig Stadler, 210, Floyd, 210, Ballesteros, 212 and Watson 212. All were former winners, Stadler the defending champion.

With four shots saved, Seve flashed past Stadler and Floyd in a twinkling. His eight iron approach at the first hole gave him a six-foot birdie. He saved two shots at the next, 555 yards, his three wood approach offering a ten-foot eagle putt.

He was not far away from another birdie at the third, and did get one at the 205-yard fourth, his four iron coming to rest inches from the pin.

No challenge to the charging Spaniard was forthcoming until Watson's 40-foot eagle putt went in at the eighth, perhaps the only genuine par five on the course for the leading players. Watson at once threw away these strokes by three-putting the next three greens.

Next, Stadler seemed to have a chance, but bogeyed holes 11 and 12. Floyd lost ground, Watson had a six on the par-four 14th and Crenshaw and Kite, 68 and 69 respectively, had not done nearly enough.

Though Ballesteros nervily dropped shots at the 10th and 11th, his 31 over the first half enabled him to relax, and he tried nothing fancy over the water at the 15th, finishing in 69 for a four-stroke win over Crenshaw and Kite.

Soon Stadler was helping him into his second green jacket in four years, Ballesteros having taken on the best of the Americans and left them trailing.

**Ben Crenshaw: final 68 at Augusta not enough.**

# Parkin ends US sequence at Turnberry

NOT FOR 20 YEARS, since 1963, had an American not won the British Amateur title in a Walker Cup year in Britain till Phillip Parkin ended the sequence at Turnberry. His triumph came just one week after his excellent showing in the Walker Cup at Hoylake, where he won two of his three matches.

In a break with tradition, Medal qualifying was introduced: Parkin led the 64 who reached the match play stages over the Ailsa course. One round of qualifying had been played over the neighbouring Arran course.

Parkin was outstanding. He was never pressed in any round and outplayed Jim Holtgrieve of America in the final, 5 & 4.

**Seve Ballesteros: fast start in Masters finale and never subsequently under pressure.**

## SHORT PUTTS

● Jack Newton, runner-up to Tom Watson at Carnoustie in 1975, lost his right eye and right arm and suffered severe abdominal injuries when he walked into an aircraft propeller at Sydney airport. He needed eight hours of surgery to stabilize his condition.

● The deaths occurred of two golfers who, like Newton, were Open runners-up: Dai Rees, captain of Great Britain in one of their rare (1957) Ryder Cup wins, and the amateur, Roger Wethered.

● Jan Stephenson, the beautiful blonde from Australia and US Open champion, found a second flourishing career as a model.

● Isao Aoki, first Japanese golfer to win on the American circuit, did so in February by means of holing a pitch shot from 80 yards on the 72nd hole of the Hawaiian Open. His eagle three at this 539-yard hole robbed Jack Renner of victory more quickly than it takes to tell.

● The top 125 in last year's US money-list played on an all-exempt tour, ending the practice of the weekly Monday qualifying rounds.

● The British Women's Open was not played for the first time since it was inaugurated in 1976, for lack of a sponsor.

**Jan Stephenson: glamorous US Open champion.**

## Singles stress beats Britain

WITH THEIR usual flair for withstanding the tension of the last nine holes, the US amateurs kept their grip on the Walker Cup with a 13 1/2 to 10 1/2 victory, their 26th in the series, at the Royal Liverpool Club, Hoylake. By lunchtime on May 26, Britain and Ireland had drawn level at 8-8, thanks to a 3-1 victory in the second set of foursomes.

Shortly after lunch, Philip Walton, first man to play top for Britain four times, was three up in three holes against Willie Wood, and four of the other seven members of the home team had won their first hole. But soon the Americans had taken the strain and, large as the crowds were, they were reduced almost to silence as Jay Sigel's team ground out a 5 1/2 to 2 1/2 win.

Walton held on to win 2 & 1 against Wood, but Andrew Oldcorn was the only other British winner, beating Jim Holtgrieve 2 & 1. Sigel finished the match off with a 3 & 1 win over David Carrick.

Nat Crosby played a single, which he lost against Phillip Parkin, by 6 & 4, and a foursome, in which he and William Hoffer beat George McGregor and Walton, who was otherwise 100 per cent, by two holes.

# Larry Nelson's blistering last 36 wins test of nerve and US title at Oakmont

LIKE THE MASTERS, the US Open at Oakmont, Pennsylvania, came in for brutal weather, and subjected Larry Nelson to a most searching test of nerve. The title was not settled until Monday, June 20. At ten that morning a siren sounded for play to resume, following a storm on Sunday. The leaders had only a handful of holes left to play.

There had been a potentially more dangerous interruption during the second round, when two spectators were struck by lightning, but they were released after hospital treatment. Play was held up for two and a half hours.

The final round had begun with Seve Ballesteros and the champion, Tom Watson, leading with 212, one ahead of Nelson and Calvin Peete, and two ahead of Ray Floyd.

The dashing Spaniard Ballesteros had made his best start to a US Open, with a 69 to share the lead, falling back with 74 on the second day, though that was still five ahead of Nelson, whose 65 on Saturday turned the tournament around.

Watson, with six birdies on the first nine on Sunday, looked a good bet to retain his title, but Nelson was out in 33, Watson faltered after the turn and Nelson caught him with a birdie on the 14th. One hole later the storm began, flooding the course.

Nelson's very first blow next morning, a three wood, to the short 16th, left him with a putt recorded by the USGA at 62 feet. Nelson holed it.

Watson, on the 14th, two-putted from 35 feet. Nelson was in front, but his trials were not at an end, for he three-putted the 72nd and his shoulders dropped in disappointment as he retrieved his ball from the hole. Almost at the same moment Watson missed his par putt on the 71st hole, and this was enough to give the title to Nelson, at four under par.

The most remarkable feature of his play was the accuracy of his iron shots over the last half of the Open. He began it 75, 73, then with 65, 67 broke, with 132, the 36-hole record set at 136 by Gene Sarazen 51 years ago and equalled six times since.

Larry Gene Nelson seems never to have gained the fame of his leading contemporaries, perhaps because his golf did not "travel" well. Most of his successes, apart from this Open and the Western Open in 1979, were gained in America's southeast (he was born in Georgia).

This is a flaw which opposing Ryder Cup players would not recognize, since his Cup record, as of June 1983, was nine starts, nine wins, four of them in England.

Few top-class golfers, apart from Walter Travis, started the game so late as Nelson, at 21, and fewer still can have qualified for the tour so quickly and begun to earn money so regularly, thanks in his case to his straight, though not over-long, driving and, as at Oakmont, occasional bouts of precise iron play and putting brilliance.

In a tournament of records, concerning play and interruptions, there was one for Arnold Palmer. By competing in his 31st consecutive US Open, he equalled the record of Gene Sarazen. It was Palmer's fourth Open at Oakmont.

# Jay Sigel, true-blue amateur, repeats at North Shore

FOR THE second year in succession Jay Sigel took the US Amateur. Few players of his class do not turn professional these days, and at 39 Sigel, a Pennsylvanian, became the eighth man to land consecutive titles.

He beat Chris Perry, from Minnesota, son of a major league baseball pitcher, 8 & 7 at North Shore CC, Glenview, Illinois, after a rocky road to the final, for Sigel was twice taken to extra holes. Perry had been used to extra time, too, winning three times at the 19th en route to the final. But there was no holding Sigel in the final. He was out in 33 in the afternoon. Harvie Ward in 1955-56 was the last successfully to defend the crown.

# Watson joins the Nap Hand club

WITH THE SHOT of a mature champion, Tom Watson struck a two iron to the last hole of the British Open at Birkdale and put himself alongside J.H.Taylor, James Braid and Peter Thomson

**Tom Watson: fifth British Open, but his first in England.**

as a five-time winner of the oldest Open. He remained a rung below Harry Vardon, six times a champion.

Hale Irwin was second by a stroke, with Andy Bean, and will forever rue the careless flick he took at a two-inch putt on the 14th green in the third round. He completely missed the ball, which would make it, millimetre for millimetre, about the most expensive putt for its length in the history of golf.

That is to suppose that all other things remained equal, which they seldom do in golf, and in any case none can deny Watson's right to a fifth title. He would have been playing for a repeat of his British-American Open double of 1982 but for Larry Nelson's Monday morning resistance at Oakmont two weeks earlier.

Tom Watson, a complete convert to the fascinations of British linksland, did not approve of the receptive greens that Birkdale offered, believing that it was a mistake to go over to American-type greens. Scoring, despite plenty of rough, was excellent thanks to benevolent weather and those greens, which also putted very truly.

A sign of changing times was that the favourites were European – Nick Faldo and Masters champion Seve Ballesteros. Faldo had not got the better of Ballesteros in May at Royal St George's in the increasingly significant PGA championship, now sponsored by Sun Alliance, but he had already won the French Open, Car Care Plan International and Lawrence Batley International.

Craig Stadler had the last laugh on day one, for he was round in 64, and could have had an all-time major record of 62 but for failing to birdie the reachable par-five 17th and par the last.

Denis Durnian, a club pro who was once a merchant sailor, certainly found his sea-legs among the rolling sandhills of Royal Birkdale. Soon after Trevino covered the first nine in 30 strokes, Durnian went even better. He did it in 28, and missed a ten-footer for 27 at the ninth into the bargain.

This was the lowest nine-hole score in any of the four majors. His total was 66, his self-possession collapsing, possibly under the enormity of his success: 27 had been achieved on both the European and American tour.

Eight players, headed by Watson, Bill Rogers, and the German, Bernhard Langer, were within four shots of Stadler, who was still ahead at halfway, but with Trevino, Watson and Faldo all closing in.

Watson was ahead on the final day, reassuming the role of favourite, and along came Graham Marsh with another 64 (32 out, 32 in) to set an early target of 277. It was not good enough, and with that cast-iron par at the last for a final 70 Watson had done it again, i.e. a wonderful record of five wins in nine tries.

He got £40,000 of the £410,000 purse, and the Royal & Ancient, with Keith MacKenzie officiating at his last Open as secretary before Michael Bonallack took over, drew their biggest gate: 142,894.

Apart from the support of Arnold Palmer (who scored 68 in the third round this year at age 53) and other stars, MacKenzie, a former Shell Oil executive, did more than most to revivify the Open Championship.

**Arnold Palmer: crucial support for British Open.**

---

## SCORECARD

**British Open** (Royal Birkdale, Merseyside)
T Watson 67 68 70 70 275
H Irwin 69 68 72 67 276
A Bean 70 69 70 67 276
G Marsh 69 70 74 64 277
L Trevino 69 66 73 70 278

**US Open** (Oakmont CC, Pa)
L Nelson 75 73 65 67 280
T Watson 72 70 70 69 281
G Morgan 73 72 70 68 283
C Peete 75 68 70 73 286
S Ballesteros 69 74 69 74 286

**Masters** (Augusta, Ga)
S Ballesteros 68 70 73 69 280
B Crenshaw 76 70 70 68 284
T Kite 70 72 73 69 284
T Watson 70 71 71 73 285
R Floyd 67 72 71 75 285

**US PGA** (Riviera, Cal)
H Sutton 65 66 72 71 274
J Nicklaus 73 65 71 66 276
P Jacobsen 73 70 68 65 276
Leading US money-winner: H Sutton $426,668; Europe: N Faldo £140,761

**British Amateur** (Turnberry, Scot)
P Parkin bt J Holtgrieve 5 & 4

**US Amateur** (N Shore CC, Glenview, Ill)
J Sigel bt C Perry 8 & 7

**US Women's Open** (Cedar Ridge CC, Tulsa, Okla)
J Stephenson 290

**British Women's Open:** not played

**British Women's Amateur** (Silloth, Cumbria)
J Thornhill bt R Lautens 4 & 2

**US Women's Amateur** (Canoe Brook CC, NJ)
J Pacillo bt S Quinlan 2 & 1

**World Cup** (Pondok Inah, Jakarta, Indonesia)
US (R Caldwell & J Cook) 565;
(Individual) D Barr, Canada 276

**World Match Play** (Wentworth:, Surrey)
G Norman bt N Faldo 4 & 2

**Walker Cup** (Royal Liverpool, Merseyside)
GB & Ireland 10 1/2, US 13 1/2

---

**Prince Andrew (left) and new R & A secretary Michael Bonallack.**

# Fuzzy Zoeller cleans up in white towel Open

FUZZY ZOELLER, at 32, enjoyed his greatest triumph and endured great trauma. He defeated Greg Norman from Australia by eight shots in a play-off for the US Open, so his major play-off record was perfect. His only previous win at that level, in the 1979 Masters, was also in a play-off, though that was by sudden death.

This well-built, easy-going man was ever a favourite with galleries. His nickname is derived from his initials, his full name being Frank Urban Zoeller. His crouching style is not the most graceful to be seen, but at his best few could out-hit him. He added to his likeable legend by his sporting move as he watched from down the 18th fairway at Winged Foot, New York, to see Norman hole a 45-foot putt on the 18th.

The pair of them were level off the last tee, but Norman put his second into a grandstand. He got a free drop, and needed that long putt for par. The roar that greeted it was followed by the sight of Zoeller waving his towel in mock surrender. The gesture was a brave one, since Zoeller thought the putt was for a birdie, which would have made his chances marginal. Then he got down over his approach shot, landed it behind the pin and, by now aware of the true situation, two-putted to force a tie.

Next day Zoeller ran away with the title. In seven previous attempts at the National Open his best finish had been 15th. The afternoon was overcast and steamy, and the play an anticlimax, for Zoeller's 67 was far beyond Norman, who had excited the galleries the previous day. His most embarrassing problem was that he frequently reproduced the sort of wayward second shot that he had played on the 72nd hole the day before, and was in bunker after bunker with his approaches. That was on top of the three putts he took three times in the first five holes.

Both men started as if a battle of titans was in prospect, with birdies on the first hole. In Norman's case this was an illusion. On the second hole (411 yards), he was in the right rough, had to lay up because a tree was in the way and had a putt for par. Zoeller had a 60-foot putt for a birdie, and so fast are these Winged Foot greens that an estimate of the time it took to disappear underground is ten seconds. But disappear it did, upon which Norman missed his par putt and, catastrophically, the one back, so running up a six.

Norman did not win a hole till the sixth, but made chipping and putting errors, notably on the long, long fifth where he putted away a fine birdie chance. Bunkered at the eighth, he fell five behind and, remorselessly, Zoeller allowed no way back, finishing three under par on this most punishing of Open courses. Norman was five over.

The Australian is not short of a sense of humour: he produced his own white towel on the final hole of the play-off.

Hale Irwin had been the early front runner with two 68s, and Jay Sigel had flown the amateur flag with a 69 in round one. But neither Curtis Strange, a name recurring of late in high-finishing positions, Johnny Miller, Irwin nor Fred Couples could get within five shots of Zoeller or Norman by the 72nd hole.

The trauma for Zoeller started in August. When the US PGA championship began his business manager reported that Zoeller, who had gone across to the St Andrews Open, was in hospital with a career-threatening back problem. An old basketball injury had flared up. Eventually a delicate and complicated operation was imperative.

Greg Norman: returned the white towel compliment.

Fuzzy Zoeller: ran away with US Open play-off.

Curtis Strange: beginning to finish high in major events.

# Crenshaw's popular Masters crown

AUGUSTA belonged to Ben Crenshaw. He had been popular ever since he joined the US PGA tour. He headed his qualifying school by 12 shots after a sparkling amateur career, and scored 65 in his very first tour round in the Texas Open, which he won. This softly spoken Texan with the winning manner had not extended his winning to major events. He had been runner-up five times in major tournaments,

so his victory at the Masters by two strokes (and from Tom Watson, too) was greeted with acclamation.

His swing, many thought, was a trifle overdone, and led to fatal error from the tee. His putting stroke was universally envied, and the 60-footer he sank as he began the back nine on the last day at Augusta was the coup that pushed him forward to success.

Crenshaw was also respected

among the game's enthusiasts for his role as golf historian. He collected antique equipment and books, and got himself into trouble at Muirfield after the Open of 1980 by playing with Tom Watson after hours on the Open course with old clubs and balls.

Nick Faldo was only two behind the leader as the fourth round began, but faded to 76, eight behind. He took 40 to the turn, after 70, 69, 70, for 54 holes.

# Tales of high flyers and low lifers

SPACE-AGE TECH, a ticking-off and two expensive tickets preceded the British Open. American stars landed by Concorde at Leuchars airfield within sight and sound of the Old Course at St Andrews.

Twenty players who didn't come at all were attacked as "selfish men" by Royal & Ancient secretary, and former British Amateur champion, Michael Bonallack.

All but five of the absentees were American. Their sin was not

to turn up for the qualifying rounds at Ladybank, Leven, Lundin and Scotscraig. "We did not get a word from any of them," said Bonallack.

By not informing the organizers the 20 missing players had kept out another 20 who had already tried to qualify at the regional centres.

Tommy Horton, a past-captain of the British PGA, was among the guilty ones and could, like the rest, look forward to a blast in a Royal & Ancient enve-

lope. Retiring secretary Keith McKenzie and his wife Barbara got the tickets, in the form of special silver compositive badges that would admit them to the Open for life. George Wilson, Royal & Ancient financial secretary, calculated the cost of this benefit over 20 years at £4,800 at current prices.

More people (34,897, a record for a single day) attended the Friday of the 1984 Open than attended throughout the entire 1964 championship.

**"You can't stop and play defensively at any time or people will go past you. This tour is two or three rungs higher than our tour in Europe. You have to scrap every week for every shot. Everyone is capable of shooting very low scores over here."**

NICK FALDO,
before clinching his first US tournament.

**"Good morning, doctor."**

HALE IRWIN,
to Jack Nicklaus, during practice for the British Open, after Nicklaus had been awarded an honorary doctorate of law by the University of St Andrews.

# Consolation for Faldo

NICK FALDO recorded a long-awaited breakthrough in his quest to become one of the world's foremost players. He notched up his first US Tour victory, at Sea Pines, South Carolina, seven days after suffering the let-down of an indifferent final round in the Masters.

He was two behind Gil Morgan after the first round, but was two ahead after 36 holes.

Faldo's three under par 68 on Saturday put him four shots in front, and he took the Heritage Classic by two strokes despite a strong challenge from Tom Kite, who finished with a 66.

Faldo's total of 270 tied the tournament record set five years back by Tom Watson, and he also showed remarkable consistency by breaking 70 in every round, scoring : 66, 67, 68, 69.

# Hollis Stacy, fun golfer

HOLLIS STACY, born 30 years ago in Savannah, Georgia, completed a hat-trick of US Women's Open titles at the Salem Club, Peabody, Massachusetts.

Her liking for the big occasion is self-evident, considering that of her 16 wins to date, three are Opens. As Bobby Jones once remarked, there are winners and there are major winners.

Stacy enjoyed her golf, too, and observed the Hagen admonition to "keep laughing and smiling". Blond, she looked at 30 not greatly different from the way

she had when, at 15 years and four months, she became the youngest national Junior champion, a distinction she continues to hold.

She retained that title for the next two years. Her Salem win was reward for outlasting Amy Alcott, whom she had beaten for one of her Junior titles, and Rosie Jones.

Stacy finished with a 69, the lowest total of the four days. It was a gallant finish, enabling her to make up a three-stroke deficit at the start of play.

● Total prize money for the US PGA Tour reached new proportions. It climbed above $21 million, an increase of almost $4 million over the previous year.

● Hale Irwin's luck was in at Pebble Beach in the Crosby tournament. On the much-photographed 18th, that dog-legs along the edge of the Pacific Ocean, his ball bounced back from rocks on the beach and Irwin made the most of it with a birdie, then beat British Columbian Jim Nelford in a play-off.

● After three straight American Eisenhower trophy victories, Japan's amateur team proved the world's best at the Royal Hong Kong club. The US effort foundered in the second round, in which their total of 234 was their worst ever, the best score being 77. A late rally by the Americans could not close the gap, Japan winning 870-877, with the Philippines third and Britain and Ireland fourth.

● A Japanese, Ayako Okamoto, born in Hiroshima, set another first by winning the British Women's Hitachi Open at Woburn with a total of 289. Okamoto, 33, had already won in the two previous years on the LPGA tour in America, where she qualified for her player's card at her first attempt. 1984 was her best on the LPGA tour to date. She earned $251,108 from 27 starts, with three wins, including that at Woburn.

● Four months almost to the day after giving birth to her first child, Ashley Marie (November 7), Nancy Lopez won the Uniden LPGA Invitational. She went on to win again before the year was out.

● Another avenue of profit opened up for golf professionals and their agents, as sales of instructional video cassettes soared, with the home market expanding rapidly.

● José Maria Olazabal became Spain's first holder of the British Amateur title, at the expense of Scotland's Colin Montgomerie. A determined competitor, Olazabal was being widely touted as a world-class putter.

● Lynn Adams and Catherine Duggan set an LPGA record by completing the last round of the Sarasota Classic at Bent Tree Golf and Racquet Club in 1 hour, 35 minutes, 33 seconds. The course measured 6,124 yards. Duggan scored 72 and Adams 78.

# Seve triumphs as Tom takes the wrong Road

SUNNY SEVE of former days had become a little glum of late, and won nothing all year. But it was a buoyant Ballesteros who appeared at St Andrews for the British Open, greatly encouraged by a few tips on swinging from Jaime González and Vicente Fernandez, two South Americans. There was also the presence of his girlfriend, Carmen, to lighten the Spanish countenance.

The final image of Ballesteros in action on the 18th green will live long in the memory. His birdie putt had gone down, and it would need an eagle two at the last hole by Tom Watson, who was in the process of bogeying the 17th, the Road Hole, to rob him of his second British Open. So there Ballesteros stood, on Old Tom Morris's green, repeatedly and delightedly shaking his fist in triumph.

Ian Baker-Finch, a tall, handsome Australian, had made a great impression with opening rounds of 68, 66, 71, and was in prime position on the final afternoon as he hit his approach over the Swilken Burn guarding the first green. So crisply did he strike the ball that it pitched, checked and then screwed back into the water.

He fell away, to finish on 79, as Ballesteros, on 207, got down to the task of seeing off Bernhard Langer, his playing partner, also on 207, and, right behind him, Tom Watson who, like Baker-Finch, had started with 205.

All depended, Ballesteros had said on the previous night, on the Road Hole. If he got a par four there, he would win. If not, there would be a play-off. This proved uncannily accurate. His drive at the 17th went left, optimum position being to the right, hitting perilously close to the hotel and over the black gables erected in front of the hotel to mimic the railway engine sheds of long ago.

But Ballesteros found the green with a six iron, and two putts gave him his coveted four. Watson's drive was perfect but, taking the same two iron that had put him on the green and ensured the final step towards his fifth Open the year before at Birkdale, he went for the flag 190 yards distant, went through the green and finished near the wall across the road. He did well to get a five.

Meanwhile, Ballesteros was driving, pitching to 15 feet and holing his birdie at the last. Watson needed a two to tie and, with the wind against, could not emulate Nicklaus on this occasion and drive the green (though he had done in practice, without taking his sweater off, either). He could not manage so much as a birdie,

**Seve Ballesteros: his Road Hole prediction came true.**

and the chance of moving alongside Harry Vardon with a sixth Open was gone. The final rounds of Ballesteros and Watson were:

Seve   4,4,4, 4,4,4, 4,2,4 = 34:
4,4,4, 4,4,4, 4,4,3 = 35: 69
Par   4,4,4, 4,5,4, 4,3,4 = 36:
4,3,4, 4,5,4, 4,4,4 = 36: 72
Tom   4,5,5, 5,5,4, 4,3,4 = 37:
3,3,5, 3,5,4, 4,5,4 = 36: 73

Bernhard Langer performed superbly to finish joint second with Watson, considering that he had suffered all manner of angst before teeing off at HQ. A bad back and a debilitating virus ruined his practice plans at home in Germany, and air transport troubles lengthened his journey from Munich. It was his second runner-up spot in three years. Nick Faldo had an fine Open, except for his third round 76, his only score over 70.

What Watson thought of an article (if indeed he read it) published in the Daily Telegraph before the Open began, about the Road Hole, and how it was no longer the holy terror it used to be, one hesitates to think. It quoted Nicklaus as agreeing that it was now no great difficulty to use a putter to run the ball from the road smoothly up the bank.

Moreover, according to Byron Nelson, improvements in the Road bunker meant that it was "a piece of cake", for instead of being a sickening little hollowed-out pit of compacted sand, from which it was difficult to emerge in one stroke, it now had at least a foot of sand put into it, with a level, soft floor.

**Vicente Fernandez: his swing tips helped Ballesteros at St Andrews.**

**Bernhard Langer: caught Watson but not Ballesteros.**

# US edge Curtis Cup thriller

**Vicki Thomas: like Jody Rosenthal of the US, the only unbeaten player in the Curtis Cup.**

THE HALVED MATCH fought out by British champion Jill Thornhill and her American counterpart, Joanne Pacillo, on the first day of the 1984 Curtis Cup at Muirfield was typical of the whole contest. America led by a point as day two began, and managed, by virtue of a missed four-foot putt by Penny Grice against Dana Howe in the deciding match, to stay ahead by that narrowest of margins – 9½ to 8½.

Thornhill, who had been a Curtis Cup reserve 20 years earlier, and out of the game for the past four years, also halved her first day foursomes, playing with Grice against Lancy Smith and Jody Rosenthal.

Next day Thornhill lost the battle of champions against Pacillo 3 & 2. Laura Davies made her first appearance at age 20 and, though she lost her foursome in company with Mary McKenna, she won her only other match, in the final singles series, against Anne Sander, who was making her seventh Cup appearance, against eight by McKenna. Jody Rosenthal and Vicki Thomas from Wales were the only players on either side not to suffer defeat in a hard-fought match, Diane Bailey leading the home side, Phyllis Preuss the United States.

Rosenthal beat Julie Brown for the British Amateur title at Royal Troon, but lost in the semifinal of the American event, near Seattle, where Deb Richard from Manhattan, Kansas, beat Kimberley Williams at the 37th in the final.

**Laura Davies: her first Curtis Cup brought victory over veteran Anne Sander.**

# Trevino ends barren spell with PGA title

LEE TREVINO, 44, disproved the old sporting saw about they never come back by winning the US PGA championship, his first major for ten years, at Shoal Creek, Alabama. Gary Player, 48, without a win in America for six years, gave the young idea a shock, too: he recorded a nine under par 63 in the second round, equalling the event record. It did not give him the lead, though. Also well placed were Lanny Wadkins, Dan Pohl and Seve Ballesteros who, at 27, said of Player's round: "A 63 is unbelievable on this course, at any age."

Shoal Creek had narrow fairways and thick rough. None of this worried Trevino, with four rounds all under 70. He started his final round with a 15-yard birdie putt and finished it with a birdie on the final hole, four clear of Player and Wadkins. Nick Faldo was 13 adrift, and Tom Watson and Greg Norman were 18 off the hot Trevino pace.

This was Trevino's sixth major title, and 27th tour victory. Only Jack Nicklaus and Tom Watson had won more than his £2.3 million.

# Late Langer spurt earns Masters' green jacket

THOUGH SANDY LYLE from Scotland got up among the halfway leaders at Augusta with a superb 65 in the second round, Bernhard Langer from Germany made the late pace to win the Masters, his first major championship. In two weeks he had progressed from being fined for slow play to his greatest golfing achievement, coming as he does from a country with only 100,000 players and 200 clubs.

Langer's US visit had struck trouble at Sawgrass, where the fine (£400) was imposed. This problem was a sore point with tour officials and television. CBS had five times this season been forced to leave tournaments before the final round finished in order to move on to their next scheduled programme. Langer was not the only guilty one.

Slow play was troubling the European tour also, with discussion pending on whether to return from three-ball play, which had not improved matters, to two-balls in the second half of events. The disease of the four-hour plus round was spreading outside the professional game, with amateurs and clubs looking on four hours as acceptable.

Lyle's second round 65 was his first under 70 in four starts at Augusta. His first round was a disastrous (or so it seemed at the time) 78, following which he found it difficult to speak to anyone for 20 minutes until his anger subsided. He almost equalled the course record on the second day, for he bunkered his drive at the 18th, but still gave himself a 12-foot putt for a birdie. The ball stopped on the lip.

All the Europeans engaged qualified, a cheering thought for captain Tony Jacklin with the Ryder Cup coming up at a new venue, The Belfry in the West Midlands, in the autumn. Nevertheless, 1982 champion Craig Stadler added a 67 to a 73, giving himself a three-stroke lead from Seve Ballesteros and Lyle. Langer (72, 74), the Scot, Sam Torrance (in his first Masters), and Nick Faldo all trailed six behind Stadler, who had moved imperiously clear with five birdies in his last eight holes.

Langer's experience of twice finishing second in the British Open stood him in good stead when the tournament heated up over the last nine holes. At the turn on the final day Langer was four strokes in arrears. He was also playing with Ballesteros, who bested him at St Andrews and in the World Match Play last season.

Langer's biggest problem had been his putting, but he proved at Augusta that Henry Longhurst's dictum about the "yips" that, "once you've had 'em, you've got 'em", was not necessarily so. He was now cross-handed on shorter putts, but on these slippery slopes his stroke proved sound.

Langer covered the last 36 holes in 136, and the last 30 in ten under par, making up five shots in seven holes on Curtis Strange, who was in the water at the 13th and 15th, and failed to get the birdie at the last that he needed to tie. Indeed, he took five, as did Langer, which made his wait for Strange to finish more uncomfortable than it need have been, for he had kept Ballesteros safely at bay. The Spaniard finished joint second with Strange and Raymond Floyd, two behind the German who, with a £400 fine paid, was now £100,400 better off. Faldo and Lyle failed to finish in the top 24 by a stroke which would have given them automatic entry next year. Torrance was wider of the mark.

The following week Langer beat Bobby Wadkins, Lanny's brother, in a play-off for the Sea Pines Heritage Classic. This was definitely his month.

*Bernhard Langer: beat the "yips" for Masters triumph.*

# Andy North bogeys another US Open

NOT MANY US OPEN champions in modern times have been able to afford the luxury of a bogey on the last hole. Andy North, 35, won at Oakland Hills in Michigan despite committing this error, just as he had at Cherry Hills in 1978. His last round on both occasions was 74. North had now won three tour events, two of them Opens, which is one more than Arnold Palmer achieved (at Cherry Hills with a final 65). The new champion was at least under par this time, by one shot, thanks to excellent earlier rounds: 70, 65, 70.

A slim Taiwanese player named Tze-Chung Chen, aged 26 and known affectionately to all and sundry as "T.C.", did not quite become "Top Cat", for he finished with Denis Watson, South Africa, and Dave Barr, Canada, one behind North, but won a great many friends in the process.

His second hole of all at Oakland Hills he completed in two strokes for the Open's first double eagle (albatross on the eastern side of the Atlantic) but three under par in any language. He went on to lead on 65, one better than Fred Couples. He followed with a 69, North closing with a 65 of his own. Early in the final round Chen, the best-known Chinese player since Mr Lu, led North by four strokes and looked a good bet to be Asia's first major winner, but a most bizarre disaster overtook him at the fifth hole. He struck the ball twice in playing a chip and compiled an eight, twice the par figure.

Both Chen and Mr Lu charmed the galleries and both were coached by a Mr Chang, reportedly against a musical background. Peter Thomson, who had been a major influence in setting up the Asian tour, and was now winning large sums on the Seniors tour in America, was delighted.

It was a discordant Open for Jack Nicklaus, who did not make the cut, ending a run of 21 72-hole Opens.

**Andy North (left): profited from T.C. Chen's double hit.**

# Lyle's Open stock matures with Sandwich win

THE ITALIAN LIRA was devalued by seven per cent over the weekend of the British Open, "to prevent undue speculative pressure on the European monetary snake" but Sandy Lyle's valuation soared, thanks to his victory at Royal St George's. Lyle, 27, could be sure Mark McCormack, his manager since 1983, would make the most of the opportunities.

A British winner and the third biggest attendance ever (138,027 despite poor weather) was a fine result for the Royal & Ancient, too, though there were traffic jams on the first day, eradicated when the original routing system, the one developed for the successful return of the Open to Sandwich in 1981, was re-employed. Prize money in dollar terms ($728,000/£530,000) exceeded the purse for both the US Open ($650,000) and the Masters ($700,793).

Lyle, though a Scot, lives at Wentworth in Surrey, so it remains true that no resident Scot has won the Open since Willie Auchterlonie in 1893.

The American entry was smaller than usual, perhaps because Sandwich is a humps and bumps course demanding modifications in target golfers' tactics, but also because of the qualifying hurdle for the non-exempt. Mark O'Meara suggested that the Royal & Ancient and USGA should evolve a scheme for both Opens which would allow qualifying without crossing the Atlantic.

Two most fancied players were Europeans, Masters champion Bernhard Langer, and defending champion Seve Ballesteros. Irishman Christy O'Connor junior made the early headlines, with a 64 on day one, with seven consecutive birdies from the fourth. On day four Lyle, like Langer at Augusta, had an uncomfortable wait after finishing his round because he had made victory less likely with a bogey on the final hole. He had suddenly opened a gap on the 14th and 15th. The former, 508 yards over the "canal", he eagled with a drive, two iron and 15-yard putt. The next he birdied, with a six iron to 12 feet, parred the short 16th and putted up the slope well for his par at the 17th.

The 18th at 458 yards, par 4, is one of the most forbidding finishes in world golf. After a long, straight drive the second must stay on the right-hand side of the green, which slopes down towards fluffy grass on the left. Lyle's ball went left, far enough to demand a firm little chip, which it did not receive, trembling on the slope before rolling back to the left edge. He needed two more to get down, so his total was 282 with his final 70, much less confidence-building than the 69 he "should" have returned.

It provided a total a shot better that of a a new challenger from America, Payne Stewart, whose final 68 was equalled by José Rivero, Phil Parkin and Eamonn Darcy. Stewart's attire, plus-twos, was an echo from the past on this oldest of English open courses. David Graham and Bernhard Langer, out last, started with a bogey apiece, and seldom regained their form of the first three days, finishing two behind.

## SHORT PUTTS

● José-Maria Olazabal's victory in the British Youths' championship at Ganton, Yorkshire, made this 19-year-old Spaniard the only player to have landed the treble of Boys'(1983), British Amateur (1984) and now Youths' championships.

● The back problems of Fuzzy Zoeller, who started a week in hospital when he should have been teeing off in last year's US PGA championship, became worse a month later. Surgery followed and in February he was back on the tour, grateful to finish tied at 46th in the Doral-Eatern Open. Two weeks later he was in full working order, winning the Hertz Bay Hill Classic.

● Mark O'Meara won the final Bing Crosby at Monterey. AT & T were to take it over, and the singer's widow would not allow his name to remain as title.

● One of the world's most beautiful courses, Royal Dornoch, staged its first significant event, the British Amateur, won sweepingly by Garth McGimpsey from Ireland. Joyce Wethered had learnt to play at Dornoch, so remote in the north of Scotland as to preclude most important events.

● South African teams were excluded from the World Cup because of the Republic's apartheid policy.

**Christy O'Connor: shook Sandwich field with opening 64, which featured seven successive birdies from the fourth.**

## SCORECARD

**British Open** (R St George's, Sandwich, Kent)
S Lyle 68 71 73 70 282
P Stewart 70 75 70 68 283
J Rivero 74 72 70 68 284
C O'Connor Jnr 64 76 72 72 284
M O'Meara 70 72 70 72 284
D Graham 68 71 70 75 284
B Langer 72 69 68 75 284

**US Open** (Oakland Hills, Mich)
A North 70 65 70 74 279
D Watson 72 65 73 70 280
D Barr 70 68 70 72 280
TC Chen 65 69 69 77 280
L Wadkins 70 72 69 70 281
P Stewart 70 70 71 70 281
S Ballesteros 71 70 69 71 281

**Masters** (Augusta, Ga)
B Langer 72 74 68 68 282
C Strange 80 65 68 71 284
S Ballesteros 72 71 71 70 284
R Floyd 70 73 69 72 284

**US PGA** (Cherry Hills, Col)
H Green 67 69 70 72 278
L Trevino 66 68 75 71 280
A Bean 71 70 72 68 281
TC Chen 69 76 71 65 281
N Price 73 73 65 71 282
Leading US money-winner:
C Strange $542,321;
Europe: S Lyle £199,020

**British Amateur** (Royal Dornoch, Scot)
G McGimpsey bt G Homewood 8 & 7

**US Amateur** (Montclair GC, West Orange, NJ)
S Randolph bt P Persons 1h

**US Women's Open** (Baltusrol, NJ)
K Baker 280

**British Women's Open** (Moor Park, Herts)
B King 300

**British Women's Amateur** (Ganton, Yorks)
L Behan bt C Waite 1h

**US Women's Amateur** (Chapel GC, Pittsburgh, Penn)
M Hattori bt C Stacy 5 & 4

**World Cup** (La Quinta, Cal)
Canada (D Halldorson & D Barr) 559;
(Individual) H Clark, England 272

**Dunhill Nations Cup** (St Andrews, Scot)
Australia (G Norman ,G Marsh, D Graham) bt
US (M O'Meara, R Floyd, C Strange) 3-0

**World Match Play** (Wentworth, Surrey)
S Ballesteros bt B Langer 6 & 5

**Walker Cup** (Pine Valley GC, NJ)
US 13, GB & Ireland 11

# Ryder Cup reward for European unity

THE UNITED STATES were parted from the Ryder Cup for the first time since Dai Rees's Britain and Ireland team did the trick in 1957. The decisive moment came on September 15 at five past four on the 18th green of the latest Ryder Cup venue, The Belfry, next to PGA headquarters in the West Midlands.

Sam Torrance stood arms outstretched in triumph as his birdie putt dropped to give him victory over American Open champion Andy North, who had put his first drive in the water, which is also a hazard for the second shot. Europe went on to win 16½ to 11½, only the fourth time in 26 matches that America had lost.

The celebrations, with a 27,000 crowd, mostly European, were thunderously augmented by Concorde flying past in salute. The aircraft was one example of successful European cooperation, the Ryder Cup another, though doubts abounded about the European Community itself.

Nevertheless, the Jack Nicklaus/Lord Derby backed notion that the European option could make a contest of the Cup was borne out at the fourth time of asking. Of the value of the European recruits there could be no doubt, thanks to Bernhard Langer and four Spaniards, Seve Ballesteros, José-Maria Canizares, Manuel Pinero and José Rivero.

This last selection, even more than the choice of Nick Faldo, not in his best form this season, was controversial. Rivero had won only a single European event, though he had done so at The Belfry, but he had finished joint third in the Open at Sandwich in the most exalted company. "He had bottle", said Jacklin, and Rivero was to prove that his Open finish was no fluke.

Europe, with six major titles between them, led by (non-playing) Tony Jacklin, started hesitantly against a team who shared 12 majors and were led by (non-playing) Lee Trevino, who had more majors than any of the contestants. The United States led 4½ to 3½ on the first day, but the European counterattack on the second put them 9-7 ahead, with Rivero brought in for the first time alongside Canizares. The Spanish pair beat Tom Kite and Calvin Peete. Ballesteros and Pinero won in three of their four outings together, so nearly half

**Howard Clark: cemented Europe's win with a last hole win over Mark O'Meara in the singles at The Belfry.**

**José Rivero: controversial Cup choice by Tony Jacklin.**

**Trevino: disappointment in his role as US team captain.**

**Manuel Pinero: three points out of four in partnership with Seve Ballesteros.**

Europe's points before singles battle was joined were made in Spain. A momentary lapse in the last four-ball of the second morning cost America dear. Langer and Sandy Lyle were dormy two down to Craig Stadler and Curtis Strange. Lyle holed a huge birdie putt at the 17th, and Stadler missed a two-foot putt on the 18th to concede a half. Not a lot went right for Trevino's side after that.

Moreover, on the final day Pinero gave Europe a flying start towards the 5½ points they needed for victory by beating Lanny Wadkins, considered by Jacklin to be the strongest opposition match-player, 3 & 1. Paul Way beat Ryder Cup stalwart Raymond Floyd, Ballesteros got a half from Kite, Lyle beat Peter Jacobsen and Langer beat Sutton. That set the stage for Torrance, who had got back to level against North after trailing by three holes. His drive over the lake at the 18th was long even for this big hitter. His approach over the other body of water fronting the three-tier green was solid, and Europe had got their winning margin with five singles still to play, of which Canizares and Howard Clark won two.

There were grumbles, it is true, about the inadequate viewing facilities on this flat course, which was not of 100 per cent championship quality, and about the overly partisan behaviour of some of the crowds. But critics of Europe's leadership and rank and file there were very few.

## RYDER CUP

(The Belfry, West Midlands) Europe 16½, US 11½
Captains: Europe T Jacklin; US L Trevino

**FIRST DAY Foursomes: Morning**

| Europe | | | US | |
|---|---|---|---|---|
| S Ballesteros & M Pinero 2 & 1 | 1 | | C Strange & M O'Meara | 0 |
| B Langer & N Faldo | 0 | | C Peete & T Kite 3 & 2 | 1 |
| S Lyle & K Brown | 0 | | L Wadkins & R Floyd 4 & 3 | 1 |
| H Clark & S Torrance | 0 | | C Stadler & H Sutton 3 & 2 | 1 |

**Four-balls: Afternoon**

| | | | | |
|---|---|---|---|---|
| P Way & I Woosnam 1h | 1 | | F Zoeller & H Green | 0 |
| S Ballesteros & M Pinero 2 & 1 | 1 | | A North & P Jacobsen | 0 |
| B Langer & JM Canizares | ½ | | C Stadler & H Sutton | ½ |
| S Torrance & H Clark | 0 | | R Floyd & L Wadkins 1h | 1 |

First day: Europe 3½; US 4½

**SECOND DAY Four-balls: Morning**

| | | | | |
|---|---|---|---|---|
| S Torrance & H Clark 2 & 1 | 1 | | T Kite & A North | 0 |
| P Way & I Woosnam 4 & 3 | 1 | | H Green & F Zoeller | 0 |
| S Ballesteros & M Pinero | 0 | | M O'Meara & L Wadkins 3 & 2 | 1 |
| B Langer & S Lyle | ½ | | C Stadler & C Strange | ½ |

**Foursomes: Afternoon**

| | | | | |
|---|---|---|---|---|
| JM Canizares & J Rivero 7 & 5 | 1 | | T Kite & C Peete | 0 |
| S Ballesteros & M Pinero 5 & 4 | 1 | | C Stadler & H Sutton | 0 |
| P Way & I Woosnam | 0 | | C Strange & P Jacobsen 4 & 2 | 1 |
| B Langer & K Brown 3 & 2 | 1 | | R Floyd & L Wadkins | 0 |

Second Day: Europe 5½; US 2½
Match aggregate: Europe 9; US 7

**THIRD DAY Singles**

| | | | | |
|---|---|---|---|---|
| M Pinero 3 & 1 | 1 | | L Wadkins | 0 |
| I Woosnam | 0 | | C Stadler 2 & 1 | 1 |
| P Way 2h | 1 | | R Floyd | 0 |
| S Ballesteros | ½ | | T Kite | ½ |
| S Lyle 3 & 2 | 1 | | P Jacobsen | 0 |
| B Langer 5 & 4 | 1 | | H Sutton | 0 |
| S Torrance 1h | 1 | | A North | 0 |
| H Clark 1h | 1 | | M O'Meara | 0 |
| N Faldo | 0 | | H Green 3 & 1 | 1 |
| J Rivero | 0 | | C Peete 1h | 1 |
| JM Canizares 2h | 1 | | F Zoeller | 0 |
| K Brown | 0 | | C Strange 4 & 2 | 1 |

Singles: Europe 7½; US 4½

## TEE TALK

**"I cried all the way from the 18th tee to the green. I knew I had won the [Ryder] Cup for us when Andy North drove into the water. I have dreamt of this all my life."**

SAM TORRANCE.

**"Sometimes I think that the only way the Spanish people will recognize me is if I win the Grand Slam and then drop dead on the 18th green."**

SEVE BALLESTEROS.

# Rich Dunhill Cup goes to Greg & Co

GREG NORMAN'S 65 on the last day of the inaugural Dunhill Nations Cup (for which 16 countries competed at St Andrews) equalled the Old Course record, and inspired a 3-0 win in a surprisingly one-sided final over the United States, represented by Mark O'Meara, Curtis Strange and Raymond Floyd.

Norman's colleagues were Graham Marsh and anchorman David Graham, who got the better of the leading American Tour money-winner, Strange.

The winning trio each earned £72,000 from the richest tournament ever held in Britain, worth a million in dollar terms.

For Marsh, 41, a former maths teacher, it would be his richest-ever pay-day. He notched up over 30 wins as one of the world's most travelled players. Marsh is one of the few Australian golfers to have received an MBE.

**Graham Marsh: joined Greg Norman and David Graham in a sweeping Dunhill Cup victory for Australia.**

# Sigel: British challenge is getting better

US WALKER CUP captain Jay Sigel was unsure what was happening: either his team were getting worse, or Britain and Ireland better. He suspected the latter and, indeed, had it not been for the visitors' fade-out in the second series of foursomes, they might have won the most closely fought matches to date in America, at Pine Valley, New Jersey, which ended 13-11.

John Hawksworth's reputation was much enhanced by his 4 & 3 win over Sigel, the outstanding American amateur of recent years.

But this win gave America a 27-2-1 record in the series, Scott Verplank being unbeaten on his Cup debut.

**Sandy Lyle: uncomfortable wait for first major win to be confirmed.**

# Spurned Nicklaus again proves the Master

A CLOSE FRIEND (he must have been) in mischievous mood stuck a newspaper article on the refrigerator in the house where Jack Nicklaus stayed during the Masters. It was from the Atlanta Constitution, and said that Nicklaus was "done, through, washed up and finished" and that he had little business playing the Masters at all. Nicklaus admitted that: "It made me stew for a while, but in the end I thought that maybe the writer, Tom McAllister, has a point. I'll show him."

This the Golden Bear proceeded to do, with an emphatic finale, making light of his 46 years and showing up the fallibility of youths such as Greg Norman, Sandy Lyle and Seve Ballesteros. Norman had taken a one-stroke lead on an overcast humid Saturday from Nick Price, Bernhard Langer the defending champion, Donny Hammond and Ballesteros. Price had lowered the course record with a 63 on the Saturday, but was saddled with the burden of a 79 in round one.

The fourth round was blessed with sunshine, in which Jay Haas, nephew of Bob Goalby who won in 1968 when Roberto de Vicenzo sabotaged his hopes by signing a wrongly completed card, set a target of 283 with a 67, a disappointment perhaps, considering he reached the turn in 31 strokes with five birdies.

Tom Kite, Price and Langer were all hovering behind the leaders, Norman and Ballesteros, who had caught the Australian, then holed a 45-yard pitch at the eighth for an eagle three.

At this point the youthful indiscretions began to multiply. Norman got away with a hooked drive at the eighth, but at the tenth the second of two errant shots put him into deep trouble and he took a six.

Nicklaus was partnered for the first time by Lyle and got in a promising run of three birdies from the ninth to move within two shots of the lead, but 35 to the turn was scarcely spectacular. Indeed, he had to scramble a remarkable par from deep in the bushes at the ninth and this appeared to spur him on.

Ballesteros, meanwhile, eagled the 13th, with a medium iron to six feet, only to hit a limp shot into the water at the 15th, where he had driven splendidly and all but claimed the title. Kite and Nicklaus were now level with

Ballesteros, and the moment had come for Nicklaus. A drive and four iron offered an eagle putt at the 15th, which he holed. The short 16th by the lake he birdied with a five iron and a three-foot putt, the 17th with a drive and wedge to ten feet.

Though his putt at the last, to come home in 29 strokes, was huge, he went close. Home in 30 for 65 and a 279 total was good enough by one from Norman and Kite who both missed tying putts on the 18th. Norman had got back into position to win or tie with four birdies in a row, then played another of his major-losing loose shots into the gallery on the right and bogeyed.

Only Gary Player, with 64 in 1978, had won the Masters with a lower fourth round. Nicklaus was the oldest winner of the Masters, his sixth. He was not the oldest winner of a major, though, for Julius Boros was 48 when he won the PGA in 1968. However, Nicklaus's 18 major professional championships in 24 years was beyond all comparison.

What made the success all the more memorable for Nicklaus was that his son, Jack Jr, was there, caddying for him.

**Jack Nicklaus: cheered up the over-40s with his sixth Masters win.**

# Floyd keeps up old hands' run

TWO MONTHS after Jack Nicklaus's triumph at Augusta aged 46, at Shinnecock Hills, Long Island, Ray Floyd became the oldest US Open champion when three months short of his 44th year, five months older than Ted Ray when he won in 1920. There have also been of late PGA

champions at 44 (Lee Trevino), at 39 (Hubert Green) and an Open Champion of 35 (Andy North).

Floyd finished with a flourish, 66, but counted his first round of 75 in dreadful weather as crucial to his success. "That was the survival round. It was windy, cold and wet and I had no feel for my

shots and it was only my short game that saved me." The Open had been a barren exercise for Floyd until now. For Greg Norman it was another opportunity missed, for he had led after 36 and 54 holes, before crashing to a 75. Lanny Wadkins contrived a superb, but fruitless, closing 65.

**Ray Floyd: oldest US Open champion at 43.**

**Wadkins: 65 was in vain.**

# Greg Norman's luck turns at Turnberry

DO SPORTSMEN always tell the truth when asked, as they so often are, what they were thinking when they won (or lost) this or that? It is doubtful, but the author is certain, remembering his earlier disappointments, that Greg Norman was telling the truth about what was running through his mind as he waited to be presented with the silver claret jug for his British Open victory on July 20 at Turnberry.

"I was so scared I had done something wrong with the card. I just knew somebody was going to walk up and say: 'Gee, I'm sorry, Greg, but we can't give you this after all.'"

This ultimate, unthinkable misfortune did not happen. Most other things had, for Norman had won two tournaments since his Masters and American Open misadventures, which had included,

at the latter, a confrontation with a spectator who accused him of choking. At Turnberry he achieved all sorts of wonders, including a 74 in the gales of day one, 63 in the second round which included three putts on the 18th and, most miraculous of all, a 74 in round three in which he was among the late finishers who had to play the tough final stretch in wind and horizontal rain that made standing up, let alone golfing, an athletic event.

The author will not easily forget watching Norman trying to shelter behind waterproofs on the long 17th, the wind snatching and tearing at the garments. Somehow he scored a par five. Strength and stamina were prime considerations on the first and third days, and so was luck with the bounce on the narrow fairways, which brought protests from Jack Nicklaus and Tom Watson. This was the lost-ball Open. Michael Bonallack, the Royal & Ancient secretary, could not remember an Open in which so much ammunition was mislaid. Ball-hunts do not help the pace of play.

The 455-yard ninth, Bruce's Castle, by the lighthouse, was a particular problem. In one tilt at this hole, where the drive is played from a headland over a

rocky little bay, Norman hit the hog's-back fairway, and the ball bounced sideways into long grass. For "long" read two feet, wet and bent over in the wind. A mighty blow was required from Norman to loosen the rough's grip and move his ball on to the fairway, about as far as he could throw a small caddie. A steward's count had it that on the first (windy) day only six players from a field of 153 got their ball to stay on that fairway with their drives.

His 63 on the second day, equalling the championship record, will no doubt be remembered by Norman with a tinge of disappointment, for though he got his birdie on the 508-yard 17th, he dropped a stroke on the par four 18th, missing a three-foot putt. At halfway Norman led by two from Gordon J.Brand, and four from Tommy Nakajima and Nick Faldo, with Bernhard Langer, another stroke away, fifth. The record-equalling round was as follows:

Norman  4,3,3, 2,5,3, 3,5,4 = 32:
           3,2,4, 4,3,3, 3,4,5 = 31:63
Par     4,4,4, 3,4,3, 5,4,4 = 35:
           4,3,4, 4,4,3, 4,5,4 = 35:70

Nakajima, round shouldered and wearing glasses and looking more like a Tokyo banker than a golfer according to the "Daily Telegraph", was closest to

Norman (211-212) on the final morning, when the weather relented. The state of mind of the Japanese in challenging the big, blond Aussie was demonstrated right away at the first hole, where he missed the green, made a good fist of the chip, then three-putted from six feet. His eventual 77 plunged him to joint eighth while Brand, sticking to it manfully, achieved his finest moment as Open runner-up, though five behind Norman's finishing 67 for 280. Only the winner equalled par. Langer and the increasingly prominent, long-hitting Welshman, Ian Woosnam, shared third place, with Faldo fourth on his own (and earning £25,000 against Norman's £70,000).

Norman was the first Australian since Peter Thomson in 1965 to win the title. His first major had been long in coming. Wildly off-line shots at the crunch in Masters and US Open had stimulated much chatter about Norman's nerve. It held firm at Turnberry in the face of brutal weather and a course set up in a way Tom Watson considered unfair. At 31 Norman was three years younger than Ben Hogan when he won his first major title. On the other hand, Jack Nicklaus had won eight majors by his 31st birthday.

## SHORT PUTTS

● Cambridge University undergraduate Fiona Macdonald, 20, of the Frinton-on-Sea club in Essex became the first girl to be awarded a blue for golf in the 108-year history of the university match between Oxford and Cambridge. Oxford won this the 97th match in the series at Ganton in Yorkshire.

● The World Cup, lacking sufficient financial support and facing competition from rich events like the Dunhill Nations Cup, was not held – for the second time in the 1980s. The International Golf Association, a non-profit-making organization, decided to regroup under new director Burch Riber, and Parallel Media Group of London put in £1 million towards a 1987 revival of the event, which was the brain-child in the 1950s of Canadian John Jay Hopkins.

● Arnold Palmer scored a hole in one on consecutive days at the same hole with the same club (the 187-yard third hole), with a five iron at the New Tournament Players' Club, Avenel, near Washington. He did so on the first two days of the Pro-Am in the Senior PGA tour's inaugural Chrysler Cup. But this was a rare winless year for Palmer.

● Mac O'Grady called tour commissioner Deane Beman a "little Hitler" after being fined $500. Beman responded with a six-week suspension on O'Grady, who went to law, but lost his case.

**Greg Norman: beat the elements and the Ailsa course at Turnberry to claim Open crown.**

# Tway trap shot reopens old wounds

GREG NORMAN was in fine position after 54 holes of the US PGA at Inverness, Toledo, to double his major title collection, which he had been so long in starting. Despite closing errors in the Masters and US Open, his form since Augusta, and notably in the British Open, gave him a stroke average of 69.60.

He had had a little luck here and there in the first three rounds, chipping in three times. His total as he set out on his final round was 202, 11 under par, and four ahead of Bob Tway, 27, from Oklahoma City, who stood three inches taller than the Australian and was on his second year on the PGA Tour.

It proved a rich one, with victories in the Andy Williams Open, Westchester Classic and Atlanta Classic.

Tway was the only player who could realistically hope to challenge Norman, barring accidents to the British Open champion or miracles from Peter Jacobsen, who was six behind, or from others such as Payne Stewart and Jack Nicklaus, included among those who trailed by anything up to eight strokes.

Norman started his last round by rescuing his par four after driving behind a tree and that was it for the day as heavy rain began to flood the Inverness course.

Getting out of trouble on Monday proved far more difficult for Norman, but Tway committed errors, too, and after making inroads on Norman's lead, Tway's six on the ninth, against a birdie three by Norman, put him four behind again.

By the 14th more big exchanges of strokes put Tway level, and that was how the pair stood on the 18th tee, still without a challenge from the rest of the field.

This last hole ("The hardest easy hole I ever played", according to Jack Nicklaus) stunned Norman.

"I hit a good shot with a bad result," he said of his wedge approach, which had so much spin on it that it backed up about a foot into the deep collar around the green. Tway's sand wedge from a greenside trap caused him to make a convincing attempt at the world standing high-jump record, for he blasted straight into the cup for a birdie.

Norman was left with little chance for his birdie. His wedge missed and he two-putted. A 76 against Tway's one-under-par 70 meant defeat by two strokes. Was he going to be a master of runner-up-ism of the quality Sam Snead demonstrated so often in the US Open?

Norman's consolations for leading all four 1986 majors after 54 holes but winning only one included beating Sandy Lyle in the World Match Play and being top earner on the tour in America at the year's end. Tway was second this time, but by only $516. He also became player of the year in America.

Norman was acclaimed as sportsman of the year back home in Australia, though home for Norman, his wife and two children was now Florida.

**Bob Tway: his bunker shot stunned Norman in US PGA climax at Inverness.**

## Geddes wins eventful Open at Dayton

IT WAS not unusual for the US Women's Open to be a career-first tour victory, for 11 players had done it (three in the last five years) before Jane Geddes, a blue-eyed blonde, carried off the $50,000 prize first try at the National Cash Register club in Dayton, Ohio.

What was unusual was the rain, of monsoon intensity, which several times stopped play, the train on a nearby track that burst into flames, not to mention an earth tremor on the third morning.

Ayako Okamoto and Betsy King finished only one stroke out of the play-off in which Geddes beat Sally Little. New Englander Pat Bradley, Open champion of 1981, started badly this time, but recovered to within three of the play-off.

Bradley in this year became the first LPGA player to pass the $2 million mark in prize money earnings.

## Sony launch rankings

LAUNCHED at the time of the Masters, the Sony Ranking is an attempt, based on computerized data, to place the world's leading players in order of merit.

Results from official tour events round the world are evaluated and points are then awarded which reflect the quality of the event.

The system rolls over three years, but more recent results gain greater weight. The number of events in which players take part is also a factor.

**TEE TALK**

**"Somebody did not use their head over the fairways. It is just we should have somewhere to hit the ball with the driver."**

TOM WATSON,
apropos the elusive fairways at Turnberry.

# British experience counts in Curtis Cup

AFTER 12 consecutive US victories in the Curtis Cup, Diane Bailey was surprisingly confident about the outcome of the match starting on August 2 at Prairie Dunes, Kansas.

This faith in a Britain and Ireland win (which would be their third in 24 starts and the

**An emotional moment as Diane Bailey collects the cup.**

first in 30 years) was based on three factors. America had won by only a point at Muirfield last time out and all Judy Bell's team were new to the Cup. She said she knew Bailey's players better than her own. Thirdly, the Bailey line-up had an average age of 31 with a wealth of experience, notably in the cases of Belle Robertson, 50, Jill Thornhill, 43, and Mary McKenna, 37.

But the American knack of producing young players when required had to be recognized. The conveyor belt was for once seen to lack something on the first morning, when all the foursomes went the Bailey way and, while Bell's girls lost the afternoon singles by only a point, the United States trailed 6½ to 2½ at halfway.

The visitors, unsurprisingly, kept the same pairings next day. Trish Johnson and Karen Davies won again, so did Lilian Behan and Jill Thornhill, while Robertson and McKenna halved: aggregate 9-3 and a half-point needed for the first Britain and Ireland win on American soil.

Johnson provided the win-

ning touch, and completed the only 100 per cent performance of the match when she holed a ten-foot putt on the 15th against Kathleen McCarthy. Johnson was three under par for the holes played.

The final reckoning was 13-5, for Vicki Thomas and Claire Hourihane, the only visitors to lose on the first day, atoned with wins out in the country in the second singles series.

Diane Bailey had emulated Jacklin in her attention to detail, being careful to make available the right food and drink to sustain her flock in the 100-degree heat.

A leaf was taken from the US book in her insistence that first holes must not be lost and none were until the second series of foursomes, in which America needed a clean sweep merely to

tie the match. Instead, Kim Gardner was their sole winner.

Last holes were just as significant. Eight games reached that point and Bailey's team did not lose any of them.

No one but Belle Robertson had ever played Ryder Cup at 50. Enid Wilson, former British champion and "Daily Telegraph" golf writer, called it "raking out the dead". In the event, Belle Robertson, not to mention her mature colleagues Jill Thornhill and Mary McKenna, proved lively corpses.

Or so their young opponents must have thought when Robertson, in her seventh Curtis Cup match, sank a ten-yard putt to win on the first morning, and a ten-footer to get a half with McKenna on the second, and Thornhill emerged with three and a half points out of four.

**Diane Bailey: conquering Curtis captain at Prairie Dunes and, as she was (as Diane Frearson), on her Cup debut in 1972.**

## SCORECARD

**British Open** (Turnberry, Scot)
G Norman 74 63 74 69 280
GJ Brand 71 68 75 71 285
B Langer 72 70 76 68 286
I Woosnam 70 74 70 72 286
N Faldo 71 70 76 70 287

**US Open** (Shinnecock Hills, NY)
R Floyd 75 68 70 66 279
L Wadkins 74 70 72 65 281
C Beck 75 73 68 65 281
L Trevino 74 68 69 71 282
H Sutton 75 70 66 71 282

**Masters** (Augusta, Ga)
J Nicklaus 74 71 69 65 279
T Kite 70 74 68 68 280
G Norman 70 72 68 70 280
S Ballesteros 71 68 72 70 281
N Price 79 69 63 71 282

**US PGA** (Inverness, Ohio)
R Tway 72 70 64 70 276
G Norman 65 68 69 76 278
P Jacobsen 68 70 70 71 279
DA Weibring 71 72 68 69 280
Leading US money-winner:
G Norman $653,296;
Europe: S Ballesteros £259,275

**Sony World Ranking** (inaugurated at Masters in April)
First Ranking: 1 B Langer, 2 S Ballesteros, 3 S Lyle
Positions at end of 1986: 1 G Norman, 2 Langer, 3 Ballesteros

**British Amateur** (Lytham, Lancs)
D Curry bt G Birtwell 11 & 9

**US Amateur** (Shoal Creek, Ala)
B Alexander bt C Kite 5 & 3

**US Women's Open** (NCRCC, Dayton, Ohio)
J Geddes 287;
(Play-off) Geddes 71, S Little 73

**British Women's Open** (Royal Birkdale, Merseyside)
L Davies 283

**British Women's Amateur** (Pulborough, W Sussex) M McGuire bt L Briers 2 & 1

**US Women's Amateur** (Pasatiempo GC, Cal)
K Cockerill bt K McCarthy 9 & 7

**Dunhill Nations Cup** (St Andrews, Scot)
Australia (R Davis, D Graham, G Norman) bt Japan (T Osaki, N Osaki, T Nakajima) 3-0

**World Cup:** not played

**World Match Play** (Wentworth, Surrey)
G Norman bt S Lyle 2 & 1

**Eisenhower Trophy** (Caracas, Venezuela)
Canada 860

**Espirito Santo** (Caracas)
Spain 580

**Curtis Cup** (Prairie Dunes, Kansas)
US 5, GB & Ireland 13

**Rodger Davis: one of the triumphant Australian trio in the Dunhill Cup.**

# Greg Norman, target for thunderbolts

A deservedly popular player and all-round sportsman who after early triumphs took bad luck in his stride and has won his way back to the top

**SCORE CARD**

British Open 1986 & 1993
64 tournaments worldwide
Best stroke average on US tour 1989-90
Born Mount Isa, Queensland, Australia,
February 10, 1955

IT IS Greg Norman's fate to be a spectacular golfer and a favourite target for gob-smacking coups by opponents at inconvenient moments. His disappointments would have broken a lesser man.

Yet he is not the type to waste time in self-pity and recrimination, and finally plucked down a second major title at Royal St George's with a display which caused him to say, without an ounce of bravado, that he was in awe of himself. The rest of us were, too.

## A high flyer

Lady Luck has been fickle with Norman, but the camera has always loved him. From the word go the reports coming in from Australia sketched in the sort of golfer the galleries, the writers, the picture editors and the television directors adore.

Here are a few phrases from the Daily Telegraph in the 1970s. "A Queenslander with sun-bleached hair and the shoulders of a stevedore" ... "the rugged blond looks of a surfboard rider"... and: "He struck the ball like a thunderclap." No exaggeration here, for this trainee pro of 16 months, who had not picked up a club till he was 17, opened with a 64.

He won that tournament, the West Lakes Classic in Adelaide, by five shots from Graham Marsh and David Graham, at that time the superstar of Australian golf. Bruce Crampton and Bruce Devlin were also labouring in Norman's wake.

Graham had just beaten Hale Irwin in the World Match Play final and greeted that 64 with the words: "He must have been unconscious." There followed just a hint of future problems for, after diving 16 under par by adding a 67 and 66 to his opening 64, Norman dropped strokes at each of the last three holes in a three-over-par 74.

## All-round talent

Welcoming Norman's victory, Graham said: "He had 27 birdies. It might have destroyed him for ever if he had blown a ten-shot

**First pro victory as a teenager – by five shots – started with a 64.**

lead." How little Graham knew of the resilience of this athlete who is the complete outdoorsman, hunting (crocodiles, sometimes), shooting, surfing and scuba diving, when he is not building up his collection of sports cars, or watching his friend Nigel Mansell burning up the track. He also represented Queensland at Rugby League and Australian Rules football in his schoolboy days.

Norman credits his father, a mining manager, with eradicating his early tendency to throw clubs. Like everyone else,

Norman still gets angry, but has turned anger to account because, after playing a bad shot: "Now I am looking for a birdie, and expect to get it *immediately.*"

Peter Thomson made a plea to the Australian PGA after his 1976 West Lakes victory for special permission for Norman to play overseas. Before the end of the year Norman was representing Australia (after playing in only four professional events) in the World Cup in California.

Next summer Norman won his first European event and showed he could finish well, too,

scoring a final 66 to take the Martini International at Blairgowrie. The weather was scarcely welcoming for a tanned Queenslander, with a biting wind coming out of the north where even the lesser mountains could be seen capped with snow – in mid-June.

In 1978 Norman and Wayne Grady were runners-up to the United States in the World Cup in Hawaii, and Norman was soon deciding to cut his European appearances in favour of Japan, for he had become a big hit with galleries there after toppling local heroes Isao Aoki and Masashi "Jumbo" Ozaki in the Australia versus Japan match in Tokyo. He also won in Fiji.

## Early successes

Here was Australia's tall, blond answer to South Africa's man in black, Gary Player, as world golfer. His ultimate target had to be the United States, and he was ever more regularly in the headlines as he planned to try for his PGA Tour card in 1980, for he reckoned that the long American courses with their receptive greens would suit a high-ball player like himself.

Just after he won the Martini again (not to mention the Hong Kong Open) in 1979, there were stories about his dates with the British lawn tennis player, Sue Barker. "Just good friends" was Norman's line. Their talk, when they were both on the same continent, was mainly about winning, he said.

Even his taste in hats interests the media. The Aboriginal word for headgear is the origin of the name of the Akubra hat, as worn by Crocodile Dundee, Prince Charles, President Reagan and (in powder blue) Bo Derek, but not, it seems, Dame Edna. The Australian army were chief customers. Each hat requires

Greg Norman with daughter and baby son at Wentworth, in Surrey, where he beat Sandy Lyle in the 1986 World Match Play final.

nine rabbit skins and takes six weeks to finish, and Norman did his patriotic bit to keep the wild rabbit shooters busy in the New South Wales outback.

## Highly marketable

By the beginning of the 1980s Norman was established, in all but the crucial matter of success in major championships, as a highly marketable personality. Not only that, but he was popular, notably with his galleries, and perhaps the first man since Arnold Palmer to manage 999 times out of 1000 to say and do the right thing in public.

Company days with Norman are a mixture of fun and of being impressed by his physical presence and technical ability. His enormous strength has not lessened with the years. His short game, first seriously monitored by Norman von Nida, has been radically improved. He credits the American coach, Butch Harmon, with helping him to get rid of the right-ward tendency that has cost him dear over finishing holes.

In 1984, after a quiet start on the American PGA tour, Norman won $310,230 in his second season, which included two wins – at the Kemper Open ("Kemper" must be among his favourite words) and that "near" major, the Canadian Open. He had already won his own National Open.

By now there was a Mrs (Laura) Norman, and the family were based in the United States, with children arriving in 1982

and 1985. Norman responded to budgetary needs with 653,296 tour dollars in 1986 to head the money list but, even more lucratively, by winning his first major by five shots at Turnberry, despite the fact that his start times sentenced him to plenty of brutal weather.

His earnings, which were to reach $1 million on the PGA Tour alone in 1990, contrasted with his failures in the majors and led to the posing of a question often asked in the 1970s apropos Tony Jacklin. In Norman's terms, given his nickname, the question was: "Has commercial success taken the bite out of the great white shark's game?"

## Fluctuating fortune

The shark's teeth were blunted in the majors: wild shots on closing holes, the Bob Tway bunker shot that robbed Norman of a second major in 1986, the outrageous chip-in by Larry Mize that cheated Norman in the very next major, the Masters of 1987 – all had their effect.

There was even a threatening 27-month drought of wins on the American tour, which was ended with victory in the Canadian Open of 1992.

The year 1993 began with first place in the Doral Open and ended with $1,359,653 more in the bank and, on the way, his sweetest win yet, at Sandwich, 13 under par and with a final round of 64. Gene Sarazen called it "the greatest championship in all my 70 years in golf". That sweet must be followed by bitter in

Norman's career seems obligatory, and the following month he completed what must be for him an abominable quadrilateral.

He lost a play-off for the US PGA championship to Paul Azinger, and has now lost play-offs in all four majors.

A second career as a course architect (a strain of grass has been named after him), keeps him flying around the world in his private jet. A sore back led to his long lay-off as a pro between the 1996 and 1997 season, but subsequent shoulder surgery did not keep him off the tee for long. He shot final rounds of 64 and 67 at Royal Sydney where he was looking for his fifth Australian Open late in 1999. His competitive spirit was clearly undimmed as, at 44, he faced up to the third Millennium – but his score was

two short of holding off a new Australian phenomenon, an 18-year-old amateur named Aaron Baddeley.

Good at public relations too.

# Chip in time saves Mize

IT HAPPENED AGAIN to Greg Norman on April 12 at Augusta. Eight months and one day after Bob Tway holed a bunker shot to beat the British Open champion on the final hole of the US PGA championship at Inverness, Larry Mize, 28 and Augusta-born, chipped in from 35 yards on the second sudden-death hole of the Masters.

Mize and Norman had tied with Seve Ballesteros, with 285 strokes. At the first extra hole Mize outdrove them both and came within a whisker of settling matters there and then, so close was his birdie putt from ten feet. Norman parred, but the Spaniard three-putted the first extra hole, and at once departed the scene, cheeks stained with tears.

On the second extra hole Mize was wide with his second. His chip rolled at a fair pace to its target and dropped in, leaving Norman, as at Inverness, with a sizeable birdie putt he could not make.

His reaction was, as befits an Australian with an image as macho yet as mannerly as you can get, to take this latest hammer blow on the chin. He even, to his undying credit, brought this off with a smile, for when he entered the press interview room, his first words were: "Just clear the women right out of here." The general feeling was that this time sudden death had inflicted a most undeserved defeat on a greatly admired sportsman. Even in Mize's native land his win was looked at askance.

"Daily Telegraph" correspondent Michael Williams reported that the reaction of an American colleague to the "Augusta Chronicle" headline "Mize Loses Reputation As Choker" was that he was unaware Mize had a reputation.

Norman had avoided the self-destruct shots that had so often spoilt his chances in the majors. He had seemed out of contention after 11 holes, but holed three birdies in four holes from the 12th, only to take three putts from the back of the short 16th. Undeterred, he birdied the 17th just as he had 12 months before in pursuit of Jack Nicklaus, which meant that another birdie at the 18th would give him the lead. As it turned out, it would also have given him the title.

He played the hole well this time. His birdie putt veered away from the hole at the last fraction of a second. If it had gone in or if Mize had sunk his birdie putt on the first extra hole, it is unlikely that there would have been any recriminations about sudden death.

● Ian Woosnam enjoyed a great year. Besides being part of the Ryder Cup win in Ohio and player of the year and top earner in Europe (£439,075), he and David Llewellyn won the World Cup in Hawaii in a play-off with Sandy Lyle and Sam Torrance of Scotland. Woosnam was individual World Cup winner, too, and he also beat Lyle in the World Match Play at Wentworth.

● Bobby Locke died aged 69 on March 9. A serious car crash had scarred his declining years. Born Arthur D'Arcy Locke, in the Transvaal in 1917, he is best remembered as one of the finest ever chippers and pitchers, and for his unusual if effective putting stance. He was particularly adept at holing putts from long range. In 1947 he played a 16-match series in South Africa against Sam Snead. Locke won 14 to Snead's two.

● Henry Cotton, three times British Open winner, died aged 80 on December 22, a few days before his knighthood was gazetted, an honour of which he was aware.

● A record £4,500 was paid for a mint Gourlay feathery ball in Phillips sale.

● Judy Bell was appointed first woman member of USGA executive committee.

● Fiona MacDonald played in her second University match, winning all her matches for Cambridge, who beat Oxford.

**Bobby Locke: death at 69.**

**Larry Mize: killer chip beat Greg Norman at Augusta.**

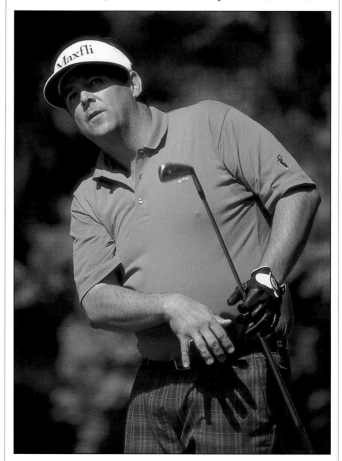

**David Llewellyn: partnered Ian Woosnam to World Cup win.**

# Nick Faldo pars his way to the Open

NICK FALDO gave himself a golfer's dream of a birthday present (he was 30 on the third day of the championship) by parring his way to the Open at Muirfield. He thus became only the sixth Briton to take the National Open since the war, though Sandy Lyle had been the fifth just two years earlier.

Eighteen pars to win by a stroke from Paul Azinger was Faldo's "modus operandi". This was not a day to encourage spectacular scoring, for Muirfield was in a distinctly unwelcoming mood, deploying a cold wind and mist that seemed to get into one's very bones. It was difficult, especially on the Saturday, to find a place to put a foot in less than a couple of inches of mud, and the total attendance was 131,142, or 3,000 fewer than at Turnberry, which was wet and windy enough in all conscience.

Faldo, drawn into golf through watching Jack Nicklaus and Co. on television, was 11 years into his professional career, which followed a distinguished record in the amateur field: the year before he turned pro he was British Youths' and English Amateur champion.

This Open also brought runner-up Paul Azinger into international prominence, though he was forced to share second place because Rodger Davis, the 36-year-old Australian, had finished with a 69, the best score by those in contention, apart from Ben Crenshaw's 68 which gave him joint fourth place with Payne Stewart.

Azinger, 26, a tall, slender New Englander, known back home as "Zinger" or the "Gee Wiz Kid", had suddenly begun to win tournaments on the tour (three of them before coming to Muirfield) after four winless but increasingly lucrative years since he got his tour card, at the third attempt. Azinger was no child golfing prodigy, but he was learning fast.

This was his first significant venture to foreign parts and he made a good start with two 68s to lead after 36 holes, one ahead of Faldo (who had followed his opening 68 with 69), Stewart,

Davis and fellow Aussie Gerard Taylor. Saturday's weather was wild and wet. There was not a single score under 70, 40 scores of 75 or worse and 12 which strayed into the 80s.

Four heroes beat the par of 71. One such was David Frost, from South Africa, whose 70 enabled him to join Faldo in second place one behind Azinger, who held on manfully with 71, which was also Faldo's score. The other par-breakers were Raymond Floyd, three behind Azinger, Ken Brown, five behind, and José Maria Olazabal, six behind.

Jack Nicklaus and Tom Kite, who was rapidly overhauling the Golden Bear in the prize money stakes, had suffered to the extent of 81 strokes in the third round, and reposed 19 strokes down the field. Tom Watson, Craig Stadler and Payne Stewart were a stroke behind Faldo and Frost, but the ante-post favourite, Langer, was seven shots adrift, two better than Greg Norman, whose convalescence from US PGA and Masters trauma was clearly not far advanced.

Frost and Azinger were the final starters as the last round began, Faldo and Stadler in front of them. The tension never relaxed for any of the principals, with Faldo straining every nerve for a birdie that would catch Azinger. It would not come. Indeed, Azinger reached the turn in 34, thanks to a two at the short fourth, birdie four at the long fifth and birdie three at the eighth, dropping only one shot, at the sixth.

He was now three ahead of Faldo but, while the Englishman continued relentlessly to equal par on every green, Azinger failed on both the 10th (bunker trouble) and 11th (three putts). There was one shot in it, and that was how it went all the way to the 17th, with pars by both players.

Par again for Faldo (of vital importance) and back on the tee Azinger was driving into the bunker from which Lee Trevino had escaped none too well but had recovered to beat Tony Jacklin 22 years ago. Faldo's drive on 18 was good: his second shot with a five iron was as solid as any he had ever hit. Though he putted four feet past the hole, he hit the one back firmly and set the target at 279, five under par. At that moment the huge scoreboards on either side of the 18th put up six against Azinger's name

for the 17th, where he could conjure no saving chip. It was all square and Azinger was in need of a birdie to win.

Faldo could not bear to watch Azinger on the 18th, but sat in the clubhouse with his wife and daughter, who was far more interested in where her next meal was coming from than the golf.

Azinger's final drive was with an iron, which he later said was an error. It left him 200 yards from the green, and the odd expletive was not deleted as his ball finished in an unhelpful lie in the left-hand bunker. Despite Azinger's wonderful touch with a wedge he came out short and two-putted.

" ... and then comes this vital shot and you can't think about it. You have to hit it from memory. Then I had and it was straight on the flag, and I wanted to shout out 'Cor, look at that.' I went hot and cold all at the same time and then it was all over."

NICK FALDO,
of his final five iron in the British Open.

## Laura Davies celebrates US Open title

NINE DAYS after Nick Faldo kept the British Open trophy at home, Laura Davies, 23, made plans to show off the American Women's Open trophy back in England. She beat off the challenge of Ayako Okamoto by two strokes and JoAnne Carner by three in a play-off for the title at the Plainfield club in New Jersey. Davies is the fourth foreign golfer to win the Open. Carner missed a four-foot par putt to win outright on the 72nd, which led to the first three way play-off of the event in Open history.

Nick Faldo: set Open target as Paul Azinger began to lose his way.

# Jacklin's men beat off US Ryder rally

"INTENSE" IS a weak, inadequate word to describe the excitement of the last hours of the Ryder Cup match which Europe won 15-13 on Jack Nicklaus's first essay in course building, Muirfield Village, not far from his birthplace in Columbus, Ohio. Jack was home team captain, too, as Europe registered their first victory on American soil. The United States had still lost only five times in 27 matches.

Perhaps the final accolade for the new-found vitality of the Ryder Cup, now that the recruitment of continental players had made it a genuine contest after years of American dominance, was the first live television coverage in America, by ABC, of an event that had occasioned no great media response in previous years. Not only that, but there was for the first time an all-ticket crowd, numbering 25,000, on a beautifully prepared course.

In the crowd there were said to be up to 3,000 supporters from across the Atlantic. Europe certainly took plenty of support with them. Apart from independent travellers there were newspaper competitions with prizes of trips to the match. The "Daily Telegraph" first prize, underwritten by Premier Investment Management Services, since the Cup was now a high-profile sponsorship target, was a trip on Concorde with Tony Jacklin's team.

European successes in recent major events had been coming thick and fast, so a close battle was expected as the Americans strove to regain the golden cup, but the surprise of the first two days was the relative weakness of the US challenge. Yet there was no doubting the fierceness of their third-day fight-back.

The morning foursomes assumed a most curious pattern, America soon leading every one. But, as can be seen in the table, they won only two, because Seve Ballesteros and José Maria Olazabal recovered from being two down against Payne Stewart and Larry Nelson, who had won the US PGA championship the

**Gordon Brand junior: final half in singles to bring up 15-13 European win at Muirfield Village.**

previous month, but was now to suffer his first Cup reverse in ten starts. Nick Faldo and Ian Woosnam brought off a most spectacular recovery from four down against Lanny Wadkins and Larry Mize, Woosnam playing out of his skin over the last nine holes.

Europe won all the afternoon four-balls, only one of which went to the last hole and which, as expected, finished almost in the dark.

Sandy Lyle was a key figure in this whitewash, hanging on with Bernhard Langer till Andy Bean and Mike Calcavecchia handed them victory by failing to get a par between them on the last two holes. Woosnam's luck was in when his shot to the 11th flew wide, hit a tree, and dropped on the green, where he holed for an eagle.

Ballesteros had much to do to shore up his partner's lack of form, but next morning he and Olazabal were together again and winning their third point in a 2½ to 1½ European foursomes victory. The United States managed equality in the four-balls after lunch, but still trailed 10½ to 5½ when the third day dawned.

Nicklaus's men required 9 points out of 12 to win, and they made a great run at it, and for hours Jacklin was in torment, wondering from where the four points Europe needed were to come. To start with, two of his in-form players, Langer and Lyle, were soon struggling.

How grateful then, after Howard Clark had beaten Dan Pohl at the last, was Jacklin to see

**Ballesteros and Olazabal: Seve and Ollie, a potent Ryder Cup pairing.**

Sam Torrance hold on to a half against Masters' champion Mize, for down went Faldo, Olazabal, José Rivero and Lyle in the next four matches.

Ireland's Eamonn Darcy, in his fourth Cup match, now came to the rescue with his idiosyncratic swing and his one and only win in 11 Cup starts. He beat Ben Crenshaw with a superb six iron setting up a birdie at the 17th, followed by a nasty downhill four-footer to win at the last.

That put the minds of visiting supporters at rest, for Langer recovered to halve with Nelson, who had suddenly lost his old flair for Ryder Cup points. Ballesteros came through against Curtis Strange and Gordon Brand added a half to bring up 15-13.

**Eamonn Darcy: set European minds at ease with a key birdie at 17th.**

# Scott Simpson quells Watson revival to lift US Open title

TOM WATSON said after Scott Simpson edged him out of a second US Open in San Francisco: "There's a lot of golf left in Tom Watson."

It was also clear after Simpson's one-stroke win at the Olympic Club that new talent was emerging, with the second major of the year falling to just as surprising a champion as did the first. The last 16 majors had been won by 16 different players.

Simpson, 31, a grave and dignified Californian from down the coast at San Diego, who twice failed in PGA Tour qualifying attempts before establishing himself, attends the Tour bible classes and, like many another golfer, thanks God for the beauty of golf courses and the opportunity to compete. He did so to some pur-

pose at Olympic, holing three birdies in a row from the 14th, while Watson could make only one. But Watson had already gravely weakened his case by dropping three shots over the first five holes. It was Watson's best US Open finish since his second place at Oakmont in 1983.

From then on it was ten pars and three birdies, but the self-imposed handicap was too heavy, with Simpson calmness itself on the brink of his first major, finishing in 68.

The pair finished four shots clear of Seve Ballesteros, who was betrayed by his second round of 75. He was in the process of enduring a rash of second and third places, eight in all in Europe and America, with only one win.

**Scott Simpson: dignified and devout US Open champion.**

## RYDER CUP

(Muirfield Village, Dublin, Ohio) US 13, Europe 15
Captains: US, J Nicklaus; Europe, T Jacklin

**FIRST DAY Foursomes: Morning**

| US | | Europe | |
|---|---|---|---|
| C Strange & T Kite 4 & 2 | 1 | S Torrance & H Clark | 0 |
| H Sutton & D Pohl 2 & 1 | 1 | K Brown & B Langer | 0 |
| L Wadkins & L Mize | 0 | N Faldo & I Woosnam 2h | 1 |
| L Nelson & P Stewart | 0 | S Ballesteros & JM Olazabal 1h | 1 |

**Four-balls: Afternoon**

| | | | |
|---|---|---|---|
| B Crenshaw & S Simpson | 0 | G Brand Jnr & J Rivero 3 & 2 | 1 |
| A Bean & M Calcavecchia | 0 | B Langer & S Lyle 1h | 1 |
| H Sutton & D Pohl | 0 | I Woosnam and N Faldo 2 & 1 | 1 |
| C Strange & T Kite | 0 | S Ballesteros & JM Olazabal 1h | 1 |

First Day: US 2; Europe 6

**SECOND DAY Foursomes: Morning**

| | | | |
|---|---|---|---|
| C Strange & T Kite 3 & 1 | 1 | J Rivero & G Brand | 0 |
| H Sutton & L Mize | ½ | N Faldo & I Woosnam | ½ |
| L Wadkins & L Nelson | 0 | S Lyle & B Langer 2 & 1 | 1 |
| B Crenshaw & P Stewart | 0 | S Ballesteros & JM Olazabal 1h | 1 |

**Four-balls: Afternoon**

| | | | |
|---|---|---|---|
| T Kite & C Strange | 0 | I Woosnam & N Faldo 5 & 4 | 1 |
| P Stewart & A Bean 3 & 2 | 1 | G Brand & E Darcy | 0 |
| H Sutton & L Mize 2 & 1 | 1 | S Ballesteros & JM Olazabal | 0 |
| L Wadkins & L Nelson | 0 | S Lyle & B Langer 1h | 1 |

Second Day: US 3½; Europe 4½
Match Aggregate: US 5½; Europe 10½

**THIRD DAY Singles**

| | | | |
|---|---|---|---|
| A Bean 1h | 1 | I Woosnam | 0 |
| D Pohl | 0 | H Clark 1h | 1 |
| L Mize | ½ | S Torrance | ½ |
| M Calcavecchia 1h | 1 | N Faldo | 0 |
| P Stewart 2h | 1 | JM Olazabal | 0 |
| B Crenshaw | 0 | E Darcy 1h | 1 |
| S Simpson 2 & 1 | 1 | J Rivero | 0 |
| T Kite 3 & 2 | 1 | S Lyle | 0 |
| L Nelson | ½ | B Langer | ½ |
| C Strange | 0 | S Ballesteros 2 & 1 | 1 |
| H Sutton | ½ | G Brand | ½ |
| L Wadkins 3 & 2 | 1 | K Brown | 0 |

Singles: US 7½; Europe 4½

## SCORECARD

**British Open** (Muirfield, Scot)
N Faldo 68 69 71 71 279
R Davis 64 73 74 69 280
P Azinger 68 68 71 73 280
B Crenshaw 73 68 72 68 281
P Stewart 71 66 72 72 281
D Frost 70 68 70 74 282

**US Open** (Olympic, San Francisco, Cal)
S Simpson 71 68 70 68 277
T Watson 72 65 71 70 278
S Ballesteros 68 75 68 71 282
Wadkins 71 71 70 71 283
C Strange 71 72 69 71 283
B Langer 69 69 73 72 283
B Crenshaw 67 72 72 72 283
L Mize 71 68 72 72 283

**Masters** (Augusta, Ga)
L Mize 70 72 72 71 285
S Ballesteros 73 71 70 71 285
G Norman 73 74 66 72 285
(Mize won play-off at second extra hole,
Ballesteros eliminated at first)
B Crenshaw 75 70 67 74 286
R Maltbie 76 66 70 74 286
J Mudd 74 72 71 69 286

**US PGA** (Palm Beach, Fla)
L Nelson 70 72 73 72 287
L Wadkins 70 70 74 73 287
(Nelson bt Wadkins in play-off)
S Hoch 74 74 71 69 288
DA Weibring 73 72 67 76 288
Leading US money-winner: C Strange
$925,941; Europe:
I Woosnam £737,977

Year-end Sony Ranking: 1 G Norman, 2 S Ballesteros, 3 B Langer

**British Amateur** (Prestwick, Scot)
P Mayo bt P McEvoy 3 & 1
S Amateur (Jupiter Hills, Jupiter, Fla)
B Mayfair bt E Rebmann 4 & 3

**US Women's Open** (Plainfield CC, NJ)
L Davies 285;
(Play-off) Davies 71, A Okamoto 73,
J Carner 74

**British Women's Open** (St Mellion, Cornwall)
A Nicholas 296

**British Women's Amateur** (Harlech, Wales)
J Collingham bt S Shapcott 19th

**US Women's Amateur** (Rhode Island CC, Barrington, RI)
K Cockerill bt T Kerdyk 3 & 2

**World Cup** (Kapalua, Hawaii)
Wales (I Woosnam & D Llewellyn) 574 bt
Scotland (S Torrance & S Lyle) in play-off;
(Individual) Woosnam 274

**World Match Play** (Wentworth, Surrey)
I Woosnam bt S Lyle 1h

**Dunhill Nations Cup** (St Andrews, Scot)
Final: England (N Faldo, G J Brand, H Clark) bt
Scotland (S Lyle, S Torrance, G Brand Jnr) 2-1

**Walker Cup** (Sunningdale, Surrey)
US 16½, GB & Ireland 7½

# Sandy Lyle's Mastery is complete

VICTORY at the Masters for Sandy Lyle was scarcely a surprise on either side of the Atlantic, since the Scot had already won two PGA Tour events when Augusta time came round in April. The manner of his victory was on a par with Gene Sarazen's epoch-making four-wood double eagle in the second Open of all, or Tom Watson's perfectly engineered chip-in at Pebble Beach six years back.

Jack Nicklaus has described the moment of having two holes left to play and needing a birdie to win a major championship as the greatest feeling life has to offer. Lyle had three holes to play and needed two birdies. He had led Mark Calcavecchia and Ben Crenshaw by two shots overnight, but had fallen behind with errors on the 11th, 12th and 13th holes on as exciting a Sunday afternoon as the Masters has ever offered.

His tee shot on the 170-yard 16th left him with a curling 12-foot putt and down it went, giving Lyle a share of the lead with Calcavecchia.

Par four at the 17th left him still in need of a birdie and he decided to use a one iron from the 18th tee. Lyle's power was a byword, but he was obviously convinced that a one iron was guaranteed not to reach fairway bunkers 256 yards away uphill. But his iron tee shot did reach the trap at that hard-to-credit range, pitching on the up slope of the sand. From there, with a seven iron, Lyle hit his career shot: it soared straight over the top of the flag, about another 140-odd yards further on, stopping 15 feet beyond the hole. From there it rolled back, leaving an eight-foot downhill putt for his second major championship and down this one went too.

Lyle, who had been at or near the head of the field once he overtook first-round leader Larry Nelson with his second round of 67, is thus enshrined as the first Briton to win the Masters. He also drew his second $100,000 cheque in a week, having won the Greater Greensboro Open, and that on top of his Phoenix Open play-off victory against Fred Couples at the third extra hole.

Lyle rose to second place in the Sony Ranking behind Greg Norman, followed by Seve Ballesteros, Bernhard Langer and Ian Woosnam, which meant that the first five positions continued to be held by non-Americans. Norman had languished 11 shots behind leader Lyle after 54 holes, then got back into the eye of the cameras, if not of the battle, with an outward half of 30.

He reverted to mundane par for a while on the way home, but then birdies at the last two par fives momentarily opened the door to thoughts of another couple of birdies, a 62, errors by the leaders and a turnabout to end all turnabouts.

But a 64 was the answer, and joint fifth place behind Lyle, whose burst of white-hot form was, according to the man himself, a result of a point an American teacher, Jimmy Ballard, had been making to Hubert Green during the previous winter tour. This was based on the principle that cricket, or baseball, demands that an out-fielder get everything behind the ball going back, and move everything through as the ball is hurled back to the wicket-keeper or shortstop. Lyle took Ballard's counsel and soon afterwards won the Tournament Players' championship.

Sandy Lyle at Augusta: three holes, two birdies and one green jacket.

# Diane Bailey's team win at home at last

GREAT BRITAIN and Ireland followed their first away win in the Curtis Cup (which was also their first win anywhere in 30 years) with their first home win in 32 years.

Their victory at Royal St George's by 11-7 matched the two successes by Tony Jacklin's Ryder Cup team.

Diane Bailey gave up the captaincy after this win, her second following the narrow defeat at Muirfield in 1984, which was the United States's 13th victory in a row. There was still much catching up to do.

For the present, Vicki Thomas's fast start on the last afternoon was reassuring, for it meant that one point was a virtual certainty and only a half was then needed.

In the event Susan Shapcott (who had three points out of four overall) beat Caroline Keggi 3 & 2 and Linda Bayman won at the last against Pearl Sinn, to retain their side's four-point margin.

It had been a testing time for Bayman, 40 on the eve of the match. Her husband, John, is chairman of the host club's greens committee, and the garden of their home backs on to the course.

Thus the locals expected much of her, and she did not disappoint. The home side were 6-3 up on the first day, cheered greatly by the half Bayman extricated from her match with Tracy Kerdyk, holing a 25-yard shot from off the green for an eagle.

Enid Wilson, former "Daily Telegraph" golf writer, who had seen almost every Cup match since the series started in 1932, said: "I never thought I would live to see the day when British girls outplayed the Americans on and around the greens."

# Strange beats Faldo in US Open play-off

ONE OF THE safest bets at the Country Club, Brookline, Massachusetts, on June 16 when the US Open championship began, was that a highly likely outcome of the 72 holes of regulation play would be a tie. That was the way Brookline's two previous Opens ended, and in three-way affairs, too. In neither case was the eventual winner, Francis Sales Ouimet and Julius Boros, the favourite.

Sure enough, there was a third tie, but only two players were involved this time, Curtis Strange outplaying Nick Faldo over 18 extra holes on the Monday. No one could know whether or not Strange was to be the successor to the three great US players of recent history, Jack Nicklaus, Arnold Palmer and Tom Watson, but he did at least quell American fears that their National Open would fall, as the Masters had, to one of the cosmopolitan bunch at the head of the world rankings – an Australian, a Scot, a Welshman, a Spaniard and a German.

Strange was certainly not looking for any excuses over the state of the course, about which he waxed lyrical: "The course just seems to flow. It's all so natural, just beautiful and real fun to play, the best since Pebble Beach in 1982."

Brookline, which for the Open is a composite of 18 holes from the 27 available, certainly does not lack for length at 7,010 yards (par 71). Moreover, the greens can be relied upon to reach lightning speed, while there is hope for the wayward in that the fairways are not as narrow as the USGA often makes them at the Open.

Strange was intent on making friends and influencing people, particularly in the matter of competing in the British Open next month, his past non-attendance having produced some animus against him as a leading US player who, by the way, was the first

## "I want a ruling. I want to know which club to hit this guy with."

HUBERT GREEN,
after a television buggy driver had run over his ball.

**Curtis Strange: outplayed Nick Faldo in Brookline Open play-off.**

for 16 years to hole in one at the Masters, a feat he brought off in April at one of golf's most feared one-shotters, the 12th across Rae's Creek.

Curtis Northrop Strange, 33, a Virginian and the son of a high-class amateur, had never failed to win less than $200,000 each year in the 1980s, and headed last year's money list with close on $1 million. Moreover, he held the St Andrews Old Course record with 62, scored all in vain as England carried off last season's Dunhill Nations Cup.

His duel with Faldo, until the very last stages of the play-off, could scarcely have been closer. He was two ahead of Faldo in the first round, stayed that way when both had 67s in the second round, and was only one ahead after 54 holes, Faldo scoring 68 to Strange's 69. The Englishman closed right up on Strange on the Sunday, the pair of them finishing six under par at 278.

Faldo's prospects of emulating Tony Jacklin's tenure of British and US Opens at the same time looked splendid as Strange

showed early signs of nerves, driving short to the 185-yard second and going through the third green, which handed the lead to Faldo.

Faldo could not break clear of his Muirfield vein, having parred every hole on the front nine. Strange holed a long putt across the seventh green for a two, and got in front at the 10th, but three putts at the 17th from not very far checked him again. Faldo made the green at the 18th, no small task over the cross bunkers, with a four iron. Strange was in a trap, but a superb splash-out left matters square, with 18 holes to come.

Strange met Faldo's play-off challenge with accomplished par golf, four strokes better than the Englishman could achieve on a warm yet blustery day. Faldo was missing too many greens and having to rely too much on his short game, and when he ran through the 17th to record a five against Strange's par four there could be only one result, and the margin of Strange's victory was swollen to four by another Faldo

bogey at the last. Apart from Faldo the visiting contingent did not prosper, in particular the bookmakers' favourite, Greg Norman, whose chances vanished with a tendon injury to his left wrist. His club had struck into a hidden stone. He withdrew from the British Open at Lytham.

**British Open** (Royal Lytham, Lancs)
S Ballesteros 67 71 70 65 273
N Price 70 67 69 69 275
N Faldo 71 69 68 71 279
F Couples 73 69 71 68 281
G Koch 71 72 70 68 281

**US Open** (Brookline, Mass)
C Strange 70 67 69 72 278
N Faldo 72 67 68 71 279
(Play-off) C Strange 71, N Faldo 75
S Pate 72 69 72 67 280
M O'Meara 71 72 66 71 280
DA Weibring 71 69 68 72 280
P Azinger 69 70 76 66 281
S Simpson 69 66 72 74 281

**Masters** (Augusta, Ga)
S Lyle 71 67 72 71 281
M Calcavecchia 71 69 72 70 282
C Stadler 76 69 70 68 283
B Crenshaw 72 73 67 72 284
D Pooley 71 72 72 70 285
G Norman 77 73 71 64 285

**US PGA** (Oak Tree, Edmond, Okla)
J Sluman 69 70 68 65 272
P Azinger 67 66 71 71 275
T Nakajima 69 68 74 67 278
T Kite 72 69 71 67 279
N Faldo 67 71 70 71 27
Leading US money-winner: C Strange
$1.147.644; Europe S Ballesteros £502,000
Year-end Sony Ranking: 1 S Ballesteros, 2 G Norman, 3 S Lyle

**British Amateur** (Prestwick, Scot)
PM Mayo bt P McEvoy 3 & 1

**US Amateur** (Virginia G & TC, Hot Springs, Va)
E Meeks bt D Yates 7

**US Women's Open** (Baltimore CC, Md)
L Neumann 277

**British Women's Open** (Lindrick, Yorks)
C Dibnah 296 (Dibnah bt S Little at 2nd hole of play-off)

**British Women's Amateur** (Deal, Kent)
J Furby bt J Wade 4 & 3

**US Women's Amateur** (Minikahda, Minn)
P Sinn bt K Noble 6 & 5

**Dunhill Nations Cup** (St Andrews, Scot)
Final: Ireland (D Smyth, R Rafferty, E Darcy) bt Australia (R Davis, D Graham, G Norman) 2-1

**World Cup** (Royal Melbourne, Australia)
US (B Crenshaw & M McCumber) 560
(Individual) Crenshaw 275

**World Match Play** (Wentworth, Surrey)
S Lyle bt N Faldo 2 & 1

**Eisenhower Trophy** (Ullva, Sweden)
GB & Ireland 882

**Espirito Santo** (Drottningholm, Sweden)
US 587

**Curtis Cup** (R St George's, Sandwich, Kent)
GB & Ireland 11, US 5

# Ballesteros trumps Price's courageous 69

**Gary Player: critical of the green keepers at Royal Lytham.**

**Nick Price: courageous final 69 but still no luck in British Open.**

NICK PRICE had the consolation at Royal Lytham, after his second near miss in the British Open, that he did not lose it. Seve Ballesteros won it with a scintillating display. Price led by two strokes at 54 holes, scored a final 69 over Royal Lytham, not the easiest championship course on the Open circuit, yet had to give best to the artistic stroke play of the Spaniard, whose third Open and fifth major title this was.

The pity was that so many would-be spectators had to miss the climactic duel between the two, who were partners in the last round, because rain had washed out the third-round play on the Saturday. With the fourth round having to be played on the Monday, many spectators could not stay over. It was comfortable, uncrowded watching for those who could.

The stoppage was puzzling to players still on the first nine. The greens after the turn were worst affected by the rain, however. Ian Woosnam and Gary Player were among those critical of the decision, Woosnam scornful of the fact that the backs of rakes had been used to clear water from the greens. This was the first day's play to be lost since Arnold Palmer's first Open victory in 1961 at Birkdale, just along the coast from Lytham.

Shocks had started early, with Barry Lane, winner the previous week of the Scottish Open, missing the cut with a second-round 85. Lee Trevino missed it by one and David Graham and Ray Floyd also made early exits. Price reached halfway a stroke clear of Ballesteros, and three clear of defending champion Nick Faldo and Craig Stadler. The attendance on the second day was a record 43,101, beating St Andrews's one-day total of 1984 by more than 3,000.

A staunch 69 by Price when play resumed early on Sunday with the players going out in threes increased his advantage to two shots over Faldo and Ballesteros. They stood one ahead of Sandy Lyle, whose prediction was that the relative inexperience of the Zimbabwean was a potential flaw and that par golf would not be enough to win. Lyle said: "Someone will have to shoot 68 or 69", which was an underestimate of the talent on show on a marvellous Monday of golf.

Ballesteros's final 65 equalled the lowest winning round in the 117-year history of the Open. Tom Watson set the mark at Turnberry in that never-to-be-forgotten duel with Jack Nicklaus. There was no doubting the truth and sincerity of Ballesteros's tribute to Price's 69: "Nick played like a champion." But there was no holding Ballesteros back from his second Lytham triumph, which ended a four-year drought in major titles.

Lyle was the first to fall back, then Faldo, who was in the final threesome with Ballesteros and Price, allowed his concentration to be disturbed by a passing train at the seventh and scored only a disappointing par five. From then on, he could not make a run at his two companions, both aged 31, whose hole-by-hole scores indicate the intensity of their struggle, played in (overdue) pleasant warm weather:

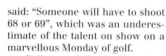

Seve  3,4,4, 4,3,4, 3,3,3 = 31:
     3,4,4, 3,5,4, 3,4,4 = 34: 65
Par   3,4,4, 4,3,5, 5,4,3 = 35:
     4,5,3, 4,4,4, 4,4,4 = 36: 71
Price  3,5,4, 4,3,4, 3,4,3 = 33:
     3,5,3, 3,5,4, 4,4,5 = 36: 69

Ballesteros caught Price with a birdie three at the eighth hole, by which time he had birdied the sixth and eagled the seventh, as did Price, both striking accurate long-iron approach shots. Both players birdied the tenth, then exchanged birdies, so to speak, at the next two holes. Both bogeyed the 14th, and were still locked together when Ballesteros produced another gem at the 16th, scene of his crucial car-park shot in the 1979 Open.

No miracle recoveries needed this time – instead, a nine iron that settled inches from the pin, putting the Spaniard one ahead. Shades of Bobby Jones's marvellous shot from sand in 1926 at the 17th, where Price conjured the bravest of pars from the rough! But Price was still one down and dropped another shot at the last, where Ballesteros added a final grace note with a delicate chip from the fringe that all but fell into the hole.

**Seve Ballesteros: artist's touch to the end at Lytham.**

# Dibnah shocks in extra time

Sally Little: voted comeback player of the year in America, but lost British Open in play-off with Corinne Dibnah.

CORINNE DIBNAH found sudden death at the climax of the British Women's Open a trial in more ways than one. She and Sally Little had squeezed past the defending champion, Alison Nicholas, with threes at the final hole.

Both Dibnah, from Australia, and Little, born in Cape Town but a veteran of the American tour, with an LPGA title and more than a dozen other tournaments won, played nervously off the tee of the first extra hole. Their drives carved out to the right, Little's landing in rough. Dibnah's caused her even more concern, for it struck a spectator in the face, breaking his glasses.

The St John's Ambulance were right on the spot and cleaned up the injury before Dibnah arrived for a long and worried examination of the damage she had done. Hopeful that no lasting harm had been caused, Dibnah nevertheless found her hands shaking as she tried to sink a decisive four-footer on the green. Unsurprisingly, she missed. At the next hole her eight iron approach gave her another chance to clinch the title, from six feet, and this time she stroked a winner into the cup.

Liselotte Neumann from Sweden, a rookie on the LPGA tour, but for years a winner on the European tour, won the US Women's Open by three shots from Patty Sheehan.

# McEvoy the inspiration

BRITAIN AND Ireland won their third Eisenhower Trophy Amateur team title at Ullna, Sweden, just holding off the United States by 882 to 887. Peter McEvoy was best individual with four under par 284; Garth McGimpsey, Jim Milligan and Eoghan O'Connell were the winning quartet. Kevin Johnson, Eric Meeks (American Amateur champion), Jay Sigel and Danny Yates represented the United States.

● Jeff Sluman brought off one of the great finishing rounds in a major championship at Oak Tree, Oklahoma. He won the US PGA title with a final 65 in high temperatures, starting three behind Paul Azinger and finishing three in front.

● The Irish had their best moment in professional golf for 30 years when their trio won the Dunhill Nations Cup at St Andrews. Des Smyth beat Rodger Davis, Ronan Rafferty beat David Graham and their only loser was Eamon Darcy, who had to give best to fit-again Greg Norman's 63.

● Curtis Strange finished his greatest year of achievement with his third Arnold Palmer award as leading money-winner, accomplished with the first total to exceed $1 million. His biggest haul ($360,000) came in the Nabisco championship. He was also voted player of the year by both the PGA and the Golf Writers' Association.

● Littlestone, Kent, reached their centenary. Never short of influential members, they had, early this century, the PM (Asquith) as captain, and, as Club President, the Leader of the Opposition (Balfour) at one and the same time.

Jeff Sluman: great finishing round in US PGA championship.

# Seve Ballesteros – the unique and natural

Seve Ballesteros: possessed of a magical short game that has been one of his enduring hallmarks.

TO Severiano Ballesteros's five major championships and 48 titles on the European Tour should be added four other American Tour wins, six victories in Japan, two in the South African Million Dollar Challenge and one each in New Zealand, Australia and Kenya, not to mention his often inspirational part in nine Ryder Cup matches, the last as captain. His Cup playing record is played 37, won 20, lost 12, halved 5). Only Nick Faldo has won more (23), but from 46 starts, and only three Americans – Arnold Palmer, Lanny Wadkins and Billy Casper – have won 20 times or more. On top of all this, Seve has won the World Cup twice for Spain, with Manuel Pinero (1976) and Antonio Garrido (1977).

## Early successes

Ballesteros won at least one tournament a year on the European Tour from 1976 to 1992, but since then has struggled, never more so than in the 1993 Ryder Cup when, to general

**From humble beginnings he rose rapidly to fame, became noted for his ability to produce spectacular recovery shots, was the first European to win the US Masters and has been three times British Open champion**

astonishment, he asked to be left out of the final four-ball and lost his single to Jim Gallagher, a worthy US tour professional who ten years earlier would have had to hit a purple patch in order to trouble Seve. It had been a highly frustrating year by the time of the autumn Cup match, with only three near-misses to sustain him, namely ties for second, third and fourth places.

It is unfortunately true that he has been troubled by back problems since his earliest tournament days, yet he is still only 42, and has the example of Ray Floyd, the 51-year-old hero of the

US 1993 Ryder Cup team, and winner of Senior and regular tour events in that year, to sustain him, not to mention his family – his wife, Carmen, and two young sons, Baldomero and Miguel.

Seve's consolation was in the 1997 Ryder Cup match. He led Europe to victory, his non-playing role carried out with obsessive zeal: he was everywhere.

## Enormous appeal

A mere litany of the triumphs of this tall, dark, powerful and undeniably handsome Spaniard does not convey a tithe of his

One club start led to heights.

appeal to followers of the game. He is not a Basque, as many people imagine, but a Cantabrian, a farmer's son, a member of a family that lived on the first floor of their home, with the animals beneath on the ground floor. His elder brothers, Baldomero, Manuel and Vicente, have always been supportive of his career and business interests, Manuel's own career as a tour professional being curtailed by his labours on Seve's behalf as the latter's prospects brightened.

At seven, Seve fitted a shaft to a three iron head and began knocking first stones, then a ball

"I'll just have to agree with Seve. Have you ever tried disagreeing with him?"

JOSÉ MARIA OLAZABAL, on being told that Ballesteros had once described their partnership as unbeatable.

"Trying to catch Seve is like a Chevy pickup trying to catch a Ferrari."

TOM KITE, at the Masters.

about, on a roughly constructed little course. Later, working as a caddie at Pedrena, he got a real three iron, complete with shaft, from Manuel. This now legendary three iron had to do duty for all the other clubs, too. His career since then suggests that he induced that three iron of his to be staggered by its own versatility.

Armed with the luxury of a full set, he is even more the master of flight and spin with variation with wooden and iron clubs, and an artist with pitching and sand wedge.

To watch him going through his chip-shot repertoire from the side of a practice green is to understand how he compensated for his early wildness through the green. Low-flying chips that pull up sharply, others that don't,

Spanish stroke-miser: master of the up and down.

chips that climb, then land softly – he has them all.

His sense of the dramatic extended, in one clinic the author saw him conduct, to landing on the practice field by helicopter. Watching him shape shots this way and that (left to right and right to left have been more at his command than with most of his rivals) is a sure-fire route to feelings of total inadequacy.

## Latin moods

Seve and Lee Trevino are very different men, apart from their Latin blood, but one thing they have in common is an unmatched skill in manoeuvring the ball close to the pin. Both are exceptional putters, and the combination of these two factors has given them a fine record in keeping down their stroke averages. Trevino won five Vardon Trophies in America for best stroke average, Seve six in Europe.

When the European Tour conducted a survey in which the professionals were handicapped over a number of rounds on the same basis as club golfers, Ballesteros emerged as the best player with a handicap of plus four.

Like Ben Hogan, both Ballesteros and Trevino worked out their method for themselves, Trevino admittedly after a good look at Hogan. This groundwork of self-education in the game explains why Ballesteros called his instructional book Natural Golf.

His entry into the championship scene was explosive. At 19 he was two ahead of Johnny Miller going into the last round of the Open at Royal Birkdale. He should have been three ahead, but inexperience led him to try to putt through some wet grass at the 54th hole.

Though he managed to rescue a potentially disastrous final round with five birdies in his last six holes, he still lost to the big blond Californian, but transmitted so much enjoyment in his play and flashed his irresistible smile all around so charmingly as to reinvent himself into a golfing goldmine.

## Memorable round

The mother lode was struck in 1979, when his first British Open win at Lytham was built on a second-day performance which Mark McCormack has described as possibly the greatest round ever in the Open in all its long

history since Young Tom Morris played the 12 holes of Prestwick in 47 strokes in 1870. It was a 65, played in a bitterly cold wind, everyone permanently wrapped in waterproofs, and McCormack explains the superlatives he lavishes on it by saying that though Bill Longmuir had scored 65 on the first day, "it is an entirely different matter for an established player [which Seve was by then], one of the favourites for the title, to produce such a score". When Hale Irwin heard about it, he said: "He must have cut out some holes!" What Seve had done was to play the final five holes in 3,3,4,3,3, four under par, though most players reckoned the true par, considering the conditions, was 4,5,4,5,4. This was the Open of his celebrated car park shot, and he enjoyed his little joke when he recalled that saving birdie after a wayward drive by striking a ball from the car park of a football stadium in Madrid over the grandstand and on to the pitch.

His Lytham heroics made him the youngest Open winner since Young Tom. He was also the youngest winner of the Masters.

## Worldwide fame

Six times head of the order of merit, he became Europe's first £3 million prize-money winner in 1992. He has not gained the same renown as Gary Player for being a "world golfer", but the geographical spread of his successes summarized above justifies Ballesteros's claim to the title. Significantly, Ballesteros was the first to earn £1 million and $1 million.

For many followers of golf, Ballesteros is most respected for his ability and eagerness to take on and beat Americans, particularly in the Ryder Cup, which he more than any man has helped to make into a contest, for which both sides are duly grateful, not least at the turnstiles and sponsorship negotiations.

A great change that Ballesteros initiated was radically to improve American appreciation of European pros. Previously, only Tony Jacklin had made any impression in the United States, and American stars wanted appearances money to cross the Atlantic. Ballesteros wanted it in Europe, too, considering himself with some reason to be as good as, if not better, on his day than any American, and so quarrelled with the European Tour, even resigning at one point. He knew his worth and

Truly inspirational putter.

stubbornly refused to be undervalued. This, and the other players' feelings that he was not sufficiently supportive of the tour, was why he did not play in the 1981 Ryder Cup.

Once Jacklin was in charge and persuaded Ballesteros back into the fold, the Ryder Cup situation was radically altered, and Europe lost by only a point in 1983, their last defeat before 1991, again by a point.

## The desire to win

Beneath the smile, not so often seen of late, for men of his stock are swayed by intense emotion, either up or down and lately he has been down, still smoulders a firebrand of a competitor. His desire to succeed made a deep impression on Colin Montgomerie when the Spaniard beat him at the first extra hole of the Volvo PGA championship in 1991 by dint of hitting a five iron from the rough to three feet.

"Seve was so determined it was unbelievable. On the first tee he hardly shook my hand and called 'tails' without being asked when we tossed for honour. I thought to myself 'Hang on, am I here?' Five minutes later it was finished. I was left behind by his experience, his determination to win. It was a unique lesson because he's unique."

### SCORE CARD

British Open
1979, 1984, 1988

Masters
1980, 1983

Born Pedrena, northern Spain, April 9, 1957.

# Faldo's shot in the dark earns green jacket

SANDY LYLE, a rival of Nick Faldo from their earliest golfing days, helped him on with his first green jacket at the Masters, a title the Scot failed to retain because of a dreadful start with a 77.

Ironically, Faldo won despite returning that very same score in round three (the round the pros

Nick Faldo: 77 in "money round" but still won Masters.

call the money round), which was finished on Sunday because of rain. His response was a brilliant putting streak with eight birdies, four in the last six holes, for a score improved by 12 shots and a tie with Scott Hoch, whom he then beat at the second hole of a sudden-death play-off.

Hoch had what looked at first glance like a tap-in to win at the first extra hole, the tenth at Augusta National. It was a putt of no more than two feet, though it must be said that, as his approach came to rest, an American television commentator at once said: "That putt isn't in yet", for the putt was fast, tricky, and called for a cool nerve.

Hoch spent a long time over it. Just as Doug Sanders had done at St Andrews nearly a quarter of a century ago when he had about twice as long a putt to win the British Open, Hoch hesitated. Then he bent to pick some fragment, real or imagined, from his line. Faldo, who had already bogeyed the hole via a bunker showed absolutely no sign of surprise as Hoch missed. No one could remember a shorter putt being missed for a major title.

Faldo made the most of the let-off by producing a shot of great quality to set up his first Masters title. On the 11th, the second extra hole, he had 209 yards to go to the pin and got a perfect contact with a three iron, though by now it was so gloomy that he could not see his shot land. It stopped about 15 feet from the pin, and Faldo holed it for an unanswerable birdie and his second major title. The final round was as follows:

Faldo 3,4,4, 2,4,3, 3,5,4 = 32:
    4,5,3, 4,3,5, 2,3,4 = 33: 65
Par (6,905 yards)
    4,5,4, 3,4,3, 4,5,4 = 36:
    4,4,3, 5,4,5, 3,4,4 = 36: 72

Faldo's inspired putting had been the key, but so too had been his thoroughness and dedication. Often after four and a half hours on the course, he would walk off to the practice ground, known as Maniacs' Hill, to work on some aspect of his game.

## Strange in a classy half-dozen

CURTIS STRANGE won his second US Open in a row at Oak Hill, Rochester, New York State, the sixth man to successfully defend the title in 89 championships. Ben Hogan had been the last, 38 years before.

For the second year a Briton challenged strongly. Ian Woosnam, the farmer's son from Wales in his first American Open, finished a shot behind Strange in company with Ryder Cup candidates Mark McCumber and Chip Beck.

The champion scored an opening 71, which left him five behind the hot pace set by Bernhard Langer, Jay Don Blake from Utah and Payne Stewart. Nick Faldo had a useful 68, but a sore throat was not helping. The going was more difficult on day two, with only 15 scores under the par of 70, on a course (at 6,902 yards) only three yards shorter than Augusta National, where the par is 72.

One of the players to beat par was Strange, whose 64 was a clear message to the rest not to be too sanguine about their chances.

Despite morning delays while water was cleared away, the third round was completed, Strange off key with three bogeys and no birdies, and finishing third, three behind Tom Kite. Strange could do no better than par in the final round, but the effect of his 64 lingered on.

Tom Kite: helped regain Dunhill Cup for America at St Andrews.

# Calcavecchia's Open finish is impeccable

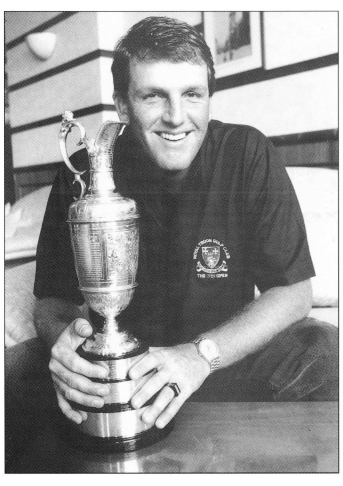

**Mark Calcavecchia: stylish finish in British Open play-off at Troon.**

NOT SINCE Tom Watson at Birkdale six years back had an American won the British Open, and Mark Calcavecchia's win at Troon was achieved with not one, but two nerveless finishes, for he tied Australians Wayne Grady and Greg Norman with a perfectly judged eight iron and single putt on the 72nd hole, then did it again from the rough with a five iron in a triple play-off.

Unexpected his victory may have been, neat it certainly was, as he followed an opening 71 with three 68s. Nothing can take the glory of a British Open from a player, but the fact that Greg Norman lost again after a prodigious last round will be a clearer recollection in many minds.

The author had not intended on the final day to watch Norman, who was far down the field after three rounds, and was setting off ten couples behind the pairing of his fellow countryman, Grady, who was seven shots in front of Norman.

But there he was about noon, swishing his driver on the first tee with intent, as you might say. So, along with a rapidly swelling crowd, the author followed him .

He birdied the first six holes, including a gigantic putt for two across the fifth green and, when he went through the seventh green, almost saved a seventh stroke from the back fringe.

That was all the author saw

of his round. At the next he missed the sliver of green between cavernous bunkers known as the Postage Stamp, and his bunker shot was not close enough to save par. He finished in eight under par 64, all the same.

At times like this Norman is an elemental force, but two simple errors undid him in the four-hole play-off over the 1st, 2nd, 17th and 18th.

At first he continued in irresistible vein, again making birdies at the first and second. Calcavecchia did not even blink and sank a birdie of his own at the second.

Grady was now just two behind Norman, who next misjudged his chip at the short 17th, and was square with the American.

Like Sandy Lyle in the Masters of the previous year, he underestimated the power lent even to his mighty frame by the excitement of the moment and found a bunker at the 18th generally thought to be out of reach from the tee.

Unlike Lyle, who birdied and so beat this same Calcavecchia by one at Augusta, Norman then found another and now went out of bounds. Calcavecchia's five iron from the right rough gave him a birdie chance he took to finish with style and end America's barren Open run.

# Stewart promise at last fulfilled

PAYNE STEWART'S steady advance up the finishing order of one major championship after another reached its climax at Kemper Lakes near Chicago with victory in the US PGA. Stewart was 24th in Nick Faldo's Masters, 13th in Curtis Strange's Open and eighth behind Mark Calcavecchia.

There was a common factor in all four of 1989's majors. The winners owed their success to some extent to the fact that better-placed rivals could not stand the heat over the final holes. The most spectacular collapse of all was by Mike Reid, 35, from Utah, who had won twice on tour in 12 years.

Despite a course-record first round of 64 by Craig Stadler, Reid led at 36 holes as he added a 67 to a 66. He was still three strokes ahead (13 under par) as the event

reached its final afternoon, and in some comfort until the 70th hole. Here he hit into the water, then took four to get down from about ten yards at the 17th, with a fluffed chip and three putts. He played the 18th remarkably well in the circumstances, with a five iron to six feet. A birdie here would rescue his chances, at least to the extent of a play-off, but as Stewart mentally prepared himself for the next stage, Reid missed again.

Reid's collapse meant that several players other than Stewart came into the reckoning, Andy Bean and Curtis Strange sharing second place with Reid, one behind Stewart, who won $200,000. Ian Woosnam, second behind Strange in the Open at Rochester, had another good payday ($40,000). Nick Faldo finished with Tom Watson, five shots

adrift. Stewart's clothing contract specified that he appear in sets of plus-twos and tops in the club colours of the various American football teams. Many considered this a little beneath the dignity of a top-class professional, even one with Stewart's easy southern charm. One writer said his clothers were suitable for burial at sea.

Ray Floyd, the American captain, was working on the selection of his last two Ryder Cup men at Kemper Lakes and, after the PGA championship, chose Tom Watson and Lanny Wadkins to go with the ten automatic choices on points. He doubtless felt that his five newcomers (Azinger, Beck, Couples, Ken Green and McCumber) were numerous enough. The Ryder team had become a matter of great moment in America.

**Payne Stewart: climbed to top of "majors" ladder at US PGA.**

# Europe keep Ryder Cup in cliff-hanger tie

**Christy O'Connor: career shot across the lake to 18th at The Belfry.**

ONE CLOSE struggle after another in recent years prompted Michael Williams, the "Daily Telegraph" correspondent, to prophesy a tie in the 28th Ryder Cup match, played at The Belfry on September 22, 23 and 24. And that is what happened for the second time in 20 years and you could get 12 to 1 about the tie, even after the first day.

Tony Jacklin made it clear that this was to be his last match as (non-playing) captain. Since the heady days of 1987 he had lost his wife, Vivien, who collapsed at the wheel of her car, and had been the target of tabloid press stories about a relationship with a girl half his age. He then married a Norwegian divorcee, Astrid Kendall, who had the difficult task, in the circumstances, of striking up as good a relationship with the player's wives as Vivien had enjoyed. To add to Jacklin's problems, Sandy Lyle, totally out of form, asked Jacklin not to select him. The vote went to

Bernhard Langer. The match turned into several sessions of catch-up, for the Americans did not lose a foursome on the gloomy first morning, when they won two and halved two. Then, in a repeat of events at Muirfield Village, Europe won all the four-balls after lunch. Tom Watson and Mark O'Meara ran into a rampant Seve Ballesteros and José Maria Olazabal, who won all the first five holes. An eagle two at the short, par-four tenth, 275 yards down the hill and over a lake, by Ballesteros was followed by three more birdies in a row for a 6 & 5 victory.

The second day summed up the match, 2-2 both sessions, leaving Europe still two ahead at 9-7. Most disappointed man on the day was Christy O'Connor, who had waited since 1975, when he was winless from two starts, for another crack at the Cup, and now lost his only match so far. Beck and Azinger were two hot golfers against Faldo and Woosnam, out

in a better ball of 30. The US response in singles, with a world-wide television audience of up to 200 million looking on, was riveting. Azinger and Beck, each already with two points out of three, levelled the score at 9-9 by beating bankers Ballesteros and Langer respectively. At one time only Mark James was ahead. Azinger's win, at the 18th, was Homeric, for he was in the water but played a career shot from a soggy spot over the lake into a bunker and still got a bogey five, which was as much as Ballesteros, also in the lake, could do.

Where, then, were the five points Europe needed to tie and keep the Cup to be gleaned? Olazabal and Rafferty got the first two, Stewart and Calcavecchia both finding the lake at the last. James beat O'Meara, and it was

now that the two oldest Europeans made their indelible mark.

O'Connor would not submit to Couples, the man many were looking to as the next dominant world golfer, and hit his career shot over that daunting carry to the 18th green – a two iron to four feet be it said. Couples, after a huge drive, missed the green with a nine iron.

The oldest of Jacklin's men, José Maria Canizares, round in 68 like his opponent Ken Green, got the final Cup-saving point with a finely judged putt to hole-side from the back of the 18th, upon which surface the American three-putted. All the last four Europeans lost, Watson and Wadkins repaying Floyd's faith in them. Three of the United States's last four wins were by one hole. It was as close as that.

**José Maria Canizares: old head beat three-putter Ken Green at the death in Ryder Cup to land the trophy for Europe.**

## RYDER CUP

(The Belfry, Sutton Coldfield, W Midlands) Europe 14, US 14
Captains: Europe, T Jacklin; US, R Floyd

**FIRST DAY Foursomes: Morning**

| Europe | | US | |
|---|---|---|---|
| N Faldo & I Woosnam | ½ | T Kite & C Strange | ½ |
| H Clark & M James | 0 | L Wadkins & P Stewart 1h | 1 |
| S Ballesteros & JM Olazabal | ½ | T Watson & C Beck | ½ |
| B Langer & R Raffery | 0 | M Calcavecchia & C Beck 2 & 1 | 1 |

**Four-balls: Afternoon**

| | | | |
|---|---|---|---|
| S Torrance & G Brand Jnr  1h | 1 | C Strange & P Azinger | 0 |
| H Clark & M James 3 & 2 | 1 | F Couples & L Wadkins | 0 |
| N Faldo & I Woosnam 1h | 1 | M Calcavecchia & M McCumber | 0 |
| S Ballesteros & JM Olazabal 6 & 5 | 1 | T Watson & M O'Meara | 0 |

First Day: Europe 5; US 3

**SECOND DAY Foursomes: Morning**

| | | | |
|---|---|---|---|
| I Woosnam & N Faldo 3 & 2 | 1 | L Wadkins & P Stewart | 0 |
| G Brand & S Torrance | 0 | C Beck & P Azinger 4 & 3 | 1 |
| C O'Connor Jnr & R Rafferty | 0 | M Calcavecchia & K Green 3 & 2 | 1 |
| S Ballesteros & JM Olazabal 1h | 1 | T Kite & C Strange | 0 |

**Four-balls: Afternoon**

| | | | |
|---|---|---|---|
| N Faldo & I Woosnam | 0 | C Beck & P Azinger 2 & 1 | 1 |
| B Langer & JM Canizares | 0 | T Kite & M McCumber 2 & 1 | 1 |
| H Clark & M James 1h | 1 | P Stewart & C Strange | 0 |
| S Ballesteros & JM Olazabal 4 & 2 | 1 | M Calcavecchia & K Green | 0 |

Second Day: Europe 4;  US 4
Match aggregate: Europe 9;  US 7

**THIRD DAY Singles**

| | | | |
|---|---|---|---|
| S Ballesteros | 0 | P Azinger 1h | 1 |
| B Langer | 0 | C Beck 3 & 2 | 1 |
| JM Olazabal 1h | 1 | P Stewart | 0 |
| R Rafferty 1h | 1 | M Calcavecchia | 0 |
| H Clark | 0 | T Kite 8 & 7 | 1 |
| M James 3 & 2 | 1 | M O'Meara | 0 |
| C O'Connor Jnr 1h | 1 | F Couples | 0 |
| JM Canizares 1h | 1 | K Green | 0 |
| G Brand Jnr | 0 | M McCumber 1h | 1 |
| S Torrance | 0 | T Watson 3 & 1 | 1 |
| N Faldo | 0 | L Wadkins 1h | 1 |
| I Woosnam | 0 | C Strange 2h | 1 |

Singles: Europe 5;  US 7

# Milligan, Walker Cup saviour as Europe complete sweep

**Peter McEvoy: stalwart display in Walker Cup.**

BRITAIN AND IRELAND won the Walker Cup on American soil for the first time with a singles performance on the second day that looked like a rout but was, thanks to earlier excellence just enough, at 1½ points out of 8, for Geoffrey Marks's team to do the trick. Marks had been on the winning 1971 team.

The deed was done at Peachtree, Atlanta, Bobby Jones's "other" creation. The clubhouse was once headquarters during the Civil War for General Sherman – he who marched so destructively through Georgia.

Peter McEvoy and Eoghan O'Connell were the inspirations on the first day, winning together and in singles.

Despite the presence of such Cup stalwarts as Jay Sigel and interesting newcomers like left-hander Phil Mickelson and Danny Yates, nephew of Charlie Yates, the 1938 British Amateur champion, the United States's points total when the second day dawned was 4½, against the visitors' 7½.

By lunch it was 11-5, Robert Gamez and Doug Martin halving with McEvoy and O'Connell to avoid a whitewash.

America, 5-11 down, hit back hard in the final singles, at one point leading all eight. They emerged unbeaten but Andrew Hare, O'Connell and Jim Milligan scrambled the three halves that took the Cup to Britain. Sigel of all people fluffed three chips at the last three holes.

Milligan did once, but in went the next, and Sigel's failure to chip close at the last was decisive. For the first time ever, the Ryder, Curtis and Walker Cups were all in European hands.

**Bob Charles: still going strong with Senior British Open title.**

# Nick Faldo's double first at the Masters

SEVEN BEHIND the leader after 18 holes, five behind after 36, three behind after 54, Nick Faldo forged ahead to gain his second Masters title in a row, a feat previously achieved only by Jack Nicklaus in 1965 and 1966. Faldo had to survive another play-off, this time against Ray Floyd, to get his second green jacket.

Mike Donald was the surprise first-round leader, with a 64. This fine score by Donald, and a 66 by second-placed John Huston, disproved the generally held belief that players competing at Augusta for the first time stood little chance. Donald's 64, "the round of my dreams" and one more than the course record, equalled the best previous "first-time" round by Lloyd Mangrum half a century ago.

Much was expected of Greg Norman (who had recently won the Doral Open at the first extra hole after a final round of 62) and of Faldo. Seve Ballesteros was also fancied, along with Ian Woosnam, the 1989 US Open runner-up. In the event, Norman had another of his bad Augusta first days. His 78 followed this three previous first-day scores: 73, 77, 74. Woosnam managed a 72.

The blustery conditions on day two made all good scoring harder. Donald averaged one more shot per hole as he carded an 82, while Faldo returned a 72 to close the gap on new overnight leader Raymond Floyd, who was two ahead of Huston. Faldo's third round 66 looked potentially lucrative, getting him to within three of Floyd, who had a second straight 68. Huston matched Floyd to remain behind by two.

The story of the last round is one of disappointment for Floyd and dogged pursuit by Faldo, despite a double bogey six on the first hole. He responded with a birdie at the second, but Floyd moved four clear of Faldo with a birdie two from the back fringe of the 12th. "I did not think I could lose," he said afterwards. Floyd, trying, at 47, to become the oldest Master ever, felt that if he could par in, the chances of any of the chasers shooting a 31 were poor on a superb sunny afternoon.

Despite that double bogey, Faldo returned a 69 to catch Floyd, who found par on the remaining holes beyond him and could not capitalize on the two reachable par fives, three-putting the 17th. Faldo, by contrast, after scrambling par via a bunker and an 18-foot par putt at the 12th, was on the long 13th for a two-putt birdie, and chipped and putted another birdie four from over the back of the 15th. A further birdie from 20 feet at the 16th turned out to be the crucial blow. An inward half of 34 gave Faldo the play-off with Floyd.

Matters ended limply for Floyd at the second extra hole, where he found the water with his second shot, and Faldo's par four was enough.

Nick Faldo: on his way to a follow-up Masters victory.

# Faldo breaks Norman and everyone else at HQ

WINNING THE OPEN at the home of golf, the Old Course at St Andrews, is for the golfer what the great English novel is for the writer. For a chef, it's a rosette in the Michelin Guide. Nick Faldo won his second Open, and second major of the year, in the grand manner, burning off Greg Norman in round three and finishing five strokes ahead of the joint runners-up, Mark McNulty of Zimbabwe and the elegantly kitted out Payne Stewart, though some found the American Football club colours that he flaunted a little overpowering.

Faldo's total of 270 was six better than the previous Open best, set by Seve Ballesteros in 1984. He had been within a putt of the American Open play-off a month earlier, so his majors score for the year was 1,3,1, and a career total of four.

A record first-day crowd watched Norman make his fastest start for some time in a major, sharing the lead with Michael Allen, a much lesser known American tour player, as yet without a win. Faldo was only one behind and the golf connoisseur's dream came true in the second round, which left Norman and Faldo together on 132, four clear of Norman's countryman, Craig Parry and Stewart.

Perhaps the most satisfied golfer on the Friday evening was Jamie Spence, a 27-year-old pro from Kent, who had battled through qualifying, had shaken off food poisoning which rendered his trousers much too big round the waist, and then captured the complete attention of the media by equalling with 65 the best score returned in 24 Opens at St Andrews. This had been set 20 years ago by Neil Coles and equalled since by Nick Faldo.

The 65 mark did not last long, and neither did the test of nerve between Faldo and Norman, who subsided to 76 after his opening volley of two 66s. Five fives in a row appeared against Norman's name as Faldo ground relentlessly on to another 67, to a never-before-achieved total at 54 holes of 199, five ahead of Ian Baker-Finch and Payne Stewart with a round to go.

The fresh assault on the Old Course record was mounted by Paul Broadhurst, 24, a Midland pro who had the advantage of another perfect golfing day and a number of not unfriendly pin positions. Of both he took full advantage, with birdies from the fifth to the tenth, having already birdied the first and third. He used only 12 putts on the first nine holes, which he covered in 29 shots, the mark set by Tony Jacklin before the storm of 1971 that cost him so dear.

He parred in from the tenth, till a nine iron to 18 inches at the last gave him his ninth birdie, and that 63. Maybe this rush of birdies had something to do with the telephone box door that had split Broadhurst's eyebrow the day before as he rang to discover whether he had qualified for the final 36 holes. Faldo gave his pursuers few discernible flickers of hope on the final afternoon, though he admitted: "It was scary. There are deep bunkers out there. If I had lost it, it would have been a big blow-out."

The author's colleague on the "Daily Telegraph", John Reason, more usually to be seen in Rugby Union press boxes, gave it as his opinion on the last day that bunkers were ignored by the leading players, and like the Valley of Sin, the little dip in front of the 18th, back into which many an approach to the pin has rolled, had been made irrelevant by modern equipment.

Bunkers were clearly not ignored by Faldo, and Stewart's promising run at Faldo in the later stages of the final round (he was as close as two strokes) came to a juddering halt ... in a bunker on the 13th. He also went on to the Road at the 17th and took another five from the Valley of Sin.

# Irwin's monster putt trumps Donald

THE SECOND major championship of the year ended like the first, in a tie, and as it was in the US Open this one was settled over 18 holes, or rather 19, since a full round was not enough to separate Hale Irwin and Mike Donald after they tied on 280 over 72 holes.

Donald had gained only one victory in 11 years on the PGA Tour, but again demonstrated his hunger for a more high-profile reputation, since he had led in the Masters before subsiding to 82 in round two. This time there was no falling away, but Irwin's experience gained the day at that 19th, where he holed an eight-foot putt for a birdie after he and Donald had covered the play-off round in 74 at Medinah, Illinois.

Donald can scarcely have been surprised to see Irwin hole that putt. On the 72nd Irwin holed a putt right across the green. It was reckoned at about 60 feet or, as Irwin put it, "about four times as long as any other putt I made all week".

Irwin is not the most demonstrative of men, but he galloped a lap of honour round the green, and repeated this manoeuvre at his press conference later. He had come back in 31 shots, putting beautifully on the frighteningly fast

Hale Irwin: displaced Ray Floyd as oldest US Open champion.

Medinah greens and graciously crediting Greg Norman's 32 over the first half as his inspiration. All these birdies and victory runs did Irwin credit, for he was now, at 45, the oldest Open champion of them all, Ray Floyd having been 43 when he won in 1986.

Irwin's final putt vanished from sight two hours before the last group came up the 18th fairway. Of all those who followed Irwin in, only Donald could match his 280, though Nick Faldo had a birdie putt for that total which caught the edge of the hole but would not drop.

It had been a victory every bit as hard fought as his US Open triumph at Winged Foot in 1974, where he shot seven over par and yet won by two shots.

Ian Woosnam, a favourite with American galleries, had been sailing along serenely in round two when, at the short 17th, he babied a chip and left it in the fringe grass, got to within three feet with his next effort and then three-putted.

This hole had troubled Faldo, too, costing him a four on each of the first two days. On the second he required a two with his second ball to achieve his bogey, having hit his first into the water guarding the green.

---

# Spencer-Devlin returns to action after being disqualified for pre-tournament tirade

MUFFIN SPENCER-DEVLIN, disqualifed from the Ford classic at Woburn in April following a volley of bad language during the pre-tournament dinner, was back in action at Woburn in the Weetabix British Women's Open. She shot a first-round 71, two behind the leader, Kitrina Douglas. This was Spencer-Devlin's best score since returning to competition after a spell in a London psychiatric clinic.

Joe Flanagan, director of the women's European tour, said nothing had impressed him half as much as the way in which the American woman had done everything in her power to make up for the goings-on in April and

that he would be very happy to have Spencer-Devlin back on the European Tour.

Helen Alfredsson became the first Swede to win the British Open, beating Jane Hill at the fourth hole of a sudden-death play-off. Both players had recorded four-round scores of 288.

The US Women's Open went for the second year to Betsy King, at Atlanta Athletic Club. King did not win on Tour for seven years after joining it in 1977, but made up for that from 1984, with at least $200,000 a year, surpassing half a million in her two Open title years.

Blue-eyed and blond, Betsy stands only five feet six inches.

# Groove Wars: let-off for the R&A

THERE WAS good news for British golf from an American judge who ruled that a court in Arizona had no jurisdiction over the Royal & Ancient.

This looked like the beginning of the end of the Groove Wars, declared when Karsten Solheim served writs against the USGA and Royal & Ancient following their rulings that his Ping Eye-2 clubs were illegal.

The two ruling bodies objected to the shape of the Ping Eye-2 iron grooves, square rather than the traditional V-shape.

These put more spin on the ball, giving greater control with pitch shots to the green, at least for expert players. The benefits would be more marginal for average players.

Solheim's contention that the method of groove measurement was changed without the makers' knowledge was negated by the USGA catch-all clause which stated that the advice of

the association should be sought by any manufacturer in doubt about such matters.

The Arizona court's decision certainly let the Royal & Ancient off the hook, and the offending clubs were henceforth illegal at all championships under R&A jurisdiction, including the Open championship at St Andrews. The USGA had been forced to proceed more circumspectly, remembering the $4 million it cost them when they outlawed the Polara ball, which was designed not to hook or slice. This was of doubtful value to competent players in any case, since they needed to shape their shots and work the ball with draw or fade.

The USGA and Karsten Manufacturing settled out of court. Existing Eye-2 irons were deemed legal, but future clubs must conform to the standards of the USGA, who thus retained their traditional control over equipment.

# Grady makes mark as Shoal Creek gets the wrong headlines

WAYNE GRADY, 33, the Queenslander who was clearly majors material after holding on so staunchly and so long in the British Open at Troon 12 months previously, held on too tightly even for an improving Fred Couples at Shoal Creek, Alabama, and won the US PGA championship by three strokes.

Nick Faldo, burning with ambition to equal Ben Hogan's three majors in a year, finished well back, having slumped to 155 strokes for the middle 36 holes. He was 13 strokes behind Grady, in the good company of Tom Watson and Greg Norman.

This was a win of grinding application by Grady on a course which allowed only him, Couples and Gil Morgan to finish under par because (according to professional opinion) no one could predict how the ball would act on hitting the greens.

Some balls stopped, some went on. But there is always someone who can play the course (shades of Tony Jacklin at Hazeltine in 1970!).

The event, or rather the host club, had been making headlines for weeks before tee-off time. The fires of controversy were lit by the words of Shoal Creek founder Hall Thompson in a newspaper article: "I think we've said that we don't discriminate in every other area except the blacks."

Many other clubs had the same attitude, including Augusta, but none had come out with the bald statement that they would not admit blacks.

Picketing was the least the club could expect. Even more effective, in the market-led way of 20th-century politics, was the decision of most sponsors of the ABC telecasts of the US PGA to drop out.

The three major golf authorities, the PGA, the Tour and the USGA, also reacted quickly. None of their events would be staged at clubs that discriminated in word or deed.

Less than two weeks before the start of the championship, Louis Willie, a local businessman, was made an honorary member of Shoal Creek.

By contrast, nine clubs, including Merion, Cypress Point, Chicago, and Aronimink, would not comply with the spirit of the ruling made by American golf's ruling bodies.

Wayne Grady: US PGA consolation at Shoal Creek for Troon defeat.

# Solheim Cup goes to US by seven points

Nancy Lopez: crushing last-day win in first Solheim Cup.

KATHY WHITWORTH, winner of 88 LPGA tour events, led her team of eight American professionals to victory by 11-4, with one match halved, in the inaugural Solheim Cup contest against Europe at Lake Nona, Florida, in mid-November.

The win was gained on all fronts: 3-1 in foursomes on the first day, 3-1 in four-balls on the second and 5-2 in singles on the third, plus Betsy King's half with Pam Wright.

There was no doubt about the American star of the show: Beth Daniel was the only 100 per cent player, while Laura Davies was Europe's best with a prized foursomes win, partnered by Alison Nicholas, against Nancy Lopez and Pat Bradley. She added a victory in the singles, overcoming Rosie Jones.

Nicholas said of Lopez after the foursomes win: "She was my hero when I started playing the game. To beat her is incredible."

On the third day Lopez (against Nicholas) and Daniel (playing the Swede Liselotte Neumann, the 1988 American Open champion) had the thrill of putting together the last points needed to secure the trophy (which is a crystal vase).

Lopez, housewife and superstar, said: "It is amazing how important it is to win when you are representing your country."

American putting and cool nerve at crisis points were the decisive factors, as they so often have been in Ryder, Walker and Curtis play. Pam Wright felt a little sore about her half with King, though. She had recovered from two down with six to play, and as the match went down the final fairway (the only Cup match to get that far), Wright thought she had it won as King's approach went through the green and seemed destined for "out of bounds". Then it hit a tree, rebounded on to the green, and King holed from 40 feet to secure her half.

The European Tour commissioner, Joe Flanagan, thought the gamble of taking on the might of the LPGA worthwhile. He was sure it would make women's golf easier to sell and raise its profile generally.

He said: "If people will only look at the standard of golf that was played here, they will see just how much of a draw it could be." His comments were directed mostly for the benefit of the television companies.

# US gain Curtis Cup revenge

GREAT BRITAIN and Ireland were trying for their third successive win in the Curtis Cup series, at Somerset Hills, New Jersey, a unique experience for the visiting side led by Jill Thornhill. The overall score since the series began was 19-4 in favour of the side captained by Lesley Shannon, who were, not unnaturally, thirsting for revenge.

Mrs Shannon's players were well mixed in age and experience. They did not let her down. Her new recruits were Brandie Burton, Katie Peterson and Robin Weiss, and all three, like Anne Sander who was appearing in her eighth Cup match, were unbeaten throughout the event.

Sander, still a player to be reckoned with at 52, was paired with the reigning American Amateur champion, Vicki Goetze, aged 17.

They won both of their foursomes.

Julie Hall, 1990 British champion, was one of the few visiting successes. She and Kathryn Imrie won their foursome on the first day, and she went on to beat Goetze in singles, but apart from Vicki Thomas's win in the bottom match over Carol Semple Thompson, that was the extent of British and Irish progress on day one.

As the American male teams have been known to do, the American women swept through the second-day singles, dishing out as thorough a whitewashing as ever was seen.

Only Imrie got as far as the last hole. The hope aroused by that last-gasp Thomas win, by one hole, on day one was totally extinguished. Goetze was three under par on the front nine in beating Helen Dobson

4 & 3, and Burton, never short on length, had four birdies and an eagle as she tidied up with the Cup-winning point against Catriona Lambert.

Goetze and Karen Noble of the Curtis team made up, with Pat Hurst, the US trio that won the Espirito Santo trophy at Christchurch, New Zealand. They finished on 585, 12 ahead of the home team and 20 ahead of Great Britain and Ireland, represented by Hall, Thomas and, from Ireland, Claire Hourihane.

Thirteen years after winning the British Amateur title, Angela Uzielli completed a remarkable return to top form when winning the English Amateur, at Rye in Sussex. The evergreen Uzielli overcame Linzi Fletcher in a tight match, 2 & 1.

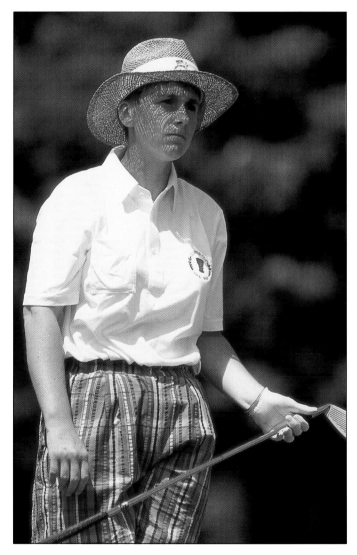

**Julie Hall: British Amateur Champion, and effective performer in the Curtis Cup, despite the visitors' sound beating.**

## SHORT PUTTS

● The growing strength of Swedish golf was amply demonstrated at Christchurch in New Zealand when Mathias Gronberg, who had earlier won the British Youths' championship (with a birdie on the final hole) at Southerness in Scotland, was leading individual as Sweden won the Eisenhower trophy from the United States and New Zealand by 13 shots. Great Britain and Ireland, the holders, were 31 shots adrift.

● Nick Faldo, winner of the Masters and British Open, was named player of the year by the US PGA.

● José Maria Olazabal, 24, of Spain won the World Series of Golf over the severe South Course in Akron, Ohio, with one of the PGA tour's greatest exhibitions of stroke play. His rounds (61,67,67,67) gave him a total of 262, 18 under par. He won by 12 shots, a record like his total, which was five shots better than the mark set by Lanny Wadkins in 1977, of 267.

● The gardener at the Old Course Hotel at St Andrews wears a tin helmet. A fair number of players are too ambitious with their line off the tee to the favoured right side of the fairway of the Road Hole.

● Lord Derby resigned as president of the PGA after he had been left to make the casting decision for The Belfry as the 1993 Ryder Cup venue, against strong claims for a Spanish course, Club de Campo, to be used. Instead, it was guaranteed. that the 1997 Ryder Cup would go to Spain.

## SCORECARD

**British Open** (St Andrews, Scot)
N Faldo  67 65 67 71  270
M McNulty  74 68 68 65  275
P Stewart  68 68 68 71  275
I Woosnam  68 69 70 69  276
J Mudd  72 66 72 66  276
I Baker-Finch  68 72 64 73  277
G Norman  66 66 76 69  277

**US Open** (Medinah CC, Ill)
H Irwin  69 70 74 67  280-73-3
M Donald  67 70 72 71  280-73-4
(18-hole play-off tied; Irwin won on first extra play-off hole)
N Faldo  72 72 68 69  281
BR Brown  69 71 69 72  281
G Norman  72 73 69 69  283
T Simpson  66 69 75 73  283
M Brooks  68 70 72 73  283

**Masters** (Augusta, Ga)
N Faldo  71 72 66 69  278
R Floyd  70 68 68 72  278
(Faldo won play-off at second extra hole)
J Huston  66 74 68 75  283
L Wadkins  72 73 70 68  283
F Couples  74 69 72 69  284

**US PGA** (Shoal Creek, Atlanta,Ga)
W Grady  72 67 72 71  282
F Couples  69 71 73 72  285
G Morgan  77 72 65 72  286
B Britton  72 74 72 71  289
C Beck  71 70 78 71  290
B Mayfair  70 71 75 74  290
L Roberts  73 71 70 76  290
Leading US money-winner:
G Norman  $1,165,477;
Europe: I Woosnam £737,977
Year-end Sony Ranking: 1 G Norman, 2 N Faldo, 3 JM Olazabal, 4 I Woosnam, 5 P Stewart

**British Amateur** (Muirfield, Scot)
R Muntz bt A Macara  7 & 6

**US Amateur** (Cherry Hills CC, Col)
P Mickelson bt M Zerman  5 & 4

**US Women's Open** (Atlanta AC, Duluth, Ga)
B King  284

**British Women's Open** (Woburn, Bucks)
H Alfredsson  288

**British Women's Amateur** (Dunbar, Scot)
J Hall bt H Wadsworth  3 & 2

**US Women's Amateur** (Canoe Brook CC, NJ)
P Hurst bt S Davis  37th

**World Cup** (Grand Cypress Resort, Orlando, Fla)
Germany (B Langer & T Giedeon)  556;
(Individual) P Stewart, US  271

**Dunhill Nations Cup** (St Andrews, Scot)
Ireland (P Walton, R Rafferty, D Feherty) bt England (M James, R Boxall,  H Clark)  3½-2½

**World Match Play** (Wentworth, Surrey)
I Woosnam bt M McNulty  4 & 2

**Solheim Cup** (Lake Nona GC, Fla)
US  11½, Europe  4½

**Eisenhower Trophy** (Christchurch, NZ)
Sweden 879, NZ 892, US 892;
(Individual [unofficial]) M Gronberg, Sweden 286

**Espirito Santo** (Russley, NZ)
US  585

**Curtis Cup** (Somerset Hills, NJ)
US  14, GB & Ireland  4

# Nick Faldo the obsessed but greatest of his era

## The outstanding talent of Britain's post-war golfing revival, three times winner of the British Open and the US Masters, Faldo has proved himself a quirky genius with an unquestioned devotion to the game

THE FACT THAT Nick Faldo got on well with Ben Hogan, renowned as not the most approachable of golfers, fits the personalities of both perfectly. There have been other obsessive practisers and seekers after the holy grail of golf perfection. Gary ("the more I practise, the luckier I get") Player springs to mind. Yet when Player approached Hogan on a technical point, Hogan asked whose clubs Player used [Dunlop] and told him to go and ask Mr Dunlop.

Hogan and Faldo are two of a highly restricted kind, however. Both men had the confidence, mental energy and sheer guts not only to refine their swing, but to make radical changes, to reinvent themselves as golfers. The effort has finished the careers of great golfers in the past, notably US Open champion Ralph Guldahl. The process of examining his own method during research for an instruction book led to paralysis by analysis, and he faded from the scene never to return.

## The search for

Faldo, like Hogan decided that his swing was not good enough and, with the help of David Leadbetter, who is British but based in Florida, got to work building a new one.

He approached Leadbetter (you can't miss him, he's almost six feet, six inches tall) in 1984. Leadbetter, born in Worthing in Sussex, played on the European Tour in the 1970s, but concluded rightly that those who can do, and those who can't (quite) teach. Nick Price and Denis Watson had prospered as Leadbetter students, hence Faldo's approach. The next year,

**Frustrating business, this putting ... Faldo feels the pain.**

Faldo entered on a complete rehaul of his *modus operandi*.

Leadbetter's method is to study, film and analyse the swings of all the best players in search of a common factor of effectiveness. He has invented a series of drills to iron out problems thus detected. The aim is consistency under pressure. Another parallel with Hogan is discernible here, for the later Hogan swing has tighter leg movement and the whole thrust of Faldo's remodelling is to give a more compact effect. He does not hit the ball so far, but his ball stays most profitably in play.

Theoretical concepts are all very well, but useless without an athlete of Faldo's stamp, with great hand and eye coordination, physical strength and endurance (he is 15 stone [210 pounds] and six feet, three inches tall). Above all, he has the grinding determination to turn learning to account, as when two birdies were required in the last four holes to win at Muirfield in 1992.

## Faldo supreme

World ranking statistics did not tell the whole story during Faldo's decade of six major wins, 1987–96, as Greg Norman's huge haul of lesser tournaments kept him on top of Sony lists for far longer than the Englishman, who nevertheless enjoyed 81 weeks at the top in 1993–94. However, achievement is measured in major events, such as stroke averages, comparison of finishing rounds, leading positions, not to mention Ryder Cup contributions, and the quality of Faldo's game at the highest level was unequalled for a decade. In the years 1987 to 1996 he made 38 starts in the four majors, winning six and finishing 18 times in the top ten. He missed only one cut. In half of his ten attempts on the British Open in those years, he was third or better. Moreover, his 23 Ryder wins from 46 starts is unequalled on either side of the Atlantic.

The bitter disappointment of his career was almost certainly Mark James's decision to select Andrew Coltart as his final wild card for the 1999 Cup match at Brookline, though Faldo's lack of an individual victory since the Nissan Open at Riviera, Los Angeles, early in 1997 and missed cuts in majors scarcely recommended him for selection – this despite his winning partnership with David Carter to take the World Cup for England at Auckland in 1998.

The success of the swing rebuilding process, which Faldo says took the best part of two years, was not immediate. Leadbetter after all is trying to make his pupils do something which, as described in his book The Golf Swing, sounds impossible. Yet tournament golfers do it regularly. The club "has to be swung at a speed approaching 90 miles an hour through an arc of approximately 18 feet. The ball is on the club face for just 0.00035 of a second and, to be hit in the desired direction, has to be launched at an angle of .2 of a degree." All the same, Faldo must have achieved this counsel of perfection now and then in gaining five majors from 1987 to 1992. His score on the European tour is 26 victories, three in the United States, including his two Masters titles, and he has won in South Africa, Jamaica and Hong Kong.

## Early achievements

His first competitive successes were in the British Youths' championship and the English Amateur, both of which he won in 1975. Like younger members of recent Ryder Cup squads, Faldo was hooked on golf by television, deciding to ditch other sports in order to focus all effort on playing in beautiful places like Augusta against the Nicklauses and the Watsons.

His success in his chosen profession was encouraged by his parents, though he did not come from a wealthy family, and his first golfing days closely resembled those of Ballesteros: with one club, donated by a schoolmaster, knocking balls he had found around a sports field.

Soon he was hot on the heels of an omnipresent rival, Sandy Lyle, in pursuit of one trophy after another, notably the Open and the Masters. Lyle helped him on with his first green jacket.

## Awkward genius

Faldo's problem seems to be an inability to cope with moments of extreme tension, success and failure. His rendition of "My Way" after his narrow escape from the greatest let-down of his golfing life at the second Muirfield Open, and his crass remarks about the media, however much some press men deserve castigation, were not wise.

Why, though, should we expect someone who is a world-class exponent of a difficult art to be likeable? Talent often brings unwanted baggage with it, notably impatience with merely

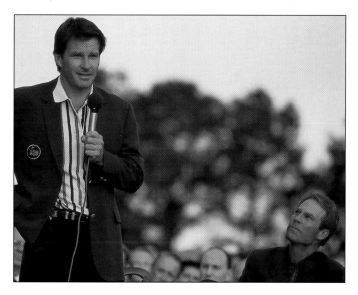

Faldo, watched by defending champion Ben Crenshaw, talks to the crowd after winning his third Masters at Augusta in 1996.

Caddie Fanny Sunesson (rear) formed a fine partnership with Faldo throughout the 1990s.

### SCORE CARD

**British Open**
1987, 1990, 1992

**Masters**
1989, 1990, 1996

Born Welwyn Garden City, Hertfordshire, July 18, 1957.

### TEE TALK

**"From being a kid it has been my dream to leave a legacy. I want people to say 'Did you see Nick Faldo play?'"**

NICK FALDO

**"Ah, glass. Good, you don't have to polish it."**

BUSH TELEGRAPH, quoting the golfer's words on receiving a new trophy in an assessment of Faldo's people skills.

**"I thank the press from the heart of my, well, bottom."**

NICK FALDO
part of his much criticised victory speech after his much admired 1992 Muirfield Open win.

Coach David Leadbetter (left) remodelled pupil Nick Faldo's swing to great mutual profit.

normally gifted mortals and an inability to see anything but the professional target, viewed down a narrow tunnel.

These traits Faldo has shown in abundance, though he has never wasted his talents in the same way as a Paul Gascoigne or misused them like a John McEnroe, and he is a man who does much for charity, once giving away a sizeable chunk of a tournament prize cheque to a worthy childrens' cause.

He does, however, seem to attract enmity at times, and Scott Hoch, beaten by Faldo in a play-off for the 1989 Masters, made no secret of the fact that he was less than happy at having been drawn with the Englishman in the first round in 1990 (when Faldo won again). Hoch, who missed a two-footer to win the play-off at the first extra hole, had afterwards called Faldo the luckiest man alive, a remark to which Faldo took great exception.

## Newspaper slurs

Later came remarks attributed to Hoch by the tabloid press, distilled in headlines to the effect that "We all hate Faldo ... he's miserable and aloof". The pair met soon afterwards at St Andrews. Faldo's version ran thus: "Hoch said to me, 'Whatever you have seen I didn't say it.' I told him, 'Don't worry, I don't read it.'" Hoch's wife Sally had it about right: "Boy, your papers are the pits."

Faldo's marital problems have attracted even more public interest. His first wife, Melanie, divorced him because of his admitted adultery with Gill Bennett, a secretary who became his second wife. Melanie's analysis of Faldo bears repeating: "Genius in any form is never comfortable to live with" ... she assessed Faldo as a 24-handicapper at small talk. He has three children. As his marriage with Gill ended in a reported £10million divorce settlement, he began a new life in America with a 20-year-old student named Brenna Cepelak. That enterprise did not last the 20th century, though Faldo declared he had unravelled the knots he had tied himself into.

His most rewarding female companion to date has been his long-time caddie, Fanny Sunesson, who had decided that her five handicap was not going to earn her fame and fortune. Faldo hired her at the beginning of 1990. Together they picked up four majors and much wealth. At the end of 1999, she left to pick up the bag of Sergio Garcia.

# Woosnam stays cool at Augusta's 18th

**Ian Woosnam celebrates as his putt disappears on the 72nd green.**

WELSHMAN IAN WOOSNAM kept his head well at the Masters to edge out José Maria Olazabal and Tom Watson, who both had chances to win there. So, after 51 years without a British Master golfer, four green jackets in a row had gone to the old country. In fact, Ryder Cup Europeans won at Augusta seven times in 12 years.

Standing only five feet four inches tall, Woosnam has the build of one his country's more durable rugby scrum-halves. He hits a prodigiously long ball with a swing so simple-looking, a dismissive swish, that it seems nothing can go wrong.

Left-handed amateur Phil Mickelson, a student at Arizona State University, had shocked the pros by winning the Northern Telecom Open at Tuscon. He returned a first-round 69, three better than his playing partner, defending champion Nick Faldo. Mickelson was only one of nearly 30 players separating Faldo and Woosnam from the leaders, Mickelson was only one of nearly 30 players separating Faldo and Woosnam from the leaders, Lanny Wadkins, Jim Gallagher junior and Mark McCumber, all on 67. A stroke behind them was a group that brought back old times, for it included Watson and Jack Nicklaus. After day two, Woosnam (with a 66), Mark Calcavecchia and McCumber all trailed by two strokes behind Tom Watson, whose second 68 suggested that he could end his four-year stretch without a win. Woosnam's improvement was very much on the greens. He used a heavier putter, feeling that the greens had slowed since the first day. He also made best use of his great length, with an eagle at the 13th and birdies at two other par fives. He reached the 555-yard second hole with a drive and a five iron.

Woosnam got a grip on the championship with a 67 to lead by one from Watson and three from Olazabal and Wadkins. Four birdies in a row from the 12th offered a fine launch pad for the last round.

Olazabal caught Woosnam with three birdies in his first seven holes but dropped shots at the next three. Woosnam reached the turn three ahead of Watson, Wadkins and Olazabal. For Watson, eagles at the 13th and 15th, after a double-bogey five at the short 12th, restored his chances. Woosnam had a six at the 13th, but never faltered at the death as Olazabal, too, birdied himself into contention.

Woosnam chose a route to the last hole that perhaps only he could have managed, walloping his drive far over the left-hand bunkers and coming in a rarely used angle. He was left with a five footer that, at this stage, could hardly have been more nerve-testing. In it went, for his first major title, with Olazabal a stroke short. For the first time, foreign golfers were first and second.

# Stewart wins at tragic Chaska

**Payne Stewart: five-round slog to win US Open.**

PAYNE STEWART, 1989 US PGA champion, beat Scott Simpson in a play-off for the US Open at Hazeltine National, near Chaska, Minnesota, his first national championship victory. It was the first time that Hazeltine had staged the Open since 1970, when Britain's Tony Jacklin recorded a rare victory for overseas players.

Stewart's 1991 fortunes up to the Open did not suggest championship form, for he had withdrawn from the Masters with a nerve injury in the neck and had to wear a brace. He came back with a fourth place in the Heritage tournament, then led or shared the lead in the Open after every round, before beating Simpson over 18 holes.

The first round was delayed for some hours because of the risk of thunderstorms, which was considerable, for lightning killed a spectator, William Fadell, during that first round on July 13. Five others were injured.

Ian Woosnam, more than usually keen to do well as he was the only player in Grand Slam mode, returned a 73, six behind Stewart, but he had been five behind after 18 holes at Augusta.

The Welshman got closer next day, with a 67, Stewart staying clear with 70 over this long (7,149 yards) par-72 course. But Welsh hopes evaporated with a 79-80 finish, Woosnam sharing 55th place.

Stewart, though was caught by Simpson. The scores (73 and 72 respectively) were not brilliant, but this is a tough course, with winds coming in off the prairie. Simpson got ahead in the final round, but he drove into the rough at the last and the five it cost him was not enough to keep him ahead of Stewart, who scrambled a four.

The high-scoring play-off, which drew a crowd of 35,000, was also close. The lead changed hands several times, until Stewart birdied the 16th against Simpson's five. Usually the steadiest of players, Simpson's hoped ended with a water-bound tee-shot at the short 17th.

# Baker-Finch is the champ at Birkdale

**Ian Baker-Finch: beat fellow Aussie Mike Harwood in British Open.**

FEW PLAYERS in any generation have ever played such a positive final round as Ian Baker-Finch, the six foot four inch Australian, achieved in winning, or rather, overwhelming the British Open championship at Royal Birkdale.

Baker-Finch had the additional satisfaction of beating a compatriot, Mike Harwood, to the championship. He started in relatively sedate fashion, like Tom Watson at 33-1 against, with 71, 71. Nick Faldo was a parsimonious 13-2 and had an opening 68, congruent with his odds, but followed with 75, which was not.

Seve Ballesteros capped the revival he had been enjoying in recent months with a splendid 66 on the first day. He had broken a 12-month drought with a pair of victories in successive weekends, in the PGA Championship at Wentworth and the Dunhill British Masters at Woburn

The second round went less well for the Spaniard, with a 73, and catastrophically for Sandy Lyle, who was not well and tore up his card before the end of it. Harwood, Gary Hallberg of the United States and Andrew Oldcorn, a British professional whose career had been threatened by a viral illness, led with 139, one up on Ballesteros and five others. Baker-Finch was still four behind.

Richard Boxall, the European tour pro, broke his leg while driving at the ninth in the third round. He was only three behind the leaders at the time and, ironically, this final tee-shot was right down the middle.

On the next day Baker-Finch made a big move, a superb 64, six under par. He began with three birdies in five holes and ended eagle, birdie. At this stage, however, he was only tied at the head of affairs with Mark O'Meara, who had improved his score each day: 71, 68, 67.

This was just as Baker-Finch had been placed, though level with Tom Watson, in 1984 at St Andrews, where his approach to the first hole in his last round had spun back into the burn, and he had faded to 79.

Now, as a much more resourceful player, he seized his chance with skill and daring. To start with, he went out in 29, which no other champion has ever done, a feat which must have thoroughly depressed his pursuers as they saw his position against par improve with almost every hole. His final round:
Baker-Finch:
    4,3,3, 2,4,3, 2,4,4 = 29:
    5,4,3, 4,3,5, 4,4,5 = 37: 66
Par: 70, 6,943 yards
    4,4,4, 3,4,4, 3,4,4 = 34:
    4,4,3, 4,3,5, 4,5,4 = 36: 70

## SHORT PUTTS

● Fred Couples won the $525,000 first prize in the inaugural Johnnie Walker World championship in Jamaica.

● Meg Mallon won the Women's Open by two shots from Pat Bradley at Fort Worth, Texas. She had already won the LPGA title, and her season's earnings were $633,802. Bradley's three LPGA wins in a month earned her a place in the Hall of Fame with the 30th victory of her career.

● Chip Beck equalled Al Geiberger's tour record 59 in the third round of the Las Vegas Invitational, with 13 birdies and no bogeys, admittedly over a course of only 6,194 yards. He received a $500,000 bonus from Hilton Hotels for beating 60.

● John Daly, US PGA champion, was named rookie of the year, his driving distance at 288.9 easily the best in the 12 years the tour had compiled such statistics.

● The world's most expensive collection of clubs was sold at a Sotheby auction in Chester, England, for £627,000. All 23 clubs sold were used by a former Open champion between 1860 and 1930, including one used by Willie Auchterlonie when he won the championship in 1893, and another made by Old Tom Morris. The buyer was unknown.

● The autocratic chairman of Augusta Golf Club Hord Hardin lost a vote of no confidence and was replaced by Jack Stephens.

● Nikki Buxton completed a rare double of English Women's Amateur and English Girls' titles.

**Nikki Buxton: both English Amateur and Girls' titles.**

## SCORECARD

**British Open** (Royal Birkdale, Merseyside)
I Baker-Finch  71 71 64 66  272
M Harwood  68 70 69 67  274
M O'Meara  71 68 67 69  275
F Couples  72 69 70 64  275
J Mudd  72 70 72 63  277
E Darcy  73 68 66 70  277
B Tway  75 66 70 66  277

**US Open** (Hazeltine National, Minn)
P Stewart  67 70 73 72  282
S Simpson  70 68 72 72  282
(Play-off) P Stewart  75, S Simpson  77
L Nelson  73 72 72 68  285
F Couples  70 70 75 70  285
F Zoeller  72 73 74 67  286

**Masters** (Augusta, Ga)
I Woosnam  72 66 67 72  277
JM Olazabal  68 71 69 70  278
T Watson  68 68 70 73  279
S Pate  72 73 69 65  279
B Crenshaw  70 73 68 68  279
L Wadkins  67 71 70 71  279

**US PGA** (Crooked Stick, Ind)
J Daly  69 67 69 71  276
B Lietzke  68 69 72 70  279
J Gallagher Jnr  70 72 72 67  281
K Knox  67 71 70 74  282
Leading US money-winner:
C Pavin  $979,430;
Europe: S Ballesteros  £744,236
Year-end Sony Ranking: 1 I Woosnam,
2 N Faldo, 3 JM Olazabal, 4 S Ballesteros,
5 G Norman

**British Amateur** (Ganton, Yorks)
G Wolstenholme bt B May  8 & 6

**US Amateur** (Honours Course, Tenn)
M Voges bt M Zerman  7 & 6

**US Women's Open** (Colonial CC, Texas)
M Mallon  283

**British Women's Open** (Woburn, Bucks)
P Grice-Whittaker  284

**British Women's Amateur** (Pannal, Yorks)
V Michaud bt W Doolan  3 & 2

**US Women's Amateur** (Prairie Dunes, Kan)
A Fruhwirth bt H Voorhees  5 & 4

**World Cup** (La Querce, Rome)
Sweden (A Forsbrand & PU Johansson)  563;
(Individual) I Woosnam, Wales  273

**World Match Play** (Wentworth, Surrey)
S Ballesteros bt N Price  3 & 2

**Dunhill Nations Cup** (St Andrews, Scot)
Sweden (A Forsbrand, PU Johansson, M Lanner) bt S Africa (J Bland, D Frost, G Player) 2-1

**Walker Cup** (Portmarnock, Ire)
GB & Ireland  10, US  14

## TEE TALK

### "I can't think what came over me."

STREAKER SHERRIE BEAVON, 16, who chased José Maria Olazabal down the first fairway clad in little more than purple eye shadow.

# Ninth alternate John Daly is surprise PGA champion

THE FIRST MAJOR of 1991 was won by a famous small Welshman who could hit the ball a long way, Ian Woosnam. The last was won by a big man who no-one had ever heard of, called John Daly, who could hit the ball a very long way indeed. Daly, a 25-year-old Californian, was still at home in Dardanelle, Arkansas, on the eve of the US PGA championship at Crooked Stick, Carmel, Indiana, more than a seven-hour drive away.

He was the ninth alternate for a place in the event, calculated according to his position on the secondary Hogan Tour, for he had got through the PGA qualifying school as recently as the previous autumn.

With 48 hours to go before tee-off time at Crooked Stick five players had pulled out and the next three alternates were all loath to chance a trip to Carmel in the hope that more vacancies would occur.

Daly, however, took that chance and, by the time he reached Carmel late on Wednesday night, South African Nick Price, the 1988 British Open runner-up, had departed because his wife was about to give birth to their first child. Daly was in.

Daly stands slightly under six feet tall, is blond and weighs 175 pounds, and took on Crooked Stick sight unseen. A lengthy course this, at 7,289 yards, suited to a man of Daly's talents. His enormous length off the tee enables him to reach par fours of around 450 yards with a drive and a shortish iron. Par fives of any description he could reach in two.

He began to attract attention only when he had added a second-round 67 to his opening 69, thus taking a lead of one shot over Bruce Lietzke.

The small man from Wales, Ian Woosnam, had led round one with 67 in company with Kenny Knox, three times a winner on the tour. Former majors winners Sandy Lyle and Craig Stadler were among those a shot behind.

Daly, hailed as "Wild Thing" and "Macho Man", became an immediate front-rank attraction as the galleries swelled to watch him bully the ball, with a long, long swing reminiscent of pictures in Victorian golf magazines, to unheard-of distances. Nor was his short game one to be sneezed

John Daly: triumph of the long-distance driver in more ways than one.

at. Like many powerful men, he had a sure touch around and upon the greens. This became clearer as he added 69 in the third round, despite dropping two shots at the eighth. He found water beyond the green, over which he flew with a sand wedge which travelled 150 yards. Nevertheless, he was three clear of Stadler and Knox.

He remained two clear at least of all challengers throughout the final round and his 12 under par total gave him $230,000 (£137,000), a lifetime exemption to the championship and a ten-year exemption on the tour. At one time he would also have earned automatic Ryder Cup selection. "I don't think I'm quite qualified," he said, "but if they were to pick me, I'd be trying, desperately."

## US regain Walker Cup

GREAT BRITAIN and Ireland's rare Walker Cup win at Atlanta was followed by defeat, at Portmarnock in Ireland, to a US team inspired by Phil Mickelson, a left-hander with delicate shot-making skills, particularly with short pitches off bare lies.

He and Bob May lost to Liam White and Paul McGinley, as the home side fought back from four points down overnight to 9-7. Mickelson then beat Atlanta hero Jim Milligan and the United States won the series 5-3 to regain the Cup 14-10.

Gary Wolstenholme restored the balance a little by beating May 8 & 6 over the 36-hole British Amateur final at Ganton, where his late father had won the Brabazon Stroke Play trophy.

"I don't even drive that far when I go on vacation."

RAYMOND FLOYD,
on John Daly.

"You couldn't sit down with a blank piece of paper and create something better. He will make millions."

HUGHES NORTON,
marketing man for Greg Norman, watching Phil Mickelson at the Masters distributing golf balls to children, whose fathers he addressed as "Sir".

"America's pride is back. We went over there and thumped the Iraqis. Now we've got the Ryder Cup back."

PAUL AZINGER.

"I saw two spike marks on my line. It looked a left, a left putt. I talked to my caddie. He said 'Hit it left centre and firm to avoid the spike marks.' That's what I tried to do. It did not go in."

BERNHARD LANGER,
speaking about that putt.

Bernhard Langer: his "Hold your breath" putt wouldn't drop and the Cup was lost.

# Langer's missed putt brings Ryder joy for US

THE BURNING desire of America's professionals to get the Ryder Cup back from Europe was exemplified, wrote Michael Calvin in the "Daily Telegraph", by a purple plastic Statue of Liberty, ten feet high, beside the practice ground at the Ocean Course at Kiawah Island, South Carolina, where the 30th Ryder Cup match was to begin on September 27. Nearby was a banner: "Ryder Cup – an American tradition", neatly ignoring the fact that Samuel Ryder was British.

No denying however, that it was an American tradition to win the Cup. The elevation of the match to the status of a sponsorship and media bonanza because of the infusion of continental Europe's finest also brought some chat and counter-chat more characteristic of heavyweight title fights.

American captain Dave Stockton implied that Europe had been wrong not to visit the course in the spring. Bernard Gallacher replied that most of the European team had never seen Muirfield Village four years before, but still won there. There were even invocations of the Gulf War successes over Iraq.

When the talking stopped and play started (to the sound of rebel yells) between, over and around the massive dunes on which Pete Dye built his (some said, monstrous) course, it was a roller-coaster of a match.

Gallacher's strategy was to lead off with Europe's most potent pairing, Seve Ballesteros and José Maria Olazabal, and anchor the foursomes and four-balls with Nick Faldo and Masters champion Ian Woosnam. This worked beautifully at the top, the Spaniards taking three wins and a half, but after two blanks, Faldo and Woosnam were split on the second day. Woosnam won with Paul Broadhurst and Faldo lost heavily with David Gilford against Paul Azinger and Mark O'Meara, Faldo's worst Cup reverse of all at 7 & 6.

The United States' Cup-wise fighters, Ray Floyd, Lanny Wadkins and Hale Irwin, were their strengths in the early stages. Floyd is unique as a former non-playing captain returning to the fray. Though Europe were 3-1 down on the first morning, they cut the deficit to 4½ to 3½.

Back came Stockton's team, working up a three-point advantage by lunch on the second day, upon which a rally by Europe secured three wins out of four in the second series of four-balls, the only pair failing to win being the Spaniards, who got a half against Fred Couples and Open champion Payne Stewart. Before this potentially life-saving series, the Spanish pair had won all but 1½ points of the European team's total of 4½.

Broadhurst had a splendid debut in the second four-balls, beating Irwin and Azinger with the help of a fine recovery to less than three feet by Woosnam out of the waste sand beside the 17th green. This was proving a daunting short hole at 197 yards, hitting the green being all but obligatory if anything was to be made of it. At this stage it was causing most bother to the home team.

Suddenly it was 8-8 going into the last-day singles, still not a happy position for Europe since, year in and year out, America had been dominant in this area, Europe's last win being in 1985, though they had held the Cup since then.

There was an additional complication in that Stockton, over breakfast, pulled out Steve Pate, who had been slightly hurt in a car crash the previous Wednesday, though he did play in the four-balls on the second day with Corey Pavin, and lost. This turned out to be an astute move, since Pate was due to play Ballesteros, who surrendered only half a point throughout. Gallacher withdrew Gilford, so the day began at 8½ points apiece with 11 singles to go.

The climax was tense almost beyond bearing. A major triumph for Gallacher was David Feherty's defeat of Stewart, hard on the heels of Faldo's win over Floyd in the top match. Azinger, Pavin and that increasingly dependable Cup fighter, Chip Beck, replied for America, while Colin Montgomerie claimed a remarkable half from Mark Calcavecchia, who had been four up with four to play, but had two triple bogeys.

Broadhurst won again and so, inevitably, did Ballesteros against Levi, and all came down to Irwin's half with Bernhard Langer. Irwin had been two up with four to play. Langer squared at the 17th, and on the 18th faced a four-foot putt to beat Irwin, who had already bogeyed, tie the match and take home the Cup. It was a "Hold your breath, this for the Cup" moment. Langer missed, right edge, and the "War on the Shore" as the hype of the day went, was won by America, 14½ to 13½.

**Lanny Wadkins (right) beat Mark James (left) at Kiawah Island.**

# Couples lays 'no goals' jibe by riding his luck to land Masters

ALL FRED COUPLES'S rivals were apprehensive about his crushing spell of form as they headed for Augusta. Two wins, two seconds, a third and sixth in six tournaments meant the 32-year-old had already pocketed over one million dollars.

There was no letting up in the Masters, Couples taking his first major by two shots from his Ryder Cup partner and mentor, Ray Floyd. Only in the final round did he fail to break 70, but for that he was gladly forgiven because he had ended the four-year domination exerted by British golfers at Augusta.

Like all champions, he had a touch of luck on the way. In the final round, his tee shot at the short 12th, Golden Bell, the graveyard of so many Masters pacemakers in years gone by, was short but stuck on the bank a foot above the water and did not drop back into the Rae's Creek.

"How that ball did not roll back in, I cannot imagine," said Nick Faldo. "It was not even as if it plugged in the bank. It even rolled back from where it had pitched."

Floyd's vast experience of such happenings brought a most philosophical approach. "Everything you do for 72 holes will not be perfect. You need to get a break at a good time." Besides, hadn't Faldo enjoyed a touch of good fortune at that very spot in his first Masters win?

**Fred Couples: hot on PGA Tour, masterly at Augusta.**

Many watchers on television thought Couples had erred in flicking a ball out of the water, bouncing it on his club, then putting it back in the creek immediately after chipping close to the flag. It seems certain this was the ball of the defending champion, Ian Woosnam, who had just passed that way. But as the ball was in a hazard, his action was not a proper stroke, said the rule-givers, and besides, he was entitled to make sure he had not played the wrong ball.

Couples had made America wait a long time for this major since he won his first significant event, the Players' Championship in 1984. He struck many of his admirers heretofore as being a little too laid back.

He recognized this failing in himself and, after his Masters win, he thanked Christy O'Connor (who beat him on the final day of the 1989 Ryder Cup because he went into the lake at the 18th and O'Connor didn't) for waking him up to reality.

He admitted he had got away with more bad shots than Australian Craig Parry, who had shared the lead with Woosnam at halfway, and led the field after 54 holes, one ahead of Couples. Perhaps, but Parry, nicknamed "Popeye" because of his giant forearms, had not putted well.

Woosnam had foundered at the 12th (part of "Amen Corner", so named because mistakes there meant "amen" to hopes of victory) and Faldo had missed a crucial putt on the ninth that would have brought him to within a stroke of Parry and Couples. Even with a final 68, Norman ended six shots shy.

Ian Ridley writing in the "Daily Telegraph" quoted Tom Weiskopf's oft-repeated view of Couples: "Great talent, no goals in life," then added: "Couples the choker had become Steady Freddie."

# Caroline Hall is Britain's Cup heroine at 18

THE "BABY" of the Great Britain & Ireland Curtis Cup team at 18 years and six months, Caroline Hall was at the climax of the most exciting month of her life as she stood 160 yards from the 18th green at Royal Liverpool on June 6 with a four iron in her hands. She had won the English Amateur title in May and was potentially one good approach shot away from the point that would regain the Curtis Cup from the United States.

Her opponent, Vicki Goetze, who had won the American Women's Amateur before her 17th birthday, had struck her approach to the last hole into a greenside trap. Caroline coolly put the most crucial shot of her young life 20 feet past the pin. Goetze came out from a nasty downhill lie in the sand 15 feet short. Hall put her putt to six inches, Goetze missed for par and the one-hole win thus gained gave the Cup to Liz Boatman's team 10-8. Caroline and Julie Hall (no relation) had won two halves together, and Caroline won both her singles: three points out of four.

Joanne Morley from Sale had also played a vital, unbeaten role. In partnership with Claire Hourihane from Ireland she had won on the first day, against Tracy Hanson and Carol Semple Thompson, and halved on the

**Caroline Hall: proud debut.**

second. Having halved her first-day single with Amy Fruhwirth, she beat her on the second day after being two down at the seventh. Morley was "Daily Telegraph" golfer of the year in 1991, when she played a key role in England's European Team championship win. Her consistent low flight with a touch of fade was well suited to the chill winds of Hoylake, where it was remarked that the Curtis Cup was better supported than the Walker Cup usually was. But then the women's side, with important help from a Scot, Catriona Lambert, and from Vicki Thomas of Wales, had now won a third Curtis match in four starts.

# Tom Kite the five-million-dollar champion

**Tom Kite: rode his luck at Pebble Beach to earn an overdue major.**

THOUGH HE HAD outdistanced all other money-winners on the US PGA circuit, with more than $6.5 million before the season began, Tom Kite was an unfulfilled golfer until Sunday, June 21, at Pebble Beach, with his 17th professional win, the US Open.

Kite, 42, was not the oldest Open winner, but had tried the patience of his keenest fans for far too long. He atoned for making his friends and admirers wait by winning against the odds on a course whose degree of difficulty on the final day was extreme.

The biggest falling off of all was to be the dreadful fate of Gil Morgan, 19 years on the tour but with only one win since 1983. He led round one with 66. Kite's one-under-par 71 left him one behind the leading visiting players, Nick Faldo and Colin Montgomerie.

Dr Morgan, a qualified optician, took a firm grip in round two with a 69 that put him on 135, three clear of Andy Dillard, and five of Montgomerie. Kite trailed by eight. Three behind him came Faldo, who crashed to 76.

Morgan, first player to be at ten under par during a US Open, moved even further ahead in round three, seven clear of the field after seven holes, then slid dramatically backwards. From his best position of 12 under par he plummeted to four under after 54 holes, still ahead of the field despite his round of 77, but by only one stroke, from Kite, Mark Brooks and Ian Woosnam.

The weather had been calm for three days, but everything changed on the fourth, blustering winds adding mightily to the difficulties of the course, notably the small greens, now faster and less receptive. There was also the matter of the rough, which had been allowed to grow long close to the greens.

Montgomerie finished three hours before the final groups, and had the best of the conditions, the wind saving its worst for the last players to tee off. Nevertheless, he had the best fourth round, 70, of any player with a winning chance. The conditions were worsening by the minute, so his total level par 288, offered a fair prospect of the title.

He had two disappointments to come, first from Jeff Sluman who just got past him with a 71, and then from Kite, whose 72 brought him victory and pushed the Scot into third place on his

**Gil Morgan: unprecedented tumble in US Open.**

first try for the title. Kite did so in a wind that tore off the Pacific and demanded skill, courage and a little bit of luck, notably at the short seventh overlooking the ocean, only 107 yards but dead into the wind. He missed the green but chipped in for a two.

The greens by now were of fierce pace, added to which standing still to putt was not easy. Kite holed a putt of 30 feet across the 12th green and got a birdie at the long 14th by aiming for the rough on the left of the green rather than going for the flag and running through into trouble. He and Sluman alone finished under par, both Woosnam and Faldo fading to the high 70s along with many others. Poor Morgan finished with an 81 for a share of 13th place.

## Sheehan hits double top

TWO YEARS after missing a wonderful chance of the US Women's Open, Patty Sheehan captured that coveted prize in a play-off against Juli Inkster, despite making a somewhat unorganized start by leaving her clubs in her hotel.

When reunited with them at Oakmont, Pennsylvania, Sheehan got round in 72, one over par, Inkster missing from about two feet twice on the second nine and losing by two. Nearly three weeks later Sheehan, 35, became the first player to complete the transatlantic double, taking the British Women's Open at Woburn by three shots from Corinne Dibnah of Australia and by five from France's Marie Laure de Lorenzo.

Sheehan's golf was something special, finishing with a record 67 round Woburn for a total of 207 and the £50,000 first prize, the total purse being £300,000.

Sheehan had focused her whole attention on rebuilding her fortunes after the San Francisco earthquake of 1989 had destroyed her home. There were record crowds of 8,000 (plus the television cameras) to watch the fireworks and Sheehan did not disappoint them.

The weather was less obliging, though, restricting affairs to only 54 holes.

● Fred Couples was fully recovered from post-Masters blues when he and Davis Love snatched the World Cup by a stroke from Sweden with a birdie apiece on the last hole in Madrid. Couples led the tour money winners, too, and his stroke average of 69.38 earned him the Vardon trophy.

● A Maori, Philip Tataurangi, was New Zealand's inspiration as they won the Eisenhower trophy for the World Amateur team title in Vancouver. In the Espirito Santo women's event Britain & Ireland lost by a stroke to Spain.

● Ray Floyd became the second man after Sam Snead to win on the PGA Tour in four different decades.

● Richard Boxall made his return to the European Tour after breaking his leg while only three off the lead in the Open at Birkdale seven months earlier with a 68 during the Turespaña Masters. "It's a minor miracle – I expected to miss the cut by plenty," he said.

● Spain (Macarena Campomanes, Estefania Knuth and Laura Navaro) overtook Great Britian and Ireland (Joanne Hockley, Joanne Morley and Catriona Lambert) to take their second Women's World Team title in four years by a stroke in Vancouver.

● Arthur Lees, four times a Ryder Cup player died aged 84 after 28 years as pro at Sunningdale.

# Faldo almost throws away The Open

A THIRD OPEN title for Nick Faldo at Muirfield took him back to the top of the world rankings. At halfway the championship looked a formality for Faldo. He had followed an opening 66 with 64. His 36-hole total of 130 lifted him three clear of Gordon Brand junior and the American, John Cook, and broke the record set by Henry Cotton at Royal St George's in 1932 and equalled by Faldo and Norman two years ago at St Andrews. Faldo reckoned this 64 "the best round of my life".

An eagle at the ninth set Faldo alight, and put him within a stroke of the leader. It was achieved with a 240-yard, three wood approach to four feet ("a career shot", said Faldo). He followed this with four more birdies.

While Faldo prospered to a total of 130, three ahead of Cook and Brand, Jack Nicklaus, though favoured with a huge ovation as he walked up the final fairway, missed the cut for only the second time since his first British Open appearance in 1962. Tom Watson, a winner here 12 years ago, Seve Ballesteros, Fred Couples and Colin Montgomerie also departed.

Faldo's third round of 69 was merely adequate, taken alongside his brilliance of the first two days, but it made his 54-hole score the daunting one of 199, four ahead of Cook and Steve Pate, and equalled the record he set at St Andrews in 1990.

For Faldo the angst was still to come. He was three strokes ahead with eight to play, then plunged to two behind Cook with four to play. Cook's chance seemed to have gone when he drove out of bounds at the ninth, where he had chipped in for an eagle on Saturday. Flurries of rain and a cold wind did not prevent Cook from saving shots at the 12th, 15th and 16th. Faldo, behind him, played "a very negative wedge" into a bunker at the 11th and took five. Three putts at the 13th and a drive into a bunker at the 14th meant three shots, and the lead, lost in four holes.

Faldo told himself that he must now play the best four holes of his life to retrieve the situation. He did. His second to the 15th offered a three-foot birdie putt. He chipped to save par at the 16th and attacked the long 17th with might and main, and got between the banks that guard the green to set up an eagle putt. He missed it, but before he tapped in his birdie putt Cook was bogeying the last hole. He had, catastrophically, missed his birdie putt of little more than two feet on the 17th.

Faldo needed to par the last hole to win the title. His second shot was a trifle long and his putt back down the slope looked to an anxious nation as if it would never get there. It got near enough for Faldo to hole out without further alarms.

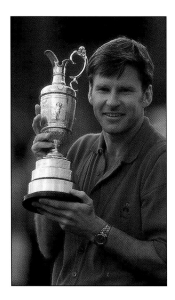

**Faldo: clinging to the Auld Mug he thought he'd thrown away.**

**John Cook looks aghast as his short putt refuses to drop.**

# Europe shock US in Solheim Cup

FIRED UP by a much-publicized comment by Beth Daniel of the United States team ("You could put any one of us in the European side and make it better") Europe's women professionals led by Mickey Walker won the Solheim Cup 11½ to 6½ on October 4 at Dalmahoy near Edinburgh.

In many ways this was the shock result of the year, since the LPGA was the richest and most talented-in-depth women's tour in the world, and by some margin, too. The Americans fielded a team of ten players who between them had won 20 major championships and 147 LPGA Tour events. But what was that about a woman scorned?

Walker had determined her tactics for the first two days weeks beforehand. The night before the match Laura Davies, again the inspiration of the Europeans, gave the thumbs up sign as she shouted from the office window of the Women Professional Golfers European Tour to Alison Nicholas that they would be playing Beth Daniel and Betsy King, first and second in the US Open.

The two Americans had beaten Davies and Nicholas in the first Solheim match and, fierce competitor that she is, Davies saw this as the key match to win. Which is what the English pair did in the top match next day, at the final hole, having gone round in 69 in miserably wet conditions.

Another flash point occurred in this match, at the par-five 11th. Greens had to be swept clear of water repeatedly, the rule being that the greens would be squeegeed only before an approach shot was played. The Americans' ball was just off the green for two, and referee David Parkin said their next would be a chip, not an approach, and refused their request for further squeegeeing. As Nicholas prepared to play her chip, Daniel and King continued their discussion on the point, and Nicholas requested quiet. This argument would run and run. Overall, Europe led 2½ to 1½ after the opening foursomes.

Next day left the Americans still one point down after the four balls, Davies and Nicholas winning again, beating Juli Inkster and Patty Sheehan at the 18th.

**Alison Nicholas (foreground) and Laura Davies.**

King and Meg Mallon also won at the 18th, against Dale Reid and Pam Wright, the other two matches being halved.

The third day singles, so often the scene of American dominance in Ryder, Curtis and Walker Cups, completed Europe's triumph, Davies leading the way with her third point in three starts, at the expense of Brandie Burton. Davies had signalled her intentions by drilling two huge wood shots 495 yards into the heart of the opening par-five green. She went on to claim five more birdies and won at the 16th, pulling up six under par.

Helen Alfredsson, Trish Johnson, Pam Wright (against Patty Sheehan), Catrin Nilsmark – who struck the winning putt before being engulfed by her joyous teammates, Lotte Neumann and Dale Reid were the other European Tour winners in a 7-3 singles victory, Daniel extracting a small revenge by beating Florence Descampe 3 & 1.

# Medlen bags another US PGA championship, this time for Nick Price

ANOTHER LATE developer, 35-year-old Nick Price, won the final major championship of 1992, the US PGA, at Bellerive, St Louis. He had earned nearly $3 million on the American tour in previous years, but had never come closer to a major title than a decade ago at Troon, where his unhappy last nine holes let in Tom Watson. That Open he lost, but Seve Ballesteros imperiously won when Price was second at Lytham in 1988.

This Durban-born six-footer was brought up in Rhodesia, which became Zimbabwe on independence. Of English parentage, he carries a British passport and lives in Florida. "I'm a bit of a hotch-potch," he will say. He served in air force signals during the hostilities in Rhodesia.

He had pulled out of this championship 12 months previously because of the imminent birth of his son, who duly arrived on the second day of the US PGA. His caddie, Squeaky Medlen, was at a loose end till the ninth alternate turned up, one John Daly. Together they carried off the prize.

No such luck for Daly this year. Medlen was restored to Price's side and Daly's game was in need of a restorative. He made the cut, but only just, and there were few to watch him putt out the 72nd hole early on the last day. Daly was battling with the media, and accused them of treating his life like a soap opera. He made a television defence of his dispute with an air stewardess, who had asked Daly and his caddie to leave her aircraft, and rejected reports that alcoholism was a problem. He wanted to put 1992 behind him. It did all sound just a little soap operatic, quite apart from disqualifications and card destruction. Price, though he did little at Muirfield, had finished joint sixth in the Masters and fourth at Pebble Beach. His putting had cost him better finishes, but he got all departments of his game working at Bellerive. This was just as well with its 7,148 yards of narrow fairways and four-inch rough. Price paced himself nicely

**Nick Price: a major title at last at the Bellerive US PGA.**

throughout the championship, starting with two 70s, to lie two under par at halfway, four behind Gene Sauers, who was having his most lucrative year to date, his ninth on the tour. Nick Faldo was two off Sauers's pace, his putting working well in round one with a 68.

Protestations by Jeff Maggert about being an average player (in his first US PGA) sounded hollow in round three, when he went round in a record 65, one better than Briton Steve Richardson had managed 24 hours earlier, but he was still two behind Sauers with a round to go. Price was coasting along on Sauers's heels, level with Maggert.

Faldo seemed out of it with a 76, still upset, perhaps, at his losing battle in the second round with the rough beyond the 17th

which cost him his birdie there. Faldo came back strongly in the final round with 67, finishing level with his Muirfield rival John Cook, Sauers and Jim Gallagher in second place behind a composed Price, whose 70 gave him a comfortable three-shot margin. His was not a spectacular victory, but his play spoke volumes about nerve and course management. He did not birdie a hole till the 11th, but dropped only one shot, with a hooked drive, at the 15th. He got it back with a birdie at the next hole. So Squeaky Medlen brought in the champion again, not to mention his share of $280,000 (£150,000).

Faldo had the satisfaction of again being the best majors performer of the year, averaging an impressive fifth.

**TEE TALK**

**"Once you only wanted to interview me after I had done a 65. Now it's a 75. I don't know how Jack Nicklaus has stood it all these years."**

FRED COUPLES,
on his post-Masters celebrity.

**"You'd think we could afford a lawn mower out here, wouldn't you?"**

BELLERIVE PRO JERRY TUCKER.

# Langer wins second Masters by four shots

DAVID LEADBETTER, Nick Faldo's coach and swing remodeller, named in the Daily Telegraph four men with the right game to win the Masters. This quartet, he said, would best meet Augusta's challenge because of their ability to move the ball from right to left off the tee and flight iron shots so that they landed softly on the treacherously contoured greens.

The four, in order of ability to fill the bill, were Nick Price, Greg Norman, Bernhard Langer and Payne Stewart. Leadbetter was right third time. The devout Langer, who often led the golfers' prayer meetings, said that Easter Day was always going to be a great day regardless of whether or not he won the Masters. As it was he donned his second green jacket eight years after the first and is the 12th man (and third European) to win two.

Since 1987, when Langer won using an orthodox putting grip, he had, and not for the first time, suffered agonies with putting. His solution was to clamp the handle of the putter with the right hand against the left forearm, thereby locking both wrists.

Langer's explanation for the European run of successes in the Masters is as follows. Unlike USGA and PGA courses, with punitive rough fertilized and sometimes raked up to impart added difficulty, the Augusta pattern is for clean lies round the greens, to which Europeans are accustomed.

Jack Nicklaus thrilled the galleries on the first day by leading on 67 in company with another former winner, Larry Mize, and (of more recent vintage)

Bernhard Langer: Leadbetter's canny Masters tip.

Tom Lehman, Corey Pavin and Lee Janzen, who had just gained his first tour victory at Tucson, 17 under par.

Langer scored 68, and was still one behind the leader, Jeff Maggert, after 36 holes, which were completed on Saturday

morning after Friday's rains stopped proceedings.

The third round was completed on a fine, sunny afternoon, but the sun shone chiefly on Langer, who alone of those in contention broke 70 in a stiff breeze. He led by four with a round to go.

Faldo was 10 over par after Saturday's 79, and made amends with a final 67, but the damage inflicted by Amen Corner in rounds two and three was irreparable. The par for the three holes of this little loop is 12. Faldo took 16 strokes in the second round and 15 in the third. Now he used only 11.

Langer was as cool as the weather was hot on the final day, his 70 giving him a four-stroke margin over Chip Beck, with a revitalized John Daly in third place two strokes further back in company with Steve Elkington, Lehman, and Lanny Wadkins. Dan Forsman, who had got to within a stroke of Langer before running up a seven with two shots into the water fronting the short 12th, tied for seventh with José Maria Olazabal on 284.

Beck, playing with Langer, got within two strokes and hit a beauty over the water to the 13th. So did Langer, who holed his eagle putt into the bargain. But Beck was castigated for his caution at the 15th where, like Langer, he laid up in front of the water, which surprised the German.

# Lee Janzen answers call for new blood

THE BEST PLAYER no-one's ever heard of: that was Lee Janzen's lot before he held off Payne Stewart hotly pursuing his second US Open title. His peers were quick to notice that he had improved each year on the tour since joining it in 1990, and he shared the first-round Masters lead in April. Bernhard Langer had come out on top then, and American golf was avidly searching for fresh talent to repel the invaders.

Janzen, 28, added his second tour victory, the Phoenix Open in January, to the Tucson Open he won 12 months earlier, and his first round 67 at Baltusrol, New Jersey, gave him a share of second place with Craig Stadler, one behind the trio in first place – Scott Hoch, Joey Sindelaar and Craig Parry the Australian. No-

one could match Janzen's pace in round two, another 67, which gave him the lead by two over Tom Watson and Payne Stewart, and equalled the 36-hole Open record.

If he had beaten it, Nick Faldo, Ian Woosnam and Sandy Lyle would have missed the cut. Faldo had endured a bad enough second round as it was, spilling much blood when his sliced second shot on the sixth fairway hit a spectator on the back of the head. The shot caused much pain to both watcher and watched. Faldo finished with a triple bogey 7.

Janzen also equalled the 54-hole Open record of 203, with 69 in the third round, but led by only one from Stewart, who reckoned his experience would see him through next day. It didn't,

Lee Janzen: clear thinker at critical moment in US Open.

because of Janzen's refusal to fall behind. He emulated Lee Trevino with his fourth sub-70 round, 69, greatly helped by a 30-yard chip-in on the 16th, for an eight-under-par total of 272, matching Jack Nicklaus's score here in 1980.

The birdie on the 542-yard 18th that gave him a two-shot margin over Stewart showed he could think constructively in a tight corner. Stewart was in position A off the tee, Janzen in the right rough, which was not of the usual USGA severity. He considered a neck or nothing shot but, two ahead, reflected that to go into the intervening water at this stage would be plain silly. So he laid up. Stewart went for it and found sand. Janzen, relieved, struck his third shot to six feet and got the putt down.

# Greg Norman's Open 'the greatest' says Sarazen

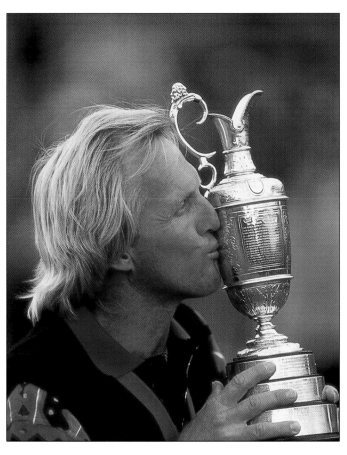

Greg Norman's second Open: relentless driving and iron play.

GENE SARAZEN is 91, with more than 70 years in and around top-class golf, including an Open of his own achieved over the fence at the Prince's course at Sandwich. So he should know, and what he said after Greg Norman's second Open championship at Royal St George's on July 18 was: "This was the great-est championship I have known. I have never seen such golf."

Two years ago, Norman, 38, the Great White Shark from Queensland, had seriously considered giving up after seeing so many big prizes disappear when almost in his grasp. Luckily for the galleries at Sandwich he didn't give up. The bald recital of what he achieved is impressive enough. His closing 64 was the lowest Open-winning final round.

His 267 total, 13 under par, beat by one Tom Watson's mark set at Turnberry in 1977. He was the first champion to break 70 in all four rounds, though Ernie Els from South Africa beat Norman to it by an hour or so. Els was joint sixth, which tells its own story about the standards maintained.

The style of Norman's victory, carrying a prize of £100,000 for the first time, was above mere figures, notably in that last round when Nick Faldo chased him with golf of the highest order, producing a 67 but falling two strokes short of a fourth Open. Payne Stewart, all too late, equalled the event record with a 63, a feat Faldo had achieved to lead by one from Bernhard Langer and two from Fred Couples, Norman and Corey Pavin in round two.

Norman, whose total was nine shots better than anyone had hitherto achieved at Royal St George's in 11 previous Opens, was close to faultless in the most vulnerable position of all, that of the leader.

His driving and iron shots were consistent, his putting hard-ly less so. He will doubtless tell his grandchildren that it should have been a 62, for he did commit two errors on the greens.

He began with a birdie, thanks to an accurate nine-iron approach, and also birdied the third and sixth. The first slip came at the long seventh. From just off the green he under-hit his approach putt, which rolled back down to his feet from the plateau of the green. He put his next close to the pin for his par five.

His relentless driving and iron play continued to give him every prospect of more birdies, and he got one at the ninth, where he put his nine-iron approach stone dead. Out in 31, he was now on his own.

A drive and a sand wedge earned another birdie at the par four 13th, and a chip from the rough at the Canal hole, the 14th, led to a birdie four. The 15th can be a tease for those who hit their second left of the green, from where to stop by the pin needs an angel's touch. Here Norman got down in two for par from the right of the green, and hit his self-assessed "shot of the day" at the short 16th, a five iron to four feet for a two.

Possibly he was thinking of his acceptance speech when he missed from two feet at the 17th, but a drive and four iron to the last, one of the most demanding finishing holes in golf, completed a true champion's round.

# Azinger is the latest to thwart Norman

WITHIN A month of his marvel-lous British Open victory, more disappointment loomed for Greg Norman as he lost a play-off for the US PGA championship to Paul Azinger at Inverness, Toledo. Norman has now, uniquely, lost play-offs for all four majors: to Mark Calcavecchia (in the British Open), Larry Mize (Masters) and Fuzzy Zoeller (American Open).

Azinger's right to this, his first major title at the age of 33, was unarguable. Vijay Singh from Fiji demonstrated how quickly he had settled down to American conditions by leading after 36 holes. He broke the course record with a 63, eight under par, to put up a halfway score of 131, 11 under par and two clear of Australian Steve Elkington and Lanny Wadkins. Norman now moved ahead, his third round of 67 giving him the lead by a stroke over Azinger, Bob Estes, Hale Irwin (now 48), Wadkins (despite his third-round shot-of-the-day eagle from 146 yards at the 14th), Tom Watson and Singh, whose third-round score was ten in excess of his second. Nick Faldo kept in close contention with 69, his third sub-70 round.

The finale was warm work, in 90-degree heat, and riveting, since 17 players were within four strokes of one another at the head of affairs.

The title finally came down to a struggle between three players, first the dogged Faldo, scoring 68 – one too many. He had broken 70 in each round, but was over-taken by Azinger, whose hat-trick of birdies from the 12th suddenly brought him to the forefront. He was followed in by Norman, who had recovered well after taking two shots in a bunker at the sixth and wasting a shot at the seventh through thinning a chip. Four birdies restored him to a 69 and a tie on 272 with the "Zinger". The first extra hole, the tenth at Inverness, was halved in fours.

At the second, the 11th hole, Norman's first putt lacked convic-tion and he missed the next after Azinger, whose approach had fin-ished closer to the cup, missed his birdie putt by a fraction, but it was enough for Paul Azinger to collect his first major champi-onship and leave Norman rueing another missed opportunity.

Paul Azinger: birdie hat-trick big help on way to US PGA title.

# US clinch another Ryder Cup thriller

ANOTHER KNIFE-EDGE Ryder Cup match before huge crowds and beside one of the biggest tented villages ever erected ended in 15-13 victory for Tom Watson's US team at the Belfry, which had greatly improved spectator facilities.

As usual, everything turned on the singles, in which the Americans have been much the stronger over the years. They went into single combat a point adrift, and this time they won often enough (7½ to 4½) to regain the Cup.

Watson's choice of Ray Floyd and Lanny Wadkins as his wild cards proved to be inspired. Floyd, at 51, lost his first match, but won the next three, including his single with José Maria Olazabal.

Wadkins had won two and lost one when he went to Watson on the eve of the singles and asked to be "the player in the envelope", which meant that if Sam Torrance, suffering from a septic little left toe, was still unable to play on the last day, Wadkins would be the man to drop out and be deemed to get a half against the Scot.

Watson appreciated the gesture. It made his decision easier, and Wadkins felt in any case that, as he had not played his way into the team, then as a "wild card" he should be the discard.

Ian Woosnam was the top scorer on either side. He halved his single with Fred Couples and was the only 100 per cent player in foursomes (winning twice with Bernhard Langer) and fourballs, winning twice with Europe's brightest new recruit, Peter Baker. A Walker Cup player at 17 in 1985, Baker, a Midlander, beat in-form Corey Pavin on the last day, a wonderful effort, considering that he spent most of the previous night at the nearby Good Hope hospital, where his daughter Georgina

had been undergoing tests for meningitis, which by tee-off time on Sunday had, happily, proved negative.

The worry for Europe's captain, Bernard Gallacher, had always been the form of the two Spaniards. Seve Ballesteros and Olazabal lost their opening foursome, but won in the afternoon and next morning, during which Ballesteros asked to be left out of the afternoon four-ball. There were diametrically opposed views as to whether Gallacher should have acceded to this request.

The upshot was that Olazabal partnered the first Swede to play in the Cup, Joakim Haeggman, and they lost. This chink in Europe's armour widened on the final day, Ballesteros losing easily to Jim Gallagher.

The crux of the battle on that day turned out to centre upon another historic debut, that of Costantino Rocca, the first Italian Ryder Cup player. Yet his unhappy last two holes against Davis Love III were placed under the microscope because the experienced European players behind him were struggling. While Haeggman won on his debut, Ballesteros, Olazabal and Langer lost, and Faldo was held by Paul Azinger, despite Faldo's hole in one at the 14th. Barry Lane, another newcomer, was three up after 13 holes, but finished 5,5,5, and lost at the last to an accomplished rally by Chip Beck, whose eagle three at the 15th trumped Lane's birdie. The final blow was Rocca's three putt on the mighty 17th, where his birdie attempt for a 2 & 1 win was too strong. He missed the one back. Love's par levelled the match. Rocca drove poorly on the 18th, was lucky to overfly the lake in front of the green, chipped indifferently, and Love's par was good enough for the crucial Cup-winning point.

**Peter Baker: from hospital to singles success.**

## RYDER CUP

(The Belfry, W Midlands) Europe 13, US 15
Captains (non-playing): Europe, B Gallacher; US, T Watson

**FIRST DAY Foursomes: Morning**

| Europe | | US | |
|---|---|---|---|
| S Torrance & M James | 0 | L Wadkins & C Pavin 4 & 3 | 1 |
| I Woosnam & B: Langer 7 & 5 | 1 | P Azinger & P Stewart | 0 |
| S Ballesteros & JM Olazabal | 0 | T Kite & D Love III 2 & 1 | 1 |
| N Faldo & C Montgomerie 4 & 3 | 1 | R Floyd & F Couples | 0 |

**Four-balls: Afternoon**

| | | | |
|---|---|---|---|
| I Woosnam & P Baker 1h | 1 | J Gallagher Jnr & L Janzen | 0 |
| B Langer & B Lane | 0 | L Wadkins & C Pavin 4 & 2 | 1 |
| N Faldo & C Montgomerie | ½ | P Azinger & F Couples | ½ |
| S Ballesteros & JM Olazabal 4 & 3 | 1 | D Love III & T Kite | 0 |

First Day: Europe 4½; US 3½

**SECOND DAY Foursomes: Morning**

| | | | |
|---|---|---|---|
| N Faldo & C Montgomerie 3 & 2 | 1 | L Wadkins & C Pavin | 0 |
| B Langer & I Woosnam 2 & 1 | 1 | F Couples & P Azinger | 0 |
| P Baker & B Lane | 0 | R Floyd & P Stewart 3 & 2 | 1 |
| S Ballesteros & JM Olazabal 2 & 1 | 1 | D Love III & T Kite | 0 |

**Four-balls: Afternoon**

| | | | |
|---|---|---|---|
| N Faldo & C Montgomerie | 0 | J Cook & C Beck 2h | 1 |
| M James & C Rocca | 0 | C Pavin & J Gallagher Jr 5 & 4 | 1 |
| I Woosnam & P Baker 6 & 5 | 1 | F Couples & P Azinger | 0 |
| JM Olazabal & J Haeggman | 0 | R Floyd & P Stewart 2 & 1 | 1 |

Second Day: Europe 4; US 4
Match aggregate: Europe 8½; US 7½

**THIRD DAY Singles**

| | | | |
|---|---|---|---|
| I Woosnam | ½ | F Couples | ½ |
| B Lane | 0 | C Beck 1h | 1 |
| C Montgomerie 1h | 1 | L Janzen | 0 |
| P Baker 2h | 1 | C Pavin | 0 |
| J Haeggman 1h | 1 | J Cook | 0 |
| M James | 0 | P Stewart 3 & 2 | 1 |
| C Rocca | 0 | D Love III 1h | 1 |
| S Ballesteros | 0 | J Gallagher Jnr 3 & 2 | 1 |
| JM Olazabal | 0 | R Floyd 2h | 1 |
| B Langer | 0 | T Kite 5 & 3 | 1 |
| N Faldo | ½ | P Azinger | ½ |

S Torrance (injured) and L Wadkins both withdrawn at start of day: half agreed
Singles: Europe 4½; US 7½

# Pyman pips Page at Portrush

MICHAEL BONALLACK, Royal & Ancient secretary and five times British Amateur champion, said that the final between Paul Page, 21, of Kent and Iain Pyman, 20, of Yorkshire was the best in his memory.

Pyman got home at the 37th at Portrush after the pair swapped birdies regularly, with

Pyman lying dormy two after his eighth birdie. Page got level, thanks to Pyman missing a two-foot putt at the 36th hole, only to miss the putt at the 37th that would have kept the final alive. Pyman was also the low amateur in the Open championship, beating Guy Wolstenholme's record 283 by two shots.

### TEE TALK

**"Arsenic."**

BEN CRENSHAW,
to a bartender asking him what drink he wanted after a 79 trying to qualify for the Britsh Open.

**"I seem to be forever surrounded by Svens."**

HOWARD CLARK,
on the rising Swedish challenge.

### SCORECARD

**British Open** (R St George's, Sandwich, Kent)
G Norman  66 68 69 64  267
N Faldo  69 63 70 67  269
B Langer  67 66 70 67  270
C Pavin  68 66 68 70  272
P Senior  66 69 70 67  272

**Masters** (Augusta, Ga)
B Langer  68 70 69 70  277
C Beck  72 67 72 70  281
T Lehman  67 75 73 68  283
J Daly  70 71 73 69  283
S Elkington  71 70 71 71  283
L Wadkins  69 72 71 71  283

**US Open** (Baltusrol, NJ)
L Janzen  67 67 69 69  272
P Stewart  70 66 68 70  274
C Parry  66 74 69 68  277
P Azinger  71 68 69 69  277
S Hoch  66 72 72 68  278
T Watson  70 66 73 69  278

**US PGA** (Inverness, Toledo, Ohio)
P Azinger  69 66 69 68  272
G Norman  68 68 67 69  272
(Azinger won play-off at second extra hole)
N Faldo  68 68 69 68  273
V Singh  68 63 73 70  274
T Watson  69 65 70 72  276
Leading US money-winner:
N Price $1,478,557;
Europe: C Montgomerie £710,896
Year-end Sony Ranking: 1 N Faldo, 2 G Norman, 3 B Langer, 4 N Price, 5 P Azinger

**British Amateur** (R Portrush:, Co Antrim, N Ire)
I Pyman bt P Page 37th

**US Amateur** (Champions, Houston, Tex)
J Harris bt D Ellis 5 & 3

**US Women's Open** (Crooked Stick, Carmel, Ind)
L Merten 280

**British Women's Open** (Woburn, Bucks)
K Lunn 275

**British Women's Amateur** (Royal Lytham, Lancs)
C Lambert bt K Speak 3 & 2

**US Women's Amateur** (San Diego CC, Cal)
J McGill bt S Ingram 1h

**World Cup** (Lake Nona, Fla)
US (F Couples & D Love III) 556;
(Individual) B Langer, Germany 272

**World Match Play** (Wentworth, Surrey)
C Pavin bt N Faldo 1h

**Walker Cup** (Interlachen, Minn)
US 19, GB & Ireland 5

# Newcomer Fisher scores double

DAVID FISHER, 21, a county player from the Stoke Poges club west of London, won both the Brabazon trophy for the English Amateur Stroke Play title, holding off Philip Tataurangi, low scorer in the 1992 Eisenhower trophy and the English Amateur championship, in rough July weather on the Devon links course at Saunton. The double had not been achieved for 25 years, since

Michael Bonallack brought it off.

Fisher did not gain a place in the Walker Cup side at Minneapolis, however, which caused controversy. It was alleged that administrative cares were put above above team selection, Fisher being apparently passed over for late selection so that information sent to the USGA for inclusion in the match programme would be up to date. The

Americans named half their team ten days before the match (August 18-19).

Fisher was seldom required to play the 18th hole at Saunton where he made good use of Bernhard Langer's anti-yip method for short putts, holding the putter well down the shaft in his left hand, and pressing the top of the grip against the left forearm with the right hand.

# US overpower GB & Ireland 'boys'

BRITAIN AND Ireland suffered their most humiliating Walker Cup defeat in 30 years at Interlachen, Minneapolis. America's blend of youth and experience proved, above all else, that players who keep their game together over the final holes carry off prizes. They won 19-5.

The visitors' average age was 21. Opposing them were young tigers like Amateur champion Justin Leonard and seasoned tournament players old enough to be their fathers, like Jay Sigel, Allen Doyle, Danny Yates and local hero John Harris, who was making his debut at 41, and won the Cup-clinching point against

British champion Iain Pyman. The following week he beat Danny Ellis for the national Amateur title.

A change in the match format, the first for 60 years, was enforced when the first series of foursomes was washed out. It was agreed to play ten singles later that day, and four foursomes and ten more singles the next, so that 24 points would still be on offer.

Early play in the first singles looked promising for Britain and Ireland, but the bottom line was 6½ to 3½ in favour of Jay Sigel's side. Typical of the pattern of play was the half rescued by Kelly Mitchum by winning the last three holes

against former English champion Stuart Cage.

Next day Pyman was beaten twice to complete an unhappy hat-trick, which was also the lot of Bradley Dredge and Raymond Russell. The United States won the foursomes 4-0 and, but for the Irishmen, would have had a clean sweep in singles. Padraig Harrington, the only visitor with previous Cup experience, halved with Brian Gay, and Raymond Burns, three down after three holes, beat David Berganio at the 18th.

Mathew Stanford, the oldest of George MacGregor's team at 24, Van Phillips and Dean Robertson were Great Britain and Ireland's other points scorers.

### SHORT PUTTS

● US PGA champion Paul Azinger, 33, began treatment for lymphoma cancer at the end of the year and will miss at least six months' competition while undergoing chemotherapy and radiation. The cancer was found in his right shoulder.

● Four British Open title-winning medals won by the late Bobby Locke were auctioned for £82,800 at a Christie's sale in London. The sale of Locke's trophies, clubs, paintings and memorabilia raised a total of £178,089. The first British Open medal Locke won, at Royal St George's, Sandwich, in 1949, attracted the highest bid – £24,150.

● Bernard Gallacher agreed in September to a third term as Europe's Ryder Cup captain.

● Unsolved mystery on day one of the Australian Open in November, wrote Bruce Critchley, the Daily Telegraph's man in Melbourne, was how, on a peerless day and a course set up to be fair with minimal rough and friendly pin posi-

tions, it still took the afternoon groups almost six hours to get round.

● Two Stoke Poges players, Charles Challen and Van Phillips, shared the "Golf Illustrated" Gold Vase at Sunningdale, where Bobby Jones won the trophy in his Grand Slam year. They played the Old and New Courses in 131, and both bettered Gary Player's record 64 over the New Course, Phillips with 63, Challen with 62.

● America finished a banner year holding the Ryder, Walker, World and Dunhill Nations cups. Corey Pavin won the World Match Play title, and Larry Mize the World championship in Jamaica.

● More than 25,000 boys and girls entered for the "Daily Telegraph" young golfer of the year competition. Georgina Simpson, 17, won the girls' event and Denny Lucas, 16, took the boys' crown.

● Shock of the Year: Scotland 1, Paraguay 2 in the Dunhill Cup.

● John Daly, named in a poll as the world's most exciting golfer, well ahead of Seve Ballesteros and Nick Faldo, was suspended in November for picking up his ball and failing to finish at a tournament in Hawaii.

**John Daly: "world's most exciting golfer" finished the year under suspension.**

# Olazabal extends European grip on Masters

José Maria Olazabal: eagle at 15th paved way to Masters win.

BY WINNING his first major title at Augusta, José Maria Olazabal not only got his own career back on track at 28 years of age, but sounded a rallying cry for European golf after America's almost complete domination of 1993.

The Masters, won nine times in 15 years by Europeans, was a different matter. As 1993 champion Bernhard Langer helped Olazabal on with his green jacket, the Spaniard became the sixth European Ryder Cup player to enjoy that ceremony (Seve Ballesteros, Nick Faldo and Langer, twice). The last American Master, Couples, was absent with back trouble. Unhappily also, Paul Azinger was undergoing chemotherapy for cancer, and Phil Mickelson was in plaster with leg bones broken in a skiing fall.

It looked for a long time as if Augusta-born Larry Hogan Mize, who had stunned the World championship field with the serenity of his stroke play in Jamaica before Christmas, would win again. He led at halfway with 139, while Tom Lehman, who had finished joint third 12 months before, Dan Forsman and Greg Norman were a stroke behind.

Sandy Lyle, Sam Torrance, Nick Faldo, Langer, Ballesteros and Ian Woosnam never seriously threatened, and Woosnam did not enjoy four rounds in company with John Daly, back after suspension, and surrounded by adoring fans.

Olazabal got within two shots of Mize by adding a 67 (five birdies and no bogeys) to his initial 74. His world had seemed to fall apart after the 18th hole disaster when Woosnam won in 1991. His driving became untrustworthy, but John Jacobs, an early teacher of Olazabal, returned to improve his shoulder turn, and he gained confidence with a gritty victory at the second extra hole against Paul McGinley in the March Turespaña Open. Even more significantly, he was second to Ben Crenshaw at New Orleans four days before the Masters.

Greg Norman laboured under a mountainous burden of hype, for he had been in Olympian form, beating off a chest infection to win on the European Tour (in Thailand!) and then stretching credulity with a 24-under-par Players championship win, a record by six shots at Sawgrass where, on his 67th hole, he

dropped his first shot in 93 consecutive competitive holes. He ran into a brick wall of frustration at the halfway stage of the Masters, finishing 75,77.

Olazabal finished 69, 69 for a nine-under-par total of 279 despite the fiendish difficulty of getting approaches close to the pin on greens so dry they took on a blue tinge.

In 1990 his former Spanish Youth Team coach told the author, with great emphasis, during the British Youths' championship, which Olazabal had won five years earlier, that this was the best putter in the world. This one was tempted to believe during a tense last nine holes on a lovely Sunday afternoon as Lehman, a devout Christian who had preached at a local church before teeing off, and Mize faltered on the greens and Olazabal

got the security he wanted with a 30-foot eagle putt from the edge of the 15th green, after his approach almost rolled back into the creek. Lehman beat his head on the ground in anguish as his eagle attempt flicked the edge of the hole.

Olazabal dropped his first shot at the 17th, cutting his lead to one, but doubled it again on the last, with a good chip and putt after Lehman was bunkered off the tee, and with an iron at that.

Olazabal is from San Sebastian in northern Spain (his father was a greenkeeper) and is managed not by a major agency but by a personal friend from his cadet days, Sergio Gómez, a choice that reflects his independent spirit. His victory to some degree legitimizes metal "woods", for he is the first to win the Masters with one.

Ian Woosnam: found it wearing to play with John Daly.

Paul McGinley: felt the power of Olazabal's return to form.

Paul Azinger: the 1993 US PGA champion was facing a far harder battle off the course.

# Azinger returns

NEW ENGLANDER Paul Azinger was robbed of the chance of extending to eight his run of at least one tournament win per year by lymphoma of the right shoulder blade diagnosed late in 1993, when he finished second on the money list.

In August 1993, he was on top of the world after capturing his first major, the US PGA championship. But within a couple of months everything was put on hold. He made defending his title a target and by August he was back on tour after chemotherapy and radiation treatment. Azinger impressed everyone by finishing joint 19th in the Buick Southern Open, and 33rd at Lake Buena Vista before back spasms cut short his come-back in San Antonio.

# Ballesteros ends two-year famine

INSPIRED PERHAPS by José-Maria Olazabal's Masters victory in April, Seve Ballesteros aged 37 ended a 26-month famine by taking the £108,330 first prize in the Benson and Hedges International on the Jack Nicklaus course at St Mellion, Cornwall. Nick Faldo was three shots adrift. British Boys champion David Howell was the only one of four amateurs to survive the cut.

# VAT rethink poser for clubs

VALUE ADDED TAX on members' fees had been paid for four years when in February Her Majesty's Customs and Excise admitted that it had been a mistake to levy the tax (at 17.5 per cent) on non-profit-making amateur clubs. Talk of a £150 million refund was bruited about, but Alan Grosset, secretary of the British Sports Forum, warned that a windfall was unlikely, though in the longer term, sport would cost people a bit less.

**TEE TALK**

**"Go there, be patient. You know what to do. you're the best in the world"**

SEVE BALLESTEROS,
in a note pinned to Olazabal's locker at Augusta.

# Fly-on-wall TV empties boardroom

EVERY DIRECTOR of a north London suburban golf club, Northwood, resigned after the club president Ken Whitaker, 72, said they felt that they had brought the club into disrepute by allowing Channel 4 television to film a fly-on-the-wall documentary.

Members felt that the film, in the Cutting Edge series, had made the club a laughing stock (which it certainly had) because it indicated they were a stronghold of male chauvinism and Freemasonry.

Reports circulated later that the film's producers had sought out a club where women members were not allowed full facilities. They had chosen well if their aim was to pillory male chauvinism. Women members were seen at a general meeting where they held only a watching brief, for they had no votes and were not

entitled to do so much as speak (nor might they play at weekends). A club official told on film at the annual general meeting what the television critic of the "Daily Telegraph" called "an absolute whopper". He denied that he had threatened to expel a member, but he also appeared in the film doing just that.

Perhaps the most amusing insight into the members' thinking was that some seemed more upset about the implied message that they were a set of geriatric hackers than they were about the lies and chauvinism.

Men are not wholly to blame for restrictions on women golfers. Wirral Ladies' Club are one of the few women's clubs that have survived, along with Formby Ladies' nearby, founded in 1896. Wirral Ladies' celebrated their centenary with an extension to their clubhouse

and, in "A Centenary Portrait", Lord Evans of Claughton tells of the way social attitudes between the wars afflicted his aunt, a skilled golfer, who had been the first lady at Aberdare GC, with the young Dai Rees as caddie. She was seeking to join Wirral Ladies' when she came north as a schoolmistress.

"My mother proposed her in the usual way. In a very short time Miss Maud Henry (the formidable ex-governess who ruled the Club with a rod of iron) asked my father to go and see her in her office and said she had noticed that my aunt, Miss Dyllis Jones, was described as a spinster. She asked my father if she had an occupation.

"When my father said she was a schoolmistress Miss Henry told him that Wirral Ladies' Golf Club did not encourage working women to join the Club."

# Double-edged libel verdict

JOHN BUCKINGHAM had a £250,000 bill awarded against him at Nottingham County Court where the jury cleared Reginald Dove and Graham Rusk, fellow-members at Sherwood Forest, of maliciously telling the club committee that Buckingham, 57, moved his ball with his foot, and dropped another ball from his trouser leg during a tournament

four years ago in 1990.

Buckingham, who had retired after selling his insurance business for £3m, failed in his libel case, brought after Dove and Rusk refused to apologize or pay his share of a £6,000 internal club inquiry which found the allegation not proven.

The jury added rider that they did not want their verdict "to be

perceived as proof that Buckingham had definitely cheated".

His counsel, Patrick Milmo, QC, suggested during the trial that he had been the victim of a group which considered Buckingham, a former miner, "riff-raff".

An appeal was not entered, because of the cost, and Buckingham resigned from Sherwood Forest.

# Chokemont? – not for 92-hole E

NOTHING CAME easily to the 24-year-old South African Ernie Els in the US Open, for he needed an extra 18 holes before he could shake off Colin Montgomerie, and another two to account for Loren Roberts in subsequent "sudden death". He is the youngest to take the title post-war, except for Jack Nicklaus and Jerry Pate who, like Els, won at only his second attempt.

The greens at Oakmont, Pennsylvania, so fast as to render the stimp meter useless, are of the score-wrecking type. A ball released from the device's metal chute here is likely to trundle on till it hits the rough, unless a sizeable flat section of putting surface can be found – no easy task.

Accurate iron play and an angel's touch on the green were clearly required, and many looked to José Maria Olazabal to provide both, as he teed off with the Masters and two European Tour wins already to his credit, including the Volvo PGA Championship. The severity of the course was reflected in the cut mark at five over par. "Toughest I've seen," said Nick Faldo – prophetic, for he was among the fallen on Friday evening after two days bedevilled by morning fog or lightning. So was Olazabal, the defending champion Lee Janzen, and his runner-up at Baltusrol, Payne Stewart, along with Ian Woosnam, Nick Price ... the carnage was great.

Tom Watson, a few months short of his 45th birthday, found that the greens "rejected the ball". But he took the heat and other weather worries in his stride, and led Jack Nicklaus, Ernie Els, Frank Nobilo and Hale Irwin by a stroke with 68 in round one, cut short by a thunderstorm with 18 players still in action. A half-inch of not unwelcome rain fell, serving to ease the greens a little. At half-way, Colin Montgomerie's 65, six under par, put him two shots ahead of Irwin, John Cook and David Edwards. Nicklaus was still only three off the lead, but Arnold Palmer, to a huge and sympathetic reception, was out.

There were no more delays during the three days remaining of the Championship, certainly not to Els's progress in round three. His 66 set him up two ahead of Nobilo. He swept to his first European Tour win at Dubai in January with a 61 in the first round, holding off Greg Norman by six shots. Two years ago he sped through the Gary Player treble of South African Open, Masters and PGA title. At 24, here was a player of vast potential. Watson took issue with those who said no-one would ever dominate the game again ... "his rhythm is beautiful ... maybe it will be Ernie Els."

Roberts admired every part of Els's game, but like Montgomerie, at 24 the same age as Els, made the going tough for the South African.

Els did not make it particularly easy for himself in round four, but then neither did his closest rivals. Montgomerie led at the turn reached in 33 shots. Curtis Strange caught Els with three birdies in a row from the third hole, then began to drop shots. Roberts closed on Els with a lengthy chip-in at the 249-yard eighth after seven pars, holed for birdie at the long ninth, and went ahead at the 13th. Roberts and Phil Mickelson vie for the title of smoothest putter on Tour, but Roberts, by his own account, pushed the six-foot putt that could have won him the Open. Montgomerie had fallen back with bogeys at 11, 12 and 13, and estimated that he had blown his chances by a stroke, despite finishing steadily with a birdie at the 17th and par at 18th for a total of 279.

Els began and ended uncertainly, hooking from the first and the last tee, where he was unaware that Roberts had dropped a shot on the green up ahead. Els's ball landed on the fifth tee. He chipped out – into a divot – and finally holed a four foot bogey putt to get into the three-way play-off. A fury of room rebooking and ticket exchanging followed.

Els's final round of 73 was his worst by far, but one shot better than the 74 he scored on the fifth day. Roberts had the same score, Montgomerie 78, for though he played the last seven holes in one under, three double bogeys had wrecked the big Scot's card. The disappointment was just as sharp as when Tom Kite and Jeff Sluman overtook him at Pebble Beach two years ago.

This was a messy play-off, and there was talk of Chokemont, Els triple-bogeying the second hole. He didn't have to play that hole again, since the sudden death climax began at the 10th, with a par four apiece. (Here came a TV pause as American stations went west to picture OJ Simpson in court on a double-murder charge.)

Roberts hit into the rough on the 11th, then into a bunker, missing his up and down for par by a whisker. Els, 15 feet away in two, lagged his approach too enthusiastically, but sank the "one back" from four feet for par and title. What with the heat and extra-extra time, celebrations with caddie and girl-friend Lizel were brief, as Els became the second South African after Gary Player and fourth foreign-born player to win the US Open since Tommy Armour in 1927.

**Ernie Els: a hard-earned US Open win at only his second attempt.**

**Loren Roberts: try as he might he could not shake off Els.**

# Both hands this time for Price

Nick Price: massive putt at the 17th proves decisive.

THE 123RD OPEN CHAMPIONSHIP at Turnberry did not start with the best of vibrations, since too many leading Americans were absent, some without a word of explanation. Among the missing were Fred Couples, Curtis Strange, Hale Irwin, Lanny Wadkins and Raymond Floyd. On the other hand, only one American – Mark Calcavecchia in 1989 – had won since 1983.

The excitement of Nick Price's eagle on the 17th that gave him the edge over Jesper Parnevik, the way the weather smiled over the last two days on the huge galleries (Jack Nicklaus attracted thousands, and that was only during practice rounds), proved that the Open had not lost its Royal and Ancient charms. Besides, Price, at 37, had

paid his dues in this event, manfully withstanding the double blows it had dealt him as he frittered away the 1982 title (Tom Watson the beneficiary) and had been hammered by Seve Ballesteros in the (rain-delayed) Monday head-to-head of 1988, despite a closing round of 69.

Businesslike, brisk, crisp and other such epithets were applied to his swing: his putting could be deadly, and was on Sunday, July 17th. Price, who had served two years in the South African Air Force, was born in Durban, but now lives in Orlando.

As the championship came down to the last nine holes, Price could be forgiven for believing that Tom Watson was again going to come between him and the Auld Mug. Greg Turner had

led on day one with a 65, but Watson took over after 36 holes, with a seven under par total of 133. Parnevik and Brad Faxon were one behind him. Things became very crowded on Saturday night, for Fuzzy Zoeller and Faxon had taken three more shots overall off par, and at 201 stood one clear of Price, Parnevik, Watson and Ronan Rafferty, Price's partner for the final round.

Watson's chances of equalling Harry Vardon's six Opens had, by the bookies' reckoning, improved in less than 24 hours hours from 50s to 16s. With 10 holes remaining, Watson, aged 44, shared the lead, and his popularity in Britain was the reason the bookies were now thinking about cancelling that Barbados holiday after all as punters plunged for the still boyish-looking Kansan. His double bogeys at the ninth and 10th as tiddler putts squirmed out led to a 74, and joint 11th place.

Parnevik, son of a renowned Swedish comedian, Bo, and to some observers a little bit of a comic himself in his cap with the turned-back peak, was by contrast sailing along. He holed birdies at four holes from the 11th to the 17th. He was concentrated on playing the course, stroke by stroke, and taking no notice of what was going on around him. He did this, fatally as it turned out, to the extent of not looking at the scoreboard on the 18th fairway. The message there was that a par four would bring a 268 total. That would, apart from last year at Sandwich, have won at least a play-off in any 72-hole Open ever played. From the roars behind him he deduced that rivals were close at hand, though some of them were the reward of saving chips and ups and downs from awkward places by Rafferty and Price.

But after five birdies in his last seven holes, despite a stiff breeze, Parnevik was thinking the positive thoughts of a 29-year-old, and sought to make it a little more difficult for the chasing pack. He went for the pin, and came up short in rough that yielded little by way of tight control on his recovery shot. His par putt from nearly three yards missed, and his total was 269.

Almost simultaneously Price had a 50-foot eagle putt to

size up on the 17th. As it curved towards its target, the ball took a tiny hop – a spike mark perhaps – but nothing prevented it racing on and diving into the hole. Price leapt in the air – and almost at once saw that Parnevik had bogeyed the 18th.

That did not stop his heart racing, he said, until his par on the last hole was completed with two iron shots and two putts, for a 268 total. Like Greg Norman, last year, he had managed four rounds in the 60s but won £110,000 – £10,000 more than the Australian.

Price thought he could not have played the last three holes better than he did, three under par. The 1993 player of the year was well on the way to a repeat performance.

Parnevik dedicated his fine performance to grandparents, who died this year. Nick Faldo had regrets too, for playing the wrong ball in round one had knocked him off balance, and he scored 75. Yet a last day 64 had brought him up into joint sixth place with Tom Kite and Colin Montgomerie.

## TEE TALK

**"In 1982 I had my left hand on the trophy. In 1988 I had my right hand on the trophy. Now, finally, I have both hands on it."**

NICK PRICE,
receiving the silver claret jug

**"Golf is indeed an honest game."**

STRATHCLYDE POLICE
after 95% of lost credit cards and wallets were handed in at Turnberry.

**"I have always looked at leaderboards"**

NICK PRICE
at Turnberry

# Price reaches top of the Tree

NOT SINCE WALTER HAGEN in 1924 had anyone won the British Open and US PGA title back to back. Nick Price did it at baking Southern Hills in Oklahoma, dubbed by some the "blast furnace championship".

Moreover, the win took Price to the top of the Sony World rankings. It also dismayed US golf from its headquarteres in Far Hill, New Jersey, to the smallest nine-hole club. Never before in modern times had all four majors gone to non-Americans.

There were precious few signs at Southern Hills of Americans or anyone else parting Price from the lead in an event he had also won in 1992. True, Colin Montgomerie did equal Price's first round 67, but he fell away as Price led by five at half-way, three after 54 holes, and six from Corey Pavin at the death.

Others finishing at a respectful distance were Phil Mickelson, seven adrift, and Nick Faldo, Greg Norman, and John Cook, joint fourth but eight off Price's pace. Price missed tieing Jack Nicklaus's championship-winning record of seven shots when his return putt on the 72nd lipped out.

The other notable winner was Arnold Palmer, making his 37th PGA start. He was presented with the PGA's Distinguished Service Award and gladly forgiven for "not playing very well" on his last try at the title – the only major he never could win.

John Daly, walking out of a tournament in Hawaii, had been suspended by the PGA and did not start the season till March, and lost his chance of repeating his 1991 PGA triumph when he failed, by a stroke, to qualify at Southern Hills.

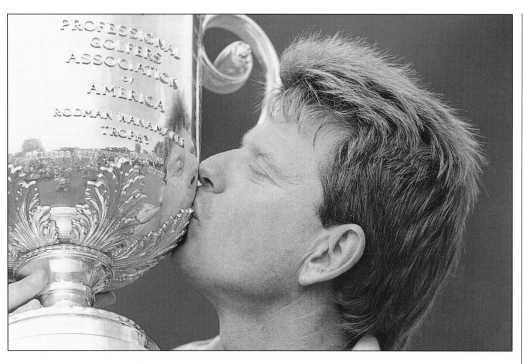

Nick Price: shades of Walter Hagen at Southern Hills.

## Greg's World Tour rattles the PGAs

THE RULING BODIES of professional golf were wrestling by year's end with a knotty problem set by Greg Norman. He, Rupert Murdoch and Fox TV were intent on setting up an eight event World Tour featuring the game's leading 40 players.

All manner of objections seethed through the minds of Tim Finchem, commissioner of the US Tour and his peers worldwide. Would these new events, for the richest purses yet, put the four majors at risk, and thrust the fixture lists on five continents in turmoil? The problem was shelved for a time at least by Finchem's declaration that joining Norman's plutocrats would mean expulsion from the US PGA Tour. Few players are willing to risk long-term prosperity for quick gains.

# Janice Moodie saviour in tied Curtis match

SINGLES, SO OFTEN the Achilles heel of Britain and Ireland in all manner of competition with America, were not the nemesis of Liz Boatman's Curtis Cup team at Chattanooga, Tennessee. True, the visitors only managed a 3-3 draw, but the overall score was tied also, at 9-9, so Liz took the trophy back to Britain.

The visitors were much in debt to Janice Moodie, 21, out last against the experienced Carol Semple Thompson, who needed only a half to regain the Cup. After three-putting away a chance to go ahead at the 17th, Moodie's six iron to 30 inches at the 18th was decisive, but she was disappointed at not being required to hole the putt: "I dreamed all my life of making a putt like that to win the Curtis Cup..."

Elsewhere, Emma Duggleby made a fairly late – at 22 – county debut for Yorkshire this year, but qualified at the third time of asking in the British Amateur at Newport, and went on to beat former French champion Cecilia Mourgue D'Algue 3 & 1. She lost the third, but was never headed from the seventh hole onward. Her opponent conceded after running through the 17th, where Duggleby hit the pin with a four iron from 160 yards.

Janice Moodie: and the "glory putt" she didn't need.

● After requiring emergency funding from the R&A to survive 1993, hopes of future prosperity for the Women's Professional Golfers European Tour, under new Executive Director Terry Coates, revived as 17 tournaments were set up. This is six more than last year. There was also the Solheim Cup to defend in West Virginia in October.

● The inaugural President's Cup match at Robert Trent Jones Club in Virginia ended in a thumping 20-12 win for the US over the International team – made up of leading players from the rest of the world apart from Europe. The event is to be played in non-Ryder Cup years.

● Relaxation of amateur rules continued. Expense payments for visiting amateurs were to be permitted. In the past such payments could be made only to representative teams.

● Tony Johnstone of Zimbabwe won his fourth South African event in a row when he took the Bell's Cup in George Cape Province, having been first in the South African Masters and Zimbabwe Open in Harare and the South African Open.

● Tony Jacklin, 50 on July 7, made his debut on the European Seniors Tour at Royal Lytham, the scene of his British Open triumph of 1969, but was disqualified in round one for signing for an incorrect score. He won at his fourth Seniors event in Grand Rapids, Michigan.

● In contrast to the drawn out political golfing battles that preceded the selection of Valderrama in Spain for the 1997 Ryder Cup, the USGA wasted no time at all in choosing the Country Club, Brookline, Massachusetts, for the 1999 match.

● Though Fred Couples and Davis Love III won the World Cup for the US in Puerto Rico, Tom Kite, Curtis Strange and Couples were surprised in the Dunhill Nations Cup final at St Andrews by Canada's Dave Barr, Ray Stewart and Rick Gibson.

**Love and (right) Couples: top of the world.**

# Hot Dottie is Solheim avenger

JOANNE CARNER'S TEAM secured thorough revenge for their Dalmahoy defeat two years ago in the Solheim Cup, routing Europe 13-7 at the Greenbrier, West Virginia. Dottie Mochrie in particular enjoyed the turn-about after her meagre haul in Scotland – half a point. In red hot form, and in a new hair colour (red) she was 100 per cent, first with Brandie Burton in four-somes and fourballs, then against Catrin Nilsmark, 6 & 5.

Yet the match was tied at five all going into the third day when, as so often in Ryder Cup play, singles proved to be the US forte. Only Alison Nicholas and Helen Alfredsson turned back the American tide but Laura Davies, with whom Nicholas won and then lost on the first two days, was crucially beaten by powerful Burton, who gained her own back for Dalmahoy after the English girl's ball got wet on the 16th. Davies's consolation was being at the top of the world rankings.

The 1996 Cup match at St Pierre in Wales is to feature teams of 12, with a format closely resembling Ryder Cup play. The galleries will hope not to see Mochrie whooping in delight and pumping her fist in the air as she did when Laura Davies missed a putt at the Greenbrier.

**Lotte Neumann: key European player and British Open champion.**

**British Open** (Turnberry, Scot)
N Price 69 66 67 66 268
J Parnevik 68 66 68 67 269
F Zoeller 71 66 64 70 271
A Forsbrand 72 71 66 64 273
M James 72 67 66 68 273
D Feherty 68 69 66 70 273

**Masters** (Augusta, Ga)
JM Olazabal 74 67 69 69 279
T Lehman 70 70 69 72 281
L Mize 68 71 72 71 282
T Kite 69 72 71 71 283

**US Open** (Oakmont, PA)
E Els 69 71 66 73 279 *74
L Roberts 76 69 64 70 279 *74
C Montgomerie 71 65 73 70 279 *78
Els won second hole of sudden-death play-off
C Strange 70 70 70 70 280

**US PGA** (S. Hills, Tulsa OK)
N Price 67 65 70 67 269
C Pavin 70 67 69 69 275
P Mickelson 68 71 67 70 276
N Faldo 73 67 71 66 277
G Norman 71 69 67 70 277
J Cook 71 67 69 70 277
Leading US money-winner N Price $1,499,276: Europe
C Montgomerie £920,647. Year-end Sony ranking: 1. N Price, 2. G Norman, 3. N Faldo

**British Amateur** (Nairn, Scot)
L James bt G Sherry 2 & 1

**US Amateur** (Sawgrass, Fl)
T Woods bt T Kuehne 2h

**US Women's Open** (Indianwood, Mich)
P Sheehan 277

**British Women's Open** (Woburn, Bucks)
L Neumann 280

**British Women's Amateur** (Newport, Gwent, Wales)
E Duggleby bt C Mourgue d'Algue 3 & 1

**US Women's Amateur** (Hotsprings, VA)
(W Ward bt J McGill 2 & 1)

**World Cup** (Durado Beach, Puerto Rico)
US (F Couples & D Love III) 536
(Individual Couples 265)

**Dunhill Nations Cup** (St Andrews, Scot)
Canada (D Barr, R Gibson, R Stewart) bt US (T Kite, C Strange, F Couples) 2-1

**World Match Play** (Wentworth, Surrey)
E Els bt C Montgomerie 4 & 2

**Curtis Cup** (Honours Course, Chattanooga TN)
US 9, GB & Ireland 9

**Eisenhower Trophy** (Paris, France) US 838

**Espirito Santo Trophy** (Paris, France) US 569

# Watch out, there's a Tiger about

ELDRICK WOODS, from Stanford University, California, beat Trip Kuehne by two holes in the US Amateur Championship final. Woods is not only the youngest to win the title, but the USGA think he staged the biggest come-back ever in the final. Six down at one time in the 36-hole match, he took the lead for the first time with a 12-foot putt for a birdie two on the 35th hole, having escaped the guardian lake by a foot. He was Junior champion in 1991-92-93. Woods's father is an African American and his mother a Thai, and he is nicknamed Tiger after a Vietnamese soldier venerated by his father who served in the US Army in Vietnam.

Travelling US amateur teams had a good year. The World Amateur team trophy fell to Woods, Allen Doyle, John Harris and Todd Demsey and the women's event to Sarah LeBrun Ingram, Carol Semple Thompson, and Wendy Ward, US Amateur Champion. Both events were held at Versailles, France.

# Remembering Harvey at Augusta

ABOUT THE ONLY golfing personality missing as the good and great and merely hopeful assembled at Augusta for the 59th Masters was a reliable tipster. Certainly the chances of the 1984 winner Ben Crenshaw were not discussed at any length, if at all, in the public prints. The oldest winner, Jack Nicklaus was there, buoyed up by a play-off victory over Isao Aoki in The Tradition tournament four days back, so too the youngest, Seve Ballesteros, re-invigorated by a recent high finish on either side of the Atlantic.

David Love III was there, thanks to last-gasp qualification with his play-off victory against Mike Heinen on the last PGA Tour stop at New Orleans. Who could have kept Nick Price away? He had won the last two majors, at Turnberry and Southern Hills. Three in a row would be beyond price for Price's CV. It turned out to be beyond Price: he missed the cut, with exactly the same scores as Gary Player, and said that the way he was playing, he'd rather watch on TV. Disappointing indeed for someone who set the course record (63).

A prescient tipster was not the only person missing: Harvey Penick, teacher to so many players, died aged 90. Crenshaw, who greatly revered him, flew back to Texas to act as a pall-bearer.

Scarcely surprising then that Crenshaw, aged 43, was in tears as he inserted his 274th stroke to beat Love by one and Jay Haas and Greg Norman by three, for his 19th Tour victory.

Love, whose final 66 was Sunday's best, had not made it to the top 10 in a major before. His late father was a Penick friend, too. Crenshaw named Harvey, author of the best-selling little red books of golfing instruction, as the 15th club in his bag.

Crenshaw's second green jacket was among other things the reward for doing what he excels at – putting. It is true that 72-hole tournaments have been won with fewer putts than the 110 Crenshaw took here, but in round four his birdie putts from two yards on the 16th and four on the 17th were crucial, especially on account of his bogey on the 18th – his only bogey on the last nine holes all week. This Masters was always tight at the top. Defending champion José Maria Olazabal, David Frost and Phil Mickelson led by one with 66s on day one, with Nicklaus among those one adrift. Haas was one ahead at half-way from Scott Hoch and John Huston. The

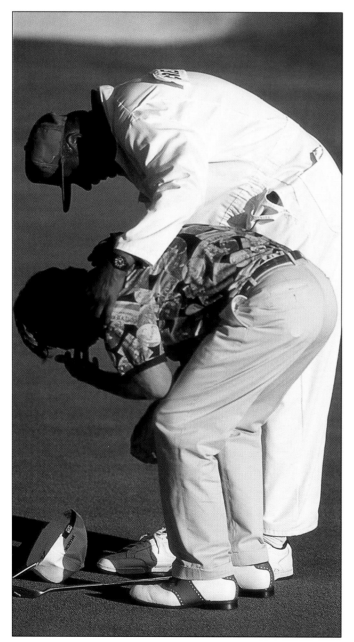

**Ben Crenshaw: bitter-sweet finale at Augusta National.**

eventual winner and Brian Henninger were top, by one over Hoch, Haas, Steve Elkington, Mickelson and Fred Couples on Saturday night.

Nick Faldo, announcing that he would keep up his home in England with wife Gill, fell from grace with a final 75, Colin Montgomerie blew it with a third round 76.

Olazabal helped Crenshaw into his second green jacket: Spain's other golfing hero, Ballesteros, had done the honours for Crenshaw in 1984. Moreover, an American had won a major after a blank 1994.

# Pavin's game takes to the Hills

THE USUAL PROSPECTS led the betting for the US Open at Shinnecock Hills on Long Island, notably Greg Norman, Nick Faldo, Nick Price, and Ernie Els. Double Masters winner Bernhard Langer was also fancied. He had just won twice in succession, the Volvo PGA Championship at Wentworth and, as usual, almost any event in his native land, this time the Deutsche Bank Open.

What the punters should have been looking for was a smallish (5ft 9in), in-form, experienced (12 wins in 14 years), mustachioed, innovative chip-and-putt artist – such as Corey Pavin, ranked 155th in Tour driving statistics. In February he won the Nissan Los Angeles Open at Riviera for the second year running: only Arnold Palmer and Ben Hogan managed that. He took Lee Janzen to a play-off in the Kemper Open four days before teeing off at Shinnecock, where the second US Open of all was played in 1896, a one-day event to follow the far more highly regarded four-day Amateur Championship.

Under sun and wind 99 years later, this most slippery of courses made ball control more difficult day by day, and the par of 70 was no gift at a chip-shot short of 7,000 yards. Only Pavin equalled it over 72 holes.

As the calming effects of rain that fell before the Open began to fade, Shinnecock got really objectionable ("an absolute bitch," said Greg Norman) on the third day, and the swaying rough brought memories of Muirfield in its hayfield mode. Tom Kite returned 82. Best of day was 67, by Tom Lehman, highly commendable, considering he had recently undergone stomach surgery. Only Ian Woosnam and Gary Hallberg, with 69 apiece, also broke par.

A more exciting last round can scarcely be imagined, as six players, led by Greg Norman and Tom Lehman initially, struggled to keep both the score decent and frustration at bay. Phil Mickelson and Bob Tway were closest at first, but Davis Love III and finally Pavin challenged as the wind rose.

Pavin came so close to a major last August, PGA runner-up to Nick Price, who could not get near par after a first round 66 here. Now Pavin's skill at enlist-

**Corey Pavin: shot to savour at Shinnecock's final hole.**

ing the help of speedy slopes and gusting wind reached new heights. He drew a four wood low more than 220 yards to within four feet of the 18th hole, surely one of most decisive and magnificent single shots ever played at the climax of a major championship. Pavin ran up the slope after it and saw it settle close in. He had two putts for a 68 and the title. His first effort was none too convincing, yet Norman was bogeying the 17th, and that was that, barring a two at the last. Yet another major had eluded him despite a gutsy scrambling display, yielding but

## TEE TALK

**"Never had a headache when I drank. Now I get them all the time."**

JOHN DALY,
discussing his various addictions

**"Sick players are the ones to watch"**

JACK NEWTON,
on ailing fellow Aussie Steve Elkington at the US PGA

## Woods gains second Amateur

TIGER WOODS, 19, WHO HAD seized the attention of Nick Price and Ernie Els at the US Open two months back ("he kept driving 40 to 50 yards past me. Ernie and I felt powerless...") won his second US Amateur title at Newport, Rhode Island, where the championship started a century ago. His two-hole final win over Buddy Marucci from Philadelphia was like his first, gained at the last hole. He was three down after 12, and two after 19, but kept ahead from the 30th. As at the Open, the fairways were fast (and unwatered), temperatures high, and the going tough. Woods and Marucci earned Walker Cup places for the match at Porthcawl in September.

one birdie over the last 36 holes.

Amateur Champion Tiger Woods, widely touted as one to watch, had to retire after damaging his left wrist. He made many news pages with his statement about his race: some, he said, thought him African American, some believed he was Asian. "In fact, I am both ... On my father's side I am African-American, on my mother's said I am Thai ... The bottom line is I am an American, and proud of it. I hope I can just be a golfer and a human being."

# Daly survives Rocca's late thrust

ST ANDREWS called up heavy winds each day to ensure that no liberties would be taken at the 124th British Open Championship – the 25th at golf's HQ. John Daly was the winner, and how typical of the switch-back career of this most unpredictable of golfers that this should be his only victory of the year. Typical, too, was the way it came about. He beat Costantino Rocca in a four hole play-off, forced by the Italian in a few seconds that changed thoughts of "Great, I'm the champ" to "Oh no, I'm not," for the American. It might have destroyed a man less assured of his talent.

To gasps of disbelief, Rocca drew level with Daly's six under par total of 282 after utterly fluffing his chip to the 18th (cue for a Daly smile and hug from wife Paulette). Rocca righted the ship with a 15-yard birdie putt up from the Valley of Sin in front of the 18th green. Daly, without a tremor, marched off for the play-off. He completed it (over St Andrews' first and last two holes) in 15 strokes, four better than Rocca – all the more fun because he hit the 17th green in two for the first time in five tries.

Domestic conflict, theatrics on and off the course, this addiction or that ... Daly, now 29, is seldom free of some such alarums. His number with the bookies was higher even than the wind-speed, at 66 to 1 against. Nick Faldo and Bernhard Langer were the favourites, and this was to be Arnold Palmer's last stand at the Open. Back problems threatened Greg Norman's chances of completing the seductive progression of Masters third, US Open second and ...

How untypical of Daly, "The Wild Thing" and recovering alcoholic, was his method of dealing with the problems set by the Old Lady. No more "Grip it and rip it" ... instead, and despite his long swing that might have been thought a handicap, he used the latest weapon, the Invex driver, made by his sponsors, Wilson. It helped him hit straight and low under the wind. He was, also, outstanding with his approach putts, often a couple of cricket pitches long at St Andrews. The ability to do both was, with four days of cool windy conditions and St Andrews' huge,

John Daly: final lap at St Andrews and (below) a kiss for Mrs D.

undulating greens to deal with, as sure a route to success as any.

The top of the leaderboard was even more crowded each day than it was at the US Open, certainly on day one, when Daly led with a 67, but with Tom Watson, Ben Crenshaw and Mark McNulty for company. David Feherty, Vijah Singh, Bill Glasson and Matts Hallberg were all a stroke away, and nine more, including Corey Pavin, only two strokes adrift. Hell bunker began a destructive few minutes for Jack Nicklaus. He took four strokes to escape it, 10 to hole out.

At least his 78 beat Palmer's 83, and he qualified next day eight strokes better, but 10 behind Daly, Brad Faxon and

Katsuyoshi Tomori, who led one clear of a gaggle of six including Pavin and Ernie Els.

The young New Zealand Michael Campbell moved into prime position in the "money round" – the third – with 65, but his game wavered on Sunday as Daly coped wonderfully well in the wind – till the 17th, where he was up against the face of the Road Bunker. Doing well to drop only one shot here, he parred the last, and waited. Rocca got his four at the 17th thanks to a masterly putt off the road beyond the green, and while he must have been confident of his ability to birdie the 18th and tie with Daly, the way he did it induced a few tears and a brief prostration in front of the old club house.

# Elkington steals Montgomerie's line

COLIN MONTGOMERIE moved to the head of the queue, recently vacated by Corey Pavin, of great players who had never won a major. He lost a sudden-death play-off to Steve Elkington of Australia in the US PGA Championship at Riviera, Los Angeles. Both men totalled 267, 17 under par, equalling Greg Norman's lowest aggregate in a major, at Sandwich in 1993. Elkington had finished first, with a seven under par 64, with never a shot dropped.

Montgomerie required birdies at each of the last three holes for a 65 to catch the Australian, who watched as the Scot lined up a 20 foot putt on the 18th to complete the birdie hat-trick he craved. In it went, and when the pair started sudden death at the 18th, Elkington was left with the same birdie putt, as far as he could judge, that Montgomerie had holed. Half a cup wide, Elkington thought, like Monty's. He was right, and his opponent, was left with a play-off record of 0 for 5, and a clutch of comforting statistics, such as 83.3% Riviera greens in regulation. He could only console himself with the thought that he had not lost the title, as Ernie Els certainly had with a final round of 72 after breaking the 54-hole majors record with 197. No, Elkington had won it.

He had not enjoyed a healthy year. Sinus problems, accentuated by an allergy to grass of all things for a golfer, had been dealt with, he hoped, by surgery last year, during which surgery was needed earlier to have a cancerous growth removed from his shoulder. A bug contracted at St Andrews (where he missed the Daly-Rocca play-off by two shots) ruled him out of the Buick Open the week before Riviera, at which he arrived short of practice and feeling far from his best. Now he could sit his five-months-old Annie in the huge Rodman Wanamaker Trophy and enjoy the title that was one step further than his previous most significant victory, in the 1991 Players Championship at Sawgrass.

**Steve Elkington: health problems forgotten at Riviera.**

## Europe's Ryder Cup woes

QUITE APART FROM Montgomerie's near miss, the PGA Championship did not improve European morale for the Ryder Cup, 40 days away, at Rochester in New York state. Most damaging of all were reports that José Maria Olazabal might be out of the Cup because of persistent foot trouble. It did not affect his golf, but his limp was getting worse. There were doubts that he could walk the 36 holes in a day that the Cup can demand of a player of the Spaniard's class. His manager, Sergio Gomez, said that if the decision was his "Olly would not play".

Moreover, while only two of the 12 Europeans at Riviera missed the cut, those two were Ian Woosnam and Seve Ballesteros. Still, Nick Faldo's chances of a wild card from Bernard Gallacher were not damaged by his final 67, his best round. The US captain, Lanny Wadkins, drew criticism after he chose Curtis Strange and Fred Couples to join the 10 players who had qualified as of right, and not Lee Janzen, with the Players Championship and Kemper Open to his credit already this year. Neither Strange nor Couples had achieved a Tour win this year, though there was no doubt about the depth of their Cup experience.

# Walker win No 4 is biggest

THE IRISH CONTINGENT took a lot of beating in a damp Walker Cup match at Royal Porthcawl. Indeed Jody Fanagan was 100 per cent, he and Padraig Harrington contributing four points towards Great Britain and Ireland's 14-10 victory, the reverse of the score in Dublin four years back, and some consolation for the record beating the United States handed out (19-5) in Minnesota in 1993. Harrington's only defeat, by the experienced John Harris, came when the match as a contest was over – giving the home team their third win in 73 years; not the Walkover Cup for once.

Gary Wolstenholme's match against double US Champion Tiger Woods on the first day explained to some degree why this Walker battle was such a crowd puller. Forecasts were greatly exceeded, with 7,000 on day one, and 9,000 as the rain battered down relentlessly on Sunday.

The legend of Woods the mighty hitter, only 19 but already with five USGA titles to his name, took a tumble in the last single on the first day. Wolstenholme is a relatively short hitter, but is very straight and can putt an opponent to distraction. He was never headed, and Woods handed him the match by hitting his approach to the 18th into an out of bounds trench.

That put Great Britain and Ireland 7-5 ahead overall, an advantage preserved in the last foursome on day two by Harrington and Fanagan against Harris and Woods, who bogeyed the last three holes. Four straight wins in singles followed to settle the issue – by the 6ft 8in British champion Gordon Sherry, David Howell over the Native American Notay Begay, Stephen Gallacher, and Fanagan. Woods got his revenge over Wolstenholme, but it was too late. Ryder Cup captain Bernard Gallacher, who had helped in Walker Cup training, was suitably encouraged.

Gordon Sherry and caddie: plotting a line to retrieve the Cup.

Gary Wolstenholme: congratulations from the Tiger (left).

## Olazabal career in peril

JOSÉ MARIA OLAZABAL is not looking forward to 1996 with any confidence. His game, particularly his irons and his putting, looks as secure as ever, his form on the practice tee impressive. But his admission to Bernard Gallacher that he gets tired towards the end of a round through agonising pain in his feet is a depressing one: 36 holes was out of the question, hence his withdrawal from the victorious Ryder Cup team and the Alfred Dunhill Cup. Nor could he defend the Volvo Championship at the end of the season.

He had limped to claim the best European place (14th) as he tried vainly to claim another green jacket at Augusta, and he helped Seve Ballesteros win the Tournoi Perrier de Paris: but his best finish in Europe was 10th.

He was able to play in only seven European Tour events, though his playing status for 1996 was protected on health grounds. Being able to take advantage of this was doubtful.

Christmas was spent crawling round his home in northern Spain, the few feet from bedroom to bathroom frequently the limit of his mobility. Specialists diagnosed rheumatoid arthritis – for which there is no cure – and Morton's Neuroma among other things. Various remedies and treatments gave temporary relief, but no certainty that he would be able to resume his career, which had brought him more than £3million in prize money alone in 10 years.

# Europe's Cup, Pavin's glory

FORMER EUROPEAN RYDER CUP captain Tony Jacklin gave it as his opinion that Bernard Gallacher's European team to met the United States at Oak Hill, Rochester, New York, on the shores of Lake Ontario in late September, was not good enough. Certainly it lacked a European banker in José Maria Olazabal, who asked to be omitted because of his painful feet. Curtis Strange, Lanny Wadkins' wild-card selection for the American team alongside Freddy Couples, said he would 100 times rather win a Tour event that make the Ryder team.

Jacklin was wrong, and Strange may have wished momentarily that he hadn't made the team. He lost in all his outings, notably as he was overtaken and beaten by Nick Faldo in a crucial single that left Europe needing a point to regain the Cup after two defeats. Philip Walton, said to have backed his team with £1,000 at 5 to 2, soon provided that with the five-yarder he rolled dead at the 18th against Jay Haas.

This was not a typical Ryder Cup performance by Europe, in that they trailed after the foursomes and four-balls 9-7, then won the singles 7-4 with one match halved. David Gilford, in his second Cup match, won three of his four matches, Costantino Rocca, atoning for his 1993 lapse against Davis Love III, won three from five, as did Sam Torrance, giving him even greater cause for rejoicing because, aged 42, he was £30,000 ahead of Colin Montgomerie in the European Order of Merit, in which Montgomerie was looking to land a hat-trick.

The outstanding player at Oak Hill was easily identified. Fittingly, it was the US Open Champion, Corey Pavin. His captain called upon him to play in every series of matches. In the first two days Pavin, partnered by Tom Lehman, Phil Mickelson, Lehman again and Loren Roberts, lost only once, with Lehman in Saturday's foursomes, to Bernhard Langer and David Gilford. The third of these points, gained in the last fourball with Roberts, was snatched with a last-hole coup to rank alongside his four-wood heroics at Shinnecock. Faldo and Langer had never led against the US pair, but were level on the 18th tee. Faldo found the fairway, and his approach finished 17 feet from the flag. From the rough, Pavin overshot the green, so Europe looked likely to go into the singles level-pegging at 8 all.

Pavin then chipped in for a birdie three that Faldo could not answer, giving Wadkins a 9-7 launch-pad for the final day. Lehman soon made it 10-7, routing a wayward Ballesteros, who had to call too often on his power of recovery, a talent that nevertheless still amazed.

In the next eight singles, Europe scored six points and a half – by Ian Woosnam, still without a Ryder singles win in seven attempts. This was achieved entirely by British Isles players, since all the continental players lost. Pavin didn't, it almost goes without saying. But the Cup tide flowed vividly the other way as Howard Clark scored an ace in beating Peter Jacobsen (Rocca did it on Saturday). Mark James, Gilford, Montgomerie, Torrance and Faldo followed up. Faldo's wedge and four foot par putt at the last to turn the tables on Strange was crucial – for in match 11 Philip Walton from Dublin was dormie three up on Jay Haas.

Shakily enough he came up with Europe's seventh, decisive win. Had Haas's third shot not spun back off the green at the 18th, Walton, might not have made it. But he and, at the third attempt, Gallacher, did.

## RYDER CUP

(Oak Hill CC, Rochester NY) US 13 ½; Europe 14 ½
Captains (non-playing) L Wadkins (US), B Gallacher (Europe)

### FIRST DAY Foursomes: Morning

| US | | Europe | |
|---|---|---|---|
| C Pavin & T Lehman 1h | 1 | N Faldo & C Montgomerie | 0 |
| J Haas & F Couples | 0 | S Torrance & C Rocca 3 & 2 | 1 |
| D Love III & J Maggert 4 & 3 | 1 | H Clark & M James | 0 |
| B Crenshaw & C Strange | 0 | B Langer & PU Johansson 1h | 1 |

### Four-balls: Afternoon

| | | | |
|---|---|---|---|
| B Faxon & P Jacobsen | 0 | D Gilford & S Ballesteros 4 & 3 | 1 |
| J Maggert & L Roberts 6 & 5 | 1 | S Torrance & C Rocca | 0 |
| F Couples & D Love III 3 & 2 | 1 | N Faldo & C Montgomerie | 0 |
| C Pavin & P Mickelson 6 & 4 | 1 | B Langer & PU Johansson | 0 |

First Day: US 5; Europe 3

### SECOND DAY Foursomes: Morning

| | | | |
|---|---|---|---|
| C Strange & J Haas | 0 | N Faldo & C Montgomerie 4 & 2 | 1 |
| D Love III & J Maggert | 0 | S Torrance & C Rocca 6 & 5 | 1 |
| L Roberts & P Jacobsen 1h | 1 | I Woosnam & P Walton | 0 |
| C Pavin & T Lehman | 0 | B Langer & D Gilford 4 & 3 | 1 |

### Four-balls: Afternoon

| | | | |
|---|---|---|---|
| B Faxon & F Couples 4 & 2 | 1 | S Torrance & C Montgomerie | 0 |
| D Love III & B Crenshaw | 0 | I Woosnam & C Rocca 3 & 2 | 1 |
| J Haas & P Mickelson 3 & 2 | 1 | S Ballesteros & D Gilford | 0 |
| C Pavin & L Roberts 1h | 1 | N Faldo & B Langer | 0 |

Second Day: US 4: Europe 4
Match aggregate: US 9; Europe 7

### THIRD DAY Singles

| | | | |
|---|---|---|---|
| T Lehman 4 & 3 | 1 | S Ballesteros | 0 |
| P Jacobsen | 0 | H Clark 1h | 1 |
| J Maggert | 0 | M James 4 & 3 | 1 |
| F Couples | ½ | I Woosnam | ½ |
| D Love III 3 & 2 | 1 | C Rocca | 0 |
| B Faxon | 0 | D Gilford 1h | 1 |
| B Crenshaw | 0 | C Montgomerie 3 & 1 | 1 |
| C Strange | 0 | N Faldo 1h | 1 |
| L Roberts | 0 | S Torrance 2 & 1 | 1 |
| C Pavin 3 & 2 | 1 | B Langer | 0 |
| J Haas | 0 | P Walton 1h | 1 |
| P Mickelson 2 & 1 | 1 | PU Johansson | 0 |

Singles: US 4 ½: Europe 7 ½

Colin Montgomerie: led
British singles charge.

## TEE TALK

### "My legs were shaking so much up the last that I thought they belonged to someone else – John Travolta maybe"

PHILIP WALTON
- at the Oak Hill Ryder Cup

# Faldo's six of the best

NICK FALDO, racking up his third Masters and sixth major title, and Greg Norman, second again, and second again more catastrophically than ever before even for him, embraced on Augusta National's 18th green. All present and the vast TV audience knew that this was an image that would endure. The man who on the first day equalled the course record of 63, nine under par, set by Nick Price a decade ago, had lost an overnight six-stroke lead and then the tournament by five – a swing of 11. Instead of donning the club's green jacket at this Diamond Jubilee Masters, Norman was relegated to his third second place. He had also been third twice.

Norman began his fourth round with a hook into the crowd. His next was into a bunker. He took three more to hole out. As his lead dribbled away, the atmosphere became almost surreal. Though Faldo dropped a shot at the fifth, his two at the next, with a seven iron to 4 feet, renewed his momentum.

The unthinkable became inescapable. Norman scored five at every hole from the eighth to the 12th. Only one was a par five, the eighth, which Faldo birdied. Immediately after missing his par from two feet at the 11th, where his birdie effort from 10 feet had burned the edge of the hole, Norman was in Rae's Creek at the 12th. That cost a double bogey, giving Faldo a two-stroke lead.

His composure was exemplary, a blend of steely resolve and almost flawlesss course management despite what must have been increasing unease at the scale of the calamity being acted out in front of him. After all Faldo, at 38, and Norman, 41, had been on the major tours for 20 years.

At the 13th, where Norman laid up, Faldo was on in two thanks to what he considered his best shot of the day, with a two iron. Both players got birdie fours though, and Norman came close to getting back into the match – which is what it had become – when his eagle chip from below the 15th green missed by a fraction. Again, both birdied the hole, Faldo with an up and down from beyond the green. The short 16th settled the issue, Norman hooking into the

water. Faldo's par three put him four ahead, a lead he augmented with a birdie three at the last – quite a flourish achieved à la Sandy Lyle from a fairway bunker.

The margin of Norman's defeat took some believing. Faldo's scintillating fourth round 67, almost flawless through the green, included 31 putts. Norman needed only 30, though overall, he took five putts more. The glaring difference between the two was in greens reached in regulation – Norman did so eight times, half as many as Faldo. Overall, Norman had hit marginally more greens than his opponent, 50 to 49. In retrospect, nothing Faldo has ever achieved in golf is worthier of admiration than the style of his third Masters victory, just as nothing was more deserving of condemnation than his thanks to the Press after his third Open victory "from the heart of my bottom". A complicated character this, who began his celebrations by telling Norman that he did not know what to say, but just wanted to hug him. Eyes were brimming all around as he turned to his faithful bag-carrier, Fanny Sunesson, and, having left his wife Gill last year, new girlfriend Brenna Cepelak. It had been three years since he was last in contention in a major.

It is not Norman's style to make excuses, and he did not this time. Hitting rock bottom must have hurt all the more keenly three days after one of the greatest scores of his career – he compared it to his 64 to win his second British Open. His opening marvel of 63 was performed on as lovely and azalea-bedecked an opening day of the Masters as anyone could remember, though there was a chilly start. Beginning with a sober six pars, Norman then birdied nine of the remaining 12, sinking a 24-foot birdie putt at the last. He led Phil Mickelson by two, Scott Hoch and Bob Tway by four, and Faldo and David Gilford by six, Faldo with his best opening round since his first success at Augusta seven years ago.

Gilford looked good for a 67 when his tee shot on the 16th landed 30 feet from the flag, back right at the top of a slope. His chances looked even better when his approach putt seem-

**Nick Faldo: performance of remarkable composure as Greg Norman fell apart.**

ingly pulled up two feet below the hole. Then it inched back, gathering speed till it was 40 feet away. Regular watchers at the 16th never rule out a four putt in such situations, and so it proved, though Gilford, who had shingles last winter, responded staunchly with a birdie at the 17th.

But next day he plunged out with a 78, and so did Sam Torrance, seven over par. Curtis Strange was also among the fallen, with Sandy Lyle, Payne Stewart, Arnold Palmer, two-time winner Ben Crenshaw and the two amateur champions Tiger Woods and Gordon Sherry. Faldo apart, it was not an encouraging event for Ryder Cup captain Seve Ballesteros, who returned 299, finishing 43rd, one place behind Jack Nicklaus, but one above tail-ender Alex Cejka, who gained his first three European Tour wins last year. Ian Woosnam, joint 29th, Bernhard Langer, in a tie for 36th, and Colin Montgomerie, joint 39th, were the only other Cup candidates to qualify.

Steve Jones: Artesian man who used a new grip to get his hands on the US Open trophy.

# Qualifier Jones gets the big one

NOT SINCE JERRY PATE 23 years back has a sectional qualifier won the US Open title. Steve Jones, via final qualifying at Columbus Ohio a week ago, repeated Pate's feat over the difficult Oakland Hills Course outside Detroit, by a stroke from Tom Lehman and Davis Love III, now disputing with Colin Montgomerie the deeply coveted spot of best golfer without major success. A bogey on the short 17th, and another on the 18th, cost him the title. He was too cautious with his birdie putt from above the 18th hole, and (shades of Sanders at St Andrews) missed the next downhiller – from 24 inches – and could only wait as Lehman and

Jones came down the last. Lehman drove into a bunker and dropped a shot, Jones got a straight-down-the-middle par four, calmly negotiating the two putts he had for victory.

Jones, a 6ft 4in son of Artesia, New Mexico, had four Tour victories on his CV, but none for the past four years, because of a 1991 dirt bike crash. A damaged shoulder and ankle healed well enough, but the ring finger of his left hand – one of the three that does most to secure the club, would not. Finally, by taping the damaged digit to another, and using a reverse overlap grip for play through the green, Jones got back into shape for his $425,000

triumph at Oakland Hills.

Montgomerie stayed in contention till overshooting the short 13th into rough. His chip jumped on him, running far down the green, and a five resulted. He still finished leading Briton, five off Jones's pace, with the double accolade of most accurate driver and best at greens in regulation, which was almost becoming his trademark. Nick Faldo's last round was his best, but good only for a share of 16th place, whereas Jack Nicklaus, at 56, confirmed his entry for Royal Lytham, feeling that his share of 27th place showed he could still compete at top level.

Oakland Hills recently suffered an embarrassment caused

by the eagerness of male members to make the Grill Room a no-go area for ladies, following State of Michigan legislation to forbid discrimination in private clubs. To this end they made the Grill an integral part of the men's locker room. This cost the waitresses their jobs. They sued, and won. Their lawyer found the club had no full lady members and no blacks, obligatory for clubs staging major championships. Not only had that to be put right, but the club were led to understand that a liquor licence, without which most Grill Rooms would not bother to open their doors, was unlikely to be granted to a lavatory. Result: status quo ante.

# Lehman atones for the US Pro

**Tom Lehman: crowd magnet and record-breaking British Open champion.**

THAT AN AMERICAN should win the British Open is scarcely a novelty, but Tom Lehman's £200,000 victory at Royal Lytham was a first for a US professional on that course, though the greatest amateur of all, American or otherwise, Bobby Jones, did it for nothing in 1926. Despite a last round 73, the only time he was over par, Lehman's victory was assured and almost inevitable. On the third day he broke clear of his nearest rival, Nick Faldo, by six strokes. This he achieved with a course record 64, putting especially rock solid, setting up another record, 198 for 54 holes. Lehman, who began tidily with two rounds of 67, prospered because he more than any other player coped better with the last five daunting holes, three under against next best Faldo, one under. This time there was to be no Normanesque collapse. Indeed, though Faldo had scored 68 in each of the first three rounds, his final 70 earned him only fourth place, as Mark McCumber (66) and Ernie Els (67) got to within two of Lehman's 271. Jeff Maggert climbed to joint fifth behind Faldo with the best final round, 65.

"Not pretty, but gritty," was Lehman's view of his struggle in the final round. Faldo, last out with Lehman, had played "awfully well, but did not make any putts whatsoever" said Lehman, who after years of struggle in less elevated company had reached the heights at the same age (37) as new US Open Champion Steve Jones. He had been close to success in several recent majors, notably when second to Jones last month. He made a accomplished acceptance speech too, as befits a lay preacher.

There was no doubt about who would take the silver medal for leading amateur, since Tiger Woods was the only unpaid competitor to make the cut. He achieved that with a second round 66, and went on to equal Ian Pyman's low amateur total of 281 in this money-spinning event, more than 20,000 watching the last day of practice, the championship itself 190,000. It was often shoulder to shoulder to glimpse Woods, never mind the leaders, and around the sun-baked course folk wondered about when Woods would turn pro, and how huge would be the sponsorship deals he would attract. Leading players were in general agreement that he would prosper mightily on Tour. Michael Welch, a former Telegraph Junior Golfer of the Year, had not made headlines as a pro, but had the enormous satisfaction here of beating Woods' score by a stroke, with a final 68.

# GB&I again – no blarney!

HARD FACTS REMAIN, such as United States 20 wins, Great Britain and Ireland 6, but Curtis Cup fortunes have turned against America in recent years. Since GB&I's away win in Kansas 10 years ago, the US have won but once. The winning coach at Killarney, Mickey Walker, thought that the increasing number of players from the British Isles taking up scholarships, and enjoying excellent coaching at US colleges, was part of the reason for the change of fortunes in the series for the Cup put up by the Curtis sisters.

GB&I came close to their biggest win in Killarney, with a 10-5 margin, and three matches halved. Alison Rose from Scotland won all four of her matches, one of them the Cup-clincher. Julie Hall, to everyone's stupefaction, lost all of hers. This was a novelty indeed, and besides, in five Cup appearances her team had lost only once. Hall was retiring from international play, to concentrate on duties at the Ladies Golf Union. The Scottish contingent, of Rose, Janice Moodie, who dropped only half a point, and Mhairi McKay, who lost only once, was the backbone of the team, which

**Alison Rose: 100% Scot who clinched Killarney victory.**

had no Irish member, though non-playing captain Ita Butler, who is Irish, could justly claim she had the best eight players.

US Amateur Champion Kelli Kuehne was keen to avenge her brother Trip's Walker Cup defeat, and was chief US points scorer, but the Cup was lost. Kuehne had a wonderful 1996 for all that, completing the rare women's trans-Atlantic double. She gained her second US Amateur title in Lincoln, Nebraska, beating Marisa Baena 2 and 1 in the final over Pete Dye's 6,077 yard Firethorn course. That gave her a hat-trick of titles, for she won the Junior championship in 1994. The British Amateur fell to her also, when she got the better of Becky Morgan 5 and 3 at Hoylake.

**Kelli Kuehne: Amateur double, but no Curtis Cup to take home.**

● Arnold Palmer's US team won the second President's Cup match against the Internationals by Lake Manassas, Virginia, but only by a point, 16½ – 15½, and that thanks to a 30 foot birdie putt that Fred Couples sank on the 17th to beat Vijay Singh by 2 and 1. The US lead the series 2-0: the next Cup match will be in Australia in 1998.

● A letter to The Daily Telegraph declared that the BBC coverage of Faldo's Masters was poor value for the viewers. Jonathan Martin, head of BBC Sports and Events, pointed out that 10 hours action in prime evening viewing hours was provided. It was, also, all that Augusta National would allow, even to the host TV company, CBS – 2½ hours on the first three days, 3 on the last, when 7 million watched. The club took the view that people travelling to the course and buying tickets should get more than the TV audience.

● Autograph hunters could make life difficult for players, especially when on their way to tee off, or needing a few moments of contemplation after a difficult or brilliant round. The US PGA introduced an attempt at a best-of-both-worlds system. Players were allocated a specific time and area where signing could take place in an orderly and unstressful manner.

● Greg Norman's caddie Tony Navarro wrestled a drunk to the ground at Hilton Head the week after the Masters when he accused Norman of choking, complaining "You cost me money". Police removed him to a detention centre together with several other over-imbibers. At British Open time, Norman signed a contract (his biggest yet) to play the new Maxfli XS ball. Asked if $10million was near the mark, he said: "I think you can start higher if you want to."

# Hat-trick Woods soon in the money

THOUGH HIS PATH to victory in the final was tortuous, Tiger Woods, 20, became US Amateur Champion for an unprecedented third time in a row at Pumpkin Ridge, Oregon, from a total entry of 5,538. He at once turned pro, signing a five-year deal with the Nike clothing and shoe company and Titleist clubs for sums that

were said to add up to tens of millions of dollars. Six figure appearance fees were clear possibilities.

Woods had held USGA titles for six years, three Juniors and now three amateurs. Bobby Jones managed nine USGA titles in eight years. Woods joined Jack Nicklaus, Bob Murphy and Phil

Mickelson in winning the Amateur and National Collegiate Athletic Association Championship in the same year.

Steve Scott, 19, his final opponent, did not surrender easily. He was five up after 18 holes, and two up with three to play, and lost only at the second extra hole.

# Brooks defeats local heroes

NO-ONE EXCEPT THE architect Jack Nicklaus, knew a great deal about the Valhalla course. It had never been used previously in a significant event. Nicklaus built it outside Louisville, home of the Kentucky Derby, never won by a British racehorse, and of Muhammad Ali, destroyer of the championship hopes of Henry Cooper and Brian London, among others.

Colin Montgomerie thought that all round course ignorance gave European visitors a better chance, but Texan Mark Brooks disproved that theory, beating a Kentuckian, Kenny Perry, with a birdie on the first play-off hole, the lengthy 18th. He had forced the play-off for his first major with a birdie on the same hole (out of a bunker) to dash the hopes of Perry's Kentucky fans.

During its first important event, the US PGA Championship, temperatures varied. It sometimes offered Kentucky fried fairways, even after a downpour and lightning fragmented round one. A different player led after each of the first three rounds – Perry, Phil Mickelson and Russ Cochran in that order.

Cochran, another Kentuckian, from Paducah, and a left-hander, thrilled the locals with a course record 65, seven under par, to lead. Cochran had to re-qualify for the Tour last autumn, and had only one Tour victory to his credit, gained five years ago. A real curio now became a possibility: an all southpaw battle for a major title, since Mickelson was only three shots off Cochran's pace.

But right-handers ruled on the final afternoon, Mickelson, of all people, putting poorly in returning par 72, Cochran crashing to to 77. Montgomerie, like the architect, did not qualify, but Tommy Tolles with a final 67 and Steve Elkington, the defending champion, were only one shot out of the play-off.

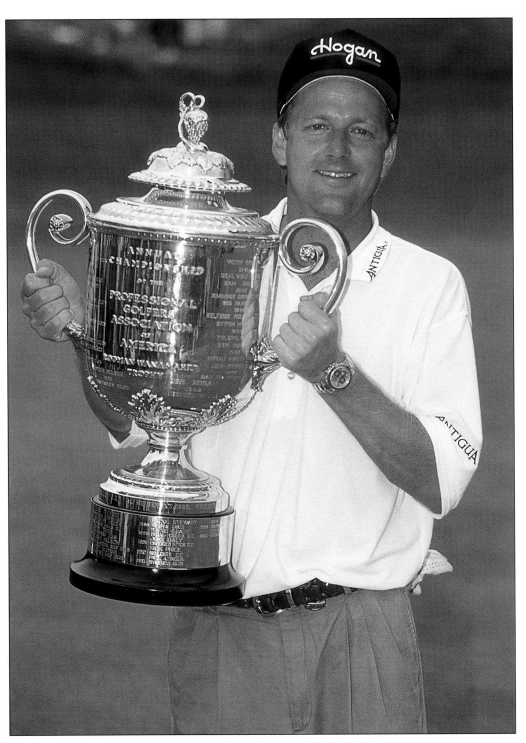

**Mark Brooks: birdie double did the trick on Valhalla's final hole.**

# Woods and Lehman in ascendant

WHEN THE PRIZES were handed out at the end of the year, Tiger Woods had in a few short months revitalised the US Tour, whose members were at once aware that he could seriously cut into their sources of income – though he would increase them. He played in eight events, made the cut in each, and won two. He had no rival as Rookie of the Year, and Tom Lehman walked away with Player of the Year.

A slimmer Colin Montgomerie led on the European Tour for the fourth year, and world-wide earned more than $3million – including victory over Ernie Els at the third extra hole of the Sun City Million Dollar Challenge, partial revenge for defeat in the US Open play-off. Els brought off a late season double – the World Cup with Wayne Westner in Cape Town, and the World Match Play, beating Vijah Singh 3 and 2 at Wentworth.

# Rankin's dozen destroy Europe

## Olazabel strides out to fitness

APPALLED NO DOUBT by the thought of the Solheim Cup staying on the eastern side of the Atlantic along with the Ryder, Walker and Curtis Cups, Judy Rankin's Solheim Cup team made mince-meat of Laura Davies and company at St Pierre in Wales. The deed was done in a 10-2 singles massacre, after Europe had led by two despite gaining only a half point out of four in the first morning's foursomes. Annika Sorenstam, who had landed her second successive US Open title at Pine Needles in North Carolina three months ago, was unbeaten throughout, and Europe's only winner in singles. Sorenstam stood second to Davies in the world rankings. Both had three wins. Liselotte Neumann was third, but won only once.

So Rankin's team ended (by 17-11) the pattern of the first three Cup games, which all went to the home side, and the US lead the series 3-1. A wasp sting next to Europe captain Mickey Walker's left eye on the second day proved to be an ill omen. So did the domination Michelle McGann achieved in the third single against Davies, usually the inspiration of her team, but who also lost to McGann in the State Rail Farm Classic play-off last month.

Dottie Pepper, who had reverted to her maiden name after divorcing Doug Mochrie, was now a blonde again, having forsaken the fiery red which tended to match too many of her moods. Rankin said that she had had a word with Pepper ... "she had the temperament of a redhead and now she's blonde and very charming."

DECEMBER WAS A MONTH of hope and revival for José Maria Olazabal, as he strode through the waves at the edge of Fuerterrabia Beach, 4 x 1,200 metres each day a few weeks after becoming a patient of Dr Hans-Wilhelm Muller-Wohlfahrt – or Dr Feelgood as he was becoming known to relieved athletes, such as skater Katarina Witt and athlete Daley Thompson, not to mention tenor Luciano Pavarotti.

A former decathlete, he had been team doctor for Bayern Munich, and was criticised by some of his peers for secretiveness and unusual methods and remedies, such as calf foetus parts. Olazabal spent weeks at his new doctor's Munich clinic, and warm baths, massage and other treatments brought improvement in a painful foot condition the German identified as a spinal hernia. Sergio Gomez, Olazabal's manager, had described the golfer thus at the beginning of the year: "He's 30, and feels disabled." His ball-striking skills had not deserted him: his ability to walk after the ball certainly had.

January was not kind to Olazabal. Opening the box in which he expected to find a pair of shoes designed to make walking easier, he found nothing. A thief had taken them. A bout of influenza did not improve his morale. He had his tonsils removed, to eradicate a possible source of infection. Two sporting goods companies, Lacoste and Titleist, kept alive their sponsorship contracts with him, hoping for better days. Visits to the Mayo Clinic, taking methotrexate, which extended Andrew Murray's career, homeopathy, avoiding this, that, and the other food – nothing had worked – until Munich.

Dottie Pepper: "blonde charmer" (left) celebrates.

Hands-on team: United States confirm Solheim control.

# Masters provides another milestone

TIGER WOODS AT 21 became the youngest Masters Champion, taking over from Seve Ballesteros, who won aged 23 in 1980. He did so with a record score of 18 under par, winning by 12 strokes from Tom Kite. That was three better than Jack Nicklaus's record margin of 1965, when Nicklaus outpaced Arnold Palmer and Gary Player.

Only Young Tom Morris, stands as a younger major winner, at 17. Some of his later British Open scores were not equalled for 30 years, till the coming of the Haskell ball. Twentieth century advances in equipment and sheer weight of competition suggested that Woods's figures would not last that long.

Having shaken the golfing firmament Woods, with the Mercedes Championship that opened the year already under his belt, was clearly destined to shake up the game's finances, swelling gate money, purses, sponsorship, and TV interest to the advantage in particular of his peers on Tours from Georgia to Taiwan. The words of Gene Sarazen about Walter Hagen came to mind: that every pro should thank the great showman every time they stretched a cheque between their fingers.

Phil Knight, founder of Nike, predicted a 60 per cent increase in sales because of his company's deal with Woods: "They laughed when we paid $25million. Now the deal is worth $250million." Knight also got to the kernel of Woods's appeal. It was the way he made such dramatic shots.

Colin Montgomerie agreed. He achieved his best round in six visits to Augusta with his 67 on Saturday, and was paired with Woods for the third round. "I knew that he hit the ball for miles and was magic with his irons. What I didn't appreciate was how well he putted. He's nine shots clear now, and he'll be further ahead at the end." Playing with Woods had a debilitating effect on Britons: both Montgomerie and Nick Faldo, the defending champion, scored 81 the day after they accompanied him.

Besides, Woods's ethnic background would give him a power no other golfer possesses: a high profile in Asia, the biggest and least developed market of all.

His mother, Kultida, is half Thai, quarter Chinese and quarter white, his father, Earl, half African-American, quarter Native America (Cherokee) and quarter Chinese. Cablinasian was the portmanteau word for the mixture.

His father had determined Tiger should have early training in the field of self-control in the face of provocation. He would rattle coins in his pocket on Tiger's back-swing, roll balls across greens while he was putting, and stand in the line of fire as his son hit wedges. Woods's power of concentration were soon a subject of awe.

As part of such a headline-grabbing performance, Woods's start at Augusta in pleasant golfing weather was dire – 40 to the turn, making a fourth Tour win since he turned pro last year look unlikely. A long iron shot from the 10th tee settled him down, and he came back in 30, finishing two under par, but five behind Nick Price. His next two rounds of 66 and 65 spreadeagled the field, and a final 69 broke the record. A seven iron was his biggest club to any par four throughout. A wedge was usual. He never three-putted.

Woods looked beyond the kudos and the cash (he is reputed to have paid cash to purchase the fastest corporate jet on offer: Greg Norman bought a modified Boeing 737). Woods's dearest wish was that the golf programmes for inner-city children should be a success. The experience of Carl Jackson, a caddie at Augusta, does not suggest that great golfing benefits will quickly accrue for black children. His difficulties in launching his son Andrew in the game, and inquiries at various stops on the Tour led him to say: "The sum total of what most kids are getting is two or maybe three outings to a driving range in their summer holidays."

Tiger Woods: a green jacket (courtesy of Nick Faldo) and plenty of greenbacks to go with it.

# Olazabal back: Faldo too

A CHEQUE FOR £10,605 was José Maria Olazabal's reward for joint 12th place in the Dubai Desert Classic. It must have felt like a billion. Last year Dr Hans-Wilhelm Muller-Wohlfahrt diagnosed a spinal hernia as the cause of the painful feet that cost Olazabal his Ryder Cup place in 1995, and threatened to end his career – a thought, said Olazabal, that was the worst strand in his suffering. The Spaniard had obtained all manner of opinions and treatments, but only the Muller-Wohlfahrt way worked.

This was Olazabal's first tournament since the Lancôme a year ago last September. Ian Woosnam should have won it. He fluffed a wedge into the water in front of the 18th. Left-hander Richard Green of Victoria was the beneficiary, beating the golfer he most revered, Greg Norman, and Woosnam in a play-off.

Dubai was less reassuring for David Carter. Two days before the Classic he was found unconscious in his hotel room. He underwent an operation to remove fluid from his brain and was soon playing again.

Nick Faldo provided Ryder Cup captain Seve Ballesteros, who did not qualify at Dubai, another good reason for blessing Sunday, March 2, the day Olazabal started to earn money again. He won the Nissan Open in Los Angeles. A month later, Olazabal won the Turespaña Masters.

# Big Easy edges big Monty

ERNIE ELS FROM Johannesburg set no records in the US Open at Congressional, Bethesda, but Jack Nicklaus and son Gary, a qualifier, did – the first father and son to play in the event. What Els did achieve was to give notice of another young golfer on the scene with huge length and piercing irons, not to mention a chipping flair that could hurt – and did, as the final nine holes began.

All the same, Tiger Woods remained at the head of the world rankings after Bethesda. He had best scoring average, the longest tee-shots, and most winnings, at close to $1.4 million. Woods no doubt had something to do with the $6.5 million ticket sell-out. He did not greatly enthuse those fans, breaking par but once. The critics had been quick to point out that he might not thrive on a tight USGA Open course, radically different with its deep rough to the open spaces of Augusta, where the greens are the course's chief defence.

Winning his second US Open in four years was Els's reward for keeping focused in a four-way, last-day battle with Tom Lehman, Jeff Maggert and World No 3, Colin Montgomerie, who was first to drop out in his three-way play-off against Els and Loren Roberts in 1994. Els chipped in at the 10th to draw level with the other three.

"Big Easy" Els, who never needed a hammock to look laid-back, closed in on victory with a soaring five iron that finished five yards beyond the pin on the 480-yard 71st green. No harder par four in the world than this hole, thought Els, who played it four times in par. Montgomerie dropped a shot there every round, even during his opening 65.

The last two greens are in a vast stadium-like bowl. Montgomerie's six iron to the 17th leaked into the rough. After chipping to six feet, he waited for five minutes for the 20,000 crowd to settle before he struck the most important putt of his career to date. It grazed the hole. Both men hit the short 18th, where Els's return putt of five feet for par was a nerve shredder, but he was equal to it. The Scot had won on the European Tour the previous week, but now finished in tears at the frustration of another near miss at the event he thinks most difficult to win.

He had withstood a renewed outbreak of hooligan behaviour from galleries sprinkled with foul-mouthed louts attracted perhaps by the spectacular new stars of the game, but totally removed from the informed and appreciative watchers who for so long had contributed to golf's good name above all other major sports.

"Big Easy" Ernie Els: towering five iron the master stroke to capture second US Open title.

# Nicholas shatters Lopez dream

**Alison Nicholas: only sixty inches high, but unyielding at climax of Battle of Pumpkin Ridge.**

NANCY LOPEZ, MORE than any golfer than perhaps Babe Zaharias, sold women's golf to the American public. She had won 48 tournaments, including three majors, when she teed off in the US Open at Pumpkin Ridge, Oregon. She became the only woman in Open history to put up four scores in the 60s – yet still failed to gain the one title she coveted above all others.

Alison Nicholas, 35, resident in the English Midlands but Gibraltar-born, was as firm as that rock in withstanding the consistent pressure applied by Lopez and surging support of a huge crowd. Nicholas, only five feet tall, built her success on her mid-dle rounds of 66 and 67. A 60-yard pitch for an eagle in the final round at the fourth where Lopez had put her third a foot from the pin was a great morale raiser. Despite a double bogey at the 14th, where she overshot into deep trouble, Nicholas held on to take the $232,500 first prize by a stroke from Lopez, who had talked Nicholas into trying again in America when her career was not going well.

The British Women's Open, in which Nicholas missed the cut, went for the second time in three years to Australia's Karrie Webb, fourth at Pumpkin Ridge. Webb had edged up to second place in the tours on either side of the Atlantic.

## Quick kill at Quaker Ridge

THE END FOR GB & Ireland's Walker Cup team at Quaker Ridge, near Scarsdale, New York, was quick and clean. To the

**John Harris: Cup clincher.**

delight of those who had reached the age of discretion, it was not imposed by a youngster such as was dominating the major championships of 1997, but by John Harris, 45. His was the best record in Cup competition (P11 W10). He had also got the winning point in despatching the visitors at Interlachen in 1993, a record 19-5 US victory. Only 18-6 this time, but splendid revenge for Downing Gray, losing captain at Royal Portcawl two years ago. Justin Rose, just 17, provided consolation for the visitors. The youngest ever Cup player, he won two points out of four.

# Leonard turns Troon around

BY TURNING A FIVE-stroke, third-round deficit into a three-stroke victory over Sweden's Jesper Parnevik and Ireland's rapidly maturing Darren Clarke, Justin Leonard, 25, from Texas became the third successive US winner of the British Open. Americans had also won on the last five occasions the Open was staged at Royal Troon. Arnold Palmer started the sequence in 1962. Not a particularly long hitter, Leonard's game was strong around and in particular on the greens. At an unusually benign and fast-running Troon that made the difference over the last nine holes. Leonard held on well on a windy first day, and again when his putting stroke was fallible on the second day.

The title had seemed to rest between Clarke and first one American, Jim Furyk, then another, Leonard, until the Swede moved ahead in round three, with Clarke, Freddie Couples and Leonard in close attendance. Leonard's birdies at two of the last three holes ensured victory, his final round of 65 the best since Greg Norman's 64 four years ago.

Apart from the claret jug, Leonard's immediate reward was a Ryder Cup place in September. He rewarded the crowd, a little disappointed perhaps that one of the Europeans had not held on, with an impeccable acceptance speech, including a plea for a moment to enjoy the moment.

Ayrshire was again unkind to Parnevik, who crucially pushed wide his short birdie chance at the 16th. His shaky last two holes reflected how deeply he was unnerved by this and Leonard's birdie up ahead at the 17th (Parnevik was now checking scoreboards after his Turnberry trauma). Troon, said the Swede, was more painful than Turnberry, because he felt confident at Troon.

Tiger Woods was nervous about security, for he was the autograph hunters' chief target, and that of the hate letter-writers, too. Well off the pace at half-way, like many other fancied runners such as Payne Stewart, Colin Montgomerie and Nick Faldo, a 64 (including two bogeys) in round three put him in with a chance, but he was ten strokes worse on the final day, when that tiny menace, the Postage Stamp, Troon's eighth hole, exacted a triple-bogey six. Woods was still world number one.

Justin Leonard: sure touch on greens richly rewarded.

# Love's major a family affair

A GREAT DEAL HUNG on the US PGA Championship at Winged Foot, in New York's suburbs, a course which defending champion Mark Brooks said comprised six difficult holes, six very difficult, and six impossible. Correct for him anyway, for he missed the cut along with Jack Nicklaus, Nick Faldo, Hal Sutton, José Maria Olazabal and Darren Clarke. The US Ryder Cup team was to be announced by captain Tom Kite after the event. A win here or a high finish could catapult contenders into the team as of right, or cajole Kite into awarding a wild card.

Davis Love III had been at a nervous 10th place in Cup standings, so his three-stroke win from Justin Leonard not only confirmed that the best-player-not-to-have-won-a-major millstone was now firmly round Colin Montgomerie's neck, but ensured a ticket to Valderrama. Jeff Maggert's third place (he had been 11th in Cup standings) did so too, while the wild cards went to Lee Janzen (fourth, a stroke better than captain Kite himself) and Freddie Couples who was 29th at Winged Foot.

So was Tiger Woods after a last round 75. Having finished 29th at Troon too, and 19th at Congressional, Woods's perennial favouritism was remarkably resilient, despite accusing fingers pointing at his rash of double bogeys; he was still firmly World No. 1. He and Leonard, Tom Lehman, Jim Furyk, Phil Mickelson, Mark O'Meara, Scott Hoch and Brad Faxon made up Kite's dozen. Europe's selection was stilled dogged by controversy about the wrist injury to Miguel Angel Martin, who looked unlikely to gain the place to which his record entitled him.

Love, at 33, and by six years the oldest major winner of the year, gained his first major with a flourish by five strokes, at 11-under par. His final round was his third 66 of the Championship, his technique and nerve proof against rain, humidity and heat. Leonard applied heat of his own, but to no avail. The new champion's father was a respected teaching pro, but never a Tour star. After his death in a 1988 air crash, his widow nurtured the career of the third Davis Love, who also had his brother – and caddie – Mark to thank, especially as Mark had given up his original intention to follow his father as a teacher to carry Davis's bag. Loves find a way, so to speak.

Davis Love III: US PGA No. 1.

# Europe walk singles tightrope again

SEVE BALLESTEROS HAD long despaired of his countrymen ever taking much notice of his or any Spaniard's golfing feats ("A rich man's game" scoffed a Spanish premier). He could rest assured that they would let him know about it if, under his captaincy, Europe failed to retain the Ryder Cup at Valderrama, the pride and joy of the Bolivian millionaire Jaime Ortiz-Patino, reputed to have spent $35 million to transform it to Championship standard. Hence perhaps the obsessive Ballesteros preparations and his highly mobile on-course behaviour which amounted, some thought, to paranoia.

Whether or not these factors helped or hindered Europe's victory by one point (14½ – 13½) was of no great consequence once

Colin Montgomerie played what won him a the shot of the year award off the 18th tee. Soon he was conceding Scott Hoch's putt. That made their match a half (to the disgust of those who had backed the Scot), and retained the Cup for two more years. Jets of champagne drenched Europeans already soaking happily in a final day downpour. Since Jack Nicklaus and Lord Derby had set in train the substitution of Europe for Great Britain and Ireland to improve Ryder Cup competitiveness, each side had won or retained the Cup five times; in short, a money-spinner.

Though Montgomerie was the chief European points scorer, at three out of five plus the Hoch half, the victory, unlike that at

Oak Hill, owed most to continental skill. Costantino Rocca, Bernhard Langer and José Maria Olazabal had eight wins between them, while Per-Ulrik Johansson won his only two matches – his single against PGA Champion Davis Love III and his four-ball with Jesper Parnevik.

That did not exculpate Europe from their by-now-almost-traditional singles ordeal. With a five-point lead, and needing four more from 12 singles, problems seemed few. Nevertheless in the final single to finish, Montgomerie, followed by a fair proportion of the 30,000 crowd, was hard-pressed by Hoch, who set up a two-hole lead. Freddie Couples, Phil Mickelson, Mark O'Meara, Lee Janzen, Jeff Maggert, Jim Furyk

and Tom Lehman had all won, and Justin Leonard had halved with Thomas Bjorn, whose obdurate play, capped by a brilliant birdie at the perilous and contentious 17th, was crucial to out and out victory.

Kite's three major champions were among his least effective players. Tiger Woods had one win, aided by his near neighbour and mentor O'Meara. Apart from that there was only a half with Leonard, so Leonard could offer only two halves. Love lost four out of four.

Ian Woosnam, still without a singles win, had a win and a loss at Valderrama, Ireland's Darren Clarke did likewise, but doubtless planned to do better in 2005, when the Cup was at last to be staged in his native land.

## RYDER CUP

(Valderrama, Spain) Europe 14½; US 13½.
Captains (non-playing) Europe: S Ballesteros, US T Kite.

**FIRST DAY Four-balls: Morning**

| Europe | | US | |
|---|---|---|---|
| JM Olazabal & C Rocca 1h | 1 | D Love III & P Mickelson | 0 |
| N Faldo & L Westwood | 0 | F Couples & B Faxon 1h | 1 |
| J Parnevik & PU Johansson 1h | 1 | T Lehman & J Furyk | 0 |
| C Montgomerie & B Langer | 0 | T Woods & M O'Meara 3 & 2 | 1 |

**Foursomes: Afternoon**

| | | | |
|---|---|---|---|
| C Rocca & JM Olazabal | 0 | S Hoch & L Janzen 1h | 1 |
| B Langer & C Montgomerie 5 & 3 | 1 | M O'Meara & T Woods | 0 |
| N Faldo & L Westwood 3 & 2 | 1 | J Leonard & J Maggert | 0 |
| J Parnevik & I Garrido | ½ | T Lehman & P Mickelson | ½ |

First Day: Europe 4½; US 3½.

**SECOND DAY Four-balls: Morning**

| | | | |
|---|---|---|---|
| C Montgomerie & D Clarke 1h | 1 | F Couples & D Love III | 0 |
| I Woosnam & T Bjorn 2 & 1 | 1 | J Leonard & B Faxon | 0 |
| N Faldo & L Westwood 2 & 1 | 1 | T Woods & M O'Meara | 0 |
| JM Olazabal & I Garrido | ½ | P Mickelson & T Lehman | ½ |

**Foursomes: Afternoon**

| | | | |
|---|---|---|---|
| C Montgomerie & B Langer 1h | 1 | L Janzen & J Furyk | 0 |
| N Faldo & L Westwood | 0 | S Hoch & J Maggert 2 & 1 | 1 |
| J Parnevik & I Garrido | ½ | J Leonard & T Woods | ½ |
| JM Olazabal & C Rocca 5 & 4 | 1 | D Love III & F Couples | 0 |

Second Day: Europe 6, US 2
Match aggregate: Europe 10½; US 5½

**THIRD DAY Singles**

| | | | |
|---|---|---|---|
| I Woosnam | 0 | F Couples 8 & 7 | 1 |
| PU Johansson 3 & 2 | 1 | D Love III | 0 |
| C Rocca 4 & 2 | 1 | T Woods | 0 |
| T Bjorn | ½ | J Leonard | ½ |
| D Clarke | 0 | P Mickelson 2 & 1 | 1 |
| J Parnevik | 0 | M O'Meara 5 & 4 | 1 |
| JM Olazabal | 0 | L Janzen 1h | 1 |
| B Langer 2 & 1 | 1 | B Faxon | 0 |
| L Westwood | 0 | J Maggert 3 & 2 | 1 |
| C Montgomerie | ½ | S Hoch | ½ |
| N Faldo | 0 | J Furyk 3 & 2 | 1 |
| I Garrido | 0 | T Lehman 7 & 6 | 1 |

Singles: Europe 4, US 8

**Colin Montgomerie: congratulations from captain Seve (centre).**

## SCORECARD

**British Open** (R Troon, Scot)
J Leonard 69 66 72 65 272
D Clarke 67 66 71 71 275
J Parnevik 70 66 66 73 275
J Furyk 67 72 70 70 279

**Masters** (Augusta)
T Woods 70 66 65 69 270
T Kite 77 69 66 70 282
T Tolles 72 72 72 67 283
T Watson 75 68 69 72 284

**US Open** (Congressional, Bethesda, Md)
E Els 71 67 69 69 276
C Montgomerie 65 76 67 69 277
T Lehman 67 70 68 73 278
J Maggert 73 66 68 74 281

**US PGA** ( Winged Foot, NY)
D Love III 66 71 66 66 269
J Leonard 68 70 65 71 274
J Maggert 69 69 73 65 276
L Janzen 69 67 74 69 279
Leading US money-winner PGA Tour T Woods
$2,066,833 (on US Seniors tour: H. Irwin
$2,343,364); Europe C Montgomerie
£1,034,752. Year-end Sony ranking:
1. G Norman, 2. T Woods, 3. N Price

**British Amateur** (R St Georges, R Cinque
Ports)
C Watson bt T Immelman 3 & 2

**US Amateur** (Cog Hill, Lemont, IL)
M Kuchar bt J Kribel 2 & 1

**US Women's Open** (Pumpkin Ridge, OR)
A Nicholas 274

**British Women's Open** (Sunningdale, Berks)
K Webb 269

**US Women's Amateur** (Brae Burn, MA)
S Cavalleri bt R Burke 5 & 4

**British Women's Amateur** (Cruden Bay, Scot)
A Rose bt M McKay 4 & 3

**World Cup** (Kiawah Is. SC)
Ireland (P Harrington & P McGinley) 545.
(Individual) C Montgomerie 266

**Dunhill Nations Cup** (St Andrews, Scot)
S Africa (R Goosen, D Frost, E Els) bt Sweden
(J Parnevik, PU Johansson, J Haeggman)
2-1

**World Match Play** (Wentworth, Surrey)
V Singh bt E Els 1h

**Walker Cup** (Quaker Ridge, NY)
US 18 GB & Ireland 6

Paul McGinley and (right) Padraig Harrington: Kiawah coup.

## SHORT PUTTS

● Fuzzy Zoeller from Indiana ruffled feathers when he hoped that Tiger Woods would not use the winners privileges at the celebratory Masters dinner to "order fried chicken and collard greens or whatever else they eat". The dismissive quality of the word "they", whether Zoeller realised it or not, could not have pleased Woods, who clouded his own image with off-key jokes in a magazine interview.

● Juniors were admitted free at the Troon Open.

● After playing 86 US Tour events with seven second places but no wins, David Duval won his final three starts in 1987, taking a week off after the first two before winning the Tour Championship at Houston: $1,269,000 for the month.

● Paul McGinley and former Walker Cup hero Padraig Harrington won the World Cup of Golf for Ireland at Kiawah Island, South Carolina, with Colin Montgomerie and Raymond Russell second for Scotland, pushing four-time US winners Freddie Couples and Davis Love III into third place. Montgomerie, still without a major victory to his name, picked up the individual award with a total of 266.

## TEE TALK

### "I call them melons – green on the outside, red on the inside"

JAIME ORTIZ-PATINO
on his doubts about Spanish Green Party's political orientation and their objections to golf courses

# Death of three Ryder captains

BEN HOGAN AT 84, Jay Hebert 74, and Dave Marr 63, all died in 1997. Hogan, widely thought to be the most masterful ball-striker of them all, and winner of nine majors, was, like Hebert and Marr a victorious Ryder Cup captain.

Hebert, a Purple Heart winner at Iwo Jima, and Marr were both US PGA Champions. Marr became a much admired TV commentator with a wry turn of Texan phrase, as in "that old dog can still hunt" of a mature competitor.

Michael Williams, Daily Telegraph golf correspondent since 1971, collapsed and died while playing at his club at Chelmsford a few days after reporting Tiger Woods's Masters triumph. Cancer claimed the respected writer Dick Taylor in America.

At year's end at the age of 96 died the player said by Bobby Jones to be the best, man or woman, he had ever seen, Lady Heathcoat Amory. The former Joyce Wethered won the English Amateur five years running, and the British Amateur four times.

## TEE TALK

### "He could sort out the men from the boys like a 50 mph wind"

BRIAN HUGGETT
of the late Michael Williams, Daily Telegraph correspondent

# Tiger Woods, a global star

by Lewine Mair

**Tiger Woods's background – a black golfer in what is still predominantly a white man's game – has maybe played its part in his resolve to become, in coach Butch Harmon's words, "the best player ever to walk the planet."**

The late Gene Sarazen was the man who came up with the first put-down for Tiger Woods. When, on the eve of the 1997 US Masters, people were asking the old gentleman what he thought of the game's latest whiz-kid, Sarazen looked up, with mingled mischief and innocence in his eyes, and called for confirmation of the young man's age.

"Twenty-one," came the reply. "By the time I was 21," said Sarazen, "I'd already won a major."

In the wake of that Masters, which Woods won by a record 12 shots with a record aggregate of 270, nobody was so dismissive again.

"Tiger humiliated us all," said Colin Montgomerie, who is never less than honest. He was among those who consoled themselves with the thought that Augusta was Augusta, and that Woods was unlikely to be so effective amid the rough of our Open or a US Open. "If he is," surmised the Scot, "we're all in trouble."

To their temporary relief, he was not. Not until the 1999 PGA Championship at Medinah did Woods win his second major. Yet, on the occasion of this second such triumph, Woods was an altogether better player than he had been two years earlier.

## Still improving

Instead of sitting back as the rest strove to catch him, he had worked as hard as any of them. Firstly, he and his coach, Butch Harmon, had arrived at a slightly flatter swing than the one that had served so well in junior days. Again, he had increased his repertoire of strokes, with his newly honed approaches verging on the sensational.

Though there is nothing like exaggerated backspin to have the crowds in raptures, Woods's shorter irons were now tending to drop and stop like so many bags of sugar. Except, of course, when it came to the 17th green at Valderrama on that November day in 1999, when he tied up what was his second US money-list. Then, with the combination of wind and pin position having rendered the green almost

Tiger Woods: model prize for model golfer at Augusta National.

unplayable, his ball landed past the flag but rolled all the way back down the slick and slippery surface into the water. It was an unavoidable mishap which led to that dramatic play-off with Miguel Angel Jimenez.

Valderrama, one of the new World Golf Championship events in which the prize-money counts on both the US Tour and its European equivalent, represented the end of a season in which Woods had won eight times in 11 starts.

## $6million man

His season's earnings were by then up to $6,616,585 million which, as everyone was quick to point out, was more than David Duval, who finished second, and Davis Love, who finished third, had won between them. It was also more than Jack Nicklaus had won in 38 years at the top.

Yet, though most would agree that nobody, not even Ben Hogan or Bobby Jones, touched greater heights in the 20th century than Woods, the jury must remain out on whether he is the best player of all.

Too many facts and figures still have to be entered into the computer, not the least of which centre on the player's golfing longevity.

## Longevity questions

Woods, at 23, has won two of the professional game's majors in three years. Nicklaus, on the other hand, won 18 professional majors over 25 years, 1961–86. What is more, as recently as the 1998 Masters, the by-then 58-year-old Nicklaus was still very much in the hunt with nine holes to play.

Though the gods had done nothing to douse his competitive fire, Nicklaus had joints in keeping with one who had spent half a century hitting golf balls and hitting them hard. As he came down the stretch, he was competing not just against Mark O'Meara and the rest, but against a hip joint which would shortly have to be replaced It was exhaustion, more than anything, which did for Nicklaus that day.

The general consensus of opinion, backed up by fact, is that a man's keenest competitive edge seldom lasts longer than ten years. Gary Player, in terms of retaining the ability to win majors, was in much the same enduring class as a Nicklaus, having won his maiden Open at Muirfield in 1959 and his farewell Masters in 1978. Again, both Walter Hagen's and Lee Trevino's "major" careers spanned closer to 20 years than ten at that lofty level, though Bobby Jones retired as a competitive golfer when 28. Seve Ballesteros and Nick Faldo were two more great champions who remained at the top for no more than eight years. Arnold Palmer had seven years separating his first major and his last.

The career of Joyce Wethered who, in the opinion of

Jones, had the best swing of any golfer, man or woman, he saw, was along much the same concise lines. She won five English championships in a row from 1920, and four of the six British women's championships in which she played between 1922 and 1929.

## Living in the spotlight

A potential problem for Woods is that he has been in the wearing glare of the spotlight since he started to walk. In a chronology drawn up by Mark McCormack's IMG, for example, the first entry concerns his performances from the age of two to five;

- Aged two, appeared on CBS News and Mike Douglas Show putting with Bob Hope;
- Aged three, shot 48 for nine holes at Navy Golf Club in Cypress, California;
- Aged five, appeared on That's Incredible.

Between the ages of six to 13, Woods won four Optimist international Junior World championships. At 15, he was the youngest winner of the US Boys' Championship, the Orange Bowl World Junior International Championship and a host of other major under-18 events.

At 18, he won the first of three successive US Amateurs, the Western Amateur, the Southern California, the Pacific Northwest, and the Jerry Pate Invitational. He also bagged his opening college event at Stanford, the William Tucker invitational.

His two years at Stanford, though packed with college golf, gave him something of a break, but who can tell whether such high-powered junior activity will eat into his span in the professional arena?

When he won the Masters, his father prophesied that the only thing which could "ruin everything" for his son would be "the wrong broad". Indeed, it would be interesting to speculate on how Earl Woods would react were his son to do a Phil Mickelson and announce that he would happily abandon a winning position in the US Open to be with his wife while she was giving birth. Woods could well turn into the same species of hands-on father as Mickelson but, to date, none of his girlfriends would seem to have impinged on his golfing ambitions.

## Leaving nothing to chance

Though Trevino once said that no golfer has everything, and that the deity always keeps something back, Woods has the lot and he wants more. Recently, in a decision which set others blinking, he had laser treatment

**World champion: Valderrama victory in Amex play-off.**

on what had seemed to be a perfectly good pair of eyes.

Where most of us, in this game of handicaps, would have deemed it fairer if he had taken to the course blindfold, he in fact emerged from the treatment warning "the ball looks bigger, the hole looks bigger".

Yet, in spite of everything, he is well liked by his fellow players. Other Americans may have gone overboard in that never-to-be-forgotten Ryder Cup at Brookline, though Woods, like his old friend O'Meara, was never guilty on that score. Though there is no false modesty about him and he talks, cheerfully, of how he expects to win every tournament in which he plays, he is always extraordinarily well versed in the feats of others. He has a genuine respect for their achievements.

At the end of 1999, when he met Montgomerie in some far-flung place, he broached the subject of how, at Valderrama, he had been winning his second American money-list whereas the Scot had brought his tally of European money-lists up to seven in a row.

**Golf Family Woods: Kultida, winner Tiger and Earl at Johnny Walker Classic in Thailand.**

| SCORECARD | |
|---|---|
| **Masters** | 1997 |
| **USPGA** | 1999 |
| Born Stanford, California, December 30, 1975. | |

# Age will have its day

AFTER THE SUCCESS OF (relatively) callow youth in the majors of 1997, a fast finish by Mark O'Meara, 41, at the Masters of two birdies in the last three holes robbed Freddie Couples of a second victory and David Duval of his first. Defending champion Tiger Woods was soon helping his Florida neighbour on with his first green jacket. He didn't perform the ceremony all that smoothly, O'Meara pointing out that at 41 he couldn't lift his arm "up there".

He no doubt found lifting the prize cheque easier. The Masters' purse had edged over $3million. O'Meara's reward for winning a major at his 57th attempt amounted to $576,000.

Further lustre was added to Tour sages by Jack Nicklaus's feat of beginning to weigh on the last-round nerves of the one-time leader, as Fred Couples admitted later. Now 58, Nicklaus walked with less than military snap, indeed with a hint of a limp, and his waistline shows no sign of receding. He was two under par after two holes, saving a stroke with his chip at the third.

The happy holders of Augusta badges (retailing at $10,000 in the free market as against $100 charged by the club), have never considered "impossible" and "Nicklaus" to be related expressions, and cheered him from the facilities before he took on the sixth hole, where he missed the birdie offered by his accurate six iron approach. He made no such mistake at the next, moving to two off Couples's pace. He was greeted by standing ovations at all points. A birdie from sand at the 13th was his final thrust so, at his 40th Masters, Nicklaus finished joint sixth with young David Toms, at five under. (Toms's 64 included a record-equalling six birdies in a row). Both were four adrift of O'Meara, who was nine under par for his final two rounds.

Couples was five ahead of O'Meara at half-way, but only two when round four began. His putting, never a strength in previous tussles with the lightning greens of Augusta, buoyed up O'Meara this time, notably with the 10-footer he drained on the 72nd green. Couples lost his way on the par five 13th, ironically the easiest hole on the course with an average of 4.414, by pulling his tee shot into the trees.

A greater contrast to the whizz-kid winner of the previous year could scarcely be imagined: O'Meara the family man, Woods the "Phenom" (enon) not long out of his teens. Yet the one encouraged the other, practising together, and the younger profiting from the elder statesman lore of his friend. For such a young man, Woods dealt adequately with the burden of his suddenly acquired fame. On course, his progress had stalled a little, without a win for nine months, apart from making up an eight shot deficit and beating Ernie Els in for the Johnny Walker Classic. But that was in Thailand, where he was awarded citizenship.

He never managed to break 70 in defence of his Masters title, finishing joint eighth, level with the British Open Champion, Justin Leonard, and the best of the invaders, Colin Montgomerie and Darren Clarke. In joint 12th place José Maria Olazabal, Per-Ulrik Johansson, Jay Haas and Phil Mickelson won $64,800 apiece.

Mark O'Meara: due deference to a mature Master golfer from old greenjacket Freddie Couples.

# Janzen's Open: Olympic's brickbats

CHARGES OF UNFAIRNESS against US Open courses are legion. Olympic at San Francisco came high-up in the hate-list of the world's leading players. Some thought 60 was on the cards if the rough had been cut back on this 6,797 par 70 course. Tiger Woods spoke of "border-line-illegal" pin positions. Tom Watson plaintively remembered when drivers were the norm off tees. Colin Montgomerie, renowned as the straightest off the tee, never used his driver in the first three rounds. Lee Janzen gained his second US Open for all that, overcoming a five-shot deficit to win on level par by a stroke from Payne Stewart.

Indeed Janzen dropped strokes at two of the first three holes to drive home his disadvantage against Stewart, who looked to repeat his 1991 feat at Hazeltine National, where he was never headed. So Janzen had to do what Billy Casper achieved at Olympic in 1966, when he overcame Arnold Palmer from the same margin of seven strokes back.

He did it with more than one stroke of good fortune, but any amount of cool nerve. He thought he had lost his ball up a tree at the fifth, and he had – until the wind dislodged the ball as Janzen trekked back to the tee. He chipped to the fairway, overshot the green – then chipped in for par.

Six holes later he got a bounce from rough to green, and holed his birdie putt. This was one of four birdies in a steadfast last 15 holes. A divot, filled with sand, tripped up Stewart at the 12th, bringing Janzen level. Stewart was further disturbed at this turning point by a slow-play warning as he agonised over escape routes.

The 18th green completed his torment, as his firm attempt at an 18-foot putt to tie slipped across the front of the hole. His playing partner Tom Lehman, in the last group for the fourth year running, four putted it. John Daly thought this pin the single most ridiculous thing he had ever seen in golf. It cut Stewart's lead from three to one in round two when it was in an even more impossible position: a player who missed by a fraction putting up the green was likely to get the ball back at his feet.

Montgomerie's 69 on the last day included a lengthy birdie putt at the 18th. He was accompanied by two uniformed policemen. He was the butt of much abuse, not diminished by the example of name-calling in the local press. He was joint 12th, a stroke behind one of the hits of the championship, smiling Matt Kuchar, Tiger Woods's successor as Amateur Champion. Casey Martin, using a caddie car following his appeal under the Disabilities Act, won $34,043. It was a thought provoking pairing that sent him out one day with José Maria Olazabal.

Matt Kuchar: top Masters amateur - and at US Open, too.

Lee Janzen: touch of luck helped towards second US Open title.

# O'Meara double, Rose flowers

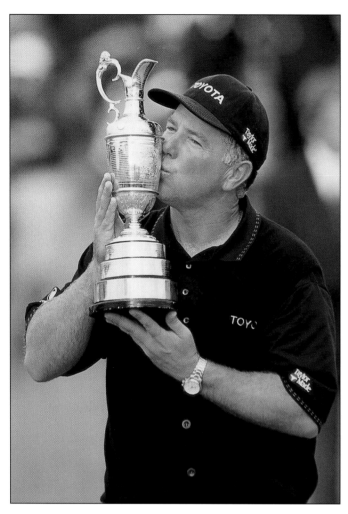

**Mark O'Meara: serene in play-off against "unknown" Brian Watts.**

MARK O'MEARA AGAIN proved that grey hairs do not an also-ran make, landing the rare double of Masters and British Open. The two middle days of the event were wild and often wet, Friday's 40 mph gusts halting play for half an hour at Royal Birkdale.

O'Meara had to share the headlines with Justin Rose, a 17-year-old amateur qualifier from Hook in Hampshire, and the youngest of Walker Cup players. The silver medal for the unpaid had never been more spectacularly won. Rose finished with a pitch out of the rough from close on 50 yards on the 72nd hole that climbed over the bunkers and trickled in for a birdie and a final 69 for joint fourth. The noise was deafening. Across came Sergio Garcia, winner of the British Amateur last month and everyone's favourite to become a latter-day Seve Ballesteros, to shake Rose's hand.

The player one stroke ahead, with a final 66, a score Rose himself had put up in round two, was Tiger Woods, one over par on 281. Two ahead and heading for the British Open's four-hole play-off tie-breaker were O'Meara and another headline maker in Brian Watts, born in Montreal 32 years ago of an English mother and a German father. He had made a deal of money playing in the Far East, but few waves anywhere else – till now.

Even then, few recognised him in and around the nearest town and quintessential English seaside resort, Southport, and he had the idea that no-one had noticed he was winning the Open – which he was on Friday and Saturday nights. He played with a calm demeanour, his swing seldom hinting at anxiety. So well did he hold his game together that, with due respect to Rose's 72nd hole coup, he played the shot of the championship at that same hole, even more meritorious since he was in such close contention with O'Meara. His second had left him with a bunker shot from the back of the hazard, right foot on grass well above the sand, left foot in the sand, but 12 inches lower than his right. O'Meara led the applause when the ball finished inches away from a birdie.

Watts lost the play-off by two strokes. O'Meara at once took the lead with a birdie four on the 15th, and held on with the same good sense he had displayed at Augusta.

Nick Faldo, Bob Tway (third at Olympic), Colin Montgomerie, Seve Ballesteros, and Darren Clarke, all missed the cut. So did Tom Watson at this, the scene of his fifth Open victory. Greg Norman, in need of shoulder surgery after he failed to qualify for the Masters, did not enter: the most notable absentee was unfit Jack Nicklaus, after 146 consecutive majors, 153 starts in all.

# Rose cashes in

JUSTIN ROSE WOULD HAVE won well over £50,000 at Birkdale if he had turned pro before the championship. As it was, he and father Ken accepted some of the offers of sponsorship that flooded in, and he turned pro immediately, entering the Dutch Open the following week.

He did not make the cut. Stephen Leaney won the event, at Hilversum. He had practised with fellow Australian Stuart Appleby at Birkdale, so was all the more affected by the death in a road crash days earlier of Renay, 25, Appleby's wife, on her way to their second honeymoon in Paris.

Alan Shepard, 74, has also

died: the first extra-terrestrial golfer. Twenty-seven years ago he took a six iron on board an Apollo mission and two balls. The first he shanked into a crater then, swinging slower, he hit the second about 200 yards: he had calculated that with the same club-head speed, a ball must go six times as far on the Moon. His TV audience was immense. The deaths were also announced of two distinguished Americans in twice US Open champion (and qualified dentist) Cary Middlecoff and Gardner Dickinson, a leader of the Tour pros in their struggle to free themselves from (as they saw it) the tyranny of the PGA.

**Justin Rose: at concert pitch holing out at the 72nd.**

# Vijay on heavenly US PGA ground

VIJAY SINGH, THE GREAT practiser, made his labours pay off in major terms for the first time beating Steve Stricker by two and Steve Elkington, a US PGA specialist, by three at Sahalee, Washington State, near Seattle in America's Pacific North-west. The first Asian to hit the heights, if Tiger Woods's claims to be both Asian and African American are disregarded, Singh, of Indian lineage, hoped there would be a TV feed to his people in Fiji. He was disappointed, the news of his US PGA victory reaching "home" – Singh is based in Florida – through telephone calls to such as Sir Timoci Tuivaga, President of Fiji Golf Club and Chief Justice of Fiji. Ironically, the Prime Minister, Sitiveni Rabuka, has been criticised of late for spending too much time on the

golf course. There are ten courses on Fiji, 2,000 players and 19 pros, which might change if golf mania were to bite into Fiji's dominant sport, rugby.

Important golf events close to Seattle are almost as rare as Fijian champions, but Sahalee (the word is Chinook, meaning high, heavenly ground) became paradisiacal for Singh as he threaded his ball between its immense stands of tall trees, demanding not just accuracy, but shaped, customised shots from the tees.

Tiger Woods started round one by pushing a two iron at breakfast-time into the right rough. That cost a bogey. Woods then broke the course record with a 66. He was from that point increasingly on the periphery of the event, as Singh worked

through one sub-70 round after another. The record passed to Greg Kraft with a 65 on the second day, and Nick Price got within five of Singh's nine under par 271, with another 65 on the final day. O'Meara never exceeded par, but his hopes of a third 1998 major foundered five behind the tall, slim but big-hitting Fijian. Stricker, whose wife Niki was expecting their first child, had been enduring a thin time since his two wins in 1996, had the consolation of a $324,000 cheque.

Singh was full of praise for his caddie, Dave Renwick, from Scotland, who carried winning bags for José Maria Olazabal (Masters) and for Elkington (US PGA). Colin Montgomerie, one behind Singh at half-way, had a shocking weekend, 11 over par.

Vijah Singh: paid tribute to his "major" bag-carrier, Dave Renwick.

### "It's like playing down a cathedral aisle"

**PAUL RUNYAN**
of the fairways lined by the mighty cedars of Sahalee, the US PGA Championship course.

# Se Ri Pak, serious golfer

**Se Ri Pak: escape from water hazard in US Open play-off.**

IN A ROOKIE YEAR THAT more than stood comparison with Tiger Woods's startling apprentice efforts, Se Ri Pak, stocky, strong, Korean, and 20 years old, won the US Open after a marathon struggle at Black Wolf Run against amateur Jenny Chuasiriporn, of Thai descent.

She won at the second sudden-death hole after an 18-hole play-off, at the end of which Si Re Pak had to go paddling to recover from the edge of a water hazard. It cost a seemingly fatal bogey, but her opponent chipped and two-putted for a bogey also. A week after the Open, Si Re Pak returned a 61, the lowest ever LPGA score, in winning the Jamie Kroger Classic, by nine shots. Back in May she won her first major, McDonald's LPGA Championship.

Chuasiriporn went on to reach the US Amateur final, only to fall to another Korean, Grace Park, 19, by 7 and 6 at Barton Hills, Michigan.

# Deep South Double

NOVEMBER 22 WILL ever be remembered as a golden day of multiple success for players from the British Isles. Peter McEvoy led Gary Wolstenholme, Luke Donald, Lorne Kelly, and Paddy Gribben to Great Britain and Ireland's fourth Eisenhower Cup victory in Santiago, Chile. In 1964 he was best individual in the team that won in Rome; he is the only man to win as both player and captain.

Key to the four stroke win over Australia was Wolstenholme's final four-under par 67, with no bogeys, at the Los Leones club. Because of possible repercussions after the arrest in London of the former Chilean President, General Pinochet, McEvoy's team made the trip only at the last minute. The women's team stayed away from Chile, where Jenny Chuasiriporn was consoled for her US Amateur defeat by returning a record low individual score as the US won the Espirito Santo Trophy by 21 shots from Italy and Germany.

As McEvoy's team edged ahead in Chile, Nick Faldo and David Carter beat Costantino Rocca and Massimo Florioli of Italy by two shots at windy Gulf Harbour, Auckland, New Zealand in the World Cup of Golf. John Daly and Scott Verplank were third two shots further back for the US. Faldo parted from the coach who remodelled his swing, David Leadbetter, now coaching a woman for the first time – Si Re Pak.

On the same day, there were three more English winners round the world: Lee Westwood – Dunlop Phoenix in Japan: David Howell – Australian PGA title, Brisbane: Laura Davies PageNet LPGA Tour Championship, Las Vegas. Davies netted $215,000.

## TEE TALK

### "One stops a fade and the other a hook"

**TONY EDLUND**
explaining why he wore one black shoe and one white.

# US women clean up Cups

EUROPE IN THE SOLHEIM Cup, and Great Britain & Ireland in the Curtis Cup, seldom looked capable of blocking a US Pro-Am double in team competition. Judy Rankin was again the winning US captain, and Dottie Pepper again irritated the visitors to Jack Nicklaus's Muirfield Village course with what they considered gestures to incite the gallery.

The US margin was 16-12, Europe's only ray of hope coming when Laura Davies, Helen Alfredsson, Annika Sorenstam and Liselotte Neumann won the top four singles, almost levelling the overall score. Pepper's win over Trish Johnson began a US singles rally that proved decisive.

Brenda Corrie Kuehn with a 4-0 record was at the centre of America's 10-8 Curtis Cup victory at Minikahda, Minneapolis, the US edging ahead at every session except the last singles series, but a one point margin there was too little and too late for Ita Butler's team, for whom that straight hitter from Wheatley in Yorkshire Rebecca Hudson dropped only half a point from four starts.

## SHORT PUTTS

● R&A Rules Secretary David Rickman held that a hat invented by Ray Halle, an Australian engineer, weighted with a copper band to help players keep their heads still, was illegal under Rule 14-3: Artificial Devices and Unusual Equipment.

● It took Phil Mickelson seven months to complete his AT&T win at Pebble Beach, where rain postponed the final round till August.

● Annika Sorenstam became the first woman ever to post a stroke average of less than 70 – a tight squeeze at 69.99 – over the LPGA Tour year. Despite Si Re Pak's explosion on to the scene, Sorenstam was again world No. 1.

● The British Amateur Championship threw up a budding new superstar from Spain. Sergio Garcia, aged 18, crushed Craig Williams 7 & 6 in the final at Muirfield.

**Sergio Garcia: closing in on British Amateur title at Muirfield.**

# US down down-under

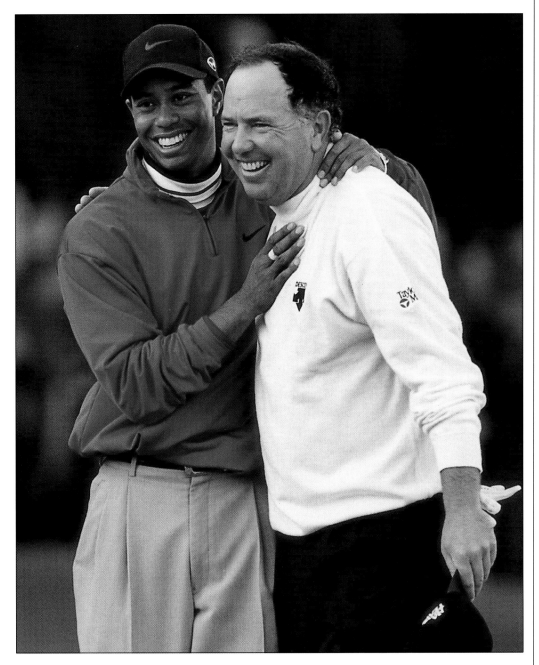

Tiger Woods and Mark O'Meara: friendly World Match Play rivals - but losers in Melbourne.

NARROW DEFEAT IN THE second President's Cup match (effectively US v The World, less Europe) was avenged by thumping victory by the Internationals, led by Peter Thomson, on the magnificent Royal Melbourne course. After this depressing year's ending for US Tour pros, led by Jack Nicklaus, US PGA Tour commissioner Tim Finchem talked of the "urgent need" for the US to win next year's Ryder Cup.

He intimated that more US diligence was needed in foursomes and fourballs. The Internationals won them by nine points, so only two singles wins were needed for victory. Nicklaus put his heavy hitters out last: Mark O'Meara, US Golfer of the Year, world No 1 Tiger Woods, and reliable Freddie Couples. The trio got two wins and a half – all in vain, since Craig Parry trounced Justin Leonard 5 and 3 in the top match and Nick Price

beat leading US money-winner David Duval at the 17th to ensure victory. Greg Norman was back after six months off for shoulder repair and lost only once – to Woods in that dead (penultimate) match.

To the team's back-bone of Australasians and South Africans were added talents from Paraguay, Fiji, and Japan – from whence came, outstandingly, Shigeki Maruyama, who won every match he played.

## Lightning shot hits golfers

LORD JUSTICE SIMON Brown ruled that a golfer is liable for any injuries caused by mis-hit shots, however small the perceived risk to other players. Three Appeal Court Judges disallowed the appeal of Anthony Lightning, whose sliced shot at Dunwood Manor, Hampshire, ricocheted off a tree and hit John Pearson in the eye. Pearson was awarded damages. He was standing on another fairway when the incident occurred, six years ago, and suffered retinal damage. He has not played since. Some household policies would cover public liability. Cover for £1million or more was available through special golfers' policies. Golfers feared a flood of actions for damages now that the Lightning decision made a player's duty of care more strict.

### TEE TALK

## "Shouting 'Fore' is not enough."

**ADVICE TO HACKERS**
after court awarded of damages to a golfer hit by a stray shot.

## Kuehnes pile it on

HANK KUEHNE ADDED to his family's USGA trophies (sister Kelli won the US Junior and two US Amateurs, not to mention the British Amateur) with a 35th hole US Amateur final victory over Tom McKnight. At 44, McKnight is exactly twice Kuehne's age. Hank is a recovering alcoholic: brother Trip caddied for him, at Rochester, New York. Trip was runner-up to Tiger Woods in the 1994 final.

Trip and (right) Hank Kuehne: adding to the family silver.

# Masterly Olly/Sergio double

José Maria Olazabal: hot round on chilly Friday at Augusta National set up second green jacket.

JOSÉ MARIA OLAZABAL (50-1) was according to the bookmakers ten times less likely to win at Augusta than David Duval, who in January had won the Bob Hope Chrysler Classic with a closing 59, never achieved before to win a tournament. Olazabal was rated as eight times as unlikely to win as Tiger Woods.

Duval looked a good thing. Starting the year with victory in the opening Mercedes Championship in Hawaii, and in the Bob Hope a fortnight later, he went into the Masters after back-to-back victories, in the Players' Championship and the Bell South Classic. This last effort gave him the world No. 1 ranking enjoyed by Woods since last June. The world was Duval's oyster ... and father Bob gained his first Senior PGA title hours before Duval's Bell South success.

Not only did Olazabal win, but his second Masters at 33 was half of a unique Spanish double, for Sergio Garcia (295, tied for 38th), beat Americans Tim McKnight (297), Matt Kuchar (299) and South African Trevor Immelmans (305) to the amateur prize. Was this 19-year-old, the European captain Mark James must have mused, to be the long-coveted future Ryder Cup replacement partner for Olazabal? The old partner, Seve Ballesteros, missed the cut. Jack Nicklaus, ruled out by a hip injury, defiantly determined to enter for the St Andrews 2000 Open.

Olazabal's ploy to gain his second Green Jacket was to advance the "money-round" – usually the Saturday – to chilly Friday, when his 66 put him eight under par, one ahead of Norman at half-way: 73-71 at the weekend kept him eight under, beating Davis Love III by two shots and Greg Norman by three. Despite the novelty of rough at Augusta, a windy, hot final day meant that chipping and putting were fiendishly difficult. They are Olazabal's forte: key to his win also was his par-saving bunker shot at the 12th to within inches.

Only Duval among those in contention beat Olazabal's final 71, by a stroke, but he finished five behind the Spaniard. Woods, equipped with a flatter swing, already had a first, second and third and $1,315,115 on his 1999 record, but faded to a final 75.

## Garcia takes the plunge

FIVE DAYS AFTER THE Masters 1998 British Amateur Champion Sergio Garcia, nicknamed "El Niño", who earned a scratch handicap aged 13, six years ago, has turned pro. He had played in a number of pro events while polishing his game. Moreover he had the trick, still eluding Colin Montgomerie, of recruiting fans wherever he played. Justin Rose, nine months after turning pro at 17, missed his 17th cut.

# Stewart unpicks Ross lock

**Payne Stewart: crucial putt at US Open's 72nd hole drops this time.**

PAYNE STEWART, ALL patience and willpower, putted with tireless resolution to hold off Phil Mickelson on Donald Ross's celebrated 92-year-old Pinehurst No. 2 course, hosting its first US Open (the 99th: the 100th is Pebble Beach's Year 2000 prize).

Rough at Augusta for the first time was followed by not much rough at Pinehurst, because of drought. That was a relief, because the parched and indecently quick crowned greens are, as on many older courses, small. Finishing near the flag requires perfection in placement and spin, otherwise the ball trundles off and a nerve-racking chip presents itself.

In the North Carolina sandhills it was easy to fall victim to a malady similar to the curse of the Foreign Legion, cafard – French for the blues. Masters Champion José Maria Olazabal got them bad. So put out was he by his opening 75 that he punched his hotel room wall, which retaliated by breaking a bone in his right hand. He had to withdraw. John Daly was also afflicted: he angrily thumped his ball off the eighth green in the third round, scored 11, and finished last with 309.

Stewart, looking on a dampish final day for his second US Open eight years after his first, wore a waterproof top with the sleeves torn off, to free his swing. Putts of 25, 6 and 18 feet at the last three holes held off Mickelson, who fractionally missed a birdie putt on the 17th just before Stewart holed his. His par on the last secured the $625,000 first prize by one stroke: 12 months ago, on the "crazy golf" slopes, as some called them, of the 18th at Olympic, he missed the putt that would have given him a play-off with Lee Janzen.

Thomas Björn (playing with an old set of clubs because someone threw his new ones into a lake in Copenhagen), Ben Crenshaw, Ernie Els, Nick Faldo, and Scott Hoch were among the baker's dozen who missed the cut by one with 36-hole totals of 148, eight over par. The course has negligible water hazards, but is 7,175 yards long and the par, said Colin Montgomerie, should have been 72, not 70. The USGA must have gained deep satisfaction at Stewart's win: only he finished under par. Tiger Woods and Vijah Singh were one over: Jeff Maggert, world matchplay champion, finished joint seventh alongside David Duval, still World No. 1, who finished 75, 75.

# World Championship refined

GREG NORMAN FIRST floated the idea of a world championship series late in 1994: eight events for the world's leading 40 players. To minimize upsets to existing sponsors, the 1999 programme was four events. Jeff Maggert carried off the million dollar first prize for the opener, a full 64-draw, 18-hole matchplay version of the invitational Andersen Consulting event.

Maggert beat Andrew Magee with a chip in at the second extra hole of final at Carlsbad, California, beating Tiger Woods, Nick Price and Bernhard Langer along the way. Extensively televised, the event did not reverberate long beyond the next day's newspapers.

That left the upgraded World Series at Akron (the old NEC Invitational), the American Express title at Valderrama (the first WGC event to be played in Europe), and the EMC World Cup of Golf, with the traditional two-man national teams. Purses for the four totalled more than £9million.

# Lawrie keeps right on

TO THE GIFT OF devolved government for Scotland was added at the 128th Open the nation's first home-based Champion since Willie Auchterlonie 106 years ago: Paul Lawrie, 30, a resident of Aberdeen, where he was born. His last round of 67, four under par, was best of the day by two shots. His composure in the four-hole play off with Jean Van de Velde, a Frenchman based in Geneva, and Justin Leonard (US) was admirable, in sharp contrast to the undignified scrambling of the last hours of the Championship.

Auchterlonie won at Prestwick, a course not used for the Open these 54 years, Lawrie won in a four hole play-off at Carnoustie, not used since Tom Watson's first success in 1975. Since then accommodation and the other essentials for a major championship had been greatly improved.

Chances of hitting the fairways were definitely not improved, and the rough was penal. Michael Bonallack, the R&A Secretary, said that it was too late to widen the fairways after much rain, but general consensus was that the heavy rough should have been thinned out. Letters to The Daily Telegraph. spoke of lottery, farce, and crazy golf. The R&A were accused of showing the course little respect, and not allowing it to rely on its natural defences. Of these, it had plenty, for the weather was far from clement, though the wind eased on day four.

Sergio Garcia, winner of his first European Tour event two weeks ago, was in tears after his 89, 83 start, finishing dead last of the non-qualifiers who completed 36 holes. He had a 62 last week at Loch Lomond. Tom Watson headed the non-qualifiers: the cut came at 12 over par, which says it all.

The climax had three acts. The first, Lawrie's 67, in the circumstances the best round he is ever likely to play, was not immediately appreciated. He and Justin Leonard, who scored a final 72, were together on 290, looking sure things to tie for second place (and £185,000). Craig Parry, Angel Cabrera, Greg Norman, Tiger Woods, and David Frost had all threatened. But Van de Velde, who started five ahead, surely destined to be the first Frenchman to win since Arnaud Massey in 1907, came to the last wanting a six to win his first major – like Lawrie he had won but one four-round Tour event. Careful avoidance of the Barry Burn would surely bring a bogey and victory by two.

In a bizarre act two, he took seven. His driving had scarcely entitled him to be in contention at all, but by élite scrambling got one hand on the auld mug. His drive went well right, but into short grass near the 17th fairway. Two cautious irons must have secured a five. Instead Van de Velde went at it with a two iron: caddies everywhere blenched. The ball hit a grandstand, ricocheting back over the Burn into long grass. From there, he hit into the Burn. The player himself, shoes and socks off, waded in. "Wait a few minutes and the tide

Paul Lawrie: got the better of Carnoustie's perilous 17th and 18th.

might have gone out," was Parry's advice to Van de Velde. Instead he took a drop, hit into sand, but got up and down from five feet.

Act three, the play-off, dark and damp, began messily – Van de Velde six to his opponents' fives on the 15th. All were one

over on the short 16th. Now Lawrie took hold, with his second birdie of the day on the 17th (par four with a Championship average of 4.57). The Frenchman got a birdie too, but there was no stopping the Scot, and Leonard found the Burn on the last for the second time in a day. From 220 yards on the 18th Lawrie hit a four iron to little over a yard. In went the putt, and Lawrie had won the play-off by three. He had played the perilous 17th and 18th holes twice in three under par. Lawrie is the only qualifier ever to win since the present system was introduced.

Jan Van de Velde: bizarre choice of clubs on 72nd hole led to watery disaster.

### "More Jacques Tati than Jack Nicklaus"

PETER ALLISS
Describing the events at the 72nd hole at the Carnoustie Open.

# Woods's PGA, but Garcia plays "The Shot"

THE 81ST US PGA Championship was the Tiger Woods and Sergio Garcia Show. Their shoot-out at Medinah, Chicago, brought victory to the American, his fifth of the year world-wide, but the shot of the tournament was played (and will be played and replayed for ever and a day on TV) by the Spaniard.

Woods was five ahead with seven holes remaining, but bogeyed the 12th. In the penultimate group up ahead of Woods, Garcia holed a huge putt for a two. Woods was less adept – too long with tee-shot and chip back, he double-bogeyed. Garcia was soon two behind again, bogeying the 15th.

Facing a shot of almost 200 yards to the next, his ball hard up against a tree, he risked all, including wrists and club, by taking aim with a six iron, and closing his eyes on impact, and jumping away. He bounded after the shot to watch it slice mightily – bending over 50 yards – on to the green. His par four was pure early Ballesteros. Woods coming up behind could not equal it: one shot between them.

Garcia's pars at the final two holes were not enough to defeat Woods, back at No. 1 again, and rejoicing at his second major if only because charges of being a one major miracle must be dropped. Garcia looked good for a Ryder Cup place.

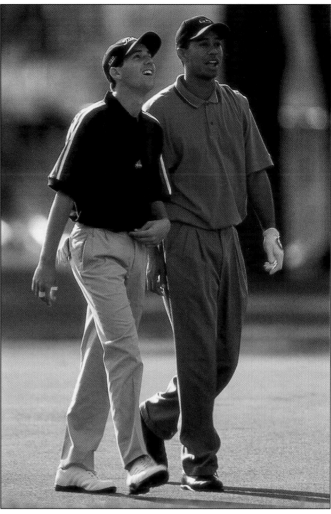

Young gladiators: Sergio Garcia (left) chased Woods all the way.

Tiger Woods: came so close to losing five-stroke lead.

## SHORT PUTTS

● Nonagenarian Ian Patey, former England international and English Amateur Champion in 1946, got married to a nurse aged 41 to avoid inheritance tax. Patey, of the Hayling club near Portsmouth in Hampshire, and a Halford Hewitt stalwart said: "The Government would get £150,000 if I died tomorrow, but if I marry they don't get anything. I don't like this Government."

● Losers, they say, are soon forgotten. Yet a Carnoustie Hotel suite was named after Jean Van de Velde: true, he did lose big. As the hotel manager put it at a dinner in honour of the Frenchman (whose website is www. allezjean.com): "What you did in the Open, we're still living on it."

● A 10-year partnership ended as Nick Faldo's caddie Fanny Sunesson joined Sergio Garcia. Faldo, devastated that he did not get a Ryder Cup wild card and Andrew Coltart did, planned to marry Valerie Bercher, a Swiss. Former girlfriend Brenna Cepelak reportedly attacked one of his Ferraris with a wedge.

● Marine Monnet, French winner of the British Girls title three years ago, completed the double at Birkdale with the British Amateur, though Rebecca Hudson from Yorkshire took her to the final green. California's Dorothy Delasin turned pro after winning the US Amateur from Jimin Kang 4 & 3 over a Donald Ross-designed course at Biltmore Forest in North Carolina.

# US conquer in Rowdy Ryder

BEN CRENSHAW'S MEN made a positive response to PGA Commissioner Tim Finchem's urgent plea for a Ryder Cup victory after the President's Cup rout in Australia last year. Miguel Angel Jiménez's verdict was succinct. The Americans wanted to win at any cost. The price of this was, the Spaniard said after his first Ryder Cup appearance: "their dignity and our respect." The Ryder Cup venue was Brookline, near Boston. The result rested, as usual, on an American rally in singles. Europe needed only four points out of 12 to retain the Cup, but fell half a point short.

What had most upset Jiménez was what the Europeans considered incitement of the crowd by Ben Crenshaw's team, and much abuse of Colin Montgomerie as the day grew older and alcoholic intake of the new breed of fans attracted by the Tiger phenomenon undoubtedly increased. Colin's father left the course when he felt he could stand no more. His opponent, Payne Stewart, was clearly embarrassed. But there was no mistaking the explosive power of the US blitzkrieg in singles. The smallest winning US margin in the top six matches was 3 & 2.

The major flash-point was the invasion of the 17th green after Justin Leonard holed a monster putt at the climax of a charging rally. José Maria Olazabal was left with one almost as big to stay level – this after losing a four-hole lead. Before he could proceed, Leonard, dashing about rejoicing, arms aloft, was joined on the green by a scrum of US players, caddies, wives etc. This from a player who objected to Matt Kuchar and his father exchanging high fives during the US Open last year. Tom Lehman afterwards claimed the right to celebrate as the Europeans had done in Spain.

The European view was: "Not while the match is still in progress." When it at length resumed, Olazabal missed his birdie putt, but holed a sizeable one on the 18th to force a half with Leonard. That meant defeat for Europe, though Padraig Harrington had beaten Mark O'Meara and Montgomerie and Paul Lawrie won two of the last three matches while Jim Furyk mastered Sergio Garcia 4 & 3. Lawrie finished an excellent Cup debut by defeating the world matchplay champion, Jeff Maggert, 4 & 3.

The right response, veteran golfer Lord Deedes concluded in The Daily Telegraph, was to "shrug our shoulders". US emotions were strong – but scarcely disgusting, as the British Prime Minister declared. Older Americans perhaps remembered Tommy Bolt's remark about the behaviour of the enormous crowds who encouraged Dai Rees's team at Lindrick to inflict a (then) rare defeat on the US: "Good relations – don't make me sick."

Stampede begins: American reaction to Leonard's putt.

Sergio Garcia and (right) Sam Torrance: taking a dim view.

## RYDER CUP

(Brookline Country Club, Boston, MA). US 14½: Europe 13½.
Captains(non-playing): US B Crenshaw: Europe: M James

**FIRST DAY Foursomes: Morning**

| US | | Europe | |
|---|---|---|---|
| D Duval & P Mickelson | 0 | C Montgomerie & P Lawrie 3 & 2 | 1 |
| T Lehman & T Woods | 0 | S Garcia & J Parnevik 3 & 2 | 1 |
| Davis Love III & P Stewart | ½ | MA Jimenez & P Harrington | ½ |
| J Maggert & H Sutton 3 & 2 | 1 | L Westwood & D Clarke | 0 |

**Four-balls: Afternoon**

| | | | |
|---|---|---|---|
| P Mickelson & J Furyk | 0 | J Parnevik & S Garcia 1h | 1 |
| D Love III & J Leonard | ½ | C Montgomerie & P Lawrie | ½ |
| H Sutton & J Maggert | 0 | JM Olazabal & MA Jimenez 2 & 1 | 1 |
| D Duval & T Woods | 0 | L Westwood & D Clarke 1h | 1 |

First Day: US 2 Europe 6

**SECOND DAY Foursomes: Morning**

| | | | |
|---|---|---|---|
| H Sutton & J Maggert 1h | 1 | C Montgomerie & P Lawrie | 0 |
| J Furyk & M O'Meara | 0 | L Westwood & D Clarke 3 & 2 | 1 |
| T Woods & S Pate 1h | 1 | MA Jimenez & P Harrington | 0 |
| P Stewart & J Leonard | 0 | S Garcia & J Parnevik 3 & 2 | 1 |

**Four-balls: Afternoon**

| | | | |
|---|---|---|---|
| T Lehman & P Mickelson 2 & 1 | 1 | D Clarke & L Westwood | 0 |
| D Duval & Davis Love III | ½ | J Parnevik & S Garcia | ½ |
| J Leonard & H Sutton | ½ | MA Jimenez & JM Olazabal | ½ |
| S Pate & T Woods | 0 | C Montgomerie & P Lawrie 2 & 1 | 1 |

Second Day; US 4 Europe 4
Match Aggregate: US 6 Europe 10

**THIRD DAY Singles**

| | | | |
|---|---|---|---|
| T Lehman 3 & 2 | 1 | L Westwood | 0 |
| H Sutton 4 & 2 | 1 | D Clarke | 0 |
| P Mickelson 5 & 3 | 1 | J Sandelin | 0 |
| Davis Love III 6 & 5 | 1 | J Van de Velde | 0 |
| T Woods 3 & 2 | 1 | A Coltart | 0 |
| D Duval 5 & 4 | 1 | J Parnevik | 0 |
| M O'Meara | 0 | P Harrington 1h | 1 |
| S Pate 2 & 1 | 1 | MA Jimenez | 0 |
| J Leonard | ½ | JM Olazabal | ½ |
| P Stewart | 0 | C Montgomerie 1h | 1 |
| J Furyk 4 & 3 | 1 | S Garcia | 0 |
| J Maggert | 0 | P Lawrie 4 & 3 | 1 |

Singles: US 8 ½; Europe 3 ½

# Stewart killed in aircrash

PAYNE STEWART, 42, DIED in a private jet crash a month after his fifth Ryder Cup match. The jet took off from Orlando for Dallas, to pick up Justin Leonard en route to the Tour Championship at Houston.

While it was still over Florida oxygen starvation is believed to have killed the crew and passengers, including agents employed by US Open Champion Stewart and Paul Azinger. The aircraft flew on at great height, tracked by military aircraft after flight controllers lost contact. Service pilots could see no sign of life on board. Not until many states had been crossed and its fuel was exhausted did the jet come down.

Stewart, a striking figure in his plus twos – he had his own clothing label – had won three majors and won more than $11million on the US Tour. He leaves his wife Tracey and a son and daughter.

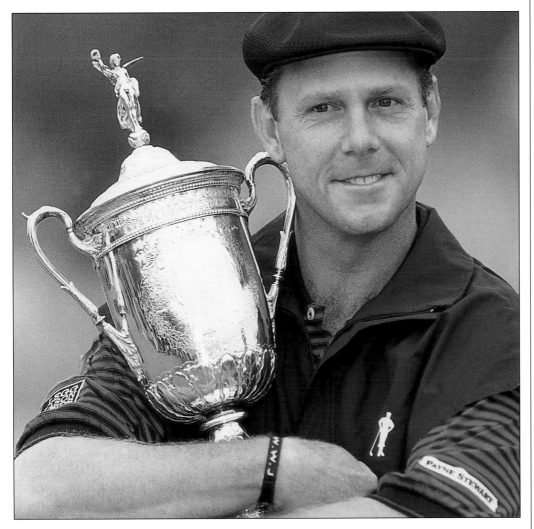

**Payne Stewart and US Open trophy: bizarre aircrash death at the summit of his fortune and fame.**

# GB & I – 19-5 'home banker'

GB AND IRELAND regained the Walker Cup at Nairn by their biggest ever margin, 15-9, still way short of the fanciest US scores, such as 11-1 (1961) and 19-5 (1993). The series is becoming one of home bankers: not since Atlanta ten years ago and Portmarnock two years later has the visiting team won.

At Nairn, Peter McEvoy's team were two adrift on the first day, but romped in with a 7-1 singles result at the death. McEvoy's faith in Graham Rankin was rewarded after a losing first day with two wins, the second against Steve Scott, who gave Tiger Woods such a hard time in his third US Amateur final.

England boys, led by Lancashire's Nick Dougherty, added the Home Internationals title to the World Junior title gained in Japan, and the European in Sweden – a dividend for 25 years of service to junior golf by Roy and Jean Case. Dougherty was best individual in the World Juniors.

# Junior Golfers

So, in a week of the golden summer in 1994 at Little Aston, I watched this slight schoolboy reach the last eight of the British Boys' Championship – and realised he was something special. That is the wonderful thing about covering junior sport. Exciting as it is to watch the giants of the game, there is nothing as certain to make the heart miss a beat or cause a gallery to catch its collective breath more sharply than a fresh young talent.

There is something about them which suggests success. And, after more than a quarter of a century of reporting amateur golf for The Daily Telegraph, I have felt that tingle down my spine on several occasions. Garcia remains firmly in the memory. So does Lee Westwood. He was a confident, friendly young man of 18 when he proved in the 1991 Peter McEvoy Trophy at Copt Heath that he had what it takes to reach the top. I recall that he started with an 80 in a bitingly cold April wind, and was seven strokes behind the leader. After a second-round 77 he was trailing by no fewer than nine strokes at the end of the first day.

It was then that Westwood showed a glimpse of the magic that was to shoot him to world fame within a few years. A second-round 70 was followed by a remarkable 69, when he was out in 32 and edged a stroke clear of the field.

He told me then: "I have set my sights on a Walker Cup place and then turning pro." The Walker Cup dream never came true, but Westwood turned pro at the end of the 1993 season and has never looked back.

## Justin Rose

Then there was the young Justin Rose. In July 1995, before his 15th birthday, I watched him win the English Under-18 strokeplay title at Burnham & Berrow. Three years later he finished fourth in The Open at Royal Birkdale. I remember Rose sitting in the clubhouse at Burnham after two amazing rounds of 71 and 69 on a final day when the wind swirled in every direction off the Somerset coast. With Graeme Storm still out on the

Sergio Garcia: an obvious candidate for the game's top rank when scarcely into his teens.

They told me he was good, writes Bill Meredith. They were right. "Look out for a young Spaniard," they said. "He's only 14 but he's going to be great. Name of Garcia."

course and needing a birdie at the last to tie, Rose was quietly sipping a glass of Coke.

When I told him that Storm had missed his birdie, Rose celebrated – with another Coke. There was something special about him then. Not only his golf, but also his whole demeanour. Quiet, unassuming – yet completely confident. Even at 14 he could stand up and give a charming off-the-cuff "thank-you" speech.

Now that he has weathered the awkward couple of years since that memorable Open at Birkdale, I am sure Rose will prove himself on the European Tour. He was seven under par in his six rounds at the qualifying school at San Roque in 1999, and said afterwards: "I am ready for it. I know my potential and what

I can do." It was good, too, to see Nick Ludwell qualify for the Tour. Ludwell, now 26, from Selby, was The Daily Telegraph Junior Golfer of the Year in 1989, when he was 17. Now he has made it after ten years of hard graft and Yorkshire grit.

At Penina back in 1989, Ludwell told me: "I know I have a long, long way to go." He could hardly have realised just how long. At the time, though, I wrote: "He has the look of a boy who could be going places." Ludwell could yet prove me right.

## Budding female talent

The Daily Telegraph Junior Championship, now stoutly supported by Center Parcs, has been

a wonderful source of young talent over the past 30 years or more. Take Mhairi McKay, our champion back in 1991 when she was 16. Tony Jacklin described her then as "the best I have watched since Seve Ballesteros as a 17-year-old. She has something special. The sort of thing which only happens every ten years or so."

McKay went on to play twice in the Curtis Cup and is now on the US Women's Tour after a spell at Stanford University, where she was a fellow student of Tiger Woods. Another of our champions, Rebecca Hudson, also looks booked for fame on the women's circuit. Hudson first reached the Telegraph/Center Parcs junior finals when she was 14, and finished fourth. The next year she was back to win the first

Yorkshire's Rebecca Hudson: strong showing in Curtis Cup.

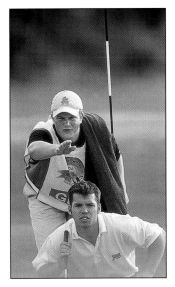

Paul Casey: masterly at
tough St. Mellion.

young player who made his name in our junior finals.

Other names to note for the future are Paul Casey, the young man from Burhill in Surrey who won the English Amateur in such fine style at St Mellion, Philip Rowe and Luke Donald, who are all honing their talents at American universities.

## The next Nick Faldo?

Graeme Storm, the Amateur champion from Durham, also has the ability to carve his name with some pride on the leaderboards of the world. His success at Royal County Down earned him an automatic place in the 2000 Masters at Augusta. The next Nick Faldo? That could be another Nick – Nick Dougherty, a tal-

ented teenager from Shaw Hill in Lancashire, who won the individual World Junior Championship in Japan in 1999 and was a highly successful captain of the British boys' team.

David Porter, from Justin Rose country in Hampshire, is another to keep an eye on. At 16 he won both the Peter McEvoy and Carris trophies – a unique double. He is built like a rugby forward and hits the ball a mile. Ask the other finalists in the Telegraph/Center Parcs finals of 1999. Even so, after an incredible first-round 69 at Ocean Forest in Georgia, Porter could finish only fourth, behind winner David Skinns.

That shows the depth of talent in junior golf. Perhaps my only regret is that not so many girls seem to be coming into the game. Two who could make their mark, though, are Louise Kenney, a Scot with skill and tenacity, and Rachel Adby, from Alsager, Staffordshire. Both have been Telegraph/Center Parcs champions.

The Masters, The Open, the Ryder Cup ... they are watched by millions throughout the world. They show the thrills and skills of the most highly gifted golfers in the game. For real excitement, though, try a bleak April day at Copt Heath in Solihull, where more than 100 young players, ranging in age from 14 to 18, tackle 72 holes in two days.

The glimpse of something special can send a tingle up your spine. It is a mixture of talent and tenaciousness; of skill and stamina. It is something indefinable. But it is something that Lee Westwood had; even in the cold at Copt Heath.

of her three Telegraph titles at San Lorenzo. Hudson, from Wheatley in Yorkshire, played in the 1998 Curtis Cup clash against the United States and won two of her three matches.

## Andrew Coltart shows the way

I first met Andrew Coltart on a bleak, wet day at The Belfry in 1986 when he was 16. In constant rain and in the face of a raging wind he managed a 76, only three over par, to win the Telegraph junior crown. In 1987 he qualified for our finals again, but had to be satisfied with the runner-up spot.

Coltart, though, was obviously a special talent, and he went on to become a Scottish amateur international and Walker Cup player before turning professional. He eventually established himself as a leading member of the European Tour and, in 1999, made the Ryder Cup team.

Year after year the young golfers come bursting through. In the triumphant Great Britain & Ireland Walker Cup side of 1999 there were no fewer than seven players in their early 20s, many of them ready to stake a claim in the professional game. Not surprisingly two of them are from Yorkshire – Simon Dyson and Ben Mason, yet another

Nick Dougherty: the pride of Lancashire, with Nick Faldo.

# The different worlds of golf

I n a few years, who knows whether someone else will be making Tiger look like a five handicapper? The young amateur who won the Australian Open, Aaron Baddeley, perhaps, or maybe Luke Donald, the star of Britain's crushing Walker Cup victory over the United States.

The chasm between top-level professional golf nowadays, and the game you and I play on a Sunday morning, is now so wide as to constitute a totally different sport. Imagine taking part in a Formula One Grand Prix behind the wheel of a split-screen Morris Minor, and you've just about got the size of the gap.

Armed with his space-age equipment, the modern professional now routinely drives the ball 300 yards, and if he has a good day with the putter, he's looking to break 60 rather than 70.

## High cost of saving shots

The club golfer, on the other hand, forks out hundreds of pounds for his Titanium, fat-shaft, bubble burner, extra-oversize, biggest-ever bertha, and a peripheral weighted, laser sighted, concentrated, sweet-spot putter. Yet he still goes out and shoots the same 92 his dad used to do with those flaky old wooden things with the bits of twine unravelling from the clubhead.

This has something to do with money, of course, and with the rewards so high – the lucrative US tour, which makes millionaires out of the Fred Funks of this world, already has bumped up its year 2000 purses by another 30 per cent – the players are never off the practice ground. The days of Christy O'Connor Snr taking a flask laced with brandy around with him, or Brian Barnes taking a fold-up chair as a protest against slow play, probably are gone for ever.

The gulf between the very best professionals and the journeymen is now so vast that when Tiger Woods won the individual prize at the 1999 World Cup of Golf in Malaysia, the Jamaican occupying last place, Jimmy Campbell, finished 64 strokes adrift of him over four rounds. If the two of them came head to head in match play, on those figures Campbell would be off a 16 handicap.

Bobby Jones once said of the young Jack Nicklaus: "He plays a game with which I am not familiar," and Jack Nicklaus said much the same of the young Tiger Woods writes Martin Johnson.

Jamaica's Ralph Campbell: gap in standards under microscope at World Cup of Golf.

Brian Barnes: easing golf's longueurs with pipe and foldaway chair at the London Masters Seniors tournament.

The boom in golf has resulted in a corresponding rush of high-class club players trying to clamber aboard the pro circuit's gravy train. Around 99 per cent of them will vanish without trace. Nick Faldo said not so long ago that anyone not capable of going round his own course in five under par on a regular basis (in effect, a plus-five handicapper) should confine any thoughts about making money from the game to his regular £5 stableford on a Sunday morning. In any event, the life of a professional golfer is not quite the glamorous occupation it appears to those of us watching from outside the ropes.

Sergio Garcia has made the transition so effortlessly, that he is already starting to moan and whine about the same sort of terrible conditions endured by you and me. Such as too much sand in the bunkers, the wrong type of grass on the greens, the courtesy car not having a TV and a cocktail cabinet in back. The practice facilities are lousy as well, in that while everyone gets brand new balls to hit, they're not always of the individual's favourite brand and compression. And anyone who thinks they might have a tedious job should see these boys on the practice ground. Hours doing nothing but hitting golf balls,

and checking the video with coach or caddie to see that the left elbow is still in perfect alignment with Jupiter.

## Practice makes perfect

It is, by and large, practice which makes these players so good. There are any number of low-handicap players who strike the ball as well as a European tour pro, and some who hit it straighter as well. The difference is that they don't score anything like as well.

Professional golfers miss greens all over the place, but they get up and down for a pastime. Take bunker play. When the pro hits a ball in one (sometimes deliberately if the alternative is thick rough), he is only really happy if he holes it.

The amateur goes in and, two or three Hamlets later, the ball emerges like an under-the-radar, heat-seeking missile, almost decapitating the bloke teeing off on the next hole.

It is probably no great mystery why so many people get so much pleasure out of a game they play so appallingly badly. Everyone, at some time or other, has hit a shot that Colin Montgomerie would be delighted with, and if they don't do it again for another two years the memo-

ry – and the chance of doing it again some time before they die – always draws them back.

Tony Jacklin started the golf boom in this country by winning The Open at Royal Lytham in 1969. The following Sunday, the municipals of Britain were full of golfers wearing their customary gear (bobble hats and a pair of jeans tucked into the socks), but Jacklin introduced them to the glove hanging out of the back pocket. They'd still four putt, but they felt more like golfers.

## "Miracle" shots

Years ago, I used to play with a friend's father, who never, and I mean never, got the ball more than four inches off the ground. Wedge or driver, it was always the same trajectory. He also hit it anywhere within a 180-yard radius, so while his ball was in flight you were never at risk of decapitation, but it was never a bad idea to wear shin pads.

As for his offspring, he is comfortably the most uncoordinated man who ever played the game, who would never get through a round without spilling most of his equipment on the course, and turning over his trolley at least five times a round. He played two of the most extraordinary shots I've witnessed (not

both in the same round), firstly when he took a three wood on a spongy fairway, and drilled the ball further towards the earth's core than the green. It disappeared a foot underground and, not being in possession of a spade with which to dig it out, no-one knew the rule for proceeding.

He also recorded a birdie three at a par four, after socketing a fairway iron out of bounds. The ball hit the concrete road running parallel to the hole, bounced down it for fully 130 yards, hit a loose pebble, shot back over the fence and finished a foot from the hole. No wonder we all keep on playing.

Maybe the answer, seeing as none of us can hope to get up to the pros' level, is to make them play under the same conditions as the regulation Sunday morning hacker. OK Tiger, I'll take you on. But you've to drink ten pints of Old Dogbolter the night before, stagger out of bed a bit too late to entirely rule out an on-course accident from that late-night vindaloo, play with a ball that looks as though it's been through a butcher's mincer, pull your own trolley, and play every shot with a cry of "Fore!" on your backswing, and a nasty fizzing noise whistling past your ear on the downswing. That would even out things a little.

# INDEX

Note: Places and Clubs are in Britain unless otherwise indicated. Page numbers in bold type indicate illustration.